The Routledge Handbook of Security Studies

Focusing on contemporary challenges, this major new Handbook offers a wide-ranging collection of cutting-edge essays from leading scholars in the field of Security Studies.

The field of Security Studies has undergone significant change during the past twenty years, and is now one of the most dynamic sub-disciplines within International Relations. It encompasses issues ranging from pandemics and environmental degradation to more traditional concerns about direct violence, such as those posed by international terrorism and interstate armed conflict. A comprehensive volume, comprising articles by both established and up-and-coming scholars, the *The Routledge Handbook of Security Studies* identifies the key contemporary topics of research and debate today.

The book is divided into four main parts:

Part I: Theoretical approaches to security and different 'securities'
Part II: Contemporary security challenges
Part III: Regional security challenges
Part IV: Confronting security challenges

This Handbook is a benchmark publication with major importance both for current research and the future of the field. It will be essential reading for all scholars and students of Security Studies, War and Conflict Studies, and International Relations.

Myriam Dunn Cavelty is Head of the New Risks Research Unit at the Center for Security Studies, ETH Zurich and Lecturer in the Department of Social Sciences and Humanities at ETH Zurich, Switzerland. Her recent publications include *Cyber-Security and Threat Politics: US Efforts to Secure the Information Age* and *Securing the Homeland: Critical Infrastructure, Risk, and (In)Security* (co-edited with Kristian Søby Kristensen).

Victor Mauer is the Deputy Director of the Center for Security Studies (CSS), ETH Zurich; Lecturer in the Department of Social Sciences and Humanities at ETH Zurich; and Guest Lecturer at the Europainstitut, University of Basel, Switzerland. His recent publications include *European-American Relations and the Middle East: From Suez to Iraq* (co-edited with Daniel Möckli, forthcoming) and *Power and Security in the Information Age* (co-edited with Myriam Dunn Cavelty).

The Routledge Handbook of Security Studies

Edited by
Myriam Dunn Cavelty and Victor Mauer

LONDON AND NEW YORK

First published 2010
This edition first published in paperback 2012
by Routledge
2 Park Square, Milton Park, Abingdon, Oxon OX14 4RN

Simultaneously published in the USA and Canada
by Routledge
711 Third Avenue, New York, NY 10017

Routledge is an imprint of the Taylor & Francis Group, an informa business

Typeset in Bembo by
Taylor & Francis Books
Printed and bound in Great Britain by
CPI Antony Rowe, Chippenham, Wiltshire

British Library Cataloguing in Publication Data
A catalogue record for this book is available from the British Library

Library of Congress Cataloging in Publication Data
A catalog record for this book has been requested

ISBN 978-0-415-46361-4 (hbk)
ISBN 978-0-203-86676-4 (ebk)
ISBN 978-0-415-66472-1 (pbk)

Contents

CONTENTS

Illustrations

Figures

Tables

Contributors

Claudia Aradau is Lecturer in International Studies in the Department of Politics and International Studies at The Open University, UK.

Thierry Balzacq is Professor of Political Science at the Université de Namur and Director of Research at CECRI, Université de Louvain. He is also a Research Associate at the Centre for European Policy Studies, Brussels.

Masooda Bano is Post-Doctoral Fellow of the Economic and Social Research Council (ESRC) at the Department of International Development, University of Oxford and a Research Fellow at Wolfson College, Oxford.

Martin Beck is a political scientist and Senior Research Fellow at the German Institute of Global and Area Studies (GIGA), Institute of Middle East Studies (IMES), in Hamburg, Germany. He is also a Senior Lecturer at the Institute of Political Science at Hamburg University.

Alex J. Bellamy is Professor of International Relations and Executive Director of the Asia-Pacific Centre for the Responsibility to Protect, at The University of Queensland, Australia.

Thomas J. Biersteker is the Curt Gasteyger Professor of International Security and Conflict Studies at the Graduate Institute of International and Development Studies, Geneva and an Adjunct Professor in the Department of Political Science and the Watson Institute for International Studies at Brown University.

Arjen Boin is Associate Professor at the Public Administration Institute of Louisiana State University and an Adjunct Associate Professor at Leiden University's Department of Public Administration.

Barry Buzan is the Montague Burton Professor of International Relations at the London School of Economics and Political Science (LSE) and an honorary professor at Copenhagen and Jilin Universities. From 1988 to 2002, he was a Project Director at the Copenhagen Peace Research Institute (COPRI). Since 1998, he has been a fellow of the British Academy.

Richard Caplan is Professor of International Relations and the Director of the Centre for International Studies (CIS) in the Department of Politics and International Relations at Oxford University.

Tobias Debiel is Professor of International Relations and Development Policy at the Institute of Political Science, University of Duisburg-Essen; the Director of the Institute for Development and Peace (INEF), Duisburg; and a Member of the Advisory Board 'United Nations' of the German Foreign Office, Berlin.

Myriam Dunn Cavelty is Head of the New Risks Research Unit at the Center for Security Studies, ETH Zurich and Lecturer in the Department of Social Sciences and Humanities at ETH Zurich, Switzerland.

Magnus Ekengren is Associate Professor of Political Science and the Director of the European Security Research Program at the Swedish National Defence College.

Mark Fitzpatrick is Senior Fellow for Non-Proliferation and the Director of the Non-Proliferation and Disarmament Programme at the International Institute for Strategic Studies (IISS) in London.

Pieter Fourie teaches Politics at Macquarie University in Sydney. In 2003–4, he worked for UNAIDS in London as a researcher on a scenario-building project regarding the future impact of AIDS in Africa, and he remains involved in a number of projects on global health.

Sumit Ganguly is Professor of Political Science; holds the Rabindranath Tagore Chair in Indian Cultures and Civilizations; and is the Director of Research of the Center on American and Global Security at Indiana University, Bloomington.

Nils Petter Gleditsch is Research Professor at the International Peace Research Institute, Oslo (PRIO); the Editor of the Journal of Peace Research; and a Professor of Political Science at the Norwegian University of Science and Technology (NTNU) in Trondheim, Norway. He has served as the President of the International Studies Association (2008–9).

Mark A. Heller is Principal Research Associate at the Institute for National Security Studies, Tel Aviv University.

Jef Huysmans is Senior Lecturer in the Department of Politics and International Studies and Security Programme Director at the Centre for Citizenship, Identities and Governance (CCIG) at The Open University, UK.

Bruce W. Jentleson is Professor of Public Policy and Political Science at Duke University.

David C. Kang is Professor at the University of Southern California, with appointments in both the School of International Relations and the Marshall School of Business. At USC, he is also the Director of the Korean Studies Institute.

Barry Kellman is Professor of International Law and the Director of the International Weapons Control Center, DePaul University College of Law.

Pauline Kerr is Fellow and Director of Studies in the Asia-Pacific College of Diplomacy at the Australian National University (ANU). She is a member of the Australian component of the Council for Security Cooperation in the Asia-Pacific and of the editorial board of the ANU's Strategic and Defence Studies Centre publications programme.

Daniel Lambach is Senior Researcher at the Institute for Development and Peace (INEF) and Adjunct Professor at the Institute of Political Science, University of Duisburg-Essen.

Anna Leander is Professor at the Copenhagen Business School with special responsibilities in the area of Business in International Conflicts.

Richard Ned Lebow is the James O. Freedman Presidential Professor of Government at Dartmouth College and Centennial Professor of International Relations at the London School of Economics and Political Science (LSE).

Jeffrey Mankoff is Associate Director of International Security Studies (ISS), Yale University and Adjunct Fellow for Russia Studies at the Council on Foreign Relations.

Carlo Masala is Professor of International Relations and the Director of the Department of Political Science at the University of the German Armed Forces in Munich.

Victor Mauer is the Deputy Director of the Center for Security Studies (CSS), ETH Zurich; Lecturer in the Department of Social Sciences and Humanities at ETH Zurich; and Guest Lecturer at the Europainstitut, University of Basel, Switzerland.

Herfried Münkler is Professor of Political Theory and the History of Political Ideas at Humboldt University, Berlin and a member of the Berlin-Brandenburg Academy of Sciences and Humanities.

Rens van Munster is Senior Researcher at the Danish Institute for International Studies in Copenhagen.

David Mutimer is Associate Professor of Political Science and Deputy Director of the Centre for International and Security Studies at York University, Toronto, Canada.

Iver B. Neumann is Research Director at the Norwegian Institute of International Affairs, on leave from his professorial chair in Russian Studies at Oslo University.

Colleen O'Manique is Associate Professor in the Departments of Politics and Women's Studies, Trent University, Peterborough, Canada.

Robert W. Orttung is Senior Fellow at the Jefferson Institute and Visiting Fellow at the Center for Security Studies at ETH Zurich.

Jeronim Perovic is Senior Researcher at the Institute of History at the University of Basel and Visiting Fellow at the Center for Security Studies at ETH Zurich.

Oliver Ramsbotham is Emeritus Professor of Conflict Resolution at the University of Bradford, UK; Chair of the Oxford Research Group; and the President of the Conflict Research Society.

Mark Rhinard is Senior Research Fellow at the Swedish Institute of International Affairs, Stockholm.

David L. Rousseau is Associate Professor of Political Science at the University at Albany (State University of New York).

Amin Saikal is Professor of Political Science and Director of the Centre for Arab and Islamic Studies (the Middle East and Central Asia) at the Australian National University.

Scott Snyder is Director of the Center for U.S.–Korea Policy and a Senior Associate at The Asia Foundation and Pacific Forum CSIS. He is also an Adjunct Senior Fellow for Korean Studies and the Director of the Independent Task Force on Policy toward the Korean Peninsula at the Council on Foreign Relations.

Vicki Squire is RCUK Research Fellow at the Centre of Citizenship, Identities and Governance and at the Department of Politics and International Studies, The Open University, UK.

Gareth Stansfield is Professor of Middle East Politics at the Institute of Arab and Islamic Studies at the University of Exeter and an Associate Fellow with special reference to Iraq on the Middle East and North Africa Programme at the Royal Institute of International Affairs (Chatham House), London.

Tobias Theiler is Lecturer in the School of Politics and International Relations at University College Dublin.

Ole Magnus Theisen is a PhD student in Political Science at the Norwegian University of Science and Technology and a Research Fellow at the Centre for the Study of Civil War at PRIO.

Thomas C. Walker currently teaches international relations at Dartmouth College.

Annick T.R. Wibben is Assistant Professor of Politics at the University of San Francisco where she chairs the interdisciplinary International Studies Program. She is also affiliated with the Watson Institute of International Studies at Brown University.

Paul Wilkinson, CBE is Emeritus Professor of International Relations and Chairman of the Advisory Board of the Centre for the Study of Terrorism and Political Violence at St Andrews University, Scotland.

Phil Williams is Professor of International Security at the Graduate School of Public and International Affairs, University of Pittsburgh.

James J. Wirtz is the Dean of the School of International Graduate Studies, Naval Postgraduate School, Monterey, California.

William C. Wohlforth is the Daniel Webster Professor in the Department of Government at Dartmouth College and Editor-in-Chief of *Security Studies*.

Tom Woodhouse is the Director of the Centre for Conflict Resolution at the Department of Peace Studies, University of Bradford. He holds the Adam Curle Chair in Conflict Resolution.

Acknowledgements

A book of this kind requires commitment, patience – in the words of Ambrose Bierce, 'a minor form of despair, disguised as virtue' – enthusiasm and, occasionally, a good sense of humour. We shared all of this not only among ourselves, but also with our 50 contributors.

However, before we could turn ideas into a real project and decided to stick with each chapter along the way, there were some obstacles to be overcome. First, there were those who – without meaning to discourage us – boldly argued that they not only did not believe in the genre, but that they thought 'the web has made it obsolete'. We comforted ourselves with the notion that despite or precisely because of their advanced age, they had become carried away by their youthful excitement about the alleged importance of the worldwide web for academic writing – and decided to soldier on. Secondly, there were those who, despite their support for the project from the very beginning, identified the relatively short deadlines we set as the(ir) biggest problem. In the end, it was they who delivered their contributions first, while we kept waiting for other draft chapters we had expected to arrive early.

We are indebted to our authors, some of whom we never met, first of all, for agreeing to contribute to our joint project; secondly, for accepting the limits and constraints such a project inevitably brings about; third, for considering our suggestions and comments, some of which came in the form of penetrating criticism and – to the despair of some – in 'track changes' mode, which makes even the most elegantly argued contribution look a complete mess; and finally, for listening to our arguments, with which we suspect they did not always agree. We have been privileged to work with all of them, and the Handbook is a product of their devotion and commitment.

In addition, we wish to thank Christopher Findlay of the Center for Security Studies at ETH Zurich for his prompt and ever-cheerful academic editing skills. His editorial comments were delivered with his customary brio and insight and in addition helped us remove some errors of fact. Marion Ronca of the Center for Security Studies at ETH Zurich reconfigured all tables and graphs.

Present at the creation was Andrew Humphrys, Senior Editor at Routledge, who with the right mix of support, interest and impatience oversaw the project from beginning to end. It has been a pleasure to work with him in preparing the book for publication as well as with his assistant, Rebecca Brennan, who dealt with our requests with great efficiency.

This Handbook primarily addresses fellow academics and graduate students, but also interested policymakers. While it engages seriously with security issues, and offers assessment and critique, the individual chapters were written with a view towards avoiding technical terms, jargon and formal notation. In a venture as collaborative as this one, the scope for human error is inevitably widened. It is, therefore, to our readers that we turn to encourage them to send us their feedback and comments – this time online.

Myriam Dunn Cavelty and Victor Mauer
Zurich

Introduction

Myriam Dunn Cavelty and Victor Mauer

The aim of any Handbook should be to be as comprehensive as possible within the given space. At the same time, however, a volume such as this one can never be more than a snapshot of a rich landscape from a specific vantage point. Even with a broader panoramic format, there are limits to the details that can be shown. On the other hand, if our image were to consist of very detailed close-ups in order to be as inclusive as possible, the landscape around us would still be constantly changing while we were completing the picture. In essence, we would never finish the perfect 'shoot'. At the same time, the selection of a vantage point from where to take a snapshot, a panorama picture or several close-ups also means choosing an angle of view – and this means willingly or unwillingly including some things, while excluding others.

Therefore, this introduction aims to describe both the landscape and the reason why a specific vantage point was chosen. The language of geography, of borders and of demarcations fits this undertaking well. A recent article on the birth of International Relations (IR) theory states that 'the role of a demarcation line is to put an end to territorial conflict' (Guilhot 2008: 281). But then again, the drawing of the demarcation line is also often the main cause of conflict; the history of Security Studies can be read as one littered with territorial conflict because of such 'line drawing' and subsequent inclusions/exclusions. There is no escaping the fact that this Handbook is inadvertently part of such conflicts, be they dormant or fought in the open, by the very stance it takes.

One of the most prominent and identity shaping (though more or less resolved) conflicts in the field is what we might call the 'traditionalists vs. wideners–deepeners conflict'. This is a debate which mainly raged in the early 1990s, though earlier exponents of the debate can easily be identified (cf. Brown 1977; Ullman 1983; Matthews 1989). The main bone of contention was the move by an ever-growing group of researchers to expand Security Studies beyond 'the study of the threat, use and control of military force' (Walt 1991: 212). Traditionalists did not believe that the security landscape had changed to a degree where Walt's definition had to be adjusted, and therefore called for a continued approach to security (often labelled 'strategic studies') from the viewpoint of the nation-state and interstate war, allegedly for the sake of conceptual clarity and theoretical parsimony (cf. Mearsheimer 1995; Chapman 1992). The wideners, on the other

1

hand, have added economic, societal, political and environmental risks to the military threats that dominated classical scholarship in this field (Westing 1989; Buzan 1991). The deepeners, in turn – often the same individuals as the wideners – are concerned with adding additional units of analysis to the traditional state-centric view; most explicitly, they have introduced the idea that there are five levels of depth to security: international systems, international subsystems, units, subunits and individuals (Buzan et al. 1998: 5f.; see also Booth 1991; Falk 1995).

The lack of consensus on the meaning of security was at the heart of the line-drawing and hence at the core of the conflict between traditionalists and wideners–deepeners. Many have observed over the years that security is a contested concept or even an 'essentially contested' one (Baldwin 1997; Buzan 1991). But not only that: security is also a condition; and because it is a condition, it is imbued with values and emotions. Therefore, security is not only a contested concept, but it is also about contested values, while being a normative enterprise in itself (Kolodziej 2005: 2). Strong subjectivity is an inevitable side effect of this – and therefore, security will always mean different things to different people. In 1991, Barry Buzan identified 12 different definitions of security that important analysts have produced (Buzan 1991: 16), one of the more prominent examples being Arnold Wolfers's early definition that 'security, in an objective sense, measures the absence of threats to acquired values, in a subjective sense, the absence of fear that such values will be attacked' (Wolfers 1952: 485). Since then, the definitions of security have multiplied considerably beyond the 12 identified by Buzan; and security has fittingly been called 'a Tower of Babel' (Kolodziej 2005: 11), indicating both towering piles of texts and a great confusion as to the meaning of the conceptual foundations at the same time.

In addition, the tower continues to grow: Security Studies have not only undergone significant change during the past 20 years, they can also be said to be one of the most dynamic areas of IR today. Worldwide, there are more undergraduate and graduate students in this field than ever before, partly as a result of the 11th September 2001 attacks in the US and the ensuing 'Global War on Terror' that has led to renewed security concerns across the globe (Wæver and Buzan 2007: 384). Judging from the number of texts published in recent years, it also seems to constitute a growth market in the academic book industry.[1]

Because of the diversity of these extant definitions, the area of overlap between all of the above positions can only be a very broad and general one. It is at this very general level that the definition of security used in this Handbook is situated. Most researchers would agree that security is somehow related to a threat to a given object of protection, and that it is most often linked to a threat to survival. The concept is therefore connected to the highest possible stakes and to existential issues, which legitimizes emergency responses (Buzan et al. 1998; Wæver 1995; Huysmans 2008). Our position within the debate between traditionalists and wideners–deepeners (and other conflicts that revolve around the question of when something is or is not a security issue), therefore depends on the nature of the threat and the referent object of security that we believe constitutes the rightful topic of investigation.

As mentioned above, this particular conflict is settled and the lines have been drawn: strategic studies are considered a sub-field and a mere province of Security Studies today. The fact is that 'wideners succeeded enough for chapters on different sectors of security to be necessary' in any Security Studies volume today (Wæver and Buzan 2007: 384). Although it does not focus particularly on sectors of security like other textbooks (cf. Collins 2007a), the editors of this Handbook also believe that a comprehensive understanding of security requires the inclusion of a wide variety of threats as well as of many referent objects beyond the state.

Sitting alongside the 'traditionalists vs. wideners–deepeners conflict' there is a second academic divide that has not been, and may never be, resolved. In general, Security Studies are treated as a sub-field of IR.[2] Therefore, Security Studies – seen as a kind of province or state within the territory of IR – are directly affected by the conflicts ongoing in the field of IR. The conventional (and rarely contested) view is that the evolution of IR as a discipline is built around the 'great debates', that the field has progressed through a series of phases involving 'idealist, realist, behavioralist, post-behavioralist, pluralist, neorealist, rationalist, postpositivist and constructivist' positions (Schmidt 2002: 3).[3] In this history, the limits of rationalism are a strong and recurring theme (Guilhot 2008: 282), as is the closely related discussion over what does or does not constitute an academically or scientifically sound method of inquiry.

Currently, the field of Security Studies is criss-crossed by the respective entrenched positions defended by positivists/rationalists on the one side and what might be labelled post-positivist or 'critical/reflexive' approaches on the other. Whether the focus is on an apparent conflict between 'American' and 'European' approaches to security – the former predominantly concerned with offensive versus defensive realism; the role of power; and institutions in order/empires – or on the emergence of various critical schools such as the 'Copenhagen', 'Welsh' (Aberystwyth) and 'Paris' Schools, which are, of course, locally dispersed (C.A.S.E. Collective 2006: 444; C.A.S.E. Collective 2007: 561–65), security (meta-) theory moves to the centre stage of identity building – and thus conflict.

Indeed, 'a number of theories now compete for tackling the whole field of security' (Wæver and Buzan 2007: 384). While there is some similarity between the different schools, there is also great diversity, be it among the approaches predominantly pursued in the US, or the ones common in Europe. Rather than being a drawback, however, this has probably had a significant impact on the increased attraction of Security Studies after 9/11, since a wide range of choices is now available when thinking about security issues, providing a very rich and fertile environment for the inquisitive analyst. In this Handbook, the aim is to illustrate this diversity – not only when it comes to theoretical approaches, but also when specific issues are tackled. In fact, diversity is the key to understanding the current landscape and should be embraced to the fullest. At the same time, this diversity of valuable approaches points to the fact that neither IR nor Security Studies are 'an American social science', as was so often proclaimed (Hoffmann 1977; see also Biersteker 2009; Wæver 1998).

Of course, next to these two major conflicts, there are many other minor or middling brawls to be observed in the field of Security Studies, which we do not mention here, though many of them will continue to strongly enrich the debate in the future. One issue that we think does merit attention, however briefly, is related, once again, to the question of when something is or is not a security issue. It is also related to the security environment and the question of whether it has changed to a degree that justifies new or different approaches. Put bluntly, Security Studies are not truly international – in the sense that they are concerned with foreign affairs and global issues among states within the international system – so that we could even question whether it makes sense to call them a sub-discipline of IR. It is a truism nowadays that the forces of globalization have led to internal issues becoming externalized and external issues becoming internationalized (Collins 2007b: 2f.). Particularly when we ask ourselves why and how an issue becomes a security issue – as approaches related to the Copenhagen school do – the focus is not on the international sphere, but on domestic politics and in particular on the politics of threats and insecurity.

The new environment also forces us to take a close look at security measures and instruments, many of which are more associated with the local than the global and with the 'ordinary' rather than the exceptional. Some researchers have observed that in the current (in-)security environment, achieving absolute security is no longer possible (Kristensen 2008).[4] The logical consequence of such observations is that one has to manage the residual *risk* nationally and regionally as well as on an international level. This is a concept that clearly becomes more important for understanding the ontology of contemporary challenges (Aradau and van Munster 2007; Daase and Kessler 2007; Rasmussen 2006). In this way, security is turned from a condition that is inherently binary – meaning that either one is secure or one is not – into a future state of being that is continually approached through risk management. At the same time, many of the current security discourses are no longer primarily about threats and battles against an enemy, but they are characterized by an inward-looking narrative about vulnerabilities and protection. Such a development questions the perception of security as 'exceptional' and indicates that security is not only about 'utterances referring to dangerous futures', but also points to the technologies and strategies by means of which security is sought and produced (C.A.S.E. Collective 2006: 469).

Given this diverse and changing landscape, we decided to adopt a vantage point that allowed us to explore all the undulations that contemporary International Relations theory now entails. And as such, we believe that all theoretical approaches hold a degree of validity and certainly merit attention. We therefore left the choice of which theoretical approach to use, or whether to use one at all, to the contributors. This Handbook has four parts: the first looks at a wide variety of theoretical positions, from the historically dominant traditions to powerful critical voices since the 1980s, and focuses on specific conceptions of security. The second part addresses a number of contemporary security topics, including terrorism as well as climate change and other topical transnational issues. The third part analyses specific regional security issues, before turning to the fourth part on available tools and instruments to counter these challenges.

At the same time (as with photography, where external conditions such as the weather or the light are crucial), not everything was completely in our power. Some conditions had been predetermined, such as the maximum length of the volume or that it should be a volume on Security Studies – and not, for example, on insecurity studies (Huysmans 2006) or New Security Studies (Burgess 2010). In addition, some of the exclusions were voluntary, while others were less deliberate: in more than one case, a shadow fell on the landscape; and not everything that we thought should be included could be included. For example, Africa as a region is probably under-represented. A chapter on security in developing countries is missing, as is a chapter on homeland security. There was no space to pay tribute to the history or historiography of Security Studies, or indeed the role of religion and conflict. Some of the contributions are more timeless than others, but in any case, in the age of digital photography, corrections are possible even after the photo session. We do hope, therefore, that some of the potential omissions can be addressed in a next edition.

Notes

1 Of course, this development notwithstanding, security has always been a very prominent issue, turning it not only into 'high' politics, but actually 'the highest' politics. Or, as Der Derian puts it: 'no other concept in international relations packs the metaphysical punch, or commands the disciplinary power, of "security"' (1995: 24).

2 At times, scholars have argued that IR was in fact a sub-field of security and not the other way around, as IR was depicted as dealing almost exclusively with deterrence and compellence (Jervis 1991: 80).

3 However, this kind of historiography implies a danger of its own, as Schmidt and others like to point out. For example, through this particular writing of history, numerous theoretical insights and writings have been 'erased from memory' (Schmidt 2002: 4). In addition, simplified and simplifying historical accounts give rise to specific and fairly powerful myths regarding the evolution of the field. While we do not argue that all of these accounts are wrong, we would argue, like Schmidt, that one must be careful not to fall into the trap of simply repeating what is generally represented as historical facts – especially since this history is in need of more careful and more detailed delineation.

4 Even if we do not believe that it has ever been possible to achieve absolute security: during the Cold War, there was at least the illusion that it could be achieved.

References

Aradau, C. and van Munster, R. (2007) 'Governing terrorism through risk: Taking precautions, (un) knowing the future', *European Journal of International Relations* 13, 1: 89–115.

Baldwin, D.A. (1997) 'The concept of security', *Review of International Studies* 23, 1: 5–26.

Biersteker, T.J. (2009) 'The parochialism of hegemony: Challenges for "American" international relations', in Tickner, A. and Wæver, O. (eds) *International Relations Scholarship around the World*, London: Routledge.

Booth, K. (1991) 'Security in anarchy: Utopian realism in theory and practice', *International Affairs* 67, 3: 527–45.

Brown, L.R. (1977) 'Redefining national security', *Worldwatch Paper* 14, Washington, DC: Worldwatch Institute.

Burgess, P. (ed.) (2010) *Handbook of New Security Studies*, London: Routledge.

Buzan, B. (1991) *People, States and Fear: An Agenda for International Security Studies in the Post-Cold War Era*, 2nd edn, Boulder: Lynne Rienner.

Buzan, B., Wæver, O. and de Wilde, J. (1998) *Security: A New Framework for Analysis*, Boulder: Lynne Rienner.

C.A.S.E. Collective (2006) 'Critical approaches to security in Europe: A networked manifesto', *Security Dialogue* 37, 4: 443–87.

——(2007) 'Europe, knowledge, politics engaging with the limits: The C.A.S.E. collective responds', *Security Dialogue* 38, 4: 559–76.

Chapman, J. (1992) 'The future of security studies: Beyond grand strategy', *Survival* 34, 1: 109–31.

Collins, A. (2007a) (ed.) *Contemporary Security Studies*, Oxford: Oxford University Press.

——(2007b) 'Introduction: What is security studies?' in: Collins, A. (ed.) *Contemporary Security Studies*, Oxford: Oxford University Press, pp. 1–10.

Daase, C. and Kessler, O. (2007) 'Knowns and unknowns in the "War on Terror": Uncertainty and the political construction of danger', *Security Dialogue* 38, 4: 411–34.

Der Derian, J. (1995) 'The value of security: Hobbes, Marx, Nietzsche, and Baudrillard', in Ronnie D. Lipschutz (ed.) *On Security*, New York: Columbia University Press, pp. 24–45.

Falk, R. (1995) *On Humane Governance: Toward a New Global Politics*, Cambridge: Polity Press.

Guilhot, N. (2008) 'The realist gambit: Postwar American political science and the birth of IR theory', *International Political Sociology* 2, 4: 281–304.

Hoffmann, S. (1977) 'An American social science: International relations', *Daedalus* 106, 3: 41–60.

Huysmans, J. (2006) 'International politics of insecurity: Normativity, inwardness and the exception', *Security Dialogue* 37, 1: 11–29.

——(2008) 'The jargon of exception – On Schmitt, Agamben and the absence of political society', *International Political Sociology* 2, 2: 165–83.

Jervis, R. (1991) 'Models and cases in the study of international conflict', in Robert L. Rothstein (ed.) *The Evolution of Theory in International Relations*, Columbia: University of South California Press, pp. 61–81.

Kolodziej, E.A. (2000) 'Security studies for the next millennium: Quo vadis', in Croft, S. and Terriff, T. (eds) *Critical Reflections on Security and Change*, London: Frank Cass, pp. 18–38.

——(2005) *Security and International Relations*, Cambridge: Cambridge University Press.

Kristensen, K.S. (2008) '"The absolute protection of our citizens": Critical infrastructure protection and the practice of security', in Dunn Cavelty, M. and Kristensen, K.S. (eds) *The Politics of Securing the Homeland: Critical Infrastructure, Risk and Securitisation*, London: Routledge, pp. 63–83.

Matthews, J. Tuchman (1989) 'Redefining security', *Foreign Affairs* 68, 2: 162–77.

Mearsheimer, J. (1995) 'A realist reply', *International Security* 20, 1: 82–93.

Rasmussen, M.V. (2006) *The Risk Society at War: Terror, Technology and Strategy in the Twenty-First Century*, Cambridge: Cambridge University Press.

Schmidt, B.C. (2002) 'On the history and historiography of international relations', in Carlsnaes, W., Risse, T. and Simmons, B.A. (eds) *Handbook of International Relations*, London: Sage, pp. 1–22.

Ullman, R.H. (1983) 'Redefining security', *International Security* 8, 1: 129–53.

Wæver, O. (1995) 'Securitization and desecuritization' in Lipschutz, R. (ed.) *On Security*, New York: Colombia University Press, pp. 46–86.

——(1998) 'The sociology of a not so international discipline: American and European developments in international relations', *International Organization* 52, 4: 687–727.

Wæver, O. and Buzan, B. (2007) 'After the return to theory: The past, present, and future of security studies', in Collins, A. (ed.) *Contemporary Security Studies*, Oxford: Oxford University Press, pp. 383–402.

Walt, S. (1991) 'The renaissance of security studies', *International Studies Quarterly* 35, 2: 211–39.

Westing, A.H. (1989) 'The environmental component of comprehensive security', *Bulletin of Peace Proposals* 20, 2: 129–34.

Wolfers, A. (1952) 'National security as an ambiguous symbol', *Political Science Quarterly* 67, 4: 481–502.

Part I

Theoretical approaches to security and different 'securities'

Realism and security studies

William C. Wohlforth

It is impossible to understand contemporary Security Studies without a grounding in realism.[1] After all, many of the most influential theories that have ever been advanced about violence and security among human groups fall within this intellectual tradition.[2] Given the many scholarly criticisms of realism, ongoing debates about its place in security studies and the proliferation in recent years of such realist 'brands' as defensive, offensive and neoclassical realism, gaining such a grounding might seem a formidable undertaking. In fact, the task has been made easier by all this controversy and complexity. As this chapter shows, realist thinking is now far more robust and rigorous than ever, making it much more accessible and useful to security scholars. This chapter provides the four key elements that students of international security need to make use of realism: a simple definition of realism that distinguishes it from other approaches; an introduction to the various sub-schools of realist thought, such as neoclassical realism, which help to bring order to the daunting diversity of realist scholarship; an outline of some of the most prominent realist theories, which do the actual work of explaining puzzling real-world phenomena; and a sketch of contemporary realist contribution to Security Studies.

Defining realism

Realism is a school of thought based on three core assumptions about how the world works:[3]

1 *Groupism.* Politics takes place within and between groups. Group solidarity is essential to domestic politics, and conflict and cooperation between polities is the essence of international politics. To survive at anything above a subsistence level, people need the cohesion provided by group solidarity, yet that very same in-group cohesion generates the potential for conflict with other groups. Today, the most important human groups are nation-states, and the most important source of in-group cohesion is nationalism. For convenience, this chapter uses the term 'states'. But it is important to stress that realism makes no assumption about the nature of the polity. It may apply to any social setting where groups interact.

2 *Egoism.* When individuals and groups act politically, they are driven principally by narrow self-interest. Although certain conditions can facilitate altruistic behaviour, egoism is rooted in human nature. When push comes to shove, and ultimate trade-offs between collective and self-interest must be confronted, egoism tends to trump altruism. As the classic realist adage has it, 'Inhumanity is just humanity under pressure.'

3 *Power-centrism.* Once past the hunter–gatherer stage, human affairs are always marked by great inequalities of power in both senses of that term: social influence or *control* (some groups and individuals always have an outsized influence on politics) and *resources* (some groups and individuals are always disproportionately endowed with the material wherewithal to get what they want). The key to politics in any area is the interaction between social and material power, an interaction that unfolds in the shadow of the potential use of material power to coerce. As Kenneth Waltz put it:

> The web of social and political life is spun out of inclinations and incentives, deterrent threats and punishments. Eliminate the latter two, and the ordering of society depends entirely on the former – a utopian thought impractical this side of Eden.
>
> (Waltz 1979: 186)

Realism's most important single argument builds on these assumptions to illuminate a relationship between political order and security: if human affairs are indeed characterized by groupism, egoism and power-centrism, then politics is likely to be conflictual unless there is some central authority to enforce order. When no authority exists that can enforce agreements – in a state of 'anarchy' – then any actor can resort to force to get what it wants. Even if an actor can be fairly sure that no other will take up arms today, there is no guarantee against the possibility that one might do so tomorrow. Because no actor can rule out this prospect, all tend to arm themselves against this contingency. With all actors thus armed, politics takes on a different cast. Disputes that would be easy to settle if actors could rely on some higher authority to enforce an agreement can escalate to war in the absence of such authority. The signature realist argument is therefore that anarchy renders security problematic, potentially conflictual and is a key underlying cause of war.

This argument is not restricted to international politics. It identifies a fundamental and universal human problem that may apply to individuals as well as city-states, tribes, empires or nation-states. The point simply is that insecurity is endemic to anarchy. To be secure, people need to overcome anarchy. One way to do this is to strengthen the bonds within a group to provide governance. This is what states do – or what they are supposed to do. If they fail, then life within a state can become just as threatened by insecurity as life between states. The dilemma is that solving the anarchy problem within one group only magnifies it among groups. Much realist thought is thus focused on how the security problem manifests itself in inter-group relations, but its insights are applicable to politics at all levels of analysis.

Realism's diversity: theoretical schools

Realism today is marked by the coexistence of numerous sub-schools, notably defensive, offensive and neoclassical realism. These sub-schools are the outgrowth of sharp debates among scholars as well as unceasing efforts to check realist ideas against international political reality. It all began with classical realism – a term scholars use to describe the whole realist tradition in all its diversity as it unfolded up to the 1970s. For the subsequent development of International Relations theory, however, one classical realist text stands far above all others: Hans J. Morgenthau's *Politics Among Nations* (Morgenthau 1954). This book inaugurated the practice of seeking to translate the realist tradition of scholarship and statecraft into what Morgenthau, in the famous first chapter of his text, called 'a realist theory of international politics'.[4]

Morgenthau's major text did bring realist arguments to bear on a very large number of phenomena: war, peace, cooperation, international law, diplomacy, ethics, international organization, world public opinion and more, but it simply failed to hold together as a unified theory, at least in the eyes of his critics. Even fellow realists found Morgenthau's theory beset by 'open contradictions, ambiguity and vagueness' (Tucker 1952: 214). Key concepts such as the 'national interest' or 'the balance of power' were either undefined or defined in multiple and mutually contradictory ways. Not surprisingly, arguments deployed in different issues areas did not always cohere. By the 1960s, many scholars of International Relations had come to see the natural sciences as models for social science. For them, a 'theory' had to be a coherent set of linked propositions, preferably falsifiable and empirically verified, that explains some phenomena. In this context, Morgenthau's more modest and more humanistic understanding of what a theory of international politics can and should be seemed increasingly anachronistic (Williams 2007). And these scholarly criticisms mounted just as the world's security preoccupations were moving from the great-power contest between the US and the Soviet Union towards issues such as inequality between the wealthy north and the developing south, resource scarcity and human rights. Morgenthau's version of realism seemed out of sync with the times. Out of this first post-war 'crisis' or realism came a revival of realist thinking that came to be called 'neorealism'.

Neorealism and security studies

As scholarly criticism of realism mounted in the 1960s and 1970s and the interest in the scientific approach to the study of politics grew (especially in the US), Kenneth Waltz sought to revivify realist thinking by translating some core realist ideas into a deductive, top-down theoretical framework that eventually came to be called neorealism. Waltz (1959) held that classical realists' powerful insights into the workings of international politics were weakened by their failure to distinguish clearly between arguments about human nature, the internal attributes of states and the overall system of states. His *Theory of International Politics* (Waltz 1979) brought together and clarified many earlier realist ideas about how the features of the overall system of states affect security affairs. He presented the book as the transformation of classical realist 'thought' into a theory on the scientific model, in keeping with the contemporary expectations of the wider discipline of political science.

By restating in the clearest form yet realism's key argument about how the mere existence of groups in anarchy can lead to powerful competitive pressure and war – regardless of what the internal politics of those groups might be like – Waltz presented a theory that purported to answer a few important but highly general questions about international politics: why the modern states-system has persisted in the face of attempts by certain states at dominance; why war among great powers recurred over centuries; and why states often find cooperation hard. In addition, the book forwarded one more specific theory: that great-power war would tend to be more frequent in multipolarity (an international system shaped by the power of three or more major states) than bipolarity (an international system shaped by the power of two major states or superpowers). Events in the real world seemed to underline the salience of Waltz's seemingly abstract ideas. No sooner had Waltz published his book than the Cold War rivalry heated up, driving the world back into intense great-power security competition and reinforcing the sense that bipolarity was indeed a powerful structural force shaping international security.

Yet even in the 1980s, it was clear that neorealism left a great many questions about international security unanswered: why alliances form; why arms races begin and end; why states create international institutions; why the Cold War began; why the superpower rivalry waxed and waned; and many more. The overwhelming majority of scholars seeking to address those questions not surprisingly found Waltz's theory – constructed to address different and usually much more general questions – insufficient. Most responded by using Waltz's work as a foil for developing self-consciously non-realist explanations of specific puzzles or, more ambitiously, for developing alternative theoretical schools, most notably institutionalism (Keohane 1984) and constructivism (Wendt 1999). But some responded by developing their own realist theories even as they endeavoured to make use of Waltz's. For example, in seeking to explain alliance behaviour, Stephen M. Walt (1987) integrated insights from Waltz into a new, related but clearly distinct 'balance of threat' theory (discussed below), while Glen Snyder (1997) combined Waltz's theories with other complementary theories. In explaining cooperation, Joseph Grieco (1988) supplemented Waltz's theory with propositions from game theory. A great many scholars used Waltz's theory as part of more complex explanations for more specific puzzles or events.

Thus, even though Waltz, like Morgenthau, presented his work as a single stand-alone realist 'theory of international politics', the natural development of scholarly inquiry led to the development of neorealism as a complex sub-school within realism that encompassed many Waltz-inspired theories. What linked the research of these scholars was a common bet that Waltz's reformulation of realism was the best place to start inquiry. These links were often unclear, and the boundaries of the school debatable, but the term 'neorealism' captures the profound influence Waltz had on the thinking and research of many other realist scholars.

Offensive and defensive realism

The advent of neorealism sparked a major debate that still reverberates among scholars. The debate was well underway before the Berlin Wall fell, but the Cold War's end seemed to many scholars to undermine neorealist theory and so had the effect of intensifying critical scrutiny of Waltz's ideas. The criticisms added up to a second post-war crisis of realism that was easily as consequential as the antirealist storm that had pummelled Morgenthau in the 1960s and 1970s. While the focus at the time was on the theory's deficiencies – and neorealism has never recovered the scholarly influence it attained in the 1980s – in hindsight, it is clear that neorealism had caused scholars to think much harder and more clearly about the underlying forces that drive International Relations. Realists working with Waltz's theory discovered that, depending on how they thought about the core assumptions and what they saw as the most reasonable expectations about real-world conditions, neorealism could lead to very different predictions. Written in a highly abstract manner, Waltz's neorealism ignored important variations in

International Relations, including geography and technology. Depending on how one conceptualized those factors, the very same neorealist ideas could generate widely disparate implications about the dynamics of interstate politics. Out of this realization were born two new theoretical sub-schools, each of which built on the basic insights of neorealism: defensive realism and offensive realism.

Building on core ideas presented in Waltz's *Theory of International Politics* and, arguably even more importantly, on the pioneering work of Robert Jervis (1986) on cooperation under anarchy, defensive realists reasoned that under very common conditions, the war-causing potential of anarchy is attenuated (Taliaferro 2000/1). Proceeding from the core realist assumption about groupism, these theorists argued that the stronger the group identity is − as in the modern era of nationalism − the harder it is to conquer and sub-jugate other groups (Van Evera 1999). And the harder the conquest is, the more secure all states can be. Similarly, technology may make conquest hard − for example, it is hard to contemplate the conquest of states that have the capacity to strike back with nuclear weapons. Thus, even accepting all of Waltz's arguments about how difficult it is to be secure in an anarchic world, under these kinds of conditions, states could still be expected to find ways of defending themselves without threatening others, or could otherwise signal their peaceful intentions, resulting in an international system with more built-in potential for peace than many realists previously thought (Glaser 1994/95). The result was to push analysts to look inside states for the domestic and ideational causes of war and peace.

Offensive realists, by contrast, were more persuaded by the conflict-generating, structural potential of anarchy itself. They reasoned that, with no authority to enforce agreements, states could never be certain that any peace-causing condition today would remain operative in the future. Even if conquest may seem hard today due to geography, tech-nology or group identity, there is no guarantee that another state will not develop some fiendish device for overcoming these barriers. Given this uncertainty, states can rarely be confident of their security and must always view other states' increases in power with suspicion. As a result, states are often tempted to expand or otherwise strengthen them-selves − and/or to weaken others − in order to survive in the long term. The result is to reinforce the classic realist argument about the competitive nature of life under anarchy, regardless of the internal properties of states.

Defensive and offensive realism emerged in the 1990s as outgrowths of Waltz's neorealism. In keeping with the tradition established by Waltz and Morgenthau, many of the scholars who developed these theories saw them as articulating *the* realist theory. Thus, scholars framed much defensive realist theorizing as developments of Waltz's neorealism. In *The Tragedy of Great Power Politics*, John J. Mearsheimer portrays offensive realism as *the* successor to Waltz's neorealism, which he equates with defensive realism. But it is impossible to put the genie of realism's diversity back into the bottle. It is clear that defensive and offensive realism coexist as distinct sub-schools. And those two sub-schools hardly exhaust realism's diversity, for many other realist theories fall outside either of them.

A telling example of this diversity is the work of Waltz's contemporary Robert Gilpin, whose magisterial *War and Change in World Politics* (1981) is seen by many as a more important and lasting theoretical contribution than Waltz's (Danspeckgruber forthcoming). Written and conceived completely independently from Waltz's *Theory*, Gilpin's work was no less realist. It provided an elegant theoretical framework to explain the links between shifting power balances, order and war over centuries. Furthermore, many of the theo-retical ideas in Morgenthau's *Politics Among Nations*, particularly those relating to the analysis of foreign policy, retained potential relevance, but had fallen by the wayside in

Waltz's reformulation of realism. It was the sense that too many important realist ideas had been lost in the transition to neorealism and the closely related sub-schools of offensive and defensive realism that gave rise to the sub-school that eventually came to be called 'neoclassical realism'.

Neoclassical realism

Neoclassical realism is a problem-focused sub-school within realism that embraces rather than denies realism's diversity. Works in this sub-school share two features: a focus on the explanation of specific puzzles or events; and the effort to recapture important realist insights that were lost in the neorealists' obsessive search for the one overarching realist theory of international politics. As clear and elegant as neorealism and its immediate outgrowths were, it remained unclear just how relevant they were to any given foreign policy problem. So focused were realists on defining the single best and most universal formulation of their theory that it began to seem as if the development of realism had taken a completely different path from the analysis of foreign policy. Waltz (1996) himself famously argued that 'international politics is not foreign policy', implying that theory development and foreign policy analysis had become two distinct endeavours with little connection to each other.

Neoclassical realism seeks to rectify this imbalance between the general and the particular. It accepts from neorealism and its descendents the basic utility of thinking theoretically about the international system as distinct from the internal properties of states (Rose 1998). Having carefully specified their assessment of the international conditions particular states face, however, neoclassical realists go on to factor in specific features of a given situation to generate more complete explanations of foreign policy. They seek to recapture the grounding in the gritty details of foreign policy that marked classical realism, while also benefiting from the rigorous theorizing that typified neorealism.

Neoclassical realists are not driven by the dream of creating the one universal theory of international politics. For them, the question is: which realist school or theory (if any) is most useful for explaining a given puzzle or analysing issues of foreign policy at a given place and time? To some extent, the choice of theory is a contextual issue. For example, offensive realism provides a powerful shorthand portrayal of the incentives and constraints states faced in parts of Europe for long stretches of the eighteenth to twentieth centuries. In other periods, and for some groups of states in Europe, defensive realism arguably provides a more accurate model of the international setting.

The degree to which a theoretical picture of the international system really applies is a matter of judgement, based on the analyst's reading of the context. Neoclassical realists remain agnostic over which theoretical proposition may apply; they bring to bear those theories that are arguably relevant. While they are agnostic over which theory or theoretical school may apply, they agree that theory helps strengthen analysis. A basic question constantly recurs in Security Studies. To what extent is a given change (e.g. globalization, the spread of democracy, new norms and international institutions) changing the basic incentives for the use for force? Answering that question requires some theory about what international security would be like in the absence of the transformation in question. The key contribution of neorealism and its offshoot sub-schools of offensive and defensive realism is rigorous thinking about such a theory. For neoclassical realists, theoretical structures like offensive and defensive realism are not always and everywhere true or false. Rather, they make it easier to perform the key mental experiments that lie at the core of foreign policy analysis by helping analysts frame their assessments the external constraints and incentives states face.

Realist theories

Sub-schools within realism help the student figure out the intellectual connections between scholars, how various arguments are related and how scholarship progresses. Equally important are specific theories about the fundamental constraints and incentives that shape behaviour and outcomes in international politics. When the issue at hand is a real explanatory problem – such as the effort to explain puzzling security dynamics in a particular issue area or regional setting – analysts should take recourse to the specific theories that appear to be relevant, such as theories of the balance-of-power and balance-of-threat, security dilemma, offence–defence balance, hegemonic stability and power transition. Certainly, there are numerous other realist or realist-related theories, but even this list makes the main point: realist theories, which do the real work of explanation, are far more diverse than any one theoretical sub-school within realism.

Arguably, the best-known theoretical proposition about international relations is *balance-of-power theory*. Given the basic problem that, under conditions of anarchy, any state can resort to force to get what it wants, it follows that states are likely to guard against the possibility that one state might amass the wherewithal to compel all the others to do its will and even possibly eliminate them. The theory posits that states will check dangerous concentrations of power by building up their own capabilities ('internal balancing') or aggregating their capabilities with other states in alliances ('external balancing'). Because states are always looking to the future to anticipate possible problems, balancing may occur even before any one state or alliance has gained an obvious power edge. Thus, in the view of many historians, Britain and France fought the Russian Empire in Crimea in the middle of the nineteenth century less because they saw an immediate challenge to their position than because they reasoned that, if unchecked, Russian power might someday be a threat to them. However wise or unwise it may have been, the thinking in London and Paris at this time was entirely consistent with the expectations of balance-of-power theory.

Balance-of-threat theory adds complexity to this picture. As its name implies, this theory predicts that states will balance against threats. Threat, in turn, is driven by a combination of three key variables: aggregate capabilities (that is, its overall military and economic potential), geography and perceptions of aggressive intentions. If one state becomes particularly powerful and if its location and behaviour feed threat perceptions on the part of other states, then balancing strategies will come to dominate their foreign policies. Thus, the US began both external and internal balancing after the end of the Second World War, even though the Soviet Union remained decidedly inferior in most categories of power. Ultimately, the Western alliance overwhelmed the Soviet-led alliance on nearly every dimension. Balance-of-threat theory holds that it was the location of Soviet power in the heart of Europe, as well as the threat inherent in its secretive government and perceived aggressiveness that produced this outcome (Walt 1987).

Security dilemma theory: The 'security dilemma' is a term coined by John Herz (1950) for the argument that in arming for self-defence, a state might *decrease* its security via the

15

unintended effect of making others insecure, prompting them to arm in response. In a hugely influential article, Robert Jervis (1986) showed how this consequence of anarchy could lead security-seeking states into costly spirals of mistrust and rivalry. He argued that the severity of the security dilemma depends on two variables: the balance between offence and the ability to distinguish offence from defence. Thus, although anarchy is theoretically a constant, 'there can be significant variation in the attractiveness of cooperative or competitive means, the prospects for achieving a high level of security, and the probability of war' (Glaser 1997: 172). The article prompted a major debate among realists that eventually ended up in the two sub-schools of offensive and defensive realism. Barry Posen (1993) demonstrated how security dilemma theory can be deployed to explain ethnic conflict with states, opening a rich avenue for research relevant to state collapse and civil war.

Offence–defence theory is an offshoot of Jervis's development of security dilemma theory. As developed by Charles Glaser (1994/95), Stephen Van Evera (1999) and others (Lynn-Jones 1995; Glaser and Kaufman 1998; Brown et al. 2004), this is a set of theoretical propositions about how technology, geography and other factors affect the ease of conquest as opposed to defence, as well as the ease of distinguishing between offensive and defensive postures. Its main prediction is that militarized conflict and war are more likely when offensive military operations have the relative advantage over defensive operations, while peace and cooperation are more likely when defence dominates. Similarly, the easier it is to distinguish offensive from defensive military preparations, the greater the probability of peace and cooperation. The theory also extends to perceptions: when leaders believe offence is relatively easy, war and conflict are more likely and vice versa. This has spawned a massive literature that seeks to explain the origins of perceptions and misperceptions of the offence–defence balance (Snyder 1984; Van Evera 1999). Posen (1993) adapted offence–defence theory to help explain the intensity of competition of groups within states when faced with the security problems that may arise when state authority breaks down.

Hegemonic stability theory builds on the observation that powerful states tend to seek dominance over all or parts of any international system, thus fostering some degree of hierarchy within the overall systemic anarchy. It seeks to explain how cooperation can emerge among major powers, and how international orders – comprising rules, norms and institutions – emerge and are sustained. The theory's core prediction is that any international order is stable only to the degree that the relations of authority within it are sustained by the underlying distribution of power (Gilpin 1981). According to this theory, the current 'globalization' order is sustained by US power and is likely to come undone as challengers like China gain strength.

Power transition theory is a subset of hegemonic stability that seeks to explain how orders break down into war. Building on the premises of hegemonic stability theory, it deduces that dominant states will prefer to retain leadership, that lesser states' preference for contesting that leadership will tend to strengthen as they become stronger relative to the dominant state, and that this clash is likely to come to the fore as the capabilities of the two sides approach parity (Tammen et al. 2000). Applied to the current context, the theory posits that the stronger China becomes, the more likely it is to become dissatisfied with the US-led global order. It predicts that a war or at least a Cold War-style rivalry between the US and China is likely unless China's growth slows down or Washington finds a way to accommodate Beijing's preferences.

Contemporary realist scholarship and security studies

It has been argued in this chapter that realism is not now and never has been a monolithic and universal 'theory of international politics'. It has always been diverse, with even its grandest theories contingent in scope if not name. The chief development of the last 15 years has been a greater recognition of this fact, as well as an associated decline in realism's centrality to the discipline. With the advent of neoclassical realism, meanwhile, realist research has become more problem-focused, and its interactions with research from other traditions more complex and arguably more productive.

All of this is good news for Security Studies. The accumulation of new and important research by scholars working within the realist tradition has figured centrally in recent scholarship on international security. This includes work that seeks to account for general phenomena, such as the origins of war (Copeland 2000); regional war and peace (Miller 2007); suboptimal under-provision of security by states (Schweller 2006); great-power military interventions (Taliaferro 2004); threat assessment (Lobell 2003); the origins of revisionist state preferences (Davidson 2006); the constraints on peace settlements after major wars (Ripsman 2002); the dynamics of unipolarity (Wohlforth 1999, 2009; Pape 2005), to mention only a few. It also includes research explaining more discrete events or behaviours, such as US foreign policy in the Cold War (McAllister 2002; Dueck 2006); the end of the Cold War (Schweller and Wohlforth 2000); US, South Korean and Japanese strategies *vis-à-vis* the North Korean nuclear crisis (Cha 2000); the evolution of US monetary policy after the demise of the Bretton Woods monetary system (Sterling-Folker 2002); the origins of the Bush administration's approach to foreign policy and the invasion of Iraq (Layne 2005; Dueck 2006); and many others.

These works are eclectic. Most avoid chest-thumping advocacy on behalf of realism. Many expend considerable effort finding fault with other realist works. Nevertheless, if they had to be classified as being in one theoretical school, all would end up in the realist column. All share a sensitivity to realist core insights, a central role for the three key assumptions that define realism, and an appreciation of how neorealism and its successor sub-schools can aid in analysis. At the same time, most are open to the insights of classical realism and lack dogmatic attachment to one theory or another. While they hardly represent the last word on the respective subjects, in aggregate, they stand as testimony to the ongoing contributions of realism to Security Studies.

Conclusion

Realist theories remain an important, if insufficient, part of the Security Studies toolkit. Once we set aside the fruitless debate over which overarching theory trumps all others, the diversity of realist scholarship comes to light. The advent of new sub-schools of realist thought, such as offensive, defensive and neoclassical realism, help to organize this diversity and make sense of the many theories that have grown out of the realist tradition. As a result, it is easier for today's security scholars to make sense – and use – of realist theories than it was 10 or 20 years ago. Also, thanks in part to these developments within realism, it is much easier for realists and scholars working in other intellectual traditions to interact productively, as evidenced by a burgeoning literature that bridges realism and constructivism (e.g. Bukovansky 2002; Goddard and Nexon 2005; Sterling-Folker 2002).

Needless to say, today's complex mix of classical, great-power security issues such as the rise of China, Russia and India; equally classic but newly salient phenomena such as civil war and terrorism; and novel problems like nuclear proliferation present new challenges to scholars working within and outside the realist tradition. Realist scholarship still has not come fully to terms with research findings on the effects of domestic institutions on international conflict – arguably, the most significant development in Security Studies over the last two decades. For their part, democratic peace researchers have yet to take on board the implications of more fine-grained realist theories, which predict much more variation in states' conflict behaviour than neorealism. Both need to grapple with older theories from the classical realist tradition concerning the effect of international systemic conditions on domestic institutions. Realists are still struggling with the implications of nuclear proliferation. They remain unsure of the security implications of the spread of weak and non-survivable nuclear arsenals.

Arguably, the issue that is most ripe for more work is the interaction between international security and the global economy. Decades ago, pioneering scholars such as Robert Gilpin (1975, 1986) and Stephen Krasner (1986; 1991) explored the links between state power, international institutions and the international political economy. Many of the core ideas they propounded fell by the wayside as scholars studying security and political economy went their separate ways. But recent works have begun to re-engage this interaction. Stephen Brooks (2005) shows how the globalization of production by multinational corporations has 'changed the calculus of conflict'. Jonathan Kirshner (2007; see also Kirshner 2006) demonstrates the links between financial interests and states' propensity towards war. As these works demonstrate, in a world of dramatic economic change amid rapidly shifting interstate power balances, realist scholarship has a lot more to offer security studies.

Notes

1 This chapter draws heavily on Wohlforth (2008) and to a lesser extent on Wohlforth (2007).
2 Between 1991 and 2001, for example, citations of the chief contributions to the balance-of-power literature dwarfed those concerning all the other major propositions in conflict studies, including the notion of democratic peace (Bennett and Stam 2004).
3 Here I follow Gilpin (1996: 7f.). See Donnelly (2000: 7f.) for a good list of representative defining assumptions of realism.
4 Carr's *Twenty Years' Crisis* (1946) does seek to advance IR as a science, but does not explicitly articulate an overarching theory.

References

Ashley, R.J. (1986) 'The poverty of neorealism', in Keohane, R. (ed.) *Neorealism and its Critics*, New York: Columbia University Press, pp. 255–300.
Bennett, D.S. and Stam, A.C. (2004) *The Behavioral Origins of War*, Ann Arbor: University of Michigan Press.
Brooks, S.G. (2005) *Producing Security: Multinational Corporations, Globalization, and the Changing Calculus of Conflict* Princeton: Princeton University Press.

Brown, M.E., Coté, O.R. Jr., Lynn-Jones, S.M. and Miller, S.E. (eds) (2004) *Offense, Defense and War*, Cambridge, MA: MIT Press.

Bukovansky, M. (2002) *Legitimacy and Power Politics*, Princeton: Princeton University Press.

Carr, E.H. (1946) *The Twenty Years' Crisis, 1919–1939: An Introduction to the Study of International Relations*, 2nd edn, New York: St Martin's Press.

Cha, V. (2000) 'Abandonment, entrapment, and neoclassical realism in Asia: The United States, Japan, and Korea', *International Studies Quarterly* 44, 2: 261–91.

Copeland, D. (2000) *The Origins of Major War*, Ithaca: Cornell University Press.

Danspeckgruber, W. (forthcoming) *Grand Strategy in the Emerging International System: In Honor of Robert G. Gilpin* Liechtenstein Colloquium Report Vol. II, Princeton: Princeton University Press.

Davidson, J.W. (2006) *The Origins of Revisionist and Status Quo States*, New York: Palgrave-Macmillan.

Donnelly, J. (2000) *Realism and International Relations*, Cambridge: Cambridge University Press.

Dueck, C. (2006) *Reluctant Crusaders: Power, Culture and Change in American Grand Strategy*, Princeton: Princeton University Press.

Elman, C. (1996) 'Horses for courses: Why not neorealist theories of foreign policy?', *Security Studies* 6, 1: 7–53.

Gilpin, R.G. (1975) *US Power and the Multinational Corporation*, New York: Basic Books.

——(1981) *War and Change in World Politics*, Cambridge: Cambridge University Press.

——(1986) 'The richness of the tradition of political realism', in Keohane, R. (ed.) *Realism and Its Critics*, New York: Columbia University Press, pp. 301–21.

——(1987) *Political Economy of International Relations*, Princeton: Princeton University Press.

——(1996) 'No one loves a political realist', *Security Studies* 5, 3: 3–26.

Glaser, C.L. (1997) 'The security dilemma revisited', *World Politics* 50, 1: 171–201.

——(1994/95) 'Realists as optimists: Cooperation as self-help', *International Security* 19, 3: 50–90.

Glaser, C.L. and Kaufmann, C. (1998) 'What use the offense–defense balance and can we measure it?' *International Security* 22, 4: 44–82.

Goddard, S. and Nexon, D. (2005) 'Paradigm lost? Reassessing theory of international politics', *European Journal of International Relations* 11, 1: 9–61.

Grieco, J. (1988) 'Realist theory and the problem of international cooperation: Analysis with an amended prisoner's dilemma model', *International Organization* 42, 3: 485–507.

——(1997) 'Realist international theory and the study of world politics', in Doyle, M.W. and Ikenberry, G.J. (eds) *New Thinking in International Relations Theory*, Boulder: Westview Press, pp. 163–77.

Herz, J.H. (1950) 'Idealist internationalism and the security dilemma', *World Politics* 2, 2: 157–80.

Jackson, P. and Nexon, D. (2004) 'Realist constructvism or constructivist realism?' *International Studies Review* 2, 6: 337–41.

Jervis, R. (1986) 'Cooperation under the security dilemma', *World Politics* 30, 4: 167–214.

Keohane, R.O. (1984) *After Hegemony: Cooperation and Discord in the World Political Economy*, Princeton, NJ: Princeton University Press.

Kirshner, J. (ed.) (2006) *Globalization and National Security*, London: Routledge.

——(2007) *Appeasing Bankers: Financial Caution on the Road to War*, Princeton: Princeton University Press.

Krasner, S.M. (1986) *Structural Conflict: The Third World Against Global Liberalism*, Berkeley: University of California Press.

——(1991) 'Global communications and national power: Life on the Pareto frontier', *World Politics* 43, 3: 336–66.

Layne, C. (2005) *The Peace of Illusions*, Ithaca: Cornell University Press.

Lebow, R.N. (2003) *The Tragic Vision of Politics: Ethics, Interests, and Orders*, Cambridge: Cambridge University Press.

Legro, J.W. and Moravscik, A. (1999) 'Is anybody still a realist?' *International Security* 21, 2: 5–55.

Lobell, S.E. (2003) *The Challenge of Hegemony: Grand Strategy, Trade, and Domestic Politics*, Ann Arbor: University of Michigan Press.

Lynn-Jones, S.M. (1995) 'Offense–defense theory and its critics', *Security Studies* 4, 4: 660–91.

19

McAllister, J. (2002) *No Exit: American and the German Problem, 1943–1954*, Ithaca: Cornell University Press.

Mearsheimer, J.J. (2001) *The Tragedy of Great Power Politics*, New York: Norton.

Miller, B. (2007) *States, Nations, and the Great Powers: The Sources of Regional War and Peace*, Cambridge: Cambridge University Press.

Morgenthau, H.J. (1954) *Politics Among Nations: The Struggle for Power and Peace*, 2nd edn, New York: Alfred A. Knopf.

Pape, R. (2005) 'Soft balancing against the United States', *International Security* 30, 1: 7–45.

Posen, B.R. (1993) 'The security dilemma and ethnic conflict', *Survival* 35, 1: 27–47.

Ripsman, N.M. (2002) *Peacemaking by Democracies: The Effects of States Autonomy on the Post World War Settlements*, University Park: Pennsylvania State University Press.

Rose, G. (1998) 'Neoclassical realism and theories of foreign policy', *World Politics* 51, 1: 144–72.

Schweller, R.L. (2003) 'The progressivism of neoclassical realism', in Elman, C. and Elman, M.F. (eds) *Progress in International Relations Theory: Appraising the Field*, Cambridge: MIT Press, pp. 311–48.

——(2006) *Unanswered Threats: Political Constraints on the Balance of Power*, Ithaca: Cornell University Press.

Schweller, R.L. and Wohlforth, W.C. (2000) 'Power test: Evaluating realism in response to the end of the Cold War', *Security Studies* 9: 1: 60–107.

Snyder, G.H. (1997) *Alliance Politics*, Ithaca, NY: Cornell University Press.

Snyder, J.L. (1984) *The Ideology of the Offensive*, Ithaca, NY: Cornell University Press.

Sterling-Folker, J. (2002) 'Realism and the constructivist challenge: Rejecting, reconstructing, or rereading', *International Studies Review* 4, 1: 73–97.

——(2004) 'Realist-constructivism and morality', *International Studies Review* 6, 2: 341–53.

Taliaferro, J.W. (2000/1) 'Security seeking under anarchy: Defensive realism revisited', *International Security* 25, 3: 128–61.

——(2004) *Balancing Risks: Great Power Interventions in the Periphery*, Ithaca, NY: Cornell University Press.

Tammen, R.L. et al. (2000) *Power Transitions: Strategies for the 21st Century*, New York: Chatham House.

Tucker, R.W. (1952) 'Professor Morgenthau's theory of political "realism"', *American Political Science Review* 46, 2: 214–24.

Van Evera, S. (1999) *Causes of War: Structures of Power and the Roots of International Conflict*, Ithaca, NY: Cornell University Press.

Walt, S.M. (1987) *The Origins of Alliances*, Ithaca, NY: Cornell University Press.

Waltz, K.N. (1959) *Man, The State, and War*, New York: Columbia University Press.

——(1979) *Theory of International Politics*, New York: Random House.

——(1991) 'Realist thought and neorealist theory', in Rothstein, R.L. (ed.) *The Evolution of Theory in International Relations: Essays in Honor of William T.R. Fox*, Columbia: University of South Carolina Press, pp. 21–38.

——(1996) 'International politics is not foreign policy', *Security Studies* 6, 1: 54–57.

Wendt, A. (1999) *Social Theory of International Politics*, Cambridge: Cambridge University Press.

Williams, M.C. (2007) 'Introduction', in Williams, M.C. (ed.) *Realism Reconsidered: The Legacy of Hans J. Morgenthau in International Relations*, Oxford: Oxford University Press, pp. 1–17.

Wohlforth, W.C. (1999) 'The stability of a unipolar world', *International Security* 21, 1: 1–36.

——(2007) 'Realism and foreign policy', in Smith, S., Hadfield, A. and Dunne, T. *Foreign Policy: Theories, Actors, Cases*, Oxford: Oxford University Press.

——(2008) 'Realism', in Snidal, D. and Rues-Smit, C. (eds) *Oxford Handbook of International Relations*, Oxford: Oxford University Press.

——(2009) 'Unipolarity, status competition and great power war', *World Politics* 61, 1: 28–57.

2

Liberalism

David L. Rousseau and Thomas C. Walker

Liberalism is an expansive concept that carries a variety of meanings for students of politics. For Doyle (1997: 206), 'liberalism resembles a family portrait of principles and institutions, recognizable by certain characteristics – for example, individual freedom, political participation, private property, and equality of opportunity'. In the realm of International Relations (IR), students look to liberalism to explain how human reason, progress, individual rights and freedoms can give rise to more peaceful interstate relations. Liberals predict that stable democracies and economically interdependent states will behave differently in several respects. First and most importantly, democratic states are less likely to initiate and escalate conflicts with other states (also known as the 'democratic peace theory'). Second, democratic states are more likely to engage in international trade and investment, and the resultant interdependence will contribute to peace. Third, democratic states are more likely to seek cooperative solutions through international institutions. While there are significant differences between individual liberal thinkers, all have a general faith in the pacifying effects of political liberty, economic freedom, interdependence and international association.

Before proceeding, it is important to dispel one persistent myth that has clouded understandings of liberalism: the association between early forms of liberal internationalism and normative-laden versions of idealism. For example, Howard (1978: 11) defined 'liberals' as 'all those thinkers who believe the world to be profoundly other than it should be, and who have faith in the power of human reason and human action so to change it'. But liberal theory provides much more than imagining a world as it *should be*. Like realist theory, liberalism provides a relatively coherent set of principles and propositions that explain or predict interstate relations. By one recent account, quantitative studies testing liberal hypotheses in IR have come to outnumber realist studies (Walker and Morton 2005). Given the prevalence of empirically based liberal studies, liberalism cannot be characterized as a utopian project. Indeed, the worldwide spread of liberalism has been considered 'the defining feature of the late twentieth century' (Simmons et al. 2006: 781).

We begin this chapter by tracing the emergence of liberalism in IR to two leading thinkers of the Enlightenment: Thomas Paine and Immanuel Kant. The works of Paine and Kant highlight all the core principles of liberalism and illustrate the variation (and tensions) within the liberal tradition. After our discussion of these two strands of classical liberalism, we turn to an assessment of recent empirical research that probes the claims articulated by Paine and Kant. Does history support the liberal claims that democratic institutions, economic interdependence and international institutions facilitate peace?

The roots: evolutionary and revolutionary liberalism

Perhaps the most distinguishing feature of liberalism is the belief in a process by which human reason can promote a more prosperous, free and peaceful world. Keohane (2002: 45) noted how 'liberalism believes in at least the possibility of cumulative progress, whereas realism assumes that history is not progressive'. Although progress is not inevitable, or even easily achieved, it is possible, according to liberals. Moreover, we can empirically assess whether progress has occurred by examining evidence of increased human freedom (e.g. the percentage of humans living in democratic polities), economic prosperity (e.g. the percentage of humans suffering from malnourishment) and peace (e.g. the percentage of humans dying in interstate conflicts). Given this emphasis on progress and human reason, most liberal claims can be traced back to the Enlightenment.

In the previous chapter, Wohlforth presented variations of realist theory, including offensive, defensive and neoclassical realisms. Liberalism can also be categorized in a number of ways. Zacher and Matthew (1995: 121) present six strands of liberal international theory. Keohane (2002) and Moravcsik (1997) employ the more conventional categorization of ideational, commercial and republican liberalism. Drawing on Walker (2008), we divide the field into the evolutionary liberalism of Kant and the revolutionary liberalism of Paine. Revolutionary liberals such as Paine typically assume harmonious preferences that facilitate cooperation and progress. In contrast, evolutionary liberals such as Kant recognize a combination of shared and competing preferences that makes cooperation and progress far more difficult.

To organize this survey, we rely on a levels-of-analysis approach made popular by Waltz (1959). Waltz argued that the causes of conflict and cooperation between states can be identified along three levels of analysis: the individual, the state and the international system.

The individual level of analysis: human nature

While Waltz ultimately downplayed the importance of human nature arguments at the individual level of analysis, Lanyi and McWilliams (1966: 8) argued that '*human nature will remain, if not the basis, at least the starting point of all theories of politics*'. From game theoretic models to historical case studies, foundational assumptions about human nature inform any effort to understand politics. This is especially true for the theoretical frameworks of Paine and Kant. Different assumptions about human nature serve as the wedge that divides revolutionary from evolutionary liberalism. In *Rights of Man*, Paine (1791: 169) noted that 'man, were he not corrupted by [non-democratic] governments, is naturally the friend of man, and that human nature is not itself vicious'. Democratic revolution would free mankind from these corrupting influences and human reason would emerge quickly to transform the world. Paine (1791: 230) celebrated 'a morning of reason rising upon man on the subject of government, that has not appeared before'.

Perhaps most importantly, Paine (1791: 178) predicted that the transition to this 'morning of reason' would be swift. He was confident that Europe would be democratic and peaceful by the end of the eighteenth century. This extreme optimism remains the most distinctive characteristic of revolutionary liberal thought.

Turning to evolutionary liberals, we see a far more cautious view of human nature. Kant (1798: 181) depicted human nature as 'mixture of evil and goodness in unknown proportions'. But Kant remained optimistic about man's ability to evolve away from his crass beginnings and benefit through reason. In *Universal History*, Kant (1784: 42) argued that 'reason does not itself work instinctively, for it requires trial, practice, and instruction ... one stage to the next'. Kant (1795: 112) looked to the careful formation of enlightened government to promote man's goodness and repress the bad: 'It only remains for men to create a good organization for the state ... so that man, even if he is not morally good in himself, is nevertheless compelled to be a good citizen.' Thus, for Kant and evolutionary liberals, social forces and governmental institutions must work to compel individuals to be good. This can be a long and often arduous process.

The state-society level: democratic regimes

To best understand how liberalism influences Security Studies, we must turn to the state-society level, which examines the impact of governmental structure and society. Paine and Kant were among the first to articulate why democratic states may behave more peacefully. In *Common Sense*, Paine (1776: 80) pointed out that the republics (i.e. democracies) of the world tended to be peaceful: 'Holland and Swisserland [sic] are without wars, foreign or domestic.' According to Paine (1776: 95), this peace results from the democratic tendency to 'negotiate the mistake' rather than letting regal pride swell 'into a rupture with foreign powers'. Kant made a related claim that if

> the consent of the citizens is required to decide whether or not war is to be declared, it is very natural that they will have great hesitation in embarking on so dangerous an enterprise. For this would mean calling down on themselves all the miseries of war.
>
> (Kant 1795: 100)

Both Paine and Kant initiated the liberal claim that democracies will probably spend less on their militaries than authoritarian regimes. They shared the liberal suspicion that high levels of military spending are dangerous for both domestic and international politics. On the domestic front, they present the classic butter-or-guns dilemma while arguing in favour of butter. Kant (1784: 51) argued that as a result of high military spending, 'the world's present rulers have no money to spare for public educational institutions or indeed for anything which concerns the world's best interests (for everything has been calculated out in advance for the next war)'. To discourage deficit spending for military actions, two of Kant's (1795: 94f.) preliminary articles for perpetual peace sought to abolish standing armies and to ensure that 'no national debt shall be contracted in connection with external affairs of the state'. Paine (1791, 1807) made similar appeals to limit navies to coastal gunboats, rely on a small militia and then re-allocate resources to education and old age pensions.

The second liberal critique of high military spending warns of the dangers associated with increases in power, known widely as the 'spiral model' (Jervis 1976; Glaser 1992). This view maintains that efforts to increase security by increasing armaments may be

23

perceived as threatening by a neighbouring state. Paine (1787: 66) warned against Pitt's military build-ups because 'the sparks of ill will are afresh kindled up between nations, the fair prospects of lasting peace are vanished'. Paine's solution, and one endorsed by nearly all subsequent liberals, was arms reductions. In addition to arms control, Paine (1807) advocated the use of small gunboats that were incapable of straying far from the coastline. By emphasizing weapons that could not be used for offensive purposes, Paine was one of the pioneers of non-provocative defence (Jervis 1978; Galtung 1984).

Kant shared Paine's concerns with how increased military preparation may threaten neighbouring states. Armies, according to Kant (1795: 94), 'constantly threaten other states with war by the very fact that they are always prepared for it ... the armies are themselves the cause of wars'. Kant (1797: 168) later argued that any shift in power 'would create a threat to one state by augmenting the power of another'. Kant, however, was not so quick to endorse easy solutions like universal arms reductions. Kant (1795: 95, 1797: 167) warned that in an anarchical system with authoritarian regimes, states might be forced to either balance power or even launch 'preventative attacks' against those states undergoing rapid military build-ups. Again, Kant's evolutionary liberalism diverges from the optimism of Paine's revolutionary liberalism.

The systemic level

At the systemic level, we examine how states interact with other states in the global system. The peaceful effect of trade remains central to the liberal research tradition. Paine was one of the first popular proponents of free trade as a means of promoting peace. In the widely circulated *Rights of Man*, Paine (1791: 234) asserted that free trade creates 'a pacific system, operating to cordialize mankind, by rendering nations, as well as individuals, useful to each other ... If commerce were permitted to act to the universal extent it is capable, it would extirpate the system of war.' Paine frequently pointed to how trade promotes international understandings, thereby working to 'cordialize' mankind. Economic interaction would work to acquaint nations with one another and reduce misunderstandings that might lead to conflict. Trade not only produces wealth, but also reduces conflict by promoting understanding and unveiling the harmony of interests between all nations.

While Kant also saw trade leading to peace, his reasoning was somewhat distinct from Paine's. A less utopian and more pragmatic Kant posited that trade may lead to peace because of the vested interests of international financiers and businessmen. Kant claimed that

> the *spirit of commerce* sooner or later takes hold of every people, and it cannot exist side by side with war. And of all the powers (or means) at the disposal of the power of the state, *financial power* can probably be relied on most.
>
> (Kant 1795: 114, emphasis in original)

Kant's 'financial powers' and business interests would reduce war throughout the world. To preserve wealth generated through trade, Kant argued,

> states find themselves compelled to promote the noble cause of peace, though not exactly from motives of morality. And wherever in the world there is a threat of war breaking out, they [trading states] will try to prevent it by mediation.
>
> (Kant 1795: 114)

Trade, according to Kant's logic, would only limit wars and those high-level conflicts threatening commerce. For Paine, trade would dampen all conflicts between trading states by bringing to light that natural harmony of interests that characterizes revolutionary liberalism.

On the issue of intervention, revolutionary liberals like Paine advocate military intervention to bring freedom to all people who suffer the injustices brought about by non-democratic governance. In his 1792 dedication of *Rights of Man: Part II*, Paine promised to join the French general Lafayette in 'the Spring Campaign' that will 'terminate in the extinction of German despotism, and in establishing the freedom of all Germany'. Paine's justification for a military intervention was clear: 'When France shall be surrounded with revolutions, she will be in peace and safety.' France's national security, Paine reasoned, depended upon extending political liberty to neighbouring states, even by force of arms.

Kant, on the other hand, issued a firm warning against interventions to shape domestic political institutions. In his *Preliminary Articles of a Perpetual Peace*, Kant (1795: 96) was explicit that 'No state shall forcibly interfere in the constitution and government of another state.' Kant defended the principle on the grounds that

> interference of external powers would be a violation of the rights of an independent people which is merely struggling with its internal ills. Such interference would be an active offence and would make the autonomy of all other states insecure.
>
> (Kant 1795: 96)

Kant reiterated that even the most despotic states should be protected from outside interference. He (1795: 118) argued that 'no state can be required to relinquish its constitution, even if the latter is despotic'. Any governing constitution, Kant continued, is 'better than none at all, and the fate of premature reform would be anarchy'. As an extension of his cautious faith in democratic processes, Kant reasoned that a just society could not be imposed by forces outside the actual polity. Revolutionary liberals like Paine, however, see no virtue in patience when rights are being trodden upon.

These two variations of liberalism provide different views of international law and organization. For Paine (1801: 2), it was 'absolutely necessary that a *Law of Nations* be formed'. Towards this end, he advocated global governance complete with sanctions against any state violating freedom of the seas and generalized embargoes against belligerent powers. Kant's evolutionary liberalism was far less ambitious towards international law. Kant (1795: 113) harboured misgivings over global governance because 'laws progressively lose their impact as the government increases its range, and a soulless despotism ... will finally lapse into anarchy'. However, Kant did have greater faith in the peace-promoting powers of a voluntary confederation of republican states (Kant 1795: 104). Kant does not envision a series of temporary alliances designed to deter war. Rather, he envisions a pacific league that abolishes all wars through the establishment of norms and rules that promote cooperation within the league and that defend the league from external aggression.

Empirical tests of claims by Kant and Paine

The preceding discussion has exposed the philosophical roots of liberalism in International Relations by highlighting the works of Kant and Paine. Both authors make a series of claims about how the world actually works (rather than normative claims focusing on how they would like it to work). The three most significant claims have become the vertices of the liberal triangle of peace: (1) democracy reduces military conflict, (2) economic interdependence reduces military conflict and (3) international institutions reduce military conflict (Russett and Oneal 2001: 35). Over the last quarter of acentury, these three liberal claims have come under intense scrutiny from sympathetic liberals and sceptical realists. The empirical tests have ranged from quantitative analysis (Huth and Allee 2002) and laboratory experiments (Geva and Hanson 1999) to historical case studies (Layne 1994) and computer simulations (Rousseau 2005). In the following three subsections, we examine the balance of findings for these three central claims. Overall, the empirical literature strongly supports the three central claims of Paine and Kant.

Claim #1: Democracy reduces military conflict

Are democratic states better able to resolve international disputes without resorting to military force than non-democratic states? For realists, the answer is no. Realists predict that states will balance (e.g. increase defence spending or establish alliances) against all stronger states because these powerful agents represent a threat to a state residing in anarchy. Thus, realists predict that democracies will behave just like autocracies: They will balance against the strong and use force if the situation calls for it.

Early empirical research on the behaviour of democracies seemed to confirm the realist predictions. Wright (1942: 841) concluded that regime type has little impact on the frequency of war because democracies possess attributes that both encourage and discourage war. In an early statistical analysis of the relationship between war and regime type, Small and Singer (1976: 67) concluded that democracies had not been noticeably peaceful over the 1816–1965 period. In the following decade, Chan (1984) and Weede (1984) reached a similar conclusion using quantitative analysis techniques and large cross-national times-series data sets. Although some evidence supporting the democratic peace emerged (Babst 1972; Rummel 1983), the realist position reflected the general consensus in the early 1980s.

The realist consensus came under attack with the publication of a series of articles by Doyle (1986). Doyle reframed the debate by looking at the characteristics of both the initiator of conflict and the target of conflict. After compiling a list of liberal societies from 1700–1982 and a list of interstate wars from 1816–1980, Doyle found that no two democracies had engaged in a full-scale war. He concluded that 'liberal states have created a separate peace, as Kant argued they would, and have also discovered liberal reasons for aggression, as he feared they might' (Doyle 1986: 1151). Doyle's groundbreaking work trigged an avalanche of studies that is now collectively referred to as 'the democratic peace theory'. According to Levy (1988), the democratic peace is the closest thing to an empirical law found in the study of International Relations.

In the decades since Doyle's publication, there has been an explosion of empirical studies of the democratic peace. Although there have been some critiques of the claim (e.g. Layne 1994; Gowa 1999; Oren 2003; Gartzke 2007), most of the empirical analysis has centred on the causal mechanisms: why do democracies behave differently? The most prominent explanation starts from the interstate level of analysis and predicts that democracies are only more peaceful when engaging other democracies (referred to as the 'dyadic' democratic peace). When a dispute erupts between two democracies, each side knows that the other faces domestic constraints on the use of force. This expectation limits bluffing, dampens spirals of hostility and slows the mobilization process. Extensive empirical analysis has been produced for the dyadic democratic peace (Babst 1972; Doyle 1986; Maoz and Russett 1993; Huth and Allee 2002; Russett and Oneal 2001; Bennett and Stam 2004; Bueno de Mesquita et al. 2003; Rousseau 2005).

A second explanation starts from the state level of analysis and claims that democracies are more peaceful regardless of the opposition (referred to as the 'monadic' democratic peace). Here, the causal mechanism does not focus on expectations about the behaviour of the other party in the dispute. Rather, democracies are seen as less likely to initiate disputes and escalate crises because they are constrained by domestic institutions and norms of conflict resolution. The existence of domestic political opposition makes democratic leaders more risk-averse because foreign policy failures (and even costly successes) can be politically costly (Morgan and Campbell 1991; Morgan and Schwebach 1992; Bueno de Mesquita and Siverson 1995). Although the early research did not provide much support for this monadic argument, a number of more recent studies have produced strong statistical evidence in support of the hypothesis (Schultz 2001; Huth and Allee 2002; Bueno de Mesquita et al. 2003; Bennett and Stam 2004; Rousseau 2005). In sum, there is strong empirical evidence to support the claim by Kant and Paine that an expansion of political liberty reduces interstate conflict.

Claim #2: Economic interdependence reduces military conflict

Economic interdependence is traditionally defined as the degree to which two (or more) states are connected by flows of goods, services, capital, labour and technology. Although much of the empirical analysis of interdependence has tended to restrict its focus to the trade of goods and services (e.g. Russett and Oneal 2001: 139ff.), some researchers have emphasized the importance of including capital flows in the measure of interdependence after 1900 (e.g. Gartzke 2007). Regardless of the actual measure, realists argue that economic interdependence *increases* the probability of conflict by expanding the number of issue areas under competition (Waltz 1979: 138). For example, Gaddis (1986: 110) argues that the economic independence of the East and West, rather than interdependence, was a key element of the 'long peace' during the Cold War.

In contrast, liberals such as Paine, Kant and Cobden argue that economic interdependence decreases international conflict. There are several causal mechanisms that can explain this relationship. First, decision-makers contemplating whether to initiate a dispute or escalate a crisis must calculate the cost of such an action. If two states are highly interdependent and the leaders believe that initiation or escalation will undermine this relationship, they are less likely to use force. This does not mean that interdependence is a sufficient condition for peace. Rather, all other factors being constant (the nature of the dispute, the power of the states, etc.), a dispute between interdependent states is less likely to escalate compared with a dispute between two states with no economic ties. Second, as Kant emphasized, firms and workers with international ties (e.g. export-oriented firms or firms using imports in the production process) will pressure government representatives to de-escalate disputes that arise between trading partners. Although research has not decisively disentangled these distinct (but complementary) causal mechanisms, the empirical literature has provided significant evidence supporting the interdependence claim (Wallensteen 1973; Gasiorowski 1986; Polachek and McDonald 1992; Mansfield 1994; Russett and Oneal 2001).

Some scholars have qualified the liberal interdependence claim by specifying conditions that restrict the scope of the claim. For example, Keohane and Nye (1977: 10)

27

make a clear distinction between symmetrical interdependence (i.e. both states are equally dependent on each other) and asymmetrical interdependence (i.e. state A is very dependent on state B, but state B is not very dependent on state A). While symmetrical interdependence creates a mutual desire for continued trade and investment, asymmetrical interdependence invites attempts to exploit weakness and manipulate behaviour (see also Hirschman 1945). In a similar vein, Copeland (1996) argues that the expectation of continuing trade is the key conditional variable. Only if state leaders expect trade to continue (or increase) are they less likely to use force. Finally, Ripsman and Blanchard (1996/97) contend that interdependence will only inhibit conflict if the trade involves strategic goods (e.g. oil or nitrates) that cannot be supplied from alternative sources. If substitute goods or markets are readily available, the cost of disrupting the relationship can fall dramatically.

The claim that interdependence reduces conflict has been criticized from a number of perspectives. First, not all statistical analysis has produced strong support for the interdependence hypothesis. For example, Barbieri (1996) finds little evidence for the conflict-dampening impact of trade during the 1870–1938 period. Second, some authors believe that the empirical relationship between trade and conflict identified in some quantitative analysis may be spurious. For example, Gartzke (2007) provides statistical evidence that market openness, rather than trade interdependence (or democracy), has reduced violence in the post-Second World War era. Similarly, Kim and Rousseau (2005) find that the pacifying impact of trade evaporates when using several different measures of interdependence and a model of reciprocal causation (i.e. simultaneously testing two claims: 'military conflict decreases trade' AND 'trade decreases military conflict'). Third, the findings from qualitative case studies are often inconsistent with the general trends identified in the quantitative literature. For example, Ripsman and Blanchard (1996/97) find little concern for the costs of interdependence in their analysis of historical crises among great powers during the July Crisis in 1914 and the Remilitarization of the Rhineland Crisis in 1936. Thus, although there is significant empirical evidence for the 'interdependence causes peace' hypothesis, it is less robust than the 'democratic peace' claim, and scholars continue to investigate the conditions that might moderate the impact of trade and investment.

Claim #3: International institutions reduce military conflict

The third pillar of the liberal peace rests upon the impact of international institutions: liberals claim that international institutions decrease the probability of conflict and increase the probability of cooperation. In contrast, realists tend to view international institutions either as generally ineffective or as the instruments of powerful states (i.e. international institutions have no independent causal impact (Mearsheimer 1994/95; Organski 1968)). Although most realists and liberals would agree that the number of international institutions have grown exponentially over the last 100 years (e.g. Shanks et al. 1996), they disagree on the impact of this growth.

Early studies in this research programme tended to focus on formal 'international organizations' such as the UN. However, over time, the research programme has expanded beyond the analysis of rules, procedures and outcomes in formal institutions (e.g. UN voting patterns) towards 'international institutions' more generally and ultimately the broadest conceptualization of 'global governance'. For example, Lipson's analysis of the banking sector's response to the debt crisis in the 1980s emphasizes the 'informal' regime created by the banks seeking cooperation with each other (Lipson 1986). Following the general lead of Mearsheimer (1994/95: 9), we can define international institutions simply and broadly as a set of rules that govern how actors should cooperate and compete with each other within an issue area (see Simmons and Martin 2002). These rules govern behaviour in formal institutions such as the World Trade Organization (WTO) and informal institutions such as the debt-crisis banking regime.

International institutions promote cooperation in a wide range of issue areas, from trade and the environment to human rights and gender equality. In the more restricted domain of peace and security, how do international institutions promote peace? First, collective security organizations and alliances can promote peace by deterring aggression or intervening to halt a conflict. Second, international and regional institutions can mediate disputes (e.g. the good offices of the UN Secretary General) or provide arbitration (e.g. the International Court of Justice). Third, international regimes can monitor compliance with agreements and reduce transactions costs for follow-up accords (Keohane 1984). Fourth, international institutions can promote conflict-reducing norms and alter identities and related interests (Barnett and Finnemore 1999; Wendt and Duvall 1989). Fifth, international institutions can alter the perceived costs and benefits of military conflict by expanding areas of cooperation and establishing opportunities for repeated interaction across time to build confidence. Many international institutions reduce conflict through several of these mechanisms simultaneously. For example, the WTO and the Organization for the Prohibition of Chemical Weapons (OPCW) adjudicate disputes, monitor compliance, encourage norms (e.g. by promoting economic liberalism in the case of the WTO and by banning weapons of mass destruction in the case of the OPCW) and alter cost-benefit calculations (e.g. by increasing trade ties in the case of the WTO and by collectively punishing rule violators in the case of the OPCW).

There is extensive empirical evidence supporting Kant's and Paine's prediction that international institutions will reduce military conflict. Despite the intensity of the superpower conflict during the Cold War, new international institutions helped foster cooperation. In some cases, the link between international institutions and conflict was quite direct. For example, studies have highlighted the role of the International Atomic Energy Agency (IAEA) in curtailing proliferation among rivals such as Brazil and Argentina (Cirincione et al. 2005). In other cases, the role of international institutions was indirect (Dorussen and Ward 2008). For example, most observers credit the General Agreement on Tariffs and Trade (GATT) and the WTO with contributing to the explosive growth in trade during the post-Second World War period (Held et al. 1999: 175); the literature reviewed in the preceding subsection links the expansion in trade to a decline in military conflict among dyads. In more general terms, Russett and Oneal (2001: 170f.) find that as two states increase their membership in international organizations, the probability of military conflict declines. Huth and Allee (2002: 278) find that common security ties (bilateral and multilateral) reduce the probability of violence. Mansfield and Pevehouse (2000) find that states that share membership in a preferential trading agreement are less likely to engage in military conflict. Although no liberal would claim that international institutions are a sufficient (or even necessary) cause of peace, these institutions appear to dampen a wide variety of conflicts.

Conclusion

The purpose of this chapter has been to provide a broad overview of liberalism in International Relations by linking the writings of classical liberals with the empirical research of modern social scientists. In any brief overview, it is impossible to address all the causal claims falling within a broad school of thought such as liberalism. Several liberal claims that have sparked recent research have not been elaborated. For instance, evidence that democracies spend less on defence budgets than autocracies has been reported by Goldsmith (2003) and by Fordham and Walker (2005). Similarly, evidence that democracies are more likely to win wars because they are careful whom they fight has been elaborated by Reiter and Stam (2002).

In this review, we have attempted to show that there is strong and well-established empirical evidence for three central liberal claims: (1) democracy reduces conflict, (2) interdependence reduces conflict and (3) international institutions reduce conflict. Moreover, these three pillars of the liberal peace are interwoven. For example, democratic states are more likely to be interdependent (Mansfield et al. 2000). Similarly, democratic states are more likely to join international organizations (Russett and Oneal 2001: 170) and utilize international institutions for mediation and arbitration (Raymond 1994; Dixon 1994; Hasenclever and Weiffen 2006). Kant himself argued that only the combination of the three pillars acting in unison could provide a stable peace in the long term (Cederman 2001).

References

Babst, D.V. (1972) 'A force for peace', *Industrial Research* 14, April: 55–58.

Barbieri, K. (1996) 'Economic interdependence: A path to peace or a source of interstate conflict?', *Journal of Peace Research* 33, 7: 29–49.

Barnett, M.N. and Finnemore, M. (1999) 'The politics, power and pathologies of international organizations', *International Organization* 49, 2: 699–732.

Bennett, D.S. and Stam, A.C. (2004) *The Behavioral Origins of War*, Ann Arbor, MI: University of Michigan Press.

Bueno de Mesquita, B. and Siverson, R.M. (1995) 'War and the survival of political leaders: A comparative analysis of regime type and accountability', *American Political Science Review* 89, 4: 841–55.

Bueno de Mesquita, B., Smith, A., Siverson, R.M. and Morrow, J.D. (2003) *The Logic of Political Survival*, Cambridge, MA.: MIT Press.

Cederman, L.-E. (2001) 'Back to Kant: Reinterpreting the democratic peace as a macrohistorical learning process', *American Political Science Review* 95, 1: 15–31.

Chan, S. (1984) 'Mirror, mirror on the wall ... are the freer countries more pacific?', *Journal of Conflict Resolution* 28, 4: 617–48.

Cirincione, J., Wolfsthal, J.B. and Rajkumar, M. (2005) *Deadly Arsenals: Nuclear Biological, and Chemical Threats. Second Edition*, Washington, DC: Carnegie Endowment for International Peace.

Copeland, D.C. (1996) 'Economic interdependence and war: A theory of trade expectations', *International Security* 20, 4: 5–41.

Dixon, W.J. (1994) 'Democracy and the peaceful settlement of international conflict', *American Political Science Review* 88, 1: 14–32.

Dorussen, Han and Ward, H. (2008) 'Intergovermental organizations and the Kantian peace: A network perspective', *Journal of Conflict Resolution* 52, 2: 189–212.

Doyle, M. (1986) 'Liberalism and world politics', *American Political Science Review* 80, 4: 1151–69.

——(1993) 'Kant, liberal legacies, and foreign affairs', *Philosophy and Public Affairs*, Parts 1 and 2, 12, 3–4: 205–35, 323–53.

——(1997) *Ways of War and Peace: Realism, Liberalism and Socialism*, New York: W.W. Norton.

Fordham, B.O. and Walker, T.C. (2005) 'Kantian liberalism, regime type, and military resource allocation: Do democracies spend less?', *International Studies Quarterly* 49, 1: 141–57.

Gaddis, J.L. (1986) 'The long peace: Elements of stability in the postwar international system', *International Security* 10, 4: 99–142.

Galtung, J. (1984) *There are Alternatives: Four Roads to Peace and Security*. Nottingham: Spokesman.

Gartzke, E. (2007) 'The capitalist peace', *American Journal of Political Science* 51, 1: 166–91.

Gasiorowski, M.J. (1986) 'Economic interdependence and international conflict: Some cross-national evidence', *International Studies Quarterly* 30, 1: 23–38.

Geva, N. and Hanson, D.C. (1999) 'Cultural similarity, foreign policy actions, and regime perception: An experimental study of international cues and democratic peace', *Political Psychology* 20, 4: 803–27.

Glaser, C.L. (1992) 'Political consequences of military strategy: Expanding and refining the spiral and deterrence models', *World Politics* 50, 1: 171–202.

Goldsmith, B. (2003) 'Bearing the defense burden, 1886–1989: Why spend more?', *Journal of Conflict Resolution* 47, 5: 551–73.

Gowa, J. (1999) *Ballots and Bullets: The Elusive Democratic Peace*, Princeton, NJ: Princeton University Press.

Hasenclever, A. and Weiffen, B. (2006) 'International institutions are the key: A new perspective on the democratic peace', *Review of International Studies* 32, 4: 563–85.

Held, D., McGrew, A., Goldblatt, D. and Perraton, J. (1999) *Global Transformations: Politics, Economics, and Culture*, Stanford, CA: Stanford University Press.

Hirshman, A.O. (1945) *National Power and the Structure of Foreign Trade*, Berkeley, CA: University of California Press.

Howard, M. (1978) *War and the Liberal Conscience*, New Brunswick, NJ: Rutgers University Press.

Huth, P.K. and Allee, T.L. (2002) *The Democratic Peace and Territorial Conflict in the Twentieth Century*, Cambridge, UK: Cambridge University Press.

Jervis, R. (1976) *Perception and Misperception in International Politics*, Princeton, NJ: Princeton University Press.

——(1978) 'Cooperation under the security dilemma', *World Politics* 30, 2: 167–214.

Kant, I. [1784] (1991) 'Idea for a universal history with a cosmopolitan purpose', in, Reiss H. (ed.) *Kant's Political Writings*, Cambridge: Cambridge University Press, pp. 41–53.

——[1795] (1991) 'Perpetual peace', in Reiss, H. (ed.) *Kant's Political Writings*, Cambridge: Cambridge University Press, pp. 93–130.

——[1797] (1991) 'The metaphysics of morals', in Reiss, H. (ed.) *Kant's Political Writings*, Cambridge: Cambridge University Press, pp. 131–75.

——[1798] (1991) 'The contest of faculties', in Reiss, H. (ed.) *Kant's Political Writings*, Cambridge: Cambridge University Press, pp. 176–90.

Keohane, R.O. (1984) *After Hegemony: Cooperation and Discord in the World Political Economy*, Princeton, NJ: Princeton University Press.

——(2002) *Power and Governance in a Partially Globalized World*, London: Routledge.

Keohane, R.O. and Nye, J.S. (1977) *Power and Interdependence: World Politics in Transition*, Boston, MA: Little Brown.

Kim, H.M. and Rousseau, D.L. (2005) 'The classical liberals were half right (or half wrong): New tests of the liberal peace, 1960–88', *Journal of Peace Research* 42, 5: 523–43.

Lanyi, G. and McWilliams, W.C. (1966) 'Theories of world politics', in Lanyi, G. and McWilliams, W. C. (eds) *Crisis and Continuity in World Politics*, New York: Random House, pp. 3–8.

Layne, C. (1994) 'Kant or cant: The myth of the democratic peace', *International Security* 19, 2: 5–94.

Levy, J. (1988) 'Domestic politics and war', *Journal of Interdisciplinary History* 18, 3: 653–73.

Lipson, C. (1986) 'Bankers' dilemmas: Private cooperation in rescheduling sovereign debt', in Oye, K. (ed.) *Cooperation Under Anarchy*, Princeton, NJ: Princeton University Press, pp. 200–224.

Mansfield, E.D. (1994) *Power, Trade, and War*, Princeton, NJ: Princeton University Press.

Mansfield, E.D. and Pevehouse, J.C. (2000) 'Trade blocs, trade flows, and international conflict', *International Organization* 54, 4: 775–808.

Mansfield, E.D., Milner, H.V. and Rosendorff, B.P. (2000) 'Free to trade: Democracies, autocracies, and international trade', *The American Political Science Review* 94, 2: 305–21.

Maoz, Z. and Russett, B. (1993) 'Normative and structural causes of democratic peace, 1946–86', *American Political Science Review* 87, 3: 624–38.

Mearsheimer, J.J. (1994/95) 'The false promise of international institutions', *International Security* 19, 3: 9–12.

Moravcsik, A. (1997) 'Taking preferences seriously: A liberal theory of international politics', *International Organization* 51, 4: 513–53.

Morgan, T.C., and Campbell, S.H. (1991) 'Domestic structure, decisional constraints, and war', *Journal of Conflict Resolution* 35, 2: 187–211.

Morgan, T.C. and Schwebach, V.L. (1992) 'Take two democracies and call me in the morning: A prescription for peace?', *International Interactions* 17, 4: 305–20.

Oren, I. (2003) *Our Enemies and US: America's Rivalries and the Making of Political Science*, Ithaca, NY: Cornell University Press.

Organski, A.F.K. (1968) *World Politics*, New York: Alfred A. Knopf.

Paine, T. [1776] (1986) *Common Sense*, London: Penguin Books.

——[1787] (1908) 'Prospects of the rubicon', in Wheeler, D.E. (ed.) *Life and Writings of Thomas Paine*, vol. 9, New York: Vincent Park and Company, pp. 9–67.

——[1791] (1969) *Rights of Man*, Baltimore: Penguin Books.

——(1801) *Compact Maritime of an Association of Nations*, Washington, DC: Smith.

——[1807] (1945) 'Of the comparative powers and expense of ships of war, gun boats, and fortifications', in Foner, P. (ed.) *The Complete Writings of Thomas Paine*, New York: The Citadel Press, pp. 1072–77.

Polachek, S.W. and McDonald J. (1992) 'Strategic trade and incentives for cooperation', in Chatterji, M. and Forcey, L.R. (eds.) *Disarmament, Economic Conversions and the Management of Peace*, New York: Praeger, pp. 273–84.

Raymond, G.A. (1994) 'Democracies, disputes, and third-party intermediaries', *Journal of Conflict Resolution* 38, 1: 24–42.

Reiter, D. and Stam, A.C. (2002) *Democracies at War*, Princeton, NJ: Princeton University Press.

Ripsman, N.M. and Blanchard, J.-M. (1996/97) 'Commercial liberalism under fire: Evidence from 1914 and 1936', *Security Studies* 6, 2: 4–50.

Rousseau, D. (2005) *Democracy and War: Institutions, Norms, and the Evolution of International Conflict*, Stanford, CA: Stanford University Press.

Rummel, R.J. (1983) 'Libertarianism and international violence', *Journal of Conflict Resolution* 27, 1: 27–72.

Russett, B. and Oneal, J. (2001) *Triangulating Peace: Democracy, Interdependence, and International Organizations*, New York: Norton.

Schultz, K.A. (2001) *Democracy and Coercive Diplomacy*, Oxford, UK: Oxford University Press.

Shanks, C., Jacobson, H.K. and Kaplan, J.H. (1996) 'Inertia and change in the constellation of international government organizations, 1981–92', *International Organization* 50, 4: 593–626.

Simmons, B. and Martin, L.L. (2002) 'International organizations and institutions', in W. Carlsnaes et al. (eds) *Handbook of International Relations*, London: Sage Publications, pp. 192–211.

Simmons, B., Dobbin, F. and Garrett, G. (2006) 'Introduction: The international diffusion of liberalism', *International Organization* 60, 4: 781–810.

Small, M. and Singer, J. D. (1976) 'The war-proneness of democratic regimes, 1816–1965', *The Jerusalem Journal of International Relations* 1, 1: 50–69.

Walker, T.C. (2008) 'Two faces of liberalism: Kant, Paine, and the question of intervention', *International Studies Quarterly* 52, 3: 449–68.

Walker, T.C. and Morton J.S. (2005) 'Re-assessing the "power of power politics" thesis: Is realism still dominant?', *International Studies Review* 7, 2: 341–56.

Wallensteen, P. (1973) *Structure and War: On International Relations 1920–1968*, Stockholm: Raben & Sjogren.

Waltz, K. (1959) *Man, the State, and War: A Theoretical Analysis*, New York: Columbia University Press.

——(1979) *Theory of International Politics*, Reading: Addison-Wesley.

Weede, E. (1984) 'Democracy and war involvement', *Journal of Conflict Resolution* 28, 4: 649–64.

Wendt, Alexander and Duvall, Raymond. (1989) 'Institutions and international order', in Czempiel, E.-O. and Rosenau, J. (eds) *Global Changes and Theoretical Challenges*, Lexington, MA: Lexington Books, pp. 51–73.

Wright, Q. [1942] (1965) *A Study of War*, Chicago: University of Chicago Press.

Zacher, M. and Matthew, R. (1995) 'Liberal international theory: Common threads, divergent strands', in Kegley, C. (ed.) *Controversies in International Relations Theory: Realism and the Neoliberal Challenge*, New York: St. Martin's Press, pp.107–50.

3

The English school and international security

Barry Buzan[1]

The 'English school' and 'International Security Studies' are names that are seldom found in the same sentence. Few if any people working within mainstream international security studies would think about the English school (ES) as a body of either theory or empirical work relevant to Security Studies. If they thought about it at all, they might well see the ES, with its concerns about order and legitimacy (Bull 1977; Clark 2005), as coming from the opposite, liberal, end of International Relations theory, than from the conflict/disorder realist end of the spectrum to which International Security Studies generally relates. The classic ES approach involves seeing International Relations as composed of three elements (Buzan 2004b: 6–10): international system (realism, Hobbes), international society (rationalism, Grotius) and world society (idealism or revolutionism, Kant). These elements are in constant interplay and the nature of international relations depends on the balance between them. In principle, this opens a bridge between the ES and International Security Studies via the realism element in ES theory. In practice, however, the great bulk of ES work has focused on international and world society, and on the rules, norms and institutions that underpin the social order of international society. Few within the ES have explicitly addressed the International Security Studies agenda, and the concept of security does not play much role in ES thinking. It is therefore reasonable to ask what a chapter on the English school is doing in a volume on International Security Studies. This chapter contains three answers to this question. The next section sets out the ES as a general theoretical framing for International Security Studies comparable with realism, liberalism and Marxism. The section after that reviews the existing ES literature on international security to show where the overlaps are, and the concluding section opens up some opportunities for how the relationship might be developed further.

The English school as an approach to international security studies

As the other chapters in this section make clear, the sub-field of International Security Studies does not stand by itself. Its traditional core of strategic studies focuses on state ('national') security and sees threats and responses largely in military terms. As just noted, this traditional core is closely related to realism, whose state-centric, power-political and conflictual understanding of International Relations provides a complementary and close-fitting general framework for strategic studies. Marxism, which also features a power-political and conflictual, if not state-centric, understanding of International Relations, can also serve as a general theoretical framing for International Security Studies. So can liberalism, though with its emphasis on intergovernmental and transnational institutions, cooperation and joint gains, the framing it provides emphasizes possible ameliorations of and/or exits from the 'permanent' conflicts and security dilemmas of the realist and Marxist worlds. These various theoretical framings have all played their part in the widening and deepening of International Security Studies as a sub-field that has been going on since long before the end of the Cold War (Buzan and Hansen 2009).

The English school has not so far played much of a role in the widening and deepening of International Security Studies, but it could, and probably should, do so. What is distinctive about the ES is its focus on the societal elements of International Relations, which it approaches through history, political theory and law. Constructivists have recently moved onto this ground as well, but their approach to social processes is made mainly through ontology and epistemology. Realism, liberalism and Marxism all offer a picture of what international society does or should look like. Constructivism generally does not offer such a picture, though Wendt (1999) does give a general sketch of international social orders built around relationships of friend, rival and enemy. Because the ES comes from historical and normative roots, and makes a feature of the primary institutions[2] of international society, it offers a much more detailed picture of international society and so can more easily serve as a general framing for International Security Studies.

In a nutshell, the ES framing for International Security Studies can be set out as follows. Whereas realism sees a world of enemies and rivals running on a logic of coercion and calculation, the ES agrees with Wendt in allowing enemies, rivals and friends, and running on a logic of coercion, calculation and belief. In this sense, the ES incorporates both the realist and liberal framings, and contextualizes them in a range of possible types of international society[3] that offer much more depth and detail than Wendt's general scheme. This spectrum can be envisaged as four general types:

- *Power Political* represents an international society based largely on enmity and the possibility of war, but where there is also some diplomacy, alliance making and trade. Survival is the main motive, and few values are shared. Institutions will be minimal, mostly confined to rules of recognition and diplomacy. Quite a bit of ancient and classical history looks like this, and the units composing such a society may be empires, city-states and nomadic barbarians as well as states in the modern sense.
- *Coexistence* is modelled on the exemplar of pre-1945 Europe, meaning the kind of Westphalian system in which the core institutions of international society are the balance of power, sovereignty, territoriality, diplomacy, great-power management, war and international law. The units seek some degree of international order, but remain distinct, self-centred and not infrequently warlike.
- *Cooperative* means that the units seek a level of order sufficient to pursue some joint projects (e.g. a world economy, human rights, big science). It might come in many guises, depending on what types of values are shared and how/why they are shared, though the standard model here is based on shared liberal values. Cooperation does not require broad ideological agreement, but only instrumental commitments to specific projects. The contemporary commitment to the market is a good example,

with many illiberal and non-democratic countries willing to play by international market rules. Probably war becomes downgraded as an institution, and other institutions might arise to reflect the solidarist joint project(s).

■ *Convergence* means the development of a substantial enough range of shared values within a set of states to make them adopt similar political, legal and economic forms, and to aspire to be more alike. The usual models here are the EU, or democratic peace theory, but, in principle, any shared ideological base could underpin convergence. The range of shared values simply has to be wide enough and substantial enough to generate similar forms of government (liberal democracies, Islamic theocracies, communist totalitarianisms) and legal systems based on similar values in respect of such basic issues as property rights, human rights and the relationship between government and citizens.

It is immediately apparent from this spectrum that what type of international society one is in has huge consequences for what the agenda of international security will look like. Life within a power political international society will be extremely different from life in a cooperative or convergence one. It is also clear that these international societies represent forms of social order quite distinct from the materialist sense of order represented by the distribution of power in realism. In a sense, realist assumptions are confined within the power political and coexistence models, and pay attention only to some of the institutions that define those models. The classical ES view of coexistence international societies, like the realist one, stresses great powers, war and balance of power as key institutions of the social order. But in cooperative and convergence international societies of almost any conceivable sort, war and balance of power will be respectively marginalized or nearly eliminated as institutions. This does not, of course, mean that such societies have no security agenda. As one can see from the contemporary practice of the EU or the liberal international economic order, security concerns move away from the traditional military ones towards economic, societal and environmental ones, and the human security agenda.

International society therefore represents a type of social structure. This structure can vary in form (as above) and also in distribution (it may be universal or partial, and if universal may still have differentiations of degree within it − think of the EU within global international society). Thinking of international society in this way opens the possibility of transposing Walker's (1993) inside/outside perspective to thinking about how an ES approach frames international security. Walker's idea is that thinking about international relations and international security has been largely framed as a distinction between what goes on inside states (order, progress) and what goes on outside (or between) them (disorder and a repetitive logic of anarchy). If international society is conceived as a social structure, then it also has inside/outside qualities, and this points to at least three novel lines of thinking about international security.

1   What are the security consequences for insiders of being included within the particular set of primary institutions that defines any international society? The primary institutions of international society are the key social framework within which the processes of securitization occur. It makes a difference whether the dominant institutions are, say, dynasticism, human inequality and suzerainty, or popular sovereignty, human equality and nationalism. Likewise, the possibilities for securitization are shaped by whether the dominant economic institution is mercantilism or the

market. Some institutions have an obvious major impact on what the agenda of international security will look like (e.g. sovereignty, territoriality, colonialism, war, balance of power, human inequality, nationalism, market and environmental stewardship). Will it be a security agenda arising from classic military–political competition among states, or one more centred around interdependence issues such as economy, environment and/or identity?

2 What are the security consequences for outsiders of being excluded from international society? Insiders have to live with the consequences of being inside as in point 1. Outsiders have the problem of not being recognized as equals, or possibly not being recognized at all. Think of the era of European (or Roman, or Persian, or Chinese) imperialism with the world divided into the civilized, barbarian and savage, with few or sometimes no restraints on the 'civilized' from subordinating or even exterminating the 'lesser breeds'. As a few days in Taipei quickly reveals, non-recognition poses real security problems for outsiders. The ES view of inside/outside relating to membership of international society provides a framing for International Security Studies that makes much more sense for constructivist, feminist and Copenhagen school approaches, and puts the traditionalist, military–political approach into a wider context within which one can see whether its assumptions are appropriate or not.

3 If one puts the inside and outside perspectives together, then the institutions of international society, both individually and collectively, can become the referent objects of security. Since the institutions of international society constitute both the players and the game (think of sovereignty and territoriality and the market for example), threats to those institutions affect both the units and the social order. One of the logics behind the 'war on terrorism' is that violence-wielding outfits such as al-Qaeda threaten the institution of sovereignty. The global market easily becomes a referent object when there are threats to the rule on trade and finance on which its operation rests.

This is how the ES *could* be used as a comprehensive approach to International Security Studies, and the next section sketches out to what extent this has been done so far.

Existing English school literature on international security

Deciding what is, or is not, 'English school' literature, or indeed what is, or is not, 'international security', is hardly an exact science. Neither is it always clear how they should be linked together. There is, for example, some discussion of collective security in classic ES texts (Bull 1977: 238ff.; Hudson 1966), but this has little significance for international security because it is mainly about how to define solidarism and is not really a discussion of collective security in itself. There is also the problem of how to place the work of individuals who sometimes wrote in the ES tradition, but some of whose work is probably more correctly placed outside it: Hedley Bull's works on arms control, for example, or Michael Howard's on war.

Despite these difficulties, there is a lot that is pretty clearly both English school and international security. In some cases, ES work is explicitly addressed to security issues, but other cases require an exercise in reading ES work through security lenses. The brief survey that follows is organized along the three lines of thinking about international security within the ES sketched above, albeit not all the literature falls neatly under a particular heading. Limitations of space forbid an attempt to capture all of the literature, but the discussion below is hopefully sufficient to give an accurate sense of its general shape and orientation.

The security consequences of international society for insiders

There are two ways of approaching this topic. The first is to follow a general set of models of international society like those sketched in the previous section and analyse how their overall social structures affect the likely agendas of international security. As hinted in that discussion, the impact should be very large: there are huge security implications in the ES idea that a range of international societies is possible along a pluralist–solidarist spectrum. The classical literature had little to say on this question at the global level, but recently it has been taken up in some depth, both generally and through the idea of the security dilemma (Hurrell 2007; Booth and Wheeler 2008). This approach puts into systematic form the general proposition that there is not just one logic of anarchy, as realism suggests, but many (Buzan 1991, 2004b; Buzan et al. 1993; Wendt 1992, 1999; Clark 2005). This idea of multiple possible logics of anarchy is also explored at the sub-global and regional levels in work on security regimes (Jervis 1985), security communities (Adler and Barnett 1998) and regional security complexes (Buzan 1991; Wæver 1996; Buzan et al. 1998; Buzan and Wæver 2003) and orders (Lake and Morgan 1997; Ayoob 1999).

The second approach is to look at individual primary institutions of international society and their security consequences. The exemplar here is Mayall's (1990) discussions of how, during the nineteenth century, the rise of nationalism and the market as new institutions of international society not only changed the nature of international politics and security in themselves, but also transformed the practices associated with other institutions such as war and territoriality. There has been no systematic attempt to relate the whole possible range of ES institutions to security issues, though this would be a valuable thing to do. What there has been is quite a lot of work on some institutions, but not much on others. Much of this work parallels discussions in International Security Studies, though little of it was done with an international security audience in mind. The ES has devoted a lot of discussion to war (Howard 1966; Bull 1977; Draper 1990; Holsti 1991, 1996, 2004; Windsor 1991; Best 1994; Hassner 1994; Song 2005; Jones 2006), and there is a large body of work specifically on the laws of war by Adam Roberts (2004, 2006, 2007; Roberts and Guelff 2000). There has also been substantial ES work on the balance of power (Butterfield 1966; Wight 1966; Bull 1977; Hobson and Seabrooke 2001; Kingsbury 2002; Little 2006, 2007) and great-power management (Bull 1977; Brown 2004; Little 2006). Although the security dilemma is not considered to be an institution of international society, there have been ES reflections on that as well (Butterfield 1951; Booth and Wheeler 2007).

The other big discussions in the ES that relate to International Security Studies are those on intervention and human rights, which can be read as close to human security. The ES discussion of human rights is partly a general one about the tensions between human rights and sovereignty in relation to international order (Bull 1977, 1984b; Vincent 1986; Hurrell 2007: 143–64) and partly a more particular one about the emergence (or not) of human rights as a norm or institution of international society. There is a lot of discussion of (non)intervention generally (Vincent 1974; Bull 1984a; Roberts 1993,

1996, 1999, 2006; Vincent and Wilson 1993; Makinda 1997, 1998; Mayall 1998; Cronin 2002; Buzan 2004b), and humanitarian intervention in particular (Wheeler 1992, 2000; Knudsen 1996; Wheeler and Morris 1996; Williams 1999; Ayoob 2001; Brown 2002; Bellamy 2003; Wu 2006).

The security consequences of international society for outsiders

The only systematic general attempt to think through the security consequences of being inside or outside international society is Buzan (1996). This remains a pretty preliminary exercise, but did attempt to map out both the specific character of the spectrum of international societies on a sector-by-sector basis, and the possible security implications of these for insiders and outsiders. There has been no specific attempt to follow it up, though both Buzan (2004b) and Holsti (2004) can be read partly along those lines. Nevertheless, one of the big stories of the ES – that of the expansion of an initially European international society to global scale – is essentially about insiders and outsiders, and much of it is about the coercive imposition of European values and institutions (Bull and Watson 1984; Gong 1984; Zhang 1991; Keene 2002; Keal 2003). There are many studies in this literature of the encounters between well-armed Europeans (and later Americans) not hesitant to use force to impose their values, and a variety of non-Western cultures (mainly Japan, China, the Ottoman Empire and Thailand) forced to come to terms with the new Western order. These encounters, with their stories of unequal treaties and threats of occupation, give a stark insight into the problems of being outside international society. They also underpin the decline of a core institution of pre-1945 European international society, colonialism, which became obsolete as international society became global.

The 'expansion of international society' story is not just one of coercion, but also of the spread of particular institutions that frame security issues for all, particularly: sovereignty, territoriality and nationalism. These institutions were quickly indigenized in many places and used as defence mechanisms against ongoing Western demands. Yet insider/ outsider security dynamics are still visible. The intervention literature discussed above is relevant here inasmuch as the politics of intervention is strongly mediated by whether it is understood to be an affair among insiders (and therefore subject to the relevant primary institutions) or one between insiders and outsiders (and therefore subject only to whatever rules are thought to be universal). This dynamic plays particularly strongly in relation to institutions that are still more Western than global, most notably human rights and democracy. The West still pressures others to accept these on the grounds that they are universal rights, but there remains much resistance from many quarters to that interpretation. All of this suggests that although the idea of outsiders might appear to have lost much of its interest as international society became global, in fact it is still very much alive. It is perfectly clear, for example, that at the level of 'the street', much of the Islamic world continues to think of itself as a site of resistance to Western values.

In a global international society, or course, all are to some degree insiders, and the idea of outsiders becomes much more relative than it was during the 'expansion' story, when in and out could be pretty clearly drawn. When outsider status is relative, and contingent on one's placement in a differentiated international society (e.g. core or periphery) Wendt's (1999: 247–50) idea that social structures can be held in place by coercion, calculation and/or belief is one useful way of approaching the idea of outsiders in contemporary international society. A contemporary institution like the market is obviously held in place by a mixture: some believe in it (US), some calculate it to be in their

39

interest (China) and others are mainly bullied into it (parts of the third world). Where a particular institution is either contested, or held in place mainly by coercion, that could be seen as marking a form of outsider status.

International society as a referent object of security

This line of thinking features either the international social order as a whole (Bull 1977: 18), or individual primary institutions, as the referent objects for security. It plays to the English school's focus on social structures, and contrasts with the realist's inclination to privilege the state as the central referent object for all Security Studies. The Copenhagen school has applied its securitization theory to show how the primary (e.g. sovereignty and market) and secondary (e.g. WTO and UN) institutions of international society can be a referent object for securitization in their own right (Buzan et al. 1998).

The expansion of the international society story discussed above also implicitly features this issue. A consistent theme in the classical ES story of expansion is the consequences of the fact that as European international society expanded, it necessarily moved beyond its foundational cultural base, and absorbed non-European cultures. Much classical ES literature assumes that interstate society necessarily rests on a substrate of shared culture from which it draws the shared values that define and enable its institutions. Modern Europe could be understood as Christendom, and classical Greece could also be understood as a zone of shared culture within which a states-system operated. The concern was that a multicultural foundation would necessarily diminish the pool of shared values available for international society, and thus expansion would equate to weakening. The ongoing tensions over human rights and democracy already noted exemplify the force of this concern, although the readiness with which some institutions, notably sovereignty, nationalism and territoriality have become accepted and internalized offers some counterweight to it.

If international society can be threatened by a reduction in its cultural coherence, it can also be threatened by the interplay of institutions that pull in contradictory directions. There are several possibilities here, including the market and territoriality, and nationalism and sovereignty, but the one that has been most written about in the ES literature is that between human rights and sovereignty (Bull 1977, 1984b; Vincent 1986; Makinda 1998; Bain 2001; Bellamy and McDonald 2004). Here the problem is that if human rights are universal and rooted in the individual, then this brings sovereignty (the absolute right of the state to exercise authority within its territory) into fundamental question. That tension has large implications for the legitimacy of humanitarian interventions, and also ties into the human security agenda of how more broadly to harmonize the rights and responsibilities of individuals with those of states (Buzan 2004a; Dunne and Wheeler 2004). In considering this question, Williams (2004) makes the case for linking the more radical concerns with human rights in the ES to the emancipatory themes of Critical Security Studies to create a more revolutionist ES approach to security. Morris (2004) and Nardin (2004) address the related, but more general, question of how the structure of international society defines the legitimacy (or not) of the use of force.

Conclusions: opportunities for developing the linkage

It should be clear from the above that in terms of both general framing and specific topics addressed, there is a lot of common ground between the English school and International

Security Studies. That said, it is obvious that there is a lack of mutual awareness and interaction between them. The blindness is probably greater on the International Security Studies side, but it is equally true that ES writers need to do more to make the security dimension of ES work explicit, and to address it clearly to issues and debates within International Security Studies. Hopefully, this chapter has shown that the thinness of the contact so far hides quite rich possibilities for synergies. One of these possibilities is to focus attention more specifically on the interplay between the primary institutions of international society and security. How do primary institutions such as nationalism, territoriality, sovereignty, colonialism, human rights and suchlike both define and frame the whole discourse of security? In what sense can and do such institutions become the referent object for processes of securitization?

Another possible synergy is available in the interplay between the study of regional international societies and regional security. There is some work on this (Ayoob 1999), but so far the ES has not shown much interest in the regional level of international society, having chosen to concentrate on the global level. A good case can be made that there are distinctive regional international societies (think of the EU), and there are some studies that analyse what makes them distinct from the global level and how that distinctiveness matters (Buzan et al. 2009). From the security perspective, for example, it seems clear that within the Middle East, sovereignty is a weaker institution than at the global level, and war a stronger one. Just as a social structural perspective throws interesting light on the analysis of security at the global level, so it does at the regional one. One obvious linkage point here is the Copenhagen school, which has a particular interest in regional security (Buzan and Wæver 2003) and is also open to English school thinking. Can one, for example, theorize a connection between strong security interdependence on the one hand, and the emergence of distinctive regional international societies on the other? Does security interdependence generate the incentives for a degree of international order that underpins international societies? On the face of it, it looks a reasonable hypothesis. It fits with European history, the Middle East case lends further credence to it, and others might as well. The idea of regional international societies also plays into the discussion of intervention above, because the differences represented by regional international society could well define the terms of insider/outsider that would make intervention legitimate or not.

The English school has much to offer International Security Studies, but it needs to be considerably more proactive than it has been in making this clear to the community of International Security Studies scholars. For their part, some of the International Security Studies community need to open their eyes to the importance of international society in framing and shaping the agenda of international security.

Notes

1 I would like to thank Rita Floyd, Lene Hansen and the editors for comments on an earlier draft of this paper.
2 Primary institutions are deep, organic, evolved ideas and practices that constitute both the players and the game of international relations. They include sovereignty, territoriality, balance of power, war, international law, diplomacy, nationalism, great-power management and the market. This understanding of institutions is quite different from that used by regime theorists and liberal institutionalists who focus mainly on instrumental and constructed organizations and arrangements such as intergovernmental organizations and regimes, which are referred to in the following as secondary

institutions. Primary institutions have a history as old as human civilization, whereas secondary ones emerge only in the nineteenth century (see Buzan 2004: 161–204).

3 The ES has concentrated mainly on international society where states are the central players, and the discussion that follows mainly reflects that focus. World society, which centres mainly on individuals and civil society, is less well developed in ES thinking, and there is some tension as to whether it should be approached via the domestic reform of states or via more cosmopolitan, transnational ways of thinking. There is not space in this short chapter to address this level of complexity.

References

Adler, E. and Barnett, M. (eds) (1998) *Security Communities*, Cambridge: Cambridge University Press.

Ayoob, M. (1999) 'From regional system to regional society: Exploring key variables in the construction of regional order', *Australian Journal of International Affairs* 53, 3: 247–60.

——(2001) 'Humanitarian intervention and international society', *Global Governance* 7, 3: 225–30.

Bain, W. (2001) 'The tyranny of benevolence?: National security, human security, and the practice of statecraft', *Global Society* 15, 3: 277–94.

Bellamy, A.J. (2003) 'Humanitarian responsibilities and interventionist claims in international society', *Review of International Studies* 29, 3: 321–40.

Bellamy, A.J. and McDonald, M. (2004) 'Securing international society: Towards an English school discourse of security', *Australian Journal of Political Science* 39, 2: 307–30.

Best, G. (1994) *War and Law Since 1945*, Oxford: Clarendon Press.

Booth, K. (1991) 'Security in anarchy: Utopian realism in theory and practice', *International Affairs* 67, 3: 527–46.

Booth, K. and Wheeler, N. (2008) *The Security Dilemma: Anarchy, Society and Community in World Politics*, Basingstoke: Palgrave.

Brown, C. (2002) 'Intervention and the Westphalian order' in Norman, R. and Moseley, A. (eds) *Human Rights and Military Intervention*, Aldershot: Ashgate, pp. 153–69.

——(2004) 'Do great powers have great responsibilities? Great Powers and moral agency', *Global Society* 18, 1: 5–19.

Bull, H. (1977) *The Anarchical Society: A Study of Order in World Politics*, London: Macmillan.

——(ed.) (1984a) *Intervention in World Politics*, Oxford: Clarendon Press.

——(1984b) *Justice in International Relations*, Hagey Lectures, Ontario: University of Waterloo.

Bull, H. and Watson, A. (eds) (1984) *The Expansion of International Society*, Oxford: Oxford University Press.

Butterfield, H. (1951) *History and Human Relations*, London: Collins.

——(1966) 'The balance of power', in Butterfield, H. and Wight, M. (eds) *Diplomatic Investigations*, London: Allen and Unwin, pp. 132–48.

Buzan, B. (1991) *People, States and Fear: An Agenda for International Security Studies in the Post-Cold War Era*, Hemel Hempstead: Harvester-Wheatsheaf.

——(1996) 'International society and international security', in Fawn, R. and Larkin, Jeremy (eds) *International Society After the Cold War*, London: Macmillan, pp. 261–87.

——(2004a) '"Civil" and "uncivil" in world society', in Guzzini, S. and Jung, D. (eds) *Contemporary Security Analysis and Copenhagen Peace Research*, London: Routledge, pp. 94–105.

——(2004b) *From International to World Society? English School Theory and the Social Structure of Globalisation*, Cambridge: Cambridge University Press.

Buzan, B. and Hansen, L. (2009) *The Evolution of International Security Studies*, Cambridge: Cambridge University Press.

Buzan, B. and Wæver, O. (2003) *Regions and Powers*, Cambridge: Cambridge University Press.

Buzan, B., Gonzalez-Pelaez, A. and Jorgensen, K.E. (eds) (2009) *International Society and the Middle East: English School Theory at the Regional Level*, Basingstoke: Palgrave.

Buzan, B., Jones, C. and Little, R. (1993) *The Logic of Anarchy: Neorealism to Structural Realism*, New York: Columbia University Press.

Buzan, B., Wæver, O. and de Wilde, J. (1998) *Security: A New Framework for Analysis*, Boulder, CO: Lynne Rienner.

Clark, I. (2005) *Legitimacy in International Society*, Oxford: Oxford University Press.

Cronin, B. (2002) 'Multilateral intervention and the international community', in Keren, M. and Sylvan, D. A. (eds) *International Intervention: Sovereignty vs. Responsibility*, London: Frank Cass, pp. 147–65.

Draper, G.I.A.D. (1990) 'Grotius' place in the development of legal ideas about war', in Bull, H., Kingsbury, B. and Roberts, A. (eds) *Hugo Grotius and International Relations*, Oxford: Clarendon Press, pp. 177–209.

Dunne, T. and Wheeler, N.J. (2004) '"We the peoples": Contending discourses of security in human rights theory and practice', *International Relations* 18, 1: 9–23.

Gong, G.W. (1984) *The Standard of 'Civilization' in International Society*, Oxford: Clarendon Press.

Hassner, P. (1994) 'Beyond the three traditions: The philosophy of war and peace in historical perspective', *International Affairs* 70, 4: 737–56.

Hobson, J.M. and Seabrooke, L. (2001) 'Reimagining Weber: Constructing international society and the social balance of power', *European Journal of International Relations* 7, 2: 239–74.

Holsti, K.J. (1991) *Peace and War: Armed Conflicts and International Order 1648–1989*, Cambridge: Cambridge University Press.

——(1996) *The State, War and the State of War*, Cambridge: Cambridge University Press.

——(2004) *Taming the Sovereigns: Institutional Change in International Politics*, Cambridge: Cambridge University Press.

Howard, M. (1966) 'War as an instrument of policy', in Butterfield, H. and Wight, M. (eds) *Diplomatic Investigations*. London: Allen and Unwin.

Hudson, G.F. (1966) 'Collective security and military alliances', in Butterfield, H. and Wight, M. (eds) *Diplomatic Investigations*. London: Allen and Unwin.

Hurrell, A. (2007) *On Global Order: Power, Values and the Constitution of International Society*, Oxford: Oxford University Press.

Jervis, R. (1985) 'From balance to concert: A study of international security cooperation', *World Politics* 38, 1: 58–79.

Jones, C.A. (2006) 'War in the twenty-first century: An institution in crisis', in Little, R. and Williams, J. (eds) *The Anarchical Society in a Globalized World*, Basingstoke: Palgrave, pp. 162–88.

Keal, P. (2003) *European Conquest and the Rights of Indigenous Peoples: The Moral Backwardness of International Society*, Cambridge: Cambridge University Press.

Keene, E. (2002) *Beyond the Anarchical Society: Grotius, Colonialism and Order in World Politics*, Cambridge: Cambridge University Press.

Kingsbury, B. (2002) 'Legal positivism as normative politics: International society, balance of power and Lassa Oppenheim's positive international law', *European Journal of International Law* 13, 2: 401–36.

Knudsen, T.B. (1996) 'Humanitarian intervention revisited: Post-Cold War responses to classical problems', *International Peacekeeping* 3, 4: 146–65.

Lake, D.A. and Morgan, P. (1997) *Regional Orders: Building Security in a New World*, University Park: Pennsylvania University Press.

Little, R. (2006) 'The balance of power and great power management', in Little, R. and Williams, J. (eds) *The Anarchical Society in a Globalized World*, Basingstoke: Palgrave, pp. 97–120.

——(2007) *The Balance of Power in International Relations; Metaphors, Myths and Models*, Cambridge: Cambridge University Press.

Makinda, S. (1997) 'International law and security: Exploring a symbiotic relationship', *Australian Journal of International Affairs* 51, 3: 325–38.

——(1998) 'The United Nations and state sovereignty: Mechanism for managing international security', *Australian Journal of Political Science* 33, 1: 101–15.

Mayall, J. (1990) *Nationalism and International Society*, Cambridge: Cambridge University Press.

——(1998) 'Intervention in international society: Theory and practice in contemporary perspective', in Roberson, B.A. (ed.) *International Society and the Development of International Relations Theory*, London: Pinter.

Morris, J. (2004) 'Normative innovation and the great powers', in Bellamy, A.J. (ed.) *International Society and its Critics*, Oxford: Oxford University Press, pp. 265–82.

Nardin, T. (2004) 'Justice and coercion', in Bellamy, A.J. (ed.) *International Society and its Critics*, Oxford: Oxford University Press, pp. 247–64.

Roberts, A. (1993) 'Humanitarian war: Military intervention and human rights', *International Affairs* 69, 3: 429–49.

——(1996) 'Humanitarian action in war', *Adelphi Papers*, 305, London: International Institute for Strategic Studies.

——(1999) 'NATO's "humanitarian war" over Kosovo', *Survival* 41, 3: 102–23.

——(2004) 'The laws of war', in Cronin, A.K. and Ludes, J.M. (eds) *Attacking Terrorism: Elements of a Grand Strategy*, Washington, DC: Georgetown University Press, pp. 186–219.

——(2006) 'Transformative military occupation: Applying the laws of war and human rights', *American Journal of International Law* 100, 3: 580–622.

——(2007) 'Torture and incompetence in the "war on terror"', *Survival* 49, 1: 199–212.

Roberts, A. and Guelff, R. (2000) *Documents on the Laws of War*, 3rd edn, Oxford: Oxford University Press.

Song, D. (2005) 'The war philosophy of the English school: A Grotian interpretation', *World Economics and Politics*, 10: 26–31.

Vincent, R.J. (1974) *Nonintervention and International Order*, Princeton: Princeton University Press.

——(1986) *Human Rights and International Relations: Issues and Responses*, Cambridge: Cambridge University Press.

Vincent, R.J. and Wilson, P. (1993) 'Beyond non-intervention', in Forbes, I. and Hoffman, M. (eds) *Ethics and Intervention*, London: Macmillan, pp. 122–30.

Wæver, O. (1996) 'Europe's three empires: A Watsonian interpretation of post-wall European security', in Fawn, R. and Larkin, J. (eds) *International Society After the Cold War*, London: Macmillan, pp. 220–60.

Walker, R.J.B. (1993) *Inside/Outside: International Relations as Political Theory*, Cambridge: Cambridge University Press.

Wendt, A. (1992) 'Anarchy is what states make of it: The social construction of power politics', *International Organization* 46, 2: 391–425.

——(1999) *Social Theory of International Politics*, Cambridge: Cambridge University Press.

Wheeler, N.J. (1992) 'Pluralist and solidarist conceptions of international society: Bull and Vincent on humanitarian intervention', *Millennium* 21, 3: 463–89.

——(2000) *Saving Strangers: Humanitarian Intervention in International Society*, Oxford: Oxford University Press.

Wheeler, N.J. and Morris, J. (1996) 'Humanitarian intervention and state practice at the end of the Cold War', in Fawn, R. and Larkin, J. (eds) *International Society After the Cold War*, London: Macmillan.

Wight, M. (1966) 'The balance of power', in Butterfield, H. and Wight, M. (eds) *Diplomatic Investigations*, London: Allen and Unwin, pp. 149–75.

Williams, J. (1999) 'The ethical basis of humanitarian intervention, the Security Council and Yugoslavia', *International Peacekeeping* 6, 2: 1–23.

Williams, P. (2004) 'Critical security studies', in Bellamy, A.J. (ed.) *International Society and its Critics*, Oxford: Oxford University Press, pp. 135–50.

Windsor, P. (1991) 'The state and war', in Navari, C. (ed.) *The Condition of States*, Buckingham: Open University Press, pp. 125–41.

Wu, Z. (2006) 'John Vincent: Sovereignty, human rights and humanitarian intervention', in Chen, Z., Zhou, G. and Shi, B. (eds) *Open International Society: The English School in IR Studies*, Beijing: Peking University Press, pp. 165–77.

Zhang, Y. (1991) 'China's entry into international society: Beyond the standard of "civilization"', *Review of International Studies* 17, 1: 3–16.

4

Critical security studies

David Mutimer

'The philosophers have only interpreted the world in various ways; the point is to change it' (Marx 1888). This noted aphorism by Karl Marx may be said to mark the origin of modern critical social theory. While the point might be to change the world, it is not the only point. Marx is not suggesting abandoning the philosophers' search for understanding, but rather advocates understanding the world *in order* to change it. It is likely that most, if not all, forms of social theory would accept Marx's point. Social theory is a policy science, that is, a form of knowledge (science) that informs how we live together in political communities (polity). Even a liberal thinker such as Francis Fukuyama, who argues that the great struggles of history are over, would accept that social theory should seek to understand the operations of our now-eternal liberal democratic present to make things 'better': increase the overall wealth and freedom of the world's people, and include more and more in the virtuous circle of liberal democratic governance and market economies (Fukuyama 1992).

Liberal improvements to the state of the world, however, mark no *fundamental* change in the organization of society. They seek to improve the operation of the system as it is; certainly such improvement is change, but it is not the change sought by those who would identify themselves as critical social theorists. Social critique assumes that there are fundamental features of the world as we find it that must be changed. The job of theory is to identify and interpret those features for the purposes of animating their change. While critical theorists part ways with their liberal counterparts at this point, the conservatives and reactionaries would still be along for the ride. These latter would see the world as having deteriorated from some previous better phase, and the point of conservative theory is to identify the way those problems function in the present in order to animate a change returning society to some previous (possibly only perceived) better time.

Critical theories reject the premise that the world was fundamentally better in times past or places distant. Rather, they seek to make changes to the fundamental social organization of the present, so that future social organization frees those presently oppressed by the operation of the world as we find it. This freeing of the oppressed is termed 'emancipation' and is central to the politics of social critique; and the orientation of politics towards future improvement in social life is why this form of politics is sometimes termed 'progressive'.

What, then, are the fundamentals of society that require change to produce a progressive politics? Marx's answer was that society is fundamentally about the production of the essentials (and when that is achieved, the frivolities) of life. Political identity is determined by the individual's relation to the production process (their social class). Those who own the means of production in any society benefit at the expense of others, and so the 'point' is to reveal this fundamental organization of society, to mobilize the oppressed to change the society in their interest. However, what if society is not fundamentally about production in the way Marx suggests? What if the various identities produced in activities other than production are not subordinate to their class identity? Indeed, perhaps there is no single fundamental nature to social organization in all times and in all places, but rather the various forms of social activity and identity organize differently, contingently at different times and in different places, and so progressive social change must look to multiple sites of fundamental oppression. As industrial capitalism grew and became globalized, and particularly as capitalism became post-industrial, a body of social theory grew that made just such a claim.

What I have sketched, in admittedly a very schematic way, is the broad scope of critical social theory and its primary line of division. Those who follow Marx's theory of a fundamentally class-based society are found on one side of this division. This stream is often termed 'German', in that Marx and a good number of those that followed him were either German or based in Germany – most notably, in the twentieth century, a group of theorists gathered in Frankfurt (the 'Frankfurt School'), who coined the term Critical Theory. On the other side are those who argue that class and production are not fundamental. This second stream is often termed 'French' for the influence of a number of French thinkers in a tradition also usually labelled 'post-structural'. Foremost among these are Jacques Derrida, Michel Foucault and Jean Baudrillard. There are, of course, near infinite complexities within these broad areas of social theory, and considerable overlap at their margins. No post-structural thinker, for example, would reject the importance of the basic Marxist critique of capitalist society to understanding (and changing) the present. However, there is a significant stream of post-Marxist thinking that takes culture and ideology very seriously indeed. My objective in this chapter is to explore what has happened as critical social theory, in its many varieties, has been turned on the questions of international security to forge a field of study generally termed Critical Security Studies.

I begin with a short discussion of the origins of Critical Security Studies, as it emerged in the aftermath of the collapse of the Cold War and in response to the problems that collapse revealed with traditional security studies. Initially, the leading theoretical position identified with the term critical security was constructivism, and so I follow the discussion of origins with a short exploration of the literature on social construction. There is a real question, however, as to whether the constructivist position fits with a commitment to *critical* social theory, and so that section is followed by two that explore the deployment of first post-Marxist and then post-structural social theory to questions of security. I conclude by considering a recent attempt to bridge the divisions I sketch in the rest of the chapter, revealing in the process some of the ways that some divisions appear inescapable.

Origins

Security Studies was, in its inception and early practice, very much a 'policy science'. It grew along with the nuclear age, operating under the shadow of a future nuclear war, with the avowed commitment to prevent it if possible, and win it if necessary. The concern of Security Studies was, in the words of one of its staunchest defenders, 'the study of the threat, use and control of military force' (Walt 1991). It was concerned with interpreting the world of military strategy, not to change it fundamentally, but to make it better on its own terms. Providing direct policy advice to those in control of states' militaries, particularly to nuclear-armed militaries, was very much a part of the Security Studies understanding of its purpose. Furthermore, the depth of that future shadow, and the degree to which it represented a 'clear and present danger', served as a strong barrier to any alteration in the study of security.

By the late 1980s, however, it seemed that a change in the nuclear standoff between East and West was in the offing. Mikhail Gorbachev was making a raft of changes to Soviet policy, both domestic and foreign, including offering truly significant nuclear arms reductions (Gorbachev 1987). The end of the Cold War opened what has been termed a 'thinking space' in the study of global security (George 1994). In large part, this thinking space resulted from the manifest failure of political realism, the theory underpinning traditional Security Studies, to not only predict the end of the Cold War, but also even to account for it once it had happened (Gusterson 1999). That failure created conditions in which self-consciously critical work to questions of security could be taken seriously in the academy.

What has come to be known as Critical Security Studies grew from this moment in political and intellectual time. The term itself emerged on the margins of a conference held at York University in 1994, and served as the title for the volume produced by that conference. That book, *Critical Security Studies: Concepts and Cases*, is still seen as an important point of origin of the Critical Security Studies idea. The book and label, however, really served as a point around which a number of strands of intellectual development could coalesce. A group of graduate students working with Ken Booth at the University of Wales, Aberystwyth were bringing post-Marxist critical theory to bear on questions of security (Booth 2007: xv–xvi). A number of other scholars, mainly at the University of Minnesota and York University, were developing ideas about constructivism in relation to security (Latham 1998; Mutimer 1998; Williams 1992, 1998; Milliken 2001; Price 1997; Weldes 1999). In other places, ideas drawn from French social theory were also being turned to questions of security (Campbell 1992; Dalby 1990).

At the same time, there were at least two other strands of thought that drew on forms of social critique to think about security, but which have not subsequently been captured, by and large, by the 'Critical Security Studies' label. The first is variously known as 'the Copenhagen School' or 'securitization studies'. (See Chapter 5 in this volume). Perhaps more interestingly, many scholars were thinking about gender and international relations, including international security (Enloe 1983; Peterson 1992; Sylvester 1994; Whitworth 1998). The Feminist IR scholarship that has grown from this strand of thinking, despite significant overlaps with the work of Critical Security Studies, and severe theoretical divisions within it, continues to exist outside the ambit of Critical Security Studies.

Security and social construction

The notion of social construction was introduced to the study of international politics just as the Cold War was ending, and was quickly picked up by students of international security (Wendt 1987, 1992). The central idea of the social construction of International Relations is well captured by the title of one of the signal contributions to its development: 'Anarchy is what states make of it'. Constructivism builds on the basic notion that social life is a product of social practice. Social construction was very appealing to those seeking to rethink security with the demise of the Cold War. It suggested a context in which the rapid change brought about by the Cold War's end was conceivable (if the Cold War was a construct, it could end, where realism seemed to suggest it could not). It also suggested that the security futures were, at least in part, open, as the constitution of those futures would depend on social practice rather than immutable law.

The appeal of constructivism is reflected in *Critical Security Studies: Concepts and Cases*, and perhaps even more clearly in an article published by one of its editors the following year. In this article, Keith Krause organized the research agenda of the new Critical Security Studies under three rubrics: the construction of threats and responses; the construction of the objects of security; and possibilities for transforming the security dilemma (Krause 1998). The assumption underlying this classification is that security is about the identification of *threats* to a particular *referent object*, and the formulation of policy *responses* to those threats. Traditional Security Studies would accept this notion of security easily, but would give singular answers to each: the threats are military, the referent object is the state and the responses are the scope of strategic policy. Thinking in terms of social construction opens the prospect of other answers, as it renders the traditional answers contingent. It therefore also opens an important range of what are known as 'how' questions (Doty 1993: 298; Weldes 1999: 15f.). That is, even if the traditional answers are a correct reflection of the world as we find it, how is it that they came to be that way, given that they are constructed, contingent features of the world? These are the questions Krause argues were driving the research in his first two categories (Krause 1998: 308f.).

Krause's third rubric is of a different order. Here the concern becomes normative: how can the way in which security is practised be transformed? Indeed, this third group of work is normative in at least two ways. Not only is it concerned with a preferred future, but it is also grounded in the assumption that social norms are an important part of international political life, even international security. Some early work explored the place of normative constraints on the use of weapons (e.g. Price 1997; Tannenwald 2007). There has also been a constructivist interest in the place of norms in the end of the Cold War, and the way norms can be produced in contemporary international society to promote security (Tannenwald and Wohlforth 2005). In particular, the place of 'norm entrepreneurs' has been studied, most notably in relation to the creation of the Ottawa Convention banning anti-personnel mines (Price 1988; Finnemore and Sikkink 1998; Price and Reus-Smit 2004; Ulbert and Risse 2005).

As important as constructivism remains in the study of world politics and international security, it is an open question whether it is critical in the sense set out at the beginning of this chapter. As Krause noted, 'the use of the term "critical" as an umbrella to describe all work that falls outside the rationalist (neoliberal and neorealist) paradigm does some violence to the intellectual origins of the term'. He used it, however, because 'other currently used terms, most prominently "constructivism" ... draw upon a narrower range of perspectives' than he surveyed (Krause 1998: 299f.). The desire for breadth may be admirable, but it does not necessarily mean that the term 'critical' captures the constructivist. Clearly, critical social theory accepts the premise of social construction: were society not produced in and through its practices, transformation would not be possible. However, critical theory is aimed at producing fundamental change of a particular kind, and the possibility, let alone the necessity, of such change is not inherent in the constructivist position (Campbell 1998a: 207–27).[1]

Security and post-Marxism

There can be no doubt as to the commitment to fundamental change of those drawing their primary inspiration for rethinking security from the German, or post-Marxist tradition of critical theory. The nature of that commitment was captured early on in a signal contribution from Ken Booth, the leading scholar in this tradition of Critical Security Studies. In his 1991 article, 'Security and Emancipation', Booth set out the political goal of a post-Marxist informed Critical Security Studies:

> Security means the absence of threats. Emancipation is the freeing of people (as individuals and groups) from those physical and human constraints which stop them carrying out what they would freely choose to do … Security and emancipation are two sides of the same coin. Emancipation, not power or order, produces true security. Emancipation, theoretically, is security.
>
> (Booth 1991: 319)

Booth has spent most of the intervening 20 years working out the implications of thinking about security as emancipation, in the post-Marxist sense of the term. Many of the intellectual foundations for this work were contributed by a colleague of Booth's at Aberystwyth, Richard Wyn Jones, whose 1999 book, *Security, Strategy, and Critical Theory*, provides an exegesis of Frankfurt School Critical Theory. His object is 'to lay the conceptual foundations for an alternative critical security studies' (Wyn Jones 1999: 165). Those foundations were based on a rethinking of both security and strategy through the intellectual lens provided by the Frankfurt School. He argues that, seen in this way, security is 'deeper', 'broader', 'extended to referents other than the state' and 'focussed, crucially, on emancipation'. Furthermore, he argues that

> a critical theory influenced approach to security – critical security studies – not only encourages the development of a more analytically useful conceptualization of security but also generates a more sophisticated framework for the analysis of military force (strategy) than that utilized by traditional security studies.
>
> (Wyn Jones 1999: 166f.)

Finally, he turns to the work of the Italian philosopher Antonio Gramsci to reconfigure the relationship between security theory and practice in such a way that 'proponents of critical security studies can not only interpret the world but also play a role in changing it' (Wyn Jones 1999: 167).

In several iterations, culminating in his *Theory of World Security* (2007), Ken Booth has built on the foundations that Wyn Jones has laid to develop a critical theory of world security, which is 'both a theoretical commitment and a political orientation concerned with the construction of world security' (Booth 2007: 30). As a 'theoretical commitment', Booth's theory of world security begins – like that of Wyn Jones – with the Frankfurt School and Gramsci. However, he considers these two to be neither sufficient nor in their entirety necessary for his theoretical framework. He therefore engages in what he terms, following Hannah Arendt, *Perlenfischerei* (pearl fishing):

diving into, first, the critical tradition in social theory, and then the radical tradition in international relations theory. The goal is to find pearls of ideas that might be strung together to make a theory of world security for our time.

(Booth 2007: 40)

The theoretical framework Booth develops from his pearls defies easy summary, as it is grand in both scope and execution (Booth 2007: 209–78). He organizes the framework into three levels. The first is 'transcendental theory', or put another way, his ontological claims:

> The transcendental dimension of the overall theoretical framework … is constructed out of eight main is-propositions. 'Human sociality' is the best overall label for them, implying as it does the radical possibilities immanent in the biology of being human.
>
> (Booth 2007: 210)

He conceives human society as being constituted in our interaction, but with the individual as the ultimate referent of security. The second level is epistemological, which he terms 'pure theory', and which is a Frankfurt-inspired take on the constitutive nature of knowledge and the critical possibilities of theory. Finally, his third level is 'practical theory', which he terms 'emancipatory realism' (Booth 2007: 249–77). While the shift in Booth's terminology from 'utopian' to 'emancipatory' realism is in part due to a desire to escape the eschatological overtones of utopia (Booth 2007: 90), the ghost of the final goal clearly haunts this project. The goal in question is a communitarian one, which he derives first from Kant (Booth 2007: 80–87) and more recently from Andrew Linklater's elaborations of Jurgen Habermas's ideas (Booth 2007: 54–57). While he explicitly eschews the possibility of blueprints, Booth articulates quite an elaborate vision for an institutionalized world community based on the principles of the enlightenment (Booth 2007: 427–70, 124–33).

Theory of World Security stands as the most extensively developed contribution to the post-Marxist (German, Italian or Welsh) approach to Critical Security Studies. It is long on theoretical development and political desire, but short on engagement with the world of security. This is not to say that there is not an extensive discussion of the state of the world in Booth's text, for there is, but rather that the discussion is not clearly informed by the theory that precedes it, rather than by Booth's own insight and erudition. So, while the post-Marxist approach to critical security is beginning to articulate a political project, it is as yet deficient in turning its critical eye to the concrete questions of contemporary security on which such a project can ultimately be built.

Security and post-structuralism

For all his commitment to theoretical pluralism, there is an oyster bed of international studies into which Booth will not dive in search of his theoretical pearls, and that is the other broad division of critical social theory with which I began: post-structuralism (Booth 2007: 462, 175–78). Nevertheless, work that can be broadly classed as 'post-structural' has made a significant contribution to the critical study of security.[2] This work draws on a number of social theorists and philosophers, though a few stand out as being more widely cited than others. These are the French thinkers mentioned at the outset: Foucault, Derrida and Baudrillard. The range of themes and issues across this literature is similarly broad and varied, but there are, perhaps, three of particular significance to security: the question of identity, that of ethics and, latterly, the biopolitics of security.

The relationship between identity and security was among the first important themes considered by scholars working in the French tradition. While constructivism had raised the question of identity, those in the post-structural tradition drew on the radical notion of the performative constitution of identity, developed out of the work of Michel Foucault and others, to think about security. David Campbell's work is signal in this regard, with his two major books, *Writing Security* and *National Deconstruction*, exploring a range of questions around identity and security (Campbell 1992, 1998b). In the former, he examines the ways in which discourses of fear animate a politics of security constitutive of the US and, in particular, how difference is produced as 'other' in such discourses. In the later book, Campbell looks at the violent effects of such othering in the case of the war and its aftermath in Bosnia. Bosnia is also the location for a more recent work on a similar theme, as Lene Hansen has recently explored *Security as Practice* in relation particularly to the Western production of Bosnia (Hansen 2006); and Elizabeth Dauphinée *The Ethics of Researching War* in relation to the Bosnian conflict (Dauphinée 2008).

The importance to post-structural thinking on security of the wars in the former Yugoslavia is not accidental. The 'thinking space' brought about by the end of the Cold War into which French philosophy-inspired work entered coincided with the collapse of Yugoslavia and the return of both war and concentration camps to the European continent (George 1994). The latter were particularly important because the routine criticism of post-structuralism was that it had no politics and, particularly, had no way to stand up to 'the worst'. It should be no surprise, then, that the 'ethnic cleansing' in Bosnia, complete with the horrifying images of emaciated prisoners behind barbed wire, should capture of the attention of post-structural thinkers on questions of security. Nor should it be surprising that the turn to examine Bosnia led these thinkers to ask questions about an ethical politics: how, in a world shorn of grand narratives or a necessary grounding for ethico-political judgements, can you respond to the violent destruction of the other? Answering this question has spawned a rich literature, much of which takes its theoretical cues from the work of Emmanuel Levinas and Jacques Derrida (Campbell 1998b; Campbell and Shapiro 1999; Dauphinée 2008; Edkins 2003; Lisle 2006).

If the wars of the former Yugoslavia commanded attention in the 1990s, after the events of 11 September 2001, that attention has tended to shift to the various issues raised by the terror attacks and, in particular, the responses to them. A number of thinkers influenced by post-structural thought have explored concerns around terrorism and security, with many deploying Michel Foucault's concept of biopolitics (Dillon and Lobo-Guerrero 2008). One notable programme of research has been organized under the 'Liberty and Security' label (CHALLENGE 2008). This group, led by Didier Bigo and R.B.J. Walker, considers the relationship between security and liberty in the European response to terror as a 'technique of government', as Foucault would call it (Bigo 2000, 2006). They explore the means by which governmental practices produce acceptable images of enemy others who can be violently excluded in the name of 'security'. Indeed, the production of the violently excluded other runs through much of the post-structural work on security after 2001, with many scholars drawing on Italian social theorist Giorgio Agamben's work on sovereignty and the exception to think about contemporary practices of security (Edkins et al. 2004; Dauphinée and Masters 2007).

The post-structural work on security is permeated by a concern with the relationship between security and the production of difference as dangerous 'other'. Scholars explore the ways in which representational and other governmental practices produce some as 'secured' and others as 'excluded' from the realm of security, an exclusion that is often effected violently. The politics of such work, therefore, continues in the emancipatory tradition of critical theory: exposing and exploring the production of exclusion for the purposes of informing a transformatory politics in favour of those who are excluded. The exclusions are produced contingently, in temporally and spatially specific locations, and so 'emancipations' can only be effected in a similarly specific and contingent fashion. The uncertainty of such an approach to political change is most concisely captured by Derrida's notion of democracy that is 'to come' (Campbell 1998b: 165–244). Democracy, in Derrida's sense, is a goal that is always deferred, rather than an institutional framework that can be applied; it is an ethos that informs politics, rather than a politics itself.

Security and academic exclusions

In 2006, a group of European scholars committed to the critical study of security attempted to draw together some of the disparate approaches that I have outlined here as quite separate (CASE Collective 2006). The attempt was interesting in a number of ways. The original article was published as a collectively authored piece of work, with a potentially changeable group of authors,[3] and perhaps just as unusually, it was titled a 'manifesto', making its politics immediately apparent. That politics is set out by the collective as breaking down the competitive individualism of contemporary scholarship, and overcoming the divisions that have emerged in critical approaches to security, specifically in the collective's case among the 'Copenhagen', 'Aberystwyth' and 'Paris' schools (CASE Collective 2006: 444f.).

The attempt to overcome internecine divisions and establish a broad research programme that can accommodate the variations of approach that have developed in non-traditional security studies is certainly laudable. However, what is particularly notable is that the responses to this initiative, almost without fail, drew attention to the exclusions that were effected by the CASE Collective's attempt at inclusion. In 2007, *Security Dialogue* published four rejoinders to the CASE Collective, followed by a response from the collective itself. Two of these four take the Collective to task for its focus on Europe, and the exclusions that it thereby produces (Behnke 2007; Salter 2007). The last of the four to be published, Christine Sylvester's 'Anatomy of a Footnote', calls the Collective to account for the exclusion of feminist scholarship (Sylvester 2007).

While all of the critiques of exclusion in an inclusionary project are interesting, the question of feminist scholarship deserves considerable attention, because it is not a problem that is unique to the CASE Collective. Indeed, Sylvester makes this point quite poignantly by discussing the exclusion of feminist security scholarship with particular reference to the work of Lene Hansen. Not only is Hansen based in Copenhagen, but she has also previously written on the exclusion of feminist scholarship from the Copenhagen school of Security Studies (Hansen 2000). Copenhagen is not alone in this lacuna, as it seems that feminism is often excluded from the lists of critical approaches to security, despite the fact that by most measures, much feminist scholarship fits within the characterization of social critique with which I began. How can we account for this exclusion, and what does it tell us more generally about the constitution of 'Critical Security Studies'?

A partial answer to the question of the exclusion of feminist scholarship can be found in both its own success and its diversity. The diversity of feminist writing means that it crosses many of the same divisions as other forms of social theory: There are, for example, liberal, Marxist and post-structural feminisms, each with their own take on questions of security. Thus, for example, Ken Booth, in building his intellectual supports for a theory of world security, is willing to include some feminist work that begins from a similar post-Marxist position (cf. Whitworth 2005). Feminist work may then be hidden by the divisions within which they fall. As Sylvester notes, however, the CASE Collective appears to exclude even those feminist scholars that fit within the divisions they are drawing. The success of feminist security scholarship has led to its being identified as a separate 'approach' when such things are catalogued and discussed. In textbooks on Security Studies, and in the scholarly reviews that constitute the fields, 'feminism' tends to be accorded its own chapter or section. Neither of these explanations, however, is entirely satisfactory. Rather, they point to the ways in which inclusions and exclusions are produced and reproduced throughout the scholarship on Security Studies inspired by the range of critical social theory. Indeed, they point to the ways in which such exclusions are always present in the ways in which we engage in scholarship.

Conclusion

Despite a shared commitment to a security scholarship that informs a politics of fundamental change in the interest of those presently disadvantaged, 'Critical Security Studies' remains riven by variations in approach and attitude. The greatest of those divisions is informed by the split in the wider world of critical social theory between those of a 'German' and those of a 'French' orientation. They are joined, however, by constructivists who seem to fit neither of these geographic markers; by members of the Copenhagen school who seem at times to fit both; and by feminists whose work reaches across and beyond the other divisions. The problem may perhaps be traced back to the quotation with which I began, in which Marx articulates the point of critical scholarship to be to change the world. It has proved impossible to agree with Marx's assumption that there is a singular 'world', even a singular world of security, which is to be transformed. If the point is to change *worlds*, to achieve *emancipations*, then the multiplicity of approaches is not only to be expected, but also to be welcomed. Each in its own way focuses critical thought on different, necessary sites of change, and so they may together inform a politics of multiple transformations. As the CASE Collective learned, however, simply willing such a broad, inclusive critical security study will not make it so.

Notes

1 For a clear example of a non-transformatory constructivist theory of world politics, see Wendt (1999).

2 This body of work defies a ready label. Booth, along with many others, calls it 'post-modern', but he recognizes that those writing within these approaches generally reject the label. 'Post-structural' is a more generally accepted term, but even that is a problematic one. The difficulty is that these scholars draw on a range of social thinkers who eschew the very idea of traditions of thought, and so while they share certain theoretical reflexes, they do not fit neatly into a single tradition.

3 A response piece authored by the collective in 2007 featured a different set of authors than the original piece, although there was considerable overlap (CASE Collective 2007).

References

Behnke, A. (2007) 'Presence and creation: A few (meta-)critical comments on the C.A.S.E. manifesto', *Security Dialogue* 38, 1: 105–11.

Bigo, D. (2006) 'Security, exception, ban, surveillance', in Lyon, D. (ed.) *Theorizing Surveillance: The Panopticon and Beyond*, Portland: Willan Publishing, pp. 46–68.

——(2000) 'When two become one: Internal and external securitisations in Europe', in Kelstrup, M. and Williams, M. C. (eds) *International Relations Theory and the Politics of European Integration: Power, Security and Community*, London: Routledge, pp. 171–204.

Booth, K. (1979) *Strategy and Ethnocentrism*, London: Croom Helm.

——(1991) 'Security and emancipation', *Review of International Studies* 17, 4: 313–26.

——(ed.) (2005) *Critical Security Studies and World Politics*, Boulder: Lynne Rienner.

——(2007) *Theory of World Security*, Cambridge: Cambridge University Press.

Campbell, D. (1992) *Writing Security: United States Foreign Policy and the Politics of Identity*, Minneapolis: University of Minnesota Press.

——(1998a) *Writing Security: United States Foreign Policy and the Politics of Identity*, 2nd edn, Minneapolis: University of Minnesota Press.

——(1998b) *National Deconstruction: Violence, Identity, and Justice in Bosnia*, Minneapolis: University of Minnesota Press.

——(2002) 'Atrocity, memory, photography: Imaging the concentration camps of Bosnia – the case of ITN versus Living Marxism', *Journal of Human Rights* 1, 1: 1–33 and 1, 2: 143–72.

Campbell, D. and Shapiro, M. (1999) *Moral Spaces: Rethinking Ethics and World Politics*, Minneapolis: University of Minnesota Press.

C.A.S.E. Collective (2006) 'Critical approaches to security in Europe: A networked manifesto', *Security Dialogue* 37, 4: 443–87.

——(2007) 'Europe, knowledge, politics: Engaging the limits: The C.A.S.E. Collective responds', *Security Dialogue* 38, 4: 559–76.

CHALLENGE: Liberty and Security (2008) Available online at: www.libertysecurity.org/ (accessed 28 January 2009).

Dalby, S. (1990) *Creating The Second Cold War*, London: Pinter.

Dauphinée, E. (2008) *The Ethics of Researching War: Searching for Bosnia*, Manchester: Manchester University Press.

Dauphinée, E. and Masters, C. (eds) (2007) *The Logics of Biopower and the War on Terror: Living, Dying, Surviving*, London: Palgrave-Macmillan.

Dillon, M. and Lobo-Guerrero, L. (2008) 'Biopolitics of security in the 21st century: An introduction', *Review of International Studies* 34, 2: 265–92.

Doty, R.L. (1993) 'Foreign policy as social construction: A post-positivist analysis of US counterinsurgency policy in the Phillippines', *International Studies Quarterly* 37, 3: 297–320.

Edkins, J. (2003) *Trauma and the Memory of Politics*, Cambridge: Cambridge University Press.

Edkins, J., Pin-Fat, V. and Shapiro, M.J. (eds) (2004) *Sovereign Lives: Power in Global Politics*, London: Routledge.

Enloe, C. (1983) *Does Khaki Become You? The Militarisation of Women's Lives*, South End: South End Press.

Finnemore, M. and Sikkink, K. (1998) 'International norm dynamics and political change', *International Organization* 52, 4: 887–917.

Fukuyama, F. (1992) *The End of History and the Last Man*, New York: The Free Press.

George, J. (1994) *Discourses of Global Politics: A Critical (Re)Introduction to International Relations*, Boulder: Lynne Rienner.

Gorbachev, M. (1987) *Perestroika: New Thinking for Our Country and the World*, New York: Harper & Row.

Gusterson, H. (1999) 'Missing the end of the Cold War in International Security', in Weldes, J., Laffey, M., Gusterson, H. and Duvall, R. (eds) *Culture of Insecurity*, Minneapolis: University of Minnesota Press, pp. 319–45.

Hansen, L. (2000) 'The little mermaid's silent security dilemma and the absence of gender in the Copenhagen school', *Millennium: Journal of International Studies* 29, 2: 285–306.

——(2006) *Security as Practice: Discourse Analysis and the Bosnian War*, London: Routledge.

Krause, K. (1998) 'Critical theory and security studies: The research programme of "critical security studies"', *Cooperation and Conflict* 33, 3: 298–333.

Latham, A. (1998) 'Constructing national security: Culture and identity in Indian arms control and disarmament practice', *Contemporary Security Policy* 19, 1: 129–58.

Lisle, D. (2006) *The Global Politics of Contemporary Travel Writing*, Cambridge: Cambridge University Press.

Marx, K. (1888) 'Thesis XI', *Theses On Feuerbach*, The Marx/Engels Internet Archive. Available online at: www.marxfaq.org/archive/marx/works/1845/theses/theses.htm (accessed 12 September 2008).

Milliken, J. (2001) *The Social Construction of the Korean War: Conflict and its Possibilities*, Manchester: University of Manchester Press.

Mutimer, D. (1998) 'Reconstituting security: The practices of proliferation control', *European Journal of International Relations* 4, 1: 99–129.

——(2007) 'Critical security studies: A schismatic history', in Collins, Alan (ed.) *Contemporary Security Studies*, Oxford: Oxford University Press, pp. 53–74.

——(2008) 'Beyond strategy: Critical thinking in the new security studies', in Snyder, Craig (ed.) *Contemporary Security Studies*, 2nd edn, London: Palgrave-Macmillan, pp. 34–59.

Peterson, V.S. (1992) *Gendered States: Feminist (Re)Visions of International Relations Theory*, Boulder: Lynne Rienner.

Price, R. (1988) 'Reversing the gun sights: Transnational civil society targets land mines', *International Organization* 52, 3: 613–44.

——(1997) *The Chemical Weapons Taboo*, Ithaca, NY: Cornell University Press.

——(2004) 'Emerging customary norms and anti-personnel landmines' in Price, R. and Reus-Smit, C. (eds) *The Politics of International Law*, Cambridge: Cambridge University Press, pp. 106–30.

Price, Richard and Reus-Smit, C. (eds) (2004) *The Politics of International Law*, Cambridge: Cambridge University Press.

Salter, M. (2007) 'On exactitude in disciplinary science: A response to the network manifesto', *Security Dialogue* 38, 1: 113–22.

Sylvester, C. (2007) 'Anatomy of a footnote', *Security Dialogue* 38, 4: 547–58.

——(1994) *Feminist Theories and International Relations in a Postmodern Era*, Cambridge: Cambridge University Press.

Tannenwald, N. (2007) *The Nuclear Taboo: The United States and the Non-Use of Nuclear Weapons Since 1945*, Cambridge: Cambridge University Press.

Tannenwald, N. and Wohlforth, W. (eds) (2005) 'Ideas, international relations and the end of the Cold War', Special Issue of *Journal of Cold War Studies* 7, 2.

Ulbert, C. and Risse, T. (2005) 'Deliberately changing the discourse: What does make arguing effective?' *Acta Politica* 40, 3: 351–67.

Walt, S. (1991) 'The renaissance of security studies', *International Studies Quarterly* 35, 2: 211–39.

Waltz, K. (1993) 'The emerging structure of international politics', *International Security* 18, 2: 44–79.

Weldes, J. (1999) *Constructing National Interests: The United States and the Cuban Missile Crisis*, Minneapolis: University of Minnesota Press.

Wendt, A. (1987) 'The agent-structure problem in international relations theory', *International Organization* 41, 3: 335–70.

——(1992) 'Anarchy is what states make of it: The social construction of power politics', *International Organization* 46, 2: 391–425.

——(1999) *Social Theory of International Politics*, Cambridge: Cambridge University Press.

Whitworth, S. (1998) 'Gender, race and the politics of peacekeeping' in Moxon-Browne, E. (ed.) *A Future for Peacekeeping?* Basingstoke: Macmillan, pp. 176–91.

——(2005) 'Militarized masculinities and the politics of peacekeeping' in Booth, K. (ed.) *Critical Security Studies and World Politics*, Boulder: Lynne Rienner, pp. 89–106.

Williams, M.C. (1992) 'Rethinking the "logic" of deterrence', *Alternatives* 17, 1: 67–94.

——(1998) 'Identity and the politics of security', *European Journal of International Relations* 4, 2: 207–28.

Wyn Jones, R. (1999) *Security, Strategy, and Critical Theory*, Boulder: Lynne Rienner.

5

Constructivism and securitization studies

Thierry Balzacq[1]

The study of security is a hard case for theories of International Relations. In recent academic scholarship, 'constructivist thinking' of the subject has risen to the challenge; it has, in effect, become one of the dominant approaches for examining security practices (cf. Ruggie 1996; Wendt 1999; Guzzini 2000; Zehfuss 2002; Farrell 2002). Some observers, however, regard the boundaries of constructivism as so permeable that any alternative view – realism, postmodernism or liberalism – can easily be subsumed under its fundamental precepts. Judged by these standards, constructivism is hardly a theory in itself (Wendt 1999: 7; Wendt and Fearon 2002). In contrast, Adler (1997) claims that because constructivism sits precisely between rationalism and reflectivism, it is a distinctive theory of International Relations, though one that is still emerging. There is no need to subscribe to either of these positions, as each embodies a particular theoretical commitment, and thus advocates its own future trajectory of constructivism. In the abstract, moreover, such discussions might be justified, but they are often distracting at the empirical level.

Thus, the aim of this chapter is not to review either constructivism or securitization, but to articulate the insights of the former as they relate to the latter.[2] To put the problem in its simplest terms: securitization predominantly examines how security problems emerge, evolve and dissolve. Securitization theory argues that language is not only concerned with what is 'out there', as realists and neorealists assume, but is also constitutive of that very social reality. Buzan and Wæver (1997: 245) claim, for instance, that securitization is 'constructivist all the way down'; Wæver (1995: 204) insists, moreover, that it is '*radically* constructivist' (emphasis added). However, constructivist approaches vary widely in their nature, which challenges us to think carefully about the kind of constructivism present in securitization. The answer, this chapter argues, depends essentially on how ontology and epistemology are blended. In fact, differing mixtures compete with one another and often lead to distinct methodological commitments.

The sequence of this chapter flows from a focused discussion of constructivism's contribution to Security Studies through what is perhaps its strongest offshoot – i.e. securitization theory. It proceeds on three fronts. First, beginning with a review of the main assumptions of securitization developed in the last decade, the chapter attempts to reconcile the illocutionary force of the concept of security and its meaning through a symbolic scrutiny of security interactions. Second, it dismisses the post-structuralist link to speech act theory, which creates an inconsistent view of securitization whereby a social ontology is wedded to interpretivist relativism. This provides, third, the baseline to advance a more coherent, i.e. pragmatic, approach to securitization that corrects the inconsistencies of the speech act approach. At this point, the chapter traverses the bridge from the speech act (i.e. philosophical) to a pragmatic (i.e. sociological) model of securitization. To explore the design and evolution of security problems, the chapter sets our sights on a new framework, blending discourse analysis and process tracing. Due to limits on length, however, the research toolkit is necessarily selective (Balzacq forthcoming a).

Security and the constructivist research programme

The origins of constructivism in IR are disputed according to where the terms of the discussion are situated. As a concept, constructivism entered the discipline essentially via the work of Onuf (1989). Practically, however, constructivist ideas spawned a great deal of IR theory in three main waves. The first relates to the works of Deutsch et al. (1957), Haas (1958) and Jervis (1970, 1976) whose arguments on images, perception and misperception predate and coincide with central assumptions of the modernist constructivism research programme. The second wave is post-positivist in inspiration and refers to an eclectic body of works that constitutes the so-called 'third debate' (Lapid 1987; Ashley 1984; Der Derian and Shapiro 1989; Walker 1987; Campbell 1992). The third wave has rationalist affinities with the first and shares an anti-essentialist ontology with the second (compare Adler 1997; Wendt 1999; Finnemore 1996; Katzenstein 1996; Kratochwil 1989; Price 1995; Tannenwald 1999; Risse-Kappen 1995).

In recent years, constructivism literature has grown in breadth and depth. One of the consequences of this colossal investment is an increasingly complex differentiation between strands of constructivism. Thus, if we are to use the concept of constructivism effectively, we need to sort out what exactly we are referring to. In many ways, the dividing lines between different classes of constructivism are often overstated. However, for the sake of clarity, this chapter endorses the 'mainstream' opposition between modern (conventional) and post-modern (critical) constructivism (Hopf 1998). It focuses on their treatment of ontology and epistemology, two essential features by which theoretical contributions to IR are gauged. This is based on the conviction that each constructivism substantiates just one kind of ontology–epistemology articulation.

To a significant extent, any approach to security starts with, and rests upon, a specific ontological commitment. Literally, ontology asks questions about the entities that populate the world; it is, in short, about the study of *beings*. Theories can be committed to different kinds of ontology, but two broad categories capture the range of possibilities on offer: materialism and idealism, on the one hand, and monism, dualism and pluralism, on the other. These can be clustered in different ways, but each theory will generally embody a combination of one element of each category at a time (e.g. materialism–dualism, idealism–monism). In this respect, constructivism is committed to a pluralist–idealist ontology. This has two implications, the first of which relates to how it conceives of beings that compose world politics and the second concerns the links between these beings. On the former, constructivism is anti-essentialist; on the latter, it is committed to a relational ontology. The two are intertwined in most constructivist schools (Jackson and Nexon 1999).

57

If ontology deals with the emergence, evolution and transformation of entities – observable or not – that populate global politics, epistemology asks what kind of knowledge claims can be made about these entities and the consequences, if any, they have on practice (Wight 2006; Chernoff 2007). For Lapid (1989), epistemology underpins and informs the third debate of the discipline. In brief, the discussion pitches positivists against post-positivists.

Neo-utilitarian theories (i.e. realism, liberalism and their 'neo' variants) are commonly defined as positivist approaches; just as critical theory and post-modernism are regarded as post-positivists. But constructivism defies easy classification. Though constructivists work with largely similar basic epistemological assumptions, different strands emphasize alternative stances and inevitably discount others. Fundamentally, constructivists are united in an opposition to empiricism – meaning that experience is the final test for our knowledge claims – and behaviourism – meaning that the rationale that underpins actors' explanation of their behaviour is of no relevance (Smith 1996: 35ff.). The vast bulk of constructivists argue that 'theory does not take place after the fact. Theories, instead, play a large part in constructing and defining what the facts are' (Enloe and Zalewski 1995: 299). This erodes the difference, drawn by structural realists, between 'real' and 'perceived' facts (Buzan et al. 1993).

However, these commitments cannot bridge the gaps between modern and post-modern constructivism, as each invokes a specific epistemological argument. The post-modernist or critical variant is decidedly interpretivist, while the modernist encourages both realist and positivist epistemologies (on this distinction, see Bevir and Rhodes 2002: 131–52). Post-modernist constructivists develop a sceptical take on core notions of positivism such as truth, objectivity and reason. Following this approach, to study world politics requires students to sort out the social discourse within which actions are designed and acquire meaning. The epistemological implication is that understanding, not explaining, constitutes the primary activity of social science (Hollis and Smith 1996).

Modernist constructivism, however, is compatible, though not coterminous, with interpretivism. For instance, Fierke (1998), Kratochwil (1989) and Onuf (1989) hardly adhere to the language of causality, falsity or truth usually associated with conventional constructivism. They argue, instead, that explanation could be expressed in terms of reasons, not causes, i.e. in terms of 'how possible' claims (Fierke 2006). Within modernist constructivism, scientific realist and positivist strains occupy a distinctive epistemological space. On the one hand, those who adopt scientific realism (e.g. Wendt 1999) attempt to explain both the causal and constitutive effects of unobservables in world politics (e.g. structures or processes). In this regard, ontology predates epistemology. On the other hand, those who defend a positivist posture encourage the use of the traditional language of causality and covering-law techniques. What distinguishes a realist from a positivist approach to epistemology is thus essentially the fact that the former acknowledges the existence of unobservable entities, while the latter does not (compare Ruggie 1998; Carlsnaes 1992).

However, the boundaries between scientific realist and positivist strands are permeable. In fact, many constructivists use scientific realism and positivism; sometimes interchangeably. Wendt (1994: 75), for instance, asserts that 'constructivists are modernists who fully endorse the scientific project of falsifying theories against evidence'. More tellingly yet, modernist constructivists claim that it is plausible to mix an anti-essentialist ontology with a positivist epistemology. This has been dubbed the *view media* or *middle ground* (Adler 1997; Wendt 1999: 40f.). More recently, however, those who endorse a modernist constructivism feel increasingly uncomfortable with the 'middle ground' orthodoxy, essen-tially because it strives to combine a social ontology with a rationalist epistemology (Fierke 2006). The detrimental effects of an inconsistent mixture of ontology and epistemology are also evident in securitization theory, whereby a social ontology is wedded to an inter-pretive relativism (i.e. post-structuralism). This chapter argues, on the contrary, that the study of the discursive design of threats need not presuppose a direct or indirect com-mitment to post-structuralism, particularly when speech act theory, which does not oppose substantialism, is simultaneously invoked.

In the search for an appropriate mixture, Fierke (2006: 174) advances a 'consistent constructivism', which promotes the 'inseparability of social ontology and epistemology'. This reformulation is useful, not least because it provides a new impetus to the study of security, and demonstrates that a constructivism which is neither modernist – as it departs from rational epistemology – nor critical – as it departs from post-structural analytics – is an achievable and promising goal. Overall, the thrust of the next section is to examine this prospect through a pragmatic approach to securitization. In this chapter, it is sug-gested that securitization advances the constructivist research programme in two ways. On the one hand, it offers a creative terrain for the development of ontological and epistemological commitments of constructivism. On the other hand, securitization theory has generated substantial results that might have broad applicability across IR because they explain how public problems (not only threats) emerge, spread and dissolve. Below, the view held by the speech act model of securitization is inspected, wherein 'episte-mology contradicts ontology' (Ruggie 1996: 95). After refining its assumptions, it considers how a pragmatic approach to securitization might produce a consistent combination of ontology and epistemology.

What is securitization?

A circle of European scholars, now widely known as the 'Copenhagen school' (CS), has striven to rekindle Security Studies on the basic creed that security is a speech act (cf. Wæver 1995; Buzan et al. 1998; Buzan and Wæver 1997; McSweeney 1996; Huysmans 1998; C.A.S.E. Collective 2006). According to the CS, an issue 'shows itself' (from the Greek *phainesthai*) as a security problem through the discursive politics of security (Dillon 1996: 47). Wæver posits it in the following way:

> with the help of language theory, we can regard 'security' as a *speech act*. In this light, security is not of interest as a sign that refers to something more real; the utterance *itself* is the act. By saying it something is done (as in betting, a promise, naming a ship). ... The *word* 'security' is the *act* ... In this instance, security is an illocutionary act, a 'self-referential' practice; its conditions of possibility are constitutive of the speech act of saying 'security'.
>
> (Wæver 1995: 55)

There are difficulties with this formulation, however. The upshot is that security cannot be wholly self-referential; instead, it frequently executes a kind of reference – though this might be partial or biased (Nightingale and Cromby 2002: 705). Further, the claim that security is a speech act may be intuitively strong, but it is theoretically restrictive and meth-odologically unfruitful. In fact, what has often been taken to be the result of the performative

59

use of the concept security does not follow from that assumption. Rather, securitization results from other unarticulated assumptions about security's symbolic power. In other words, securitization is a pragmatic act, i.e. a sustained argumentative practice aimed at convincing a target audience to accept, *based on what it knows about the world*, the claim that a specific development is threatening enough to deserve an immediate policy to curb it. Thus, the CS view can be called *philosophical*, while the pragmatic approach to securitization is termed *sociological*.

Conceptually, the two models were developed in parallel, the former in Denmark and the latter in Belgium, France and the UK. Yet, given intensive cross-fertilizations, the boundaries between these perspectives are now porous, and sometimes authors seem to move from one model to another, without further clarification. However, differences between the two persist that account for the differences in how security problems are examined. Put starkly, in the CS model, philosophical speculations often triumph over sociological insights, which are at best accorded cosmetic status. By contrast, in the second model, sociological elements subsume philosophical premises. Whereas the philosophical model prefers post-structuralist methods, the sociological view proposes a pluralist approach to securitization wherein discourse analysis and process tracing work together.

The philosophical model

Many works that have come to constitute the standard argument about securitization rest upon philosophical concepts. Both speech act theory and post-structuralist concepts have thus been applied, albeit with varying success, to a broad range of substantive issues such as identity (Buzan et al. 1998: 119–40), infectious disease (Elbe 2006; Vieira 2007), transnational crime and human trafficking (Emmers 2003; Stritzel 2007; Jackson 2006) and religion (Laustsen and Wæver 2000).

But the transferability of philosophical concepts to such a spectrum of issues has a perverse effect. The problem is essentially one of consistency in their substantive assumptions, as there is a disconnect between the theoretical premises and the method that follows (Léonard 2007). Indeed, within the philosophical model of securitization, most substantive studies fall outside the framework of speech act theory (but see Vuori 2008, for an exception). In short, the philosophical model scorns methodological consistency (in substance, though not in the basic concepts used). Equally, some proponents of the philosophical approach to securitization are led to build a compromise between philosophical contents that are hardly compatible – for instance, speech act and post-structuralism (Searle 1977a). Still, others thought it useful to conflate pieces of Bourdieu's sociology and Derrida's philosophical intuitions, without consideration for the respective reservations of these authors (cf. Bourdieu 1991; Derrida 1982; Kamuf 1991; Taurek 2006).

This section revisits and rails against the conceptualization of security as a speech act. It looks in particular at the three issues at the centre of the pragmatic reformulation of securitization, including the meaning and implications of speech act theory; the conflation of post-structuralism with the speech act view of security; and the tension between what security *means* and what it *does*. Each addresses a particular vulnerability in the CS theory of securitization. First, it is argued that by mixing perlocutionary and illocutionary acts together, the CS obscures the role of audience(s) in securitization theory. Second, by following Derrida, who blends linguistic act theory with post-structuralism, the CS belies the distinctive contribution of each approach to discourse analysis. These two problems are related, because how we understand securitization will depend on two choices –

whether to focus on illocutionary or perlocutionary acts, and whether to deploy textual or practice analysis (Neumann and Heikka 2005). Specifically, a focus on the illocutionary has led the CS to skirt the distinctive role of the audience, while an emphasis on textualism has left it unable to account for the impact of context on securitization.

Speech act inquiry in brief

In essence, the basic idea of the speech act theory according to Austin is that certain statements do more than merely describe a given reality and, as such, cannot be judged as false or true. Instead, these utterances realize a specific action; they *do* things: They are 'performatives' as opposed to 'constatives' that simply report states of affairs and are thus subject to truth and falsity tests. From Austin's (1962: 95, 107) perspective, each sentence can convey three types of acts, the combination of which constitutes the total speech act situation:

(i) locutionary – the utterance of an expression that contains a given sense and reference;
(ii) illocutionary – the act performed in articulating a locution. In a way, this category captures the explicit performative class of utterances, and the concept of the 'speech act' is literally predicated on that sort of agency;
(iii) perlocutionary acts, which consist of the consequential effects or 'sequels' that are aimed to evoke the feelings, beliefs, thoughts or actions of the target audience (Searle 1977b: 59–82).

It is important to note, however, that illocutionary and perlocutionary acts diverge in terms of the direction and the nature of consequences they initiate. The first type, by convention, is bound up with effects that occur if and only if all four of the 'felicity conditions' are met:

(i) a preparatory condition determined by the existence of a 'conventional procedure having a certain conventional effect, that procedure to include the uttering of certain words by certain persons in certain circumstances';
(ii) an executive condition to determine whether the procedure has been fully executed by all participants;
(iii) a sincerity condition that posits that participants in this conventional procedure must have certain thoughts or feelings, and 'must intend so to conduct themselves';
(iv) a fulfilment condition determined by whether participants 'actually so conduct themselves subsequently' (Austin 1962: 14f.).

The second type of acts, perlocution, is 'specific to the circumstances of issuance, and is therefore not conventionally achieved just by uttering particular utterances, and includes all those effects, intended or unintended, often indeterminate, that some particular utterances in a particular situation may cause' (ibid.). Thus, if perlocution does not adhere to rules conditioning the realization of an illocutionary act, which the CS paraphrases for its definition of security and securitization, it becomes plain that viewing security as a speech act is a restrictive theoretical position. Equally, in any intersubjective process such as securitization, the purpose is to prompt a significant response from the other (perlocutionary effect); unless this happens, no securitization takes place. Necessarily, then, perlocution is central rather than tangential to understanding how a particular public issue can change into a security problem.

Difficulties with a post-structuralist speech act

The theoretical position of the CS on speech acts stems from a Derridean re-appropriation of Austin's philosophy. This is conspicuous in two respects, at least: first, because of the paucity of contextual studies; and, second, as a corollary, because of the overemphasis on textual analysis.[3] A brief look at Derrida's ideas on the matter will make this clear. According to Derrida, what is crucial in performatives is neither the context of their utterance, nor the speaker's intention, but the intrinsic attribute of the enunciation, that is, 'its iterability' or reproducibility. Indeed, performatives can be cited, extracted from their 'context of production', and grafted onto other ones with little quibble.

Hence, Derrida is amplifying two points. First, the enunciation of a performative cannot be construed as the sheer product of a speaker's intention, since the possibility of the absence of the speaker makes the intentionality claim of any given text void. Second, the possibility of the absence coupled with the iterability and citationality of performatives reveals the worthless nature of contextual analysis. This understanding of enunciation drives us in a telling direction that, if pushed to its basic assumptions, anticipates the primary error of the CS: there is nothing to get out of the text, and the act of writing, as Derrida (1977: 174) puts it, is not a vehicle 'of communication, at least not in the ... sense of transmission of meaning'. This is a central, though often confusing, claim of post-structuralism; an assumption that leads the CS to maintain that 'the defining criterion of security is textual' and 'discourse analysis can uncover one thing: discourse', as its purpose 'is not to get at something else' (Buzan et al. 1998: 76f.). On this view, it is not clear why embarking on discourse analysis is relevant at all, if everything is known before the task is undertaken. Hence, one could argue that in making the aforementioned claims, the CS further strengthens the contention that its method is wholly devoted to the study of 'lists of instances' in texts, instead of meaning.

It is not argued here, however, that a post-structuralist view of the speech act is not, in its own terms, a valid approach to security. Instead, it is claimed that the *link* between the speech act approach to security and post-structuralism – in the guise of Derrida's philosophy – creates tremendous difficulties for securitization theory. This assertion bears directly on a central problem in the epistemology of discourse analysis: to what degree do studies draw on extant theoretical categories as opposed to building conceptual tools that emerge from the relations under scrutiny? A speech act view of security believes that the first challenge is to record securitization practices deductively, i.e. with a theoretical order imposed a priori (the rules of speech act and units of analysis). For post-structuralism, by contrast, the main purpose – and the biggest difficulty – is to capture securitization processes inductively, i.e. without a theoretical scheme imposed a priori (Sarup 1993; Carroll 1990). The core of such a position is to study the topography of discourse without 'assigning ... relatively fixed labels to pieces of textual evidence (that) one assume(s) mean the same thing' (Hopf 2002: 36). If, in some sense, speech act philosophy is committed to theoretical categories that are used to structure our understanding of collected discourses (verbal and textual), then the imperative of 'non-categorization' guiding post-structuralism will not fit within a speech act model of security. Perhaps, it dovetails best with a pragmatic scheme, with the important caveat that, in contrast to the speech act view, pragmatism posits that cognitive structure – a coherent but flexible set of modes of thought, motivations and reasons for action – have a real impact on discourse (Mead 1934; Balzacq 2003).

The sociological model

The sociological model of securitization draws upon symbolic interactionism and, to various degrees, on Bourdieu's contribution to the symbolic uses of language. However, Bourdieu's central assumptions on the social functions of language themselves flow partly from symbolic interactionism, as a kind of social pragmatism (cf. Balzacq 2003; Balzacq forthcoming a and b). However, on other counts, Bourdieu's argument outperforms the latter. For instance, those who build upon Bourdieu recast in new terms how securitizing agents coalesce to form a *social field*, i.e. a configuration of social actors that generates distinctive practices and effects (Bigo 2008; Ceyhan and Tsoukala 2002; Salter 2008; Huysmans 2006; Aras and Polat 2008). The two together work on 'symbolically-mediated' interactions (Abrahamsen 2005).[4] The next section amplifies, first, the view that securitization is an argumentative process, rather than a pure speech act mechanism. It then outlines the benefits of conceiving of securitization in a pragmatic sense.

From speech act to a pragmatic act 1: definition

The use of language, we know, is an essential component of interactions. In the context of securitization, the aim of interactions, as constituted or mediated by language, is to convince or persuade an audience to see the world in a specific way and thus act as the situation commands. Securitization, like many encounters in world politics, depends on assumptions about persuasion that students of security issues far too often neglect (Crawford 2002). This is a plea for argument analysis, because the latter captures the emergence of a new social fact, i.e. a threat, through intersubjective reasoning. In short, if the theory of securitization is embedded in a matrix of persuasion, it must be grasped in terms of the rationale underlying the latter. To clarify: while a speech act can produce effects just by following rules, argument analysis holds that for a discursive process to succeed, it needs a strategy of reasoning and persuasion. Thus, the sociological model of securitization contributes a new process – persuasive argument and reasoning – to understanding securitization that explores how variations in security symbols determine the very nature and, crucially, the consequences of the political structuration of threats.

In this light, securitization is a process whereby:

- patterns *of heuristic artefacts* (metaphors, image repertoires, analogies, stereotypes, emotions, etc.),
- are contextually mobilized by a recognized agent, who
- works persuasively to prompt a *target* audience *to build a coherent network of implications* (feelings, sensations, thoughts and intuitions), that concurs with the enunciator's reasons for choices and actions, by
- investing the referent subject with such an *aura of unprecedented threatening complexion* that
- a *customized political act must be undertaken immediately* to block its development.

Drawing on Mey (2001) this can be termed a 'pragmatic act', because it devotes more attention to the context in which securitization occurs, accounts for the status of the speakers and attends to the effects that security statements provoke in the audience than does the CS model (for a discussion of this approach, see Balzacq 2005a; Roe 2008). In the sociological model, securitization does not *necessarily* lead to the adoption of exceptional measures.

The contrast between the strategic and speech act views of security parallels the difference between 'pragmatics' and 'universal pragmatics'. The first deals with language usage, including a colourful use of language to attain a goal. Universal pragmatics, by contrast, is primarily concerned with fundamental principles or rules underlying communicative action (Habermas 1984). If the rules are not followed, the communicative action is distorted, and thus not successful or 'felicitous', to use Austin's (1962) vocabulary. The speech act concept of security, which is categorized as a kind of universal pragmatics, is consequently inadequate for students of IR to deal with the 'discursive politics of security'. It is useful to think of security pronouncements not as speech acts that are successful to the extent that rules are followed by the agents, but as discursive techniques allowing the securitizing actor to 'induce or increase the (public) mind's adherence to the thesis presented to its assent' (Perelman and Olbrechts-Tyteca 1969: 4). Phrased more carefully, the critical question is not whether discourse 'does' things, but instead *under what conditions* the social content and meaning of security produces threats.

From speech act to a pragmatic act 2: constituent analytics

The concept of security as a pragmatic act (see Table 5.1) can be broken down into three closely related, but nonetheless distinct, levels, that of the *agent*, that of the *act* and that of the *context*, each in turn having interwoven facets (Mey 2001: 214; Epstein 2008).

The *agent level* includes three aspects:

(i)   the power positions and the personal identities of those who *design* security issues, which is 'a set of attributes, beliefs, desires, or principles of action' (Bigo 2005, 2008);
(ii) the social identity, which operates to both constrain and enable the behaviour of the securitizing actor(s);
(iii) the nature and the capacity of the target audience, and the main opponents or alternative voices within the relevant social field – either individual or corporate, ad hoc or institutionalized (Fearon 1999).

The *level of the act* has three sides: the first is the 'action-type' side that refers to the appropriate language to use to perform a given act – the grammatical and syntactical rules of the language. The second facet is strategic: which heuristic artefacts shall a securitizing actor use to create (or effectively resonate with) the circumstances that will facilitate the

Table 5.1 The vocabulary of the pragmatic act of security

		Constituent Analytics
	Agent	Power positions Personal and social identities Target audience(s)
Levels	Act	Action-type Heuristic artefacts Policy tools
	Context	Distal Proximate

mobilization of the audience – analogies, metaphors, metonymies, emotions or stereotypes? What is the target audience, and who are the main opponents or alternative voices within the relevant social field – individual or corporate, ad hoc or institutionalized? Which media are favoured – electronic or print media? The overarching outcome is to open up the politics and methods of creating security, since discourse involves practice and refers to variables that are extra-linguistic (Williams 2003; McDonald 2008; Wilkinson 2007). The third facet is expressed by policy tools of securitization, i.e. '*an instrument which, by its very nature or by its very functioning, transforms the entity (i.e., subject or object) it processes into a threat*' (Balzacq 2008: 80, emphasis in the original). Given the volume of security programmes, wherein discourse and ideology are increasingly entangled and differences between securitizing actors and audiences are blurred, focusing on the nature and functions of policy tools may improve our understanding of securitization in at least two ways. Politically, an approach that regards securitization as a tool is a helpful method to attend to the dynamics of securitizing practices. It not only reveals how policymakers translate intentions into concrete actions, it also shows how the life of a policy instrument is affected by social processes. Moreover, instruments convey latent developments and produce effects that are often 'more consequential than [their] ostensible goals' (Feenberg 1991: 5). Methodologically, the awareness of these dynamics will enable students to contrive explanations that, at any level, should be sensitive to the knowledge that a tool approach provides about the nature of a threat. In fact, studying the making of security problems should open up the analytical net, to account for securitizing practices that *are not*, strictly speaking, discursively mediated (Balzacq 2008).

The *contextual level* is difficult to unpack (Balzacq 2005b). Fortunately, Wetherell's (2001: 380f.) parsimonious distinction between *distal* and *proximate* contexts makes the matter more tractable. The proximate context includes 'the sort of occasion or genre of interaction the participants take an episode to be (e.g., a meeting, an interview, a summit)'. By contrast, the distal context focuses on the sociocultural embeddedness of the text. The distal context has strong *recursive effects*, meaning that persuasive arguments operate in cascade (e.g. people are convinced because friends of a friend are convinced, etc.). It refers to 'things like social class, the ethnic composition of the participants, the institutions or sites where discourse occurs, ecological, regional, and cultural settings'.

Strategies for securitization studies

The ways in which securitization occurs is ultimately an empirical question and yet students rarely discuss issues of method (Balzacq and Léonard forthcoming). This is probably so because researchers have often been divided in their speculations over whether we should pay attention to method at all (Milliken 1999: 226f.). Further, there is considerable disagreement on why and when discourse analysis is chosen, rather than content study, and what differences these choices ultimately make in grasping policy processes (Neuendorf 2002; Herrera and Braumoeller 2004: 15–39). Finally, the differences among various discursive approaches to security are compelling, so much so that the first challenge that students of securitization face is to simply make sense of this diversity (cf. Duffy et al. 1998; Fierke 1998; Hansen 2006; Hopf 2002; Larsen 1997; Milliken 1999; Neumann 2008; Ringmar 1996; Laffey and Weldes 2004). Therefore, understanding the pragmatic approach to securitization involves making hard choices about the substantive focus of the analysis.

The conventional manner in which discourse materializes is text. The CS contends that textualism is the best method for security analysis. By textualism, proponents of the CS mean Derridean post-structuralism, whereby silence, gesture and images are excluded (Hansen 2000; Williams 2003). This is unfortunate, as one of the aims of securitization research is to retrieve information that lies beyond the purview of textualism. In fact, securitization studies seek to attend to complex processes (causal and constitutive) which give rise to security problems. In this respect, this chapter has argued that speech act cannot do the job, either alone or combined with post-structuralism. The chapter proposes, by contrast, that process tracing and discourse analysis be dwelled upon to shed light on the puzzles of securitization. The aim of the sociological approach is to develop securitization studies which sit, to use Elster's (1998: 45) words, between 'laws and description'. Of course, the number of variables is potentially high. But this could be controlled by paying special attention to the research design from the outset (for a start, see George and Bennet 2005; Neumann 2008). Doing so might contribute to the transformation of securitization into a more credible theory.

Three overlapping operational 'levels' are necessary, although none is sufficient for setting about the analysis of securitization: *discourse as text, discourse as action* and the *context of production*. The argument is summarized in Figure 5.1.

Discourse as text focuses on the analysis of actualized sets of specific strings of statements, uttered by the securitizing actor, which focuses on the internal coherence of the text (intratextuality), the systematic relationships among texts dealing with the same subject (intertextuality) and the recurrent patterns of linguistic characterization that constitute the storylines. According to Hajer (1995: 56), storylines are generative narratives 'that allow actors to draw upon various discursive categories to give meaning to specific physical or

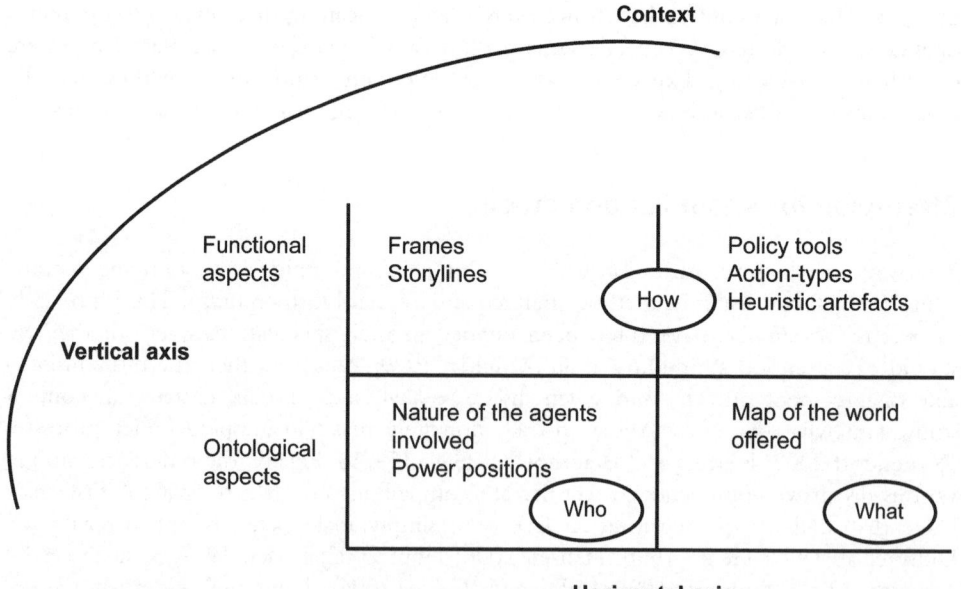

Figure 5.1 Securitization analysis in context.

social phenomena'. The storyline has three functions in discourse: first, it establishes a link among different characteristics that point toward the threatening phenomenon. Second, when reified, a storyline acquires its own momentum by contributing to a cognitive routinization. Third, storylines create contending coalitions around contrasting sets of common understandings. In other words, this textual layer – which depicts how the securitizing agent argues the security case and captures the salient characterizations of the referent object, the referent subject and the target audience, as well as agencies and interactions – belongs to the vertical axis of securitization analysis.

Discourse as action. Emphasizes the study of the performativity of the text: what kind of action does it want to achieve (assertive, commissive, expressive, directive or declarative) (Searle 1977b)? What are its communicative purposes and its domains of relevance? Which heuristic artefacts are favoured, for which meanings? What 'map' of world politics does it present? What kinds of interactions are generated? It is out of this process of considering the 'action-type' side that the horizontal axis of the analysis of security utterances arises.

The context of production. Two views of the relationship between context and discourse must be distinguished. First, the *internalist approach* argues that the context is shaped by the use of the concept of security. Thus, security, or at least its illocutionary force, remodels the context in which it occurs. What is key here is the 'abductive power' of words; that is, security utterances operate as 'instructions for the construction and interpretation of the situation. The power of words is such that appropriate conditions can be created when they are not textually or contextually erased' (Violi 2001: 187). The *externalist approach* to a context posits, on the contrary, that the success of securitization is contingent upon a perceptive – external – environment pervaded by a sense of criticality. Put differently, the context 'selects' certain features of the concept, while others are elided. Whatever the view adopted, the study of contextual implications should remain sensitive to the level of analysis (distal, proximate or both).

In sum, the pragmatic act of securitization is interested in ascertaining both the constitutive and causal effects of discourse – text and action – upon context, and vice versa. Thus, the model offered here combines the three dimensions to identify different but complementary perspectives in securitization analysis.

Each box contains different factors involved in categorizing public problems as threats. Similarly, the two axes are rough sets, not clean dichotomies. Each intersection between the two axes indicates different ways of capturing the process of discursive action, which is ultimately empirical. Although we could confine the scope of inquiry to one of the boxes or one single intersection, we need to be aware that a more credible study of securitization requires an account of all three dimensions, i.e. 'how', 'who' and 'what'. Beneath these three dimensions lies that which determines the most relevant material of scrutiny. Put differently, the three dimensions, embedded in a defined context (e.g. 'when' and 'where'), grasp the main preoccupation of securitization analysts: to understand the political structuring of a threat image. To this end, students of security discourses must initially identify the issue referred to as a threat. Three criteria, each of which is sufficient, are of operational salience: (i) the issue should be a target for parliamentary action; (ii) it should be a focus of public attention or debate; or (iii) the issue should be a target for activities related to public opinion or legal and/or political actions.

Conclusion

In recent years, there have been sustained attempts to apply, albeit with a disturbing degree of theoretical syncretism, the 'framework' of securitization to various empirical cases. However, little attention has been paid to the refinement of its theoretical premises. Some argue that because the most central tenets of securitization are now often repeated without further substantive innovation, it is time for students to turn to the examination of the consequences of securitization (Huysmans 2006). This chapter has claimed that this is misleading. In fact, even the basic assumptions of securitization remain problematic. This chapter has argued that the primary task facing students of securitization is not to add to the already long list of premises and conjectures, but instead to unpack and re-present these diverse ideas into a core of social scientific assumptions guiding empirical research. Such a research programme will necessarily address questions such as: what kind of audience(s) matter(s), in what context(s)? What are the respective powers of securitizing agents (media, political elites, think tanks, etc.)? How do we weight the respective heuristic artefacts of securitization (emotions, storylines, metaphors, pictures and policy tools)? What are the conditions of possibility for de-securitization? How cumulative is research on securitization? What kind of theory (if any) is securitization? The answer to these questions, we predict, will structure how securitization studies unfold, because they have significant conceptual, methodological, and empirical implications (Balzacq forthcoming a). Should students shy away from these challenges, securitization would be no more than an intellectual vogue.

Notes

1 I am grateful to Myriam Dunn Cavelty and Victor Mauer for their sustained effort to help me keep this work within its limits. I also thank Léon Sampana and Sandro Faes for their research assistance. Finally, I am grateful to doctoral students from the Université Libre de Bruxelles, Université catholique de Louvain and Université de Mons (FUCAM) who attended the Advanced Seminar on Constructivism and IR Theories, in 2008. Some bits of this chapter were tried on them.
2 Reviews of constructivism are numerous. A sample includes Christiansen et al. 1999: 528–44; Adler 2002: 95–118; Hopf 2002. For a bibliography on different aspects of securitization theory as they relate to critical approaches to Security Studies, see C.A.S.E. Collective 2006.
3 This is demonstrated by a closer look at Wæver's references. See, for instance, Wæver (1995: 80f., endnotes 25 and 35); Buzan et al. (1998: 47, endnote 5). Here, Austin's (1962) text is often cited in conjunction with Derrida (1977: 172–97). Interestingly, Searle's (1977a) response to Derrida, which regards this use of speech act as inappropriate, is ignored.
4 On security as a symbol, see Wolfers (1962).

References

Abrahamsen R. (2005) 'Blair's Africa: The politics of securitization and fear', *Alternatives: Global, Local, Political* 30: 50–80.

Adler, E. (1997) 'Seizing the middle ground: Constructivism in world politics', *European Journal of International Relations* 3, 3: 319–63.

——(2002) 'Constructivism and international relations', in Carlsnaes, W., Risse, T. and Simmons, B.A. (eds) *Handbook of International Relations*, London: Sage, pp. 95–118.

Aras, B. and Polat, R.K. (2008) 'From conflict to cooperation: Desecuritization of Turkey's relations with Syria and Iran', *Security Dialogue* 39, 5: 495–535.

Aristotle (1924) 'Rhetoric', trans. by Roberts, W.R. in Ross, D. (ed.) *The Works of Aristotle*, v. XI. Oxford: Oxford University Press.

Ashley, R. (1984) 'The poverty of neorealism', *International Organization* 38, 2: 225–86.

Austin, J.L. (1962) *Sense and Sensibilia*, Oxford: Clarendon Press.

Balzacq, T. (2003) *Constructivism, Pragmatism, and Security Studies*, PhD Thesis, University of Cambridge.

——(2005a) 'The three faces of securitization: Political agency, audience, and context', *European Journal of International Relations* 11, 2: 171–201.

——(2005b) 'The configuration of context and its influence on securitization', Unpublished manuscript.

——(2008) 'The policy tools of securitization: Information exchange, EU foreign and interior policies', *Journal of Common Market Studies* 46, 1: 75–100.

——(forthcoming a) *A Theory of Securitization: The Nature and Origins of Security Ideas*. Book manuscript.

——(forthcoming b) *On Securitization: A New Framework for Analysis*, London: Routledge.

Balzacq, T. and Léonard, S. (forthcoming) 'The good, the bad, and the ugly: Of methods and progress in securitization studies'. Under submission at *Security Dialogue*.

Bevir, M. and Rhodes, R. (2002) 'Interpretative theory', in Marsh, D. and Stoker, G. (eds) *Theory and Methods in Political Science*, Basingstoke: Palgrave Macmillan, pp. 131–52.

Bigo, D. (2005) 'La mondialisation de l'(in)sécurité? Réflexion sur le champ des professionnels de la gestion des inquiétudes et analytique de la transnationalisation des processus d'(in)sécurisation', *Cultures et Conflits* 58. Available online at: www.conflits.org/document1813.html (accessed June 2007).

——(2008) 'International political sociology', in Williams, P. (ed.) *Security Studies: An Introduction*, London: Routledge, pp. 116–30.

Bourdieu, P. (1991) *Language and Symbolic Power*, Cambridge, MA: Harvard University Press.

Buzan, B. and Wæver, O. (1997) 'Slippery? Contradictory? Sociologically untenable? The Copenhagen School replies', *Review of International Studies* 23, 2: 241–50.

Buzan, B., Jones, C. and Little, R. (1993) *The Logic of Anarchy: From Neorealism to Structural Realism*, New York: Columbia University Press.

Buzan, B., Wæver, O. and de Wilde, J. (1998) *Security: A New Framework for Analysis*, Boulder CO: Lynne Rienner.

Campbell, D. (1992) *Writing Security: United States Foreign Policy and the Politics of Identity*, Minneapolis: University of Minnesota Press.

Carlsnaes, W. (1992) 'The agency-structure problem in foreign policy analysis', *International Studies Quarterly* 36, 3: 245–70.

Carroll, D.R. (ed.) (1990) *The States of 'Theory': History, Art, and Critical Discourse*, New York: Columbia University Press.

C.A.S.E. Collective (2006) 'Critical security studies in Europe: A networked manifesto', *Security Dialogue* 37, 4: 443–87.

Ceyhan, A. and Tsoukala, A. (2002) 'The securitization of migration in western societies: Ambivalent discourses and policies', *Alternatives* 5, 21–39.

Checkel T. (2008) 'Process tracing', in Klotz, A. and Prakash, D. (eds) *Qualitative Methods in International Relations*, Basingstoke, UK: Palgrave MacMillan, pp. 114–30.

Checkel, T. and Moravcsik, A. (2001) 'A constructivist research program in EU studies?', *European Union Politics* 2, 2: 219–49.

Chernoff, F. (2007) *Theory and Metatheory in International Relations: Concepts and Contending Accounts*, New York: Palgrave MacMillan.

Christiansen, T., Jorgensen, K.E. and Wiener, A. (eds) (1999) 'The social construction of Europe', *Journal of European Public Policy* 6, 4: 528–44.

Crawford, N. (2000) 'The passion of world politics: Propositions on emotion and emotional relationships', *International Security* 24, 4: 116–56.

——(2002) *Argument and Change in World Politics: Ethics, Decolonization, and Humanitarian Intervention*, Cambridge: Cambridge University Press.

Der Derian, J. and Shapiro, M.J. (eds) (1989) *International/Intertextual Relations: Postmodern Readings of World Politics*, Lexington: Lexington Books.

Derrida, J. (1977) 'Signature event context', *Glyph: John Hopkins Textual Studies*, Baltimore: Johns Hopkins University Press.

——(1982) *Positions*, Chicago: University of Chicago Press.

Deutsch, K.W., Burrel, S.A. and Kann, R.A. (eds) (1957) *Political Community and North Atlantic Area*, Princeton: Princeton University Press.

Dillon, M. (1996) *Politics of Security & Towards a Political Philosophy of Continental Thought*, London: Routledge.

Duffy, G., Federking, B.K. and Tucker, S.A. (1998) 'Language games: Dialogical analysis of INF negotiations', *International Studies Quarterly* 42, 2: 271–94.

Durkheim, E. (1953) *Sociology and Philosophy*, trans. by Pocock, D.F. London: Cohen & West Ltd.

Elbe, S. (2006) 'Should HIV/AIDS be securitized?', *International Studies Quarterly* 50, 1: 119–44.

Elster, J. (1998) 'A plea for mechanisms', in Hedstroem, P. and Swedberg, R. (eds) *Social Mechanisms: An Analytical Approach to Social Theory*, Cambridge, UK: Cambridge University Press, pp. 45–73.

Emmers, R. (2003) 'ASEAN and the securitization of transnational crime in Southeast Asia', *The Pacific Review* 16, 3: 419–38.

Enloe, C. and Zalewski, M. (1995) 'Questions of identity in international relations', in Booth, K. and Smith, S. (eds) *International Relations Theory Today*, Oxford: Polity Press, pp. 279–305.

Epstein, C. (2008) *The Power of Words in International Relations: Birth of an Anti-Whaling Discourse*, Cambridge, MA: The MIT Press.

Farrell, T. (2002) 'Constructivist security studies: Portrait of a research program', *International Studies Review* 4, 1: 71–92.

Fearon, J. (1999) 'What is identity (as we now use the word)?' Unpublished Paper, Stanford University, Stanford, 3 November.

Feenberg, A. (1991) *Critical Theory of Technology*, New York: Oxford University Press.

Fierke, K.M. (1998) *Changing Games, Changing Strategies: Critical Investigations in Security*, Manchester: Manchester University Press.

——(2006) 'Constructivism', in Dunne, T., Kurki, M. and Smith, S. (eds) *International Relations Theories*, Oxford: Polity Press, pp. 166–84.

Finnemore, M. (1996) *National Interests in International Society*, Ithaca, NY: Cornell University Press.

George, A. and Bennet, A. (2005) *Case Studies and Theory Development in the Social Sciences*, Cambridge, MA: MIT Press.

Guzzini, S. (2000) 'A reconstruction of constructivism in international relations', *European Journal of International Relations* 6, 2: 147–82.

Haas, E.B. (1958) *The Uniting of Europe: Political, Social, and Economic Forces*, Stanford: Stanford University Press.

Habermas, J. (1984) *The Theory of Communicative Action*, Vol. 1, Boston: Beacon Press.

Hajer, M. (1995) *Politics of Environmental Discourse*, Oxford: Oxford University Press.

Hansen, L. (2000) 'The little mermaid's silent security dilemma and the absence of gender in the Copenhagen School', *Millennium* 29, 2: 289–306.

——(2006) *Security as Practice: Discourse Analysis and the Bosnian War*. London: Routledge.

Herrera, Y. M. and Braumoeller, B.F. (2004) 'Symposium: Discourse and content analysis', *Newsletter of the American Political Science Association Organized Section on Qualitative Methods* 2, 1: 15–39.

Hollis, M. and Smith, S. (1996) 'A response: Why epistemology matters in international theory', *Review of International Studies* 22, 1: 111–16.

Hopf, T. (2002) *Social Construction of International Politics: Identities and Foreign Policies*, Moscow, 1955 and 1999, Ithaca, NY: Cornell University Press.

——(1998) 'The promise of constructivism in international relations theory', *International Security* 23, 1: 171–200.

Huysmans, J. (1998) 'Security: What do you mean? From concept to thick signifier', *European Journal of International Relations* 4, 2: 226–55.

——(2006) *The Politics of Insecurity: Fear, Migration and Asylum in the EU*, London: Routledge.

Jackson, N.J. (2006) 'International Organizations, security dichotomies and the trafficking of persons and narcotics in post-Soviet Central Asia: A critique of the securitization framework', *Security Dialogue* 37, 3: 299–317.

Jackson, P.T. and Nexon, D. (1999) 'Relations before states: Substance, process and the study of world politics', *European Journal of International Relations* 5, 3: 291–332.

Jervis, R. (1970) *The Logic of Images in International Relations*, Princeton, NJ: Princeton University Press.

——(1976) *Perception and Misperception in International Politics*, Princeton, NJ: Princeton University Press.

Kamuf, P. (1991) *A Derrida Reader: Between the Blinds*, Columbia: Columbian University Press.

Katzenstein, P.J. (ed.) (1996) *The Culture of National Security: Norms and Identity in World Politics*, New York: Columbia University Press.

Kratochwil, F. (1989) *Rules, Norms, and Decisions*, Cambridge: Cambridge University Press.

Laffey, M. and Weldes, J. (2004) 'Methodological reflections on discourse analysis', *Qualitative Methods* 2, 1: 28–31.

Lapid, Y. (1989) 'The third debate: On the prospects of international theory in a post-positivist era', *International Studies Quarterly* 33, 3: 235–54.

Larsen, H. (1997) *Foreign Policy and Discourse Analysis: France, Britain and Europe*, London: Routledge.

Laustsen, C.B. and Waever, O. (2000) 'In defence of religion: Sacred referent objects for securitization', *Millennium* 29, 3: 705–39.

Léonard, S. (2007) 'The "securitization" of asylum and migration in the European Union: Beyond the Copenhagen School's framework', PhD thesis, University of Wales, Aberystwyth.

McDonald, M. (2008) 'Securitization and the construction of security', *European Journal of International Relations* 14, 4: 563–87.

McSweeney, B. (1996) 'Identity and security: Buzan and the Copenhagen School', *Review of International Studies* 22, 1: 81–93.

Mead, G.H. (ed.) (1934) *Mind, Self, and Society: From the Standpoint of a Social Behaviorist*, with an introduction by C.W. Morris, Chicago: University of Chicago Press.

Mey, J.L. (2001) *Pragmatics: An Introduction*, Oxford: Blackwell.

Milliken, J. (1999) 'The study of discourse in international relation: A critique of research and methods', *European Journal of International Relations* 5, 2: 225–54.

Neuendorf, K. (2002) *The Content Analysis Guidebook*, Thousand Oaks: Sage.

Neumann, I.B. (1999) *Uses of Other: 'The East' in European Identity Formation*, Minneapolis: University of Minnesota Press.

——(2008) 'Discourse analysis', in Klotz, A. and Prakash, D. (eds) *Qualitative Methods in International Relations*, Basingstoke, UK: Palgrave MacMillan, pp. 61–77.

Neumann, I.B. and Heikka, H. (2005) 'Grand strategy, strategic culture, practice: The social roots of Nordic defence', *Cooperation and Conflict* 40, 1: 5–23.

Nightingale, D. and Cromby, J. (2002) 'Social constructionism as ontology: Exposition and example', *Theory & Psychology* 12, 5: 701–13.

Onuf, N. (1989) *World of Our Making: Rules and Rules in Social Theory and International Relations*, Columbia: University of South Carolina Press.

Perelman, C. and Olbrechts-Tyteca, L. (eds) (1969) *The New Rhetoric: A Treatise on Argumentation*, trans. J. Wilkinson and P. Wæver, Indiana: University of Notre Dame Press.

Price, R. (1995) *The Chemical Weapons Taboo*, Ithaca, NY: Cornell University Press.

Ringmar, E. (1996) *Identity, Interests, and Action: A Cultural Explanation of Sweden's Intervention in the Thirty Years' War*, Cambridge: Cambridge University Press.

Risse-Kappen, T. (1995) *Cooperation among Democracies: The European Influence on US Foreign Policy*, Princeton, NJ: Princeton University Press.

Roe, P. (2008) 'Securitizing Saddam: Actor, audience(s) and emergency measures in the UK's decision to invade Iraq', *Security Dialogue* 39, 6: 615–35.

Ruggie, J.G. (1996) *Winning the Peace: America and World Order in the New Era*, Columbia: Columbia University Press.

71

——(1998) 'What makes the world hangs together? Neo-utilitarianism and the social constructivist challenge', *International Organization* 52, 4: 855–85.

Salter, M.B. (2008) 'Securitization and desecuritization: Dramaturgical analysis of the Canadian air transport security authority', *Journal of International Relations and Development* 11, 4: 321–49.

Sarup, M. (1993) *An Introductory Guide to Post-Structuralism and Postmodernism*, Hemel Hempstead: Prentice Hall.

Searle, J. (1969) *Speech Acts: An Essay in the Philosophy of Language*, Cambridge: Cambridge University Press.

——(1977a) 'Reiterating the differences: A reply to Derrida', *Glyph* 1: 198–208.

——(1977b) 'A classification of illocutionary acts', in P. Cole and J. Morgan (eds) *Syntax Semantics*, vol. 3: *Speech Acts*, New York: Academic Press.

Smith, S. (1996) 'Positivism and beyond', in Smith, S., Booth, K. and Zalewski, M. (eds) *International Theory: Positivism and Beyond*, Cambridge: Cambridge University Press.

——(2000) 'Wendt's world', *Review of International Studies* 26, 1: 151–63.

Stritzel, H. (2007) 'Towards a theory of securitization: Copenhagen and beyond', *European Journal of International Relations* 13, 3: 357–83.

Tannenwald, N. (1999) 'The nuclear taboo: The United States and the normative basis of nuclear non-use', *International Organization* 53, 3: 433–68.

Taurek, R. (2006) 'Securitization theory and securitization studies', *Journal of International Relations and Development* 9, 1: 53–61.

Vieira, M.A. (2007) 'The securitization of the HIV/AIDS epidemic as a norm: A contribution to constructivist scholarship on the emergence and diffusion of international norms', *Brazilian Political Science Review*. Available online at: http://socialsciences.scielo.org/scielo.php?pid=S198138212007000200005&script=sci_arttext&tlng=(accessed March 2008).

Violi, P. (2001) *Meaning and Experience*, trans. Jeremy Carden, Bloomington: Indiana University Press.

Vuori, J.A. (2008) 'Illocutionary logic and strands of securitization: Applying the theory of securitization to the study of non-democratic political orders', *European Journal of International Relations* 14, 1: 65–99.

Wæver, O. (1995) 'Securitization and desecuritization', in Ronnie, D.L. (ed.) *On Security*, New York: Columbia University Press, pp. 46–86.

Walker, R.B.J. (1987) 'Realism, change and international political theory', *International Studies Quarterly* 31, 1: 65–86.

Wendt, A. (1994) 'Collective identity formation and the international state', *American Political Science Review* 88, 2: 384–96.

——(1999) *Social Theory of International Politics*, Cambridge: Cambridge University Press.

Wendt, A. and Fearon, J. (2002) 'Rationalism v. constructivism' in Carlsnaes, W., Risse, T. and Simmons, B.A. (eds) *Handbook of International Relations*, London: Sage.

Wetherell, M. (2001) 'Debates in discourse research', in Wetherell, M., Taylor, S. and Yates, S.J. (eds) *Discourse Theory and Practice: A Reader*, Thousand Oaks: Sage, pp. 380–99.

Wight, C. (2006) *Agents, Structures and International Relations: Politics as Ontology*, Cambridge: Cambridge University Press.

Wilkinson C. (2007) 'The Copenhagen School on tour in Kyrgystan: Is securitization theory useable outside Europe?' *Security Dialogue* 38, 1: 5–25.

Williams, M.C. (2003) 'Words, images, enemies: securitization and international politics', *International Studies Quarterly* 47, 4: 511–31.

Wolfers, A. (1962) *Discord and Collaboration: Essays on International Politics*, Baltimore: Johns Hopkins University Press.

Zehfuss, M. (2002) *Constructivism in International Relations: The Politics of Reality*, Cambridge: Cambridge University Press.

6

Post-structuralism, continental philosophy and the remaking of security studies

Claudia Aradau and Rens van Munster

From the early 1990s, the discipline of Security Studies has witnessed the growth of a literature inspired by continental thought. Initially labelled 'post-structuralist' (Hansen 1997), this literature draws more largely on ideas and concepts from twentieth-century continental philosophy to challenge both realist understandings of security and the emerging constructivist consensus. While the term 'continental philosophy' is largely an artefact that works in opposition to 'analytic philosophy' and only entered the Anglo-Saxon world after the end of the Second World War, twentieth-century continental thought shares a series of ideas such as the historical and cultural embeddedness of subjects, the role of practice and the critique of present conditions (Critchley 1998). Drawing on continental philosophy more generally has allowed security scholars to challenge dominant understandings and practices of security and add new dimensions to the post-structuralist questions about the significance of identity construction and discourse analysis, particularly by focusing on 'unmaking security' (Huysmans 2006).

Concerned predominantly with the defence of the state, scholars in strategic studies never question the effects of framing issues in terms of national security. However, post-structuralists have pointed out that the stories produced by security scholars were not so much objective accounts about threats in the world 'out there' as a set of theoretical and political demarcations of what constitutes reality (Walker 1993). For example, Klein's (1994) seminal analysis of strategic studies showed how the latter, by taking the state as its 'natural' point of departure, contributed actively to the process of state formation and maintenance. Traditional Security Studies confirm the realist image of the international arena as an anarchic system of states where progress is an impossibility and security a necessary quest for survival. Despite its manifest discontent with the ontological and epistemological assumptions of realism, a broadly conceived constructivist approach has simply added adjectives to security, producing a 'grab bag of issue areas' (Krause and Williams 1997: 35). Societal, environmental, economic and human security have become new categories that expand the realm of security without challenging its dominant meanings. Thus, constructivist Security Studies have often run the risk of reinforcing either the extension of security (by arguing that other issues should be included as security problems) or the dominance of realism (by arguing against such extensions).

Contra these tendencies, continental philosophy has inspired an understanding of security not as 'a noun that names things', but 'as a principle of formation that does things', where the central objective is not to define security, but to enquire 'how an order of fear forms a people' (Dillon 1996: 16). Since security cannot be conceived of without a prior account of what entity or political community needs securing, representations are also always political statements about the desirable nature of the political community. Security delimits and restricts political agency by introducing a particular representation of communities, the self and alterity. One of the main concerns that emerge from the encounter with continental philosophy is how to resist security, unmake its practices and challenge its logic.

This chapter examines how security has been analysed as a principle of formation and aims to provide a broad (although necessarily simplified) account of the central themes that have shaped the literature. First, it turns to the understanding of security as an exceptional logic that constitutes the political through a binary division between friend/enemy. Bearing a strong resemblance to Carl Schmitt's theory of sovereignty and the state of exception, this has been the prevailing understanding of security. Although reformulated as a critique of security through Giorgio Agamben's recasting of Schmitt's theory of the exception, this understanding has been contested for its ahistoricity, lack of agency and erasure of the heterogeneity of power. Secondly, based in particular on Michel Foucault's work on governmentality and biopolitics, recent explorations of security have pointed out that security does not just concern the sovereign question of survival and the friend/enemy binary, but also the biopolitical question of managing the well-being and life chances of populations. Here, security establishes limits, divisions and hierarchies between different categories of the population. Concerned with the violence and insecurity that security fosters in the constitution of political communities, the final section focuses on how the logic of security can be resisted and draws on a larger body of continental thought that has addressed the possibilities of social and political transformation.

Security, sovereignty and exceptionalism

In contradistinction to the traditional concept of security that saw war as determined by the actions of pre-existing autonomous and rational states, post-structuralist studies of security discourses have shown the mutual constitution of self and other through the antagonistic logic of war and foreign policy (Campbell 1992; Hansen 2006). Security discourses depend upon and sustain particular representations of the world. David Campbell's study of American foreign policy and identity has explored how discourses of danger divide the world between a clear inside and outside, where identity is located within the political community with security practices attempting to exclude difference, heterogeneity and alterity. As the principle of formation of the modern political subject, security presupposes trust and identity between members of a community, while it relegates indeterminacy, fear and anarchy to an imaginary locus outside the social order. The metaphor of 'war' has been particularly important for the definition of security as a speech act by means of which an actor presents an issue as an existential threat that justifies extraordinary measures to neutralize that threat (Buzan et al. 1998). While the functional realm of threat management coexists with other domains of social life, security distinguishes itself from other ways of dealing with issues because of its intense relationship to an issue, which elevates it above politics and everyday haggling. This understanding of security bears a significant intellectual similarity to Schmitt's rendering of the political as the exceptional decision that constitutes the border between friend and enemy and is best captured by the metaphor of 'war' (Huysmans 1998; Williams 2003). For although war need not be actually present between friends and enemies, 'the ever present possibility of combat' (Schmitt 1996: 32) grounds the political and constitutes the authentic self-delineation of a political community.

The theory of the state of exception as reformulated by Agamben (1998, 2003) has placed many of these post-structuralist insights in clearer light. His work has added two important aspects in particular. The first is that security is an exceptional practice that draws boundaries between political life (*bios*) and abject, disqualified or bare life (*zoe*). The state of exception produces not only sovereignty and the homogeneous political community, but also its mirror image of bare life, i.e. life that can be killed with impunity. Agamben's (1998) discussion of the creation of 'bare life' as the originary gesture of sovereignty most explicitly renders the inseparability of sovereignty and the subject, and points out the ways in which sovereignty is constitutive of abjection. In a state of exception where the sovereign is exempted from all legal rules, subjects no longer enjoy the protection of the legal order. 'Bare life' is the point of internal exclusion enacted by sovereignty; it is life that is not set outside the political order, but remains included as exclusion. For Agamben, the concentration camp exemplifies the space where we find the most extreme form of 'bare life' insofar as prisoners do not enjoy legal protection against the atrocities of the guards who act as sovereigns. Construed as 'bare life', the depoliticized human, the subject of sovereign power appears as deprived of any agency.

The second point that Agamben adds to these analyses of security is that of the arbitrary sovereign decision. 'War' as the metaphor of security is the result of an arbitrary decision that simultaneously constitutes relations of power between the sovereign and the political community on the one hand and 'bare life' on the other. The sovereign decision brings to the fore the relation between democracy and security as well as that between law and security. As the state of exception is explicitly linked with fascism in Agamben's work, this raises questions about the forms of non-democratic politics that security practices instil within contemporary societies. Moreover, the theory of the exception sheds light on taken-for-granted assumptions about the constitution of political communities, and on the illusion of homogeneity prior to the threat. The imaginary of societal homogeneity that is advocated by traditional understandings of security is rendered possible only on the basis of a constitutive violence and depoliticization of 'bare life'. Agamben's observations have informed a range of analyses of the so-called 'war on terror' and contemporary security policies. The war in Iraq (Diken and Laustsen 2005; van Munster 2004); refugee camps and airport holding zones (Noll 2003; Salter 2008); humanitarian intervention (Dauphinée and Masters 2007; Edkins et al. 2004); detention centres for terrorist suspects (Neal 2006); and the shoot-to-kill policies of the London police (Vaughan-Williams 2007) have all been recognized as exceptional practices by means of which the life of some people is reduced to that of bare life.

Although Agamben's work has made more salient the exceptionalism and arbitrariness at the heart of security, his theory of the exception was thought to give a somewhat distorted picture of security as always producing a strict dividing line between inside and outside. Whatever its spatial and temporal modifications, security ultimately founds a co-constitutive relation of inclusion/exclusion, self/other and friend/enemy. Against the assumption that 'bare life' is defined exclusively through negation, thereby denying the possibility of political agency, it has been shown that camps, for example, are imbued with knowledge and technologies of governance, from ration cards and hygiene education to psychological therapy. As Fleur Johns (Johns 2005) has remarked, Guantánamo Bay is replete with administrative rules and regulations. Rather than constituting empty spaces of 'bare life', camps and other exceptional spaces are governed through bureaucratic technologies and regulations that are often reminiscent of colonial and political histories.

The understanding of security as something exceptional downplays other, more routinized forms of security. Jabri (2006) has argued that the metaphor of 'war' associated with security has become a transnational strategy of control that targets states, communities and individuals. Rather than being generalized, the state of exception is inscribed in different ways upon various sectors of society and is also experienced in different ways by particular categories of populations. Similarly, Bigo (2002), who focuses on the security experts that manage 'unease' within society on a daily basis, points out that exceptional security practices can be understood in the context of ongoing processes of bureaucratic and market-driven routinization. These processes of routinization, redeployment of knowledge and governance of life have been explored by drawing on Foucault's analyses of governmentality and biopolitics.

Security, governmentality and biopolitics

Michel Foucault has offered a rich understanding of how different regimes of power function in heterogeneous ways that go beyond the sovereign question of territoriality and that of centralized legitimate authority. Starting from the eighteenth century, Foucault has argued, sovereign power (defined by the absolute power to kill or let live) has been changing, as a new form of power, namely biopolitics, takes populations and their lives as the object of governance (Foucault 1991, 2007). The advent of the biopolitical state brings about a change in the development of the modern state from the 'city-citizen' game to those of pastoral care of life and the living (Foucault 2000). The state not only assigns membership in the political community and ensures the survival of the community, but is also in charge of the well-being of individuals (or of categories of the population). On the one hand, security is entwined with the development of the state in heterogeneous ways that go beyond the territorial and geopolitical dominant understanding of security. Security functions in ways that complexify and disturb the state's taken-for-granted 'right to kill' and the legitimacy of rule. Rather than functioning through juridical prohibition and drawing boundaries of life and death, power is deployed in much more insidious ways by disciplining subjects and governing the life of populations. On the other hand, Foucault's later concept of 'governmentality' relates security to institutions and forms of knowledge that are mobilized in the governing of societies and populations. Under liberal governance, governing security is directly related to the promotion and protection of the mobility and circulation of populations, goods and services rather than the protection of territories (Dillon and Lobo-Guerrero 2008; Dillon and Reid 2001; Duffield 2007).

Although Foucault reserved the term 'security' more specifically for the biopolitical practices emerging from the eighteenth century on, in Security Studies the concept has been analysed through the re-articulation of different modalities of power. For Foucault, governmentality was opposed both to the model of sovereignty and that of the family, taking as its subject neither the people (both subjected and the agent of popular sovereignty) nor the extended family, but the life of populations. Nevertheless, in a broad sense, governmentality is understood simply as the 'techniques and procedures for directing human behaviour' (Foucault 1997: 82). Thus, it refers to the ways in which security practices combine sovereign, disciplinary and biopolitical technologies. Individuals or populations are ordered according to a norm against which deviations can be measured. A governmental mode of analysis unpacks security as a specific type of ordering of the *polis*, an ordering based on practices of inclusion and exclusion and imbued with a mimetic desire to make its members conform to ideal images of what they should be (Hindess 1998: 59).

However, as part of this process of governing populations and securing order, boundaries are drawn, creating categories of individuals who are to be protected at the expense of the exclusion and elimination of others. Just as racial boundaries delimit and divide humankind into lives worthy of living and lives that are to be curtailed (Foucault 2004), security practices are exposed as inherently *insecuring*, dividing categories of populations and preparing some for elimination, disciplining or therapy. In Dillon's (2005: 41) words, the 'continuous biopolitical assaying of life proceeds through the epistemically driven and continuously changing interrogation of the worth and eligibility of the living across a terrain of value that is constantly changing'.

The biopolitical management of populations also introduces a specific temporal element in the analyses of security. The governmentality of populations and the conjoint betterment of life already contained an implicit temporal element. Temporality becomes explicitly problematized when scenarios of danger concern the occurrence of events in the future life of populations and sovereignties. Security practices intervene to 'tame' the future and to recuperate the temporality of progress and linearity. Whether understood through statistical calculations of probability (Lobo-Guerrero 2007), scenarios of preparedness (Collier et al. 2004), or imaginations of catastrophe and disaster (Aradau and van Munster 2007), dangerous events shift the spatial understanding of security towards the equal problematization of temporality.

Security, subjectivity and resistance

Conceptualized as an exceptional or governmental practice, the political effects of security appear equally troubling. As an exceptional practice, security works against democracy, foretells violence and enacts exclusions. As a governmental and biopolitical practice, security is entwined with bureaucratic modes of regulating populations and with separating life worthy of improvement from life that is less valuable. Even when biopolitical practices appeared as less violent and spectacular, their divisions and exclusions were inscribed in the quotidian, the everydayness of populations. Classification and categorization as well as the division of populations and forms of life are part of the concerns with the internal exclusions of security. Therefore, resistance to security has emerged as an important question in Security Studies. Drawing on diverging strands of continental philosophy, Security Studies have offered different and sometimes competing answers. Central to these approaches, however, is the attempt to transform the relationship between the self and other that security brings about. For Rob Walker (1997: 78), a critical discourse about security depends upon 'emerging accounts of who we might become, and the conditions under which we might become other than we are now without destroying others, ourselves, or the planet on which we all live'. While ethical approaches focus mostly on the *subject* of security, agency and emancipation are broadly focused on the *abject*, the other, the alterity that security practices delimit and exclude to foster the imaginary security of the self.

Ethics

Ethics attempt to resist security discourses and the logic of self/other that it brings about. An '*ethical relation* in which our responsibility to the other is the basis for reflection' (Campbell and Shapiro 1999: x) can replace the inimical and antagonistic relations that security brings about. Ethics is a practice of deconstruction (Campbell 1998), an eternal transformation of the conditions that structure our existence. Hansen (2006) has already drawn attention to the complexity of the self/other relations and the degrees of differ- ence that are constitutive of identity. Rather than necessarily being formulated as antag- onistic, the relation between self and other can be radically reformulated as interdependent. Campbell, for example, draws on Levinas's ethics of responsibility, while Judith Butler formulates an ethics based on the non-violent principle of mourning. Common to both, however, is that their ethic takes as its point of departure the self/other relationship. The interdependence between self and other is crucial, because it undermines the exclusionary logic of security by pointing to the need to recognize the fundamental ambivalence, heterogeneity and difference that contaminates all identities. Whereas dis- courses of danger portray the other as the condition of impossibility for the existence of a secure, homogeneous identity, these ethical positions stress that alterity is in fact deeply enmeshed with the subject. Rather than homogeneous and separate, self and other are inextricable.

According to Levinas's philosophy, the ethical relationship with the other is defined by responsibility towards the other. Although security may define our relationship to the other in terms of abjection, violence and domination, the structure of responsibility never- theless summons us to recognize 'the structural condition of alterity prior to subjectivity and thought' (Campbell 1999: 41). Even if we can never fully respond to the calls of others at all time, the understanding of subjectivity in terms of responsibility helps us resist discourses of security that depend on the other's suppression and domination in favour of forms of belonging that respond to the ethical call of the other.

Judith Butler comes to similar conclusions in her account of mourning that grounds subjectivity in the social vulnerability and exposure of corporeal bodies in the public sphere:

> The body implies mortality, vulnerability, agency: the skin of the flesh exposes us to the gaze of others, but also to touch, and to violence, and bodies put us at risk of becoming the agency and instrument of all these as well.
>
> (Butler 2003: 15)

Bodily vulnerability experienced in the loss of the other's life (for example, as a result of disease, death or violence) has a transformative impact on the self, which, being con- stituted in relation to the other, is no longer the same after the loss. For Butler, the experience of fragility in the context of a loss is not just a private matter, but a political principle around which social ties are reinvented and re-articulated on the basis of bodily suffering: 'To grieve, and to make grief itself into a resource for politics is not to be resigned to inaction, but it may be understood as the slow process by which we develop a point of identification with suffering itself' (Butler 2003: 19).

Responsibility and mourning imply a politics of transformation, where ethics resigni- fies and reconfigures social practices of security. Security is opposed to the principle of mourning in the sense that security practices seek to deny the vulnerable inter-human bond around which subjectivity is constituted. The other is no longer encountered as a grievable life, but as an enemy that is not worth mourning. The ethical imperative is to recognize vulnerability and to inquire into and deconstruct the social and political conditions by means of which some forms of life appear more grievable than others. For example, Edkins's (2003) writings on trauma and Zehfuss's (2007) work on memory critically examine how traumatic events related to war and suffering have entered collective memory, pointing out the significance of remembering an identity that is not derived simply from the desire to secure oneself in the face of the other.

Agency

Ethical and post-structuralist approaches have sometimes been criticized for their quasi-exclusive concern with 'we', the subject. The 'other' is often envisaged as a derivative of the constitution of 'us'. In Campbell's analysis of how US identity is reproduced through re-writings of dangers, the others who are written out as dangerous, abnormal, or risky are 'faceless faces', substitutable to one another. Even assaying the worthiness of life by biopolitical practices appears to be a consequence of the 'political rationality' of the state. Different others succeed one another, subjected to the need of identity reproduction.

Such an account is vulnerable to the critique that it cannot formulate alternatives to security because it does not take into account those who are relegated to the '"unliveable" and "uninhabitable" zones of social life which are nevertheless populated by those who do not enjoy the status of the subject' (Butler 1993: 3). The abject only exists as a constitutive outside, as the limit to the domain of subjectivity. Barkawi and Laffey have criticized Security Studies for what they saw as its Eurocentric assumptions about agency. The weak, they argue, appear as only bearers of rights and objects of emancipation rather than agents themselves (Barkawi and Laffey 2006). By focusing on agency, several scholars have attempted to recuperate the other, the abject, as something more than a blank space defined only through negation.

The constitution of the subject through discourses of danger comes up against the intransigence of political agency and the resistance of political subjects. Isin and Rykiel (2007: 184) have argued that a distinction needs to be drawn between the camp as a space of abjection where subjects were eliminated after having been stripped of citizenship, and abject spaces – spaces where people are rendered inexistent, invisible and inaudible. The difference has profound political implications: abject spaces are simultaneously spaces of resistance, where abjection is challenged and sovereign practices rendered ineffective. Agency is not only present in the refugee camp (Puggioni 2006), but informs other exceptional spaces and practices (Mezzadra 2006; Nyers 2006). Migrants and refugees, for example, engage in daily practices of resistance against securitization. Focusing on the agency of the other, Nyers (2003) rethinks cosmopolitanism from the standpoint of migrants, the cast-off of the global order. Arguing that the immigrant is the cosmopolitan figure per se, he calls for a move away from an understanding of cosmopolitanism that aims at the constitution of world citizens behind the horizon of contemporary politics towards an understanding of cosmopolitanism that is located in concrete struggles. The 'No One Is Illegal' initiative and other anti-deportation campaigns are examples of abject cosmopolitanism in action insofar as they radically call into question claims to sovereignty and principles of border control. Local struggles are the concrete situations where a democratic cosmopolitanism is enacted and establishes new forms of relationality with the other.

Emancipation

Emancipation shares some of the theoretical inspiration and focus on the abject with discussions of agency. Nyers's work, for example, is simultaneously informed by a concern with agency and resistance and by inscriptions of equality. Emancipation challenges ongoing practices of security through an 'unconditional principle', which refers to a *de jure* universality (of equality or freedom) as the reference point for emancipation. While agency could be re-appropriated within the governance of security, the principles of equality and freedom challenge the boundaries and limits of security. Drawing particularly on the work of Jacques Rancière and Alain Badiou, recent literature on emancipation and security shifts the political concerns of danger and risk towards those of equality and freedom. Rather than conceiving of order and practices in the way that many scholars of Security Studies have done, it starts with rupture, breaks and disorders that challenge the ways in which security constitutes communities and governs populations.

Rancière's (1999) view of universal rights as something that is simultaneously present (as written inscriptions) and non-present (not enacted) points at an irresolvable *aporia* that functions as the necessary background condition for any emancipatory politics of equality (rights are there to be taken). For example, most states that claim that human rights and freedom are universal values have also strengthened and securitized borders when it comes to the movement of the poor, who are today labelled 'economic refugees', 'illegal immigrants' or '*bogus* asylum seekers'. According to Rancière, the *de facto* denial of mobility to large parts of the people of the world is one of the most significant denouncements of equality in our time, which draws our attention to the fact that the universal right to the freedom of movement is only a right of those who make something of that universal inscription. Rens van Munster (forthcoming) has shown how undocumented immigrants in France, the *sans-papiers*, have appropriated for themselves the European inscription of the freedom of movement. As one of the spokespersons for the movement has argued: 'When these rights are under threat, it is legitimate to struggle to have them reinstated ... Freedom of movement is not something invented. It *confirms* an existing situation' (Cissé 1997, emphasis added).

Equality is the other principle that informs emancipatory political action. Equality as something that needs to be verified has recently been taken up by critical scholars of security, where it has been posited as an alternative to the hierarchical practices that security presupposes. Thinking of equality as a point of departure in social and political relations can help to unmake the hierarchical logic that security entails, while, at the same time, furnishing a principle upon which a new relationality with the other can be conceived (Aradau 2004, 2008).

Conclusion

With its emphasis on the importance of representation and power, continental thought has entered Security Studies as a means by which the common-sense assumptions of realist and constructivist approaches about the reality of security can be challenged. What unites the approaches that draw on continental thought is a shared preference for critique as the necessary condition of possibility for a progressive politics. However, continental thought is not a unified body, let alone a theory. There are different, sometimes irreconcilable, interpretations of security and its political effects which, in turn, inform different views of politics outside security. Nonetheless, at a time where security seems to pervade all aspects of human interaction, continental thought has proved a significant intellectual reservoir for interrogating the concept of security.

This chapter has engaged with some of the strands and representatives of continental thought and the effects of their work upon Security Studies. Unpacking security as an exceptional or governmental practice has led to complex analyses of its functioning and political effects. As security draws limits and divisions among categories of the population, and mobilizes knowledge and culture to render some forms of life inferior or 'bare', resistance has emerged as one of the most innovative areas of research. The discontent with the proliferation of security issues, the effects of practices upon political communities, the constitution of the subject, and democracy will lead to increasing interest in transformation, resistance, ethics or emancipation over order and discipline.

References

Agamben, G. (1998) *Homo Sacer: Sovereign Power and Bare Life*, trans D. Heller-Roazen, Stanford: Stanford University Press.

——(2003) 'L'Etat d'exception', trans J. Gayraud, in Badiou, A. and Cassin B. (eds) *L'Ordre philosophique*, Paris: Editions du Seuil.

Aradau, C. (2004) 'Security and the democratic scene: Desecuritization and emancipation', *Journal of International Relations and Development* 7, 4: 388–413.

——(2008) *Rethinking Trafficking in Women: Politics out of Security*, Basingstoke: Palgrave Macmillan.

Aradau, C. and van Munster, R. (2007) 'Governing terrorism through risk: Taking precautions, (un) knowing the future', *European Journal of International Relations* 13, 1: 89–115.

Barkawi, T. and Laffey, M. (2006) 'The postcolonial moment in security studies', *Review of International Relations* 32, 2: 329–52.

Bigo, D. (2002) 'Security and immigration: Toward a critique of the governmentality of unease', Special Issue of *Alternatives* 27: 63–92.

Butler, J. (1993) *Bodies that Matter: On the Discursive Limits of 'Sex'*, London: Routledge.

——(2003) 'Violence, mourning, politics', *Studies in Gender and Sexuality* 4, 1: 9–37.

Buzan, B., Waever, O. and de Wilde, J. (1998) *Security: A New Framework for Analysis*, Boulder: Lynne Rienner.

Campbell, D. (1992) *Writing Security: United States Foreign Policy and the Politics of Identity*, Manchester: Manchester University Press.

——(1998) *National Deconstruction: Violence, Identity and Justice in Bosnia*, Minneapolis: University of Minnesota Press.

——(1999) 'The deterritorialization of responsibility: Levinas, Derrida, and ethics after the end of philosophy' in Campbell, D. and Shapiro, M.J. (eds) *Moral Spaces: Rethinking Ethics and World Politics*, Minneapolis: University of Minnesota Press, pp. 29–56.

Campbell, D. and Shapiro, M.J. (1999) 'Introduction: From ethical theory to the ethical relation' in Campbell, D. and Shapiro, M.J. (eds) *Moral Spaces: Rethinking Ethics and World Politics*, Minneapolis: University of Minnesota Press, pp. VII–XX.

Cissé, M. (1997) *The Sans-Papiers: The New Movement of Asylum Seekers and Immigrants without Papers in France: A Woman Draws the First Lesson*, London: Crossroads.

Collier, S.J., Lakoff, A. and Rabinow, P. (2004) 'Biosecurity: Towards an anthropology of the contemporary', *Anthropology Today* 20, 5: 3–7.

Critchley, S. (1998) 'Introduction: What is continental philosophy?', in Critchley, S. and Schroeder, W.R. (eds) *A Companion to Continental Philosophy*, Oxford: Blackwell, pp. 1–20.

Dauphinée, E. and Masters, C. (2007) 'Introduction: Living, dying, surviving I', in Dauphinée, E. and Masters, C. (eds) *The Logics of Biopower and the War on Terror: Living, Dying, Surviving*, Basingstoke: Palgrave Macmillan, pp. vii–xix.

Diken, B. and Bagge Laustsen, C. (2005) *The Culture of Exception: Sociology Facing the Camp*, London: Routledge.

Dillon, M. (1996) *The Politics of Security: Towards a Political Philosophy of Continental Thought*, London: Routledge.

——(2005) 'Cared to death: The biopoliticised time of your life', *Foucault Studies* 2: 37–46.

Dillon, M. and Lobo-Guerrero, L. (2008) 'Biopolitics of security in the 21st century: An introduction', *Review of International Studies* 34, 2: 265–92.

Dillon, M. and Reid, J. (2001) 'Global liberal governance: Biopolitics, security and war', *Millennium: Journal of International Studies* 30, 1: 41–66.

Duffield, M. (2007) *Development, Security and Unending War: Governing the World of Peoples*, Cambridge: Polity Press.

Edkins, J. (2003) *Trauma and the Memory of Politics*, Cambridge: Cambridge University Press.

Edkins, J., Pin-Fat, V. and Shapiro, M.J. (eds) (2004) *Sovereign Lives: Power in Global Politics*, London: Routledge.

Foucault, M. (1991) 'Governmentality', in Burchell, G., Gordon, C. and Miller, P. (eds) *The Foucault Effect: Studies in Governmentality*, Chicago: University of Chicago Press, pp. 87–104.

——(1997) *Ethics: Subjectivity and Truth. Essential Works of Michel Foucault, 1954–1984*, New York: New Press.

——(2000) 'Omnes et singulatim: Toward a critique of "political reason"', in Faubion, D. (ed.) *Power: Essential Works of Foucault 1954–1984*, London: Penguin, pp. 298–325.

——(2004) *Society Must Be Defended*, trans. D. Macey. London: Penguin Books.

——(2007) *Security, Territory, Population*, Basingstoke: Palgrave.

Hansen, L. (1997) 'A case for seduction? Evaluating the poststructuralist conceptualization of security', *Cooperation and Conflict* 32, 4: 369–97.

——(2006) *Security as Practice: Discourse Analysis and the Bosnian War*, London: Routledge.

Hindess, B. (1998) 'Politics and liberation', in Moss, J. (ed) *The Later Foucault: Politics and Philosophy*, London: Sage, pp. 50–63.

Huysmans, J. (1998) 'The question of the limit: Desecuritisation and the aesthetics of horror in political realism', *Millennium* 27, 3: 569–89.

——(2006) *The Politics of Insecurity: Fear, Migration and Asylum in the EU*, London: Routledge.

Isin, E.F. and Rykiel, K. (2007) 'Abject spaces: Frontiers, zones, camps', in Dauphinée, E. and Masters, C. (eds) *The Logics of Biopower and the War on Terror: Living, Dying, Surviving*, Basingstoke: Palgrave Macmillan, pp. 181–204.

Jabri, V. (2006) 'War, security and the liberal state', *Security Dialogue* 37, 1: 47–64.

Johns, F. (2005) 'Guantanamo Bay and the annihilation of the exception', *The European Journal of International Law* 16, 4: 613–35.

Klein, B. (1994) *Strategic Studies and World Order: The Global Politics of Deterrence*, Cambridge: Cambridge University Press.

Krause, K. and Williams, M.C. (1997) 'From strategy to security: Foundations of critical security studies' in Krause, K. and Williams, M.C. (eds) *Critical Security Studies: Concepts and Cases*, London: UCL Press, pp. 33–60.

Lobo-Guerrero, L. (2007) 'Biopolitics of specialist risk: Kidnap and ransom insurance', *Security Dialogue* 38, 3: 315–34.

Mezzadra, S. (2006) *Diritto di fuga. Migrazioni, cittadinanza, globalizzazione*, Verona: Ombre Corte.

van Munster, R. (2004) 'The war on terrorism: When the exception becomes the rule', *International Journal for the Semiotics of Law* 17, 2: 141–53.

——(forthcoming) *Immigration, Security and the Politics of Risk in the EU*, Basingstoke: Palgrave.

Neal, A.W. (2006) 'Foucault in Guantanamo: Towards an archaeology of the exception', *Security Dialogue* 37, 1: 31–46.

Noll, G. (2003) 'Visions of the exceptional: Legal and theoretical issues raised by transit processing centres and protection zones', *European Journal of Migration and Law* 5, 3: 303–42.

Nyers, P. (2003) 'Abject cosmopolitanism: The politics of protection in the anti-deportation movement', *Third World Quarterly* 24: 1069–93.

——(2006) 'Taking rights, mediating wrongs: Disagreements over the political agency of non-status refugees', in Huysmans, J., Dobson, A. and Prokhovnik, R. (eds) *The Politics of Protection: Sites of Insecurity and Political Agency*, London: Routledge, pp. 48–67.

Puggioni, R. (2006) 'Resisting sovereign power: Camps in-between exception and dissent', in Huysmans, J., Dobson, A. and Prokhovnik, R. (eds) *The Politics of Protection: Sites of Insecurity and Political Agency*, London: Routledge, pp. 68–83.

Rancière, J. (1999) *Disagreement: Politics and Philosophy*, trans. J. Rose, Minneapolis: University of Minnesota Press.

Salter, M.B. (2008) 'When the exception becomes the rule: Borders, sovereignty, and citizenship', *Citizenship Studies* 12, 4: 365–80.

Schmitt, C. (1996) *The Concept of the Political*, trans. T.B. Strong. Chicago: University of Chicago Press.

Vaughan-Williams, N. (2007) 'The shooting of Jean Charles de Menezes: New border politics?', *Alternatives: Global, Local, Political* 32, 2: 177–95.

Walker, R.B.J. (1993) *Inside/Outside: International Relations as Political Theory*, Cambridge: Cambridge University Press.

——(1997) 'The subject of security' in Krause, K. and Williams, M.C. (eds) *Critical Security Studies: Concepts and Cases*, London: UCL Press, pp. 61–81.

Williams, M.C. (2003) 'Words, images, enemies: Securitization and international politics', *International Studies Quarterly* 47, 4: 511–31.

Zehfuss, M. (2007) *Wounds of Memory: The Politics of War in Germany*, Cambridge: Cambridge University Press.

7

Feminist security studies

Annick T.R. Wibben

> Until women have control over their own security a truly comprehensive system of security cannot be devised.
>
> (Tickner 1992: 30)

When feminist scholars began to make their mark on the field of International Relations (IR) in the 1980s, matters of security were at the top of their agenda. IR feminists were able to draw on a long history of writing about issues of peace, war and violence (Gioseffi 2003), largely in the form of historical or cross-cultural case studies, often involving ethnographic research (Ardener et al. 1987; Florence et al. 1987; Isaksson 1988; Nordstrom 1997). This writing (and the feminist activism it emerges from) provides the impetus and background material for the development of Feminist Security Studies (FSS) today.

The Women's International League of Peace and Freedom (WILPF), created in 1915, has been actively and publicly involved in debates about security, though not necessarily as an equal partner of policymakers.[1] What is more, in the 1960s, women (and WILPF) were involved in the creation of the International Peace Research Association. Despite their efforts, peace research became a male-dominated field, and gender remained noticeably absent even from debates about structural violence where gender should be a central category (cf. Batscheider 1993). Still, feminist peace researchers were, by the late 1960s, analysing power and emphasizing empowerment over coercion; by the 1970s, they had moved on to developing notions of security with an adversary and broadening security to include 'security against want, security of human rights, the security of an empowered civil society'.[2] In the 1980s, they focused on the linkages between war and patriarchy (Boulding 1992: 56f.).

In the early 1990s, feminists (in IR) began to phrase their insights on peace, war and violence in terms of security, thus engaging debates in Security Studies more directly. Most often, the advent of FSS is traced to Tickner's *Gender in International Relations: Feminist Perspectives on Achieving Global Security*, published in 1992 (cf. Blanchard 2003; Broadhead 2000). Almost at the same time, feminist peace researcher Reardon wrote *Women and Peace: Feminist Visions of Global Security* (1993). Both books, besides being notable in their emphasis on global security (rather than national security), draw on the long tradition of feminist engagements with issues of peace, war and violence – now framing them explicitly as security issues. In addition, many feminist insights, e.g. on alternative conceptions of power, cooperative security arrangements and non-state-centric perspectives (Brock-Utne 1989; Ruddick 1989; Stiehm 1972), have made their way into Security Studies via other alternative approaches, such as Critical Security Studies (Booth 1997; cf. Tickner 2001).

Since the turn of the century, there has been a veritable explosion of feminist work in Security Studies, to the point where one can now confidently refer to FSS as a sub-field at the intersections of Security Studies and feminist IR. FSS are interdisciplinary – with scholars trained in peace research and Security Studies, but also in anthropology, history, literary theory, philosophy or sociology. What unites these scholars are their feminist (methodological) commitments: they (1) ask feminist research questions; (2) base their research on women's experiences; (3) adopt a (self-)reflexive stance; and (4) have an emancipatory agenda (Tickner 2006: 22–29). Whereas IR, like many traditional sciences, assumes gender neutrality, feminists make gender (the socially constructed femininity/masculinity distinction) a central category of analysis. For feminists, gender neutrality is impossible, because 'gender is a socially imposed and internalized lens through which individuals perceive and respond to the world' (Peterson 1992b: 194). As a consequence, they argue that concepts and ideas as well as practices and institutions are shaped by gender and that gender analysis produces interesting new insights that are otherwise overlooked.

Adopting a bottom-up approach to security, feminist scholars pay close attention to the impact of security policies, including war, on the everyday lives of people. As such, FSS departs from a large part of traditional Security Studies research. FSS scholars challenge the notion that wars are fought to protect vulnerable populations (such as children and women) and show that civilians are often explicitly targeted (especially in ethno-nationalist wars) (Enloe 1998; Hansen 2000, 2001). Rather than offering security for all their citizens, states often threaten their own populations, whether through direct violence or through the structural violence that is reflected in its war-fighting priorities and embedded in its institutions (Enloe 1993, 2000; Peterson 1992a; Reardon 1985; Tickner 1992; Tobias 1985; Young 2003). Feminists also point out that the increasing technologization of war, from nuclear strategy to the current revolution in military affairs, depersonalizes killing, offers the illusion of clean warfare, and obscures accountability (Blanchard 2003; Cohn 1989a, 1989b; Masters 2005; Molloy 1995).

Clearly, feminist contributions to Security Studies are varied. It is not currently possible to make out a dominant position in FSS whose progressive history could be traced. Rather, different contributions exist side-by-side, often mirroring debates in feminist thought at large.[3] The next section highlights some of the contributions FSS scholars have made to date. Thereafter, attention turns in more detail to the epistemological and political commitments of feminist scholars and how they shape feminist research in Security Studies. The chapter concludes with a brief assessment of the impact of FSS in IR.

Contributions of feminist security studies

Beginning with the simple question of 'where are the women (in security)?', feminists subvert the traditional approach in Security Studies, which does not take into account women (nor men, children, or other living beings either). 'There are states and they are what is' Elshtain quips, going on to say that 'professionalized IR discourse … is one of the most dubious of many dubious sciences that mask the power plays embedded in the discourse and the practices it legitimates' (Elshtain 1987: 91). The subversive aspect of asking about women is illustrated clearly in the work of Enloe (e.g. 1990): She not only finds women in unlikely places, but also continually asks questions about why they are rarely seen in IR. Why is it that IR and Security Studies fail to notice diplomat's wives who provide friendly spaces for back-room manoeuvres, barmaids and prostitutes who serve military personnel (cf. Moon 1997), and women who fight for their cause, including in combat roles (cf. Goldman 1982; Herbert 1998; Lorentzen and Turpin 1998; Solaro 2006; Stiehm 1996)? Enloe reveals that not only are women omnipresent, but their existence is central to the workings of International Relations and security politics.

Contrary to idealized notions of women in the context of security, where women are likely to be associated with peace or as victims in need of rescue and protection (if they appear at all), feminists are showing that women's involvement in matters of international security is much broader than assumed. Just looking at the narrow conceptions of state (and military security), feminists find that governments need their citizens to accept established, gendered discourses about protector and protected that leave women in a very vulnerable position (Elshtain 1987; Peterson 1992a; Stiehm 1982; Young 2003). The relationship of protector/protected often resembles a protection racket, where the protected loses all autonomy and is dependent upon the protector who defines the threat (and the response to it). The chivalrous protector faces the dangers of the outside world, but is also burdened by the need for protection and personal liability if protection fails, in which case the protector might direct his anger at those closest – by limiting their movement and ideas or lashing out violently. Feminists also point out how armed forces need men and women to function in certain gender-specific ways that draw on existing cultural norms and structural inequalities, but also reinforce them (Cohn and Enloe 2003; Enloe 1998, 2000; Herbert 1998; Whitworth 2004). For example, states mobilize women to support wars, whether by drawing on them as mothers (Bayard de Volo 2001; Collins 1999; Haq 2007; Nikolic-Ristanovic 1998); as symbols of the nation or bearers of tradition (Yuval-Davis 1997); or by having them work in factories while the men are away (Woollacott 1998). When women accept these calls and engage in acceptable female activities, they support war by glamorizing and idealizing the role of men as just warriors and by picking up the pieces of societies destroyed by men (Boulding 1988; Elshtain 1987). For most feminists, women and men 'share complicity in warfare and militarism through their participation in the dual mythology of masculinity and femininity' (Burguieres 1990: 8).

More recently, the topic of women as aggressors (Stiehm 1988; Sylvester 1987, 1989) has again gained much attention (Hamilton 2007; Ibáñez 2001; McKelvey 2007; Naaman 2007; Nacos 2005; Sjoberg and Gentry 2007). These feminists present evidence to show that many women are violent (just as many men are peaceful), shattering the correlation between women and peace and pointing to a need to deepen the analysis beyond the relationship of both women and men to violence to analysing the gendering of violence (i.e. its association with masculinity). They point out that women who are violent are treated as outcasts, labelled 'crazy', or otherwise overlooked and considered unworthy of researchers' attention because they do not fit accepted standards of femininity. What is more, feminists who are wedded to the ideal of the 'woman of peace' (Ruddick 1998) actively discourage investigation of violent women, suggesting that 'violence, armed battle or warlike abstractions are [not] authentic' (Sylvester 1987: 496) occupations for women. Nevertheless, the association of women with peace often denies women power and devalues what they have to say about security issues.

This should not obscure the fact that women are still predominantly victims of war (and of militarized societies), a topic that has always received a great deal of attention from feminists (cf. Wibben and Turpin 2008). One of the oldest forms of victimization is rape, as Susan Brownmiller outlines in her classic *Against Our Will* (1975). Since ancient times, the rape of conquered women has been a widely accepted practice. More recently, rape as a strategy of war has achieved renewed attention due to its use as a tactic of ethnic cleansing in the former Yugoslavia (e.g., Nikolic-Ristanovic 2000; Stiglmayer 1993). It is here also that feminist scholars/activists have observed a phenomenon that is a central concern of FSS – the continuum of violence between peace and wartime (Cockburn 2004; Cuomo 1996; Reardon 1993; Wibben forthcoming). More specifically, in the case of the former Yugoslavia, Zorica Mrsevic raises the following question: 'Did the civil war … cause and increase in domestic violence, or did domestic violence cause the war?' (Mrsevic 2001: 41). She argues that the high prevalence and tolerance of domestic violence in Yugoslav society before the war 'contributed significantly to the "ease" with which young men suddenly changed from apparently decent boys to brutal perpetrators of violent acts' – the underlying cause being patriarchal society where 'aggressive masculinity is not only tolerated, but encouraged' (Mrsevic 2001: 42).[4]

Exploring the linkages of patriarchal society and aggressive masculinities with violence and militarism has been an important theme of FSS (Cockburn 2004; Cockburn and Zarkov 2002; Enloe 1987, 1998; Reardon 1985; Whitworth 2004). When performing feminist gender analysis, men and masculinity need to be analysed alongside women and femininity – and, Cockburn cautions, 'we need to observe the functioning of gender as a relation … of power that compounds other power dynamics' (2004: 25). Why is it that being male augments one's chances of becoming a killer? While there is much material to suggest a direct relationship between masculinity and violence, its form is culturally specific and always changing because gender hierarchies exist alongside intersecting hierarchies of class, nation, race or religion. Nonetheless, it is possible to say that militaries everywhere rely on male privilege and female subordination in order to function.

Theoretical commitments of feminist security studies

Within FSS, scholars embrace a variety of epistemological and political positions, all of which shed light on different aspects of the security puzzle. Feminist empiricists try to correct bias by strictly adhering to scientific norms and inserting women to form a more complete picture of the world, thus pointing out that Security Studies has many blind spots to remedy. Standpoint feminists derive more accurate forms of understanding by theorizing from the position of subjugated (and thus less corrupted) women and argue that the way in which security has thus far been conceptualized is inadequate from the perspective of women. Feminist post-structuralists are sceptical of any 'universal (or universalizing) claims about the existence, nature and powers of reason, science, language and the "subject/self"' (Harding 1986: 28), therefore, they question the entire framework/mindset of Security Studies. Postcolonial feminists, finally, point out that gender subordination is only one of a number of intersecting forms of oppression women face and that Western feminists are often guilty of bad theorizing – as in the case of Afghanistan, where the 'feminist focus on women under the Taliban rang with superior tones of enlightenment and righteousness, singling out the most exotic and distant situations, and representing the women of Afghanistan as passive victims' (Young 2003: 230).

87

These differences between feminist (security) scholars, while certainly subject to debate, are not considered a failure, but provide an impetus for continual engagement in the conversation. The open-ended debate and the continual questioning that are an essential aspect of feminist epistemologies can be in tension with the political aims of Security Studies, which often aim to create a single coherent narrative of security and solid, unwavering answers. While some commitments, such as the liberal feminist goal of achieving equality also by integrating women into the armed forces, and the anti-war feminist analysis of militaries as a central element of patriarchal control, are directly at odds with one another, most feminists see disagreement as a necessary and productive element of scholarly debate (Sylvester 1987). What is more, 'any feminist perspective would argue that a truly comprehensive system of security cannot be achieved until gendered relations of domination and subordination are eliminated' (Tickner 1992: 23). That is, the commitment to theorizing on the basis of women's experience to achieve meaningful security arrangements is common to all feminists.

Due to the centrality of women's experience, the most fundamental and far-reaching debate among feminists concerns the question of essentialism. Do women and men have underlying, universal essences – a uniquely female or male nature – that is more funda-mental than any variations among them? Feminists whose work presupposes such an essence often argue that it is rooted in biology – for them, gender difference follows sex difference. Conservatives, for their part, use claims about women's biology to argue that only men should fight wars and women should support them in distinctly feminine ways (on the home front). Cultural feminists use similar arguments, but conclude that women, as natural peacemakers, should resist war and should seek power in world affairs to make the world less violent. Liberal feminists argue that while biology might be limiting, through training, women can become more like men and thus gain equal access to public affairs and institutions like the military (cf. Solaro 2006). Feminist post-structuralists, being sceptical about any essentialist claims, argue that gender is mutable and socially, or even performatively (Butler 1990), constructed – also in the military – so that women joining the military conform to, and simultaneously challenge, institutional gender stereotypes.

This debate is important because the way feminists conceptualize gender shapes their entire analytical endeavour. In other words, when gender is the main category of analysis, what one sees depends on the type of gender-lens one adopts. Consider the following central question of FSS: are women inherently peaceful? Stereotypically, women are seen as peaceful, whether due to biology or to their social role as mothers, while men are considered the violent sex. Burguries (1990: 2–9) outlines three feminist positions with regard to this question:

1 to accept the male and female stereotypes, but try to subvert them to a feminist purpose (as cultural feminist might);
2 to reject the female stereotype and to argue that women should seek to be equal by becoming more like men (as liberal feminists would); and
3 to reject both male and female stereotypes, concluding that they are not histori-cally accurate and that the imagery of the peaceful mother and the power-seeking, violent man support patriarchy and militarism (as post-structuralists might).

Accordingly, feminist recommendations on peace, war and security issues can be expected to differ immensely:

Broadly, the goal of the first approach is peace grounded in feminine values; the second has equality for men as its main objective; and the third approach aims at peace based on a new world order centered around new gender relations and structures.

(Burguieres 1990: 9)

This multiplicity can be confusing, especially for non-feminists. However, while it might be politically more advantageous to posit women as peacemakers, and there certainly are many women peacemakers (Boulding 2000; Meintjes et al. 2001), seeing only women peace-makers is incorrect, devalues women's work in other areas and limits the field unnecessarily.

In FSS, one can find all three positions, though the trend is toward rejecting all stereotypes in favour of analysing the reality on the ground – and how it is gendered in each instance. It is the intersection of gender with other markers such as race, class, religion or nation that produce specific forms of being and leads to a variety of distinct forms of oppression. That variations among women and men are larger than those between them is also supported by historical evidence – and Sylvester warns that 'the differing lived experiences and multi-ple fractured identities women have in the contemporary era, and the many political struggles to which these identities give rise' (Sylvester 1987: 500) need to be taken ser-iously. The way in which different feminists conceptualize gender, therefore, significantly influences their assessment of security issues as well as their policy recommendations.

Other debates in FSS that reflect some of the differences in assumptions about gender (coupled with political orientations) are ongoing: are women (or men) who mother more peaceful than those who do not engage in mothering/caring practices (Ruddick 1998; Scheper-Hughes 1998)? Should women join the military and, if so, on whose terms (Goldman 1982; Isaksson 1988; Solaro 2006; Stiehm 1996)? Can wars benefit women (Enloe 1987)? Do women make different policies, and if so, when and how? Or are the institutions so deeply masculinized that their structure needs changing? What exactly are the relationships between masculinity and violence – or patriarchy and militarism? What can security mean in the midst of intersecting oppressions of class, gender, nation, race or religion? Finally, how is the entire framework/mindset of Security Studies gendered?

Some answers to these questions are being proposed: where traditional Security Studies aims to contain threats, 'feminists contest the possibility of a perfectly controlled, coher-ent security policy that could handle every international contingency' (Blanchard 2003: 1290). If survival (of the state) is seen as the ultimate goal of security efforts, feminists question the quality of survival from a feminist standpoint, particularly since women's relations to states have been historically complex. When security scholars debate ques-tions of military capabilities – and how to maintain or achieve peace through war (rely-ing on 'power over') – many feminists advocate for violence as a last resort, instead looking for common ground and ways to negotiate with the enemy (emphasizing 'power with'). As discourses about security make stark distinctions between peace and wartime and emphasize certain events (e.g. the events of 11 September 2001) as ushering in a new era, feminists locate them on a continuum that spans peace and wartime (Cuomo 1996) as well as within the struggles of everyday life.[5]

Conclusion

Notwithstanding the rich tradition of feminist work on security issues, IR exhibits a con-tinuing lack of appreciation or even knowledge of these contributions.[6] It is my contention that this is due to the difficulty of integrating them into the existing frameworks of Security Studies. While many scholars are concerned with broadening or deepening the reach of Security Studies, feminist contributions often fall under the category of 'opening' Security Studies. Scholars that work toward an opening of Security Studies ask why appeals to security are so powerful (Der Derian 1995; Deudney 1990; Edkins 2002); why particular formulations remain meaningful while others have withered over time (Burke 2002; Constantinou 2000; Dillon 1996; Rothschild 1995); and, maybe most importantly, how meanings might be challenged by addressing the political visions which underlie them (Huysmans 1998, 2006). They do not accept the 'a priori argument that proves the existence and necessity of only one form of security because there currently happens to be a widespread, metaphysical belief in it' (Der Derian 1995: 25). Feminist scholars are thus asking questions about the meaning(s) of security itself. This opening of the agenda begins by understanding how security has traditionally worked (Campbell 1998; Dillon 1996) and how meanings of security are tied to specific Security Studies frameworks (cf. Huysmans 1998; Wæver 1995). As Steve Smith rightly noted,

> the contribution of feminist writers to security studies is … both considerable and ultimately destabilizing for the subfield … looking at security from the perspective of women alters the definition of what security is to such an extent that it is difficult to see how any form of traditional security studies can offer an analysis.
>
> (Smith 2005: 48)

As such, it is understandable that security scholars would rather limit the scope of Security Studies (e.g. Walt 1991), even if they are open to widening it somewhat (Buzan et al. 1998; Krause 1998). However, simply because the focus of Security Studies lies elsewhere, the issues that feminists point to and the challenges they continue to levy will not simply disappear. Rather, the failure to engage with the insights accumulated in feminist work exhibits the limits, and even the poverty, of much of Security Studies.

Notes

1 Of course, not all women are also feminists, nor are all feminists women – but WILPF is representative of a particular, anti-war feminist stance also to be found in FSS today (cf. Cohn and Ruddick 2002).
2 Much as human security does today (Hamber et al. 2006; Hoogensen and Stuvøy 2006; Hudson 2005).
3 Furthermore, as Enloe (1987) reminds us, feminist theorizing on security takes place wherever women find themselves confronting militarization, war and violence (cf. Cockburn 2007).
4 Sharoni (1994) makes eerily similar observations for the Israeli–Palestinian conflict.
5 This summary is based on (Wibben 2002), see also (Wibben forthcoming).
6 Illustrated recently in the C.A.S.E. controversy (C.A.S.E. Collective 2006; Sylvester 2007) as well as in the lack of coverage in the top five IR security journals (with the exception of *Security Dialogue*).

References

Ardener, S., Holden, P., and Macdonald, S. (1987) *Images of Women in Peace and War: Cross Cultural and Historical Perspectives*, London: Macmillan.
Batscheider, T. (1993) *Friedensforschung und Geschlechterverhältnis: Zur Begründung feministischer Fragestellungen in der kritischen Friedensforschung*, Marburg: BdWi Verlag.

Bayard de Volo, L. (2001) *Mothers of Heroes and Martyrs: Gender Identity Politics in Nicaragua, 1979–1999*, Baltimore: Johns Hopkins University Press.

Blanchard, E.M. (2003) 'Gender, international relations, and the development of feminist security theory', *Signs* 28, 4: 1289–1312.

Booth, K. (1997) 'Security and the self: Reflections of a fallen realist', in Krause, K. and Williams, M.C. (eds) *Critical Security Studies*, Minneapolis: University of Minnesota Press, pp. 83–119.

Boulding, E. (1988) 'Warriors and saints: Dilemmas in the history of men, women and war', in Isaksson, E. (ed.) *Women and the Military System*, London: Harvester-Wheatsheaf, pp. 225–47.

——(1992) 'Women's experiential approaches to peace studies', in Kramarae, C. and Spender, D. (eds) *The Knowledge Explosion*, New York: Teachers College Press, pp. 54–63.

——(2000) *Cultures of Peace: The Hidden Side of History*, Syracuse: Syracuse University Press.

Broadhead, L.-A. (2000) 'Re-packaging notions of security: A sceptical feminist response to recent efforts', in Jacobs, S., Jacobson, R. and Marchbank J. (eds) *States of Conflict*, London: Zed Books, pp. 27–44.

Brock-Utne, B. (1989) *Feminist Perspectives on Peace and Peace Education*, 1st edn, New York: Pergamon Press.

Brownmiller, S. (1975) *Against our Will: Men, Women, and Rape*, New York: Simon and Schuster.

Burguieres, M.K. (1990) 'Feminist approaches to peace: Another step for peace studies', *Millennium* 19, 1: 1–18.

Burke, A. (2002) 'Aporias of security', *Alternatives* 27: 1–27.

Butler, J. (1990) *Gender Trouble: Feminism and the Subversion of Identity*, New York: Routledge.

Buzan, B., Wæver, O. and de Wilde, J. (1998) *Security: A New Framework for Analysis*. Boulder: Lynne Rienner Publishers.

C.A.S.E. Collective (2006) 'Critical approaches to security in Europe: A networked manifesto', *Security Dialogue* 37, 4: 443–87.

Campbell, D. (1998) *Writing Security: United States Foreign Policy and the Politics of Identity*, rev. edn, Minneapolis: University of Minnesota Press.

Cockburn, C. (2004) 'The continuum of violence: A gender perspective on war and peace', in Giles, W. and Hyndman, J. (eds) *Sites of Violence*, Berkeley: University of California Press, pp. 24–44.

——(2007) *From Where we Stand: War, Women's Activism and Feminist Analysis*, London: Zed Books.

Cockburn, C. and Zarkov, D. (eds) (2002) *The Postwar Moment: Militaries, Masculinities, and International Peacekeeping*, London: Lawrence and Wishart.

Cohn, C. (1989a) 'Emasculating America's linguistic deterrent', in Harris, A. and King, Y. (eds) *Rocking the Ship of State*, Boulder: Westview Press, pp. 153–70.

——(1989b) 'Sex and death in the rational world of defense intellectuals', in Forcey, L.R. (ed.) *Peace: Meanings, Politics, Strategies*, New York: Praeger, pp. 39–72.

Cohn, C. and Enloe, C. (2003) 'A conversation with Cynthia Enloe: Feminists look at masculinity and the men who wage war', *Signs* 28, 4: 1187–1207.

Cohn, C. and Ruddick, S. (2002) 'A feminists ethical perspective on weapons of mass destruction', in Lee, S. and Hashmi, S. (eds) *Ethics and Weapons of Mass Destruction: Religious and Secular Perspectives*, Princeton: Princeton University Press, pp. 405–35.

Collins, P.H. (1999) 'Producing the mothers of the nation: Race, class and contemporary U.S. policies', in Yuval-Davis, N. and Werbner, P. (eds) *Women, Citizenship and Difference*, London: Zed Books, pp. 118–29.

Constantinou, C. (2000) 'Poetics of security', *Alternatives* 25, 3: 287–306.

Cuomo, C.J. (1996) 'War is not just an event: Reflections on the significance of everyday violence', *Hypatia* 11, 4: 30–45.

Der Derian, J. (1995) 'The value of security: Hobbes, Marx, Nietzsche, and Baudrillard', in Lipschutz, R.D. (ed.) *On Security*, New York: Columbia University, pp. 24–45.

Deudney, D. (1990) 'The case against linking environmental degradation and national security', *Millennium* 19, 3: 461–76.

Dillon, M. (1996) *Politics of Security: Towards a Political Philosophy of Continental Thought*. London: Routledge.

Edkins, J. (2002) 'After the subject of international security', in Valentine, J. and Finlayson, A. (eds) *Politics and Post-structuralism: An Introduction*, Edinburgh: Edinburgh University Press, pp. 66–80.

Elshtain, J.B. (1987) *Women and War*, New York: Basic Books.

Enloe, C. (1987) 'Feminist thinking about war, militarism and peace', in Hess, B.B. and Ferree, M.M. (eds) *Analyzing Gender: A Handbook of Social Science Research*, Newbury Park: Sage, pp. 526–47.

——(1990) *Bananas, Beaches, & Bases: Making Feminist Sense of International Politics*, 1st US edn, Berkeley: University of California.

——(1993) *The Morning After: Sexual Politics at the end of the Cold War*, Berkeley: University of California Press.

——(1998) 'All the men are in the militias and all the women are victims: The politics of masculinity and femininity in nationalist wars', in Lorentzen, L.A. and Turpin, J. (eds) *The Women and War Reader*, New York: NYU Press, pp. 50–62.

——(2000) *Maneuvers: The International Politics of Militarizing Women's Lives*, Berkeley: University of California Press.

Florence, M.S., Marshall, C. and Ogden, C.K. (1987) *Militarism versus Feminism: Writings on Women and War*, London: Virago Press.

Gioseffi, D. (ed.) (2003) *Women on War: An International Anthology of Writings from Antiquity to the Present*, 2nd edn, New York: Feminist Press at CUNY.

Goldman, N.L. (ed.) (1982) *Female Soldiers – Combatants or Noncombatants?* Westport: Greenwood Press.

Hamber, B., Hillyward, P., Maguire, A., McWilliams, M., Robinson, G., Russell, D. and Ward, M. (2006) 'Discourses in transition: Re-imagining women's security', *International Relations* 20, 4: 487–502.

Hamilton, C. (2007) 'Political violence and body language in life stories of women ETA activists', *Signs* 32, 4: 911–32.

Hansen, L. (2000) 'The little mermaid's silent security dilemma and the absence of gender in the Copenhagen school', *Millennium* 29, 2: 285–306.

——(2001) 'Gender, nation, rape: Bosnia and the construction of security', *International Feminist Journal of Politics* 3, 1: 55–75.

Haq, F. (2007) 'Militarism and motherhood: The women of the Lashkar-i-Tayyabia in Pakistan', *Signs* 32, 4: 1023–46.

Harding, S.G. (1986) *The Science Question in Feminism*, Ithaca, NY: Cornell University Press.

Herbert, M.S. (1998) *Camouflage isn't only for Combat: Gender, Sexuality and Women in the Military*, New York: NYU Press.

Hoogensen, G. and Stuvøy, K. (2006) 'Gender, resistance and human security', *Security Dialogue* 37, 2: 207–28.

Hudson, H. (2005) '"Doing" security as though humans matter: A feminist perspective on gender and the politics of human security', *Security Dialogue* 36, 2: 155–74.

Huysmans, J. (1998) 'Security! What do you mean? From concept to thick signifier', *European Journal of International Relations* 4, 2: 226–55.

——(2006) *The Politics of Insecurity: Fear, Migration and Asylum in the EU*, London: Routledge.

Ibáñez, A.C. (2001) 'El Salvador: War and untold stories – women guerrillas', in Moser, C.O.N. and Clark, F.C. (eds) *Victims, Perpetrators or Actors?* London: Zed Books, pp. 117–30.

Isaksson, E. (ed.) (1988) *Women and the Military System*, London: Harvester-Wheatsheaf.

Krause, K. (1998) 'Critical theory and security studies: The research programme of "critical security studies"', *Cooperation & Conflict* 33, 3: 298–333.

Lorentzen, L.A. and Turpin, J. (eds) (1998) *The Women and War Reader*, New York: NYU Press.

Masters, C. (2005) 'Bodies of technology: Cyborg soldiers and militarized masculinities', *International Feminist Journal of Politics* 7, 1: 112–32.

McKelvey, T. (2007) *One of the Guys: Women as Aggressors and Torturers*, Emeryville: Seal Press.

Meintjes, S., Pillay, A. and Turshen, M. (eds) (2001) *The Aftermath: Women in Post-conflict Transformation*, London: Zed Books.

Molloy, P. (1995) 'Subversive strategies or subverting strategy? Toward a feminist pedagogy for peace', *Alternatives* 20, 2: 225–42.

Moon, K.H.S. (1997) *Sex among Allies: Military Prostitution in U.S.–Korea Relations*, New York: Columbia University Press.

Mrsevic, Z. (2001) 'The opposite of war is not peace – it is creativity', in Waller, M.R. and Rycenga, J. (eds) *Frontline Feminisms*, New York: Routledge, pp. 41–55.

Naaman, D. (2007) 'Brides of Palestine/Angels of Death: Media, gender, and performance in the case of Palestinian female suicide bombers', *Signs* 32, 4: 933–55.

Nacos, B.L. (2005) 'The portrayal of female terrorists in the media: Similar framing patterns in the news coverage of women in politics and in terrorism', *Studies in Conflict & Terrorism* 28, 5: 435–51.

Nikolic-Ristanovic, V. (1998) 'War, nationalism, and mothers in the former Yugoslavia', in Lorentzen, L.A. and Turpin, J. (eds) *The Women and War Reader*, New York: NYU Press, pp. 195–210.

——(ed.) (2000) *Women, Violence and War: Wartime Victimization of Refugees in the Balkans*, Budapest: CEU Press.

Nordstrom, C. (1997) *A Different Kind of War Story*, Philadelphia: University of Pennsylvania Press.

Peterson, V.S. (1992a) *Gendered States: Feminist (Re)Visions of International Relations Theory*, Boulder: Lynne Rienner Publishers.

——(1992b) 'Transgressing boundaries: Theories of knowledge, gender and international relations', *Millennium* 21, 2: 183–206.

Reardon, B. (1985) *Sexism and the War System*, New York: Teachers College Press.

——(1993) *Women and Peace: Feminist Visions of Global Security*, Albany: SUNY Press.

Rothschild, E. (1995) 'What is security?', *Daedalus*, 124, 3: 53–98.

Ruddick, S. (1989) *Maternal Thinking: Toward a Politics of Peace*, Boston: Beacon Press.

——(1998) '"Woman of peace": A feminist construction', in Lorentzen, L.A. and Turpin, J. (eds) *The Women and War Reader*, New York: NYU Press, pp. 213–26.

Scheper-Hughes, N. (1998) 'Maternal thinking and the politics of war', in Lorentzen, L.A. and Turpin, J. (eds) *The Women and War Reader*, New York: NYU Press, pp. 227–33.

Sharoni, S. (1994) 'Homefront as battlefield: Gender, military occupation and violence against women', in Mayer, T. (ed.) *Women and the Israeli Occupation*, New York: Routledge, pp. 121–37.

Sjoberg, L. and Gentry, C.E. (2007) *Mothers, Monsters, Whores*. London: Zed Books.

Smith, S. (2005) 'The contested concept of security', in Booth K. (ed.) *Critical Security Studies and World Politics*, Boulder: Lynne Rienner, pp. 27–62.

Solaro, E. (2006) *Women in the Line of Fire: What you should Know about Women in the Military*, Emeryville: Seal Press.

Stiehm, J.H. (1972) *Nonviolent Power: Active and Passive Resistance in America*, Lexington: Heath.

——(1982) 'The protected, the protector, the defender', *Women's Studies International Forum* 5, 3/4: 367–76.

——(1988) 'The effect of myths about military women on the waging of war', in Isaksson, E. (ed.) *Women and the Military System*, London: Harvester-Wheatsheaf, pp. 94–105.

——(1996) *It's our Military, too! Women and the U.S. Military*, Philadelphia: Temple University Press.

Stiglmayer, A. (ed.) (1993) *Mass Rape: The War against Women in Bosnia-Herzegovina*, Lincoln: University of Nebraska Press.

Sylvester, C. (1987) 'Some dangers in merging feminist and peace projects', *Alternatives* 12, 4: 493–509.

——(1989) 'Patriarchy, peace, and women warriors', in Forcey L.R. (ed.) *Peace*, New York: Praeger.

——(2007) 'Anatomy of a footnote', *Security Dialogue* 38, 4: 547–58.

Tickner, J.A. (1992) *Gender in International Relations: Feminist Perspectives on Achieving Global Security*, New York: Columbia University Press.

——(2001) *Gendering World Politics: Issues and Approaches in the Post Cold War Era*, New York: Columbia University Press.

——(2006) 'Feminism meets international relations: Some methodological issues', in Ackerly, B.A., Stern, M. and True, J. (eds) *Feminist Methodologies for International Relations*, Cambridge: Cambridge University Press, pp. 19–41.

Tobias, S. (1985) 'Toward a feminist analysis of defense spending', *Frontiers* 8, 2: 65–68.

Wæver, O. (1995) 'Securitization and desecuritization' in Lipschutz R.D. (ed.) *On Security*, New York: Columbia University Press, pp. 46–86.

Walt, S. (1991) 'The renaissance of security studies', *International Studies Quarterly* 35, 2: 211–39.

Whitworth, S. (2004) *Men, Militarism & UN Peacekeeping*, Boulder: Lynne Rienner.

Wibben, A.T.R. (2002) 'Security narratives in international relations and the events of September 11, 2001: A feminist study', doctoral dissertation, Department of International Politics, Aberystwyth: University of Wales.

——(2008) 'Human security: Toward an opening', *Security Dialogue* 39, 4: 455–62.

——(forthcoming) *Feminist Security Studies: A Narrative Approach*, London: Routledge.

Wibben, A.T.R. and Turpin, J. (2008) 'Women and war', in Kurtz L. (ed.) *The Encyclopedia of Violence, Peace, and Conflict*, 2nd edn, London: Academic Press, pp. 2456–67.

Woollacott, A. (1998) 'Women munition makers, war, and citizenship', in Lorentzen, L.A. and Turpin, J. (eds) *The Women and War Reader*, New York: NYU Press, pp. 126–31.

Young, I.M. (2003) 'Feminist reactions to the contemporary security regime', *Hypatia* 18, 1: 223–31.

Yuval-Davis, N. (1997) *Gender & Nation*, London: Sage Publications.

8

National security, culture and identity

Iver B. Neumann

As demonstrated by the chapters in this Handbook, the main theme of recent scholarship on security has been how uncertainty, particularly within the specific context of the system of states, makes for dilemmas. However, security also has social roots. Among these, questions of identity and national culture loom large. The first section of this chapter is a reminder that the theme is ancient. The second section traces its arrival in the discipline of International Relations. The third section reviews particularly relevant work on national identity, civilization, enlargement of groups, and agency. The concluding section is a call for more study of the role of security practices in instantiating identity.

Early influences

In his dialogue 'The Statesman', Plato (1997: 357–58 [311b-c]) explores what it is that is specific to the work of the statesman and, by implication, to politics. His answer is that politics is the overarching or perhaps better underpinning art of regulating the relationship between the one and the many. The polis, Plato suggests, is like a woven fabric. The calling of the statesman is to finish this weave. The resulting cloth should be a perfect mix of the bold and the prudent, with everybody included. Such a weave, such a political community, Plato concludes, would be the most shining one of them all.

To Plato, then, politics concerns tying together the threads of personal fates into a weave where they are all complementary, tied together in a community of practices and of fate. This is collective identity formation as seen from above. As seen from below, it is all about belonging and acting in accordance with pre-existing scripts. We find the theme all over the political theory canon. To the contract theorists, for example, people alienate their natural state in order to forge a community. Underlying all the questions of everyday politics, of what kind of constitution a community should have, how resources should be allocated, etc., we find the basic question of who we are. Groups are the key to human life. The larger they are, the more their cohesion depends on some kind of glue, some markers of commonness, some integration.

Why is that? Because it is impossible to act collectively without having some kind of preconceived scheme of the nature of the collective actor. This problem grows with the size of the group. The modern-day workplace features many occasions where the idea and practices of commonality are repeated over and over. On the one hand, these rituals aim to impart to employees a feeling of well-being, for it is a part of human nature that the perception of commonality makes most people feel good. But mainly, this feeling of commonality rests on a repertoire of knowledge about when and how to act together. It so happens that this knowledge is also a key part of productive power. It follows that a collective that knows itself to be a 'we' is simply more productive, it has a larger capacity for action that it would if the collective identity were weaker. Therefore, as has been pointed out since the days of Plato, a feeling of belonging to a superordinate group is generally desirable.

There are problems, however. Humans are not bees or ants and do not have a group mind that can orchestrate the behaviour of each and every individual. Given the nature of human existence, the group will necessarily be heterogeneous to some degree. This means that much of the feeling of commonality will be imagined, not actually lived. Close up, culture is not really shared. Even when we imagine that we share it, there are differences. Collective identity is furthered by their existing common practices, but these practices are common in the sense that they are *thought* to be the same, not that they *are* the same. Collective identity is imagined, and it is no less real for that.

Collective identities are also patchy. They are what social scientists call fuzzy sets or, following Ludwig Wittgenstein, family resemblances. There is no one physical or cultural trait that guarantees cultural similarity. In addition to being a question of self-identification, being a member of a group is also a question of being recognized as such a member by other members of the group, as well as by members of groups from which that group delineates itself. It follows that collective identities are also relational (see Emirbayer 1997 for a seminal discussion of relationalism). Where some groups are concerned, being a member of that group is compatible with being a member of another group. This has important consequences. If the group's relations with other groups sustain the group itself, then these groups constitute the we – the outside of the 'we' is constitutive of the inside of the 'we', as it were. This is an old insight; for example, Ibn Khaldun (1992) stressed how what we now call identity increases a group's capacity for action, particularly regarding defence and warfare. However, in the decades following the Second World War, this concept was elaborated upon in ways that made it into the very cornerstone of the social analysis of collective identity. Philosophers like Emmanuel Levinas, Simone de Beauvoir, Jacques Derrida and – earlier and with rather different political and analytical cadences – Carl Schmitt (1976) laid the theoretical groundwork. In terms of method, however, the breakthrough came within the social science that has specialized in identity since its inception, namely social anthropology. Fredrik Barth and associates published the book *Ethnic Groups and Boundaries* (Barth 1969) arguing that the maintenance of ethnic groups could be studied from its fringes, specifically in terms of the groups' characteristics that constituted them. This work was a groundbreaking effort for the field of social anthropology, and over the last 30 years, the other social sciences have followed suit.

It should now be quite clear why identity is a key precondition for the practice of security. Maintaining boundaries (territorial as well as social) is a prerequisite for maintaining identity and security. Delineation of a 'we' is inherent to any identity formation, and since this question goes to the core of who constitutes the 'we', it may at any time become a security question (cf. chapter on Constructivism and securitization studies in this volume). Identity, understood as the answer to the questions of who 'we' are, who our others are, and what kind of relations exist between us and them, is a key precondition for a polity's security politics. Until the late 1980s, however, the only interest in identity within Security Studies was to be found in the much discussed but continuously isolated work of Karl Deutsch and others on security communities.

Identity research and international relations

Authors such as Richard Ashley and Rob Walker (see, for example, reworked material in Walker 1993) returned to examine questions about identity within the discipline of International Relations once again in the late 1980s. Work by Simon Dalby (1990) and others within what was to be known as 'critical geopolitics' emerged at about the same time, suggesting that the impetus to study these questions came from changes in the security discourse itself, and not from developments internal to any one academic discipline. In a seminal contribution, William Connolly (1991) argued that identity requires difference in order to exist and that, if threatened, identity may respond by turning that difference into otherness. The identity debate in IR has focused on whether and under what conditions this hypothesis holds water. David Campbell (1992) argued in a book-length study about the US that its history was one of constant othering, which raised the question of whether difference stood much of a chance in a post-Cold War world. Campbell wrote this as an indictment of the US. He was soon joined by Samuel Huntington (1993), however, who essentialized and embraced the othering processes in question. Political implication aside, this move effectively excludes the prospect of empirical research: if we already know what identity is and how it is distributed, there is no reason why we should research those questions.[1] Ole Wæver (for example, 1998) added that it does not follow that otherness needs to be spatial. To Wæver, the other may also be a former incarnation of the self. This is a nice supplementary insight, but it hardly does away with the existence of territorial others.

Alexander Wendt (1994) denied that difference was analytically necessary for identity to exist; identity could be self-organizing. Bahar Rumelili responded:

> Wendt conflates two distinct processes here. The constitution of identity in relation to difference does not mean that the constitution of identity necessarily involves the agency and discourse of outsiders, but that it presupposes the existence of alternative identities. And no process can be self-organizing if it entails boundary-drawing because boundaries are by definition drawn between a self and an other – even though the other may not be actively participating in the boundary-drawing process.
>
> Bahar Rumelili (2007: 25)

Empirical research

This is roughly the theoretical terrain on which empirical research has taken place. Some studies were undertaken in the 1990s, but most of the work in this field has emerged during the last decade. This section gives an overview looking at the following topics: national identity, civilizational identity, enlargement of groups (security communities and regions), and agency (particularly the act of going to war).

National identity

Most studies concern how polities have othered others to remain secure. The obvious cases to study are those where othering in its extreme form – as dehumanization – is programmatic. National Socialism and Stalinism are modern cases in point. These cases are characterized by substantial use of de-anthropomorphing metaphors: humans are portrayed as being not humans, but dogs, rats, insects (roaches seem to be particularly popular), etc.; perhaps because of their obviousness, these cases have been little studied within IR, but there are voluminous literatures in adjacent disciplines (cf. Koenigsberg 1975; van Ree 1993, and references therein).

Campbell's 1991 book on US foreign policy has already been noted. A related publication by the author of this chapter (Neumann 1999) was inspired by Edward Said and discussed how Europe's 'East' was a necessary other to 'the West' (cf. Browning 2003: Diez 2004). Anssi Paasi (1996) contributed to the debate with a book on Finland's boundaries.

There have also been studies of how certain polities are framed by others (note that the question of whether a given study deals with othering or with the othered entity is a matter of writing technique as much as anything else, since the negotiations over identity are relational and so necessarily keep the identities of all parties in play). Campbell (1998) conducted an early study of Western representations of the Balkans, a dominant topic that so far has found its fullest expression in Hansen 2006 (a work that is also the best-informed study of the topic in terms of method). Kevin Dunn (2003) argued that during the 1960 Congo crisis, US policymakers acted on what they held to be knowledge of the local historical and social context of the crisis. However, Dunn argues, closer scrutiny makes clear that this 'knowledge' came largely from *Tarzan* films, texts such as Joseph Conrad's *Heart of Darkness*, Graham Greene's *A Burnt Out Case* and the comic book *Tintin in Congo*. The Congo case is a reminder that popular culture sometimes does supply the 'knowledge' upon which even political elites base their decisions. The US policymakers wanted to do what was appropriate, and in order to do that, they drew on the only sources of knowledge that were readily available to them. We are reminded here that the body of work on security in popular discourses spearheaded by Der Derian (1991) is definitely related to the topic under discussion here.

A recent study by Jackson (2006) of how West Germany was integrated into 'the West' in the wake of the Second World War set a new standard by focusing on the importance of identity not only as a preconditions for action, but also on action itself (in this case, West Germany's accession to NATO). The study drew extensively on archival researches, making it an exemplar in terms of data collection as well.

Civilizations

Since identity is relational, studies of national identity are linked not only to the delineation of identity on the level of like units (states), but also to more expansive territorial and non-territorial units. There is a body of work showing how systems of thought carry the potential for facilitating a process of othering. The literature on nationalism is an obvious case in point, but one could also mention Barry Hindess's work on liberalism. The rapidly expanding literature on empires is also of importance here (among the studies that stress questions of identity are Armitage 2000; Elias 1978; Mehta 1999; Muthu 2003; and Pagden 1995; a study of how ideal-typical security logics will be different for empires than for states is Nexon and Wright 2007).

Of most direct importance to security are perhaps IR studies of civilizations (Jackson 2006 is a study of Western civilization as well as on German identity; see also O'Hagan 2002). The term 'civilization' still usually refers to something like 'a kind of moral milieu encompassing a certain number of nations, each national culture being only a particular form of the whole' (Durkheim and Mauss 1971: 811).

Salter (2002) wrote a genealogy of civilization's other, namely the barbarian. The tenor of the book emerges clearly in its quote from Martin Wight (1991: 61): 'the deepest reason why the West was shocked by Hitler was his introducing colonial methods of power politics, their own colonial methods, into international relations'.[2] Like all classifications, that of 'barbarian' is not only dependent on antithetical concepts (savage vs. civilized), but also has effects in real life. The kind of security policy that is deemed to be appropriate and legitimate in relationship with 'barbarians' is different to a policy regarded as available and legitimate in other relationships. 'The barbarian', Salter argues, was the key target of the imperial nineteenth century identity project and of its civilizing mission. Without a civilizing mission, imperialism would have been a different phenomenon. The 'standard of civilization' was upheld by international lawyers into the twentieth century (Gong 1984). Friedrich Nietzsche's dedifferentiation of barbarianism and civilization was one force that destabilized the standard of civilization. Nietzsche's analysis of 'good Europeans' and 'new barbarians' paved the way for a German self-identification as barbarians (in the sense of being originary, autochthonous, natural etc.). The practices of the First World War, where colonial troops were used in Europe and a number of rules of engagement were regarded as 'barbarian' even by those who sustained them, served to dedifferentiate the barbarian/civilized dichotomy further. With Hitler coming to power, the celebration of barbarism reached new heights, as did the ferocity of the war and destruction that he wrought on Europeans during the Second World War.[3] Salter highlights how colonialism was a key precondition of Hitler's actions. It is well known that the practice of the concentration camp hails back to British colonial rule and colonial warfare during the Boer War. What is perhaps not so well known is how Hitler referred approvingly to British colonial policies in his table talk, and suggested that these practices should serve as an example for German rule in their *Lebensraum* to the East. Salter observes that the concepts of barbarism and civilization faded during the Cold War, only to resurface in the 1990s, when what we may for lack of a more accurate term call 'Western' discourse once again turned towards stressing the importance of what looked very much like the old 'standard of civilization'. The main effect of this development is to stress the value of 'Western' models as the norm for the historical development of any human society. In the wake of the attacks in the US in 2001, these effects include going to war.

This renewed stress on a 'standard of civilization' in Western discourse has stimulated scholarly interest in the topic of civilization. A volume edited by Hall and Jackson appeared in 2007, and another one by Marko Lehti and Chris Browning is forthcoming, as is a book-length study by Brett Bowden.

Enlargement of groups

After the end of the Cold War, the work done by Deutsch and his collaborators on security communities in the 1960s was finally followed up on. The volume edited by Adler and Barnett (1998) is first and foremost an empirical update on security communities in various states of gestation throughout the world. Drawing on Jean-François Lyotard's philosophical work on the importance of linking meanings, Janice Bially Mattern's study of how the 'special relationship' between the UK and the US was salvaged after the strains imposed by the Suez crisis in 1956 highlights the importance of power to the forging and maintenance of security communities (Bially Mattern 2004). The contrast between the volume by Adler and Barnett on the one hand and the volume by Bially Mattern on the other is an example of how identity work in the field of Security Studies exhibits the same bifurcation as non-rational work in IR generally: constructivists work on the socialization of norms, while post-structuralists work on power. The relationship between these insights has yet to be properly studied.

Surprisingly, the insights into security communities as general phenomena have yet to be linked to the insights produced by the literature on security cultures, which tend to be more specific. These are studies of how military structures (civil–military relations, power relations between services, standard operational procedures, procurement and deployment policies, tactics and strategy, etc.) differ between states (see van Evera 1984; Gray 1981; Hoffmann and Longhurst 1999; Jacobsen 1990; Johnston 1995, 1998; Kier 1999; Klein 1986; Neumann and Heikka 2005; Posen 1984; Snyder 1977).

One might have thought that the identity of NATO would have been an obvious object of study, but attempts to theorize about NATO in general are almost non-existent (but see Tunander 1997; Williams 2007). Behnke (2007) starts with the puzzle of why NATO survived the Cold War, given that political realism predicted its demise. The realist prediction rested on the assumption that, once the threat against which an alliance had been forged was gone or the gain that it was supposed to realize had been achieved or was no longer attainable – that is, once the alliance's original *raison d'être* had disappeared, the alliance would also disappear. Behnke's answer is that NATO survived the disappearance of the Soviet threat because NATO was so intertwined with the representation of 'the West' that it was able to survive and expand simply on the strength of being the West's politico-military arm. This answer is similar to one that has already been given earlier by constructivists (see contributors to the seminal volume edited by Katzenstein in 1996 – particularly Herman's (1996) contribution. Behnke's important critique is that constructivists treat this sequence simply as a case of socialization, with little attention to power. Behnke draws on Carl Schmitt to demonstrate how NATO was able to pacify framing of itself other than its own, for example, Russia's framing.

One precondition for studies of regions and security (the key work is Buzan and Wæver 2003) is an acknowledgement of the fact that regions exist in terms of the identities, just like any other political entity (for example, Browning and Joenniemi 2004). The literature on EU identity is huge; the scope of this chapter only permits a brief overview of some studies that are particularly relevant to Security Studies. Mälksoo (2007) delivers a voluminous description of tugs-of-war over what kind of role Poland and the Baltics do and should have in the framing of EU security policy. The study is an exercise in provincializing Western Europe and in providing a reading of Orientalism and responses to Orientalism in 'Old Europe's' readings of 'New Europe'. Pace (2005) is a close-up study of how these identities and practices are hybridized. In a key work, Rumelili (2007) discusses how Turkey challenged the EU's narrative of Turkey and its relationship to the EU by creating counter-narratives about the European self as an identity that possibly excluded the admission of a Muslim state such as Turkey. Turkey's counter-narrative first appeared as a potential threat to Europe's narrative of itself, and then acted as a catalyst of change to that narrative. In order to salvage an EU identity that emerged as inclusive of Turkey, the EU had to open the way for Turkish EU membership. Turkey accomplished this by actually playing up its cultural difference from Europe. There followed an internal

EU debate on whether this should be construed as a threat to European identity, in which case the appropriate response would have been to other Turkey, or whether Turkish difference could be accommodated by altering European identity.

Alexander Wendt (2004) took the notion of inclusive identities to its ultimate extreme when he argued not only in favour of a world state, but also that such an identity was inevitable. Drawing on Wæver's idea about temporal othering, he suggested that

> a world state could compensate for the absence of spatial differentiation through a temporal differentiation between its present and its past. The past here is anarchy, with all its unpleasantness. In Hegelian terms, we could say that 'history' becomes the Other in terms of which the global Self is defined.
>
> (Wendt 2004: 527)

Agency

Most of the work reviewed so far has focused on the production of amity and enmity as relations. There also exist studies that focus on how security is a precondition for a community to be able to function and act. Mitzen (2006) refers to this as ontological security. In a book-length study that builds on the work of sociologist Anthony Giddens, Steele (2006) posits that a polity needs ontological security, understood as a norm and a resource. Giddens argues that to be able to 'go on', an agent has to be able to tell a reasonably consistent story about whence it came from and where it is going; it has to have a certain bearing. When this is not the case, the agent experiences shame. Steele posits that states are rational egoists, but they base their egoism not upon (independent and exogenous) material structures, but upon the requirement for self-identity.

Ringmar's 1996 book remains the most ambitious study of how identity may inform security action. Ringmar posits a difference between constitutive stories about who 'we' are – stories about action and identity – on the one hand, and stories about actions and interests on the other. While the latter stories may be treated in rational terms, the former stories cannot be treated in this way. Ringmar also introduces a *setting* to the stories, that is, other story-telling entities. These 'others' are key *audiences* of the stories and, as such, they participate actively in the formation both of identity and interests, making both these concepts relational: 'In order to find out whether a particular constitutive story is a valid description of us, it must first be tested in interaction with others' (Ringmar 1996: 80). Confirmation cannot be given by just anybody, but only by those others that the self recognizes and respects as being kindred to itself. This set of others are referred to as 'circles of recognition'. One instance that deserves particular theoretical attention is, of course, the case where others deny recognition to the self's constitutive stories. In this case, the storied self has three options: to accept stories told about it by others, to abandon the stories that are not recognized in favour of others, or to stand by the original story and to try to convince the audiences that it is, in fact, a legitimate account. The need to obtain recognition for constitutive stories, Ringmar insists, will be greater at so-called formative moments, when new emblems, flags, dress codes, songs, fêtes and rituals are continuously invented. It will also be greater for social upstarts, such as Sweden in the 1630s. Ringmar concludes that Sweden entered the Thirty Years' War at this time to force other states to accept the story Sweden told about itself. To Ringmar, then, Hegel's story of how the slave must kill the master in order to get his recognition has been sublimated into the story of why certain states go to war at certain times (for a generalized theory of recognition, see Ringmar 2002).

Conclusion and outlook

As borne out by classic works by the likes of Plato and Ibn Khaldoun, the importance of identity for politics has been evident to theorists working in different cultural settings for a long time. Recent work has succeeded in rekindling interest in these issues. Most extant work has focused on identity as a precondition for action. Some of those actions belong to the field of security policy. The key move in making identity scholarship more directly relevant for Security Studies is to make the link from preconditions for action to security actions themselves. The security analysis is not complete without an analysis of how the identities of the involved parties were preconditions for and informed the security policy, and of the kinds of effects that the security policy that was pursued had on those identities. By way of illustration, consider the effects of the socially formed memory of the battle at Kosovo Polje in 1389 for Serbian security policy in the late 1980s and 1990s. Since identities are dependent on practices to evolve, the easiest way to move the focus closer to action is probably for analysts to frame action as events, and to demonstrate what role security practices play for those events.

Notes

1 A similar move was made by neo-realists in the early 1990s, who preserved the structural frame-work, but substituted 'nations' for 'states' as units of analysis. Like Huntington's approach, this move effectively bracketed the issues discussed here. See Posen (1993) and Van Evera (1994).
2 Wight seems to have taken this insight from Toynbee, with whom he worked for a number of years.
3 Note, however, that other groups, particularly Bolsheviks, could concurrently be framed as barbarian in the sense of being inferior.

References

Adler, E. (2002) 'Constructivism and international relations', in Carlsnaes, W., Risse, T. and Simmons, B.A. (eds) *Handbook of International Relations*, London, Sage, pp. 95–118.

Adler, E. and Barnett, M. (eds) (1998) *Security Communities*, Cambridge: Cambridge University Press.

Armitage, D. (2000) *The Ideological Origins of the British Empire*, Cambridge: Cambridge University Press.

Ashley, R. (1981) 'Political realism and human interest', *International Studies Quarterly* 25, 2: 204–36.

Barth, F. (ed.) (1969) *Ethnic Groups and Boundaries*, Oslo: Norwegian University Press.

Behnke, A. (2007) *Re-Presenting the West. NATO's Security Discourse After the End of the Cold War*, Stockholm: Studies in Politics No.120.

Bially Mattern, J. (2004) *Ordering International Politics: Identity, Crisis and Representational Force*, London: Routledge.

Booth, K. and Trood, R. (eds) (1999) *Strategic Cultures in the Asia-Pacific Region*, Basingstoke: Macmillan.

Browning, C. (2003) 'The internal/external security paradox and the reconstruction of boundaries in the Baltic: The case of Kaliningrad', *Alternatives* 28, 5: 545–81.

Browning, C. and Joenniemi, P. (2004) 'Regionality beyond security? The Baltic Sea region after enlargement', *Cooperation and Conflict* 39, 3: 233–53.

Buzan, B. and Wæver, O. (2003) *Regions and Powers: The Structure of International Security*, Cambridge: Cambridge University Press.

Campbell, D. (1992) *Writing Security: United States Foreign Policy and the Politics of Identity*, Minneapolis: University of Minnesota Press.

——(1998) *National Deconstruction: Violence, Justice and Identity in Bosnia*, Minneapolis: University of Minnesota Press.

C.A.S.E. Collective (1984) 'Critical approaches to security in Europe: A networked manifesto', *Security Dialogue* 37, 4: 443–87.

Connolly, W. (1991) *Identity/Difference: Democratic Negotiations of the Political Paradox*, Ithaca, NY: Cornell University Press.

Dalby, S. (1990) *Creating the Second Cold War: Discourse of Politics*, London: Pinter.

Der Derian, J. (1991) *Anti-Politics*, Oxford: Blackwell.

Deutsch, K.W., Burrell, S.A. and Kann, R.A. (1957) *Political Community and the North Atlantic Area: International Organization in the Light of Historical Experience*, Princeton: Princeton University Press.

Diez, T. (2004) 'Europe's others and the return of geopolitics', *Cambridge Review of International Studies* 17, 2: 319–35.

Dunn, K.C. (2003) *Imagining the Congo: The International Relations of Identity*, New York: Palgrave Macmillan.

Durkheim, É. and Mauss, M. (1971) [1913] 'Note on the notion of civilization', *Social Research* 38, 4: 808–13.

Elias, N. (1978) *The Civilizing Process*, New York: Urizen.

Emirbayer, M. (1997) 'Manifesto for a relational sociology', *American Journal of Sociology* 103, 2: 281–317.

van Evera, S. (1984) 'The cult of the offensive and the origins of the First World War', *International Security* 9, 4: 58–107.

——(1994) 'Hypotheses on nationalism and war', *International Security* 18, 4: 5–39.

Gong, G.W. (1984) T*he Standard of 'Civilization' in International Society*, Oxford: Clarendon.

Gray, C.S. (1981) 'National style in strategy: The American example', *International Security* 6, 2: 21–47.

Hall, M. and Jackson, P.T. (2007) *Civilizational Identity: The Production and Reproduction of 'Civilizations' in International Relations*, Basingstoke: Palgrave.

Hansen, L. (2006) *Security as Practice: Discourse Analysis and the Bosnian War*, London: Routledge.

Herman, R.G. (1996) 'Identity, norms, and national security: The Soviet foreign policy revolution and the end of the Cold War', in Katzenstein, P.J. (ed.) *The Culture of National Security*, New York: Columbia University Press, pp. 271–316.

Hoffmann, A. and Longhurst, K. (1999) 'German strategic culture in action', *Contemporary Security Policy* 20, 2: 31–49.

Huntington, S. (1993) 'The clash of civilizations?' *Foreign Affairs* 72, 3: 22–49. Available online at: http://history.club.fatih.edu.tr/103%20Huntington%20Clash%20of%20Civilizations%20full%20text.htm (accessed 9 February 2009).

Jackson, P.T. (2006) *Civilizing the Enemy: German Reconstruction and the Invention of the West*, Ann Arbor: University of Michigan Press.

Jacobsen, C.G. (ed.) (1990) *Strategic Power: USA/USSR*, New York: St. Martin's Press.

Johnston, A.I. (1995) 'Thinking about strategic culture', *International Security* 19, 4: 32–44.

——(1998) *Cultural Realism: Strategic Culture and Grand Strategy in Chinese History*, Princeton: Princeton University Press.

Katzenstein, P. (ed.) (1996) *The Culture of National Security: Norms and Identity in World Politics*, New York: Columbia University Press.

Khaldun, I. (ed. Dawood, N.J.) (1992) *The Muqaddimah: An Introduction to History*, trans. Rosenthal, F., Princeton: Princeton University Press.

Kier, E. (1999) *Imagining War: French and British Military Doctrine Between the Wars*, Princeton: Princeton University Press.

Klein, B.S. (1986) 'Hegemony and strategic culture: American Power projection and alliance defence politics', *Review of International Studies* 14, 2: 133–48.

Koenigsberg, R.A. (1975) *Hitler's Ideology: A Study in Psychoanalytic Sociology*, New York: Library of Social Sciences.

Mälksoo, M. (2007) *The Politics of Becoming European: A Genealogy of Polish and Baltic Post-Cold War Security Imaginaries*, D.Phil. submission, Centre for International Studies, University of Cambridge.

Mehta, U.S. (1999) *Liberalism and Empire: A Study in Nineteenth-Century British Thought*, Chicago: University of Chicago Press.

Mitzen, J. (2006) 'Ontological security in world politics: State identity and security dilemma', *European Journal of International Relations* 12, 3: 341–70.

Muthu, S. (2003) *Enlightenment against Empire*, Princeton: Princeton University Press.

Neumann, I.B. (1999) *Uses of the Other: The East in European Identity Formation*, Minneapolis: University of Minnesota Press.

Neumann, I.B. and Heikka, H. (2005) 'Grand strategy, strategic culture, practise: The social roots of Nordic defence', *Cooperation and Conflict* 40, 1: 5–23.

Nexon, D. and Wright, T. (2007). 'What's at stake in the American empire debate', *American Political Science Review* 101, 2: 253–271.

O'Hagan, J. (2002) *Conceptualizing The West in International Relations: From Spengler to Said*, Basingstoke: Macmillan.

Paasi, A. (1996) *Territories, Boundaries and Consciousness: The Changing Geographies of the Finnish-Russian Border*, Chichester: Wiley.

Pace, M. (2005) *The Politics of Regional Identity: Meddling with the Mediterranean*, London, Routledge

Pagden, A. (1995) *Lords of all the World: Ideologies of Empire in Spain, Britain and France c. 1500 – c. 1800*, New Haven: Yale University Press.

Plato (1997) [360 B.C.E.] 'Statesman', in Cooper, J.M. (ed.) *Plato: Complete Works*, Indianapolis: Hackett, pp. 294–358.

Posen, B.R. (1984) *The Sources of Military Doctrine: France, Britain, and Germany between the World Wars*, Ithaca, NY: Cornell University Press.

——(1993) 'Nationalism, the mass army, and military power', *International Security* 18, 2: 80–124.

van Ree, E. (1993) 'Stalin's organic theory of the party', *Russian Review* 52, 1: 43–57.

Ringmar, E. (1996) *Identity, Interest and Action: A Cultural Explanation of Sweden's Intervention in the Thirty Years War*, Cambridge: Cambridge University Press.

——(2002) 'The recognition game: Soviet Russia against the West', Cooperation and Conflict, 37, 2: 115–36.

Rumelili, B. (2007) *Constructing Regional Community and Order in Europe and Southeast Asia*, Basingstoke: Palgrave.

Salter, M.B. (2002) *Barbarians and Civilization in International Relations*, London: Pluto.

Schmitt, C. (1976) *The Concept of the Political*, Chicago: University of Chicago Press.

Snyder, J. (1977) *The Soviet Strategic Culture: Implications for Limited Nuclear Options*, Santa Monica: RAND Corporation, R–2154-AF.

Steele, B. (2006) *Ontological Security in International Relations*, London: Routledge.

Tunander, O. (1997) 'Post-Cold War Europe: A synthesis of a bipolar friend-foe structure and a hierarchical cosmos–chaos structure?', in Tunander, O., Baev, P. and Einagel, V.I. (eds) *Geopolitics in Post-Wall Europe: Security, Territory and Identity*, London: Sage, pp. 17–44.

Wæver, O. (1998) 'Insecurity, security and asecurity in the West European non-war community', in Adler, E. and Barnett M. (eds) *Security Communities*, Cambridge: Cambridge University Press, pp. 69–118.

Walker, R.B.J. (1993) *Inside/Outside: International Relations as Political Theory*, Cambridge: Cambridge University Press.

Wendt, A. (1994) 'Collective identity formation and the international state', *American Political Science Review* 88, 2: pp. 384–96.

——(2004) 'Why a world state is inevitable', *European Journal of International Relations* 9, 4: 491–542.

Wight, M. (1991) *International Theory: The Three Traditions*, Gabriele Wight and Brian Porter (eds) Leicester & London: Leicester University Press.

Williams, M.C. (2007) *Culture and Security: Symbolic Power and the Politics of International Security*, London: Routledge.

9

Societal security

Tobias Theiler

The concept of societal security originated in Barry Buzan's classic *People, States and Fear* (1983) and became a cornerstone of what is widely known as the Copenhagen School in International Relations (IR) (Wæver et al. 1993). In the period since, it has stimulated an impressive body of commentary, criticism and refinement. For many critics and proponents alike, societal security has become one of the most important challengers to state-centric and 'objectivist' conceptions of security in International Relations.

This chapter suggests that the societal security concept resides at the intersection of several theoretical turns in IR that had gained momentum in the early 1990s: a partial move away from the state as object of analytical and normative concern; a growing focus on identity; and, more broadly, the rise of social constructivism as an explanatory paradigm. Its absorption of such diverse theoretical movements helps account for the popularity of societal security as an analytical concept. At the same time, it exposes societal security theorists to many of the criticisms these broader theoretical movements have attracted. Many of these criticisms pertain to how terms such as 'society', 'identity' and 'securitization' should be defined, put into operation and applied to the real world.

Over the past decade, different writers have taken the societal security concept in increasingly divergent and in some cases mutually incompatible theoretical directions, with a widening gap between more post-structural and more mainstream social constructivist interpretations. This diversity has made it harder to attribute a single meaning to societal security, but it also testifies to the concept's continued theoretical vitality. In that sense, societal security represents an evolving conceptual project in IR more than a unified new paradigm.

This chapter first outlines the concept of societal security as proposed by the Copenhagen School. The subsequent section focuses on a range of theoretical gaps and ambiguities in contemporary societal security theorizing and on possible ways of addressing them. By way of doing so, it also highlights directions for further research and development.

Societal security and state security

Traditional approaches to security in IR focus on the state. Based on a classic definition of the state as a legal and political unit exercising sovereignty over a defined territory and population, they assume that a state achieves security if it can protect its sovereignty and territorial integrity. Since the main threat to these has traditionally come from physical force wielded by other states, conventional approaches to security are preoccupied with broadly defined military issues such as deterrence, balances of power, alliance formation and weapons proliferation.

Because of its focus on protecting the state from military threats by other states, this traditional security agenda has paid relatively little systematic attention to what is *inside* states – above all to *society*, defined, broadly, as the social, cultural and psychological formation that the state's political-cum-territorial shell encloses. Ultimately, of course, this is the logical result of conceiving of the international system as composed mainly of *nation*-states and of defining nation-states in ideal-typical terms as units whose social, cultural and political boundaries coincide. Where each society has 'its' state and each state 'its' society, societal security – defined as the cultural, linguistic and identitive survival of a social group – becomes the logical extension of state security.

In *Identity, Migration and the New Security Agenda in Europe* (Wæver et al. 1993) and a series of subsequent writings, societal security theorists seek to break with such a view of societal security as a simple extension of state security. Instead, they conceptualize 'society' as a potentially independent security object and societal forces as potential security actors in their own right. 'Society', for societal security theorists, is the social unit (a perceived nation, ethnic group, clan, tribe, or potentially any other communal formation) that provides a locus of identification for its members. 'Objectively', a society is signified and differentiated from other societies by markers such as language and customs. 'Subjectively', it is the repository of shared meanings and identifications for its members who share what Karl Deutsch (1957) has termed a 'we-feeling', or what social psychologists refer to as a common social identity (Hogg and Abrams 1988). For societal security theorists, what characterizes every identity community is that its members value its preservation as an end in itself rather than just as a means to achieve other ends, given that it helps sustain those parts of the self-concept that are socially rooted. In that sense, societal security is synonymous with a kind of 'identity security' for individuals (Buzan et al. 1998: 120).

'Societal security', in short, signifies the ability of an identity community to survive. In Ole Wæver's often-cited definition, it refers to 'the sustainability, within acceptable conditions for evolution, of traditional patterns of language, culture, association, and religious and national identity and custom' (Wæver 1993: 23). This implies that societal security, too, has an 'objective' and a 'subjective' dimension. Objectively, it pertains to the preservation of societal markers such as language and customs; subjectively, it entails the community's survival as a locus of identification for its members.

Nevertheless, it is precisely this identitive dimension that allows the subjective component of societal security to prevail over its objective counterpart. In different societal contexts, the same type of objective development triggers very different perceptions and reactions. For example, Austrian voters feel more threatened by immigration than their counterparts in Luxembourg, even though Luxembourg has proportionately many more foreign residents than does Austria; French elites worry more about the spread of the English language than do Dutch elites, even though English is used much more widely in the Netherlands than it is in France, and so on. The central insight here is that which

informs all broadly constructivist conceptions of social reality: social and political behaviour is generated by socially generated ideas about the material world, not directly by
the material world itself (Wendt 1999; Theiler 2005).

But why do people think of a given material development as an identity threat in
some settings and not in others? For societal security theorists, the central variable is
securitization. Securitization represents a 'speech act' with a 'specific rhetorical structure'
(Buzan et al. 1998: 26). That structure has three components: '(a) existential threats to
the survival of some kind of referent object [i.e. in this case, a communal unit] that (b)
require exceptional measures to protect the threatened referent object, which (c) justify
and legitimize the breaking free of normal [e.g., democratic] procedures' (van Munster
2005: 3). To securitize thus is to identify a threat to the social and cultural survival of a
community and a strategy to ward off that threat and thereby make society secure again.
Given that people perceive these as existential threats to something whose survival they
seek as an end in itself and afford absolute priority, effective securitization can lead to
defensive measures that violate what qualifies as politically or morally acceptable conduct
in normal circumstances. 'Identity emergencies' generate a corresponding willingness to
support extraordinary emergency measures beyond 'normal' politics.

As the next section suggests, societal security theorists disagree about the precise dynamics
of securitization. However, drawing on the philosopher John L. Austin's concept of 'performative utterances' (and later elaborations such as Pierre Bourdieu's notion of 'magic
discourse'), they agree that securitizing discourses can, up to a point, generate the very
reality they depict and in that sense become self-fulfilling. *Saying* 'X threatens Y' *makes it
so*, provided the audience accepts the statement as true and provided the threat and the
security referent are both part of social reality. At the same time, most societal security
theorists accept that securitizing discourses can only become 'performative' in particular
social conditions. For example, the securitizers (who may or may not be linked to the state)
must enjoy sufficient status and credibility among the audience. Moreover, the threats
they invoke must correspond to pre-existing suspicions and anxieties or at least must not
violate deeply rooted values and beliefs (Macleod 2004; Stritzel 2007). From this perspective, then, the observation that societal security threats are discursively constructed does
not imply that securitizers can construct them in any way they please. Nor, of course,
does it mean that efforts to securitize are necessarily successful, as is further argued below.

Securitization, finally, leads back to the relationship between society and the state. While
societal security theorists view the two as analytically distinct, they nonetheless treat them
as potentially entangled. On the one hand, actual or aspiring state elites may seek to
construct societal threat perceptions as a vehicle to further their own position. The use of
anti-immigration (and, more recently, especially anti-Muslim) themes by various right-
of-centre parties in Europe is a good example. Another example is the switch by several
Communist leaders in Central and Eastern Europe to xenophobic nationalist themes in
the 1970s and 1980 in an attempt to compensate for Communism's fading economic and
political appeal. Elsewhere, the relationship is more 'bottom-up', in that insecure societies may call on 'their' states for protection. By many accounts, this happened in the
European Union from the 1990s onwards as some national electorates opposed further
European integration on the grounds of wanting to protect national identities from supranational encroachment, while most state elites supported it for economic and political
reasons (Wæver and Kelstrup 1993).

The above scenarios presuppose that state and societal boundaries broadly coincide. In
that sense, they correspond to the nation-state logic discussed earlier. However, in many

107

states that assumption does not hold, as they are internally divided into different societal units – be they self-conceived nations, ethnic communities, or cultural or linguistic sub-groups. In such situations, societal security and state security can become mutually antagonistic. On the one hand, state institutions may seek to promote internal cohesion by trying to assimilate minority cultures into the dominant state-sponsored societal culture. On the other hand, many minority groups seek to ensure their cultural and identitive survival by demanding a state of their own, and these demands often increase as attempted assimilation at the hands of central state elites increases their societal insecurity. According to societal security theorists, a longing by insecure societies to obtain their own states contributed, among other things, to the disintegration of Yugoslavia and the Soviet Union in the 1990s (Wiberg 1993; Isakovic 2000). Three complementary strategies may help overcome such zero-sum constellations:

1 promoting an overarching state-wide societal identity that is complementary rather than competing with sub-unit societal identities;
2 a federal/devolutional arrangement that grants far-reaching cultural autonomy to the societal sub-units in exchange for political loyalty to the state; and
3 de-securitizing the threat posed by the state to societal identities in the ways further discussed below.

Questions, criticisms and theoretical developments

Criticisms of the societal security concept fall into two broad categories. A first category takes issue mainly with the use of the term 'security' when dealing with referents other than the state and threats other than physical force. These reservations often flow from a concern for the preservation of Security Studies as a clearly delineated academic field and/or from fears that too broad a concept of security might dilute the status of 'real' (i.e. physical) security as the principal focus of analytical and normative concern in IR (see Knudsen 2001). Regardless of their potential validity, these criticisms pertain more to the drawing of disciplinary and terminological boundaries than to the empirical applicability and theoretical consistency of the societal security concept itself. Because of this, the present chapter sets them aside in order to focus on a second category of criticisms. These tend to be sympathetic to expanded notions of security as well as to the incorporation of social and identity-related factors into Security Studies. At the same time, they hold that the concepts of societal security and securitization as proposed by the Copenhagen School suffer from several ambiguities and inconsistencies. Many go on to suggest ways of sharpening and amending both concepts to improve their theoretical coherence and empirical applicability. This section focuses on five central issues: the causes of societal security-seeking behaviour; the objectives of securitizing elites; the social and material context conducive to securitization; the potential for a dialectical relationship involving securitization, group formation (or strengthening) and the status of securitizing elites inside the group; and the still largely under-explored possibilities of de-securitization.

Motivation

A first question in need of elaboration pertains to the origins of societal security-seeking behaviour in individuals. Why should we assume that people strive for societal security, and why (and in what circumstances) should we presume that they place the defence of their communal identities ahead of other (e.g. economic) aspirations? This question is crucial for the theoretical credibility of the societal security project, particularly since societal security-centred interpretations of particular empirical events are themselves disputed. From anti-EU and anti-immigrant movements in Western Europe to the Central and East European state break-ups, even events that are the empirical jewels in the crown of societal security theorists have attracted alternative explanations as well as doubts regarding the extent to which the kind of identity-centred fears and reflexes postulated by societal security theorists really came into play (e.g. Gagnon 2006; Mueller 2000). The latter have frequently failed to counter these alternative accounts effectively, above all because they lack a coherent explanation for when and why societal security matters to people and shapes behaviour in particular ways. Put differently, their macro-level account lacks a micro-level foundation.

The discipline most able to offer such an account of human motivation is social psychology. From the very beginnings of their discipline, social psychologists have engaged with many of the questions that also preoccupy societal security theorists. This includes questions such as why people construct group boundaries and identify with groups, how dynamics inside groups shape relations between them (and vice versa), and how and why people perceive particular developments as threatening to their group identity (see Hogg and Abrams 1988; applied to the societal security concept, see Theiler 2003). In tackling these issues, social psychologists (especially those in the social identity theory tradition) often come to conclusions broadly similar to those of the societal security theorists, particularly as regards the importance of communal identifications to individuals. Accordingly, many of these social-psychological findings can be incorporated into a societal security framework. At the same time, social psychology also helps refine some of the societal security theorists' assumptions. This pertains particularly to the conditions under which people perceive particular developments as threatening to their communal identity and display particular kinds of defensive reactions. In short, a more systematic engagement with social psychology could provide societal security theorists with a better understanding of human motivation. It could help them complement their claim that communal identities and societal boundaries matter to people with a theoretically more coherent and firmly rooted account of how and why this is so in particular circumstances.

Securitization

A related area in need of greater conceptual clarity is securitization. Asserting that securitization, as a speech act, 'is a combination of language and society, of both intrinsic features of speech and the group that authorizes and recognizes that speech' (Buzan et al. 1998: 32), most societal security theorists already combine a broadly linguistic (or 'internalist') conceptualization of securitization with a more sociological (or 'externalist') one. As suggested, the first conception draws on those strands in the philosophy of language that centre on the 'performative', reality-generating potential of discourse. If X and Y are both discursively constructed, *saying* that X threatens Y can *make* it so. Yet, second, securitizing discourses can have this effect only in particular social and material contexts, pertaining to the securitizer, the audience and the threat. For example, the 'performative' effectiveness of the securitizing claim 'Condoms threaten Western civilization!' is bound to vary greatly depending on whether I utter it over lunch with colleagues or Pope Benedict utters it in a widely publicized papal encyclical. Even so, most societal security theorists have not systematically examined these contextual factors. Questions such as when and why particular securitization discourses emerge and find broad-based acceptance remain largely unanswered.

To fill this gap, a greater engagement with social psychology would once more be useful, especially with the social-psychological research on threat perceptions, defensive identity formation and related phenomena. In a more inductive vein, societal security theorists need to broaden their empirical focus beyond cases in which securitization appears to have been largely successful so that they can also consider a (probably much larger) range of cases in which it was unsuccessful. This combination of deductive and inductive approaches would help societal security theorists to better grasp how and why particular audiences do or do not respond to particular kinds of securitization discourses by particular elites in particular circumstances. It would help them 'conceptualize the deep embeddedness of security articulations in social relations of power without which ... [the] dynamics and *non*-dynamics [of securitization] cannot be understood' (Stritzel 2007: 365; see also Macleod 2004).

Securitizing elites

A further question linked to securitization pertains to the aims of securitizing elites. Who securitizes, when and for what purpose? An obvious answer would be that securitizers do so out of self-interest, but that leaves open the question of how, precisely, they benefit from securitization. Case studies in the societal security literature hint at several possibilities, each requiring further elaboration. Sometimes, elites seem to securitize in order to advance more 'hidden' personal or political agendas. For example, some anti-EU groups regularly invoke alleged threats to national identities, although in reality these groups are driven more by economic or ideological aims for which national mass publics might be more difficult to mobilize. Moreover, where securitizers are linked to the state, they may fuel societal threat perceptions to justify the self-serving use of state power under the guise of societal security protection, for instance to persecute internal opponents. As argued, this possibility is implicit in the very definition of securitization as a process that moves a given issue from the realm of 'normal' politics into that of emergency action where otherwise impermissible violations of established norms and practices are tolerated.

Securitization, group formation and social power

These mechanisms aside, successful securitization may also strengthen the securitizing actors in a more fundamental way, by the mere virtue of it being pursued. This bears on what is one of the most interesting theoretical avenues opened up by the securitization logic that societal security theorists occasionally hint at but again leave under-theorized: the reciprocal link between group securitization, group consolidation and the status of securitizing actors inside the group. In such a conception, securitization is not just a process as part of which an already fully constituted securitizing agent defends an already fully formed communal identity by invoking a threat. Instead, securitization can entail a reciprocal strengthening of all three: the social position of the securitizing actor, the communal identity and the threat perception (Wilkinson 2007). Linguistically, such a conception again flows from seeing discourse as 'performative', as discussed earlier. If the utterance 'X threatens Y' can bring X (the threat) into being, it can also generate or reinforce Y (the group identity) to the extent that both are discursively constituted. By extension, it can enhance the position of the securitizing agent whose authority to 'speak security' on behalf of the group strengthens as the threat that he/she/it enunciates becomes recognized as such. From a more sociological angle, this dialectical notion of securitization and societal identity formation bears strong affinities to a strand of sociological thinking that links conflict between groups to a strengthening of in-group cohesion – an idea whose roots go back to George Simmel's (e.g. 1955) pioneering work and that has started to attract growing interest in International Relations, particularly among theorists who seek to endogenize the corporate identities of communal actors into processes of their interaction (Cederman and Daase 2003; Jackson and Nexon 1999).

Such a dialectical perspective, in short, suggests that securitization may not only be defensive, but also constitutive of communal identities. This is especially important where these identities are still in their formative phase and where community-wide institutional hierarchies are initially insecure and contested. For example, only very few scholars interpret the disintegration of Yugoslavia as a process as part of which fully formed antagonistic ethnic identities 'reasserted themselves' after Communism's oppressive lid had been lifted. Most analysts instead postulate a dialectical trajectory whereby securitizing elites (Milosevic, Tudjman and others) heightened threat perceptions between the ethnic groups, hardened group boundaries, made ethnic identities more salient and mutually antagonistic, and solidified their own grip on power in the process, with each development reinforcing the others in a reciprocal fashion (see Brubaker 1996). In a different empirical vein, the EU's attempts to involve itself in societal boundary-protection issues tend to intensify precisely during periods when its internal political cohesion threatens to weaken, and/or EU institutions obtain additional powers that require legitimization. A good example are the EU's various audiovisual initiatives during the 1980s and 1990s, whose officially declared objective was to protect European culture from an allegedly devastating onslaught of US-made films and television programmes, e.g. through European content quotas and subsidies for audiovisual co-productions. Yet these (mostly ill-fated) initiatives were not just defensive, but also potentially constitutive. They emerged in the wider context of EU actors (especially the European Parliament and the Commission) seeking to persuade sceptical national elites and mass publics that 'European culture', 'European values', 'European civilization' and the like actually existed and that the EU should be seen as their legitimate representative authorized to speak and act on their behalf (see Theiler 2005). Of course, the EU experience to date also reinforces the earlier observation that the mere presence of a securitization agenda does not guarantee its effectiveness. Dialectics involving securitization and the consolidation of communal boundaries and institutional power structures may gain momentum only very slowly. In some cases (including, possibly, in the EU) they may never gain much momentum at all.

De-securitization

A final area in need of greater theoretical attention is de-securitization – broadly defined as taking a given issue 'out of the realm of security conceptualization' and moving it into the area of '*a*-security' (Wæver 1998: 81, emphasis added; see also Wæver 1995). Unlike societal security and insecurity, *a*-security refers to a condition whereby people do not interpret a given issue as having identity implications or simply do not think of it in identity terms at all. Over the past decade, several authors have highlighted potential paths to de-securitization (Roe 2004) – a debate that is still in its early stages. At one level, de-securitization is the inverse of securitization, featuring a kind of 'security grammar' in reverse. To the extent that discourse is 'performative', the utterance 'X does not threaten

Y' can de-securitize X. However, this, too, is bound to depend on social and material context, including the recognized authority of the would-be de-securitizer and the receptiveness of the audience as conditioned by pre-existing intersubjective under-standings. Two distinct strategies can lead to de-securitization. A first strategy is the direct opposite of securitization as it focuses on the presumed threat. It seeks to convince audiences either that a given development they believe to be threatening does not actually exist ('there are not as many immigrants as you think') or that the development in question, while existing, does not pose the threat commonly associated with it ('while we do have many immigrants, most integrate well'). A more indirect path to de-securitization focuses on the group rather than the threat, seeking to redefine the group's defining markers in such a way that the development in question no longer poses an identity threat. The logic here is broadly as follows: a given development threatens a group identity if people believe it to threaten something that signifies group boundaries and thereby sustains that identity. But, once the thing in question stops signifying group boundaries, a threat to it stops threatening these boundaries and the societal identifications they sustain. For instance, if being a 'white society' ceases to be a defining aspect of 'who we are', then non-white immigrants stop threatening 'our identity' and stop eliciting societal security responses. Non-white immigration thus becomes de-securitized as the white/non-white distinction loses its role in sustaining societal identifications.

Societal security theorists have yet to explore such processes of indirect de-securitization (and, for that matter, the inverse scenario of indirect securitization) systematically, though empirically they are probably as important as their more direct, threat-centred counter-parts. Doing so would require a focus on how particular symbols and signifiers become 'attached' to and 'detached' from societal boundaries. That, too, would demand a greater engagement with neighbouring disciplines, particularly with the large body of social anthro-pological research into how a group's perceived 'meaning' and signifiers can change even as the group and its boundaries per se remain intact or even grow stronger (Barth 1969; Cohen 1989). At the same time, what is true for securitization applies to de-securitization as well. In *principle*, social reality is infinitely malleable. Anything (e.g. any symbol or mean-ing) can come to signify anything else (e.g. any kind of communal identity). In *social prac-tice*, however, social understandings can become firmly entrenched and correspondingly resistant to change, at least in the short and medium term. The slowness in 'de-racializing', 'de-ethnicizing' and, up to a point, 'de-culturalizing' dominant understandings of citizen-ship and national belonging even in many Western liberal democracies illustrates that point. Like securitization, then, the concept of de-securitization points to possibilities whose actual realization in any given instance needs to be empirically ascertained, along with – once more – the broader social and material circumstances that promote or hinder it.

Conclusion

Societal security theorists seek to fashion the widely held notion that identity somehow 'matters' in International Relations into a more coherent theoretical framework that shows how, why and when this can be so. As the present chapter has argued, this has the potential to help us better understand phenomena in International Relations that eco-nomic or strategic explanations alone cannot adequately account for, ranging from the collapse of Yugoslavia and the Soviet Union to the rise of xenophobic movements in Western Europe and resistance to international integration.

However, as this chapter has also argued, the societal security concept as put forward by the Copenhagen School suffers from several shortcomings and ambiguities that reduce its theoretical attractiveness and empirical applicability. For a start, it still largely lacks a micro-foundational account of human motivation. Similarly, the dynamics of securitization and de-securitization remain under-theorized, as does the potential for a dialectical link between group securitization, group formation and the status of securitizing actors inside the group. Tackling these issues would require a wider theoretical engagement, particularly with social psychology and social anthropology. In many instances, it would also require societal security theorists to focus on a larger and more varied range of empirical cases.

In thinking about these issues, societal security theorists have increasingly reproduced the same broad theoretical division that runs through other areas of IR theorizing as well. A first group veers into more post-modern or post-structural directions, informed by a linguistic notion of securitization as 'performative utterance' and reality-generating process. A second group seeks to integrate the societal security concept into a more mainstream constructivist research agenda in IR, especially by exploring the social and material contexts conducive to securitization and de-securitization, respectively. As in other parts of IR, these meta-theoretical divisions are sometimes impossible to bridge. At the same time, the resulting theoretical and methodological pluralism also testifies to the continued vitality and adaptability of the societal security idea – be it as a conceptual cornerstone of a fully-fledged alternative research agenda in Security Studies or, less ambitiously, as another way of interpreting the meaning of security in International Relations.

References

Barth, F. (1969) *Ethnic Groups and Boundaries: The Social Organization of Culture Difference*, London: Allen & Unwin.

Brubaker, R. (1996) *Nationalism Reframed: Nationhood and the National Question in the New Europe*, Cambridge: Cambridge University Press.

Buzan, B. (1983) *People, States and Fear: The National Security Problem in International Relations*, Brighton: Harvester Wheatsheaf.

Buzan, B., Wæver, O. and de Wilde, J. (1998) *Security: A New Framework for Analysis*, Boulder, CO: Lynne Rienner.

Cederman, L-E. and Daase, C. (2003) 'Endogenizing corporate identities: The next step in constructivist IR theory', *European Journal of International Relations* 9, 1: 5–35.

Cohen, A.P. (1989) *The Symbolic Construction of Community*, London: Routledge.

Deutsch, K.W. (1957) *Political Community and the North Atlantic Area*, Princeton, NJ: Princeton University Press.

Gagnon, V.P. (2006) *The Myth of Ethnic War: Serbia and Croatia in the 1990s*, Ithaca, NY: Cornell University Press.

Hogg, M, and Abrams, D. (1988) *Social Identifications: A Social Psychology of Intergroup Relations and Group Processes*, London: Routledge.

Isakovic, Z. (2000) *Identity and Security in the Former Yugoslavia*, Aldershot: Ashgate.

Jackson, T.P. and Nexon, D.H. (1999) 'Relations before states: Substance, process and the study of world politics', *European Journal of International Relations* 5, 3: 291–332.

Knudsen, O.F. (2001) 'Post-Copenhagen security studies: Desecuritizing securitization', *Security Dialogue* 32, 3: 355–68.

Macleod, A. (2004) 'Les études de sécurité: du constructivisme dominant au constructivisme critique', *Cultures & Conflits* 54, 2: 13–51.

Mueller, J. (2000) 'The banality of "ethnic war"', *International Security* 25, 1: 42–70.

van Munster, R. (2005) 'Logics of security: The Copenhagen School, risk management and the war on terror', *Syddansk Universitet Political Science Publications*, No. 10.

Roe, P. (2004) 'Securitization and minority rights: Conditions of desecuritization', *Security Dialogue* 35, 3: 279–94.

Simmel, G. (1955) *Conflict and the Web of Group Affiliations*, New York: The Free Press.

Stritzel, H. (2007) 'Towards a theory of securitization: Copenhagen and beyond', *European Journal of International Relations* 13, 3: 357–83.

Theiler, T. (2003) 'Societal security and social psychology', *Review of International Studies* 29, 2: 249–68.

——(2005) *Political Symbolism and European Integration*, Manchester: Manchester University Press.

Wæver, O. (1993) '"Societal security": the concept', in Wæver, O., Buzan, B., Kelstrup, M. and Lemaitre, P. (eds) *Identity, Migration and the New Security Agendas in Europe*, London: Pinter, pp. 17–40.

——(1995) 'Securitization and desecuritization', in Lipschutz, R.D. (ed.) *On Security*, New York: Columbia University Press, pp. 46–86.

——(1998) 'Insecurity, security and asecurity in the West European non-war community', in Adler, E. and Barnett, M. (eds) *Security Communities*, Cambridge: Cambridge University Press, pp. 69–118.

Wæver, O. and Kelstrup, M. (1993) 'Europe and its nations: Political and cultural identities', in Wæver, O., Buzan, B., Kelstrup, M. and Lemaitre, P. (eds) *Identity, Migration and the New Security Agendas in Europe*, London: Pinter, pp. 61–92.

Wæver, O., Buzan, B., Kelstrup, M. and Lemaitre, P. (eds) (1993) *Identity, Migration and the New Security Agendas in Europe*, London: Pinter.

Wendt, A. (1999) *Social Theory of International Politics*, Cambridge: Cambridge University Press.

Wiberg, H. (1993) 'Societal security and the explosion of Yugoslavia', in Wæver, O., Buzan, B., Kelstrup, M. and Lemaitre, P. (eds) *Identity, Migration and the New Security Agendas in Europe*, London: Pinter, pp. 93–109.

Wilkinson, C. (2007) 'The Copenhagen School on tour in Kyrgyzstan: Is securitization useable outside Europe'? *Security Dialogue* 38, 1: 5–25.

10

Human security and diplomacy

Pauline Kerr

In any overview of contemporary security concepts, human security is contrasted with the traditional and dominant state-centric understanding of security. For advocates of the former concept, the referent object of security, or the entity to be secured, is the individual human being. For advocates of state-centric security, the referent object is the state – a stance encapsulated in the concept of 'national security'. Human security is now a core component of the contemporary debate about the meaning and definition of security.

The inclusion of the human security concept in the debate has much to do with a long-standing dissatisfaction with state-centric approaches among critical security scholars and with the post-Cold War reorientation towards intra-state security, the site of much human insecurity. Beyond the conceptual challenges that it presents to the state-centric understanding of security, human security is championed by many scholars and practitioners concerned with the human insecurities resulting from underdevelopment and political violence inside states.

This chapter makes two main arguments that contribute to the present debate about human security. First, there have been two waves of debate around the concept. The first, which began in the early 1990s, took place on two fronts: on the one hand, it was a dispute between advocates of human security and supporters of the traditional state-centric approach; and on the other hand, it was an argument between different schools of human security. The 'broad school' was primarily concerned with problems of underdevelopment issues, while the 'narrow school' focused on organized political violence inside states. The second debate, which has been evolving over the last few years, engages in more detail with the practical agenda for human security. This is an important development, since the value of any security concept is, in part, judged by its capacity to guide positive practical change. Within the narrow school – which is the focus of this chapter – the practical agenda has a number of dimensions; one of them is connected to the evolving practices for supporting the 'responsibility to protect' (R2P) principle and its three component parts – the responsibilities to prevent, react and rebuild. That said, in many respects, the debates surrounding R2P often overlook their fundamental intellectual and empirical connections with human security, and hence the importance of the concept is sometimes missed. The second argument made in this chapter is that the practical agenda of human security/R2P largely omits a critical discussion about the processes of implementation, in particular the role that diplomacy plays in advancing the practice of human security. Diplomacy is obviously involved in all three components of the R2P agenda, yet a critical review aimed at identifying and ameliorating shortcomings is missing. To make these two arguments, the chapter is in three parts. The first reviews the first debate; the second analyses the practical focus of the second debate; and the third outlines the importance of bringing in a debate about diplomacy and human security and suggests some directions for research.

The first debate about human security

For many, the end of the confrontation between East and West brought about a sense of optimism that state-centric security would be less important in the 'new world order' than during the Cold War, and as a result there would be a peace dividend that would transfer significant portions of funding from military budgets to the much neglected global development agenda. Evidence of this confidence could be seen in the United Nations Development Programme's (UNDP) *Human Development Report 1994*, which argued for a shift 'from an exclusive stress on territorial security to a much greater stress on people's security' (UNDP 1994: 22ff.). Human security, according to the report, means 'first, safety from such chronic threats as hunger, disease and repression. And second, it means protection from sudden and hurtful disruptions in the patterns of daily life – whether in homes, in jobs or in communities' (ibid.: 23). The report expounded a broad agenda that encompassed seven different dimensions: economic, food, health, environmental, personal, community and political security. As we will see, the UNDP understanding of human security is supported by the broad school, but contested by the narrow school.

Over the next decade, the concept was highlighted in many humanitarian forums, at the UN and in the foreign policy statements of many countries, particularly those 14 states that joined the Human Security Network (HSN), which brought together foreign ministers for annual meetings to promote the idea.[1] Human security also became a core concept around which much research and policy advice was undertaken by organizations concerned with internal political violence, the most significant and influential of which is the Human Security Report Project (HSRP) at Simon Fraser University in Vancouver, Canada (Human Security Centre 2006; Human Security Report Project 2008).

In parallel with these developments, and partly because of them, there was a revival of a long-standing debate about the meaning of security. In the post-Cold War version, the question of what was to be made secure from what, by whom and how became a major focus of critical security scholars within the discipline of Security Studies (Krause and Williams 1997; Booth 2005). While there was agreement among the advocates of human security that theirs was a concept that seriously challenged traditional notions of security, there were divisions within the ranks about the nature of the threat to human security. For the narrow school, the most serious threat to human security is political violence against ordinary individual people, particularly during internal conflicts (Mack 2004; Krause 2007). For the broad school, by contrast, the main threat consists of all the ills of underdevelopment (Thakur 2000; Thomas 2000). These different perspectives on the nature of the threat often led to claims that the narrow school correlated human security with 'freedom from fear' from political violence, while the broad school connected human security with 'freedom from want' and from the insecurities of underdevelopment.

The narrow school argued that the breadth of issues taken into account by the broad school meant that security had become a meaningless concept (Mack 2004: 367), while the broad school maintained that human security involved more than freedom from fear (Thakur 2000). Such was the diversity and intensity of the debate that the publishers of the journal *Security Dialogue* published an edition in 2004 that featured the main participants in the debate summarizing their main points (*Security Dialogue* 2004: 35(3)).

These differences in perspectives about human security are more than just conceptual debates – they have different policy implications. The narrow camp supports measures that aim to reduce the levels of violence, deaths and casualties in internal political conflict. Among the policies supported are humanitarian military interventions; capacity building of domestic law-and-order institutions; security sector reform (SSR); international regimes to address anti-personnel land mines and small arms trade; and the establishment of the International Criminal Court. The broad perspective directs policy towards the UNDP's agenda, particularly poverty reduction. However, although the debate among the advocates of human security implies an either/or approach, both conceptually and in practice, there are connections between the two approaches (Kerr 2007: 98–100). Conceptually, if violence is the dependent variable or the issue to be explained, then one independent variable can be underdevelopment and poverty. Likewise, violence can be one cause of underdevelopment. The policy implications are evident, namely, that in many situations the immediate action is to make people safe and secure, followed by measures that will prevent further violence; this in many cases is the essence of the UNDP agenda.

The other dimension of the first debate about human security pitted the advocates of human security as a group against the realist supporters of the traditionalist state-centric approach. Yet, both the human security and state-centric approaches are relevant to understanding security (Kerr 2007: 101f.). Realists cannot sustain an argument that does not recognize that the state is the means of protecting the citizens within. Unless the state provides this function, its legitimacy and purpose is questionable. Human security advocates cannot dismiss the fact that state-centric approaches are necessary in a world where conflict between states continues. Moreover, even though the state is a major cause of human insecurity either because it is unwilling or unable to conduct its protective role, there are many states that do perform this function, and furthermore, states are increasingly intervening to protect populations that are victims of political violence. Thus, states have a role in enhancing human security.

By about 2004, the two fronts of the debate had reached something of a stalemate. For their part, many human security advocates implicitly agreed to disagree about the appropriate meaning of human security and to get on with the important issue of developing better practical measures to support their respective view of human security. However, taking the narrow school as our focus, the task of devising a practical agenda for addressing political violence generated another set of debates about the appropriate means.

The second debate: practices to support the narrow concept of human security through R2P

The second wave of debate, focusing on the practical agenda, has merged with other debates about practices that manage violent conflict within states. Although nearly all

117

these practices, such as military humanitarian intervention to stop large-scale persecution of civilians, are intellectually grounded in the concept of human security, this important connection is often given only cursory mention, ignored or dismissed. Luck's reference to the concept as being too diverse and without the 'specific policy choice and instruments [of] R2P' misses the point that human security and R2P are two sides of the same coin (Luck 2008: 5).

A comprehensive exposition of R2P was provided by the 2001 report *The Responsibility to Protect*, delivered by the International Commission on Intervention and State Sovereignty (ICISS). R2P incorporates three practical responsibilities that are directly related to human security: the responsibility to prevent; the responsibility to react; and the responsibility to rebuild (see also the chapter by Bellamy in this volume). In the ICISS report, these responsibilities are linked to a broad conceptualization of sovereignty that includes not just the right of states to control their territorial borders and domestic affairs, but also their responsibility to protect their citizens from violence. Of particular concern is violence associated with large-scale and systematic human rights abuse and genocide.

Responsibility to prevent

The responsibility to prevent includes preventing the causes of political violence within states, whether it consists of civil war, communal conflict or terrorist acts. Within the academic literature, there is a robust debate about the causes of such internal conflict that highlights different and often overlapping factors – social, economic, political, geographic and psychological (Harff and Gurr 2004; Collier 2001; Brown 2001; Stein 2001). Preventing such varied causes is problematic, and although the validity of the maxim 'prevention is better than cure' is acknowledged, putting it into practice is still a challenge (Menkhaus 2004). Prevention also involves deterrent measures such as the specialist tribunals to address war crimes and the International Criminal Court, which prosecutes perpetrators of crimes against humanity. Preventive measures also include international regimes for monitoring small arms and light weapons trade (*Small Arms Survey* 2008). Nonetheless, the imperative to put preventive measures into practice faces many obstacles: for example, sometimes such practices are not even applied, while in other cases, they are applied and fail because they are not properly implemented. Given this situation, there is an imperative to react if violence does break out.

The responsibility to react

The responsibility to react to conflict inside states includes the option of military intervention for humanitarian purposes. Such intervention is guided by four precautionary principles: right intention; last resort; proportional means; and reasonable prospects (ICISS 2001: xiiff.). Notwithstanding these precautionary principles, the connection between human security and R2P's military intervention option is a point of debate (Abbott 2005). For many countries, such intervention is incompatible with the norm of sovereignty (Acharya 2001). For developing countries that are still sensitive to earlier eras of colonization, the connection is a stark and unpleasant reminder of the past. Taking these factors into account, the ICISS emphasizes the role of the United Nations Security Council, stating that 'Security Council authorization must in all cases be sought prior to any military intervention action being carried out' (ICISS 2001: 50). Nevertheless, the

ICISS, also aware that the UNSC can be a political obstacle to action, considers the possibility of other forms of authorization, such as ad hoc coalitions and individual states (ICISS 2001: 55). The issue of authorization was highlighted in March 1999 when the regional security organization, NATO, intervened in the Kosovo conflict without the approval of the UN Security Council. NATO's justification on humanitarian grounds only served to ensure that the debate about human security, sovereignty and intervention would continue.

Another dimension of the debate on the responsibility to react through military intervention, which springs from human security concerns, is the protection of the civilian population during such operations. A report by the Oxford Research Group argues that interventions cannot be deemed successful if, although they achieve the political or other goals of the intervening nations, the security of the people on the ground is not enhanced (Lamb et al. 2007). Among the report's recommendations is that 'the integration of human security principles is needed most urgently at the operational level, through training and a fundamental change of military culture ... for example every military operational plan for any unit size could include a civilian protection component' (Lamb et al. 2007: 13). The predictable counterargument is that military culture is deeply entrenched in the use of lethal force and in winning wars, and civilians are often the unfortunate casualties. Another dimension of the debate about protection concerns the protection of aid workers by military units. Many humanitarian actors argue that their impartiality and neutrality is compromised and they are then ethically and physically vulnerable (Wheeler and Harmer 2006).

Notwithstanding the various debates surrounding the issue of the responsibility to react through humanitarian intervention using force, there is evidence that such interventions and interventions more generally, usually under the UN auspices, are becoming positive practices for improving human security. Research on global trends of internal political violence shows that there is a decline in the scope of conflict and the numbers of fatalities (Human Security Report Project 2008). The explanation, according to the HSRP, is the increase in international intervention and activism; comprehensive peacekeeping operations; peace-making; and post-conflict peace building, especially by the UN. Hence, practices inspired at least partly by human security concerns help to explain the global decline in internal political violence. Nevertheless, there is a continuing need to develop better practices for ensuring human security. As the *Human Security Brief 2007* points out, 'few of the "root cause" drivers of warfare and deadly assaults against civilians – from poverty to group inequality – have improved and some have worsened' (ibid.: 7).

The responsibility to rebuild

Whether or not outside military intervention has been necessary, it is nearly always the case that states in conflict need to be rebuilt or perhaps built for the first time. The conceptualization and practical measures attached to the responsibility to rebuild are the focus of another debate. Conceptually, one of the key issues is that rebuilding usually focuses on capacity building, which raises questions about the nature of the state that is to be established and its relationship with its citizens. This can be problematic, since human insecurity is most often caused by political violence by the state. Some therefore prefer rebuilding measures based on global governance (Bellamy and McDonald 2002), international human rights regimes, and historical and cultural forms of sub-state governance (Roy 2004; Wesley 2008).

The reality, however, is that most rebuilding practices, certainly those supported by the aid departments of most governments, are directed towards capacity building for state building. The assumption is that the state will be a replica – if not immediately, then in the near future – of the liberal Western democratic model, which ostensibly supports human security. However, imposing this model on societies that have different political, cultural, economic and social histories can be inappropriate and cause further conflict. Moreover, at best, the adoption of such governance models takes a very long time, and the international community of donors and humanitarian agencies is rarely willing or able to stay the distance.

Despite the contest about the value of Western models, most donor countries and institutions are strong advocates of this type of state building. That said, there are debates over the details of appropriate state capacity-building programmes and their sequencing. Among the practices closely related to human security are law-and-order programmes – policing and the judicial system. Policing as a state institution for social order is 'a key element of any conception of human security' (Krause 2007: 8). Yet there are many contentious issues when police forces are deployed to post-conflict societies. One is the issue of which policing model best serves a particular society. Another is the fact that the police are agents of the state and may well act to protect the state or its leaders from legitimate protest by citizens whose rights are being abused. Or the police may themselves become self-serving and corrupt and operate either with or without the consent of that state. This leads into another series of debate about security sector reform (SSR) for implementing human security (Schnabel and Ehrhart 2005). Most often, the military forces, as agents of the state, are responsible for violent crimes against civilians. Finally, another debate that has its roots in human security and the responsibility to rebuild is the issue of disarmament, demobilization and reintegration (DDR) of combatants (Humphreys and Weinstein 2007).

A missing debate: implementation, human security and diplomacy

The above debates that revolve around human security and its practical agenda have quite a lot to say about the broad policies that might enhance human security, but much less to say about the processes and means for implementing these objectives. There is only minimal discussion, for example, about the role of diplomacy as a means for implementing the R2P agenda. This is a surprising omission for at least two reasons. First, it is obvious that all three components of R2P involve diplomacy. Indeed, the legitimacy of the precautionary principle of making humanitarian intervention a measure of 'last resort' depends on ensuring that all diplomatic means have been tried. Second, if one of the key explanations for the decline of global political violence is indeed international activism, then diplomacy, negotiation and mediation are among the key processes. The next sections in this chapter explore the prospects for enhancing implementation of the practical human security/R2P agenda through diplomatic means by examining the relationship between human security and diplomacy and suggesting a new research agenda.

Diplomacy and human security

The relationship between diplomacy and human security is a matter of some debate. Several points therefore need to be noted when discussing the prospects for enhancing the diplomatic implementation of the human security/R2P agenda. First, diplomats are already expanding their roles in managing internal conflict. Traditionally, the role of a diplomat has been seen as one that revolves around the representation and communication of a state's interest. In recent times, state diplomats have become involved in issues that concern not just state-to-state relations, but also intra-state relations, many of which relate to the R2P agenda of preventing and reacting to political violence inside states and rebuilding state capacities. This expansion of the role of diplomats, due to the increase in the issues and actors that they are involved and interact with, is often considered as evidence of 'new diplomacy' (McRae and Hubert 2001; Riordan 2003).

Second, however, an argument is developing to the effect that diplomats are not appropriate actors for conducting what is being called 'humanitarian diplomacy'. Minear and Smith make the case that humanitarian diplomacy is different from traditional diplomacy: 'formal diplomacy is ... focussed on state actors and perceived national interests. The humanitarian imperative has a different logic and framework, dynamic and urgency' (Minear and Smith 2007: 33). They argue that this is clear from a comparison of the functions performed by state-based diplomats and humanitarian personnel (ibid.: 9). The latter are not necessarily bound by concerns about sovereignty and diplomatic conventions, hence they improvise in ad hoc ways, are more opportunistic, less secretive and, indeed, in many instances distance themselves from the state to preserve their neutrality (ibid.: 11ff.).

However, Minear and Smith downplay several points. Human security can be implemented by state actors acting in support of state interests *and* humanitarian values, as we will see below. Therefore, humanitarian diplomacy is not necessarily the exclusive domain of humanitarian personnel. Furthermore, the notion of 'new diplomacy' incorporates the role of non-state diplomatic actors, such as humanitarian personnel, in formulating and implementing policy responses to human insecurity caused by political violence. Diplomacy today involves many state and non-state actors.

Third, although state-based diplomatic actors can be appropriate humanitarian actors, the argument that formal (traditional) diplomacy is founded on state actors and perceived national interests warrants further investigation. There are situations when it is in states' interests to intervene – diplomatically and, failing that, by military means – to prevent further bloody internal violence against individuals. The justification for such intervention is usually framed in terms of a threat to international peace and stability. A military response to such a threat can be authorized under Chapter VII (Article 39) of the UN Charter. Significantly, such responses have become more common since 1989, when the UNSC became 'increasingly willing to interpret the phase "threats to peace" broadly' (Fierke 2005: 70). Although responding to threats to peace may be motivated by state interests, these interests may well produce outcomes that are favourable in humanitarian terms. Moreover, states may be motivated by humanitarian values. As mentioned earlier, the March 1999 military intervention in Kosovo by NATO forces acting without UN authorization was justified in terms of human security values – specifically, the imperative to protect the human rights of Kosovar Albanians from Serbian military forces. Similarly, the 1999 INTERFET operation, led by Australia into East Timor – following large-scale militia violence after the results of the ballot showed the East Timorese wanted independence from Indonesia – was motivated to a large extent by humanitarian concerns (Wheeler 2000). However, the US reference to humanitarian motives only after the official justification for invading Iraq in 2003 was shown to be false shows that states can also use the pretext of human security disingenuously.

Finally, mindful of the above issues concerning diplomacy as a means for implementing human security, diplomacy remains an essential process when R2P involves the use of force, for example to stop genocide. That decision involves a prior obligation to show that every diplomatic effort has been made. The precautionary principle of the ICISS that military intervention should only serve 'as a last resort' implies an obligation to consider all other possible measures. There is significant evidence, however, that some interventions have been undertaken before all diplomatic means were exhausted. This warrants further investigation into the diplomatic processes employed in such situations.

Any investigation into improving the diplomatic implementation of human security will in part draw on principles that apply to the practice of diplomacy more generally, including the evolving notion of 'new diplomacy'. These principles include knowing the political, economic and social context and history of the conflict when negotiating and mediating with the warring parties. Improving the diplomatic implementation of the human security/R2P agenda will involve not just an investigation of these macro-processes of negotiation, for example bargaining and concessions, but also a new research agenda into the under-investigated 'micro-processes' of diplomacy, such as persuasion through socialization, framing and argumentation. The imperative for research is particularly important given the observable shortcomings of diplomacy as employed in decisions to use force as a last resort.

Human security and diplomacy: the micro-process of persuasion

Since the micro-processes of diplomacy have received much less empirical and theoretical research than the macro-processes, which are the focus of much scholarship on negotiation (Zartman 1995; Fisher and Ury 1991), this section will briefly consider whether research on persuasion might be a useful avenue for exploring better ways of implementing the human security/R2P agenda.

Examinations of the concept of persuasion are found in several disciplines, for example Psychology and International Relations. Given the disciplinary proximity of diplomacy and IR, it is useful to explore whether there are possible connections, and then to see if these are relevant for thinking about better ways of implementing the R2P agenda. The concept of persuasion has several dimensions in IR. The debate in part revolves around the question of how persuasion is brought to bear: is it through threats of use of power, as in bargaining; through shaming; through disclosure of rhetorical action (that is, trying to persuade the other that one is right); through change of identity (Savary 2008); or, as argued more recently, through pointing to certain facts that had escaped attention and which contributed to shared understandings (Savary 2008: 32)? Although there are few examples of scholars making the connection between persuasion and diplomacy (Savary is an exception), it is not difficult to see that there are links that could be investigated to see how the diplomatic implementation of human security could be advanced. Recent research findings, both qualitative and quantitative, could contribute to shared understandings of appropriate approaches to enhancing human security. Evidence-based 'facts', such as the revelation that long-term structural programmes are less important than immediate diplomatic and policy initiatives designed to stop wars, constitute just one example (Human Security Report Project (2008): 6) that could be used to persuade negotiators involved in constructing rebuilding programmes.

In the IR context, persuasion is sometimes explicitly, but often implicitly, associated with other concepts that support change – socialization, argumentation (Crawford 2002) and framing (Payne 2001). The case of socialization is an instructive one. Socialization as a process through which learning takes place is interesting to IR constructivist scholars because, in their view, change in international society is partly explained by the diffusion of normative standards, such as human rights, by norm entrepreneurs who interact, socialize and thereby persuade others to learn about and adopt new principles. International Relations scholars give most attention to institutions as agents of normative change rather than state-based diplomatic actors. Surprisingly, the field of diplomatic studies does little to investigate the role of diplomatic actors as agents of change through socialization.

However, if Nye's notion of 'soft power' has practical implications, it will include diplomats acting as agents who aim to socialize others about their country's attractiveness (Nye 2004). Attempts to encourage the populations of other states to find one's culture and values attractive are also pursued through public diplomacy programmes, which aim to influence the publics of other countries to appreciate the value of another state's normative beliefs. Hence, if diplomatic actors and public diplomacy are indeed agents and processes of socialization, that would constitute a useful observation for advancing the norm of human security.

Finally, the concepts of argumentation and framing, also explored in IR, are other micro-processes of persuasion that can provide other avenues for investigating how human security can be better implemented. Overall, the above discussion suggests that such micro-processes of persuasion are central to diplomacy, yet they are not part of the research agenda in diplomatic studies or of research into better ways of implementing human security.

Conclusion

The concept of human security, as reflected in the first debate, enables an important critique of the still dominant state-centric concept of security. Although both concepts are important for understanding the range of situations that involve security, the focus on human security correctly emphasizes individual human beings and reminds us that the state is the means to human security and not an end in itself.

The evolution of the overall debate is made clearer by the argument that the second debate around human security has focused on practical measures and policy to address organized political violence inside states. Similarly revealing is the critique that there is insufficient analysis of the processes for implementing these policies, including the role of diplomacy. Whether an examination of diplomacy's micro-processes, such as persuasion, will advance the implementation of human security is a research project waiting to happen. The future of the concept will depend not just on a continuing critique of the omission of human security by state-centric security, but also on policies and processes for implementing human security that actually work. Stand by for the third debate.

Note

1 There is some debate about the importance of the HSN. For example, Suhrke argues that none of the members of the network are major players and that even the original promoters, Canada and Norway, have a declining interest in the concept (Suhrke 2004: 365). Other scholars, for example Hubert (2004), are more optimistic about the role of the HSN. For further information about the network, see www.humansecuritynetwork.org/menu-e.php.

References

Abbott, C. (2005) 'Rights and responsibilities: Resolving the dilemma of humanitarian intervention', *Briefing Paper*, Oxfordshire: Oxford Research Group.

Acharya, A. (2001) 'Human security: East versus West', *IDSS Working Paper*, 17, Singapore: Institute of Defence and Strategic Studies.

Bellamy, A.J. and McDonald, M. (2002) '"The utility of human security": Which humans? What security? A reply to Thomas and Tow', *Security Dialogue* 33, 3: 373–77.

Booth, K. (ed.) (2005) *Critical Security Studies and World Politics*, Boulder, CO: Lynne Rienner.

Brown, M.E. (2001) 'Ethnic and internal conflicts', in Crocker, C.A., Hampson, F.O. and Aall, P.R. (eds) *Turbulent Peace: The Challenges of Managing International Conflict*, Washington DC: United States Institute for Peace, pp. 209–26.

Collier, P. (2001) 'Economic cause of civil conflict and their implications for policy', in Crocker, C.A., Hampson, F.O. and Aall, P.R. (eds) *Turbulent Peace: The Challenges of Managing International Conflict*, Washington DC: United States Institute for Peace, pp. 143–62.

Fierke, K.M. (2005) *Diplomatic Interventions: Conflict and Change in a Globalizing World*, New York: Palgrave Macmillan.

Fisher, R. and Ury, W. (1991) *Getting to Yes: Negotiating an Agreement Without Giving In*, 2nd edition, London: Random House.

Harff, B. and Gurr, T.R. (2004) *Ethnic Conflict in World Politics*, Boulder: Westview Press.

Hubert, D. (2004) 'An idea that works in practice', *Security Dialogue* 35, 3: 351–52.

Human Security Centre (2006) *Human Security Brief 2006*, Vancouver: The University of British Columbia.

Human Security Report Project (2008) *Human Security Brief 2007*, Vancouver: Simon Fraser University.

Humphreys, M. and Weinstein, J.M. (2007) 'Demobilization and reintegration', *Journal of Conflict Resolution* 51, 4: 531–67.

International Commission on Intervention and State Sovereignty (ICISS) (2001) *The Responsibility to Protect*, Ottawa: International Development Research Centre.

Kerr, P. (2007) 'Human security' in Collins, A. (ed.) *Contemporary Security Studies*, Oxford: Oxford University Press, pp. 91–108.

Kerr, P. and Williams, M.C. (1997) *Critical Security Studies: Concepts and Cases*, Minneapolis: University of Minnesota Press.

Kerr, P., Tow, W.T. and Hanson, M. (2003) 'The utility of the human security agenda for policy-makers', *Asian Journal of Political Science* 11, 2: 89–114.

Krause, K. (2007) 'Towards a practical human security agenda', *Policy Paper* 26, Geneva: Geneva Centre for the Democratic Control of Armed Forces.

Lamb, W.C., Sloboda, J., Rifkind, G. and Elworthy, S. (2007) 'What would military security look like through a human security lens', *Briefing Paper*, Oxfordshire: Oxford Research Group.

Luck, E. (2008) 'The United Nations and the responsibility to protect', *Policy Analysis Brief*, August, The Standley Foundation.

Mack, A. (2004) 'A signifier of shared values', *Security Dialogue* 35, 3: 366–67.

McRae, R. and Hubert, D. (eds) (2001) *Human Security and the New Diplomacy: Protecting People, Promoting Peace*, Ontario: McGill-Queen's University Press.

Menkhaus, K. (2004) 'Conflict prevention and human security: Issues and challenges', *Conflict, Security and Development* 4, 3: 419–63.

Minear, L. and Smith, H. (2007) *Humanitarian Diplomacy: Practitioners and Their Craft*, Tokyo: United Nations University Press.

Nye, J. (2004) *Soft Power: The Means to Success in World Politics*, New York: Public Affairs.

Payne, R.A. (2001) 'Persuasion, frames and norm construction', *European Journal of International Relations* 7, 1: 37–61.

Riordan, S. (2003) *The New Diplomacy*, Cambridge: Polity Press.

Roy, O. (2004) 'Development and political legitimacy: The case of Iraq and Afghanistan', *Conflict, Security & Development* 4, 2: 167–79.

Savary, K. (2008) 'From the art of seeing to the diplomatic art: Persuasion through paradigm change in international relations', *Journal of International Relations and Development* 11, 1: 29–54.

Schnabel, A. and Ehrhart, H. (eds) (2005) *Security Sector Reform and Post-Conflict Peacebuilding*, Tokyo: United Nations University Press.

Security Dialogue (2004) Special Section: 'What is human security?', 35, 3.

Small Arms Survey 2008, Risk and Resilience (2008). Available online at: www.smallarmssurvey.org/files/sas/publications/yearb2008.html (accessed 29 September 2008).

Stein, J.G. (2001) 'Image, identity and the resolution of violent conflict', in Crocker, C.A., Hampson, F.O. and Aall, P.R. (eds) *Turbulent Peace. The Challenges of Managing International Conflict*, Washington DC: United States Institute for Peace, pp. 189–208.

Suhkre, A.(2004), 'A stalled initiative', *Security Dialogue* 35, 3: 365.

Thakur, R. (2000) 'Human security regimes' in Tow, W., Thakur, R. and Hyun, I.T. (eds) *Asia's Emerging Regional Order: Reconciling Traditional and Human Security*, New York: United Nations University Press, pp. 229–55.

Thomas, C. (2000) *Global Governance, Development and Human Security: The Challenge of Poverty and Inequality*, London: Pluto Press.

United Nations Development Programme (1994) *Human Development Report 1994*, New York: United Nations.

Wheeler, N.J. (2000) *Saving Strangers: Humanitarian Intervention in International Society*, Oxford: Oxford University Press.

Wheeler, V. and Harmer, A. (2006) 'Resetting the rules of engagement: Trends and issues in military-humanitarian relations', *HPG Research Briefing*, March, 21: 1–4.

Wesley, M. (2008) 'The state of the art on the state of the art of state building', *Global Governance* 14, 3: 369–85.

Zartman, I.W. (1995) 'Dynamics and constraints in negotiations in international conflicts' in Zartman, I.W. *Elusive Peace*, Washington, DC: Brookings Institution, pp. 3–29.

Part II

Contemporary security challenges

11

Terrorism

Paul Wilkinson

No handbook of Security Studies would be complete without a chapter on terrorism. In the twenty-first century, the majority of scholars working in the field of Security Studies would agree with this assertion, even though there are many disputes about the under-lying causes of terrorism; its impact on nation-states and International Relations; and about the most appropriate and effective responses to terrorist challenges to democratic societies and the international community.

This chapter does not attempt to provide a comprehensive history of terrorism or an assessment of all the uses of terrorism by states and non-state actors at the beginning of the twenty-first century. It rather aims to provide an introduction to the concept of terrorism; a typology of current actors; and an analysis of the most significant recent developments and trends in terrorism. The main body of the chapter highlights some of the major debates that have preoccupied specialists in terrorism studies before and after 11 September 2001, both in relation to terrorism within Western democracies and in front-line states such as Iraq, where terrorism is accompanied by a wider insurgency or internal war. In conclusion, the chapter offers some thoughts on the future of terrorism; the unresolved issues that challenge both academic researchers and policy-makers; and the ways in which academic research and debate has influenced the practice of security.

The concept of terrorism

It is important at the outset to dispel some of the confusion about the concept of ter-rorism that has hampered the development of the systematic study of the subject (Schmid et al. 1988). Some commentators in the media, some politicians and members of the public continue to use 'terrorism' as a synonym for political violence in general, when in reality it is a special form of violence. It is a deliberate attempt by a group or by a government regime to create a climate of extreme fear to intimidate a target social group or government or commercial organization with the aim of forcing it to change its behaviour. It is generally directed at a wider target than the immediate victims and inherently involves attacks on random or symbolic targets, including civilians. It is important to note that the use of the term 'terrorism' came into the English language at the time of the Reign of Terror (1793–94) during the French Revolution (Greer 1935; Lucas 1972). In their quest to establish a republic based on the principle of 'virtu' following Montesquieu (Montesquieu 1965), the revolutionary leaders Robespierre and Saint-Just saw systematic mass terror as an emanation of virtue.

It is obvious that governments and regimes have historically frequently used the weapon of terror, and because they generally command far greater firepower and manpower than non-state groups, state terror has been responsible for far higher levels of death and destruction than have been achieved by non-state groups (Arendt 1958; Walter 1969). The notorious Roman *princeps* Nero, for example, carried the use of terrorism to such extremes that he engaged in a wholesale massacre of the nobility and wilfully set fire to the city (Suetonius 1957).

One of the earliest organized non-state groups (with some parallels to al-Qaida today) to employ terrorism systematically for a religious cause was the Shi'ite Muslim sect of the Hashshashin (Lewis 1967), who were active in the Middle East from the eleventh century until their suppression by the Mongols in the mid-thirteenth century. Another key stage in the history of non-state terrorism was the campaign of the *Narodnaya Volya* (People's Will) group (Avrich 1980; Laqueur 1977), against tsarist autocracy in late-nineteenth century Russia. The tactic it adopted was a series of assassination attempts on senior officials of the regime. In March 1881, Narodnaya Volya succeeded in assassinating Tsar Alexander II. However, although this alarmed the Russian elite, Narodnaya Volya failed to bring about any major change in the tsarist system. The main lesson of Narodnaya Volya's ultimately futile struggle is that non-state groups using terror are unlikely to succeed in overthrowing a ruthless autocracy or dictatorship that is prepared to use state terror, with all the resources of a secret police and an army of informers.

It is often assumed that terrorism today poses the greatest threat to security. This is perhaps understandable in the light of the attacks carried out in 2001 by al-Qaida terrorists against the World Trade Center in New York and the Pentagon building in Washington, DC, killing nearly 3,000 people (National Commission on Terrorist Attacks upon the United States 2004). This was the most deadly terrorist assault ever carried out by a non-state terrorist group in a single day. However, it is important to consider the terrorist threat in a wider strategic perspective. There are other, arguably far more serious threats to international security, for example the threat to our environment from climate change and the threat of conflict between nuclear-armed states escalating to nuclear war.

Typology of terrorism

Although it is wrong to equate terrorism with political violence in general, it is nevertheless a fairly broad concept. Specialists in terrorism studies have found it essential to develop typologies of the main types of terrorism (Schmid et al. 1988: 39–59). One fundamental distinction is between *state* and *non-state terrorism*. The former has been infinitely more lethal because regimes/governments generally have greater supplies of weapons and manpower at their disposal to implement policies of terror. However, although there has been some very important scholarship on state terrorism (Arendt 1958; Conquest 1968), particularly in the Cold War, the major preoccupation of specialists in terrorism studies in the late twentieth century, and particularly since September

2001, has been the threat from terrorism posed by non-state movements or groups seeking to impose their own agenda on the international system (Hoffman 1998).

A second major distinction is between *international* and *internal* or domestic terrorism. The former involves the citizens, property or international legal obligations of more than one country. The latter is confined within the borders of a single state and involves no foreign citizens or property. However, almost every major protracted internal terrorist campaign against a specific state develops an international dimension through the creation of overseas support networks designed to secure funds, weapons, recruits and supportive publicity for the struggle against their chosen 'enemy' state authorities and security forces.

It is also very useful to classify non-state terrorist groups by their predominant political motivation: *ethno-nationalist groups* (e.g. ETA and the Tamil Tigers); *ideological groups* (e.g. the Peruvian Maoist group Sendero Luminoso); *religio-political groups* (e.g. al-Qaida and Hamas); *single-issue groups* (e.g. the Animal Liberation Front); and *state-sponsored groups* (e.g. the Abu Nidal Organization (ANO), which was active in the 1980s).

Another distinction worth adding to our typology is that between potentially *corrigible groups* and *incorrigible groups*. In the case of the former, there is at least a possibility of finding a political/diplomatic pathway to lead the terrorist group out of violence and into peaceful participation in politics (e.g. the route followed by the IRA since the Good Friday Agreement of August 1998). *Incorrigible terrorism* occurs when the terrorist movement or group has such maximalist and absolutist aims and poses such a threat to innocent life that the only resource is to use all possible measures within the law to suppress the group.

Finally, we can construct a typology of the effectiveness of terrorist groups in achieving their goals. The majority of groups do manage to achieve some *tactical* or short-term gains, such as obtaining publicity for their cause through media coverage; raising more funds from supporters; and recruiting more militants who are ready to commit acts of terrorism. However, historically, very few groups have succeeded in winning their *strategic* political objectives. The exceptions mainly occurred in the era of anti-colonial struggles (e.g. the FLN against the French in Algeria and the EOKA against the British in Cyprus), but they were made possible due to special conditions in the post-Second World War period. The European colonial powers were exhausted and bankrupt after the war, and their government and citizens had little interest in seeing their police and soldiers killed to preserve a colonial rule that most of the public wished to terminate (Horne 1996; Townshend 1986).

The roots of terrorism can sometimes also be traced to mistaken policies of the major powers in the recent past. British policy-makers, for example, made some very serious mistakes in the way they ended the Palestine Mandate and British rule in India that were to cost many lives and plant the seeds of protracted conflicts between Israel and the Palestinians and between Pakistan and India over control of Kashmir, which was handed to India despite having a majority of Muslim inhabitants.

Terrorism studies: major issues and debates

Much of the early scholarship on terrorism was accomplished by historians dealing with specific terrorist movements. But there was also a flurry of interest in the field on the part of political scientists and sociologists writing about both state and non-state terrorism (Hardman 1937; Roucek 1962; Walter 1969; Arendt 1958; Conquest 1968; Thornton 1964). However, it was not until the burgeoning of international terrorism stemming from the conflict between Israel and the Palestinians in the late 1960s and the 1970s, and the emergence of the 'Fighting Communist Organizations' (Alexander and Pluchinsky 1972) such as the Red Brigades and the Red Army Faction in Western Europe, that academic interest in the subject began to increase rapidly. The growth of research and academic publications dealing with all types of international and internal terrorism in the late 1960s and the 1970s was clearly a reflection of the dramatic increase in terrorist incidents in many countries and the growing political and public debate on the subject. Major contributors to the growing literature of terrorism studies included Brian Jenkins (1975), Martha Crenshaw (1978, 1983), and historian Walter Laqueur (1977).

Difference in the US and Europe

Scholars, like policy-makers and communities, are to a considerable extent influenced by the political culture, history, traditions and dominant perceptions of national interest in the countries where they originate. This helps to explain the noticeable differences between the preoccupations of terrorism research in the US and those of European academic specialists in the study of terrorism: European terrorism experts mainly concentrated on the significant domestic terrorist movements that were also the focus of the counter-terrorism efforts of their countries' intelligence and security agencies – in the UK, the IRA; in Germany, the Red Army Faction; in Italy, the Red Brigades; and in Spain, ETA (*Euskadi Ta Askatasuna*, Basque Fatherland and Liberty). It was obvious to successive US administrations that the personnel and overseas facilities of the US as the leading superpower during the Cold War years were regarded as prime targets by terrorist groups in many countries. They were well aware that US installations in the Middle East were particularly vulnerable to attacks because the US is the key ally and supporter of Israel, the object of intense hatred in the eyes of most Middle Eastern terrorist groups. US intelligence and security agencies also invested considerable effort in monitoring, surveillance and countering of state-sponsored terrorism, a key feature of international terrorism in the 1970s and 1980s. The US government's annual reports, *Patterns of Global Terrorism*, compiled initially by the CIA and then by the State Department, provide abundant evidence of major concerns harboured by US officials concerning international terrorism. Each report includes a survey of the activities of state sponsors as viewed from Washington. It is hardly surprising that security specialists in US universities, research institutes such as RAND and think-tanks such as CSIS in Washington researched, analysed and debated similar themes.

This fundamental difference in recent historical experience of terrorism in the US and Western Europe also explained their rather different priorities in response to terrorism. The US took a leading role in drafting and promoting international measures and conventions aimed at preventing, or at least reducing, the threat of international terrorism. In addition to the diplomatic effort to secure international conventions, some of the most successful US initiatives included practical measures such as the system of boarding-gate x-ray machines and magnetometer archways, which were designed to strengthen airport security against the hijack threat and were designed and pioneered in US airports before being adopted by the entire international civil aviation community. European governments, on the other hand, challenged by significant levels of internal terrorism, understandably tended to concentrate on introducing anti-terrorism legislation to assist the police and judiciary to bring terrorists to justice in the 1970s and 1980s (Wilkinson 2006).

Issues prior to September 2001

The issues that preoccupied academic specialists in the study of terrorism prior to 9/11 included hardy perennials such as: Could generally agreed definitions for terrorism be found, and if not, should the concept of terrorism be discarded? How serious was the threat of terrorism to (a) democratic societies and (b) the international community? How should democratic governments and the international community respond to terrorism? Was it permissible to seek a political pathway out of terrorism, and if so, under what conditions (Wilkinson 1987: 453–65)? How could a peace process be initiated and sustained? How could basic human rights and freedom in a democracy be preserved in the face of clamour for more draconian counter-terrorist measures? How could a proper balance between the preservation of international security and democratic freedoms be attained? What roles were appropriate for the intelligence services, the police, and the military in combating terrorism (a) within a democracy and (b) against international terrorism?

There was also a debate about the future of terrorism, and particularly about the possible threat from terrorists using weapons of mass destruction (Taylor and Horgan 2000). This debate has remained unresolved, despite the rise of al-Qaida in the 1990s and the 9/11 attacks with their clear demonstration of al-Qaida's desire to cause mass casualties on an unprecedented scale. All these major issues and debates about terrorism remain on the agenda of terrorism studies today, some with still more relevance in the post-9/11 era. However, the rise of al-Qaida has had considerable implications for the study of terrorism.

Al-Qaida terrorism

Al-Qaida ('The Base') was founded in 1988 by Abdullah Azzam and Osama bin Laden, both of whom had been recruiting Sunni extremists to join the mujahideen fighters who successfully expelled the former Soviet Union's forces from Afghanistan. Al-Qaida believed it must establish strict Sharia religious law (Gerges 2005; Brachman 2009). It aims to expel the US and other 'infidels' from the Middle East and from Muslim lands everywhere. The network also wants to topple Muslim regimes and governments that they claim are 'apostates' betraying the 'true Islam' (as defined by al-Qaida) and collaborating with the US and its allies. Ultimately, al-Qaida aims to establish a pan-Islamic caliphate (super-state) uniting all Muslims, thus changing the entire international system. Al-Qaida has declared a jihad against the US and its allies and stated that it is the duty of all Muslims to kill US citizens – civilians and military – and their allies everywhere (bin Laden 1998).

There has been an ongoing debate about the state of the al-Qaida organization. Some commentators have argued that al-Qaida ceased to be an effective organization once the Taliban regime in Afghanistan was toppled in the autumn of 2001. In reality, there is overwhelming evidence that its core leaders re-established a base across the border in Pakistan's tribal areas and that they are still capable of giving their network of affiliates and cells ideological and strategic leadership, despite the loss of some of their top militants (Evans 2009). It is clear that al-Qaida 'franchises' have a presence in almost half the countries in the world. This gives them global reach and the ability to compensate for setbacks in one country by advances elsewhere. The group has also proved capable of adapting rapidly to changing circumstances. After being forced to move its core base from Afghanistan to the border areas of Pakistan, the jihadist network has made intensive use of the internet as a channel for propaganda; as a means of attracting and indoctrinating fresh recruits; and as a means of providing its followers with information about the construction of bombs and other practical guidance for terrorists.

The majority of specialists in the study of terrorism recognize a number of very significant differences between traditional terrorists groups and the al-Qaida network. It is explicitly committed to mounting mass casualty attacks. Brian Jenkins once accurately observed that the terrorist groups in the 1970s 'wanted a lot of people watching, not a lot of people dead' (Jenkins 1975: 4). Al-Qaida and its affiliates want a lot of people dead and a lot of people watching. Moreover, to this end, it uses coordinated no-warning suicide attacks, the most difficult type of terrorism to prevent in an 'open society', especially when, as they have demonstrated in successive acts of carnage, they are prepared to attack all types of locations where the public is likely to gather, such as hotels, shopping areas, mosques (for example, Shi'ite mosques in Iraq), public transport systems, airliners and shipping, as well as diplomatic and economic targets.

Ever since it was discovered that the members of the terrorist cell that carried out the 7 July 2005 suicide bombing on the London Underground and a London Transport bus, killing 52 members of the public were British, there has been a surge of research interest in the processes of radicalization and recruitment into al-Qaida-linked 'home-grown' terrorism in the UK. Other European countries have also been concerned about the continuing recruitment of members of their own Muslim community into violent extremism. However, the terms 'home-grown' and 'leaderless resistance' can be very misleading: The evidence from dozens of court cases shows that many of the convicted individuals had been in touch with terrorists overseas, in some cases by means of travel to Pakistan or the Middle East. Furthermore, some recruits still obtain training in terrorist training camps abroad and many have travelled to Iraq, Afghanistan or Somalia to obtain first-hand experience of terrorist tactics and methods (Evans 2009). Conversely, many of those recruits who have not travelled overseas to meet terrorist leaders and other militants were able to resort to the internet, a transnational medium of communication that provides an alternative and highly accessible source of foreign influence.

Not surprisingly, therefore, the study of radicalization and recruitment (and possible ways to prevent it) has become a top priority for researchers in the field of terrorism studies. Among the major conducive conditions for radicalization identified in recent research (Forrest 2006) are the following.

Political Factors include resentment against US foreign policies and the foreign policies of the UK and other NATO European allies that generally support US policy; extreme resentment and hatred against Israel; and resentment and anger against regimes in the Muslim world, which have, in many cases, ruthlessly suppressed fundamentalist Islamist movements and/or blocked them from gaining power via the ballot box, for example in Algeria in 1991.

There are also *religious factors* that can play an important part in the process of radicalization, such as the belief that the world of Islam is under attack by the US and its 'crusader' allies and that only al-Qaida and its affiliates can end the victimization and occupation of the Muslim world; the belief that existing Muslim regimes have betrayed their religion by engaging in friendly relations with infidel states; the belief that by waging a global jihad, al-Qaida and its franchises are carrying out Allah's will and that Allah will ensure that they will defeat the infidels; and the belief that by carrying out acts of voluntary self-sacrifice or martyrdom (i.e. suicide attacks) they will be rewarded in Paradise.

The *socio-economic and personal factors* are too numerous to mention, but they include the alienation felt by many young Muslims in the UK and other EU countries who believe they are being treated as second-class citizens and robbed of their identity, i.e. that they are no longer part of the traditional world of Islam, nor are they accepted as full citizens of the countries where they now reside; in some cases, resentment at being unable to gain employment or rise up the socio-economic ladder; peer group pressure from other young men who have joined extremist groups; and, last but not least, anger at what is seen unjust or repressive treatment of friends or relatives by the police or other agencies of the state.

Thus far, this chapter has dealt primarily with the use of terrorism unaccompanied by any insurgency or civil war. This has been the form of terrorism experienced in Western Europe since the 1970s. However, this has not been the experience of the so-called 'front-line' states in the Middle East and Asia, where terrorism has generally been accompanied by brutal and protracted insurgencies or full-scale internal wars. Iraq, Afghanistan, Indonesia and Sri Lanka have all experienced conflicts of this kind on a tragic scale. For example, the number of incidents of terrorism in Iraq during the insurgency in 2005 was 3,468. By 2006 this had increased to 6,630 – almost half the total number of terrorist incidents worldwide in that year (US National Counter Terrorism Center as quoted in US State Department Country Reports on Terrorism, 2007). The terrorist attacks involved outrages deliberately aimed at killing large numbers of people, such as car bombings in busy market places, crowded streets, and even mosques and hospitals. Such attacks are forbidden under the Geneva Conventions, which are aimed at protecting civilians, places of worship and medical facilities.[1] It would clearly be wrong to assume that all these outrages against civilians were supported or approved by all the groups involved in the insurgency: indeed, many of the attacks by al-Qaida in Iraq were designed to provoke inter-faction conflict between the Sunni and Shi'ite populations and to undermine the very fragile newly elected democratic government in Iraq. The next section looks briefly at the relationship between terrorism and war.

The relationship between terrorism and war

In Western democracies, so-called 'home-grown' terrorism is not accompanied by any wider insurgency or internal war. The overwhelming majority of the public are deeply opposed to the terrorists and will be ready to support and assist the police in their efforts to prevent attacks and to bring terrorists to justice. The same cannot be said for the 'front-line' states, such as Iraq and Afghanistan, where al-Qaida affiliates challenge the governments and their Western allies by exploiting full-scale insurgencies, which in certain circumstances can threaten the very stability and survival of the government. In the late twentieth century and the early twenty-first century, we have seen an increasing number of conflicts in which terrorism becomes interwoven with a wider war. Military and paramilitary organizations as well as terrorist groups increasingly resort to the weapon of terror as a means of breaking the will and morale of the 'enemy' populations.

The late twentieth century was replete with these 'terror wars', for example in Peru, Colombia, Algeria, the former Yugoslavia, the Caucasus, Central Africa, Palestine, Sri Lanka, Vietnam and Cambodia. A feature of these savage conflicts is that they tend to go on for a very long time. There is no easy exit from terror wars. The savagery of the conflicts, whipped up by ideologies of ethnic or religious hatred, polarizes the belligerents to such an extent that conflict resolution seems unattainable. Frequently, one (or both) of the belligerents obtains assistance from militant supporters from abroad. For example, large numbers of militant jihadis have travelled from Western countries to Iraq, Afghanistan, Somalia and other countries where they can gain direct experience and knowledge of terrorist weaponry, tactics and methods. EU governments have, with good reason, become worried about these militants bringing their practical experience and knowledge back to European countries, where they could apply their expertise.

Some thoughts on the future of terrorism and effective responses against it

At the time of writing (December 2008), there was no sign that the al-Qaida network had been put out of business. It is true that its affiliates in Iraq suffered heavy blows in 2007, largely due to local Sunni leaders and communities turning against them and regaining control of their local areas within the 'Sunni Triangle'. Perhaps the most serious of the many strategic blunders made by al-Qaida's core leadership has been to underestimate the extent of the backlash resulting from their readiness to massacre and maim large numbers of their co-religionists.

But there have also been major strategic mistakes by the US, the UK and other Western allies in the conduct of the 'War on Terror'. The most serious of these mistakes was the decision by US President George W. Bush, supported by British Prime Minister Tony Blair, to launch an invasion of Iraq in 2003 to topple the regime of Saddam Hussein, even though there was no evidence whatsoever that Hussein was involved in the plot to launch the 11 September 2001 attacks, or that he was about to launch attacks on his neighbours using weapons of mass destruction. The strategic blunder of diverting large-scale military and financial resources to the invasion and occupation of Iraq handed al-Qaida a valuable propaganda and recruitment weapon and provided them with hundreds of coalition targets (military and civilian) in Iraq. It also meant that there were insufficient military resources available to help the democratically elected government in Afghanistan to attain the level of security necessary to facilitate economic reconstruction. Most serious of all was the huge death toll of Iraqi civilians and the large number of soldiers who have lost their lives during the occupation.

One of the key lessons of the recent history of terrorism is that it is a serious mistake to believe that the use of military force alone is sufficient to eliminate a terrorist threat completely (Wilkinson 2006, 2008). When President George W. Bush stated, in the aftermath of 9/11, that the US was declaring 'war on terrorism', he misled many into assuming that the US military would be able to 'solve' the terrorism problem by defeating al-Qaida on the battlefields in the Middle East and that with its superior military force, the US would rapidly defeat terrorists who hide among the civilian population and plot secretly to carry out no-warning bombing attacks on the civilian populations.

At time of writing, it could not be said that the US and its allies were winning the struggle against al-Qaida, but it could be said that they had stopped losing it. In Iraq, the local al-Qaida franchise have suffered a crushing blow, and more leading al-Qaida militants have been killed by means of missile attacks launched from Predator unmanned aerial vehicles near the Pakistan border with Afghanistan. However, al-Qaida has been consolidating its position in Pakistan and has managed to protect the area where its core leadership is believed to be located. Al-Qaida has also been busy expanding its presence in West Africa and the Horn of Africa, while maintaining its recruitment of fresh militants among the Muslim communities in Europe.

It is reasonable to assume that the threat of terrorism from al-Qaida and its affiliates will remain for some years ahead. We are also likely to see the introduction of new al-Qaida tactics and some copying of the tactic of using mass shooting attacks to cause mass casualties as was used to deadly effect in Mumbai in November 2008. It seems likely that the use of similar tactics in other cities would also cause mass casualties, and that the police and security forces in many countries would find it just as difficult as the Indian security forces did to protect the public and capture the terrorists. It is also important to bear in mind that al-Qaida has shown great interest in acquiring unconventional weapons, such as chemical weapons and 'dirty bombs' (improvised explosives combined with radioactive isotopes). Governments, police forces and emergency services need to have contingency plans, equipment and medical supplies to deal with the consequences of this type of attack.

An effective strategy against terrorists has to be multi-pronged, involving the intelligence services, the police, the judiciary, immigration and customs services, the private sector, etc, and success in gaining support from the media and from the public, which can provide the eyes and ears to pick up information and clues to assist the intelligence-gathering by the police and intelligence services. The military can perform many valuable tasks within the framework of this multi-pronged strategy, but over-dependence on military force can become counter-productive. For example, the Israeli government's decision to bombard Lebanon in 2006 only strengthened support for Hizbollah, and Israel's massive and totally disproportionate bombardment and siege of Gaza launched in December 2008 only served to strengthen support for Hamas and created new generations of terrorists eager to avenge the deaths of the hundreds of Palestinian victims of the bombardment and invasion of Gaza.

Note

1 According to www.iraqbodycount.org, the latest figure for civilian deaths in Iraq from 2003 to 14 January 2009 is 98,605.

References

Alexander, Y. and Pluchinsky, D.A. (1972) *Europe's Red Terrorists: The Fighting Communist Organisations*, London: Frank Cass.

Arendt, H. (1958) *The Origins of Totalitarianism*, San Diego: Harcourt Brace and Company.

Avrich, P. (1980) *The Russian Anarchists*, Westport, CT: Greenwood Press.

Bin Laden, O. (1998) 'Fatwa', 23 February. Available online at: www.mideastweb.org/osamabinladen2.htm (accessed 13 February 2009).

Brachman, J.M. (2009) *Global Jihadism: Theory and Practice*, London: Routledge.

Conquest, R. (1968) *The Great Terror: Stalin's Purge of the Thirties*, London: Macmillan.

——(1978) *Revolutionary Terrorism: The FLN in Algeria, 1954–62*, Stanford: Hoover Institution Press.

Crenshaw, M. (1978) *Revolutionary Terrorism: The FLN in Algeria, 1954 – 1962*, Stanford: Hoover Institution Press.

——(ed.) (1983) *Terrorism, Legitimacy and Power*, Middleton, CT: Wesleyan University Press.

Evans, J. (2009) 'Chief warns of threat from global recession', *Daily Telegraph*, 7 January. Available online at: www.telegraph.co.uk/news/newstopics/politics/defence/4144460/MI5-chief-warns-of-threat-from-global-recession.html (accessed 13 February 2009).

Forrest, J.J.F. (2006) *The Making of a Terrorist*, vol 1 & 2, Westport, CT: Praeger Security International.

Gerges, F.A. (2005) *The Far Enemy: Why Jihad Went Global*, New York: Cambridge University Press.

Greer, D. (1935) *The Incidence of Terror during the French Revolution*, Cambridge, MA: Harvard University Press.

Hardman, J.B.S. (1937) 'Terrorism', in Seligman, E.R (ed.) *Encyclopaedia of the Social Sciences*, vol. 14, New York: Macmillan, pp. 575–79.

Hoffman, B. (1998) *Inside Terrorism*, New York: Columbia University Press.

Horne, A. (1996) *Savage War of Peace: Algeria 1954–62*, rev. edn., London: Papermac.

Jenkins, B. (1975) *Will Terrorists Go Nuclear?*, RAND paper No. P-5541, Santa Monica, CA: RAND Corporation.

Laqueur, W. (1977) *Terrorism*, London: Weidenfeld and Nicolson.

Lewis, B. (1967) *The Assassins: A Radical Sect in Islam*, London: Weidenfeld and Nicolson.

Lucas, C. (1972) *The Structure of Terror: The Example of Javogues and the Loire*, London: Oxford University Press.

Montesquieu (1965) in Ehrard, J. (ed.) *Politique de Montesquieu*, Textes choisis et présentés par Jean Ehrard, Paris: Armand Colin.

National Commission on Terrorist Attacks upon the United States (2004) *The 9/11 Commission Report*, New York: W. W. Norton.

Roucek, J.S. (1962) 'Sociological elements of a theory of terror and violence', *American Journal of Economics and Sociology* 21, 2: 165–72.

Schmid, A.P., Jongman, A.J. and Horowitz, I. (1988) *Political Terrorism: A New Guide to Actors, Authors, Concepts, Data Bases, Theories and Literature*, Amsterdam: North Holland Publishing Company.

Suetonius, G. (1957) *The Twelve Caesars*, trans. R. Graves, Harmondsworth: Penguin.

Taylor, M. and Horgan, J. (eds) (2000) *Terrorism and Political Violence*, Special Issue on the Future of Terrorism, London: Frank Cass.

Thornton, T.P. (1964) 'Terror as a weapon of political agitation', in Eckstein, H. (ed.) *Internal War*, New York: Free Press, pp. 71–99.

Townshend, C. (1986) *Britain's Civil Wars: Counterinsurgency in the Twentieth Century*, London: Faber.

US National Counter Terrorism Centre (2007) as quoted in *US State Department Country Reports on Terrorism*, Office of the Coordinator for Counter Terrorism, 21 March. Available online at: www.state.gov/s/ct/rls/crt/2006/82739.htm (accessed 13 February 2009).

Walter, E.V. (1969) *Terror and Resistance*, London: Oxford University Press.

Wilkinson, P. (1987) 'Pathways out of terrorism', in Wilkinson, P. and Stewart, A.M. (eds) *Contemporary Research on Terrorism*, Aberdeen: Aberdeen University Press, pp. 453–66.

——(2006) *Terrorism Versus Democracy: The Liberal State Response*, 2nd edn, London: Routledge.

——(2008) 'A brief assessment of US-European cooperation on counter-terrorism', in Alcaro, R. (ed.) *Re-Launching the Transatlantic Security Partnership*, Rome: Quaderni Instituto Affari Internazionali (IAI), November, pp. 63–74.

12

Weapons of mass destruction and the proliferation challenge

James J. Wirtz

On 6 September 2007, Israeli warplanes attacked and destroyed an industrial facility in the eastern desert of Syria. Although there were rumours at the time that Tel Aviv had actually carried out a preventive strike to destroy a covert nuclear reactor, another story began to emerge seven months later. The US government alleged that Syria, with the aid of North Korea, had been secretly building a reactor capable of producing plutonium, fissile material that could be used to construct a nuclear weapon. According to the White House, Syria was in direct violation of its obligations to the International Atomic Energy Agency to notify the international community about the presence of the reactor, which further suggested that the facility was not intended for peaceful purposes (White House 2008). Assuming that these reports are accurate, Syria's failed gambit to undertake a clandestine nuclear weapons programme is of more than passing interest because it highlights three important trends that shape the challenge posed by the proliferation of chemical, biological and nuclear weapons in the world today. First, Syria's effort to launch a covert nuclear programme did not involve a great power with an established nuclear industry and weapons capability. Instead, Syria received aid from North Korea, a state that is currently at odds with the international community over its own effort to build nuclear weapons and ballistic missiles. Syrian–North Korean collaboration is actually a case of 'second tier nuclear proliferation', whereby states in the developing world with limited scientific and manufacturing capabilities trade among themselves to enhance their weapons programmes (Braun and Chyba 2004). Other observers also have noted that this clandestine trade is occurring among non-state actors – criminal syndicates, commercial entrepreneurs and even terrorists – that are participating in what might be described as 'third tier' proliferation activities (Zaitseva 2008). Second, the Syrians apparently ignored their international obligations to undertake their nuclear programme inside the reporting and regulatory environment created by the non-proliferation regime. The incident not only raises doubts about the ability of the regime to slow proliferation in the face of a state or even non-state actors determined to acquire a weapon of mass destruction, but also about the ability of the regime to detect covert weapons programmes and trade in dual-use material and technologies (i.e. goods that can be used for peaceful and military purposes). Third, the Israeli preventive attack highlights the willingness of some states to take direct military action to prevent other state and non-state actors from acquiring weapons of mass destruction. Clandestine proliferation activity itself is an immediate threat to the peace because it can prompt neighbouring states to take military action to stave off nascent threats.

The remainder of this chapter characterizes the threat posed by chemical, biological and nuclear weapons. It also describes the changing nature of the domestic and international challenge posed by the proliferation of weapons of mass destruction. Because these weapons are different in terms of their manufacture, lethality, use in battle and the proliferation risks that they pose, the discussion of each weapon is used to illustrate a key facet of the contemporary proliferation problem. Evidence suggests that several highly lethal technologies are moving, or threaten to move, beyond state control.

Chemical weapons

Chemical weapons are products of the modern chemical industry, which emerged in the final decades of the nineteenth century. Chemical weapons are based upon mature technologies that are ubiquitous. Many technologies used in the chemical industry have 'dual use': processes and products that are devoted to peaceful purposes (e.g. pesticides) can quickly be modified to produce battlefield weapons (e.g. nerve agents). Many industrial chemicals are themselves highly toxic and can pose a threat to their local communities. In December 1984, for example, an industrial accident at Bhopal, India released a choking cloud of methyl isocyanate (MIC), a pesticide ingredient that is actually twice as lethal as phosgene, another industrial agent that has actually been used as a weapon on the battlefield (L'Italien 2005). Estimates of the death toll in this accident vary between 4,000 and 20,000 casualties. Observers worry that terrorists or even a deranged person could trigger an industrial accident, exploiting local materials to create death and destruction (Schierow 2005). A local chemical plant could be used to launch an asymmetric attack: a release of a lethal chemical could produce casualties and political consequences greater by orders of magnitude than the effort expended in simply attacking a facility, because operatives could use the materials contained in the chemical plant to generate hundreds of thousands of casualties.

Chemical weapons differ in their lethality and the way they cause injury. Some evaporate quickly, allowing attacking troops to move through an area soon after they are used. Area denial agents persist for a long time and are intended to prevent access to key facilities, e.g. ports, airfields and railroad terminals. Chemical weapons are extremely difficult to handle, and must be expertly employed in very large quantities to have more than a nuisance value against well-trained troops who possess modern defensive equipment and who are prepared for an attack. This probably explains why most of the world's nations have signed the Chemical Weapons Convention (CWC), pledging to destroy existing stockpiles of chemical agents and to abandon any effort to employ chemical weapons in battle. Against an unprotected civilian population, however, a well-executed attack with chemical weapons could prove highly lethal and disruptive to normal economic and social activity.

Chemical weapons are usually characterized as blood agents, chocking agents, blister agents, nerve agents and incapacitants. Blood agents, which are generally based on hydrocyanic acid (HCN), impair the body's ability to transport oxygen in the blood. Choking agents – phosgene and chlorine – produce hydrochloric acid when they are inhaled, causing blood and fluid to infiltrate the lungs. Blister agents are primarily intended to injure, not to kill, thereby stressing supporting medical services. The blister agent, sulphur mustard, exists as a thick liquid at room temperature but it can be turned into an aerosol using a conventional explosive. Injuries from mustard gas can sometimes take several hours to develop, which makes it a particularly nefarious way to contaminate people, terrain or equipment.

Nerve agents are the most lethal chemical weapons; exposure to high aerosol concentrations of nerve agents causes prompt collapse and death. These chemicals are called 'nerve agents' because they interfere with the body's neurological system. First-generation nerve agents, G-series (German) agents Tabun (GA), Sarin (GB), Soman (GD) and Cyclosarin (GF) are non-persistent agents that evaporate at room temperature. In March 1995, the Aum Shinrikyo cult simply punched holes in plastic bags of Sarin left on the Tokyo subway, hoping that as the chemical evaporated, it would contaminate nearby passengers (Stern 2000: 209). Second-generation V-series nerve agents (VX, VE, VG and VM), a product of British science, are about ten times more lethal than Sarin and are considered to be persistent agents. Less is publicly known about third-generation 'A-series' agents (often referred to as 'Novichok' or 'New Guy' agents), which were produced by the Soviet Union during the Cold War. A-series agents rely on commonly available dual-use chemicals, making them more difficult to find in the course of arms control inspections or by instruments designed to detect chemical weapons on the battlefield.

Incapacitants are used for personal protection (CN or Mace) or for riot control (CS or tear gas). They constitute a sort of grey area when it comes to the contemporary use of chemical weapons. They are generally banned from use in combat under international law, but they can be used to control domestic disturbances. In October 2002, for instance, Russian security forces used a gas or aerosol, presumably a fentanyl derivative, in an attempt to incapacitate Chechen separatists who were holding 800 hostages in a Moscow theatre. This 'incapacitant' killed 126 people due to either a lack of prompt medical attention or an overdose of this chemical (Croddy and Tu 2005: 130).

The Chemical Weapons Convention

On 13 January 1993, the Convention on the Prohibition of the Development, Production, Stockpiling and Use of Chemical Weapons and on their Destruction, often referred to as the Chemical Weapons Convention was opened for signature. As of February 2009, there were 186 states parties to the treaty, making it a virtually universal ban on the development, production, stockpiling, retention or use of chemical weapons. Moreover, each state party is required to destroy existing stockpiles of chemical agents and existing munitions. The organization for the Prohibition of Chemical Weapons, an international organization, is charged with verification of compliance by undertaking routine on-site inspections of declared chemical facilities and even so-called 'challenge inspections' if a violation of the convention is suspected (Center for Nonproliferation Studies 2009).

Although the CWC is a great achievement, more can be done to maximize the effectiveness of this international convention. Stockpiles of chemical weapons are being destroyed, but the US and Russia will be hard pressed to eliminate their chemical arsenals by the 2012 deadline set for complete disarmament. As strange as it may appear, questions also linger about what actually qualifies as 'destruction' when it comes to chemical weapons. Issues related to environmental protection and chemical weapons destruction are not trivial, either; munitions that were dumped at sea years ago are caught in fishing nets or resurface from shallow-water dumping sites, suggesting that issues related to destruction and the environment will continue indefinitely. Additionally, efforts have to be undertaken to increase the role of civil society and non-governmental organizations to increase transparency when it comes to domestic laws and international norms against the possession or use of chemical weapons by states, non-state actors and even individuals (Smallwood 2007).

The ongoing challenge posed by chemical weapons

Chemical weapons are no longer a weapon of choice for battlefield use, but they continue to pose a threat as a terrorist weapon. In 2007, insurgents in Iraq used chlorine cylinders in improvised explosive devices to attack civilians and foreign troops (Weitz et al. 2007). These attacks caused 'chemical' casualties, but were less lethal than well-positioned high explosives. The attacks in Iraq are important because they demonstrate that non-state actors have an ongoing interest in using commonly available chemicals as weapons, suggesting that reports of terrorist interest in obtaining chemical weapons are not far-fetched (Cornish 2007). The modern chemical industry itself constitutes a general threat because dual-use capabilities can be readily converted to military purposes and because chemical plants themselves can be targeted by terrorists and criminals to create highly disruptive incidents. This threat cannot be eliminated by traditional arms control measures like the Chemical Weapons Convention because state-sponsored chemical weapons programmes are not the primary threat faced by the international community. Instead, international collaboration in terms of domestic laws and surveillance is required to make sure that dangerous materials or legitimate manufacturing facilities are not being diverted or used for nefarious purposes.

Biological weapons

Not every disease can serve as an effective biological weapon. An agent's usefulness as a weapon of war or an instrument of terror is determined by its storage, delivery method, virulence, mode of transmission, resilience (i.e. how long can it survive in the environment) and potential lethality. Most military professionals believe that biological weapons are simply too unpredictable in their effects to be a reliable weapon. Most states are parties to the Biological Weapons Convention and have pledged not to develop, stockpile or employ biological agents in combat.

There are three types of biological agents: bacteria, viruses and toxins. Among the bacterial agents, anthrax is widely considered to be the perfect weapon. Its spores are extremely hardy (they can live for hundreds of years), an important quality when it comes to storing munitions for long periods. It also can be spread as an aerosol quickly across large areas, making it suitable for delivery by aircraft or by artillery shells. Anthrax is not contagious, so its effects are relatively containable and can be focused on specific targets. It also can be genetically engineered to be resistant to most antibiotics; during the Cold War, Soviet scientists apparently had great success in modifying anthrax to increase its resistance to treatment (Alibek 1999).

Viral agents also can make potent weapons. Policymakers are most worried about the threat posed by smallpox, which is no longer a naturally occurring disease. Unlike anthrax, smallpox is contagious. It has a lethality of about 30 per cent in its ordinary form. It also leaves survivors horribly scarred. Smallpox vaccination, even if administered a few days after exposure, can stop the disease, but to prevent a pandemic, millions of doses of vaccine might have to be made available quickly.

Toxins are not living organisms. Because they are by-products of metabolic activity, however, they are generally classified as biological weapons. Toxins are poisons produced by organisms. They are often used to attack an individual or to contaminate a specific target. Individuals have to be brought into direct contact with the toxin to suffer from its effects. Ricin seems to be the terrorists' toxin of choice because it can be easily manufactured with only rudimentary equipment. In the summer of 2007, for example, police discovered ricin that had been manufactured by an individual in a Las Vegas hotel room (Friess 2008).

The Biological Weapons Convention

The Biological and Toxin Weapons Convention (BTWC) was opened for signature on 10 April 1972. It prohibits the development, production, stockpiling and use of biological and toxin weapons. In a sense, the convention has been highly successful because it codifies a widespread interest in banning the use of biological weapons in war, but its continued efficiency is threatened by the failure to achieve a legally binding instrument to verify compliance and by a changing technological setting (Pearson 2005). Verifying the provisions of the BTWC is challenging because the production of agents does not require a large-scale industrial complex – the type of facility required to make significant amounts of chemical agents. An inspection regime would place commercial equities at risk: drug companies are loath to open up research and production venues to the scrutiny of potential competitors. Neither is there any way to devise an accurate list of 'suspect' facilities, since virtually any medical laboratory can potentially serve as a weapons lab.

The challenges faced by those who want to strengthen the BTWC are in some way more severe than those involved in the CWC, because experimentation with myriad pathogens is common medical practice. To become more effective, the international community thus has to reach a common understanding on strengthening the BTWC. Governments have to agree to bring domestic laws into line with international norms against the possession and use of dangerous pathogens and agents. A common regime needs to be created to secure pathogens in research and medical laboratories and to define scientific codes of conduct. International efforts to investigate suspicious disease outbreaks need to be enhanced, and general global disease surveillance is required to monitor more effectively the international ban on biological warfare (Tucker 2003).

The ongoing challenge posed by biological weapons

Biological weapons pose somewhat of an enigma as far as assessing the extent of their threat is concerned. Their destructive potential is virtually unlimited. A single virus could ultimately lead to the deaths of millions of people. Experts often express reservations, however, about the feasibility of deliberately starting a pandemic, noting that normal public health measures often do a good job at containing naturally occurring disease outbreaks. Doomsday scenarios can be easily imagined, but so far, these scenarios are predicated upon untested assumptions, weapons and techniques (Guillemin 2005).

Nevertheless, terrorists might be attracted to biological agents because they are highly lethal in small quantities. They also might be available to terrorists because any basic medical laboratory has the capability to cultivate biological agents. Small fermenters used to make legitimate vaccines could be quickly converted to produce biological agents. Experts often express doubts, however, about the ability of terrorists to carry out a biological weapons attack with maximum effect. They reason that if it is difficult for state-sponsored weapons programmes to initiate pandemics or deliver agents in a way that guarantees widespread infection, it might be even more difficult for individuals or small terror cells to use biological agents. The Aum Shinrikyo cult, for example, attempted to disseminate anthrax and botulinum toxin, but their efforts failed to have any effect. Terrorists might understand that disease outbreaks are difficult to control, and that they might affect their own followers more severely than the population living in targeted areas. In other words, the course of a disease outbreak would be determined by the availability of advanced public health services, not the characteristics of a disease agent itself. Contagious diseases would probably have the greatest impact on people living in poverty who lack basic public health systems and medical care.

Although there is scepticism about the threat posed by biological weapons, many observers worry that an ongoing revolution in genetic engineering is making it increasingly easy to manipulate naturally occurring diseases, transforming them into extremely effective weapons. These observers note that in much the same way as the information revolution transformed global commerce and communication, empowering people and self-organizing groups at the expense of bureaucracy and governments, accelerating progress in genetic engineering is about to have profound effects. Ordinary research programmes and medical laboratories around the globe will soon have capabilities that surpass those of today's leading scientists and universities. They worry that in the course of legitimate research, dangerous new substances, agents or processes might be discovered. Concerns have been raised that governments are not prepared to take steps to prevent these new discoveries from being deliberately or inadvertently used for nefarious purposes. The revolution in biotechnology could make biological weapons an even more dangerous reality than they are today (Committee on Prevention on Homeland Security, House of Representatives 2005).

Nuclear weapons

The history of physics, politics and war became intertwined in the twentieth century, ultimately producing extraordinarily destructive devices known as nuclear weapons. By the end of the nineteenth century, nuclear physics had emerged from the science of chemistry. During the 1930s, physicists made several theoretical and experimental advances, which suggested that nuclear fission could be harnessed in commerce and war. By 1945, they had not only produced a fission weapon, but the US had employed it twice in war over the Japanese cities of Hiroshima and Nagasaki. In the span of less than 50 years, a scientific community that did not understand how stars produced energy would create a weapon that produced temperatures and pressures that exceeded those found on the surface of the sun (Bernstein 2008).

When a nuclear weapon is detonated, it produces an electro-magnetic pulse (EMP), a thermal-light pulse, a blast and fallout. Military planners generally used blast effects to estimate casualty rates produced during a nuclear attack. As a rule of thumb, it was assumed that a one-megaton airburst would immediately kill or wound about 50 per cent of the people living within 7.5 km of ground zero. Over a longer term, nuclear weapons can produce casualties through radiation. Radiation exposure can occur at the instant of nuclear detonation or from fallout, which is irradiated debris lifted into the atmosphere by the nuclear fireball. Radiation can contaminate the immediate area surrounding a nuclear detonation and areas downwind from the explosion as nuclear fallout is carried downrange. An REM (roentgen-equivalent-man) is a measure of radiation energy absorbed by living creatures. A dose of 600 REM produces lethal radiation sickness, while 300 REM produces lethal radiation sickness in about 10 per cent of an exposed population. Exposure to about 250 REM, however, impedes the body's ability to heal from burns and kinetic injury, making non-lethal injuries deadly. Exposure to about 50 REM raises the incidence of cancer across an entire population by about 2 per cent.

Recently, many observers have raised concerns about the threat posed by the possibility of constructing explosive devices to disseminate radioactive material. These 'dirty bombs' rely on radiation to produce a lethal effect. A dirty bomb's lethality thus would be governed by how far radioactive materials might be dispersed by the conventional explosive and by the radioactivity of the material used in the bomb. The real threat posed by a dirty bomb, however, might not be the damage done by the radioactive material it disperses. Instead, it might create a panic that would be accompanied by a widespread disruption of everyday life.

Today, the US, Russia, the People's Republic of China, the UK, France, India, Pakistan, North Korea and Israel possess nuclear weapons. Iran is also suspected to be seeking the capability for creating a nuclear arsenal, despite widespread international condemnation of its efforts. Dozens of countries also have the necessary scientific and manufacturing knowledge to construct nuclear weapons, although these states have not chosen to exercise their 'nuclear option'. Nuclear weapons are the product of mature technologies; the scientific principles behind the physics and manufacture of simple 'gun-type' fusion weapons are well known. Only international efforts to safeguard fissile materials (e.g. plutonium and highly enriched uranium) stand as significant impediments to the manufacture of rudimentary nuclear weapons. The need to safeguard fissile materials will only grow in the future as commercial nuclear power plants proliferate in response to growing energy demands that cannot or should not be met by fossil fuels.

Over the course of the Cold War, the US and the Soviet Union constructed tens of thousands of nuclear weapons, resulting in a strategic standoff often described as Mutual Assured Destruction (MAD). Neither superpower could win a nuclear war in this situation, which over time caused them to moderate their behaviour. MAD might have even facilitated the demise of the Soviet Empire in the sense that neither Soviet nor US leaders saw military force as a viable option to preserve the Warsaw Pact or hasten the demise of the USSR.

Since the Cold War, the threat of nuclear Armageddon has receded. Over the last twenty years, the number of nuclear weapons deployed by Russia and the US has shrunk by about 80 per cent, remaining nuclear forces have largely been de-alerted, nuclear modernization programmes have been curtailed or greatly reduced in scope and ambition, and a de facto nuclear test ban has halted advances in nuclear weapons technology. Chinese, British and French nuclear programmes also are in stasis. The governments of these countries continue to highlight the importance of nuclear deterrence in their national security strategies, but their nuclear arsenals are a waning asset, based mostly on aging delivery systems and warheads.

By contrast, India, Pakistan, North Korea and Iran retain ambitious nuclear programmes, but limited nuclear capabilities. Unlike the long-established nuclear powers, these states continue to give their nuclear weapons programmes high priority. Their leaders apparently believe that nuclear weapons will provide the security, prestige, or diplomatic advantage they need in facing their neighbours or threats that emanate from outside their region. Although it is possible that the acquisition of a nuclear arsenal will quell their fears and result in regional stability, many observers worry that rapid advances in the size or capability of regional nuclear arsenals could leads to arms races, crisis, instability or war. There also are concerns about the security of nuclear arsenals everywhere, but particularly when it comes to nascent nuclear powers. Many worry that the proliferation of nuclear weapons programmes will only exacerbate the terrorist threat by making nuclear expertise, material or even weapons available to the highest bidder or subject to theft.

The Non-Proliferation Treaty

The Nuclear Non-Proliferation Treaty (NPT) entered into force on 5 March 1970. Unlike the CWC and the BTWC, its sole purpose is not disarmament. Its role is to safeguard and promote the use of nuclear technology for peaceful purposes, while promoting the eventual elimination of nuclear weapons. Its safeguards, focused primarily on monitoring the storage, transfer and use of fissile materials, are implemented by the International Atomic Energy Agency (IAEA), which was established in 1957. The NPT was originally intended to be in force for 25 years, but was extended for an indefinite duration during the 1995 review conference. Agreement to extend the treaty indefinitely, however, did little to reduce the inherent tension concerning the 'grand bargain' inherent in the NPT: nuclear 'have-nots' would be granted access to commercial nuclear technologies under IAEA safeguards; while the acknowledged nuclear weapons states (the US, Russia, France, the UK and China) would undertake a determined effort to eliminate their existing nuclear arsenals (Paul 2005).

Today, the NPT faces several challenges. First, the proliferation of gas-centrifuge devices and other sophisticated techniques and equipment make it difficult to draw a clear line between the commercial application of nuclear technology and a nascent nuclear weapons programme – existing safeguards embedded in the non-proliferation regime have not kept pace with the advance of technology. Second, the activities of the Pakistani scientist A. Q. Khan demonstrate that nuclear technology and equipment are no longer strictly controlled by state actors. Third, there are persistent reports of a black market in fissile materials, although most reports turn out to be little more than hoaxes or scams involving relatively harmless materials. Still, the prospect that highly enriched uranium or plutonium might fall into the hands of terrorist or criminal syndicates is alarming because the primary stumbling block in the construction of a primitive nuclear device is a lack of fissile material, not a lack of knowledge.

The ongoing challenge posed by nuclear weapons

The threat posed by nuclear weapons has abated over the last several decades, but the menace of proliferation and the possibility that terrorists will gain access to nuclear weapons or highly radioactive materials is emerging as the greatest security menace of the twenty-first century. As commercial nuclear power plants are constructed around the world to meet future demands for energy, the challenge of safeguarding nuclear material and expertise will become more daunting. Moreover, deterrence no longer appears to be an appropriate strategy for dealing with the problems posed by non-state actors. Preventive attacks might become increasingly frequent in international relations as governments attempt to head off nascent threats.

Conclusion: mitigating the threat posed by weapons of mass destruction

The information revolution, the biotech revolution and globalization have created new venues for the proliferation of chemical, biological, nuclear and radiological weapons. As the reports about Syria's alleged clandestine reactor, if true, would demonstrate, 'second tier' powers can collaborate to circumvent international norms against the proliferation of weapons of mass destruction. New actors, operating in what are often relatively permissive domestic environments, seem beyond the reach of the Nuclear Non-Proliferation Treaty, the CWC or the BWC. The US government has signed and adheres to the Biological Weapons Convention, for instance, but its citizens were still subjected to an anthrax attack. Individuals are now manufacturing, handling and employing deadly biological weapons and toxins for personal reasons, creating a fundamentally different type of proliferation problem. Many experts worry that it is only a matter of time before a terrorist syndicate launches a devastating a chemical, biological or nuclear attack. The threat is no longer confined to states or to the realm of international relations.

Governments have responded to this threat. In 2003, the administration of then US president George W. Bush unveiled the Proliferation Security Initiative, a voluntary international collaborative effort to stop the flow of dangerous nuclear materials, weapons components, manufacturing equipment and associated delivery systems by sea. The UN took action in April 2004. UN Resolution 1540 requires all states to undertake domestic and international measures to stop individuals and non-state actors from obtaining nuclear, biological and chemical weapons and delivery systems. Russia and the US also announced the Global Initiative to Combat Nuclear Terrorism in 2006, which aims at detecting, deterring and defeating nuclear-armed terrorists. Together, these measures constitute a new paradigm in the battle against proliferation and the threat posed by weapons of mass destruction (Kartchner 2009). Nevertheless, it remains to be seen whether international institutions, national militaries, intelligence agencies and law enforcement organizations can head off these second- and third-tier proliferation challenges. Domestic laws around the globe need to reinforce international norms, thereby increasing transparency, while international initiatives have to interdict traffic in prohibited commodities, technologies and weapons.

References

Alibek, K. (1999) *Biohazard*, New York: Delta.

Bernstein, J. (2008) *Nuclear Weapons: What You Need to Know*, Cambridge: Cambridge University Press.

Braun, C. and Chyba, C.F. (2004) 'Proliferation rings: New challenges to the nuclear nonproliferation regime', *International Security* 29, 2: 5–49.

Center for Nonproliferation Studies, Monterey Institute of International Studies (2009) 'Inventory of international nonproliferation organizations & regimes'. Available online at: http://cns.miis.edu/inventory/ (accessed January 2009).

Committee on Prevention on Homeland Security, U.S. House of Representatives (2005) *Hearing before the subcommittee on prevention of nuclear and biological attack*, One Hundred Ninth Congress First Session Serial No. 109–30, 13 July 2005.

Cornish, P. (2007) *The CBRN SYSTEM: Assessing the Threat of Terrorist Use of Chemical, Biological, Radiological and Nuclear Weapons in the United Kingdom*, London: Chatham House.

Croddy, E. and Tu, A. (2005) 'Fentanyl', in Croddy, E. and Wirtz, J.J. (eds) *Weapons of Mass Destruction: An Encyclopedia of Worldwide Policy, Technology, and History*, Santa Barbara: ABC-CLIO, pp. 129–30.

Friess, S. (2008) 'Man in critical condition in ricin case', *The New York Times*, 29 February 2008. Available online at: http://www.nytimes.com/2008/02/29/us/31cnd-ricin.html?hp (accessed 23 February 2009).

Guillemin, J. (2005) *Biological Weapons: From the Invention of State Sponsored Programs to Contemporary Bioterrorism*, New York: Columbia University Press.

Kartchner, K. (2009) 'The evolving international context for arms control: A new paradigm for cooperative security', in Larsen, J.A. and Wirtz, J.J. (eds) *Arms Control and Cooperative Security*, Boulder: Lynne Rienner.

L'Italien, B. (2005) 'Bhopal, India: Union Carbide accident', in Croddy, E. and Wirtz, J.J. (eds) *Weapons of Mass Destruction: An Encyclopedia of Worldwide Policy, Technology, and History*, Santa Barbara: ABC-CLIO, pp. 38–40.

Paul, T.V. (2005) 'Nuclear Noproliferation Treaty (NPT)', in Croddy, E. and Wirtz, J.J. (eds) *Weapons of Mass Destruction: An Encyclopedia of Worldwide Policy, Technology, and History*, Santa Barbara: ABC-CLIO, pp. 252–55.

Pearson, G.S. (2005) 'The central importance of legally binding measures for the strengthening of the Biological and Toxin Weapons Convention (BTWC)', Weapons of Mass Destruction Commission, Stockholm Sweden January 2005.

Schierow, L.J. (2005) *Chemical Plant Security*, CRS Report for Congress. Order Code RL31530 February 14, 2005, Washington: Congressional Research Service.

Smallwood, K. (2007) *10 Years of the OPCW: Taking Stock and Looking Forward*, 26th Workshop of the Pugwash Study Group on the Implementation of the Chemical and Biological Weapons Convention, Noordwijk, The Netherlands 17–18 March 2007, Conference Report.

Stern, J. (2000) 'Terrorist motivations and unconventional weapons', in Lavoy, P.R., Sagan, S.D. and Wirtz, J.J. (eds) *Planning the Unthinkable: How New Powers Will Use Nuclear, Biological and Chemical Weapons*, Ithaca, NY: Cornell University Press, pp. 202–29.

Tucker, J.B. (2003) 'Preventing the misuse of pathogens: The Need for global biosecurity standards', *Arms Control Today*, vol 33, no 5, (June 2003). Available online at: www.armscontrol.org/act/2003_06/Tucker.asp.

Weitz, R., Al-Marashi, I. and Hilal, K. (2007) 'Chlorine as a terrorist weapon in Iraq', *WMD Insights*, May 2007. Available online at: www.wmdinsights.com/I15/I15_ME1_Chlorine.htm (accessed 23 February 2009).

White House (2008) *Statement by the Press Secretary*, 24 April 2008. Available online at:www.cfr.org/publication/16102/statement_by_the_white_house_press_secretary_on_syria_and_north_korea.html?breadcrumb=%2Fregion%2F414%2Fsyria (accessed 23 February 2009).

Zaitseva, L. (2008) 'Organized crime, terrorism, and nuclear trafficking', in Russell, J.A. and Witz, J.J. (eds) *Globalization and WMD Proliferation: Terrorism, Transnational Networks, and International Security*, New York, Routledge, pp. 102–22.

13

Organized crime, drug trafficking and trafficking in women

Phil Williams

The issue of whether or not transnational organized crime is a threat to national and international security has been debated since the early 1990s. Sceptics argue that the transnational organized crime threat is overblown, only arrived on the agenda because of the paucity of military challenges after the end of the Cold War, and, at best, only plays a marginal role as a national security concern. Ironically, sceptics range from those who see military threats as the only real threats and, therefore, dismiss transnational organized crime as irrelevant, to those who contend that the whole idea of transnational organized crime is based on 'fundamental errors of logic and interpretation' (Naylor 2005: 26). R. Thomas Naylor, in an incisive critique of the whole concept of organized crime, argues that those who emphasize the threat posed by transnational organized crime are guilty of 'equating an association of criminals with a criminal association, confounding the criminal firm and the criminal industry, and attempting to convert a military or fraternal hierarchy (an extremely simplistic one) into a business structure' (Naylor 2005: 26). Others claim that crime is local rather than transnational (Hobbs 1998) and that the threat from transnational organized crime is deliberately exaggerated by the US in order to spread US laws and enforcement mechanisms around the globe (Woodiwiss 2001).

At the other extreme are those who perceive organized crime as a major global threat in which transnational criminal organizations are regarded as global criminal conglomerates, engaging in high-level meetings at which they agree on joint ventures and spheres of influence within the large and lucrative criminal markets that they control (Sterling 1994; Robinson 1999). Some even claim that the global criminal economy, which is not defined in any specific way, could be well over US$2 trillion – twice the value of global expenditure on armaments (Glenn et al. 2008: 34). The absence of a clear methodology for determining such figures does little to dent the apparent authority with which they are presented.

The analysis here stakes out a middle ground between doves who dismiss the threat posed by transnational organized crime and hawks who exaggerate it. A useful starting point for a middle position is the recognition that threats depend in large part on vulnerabilities that can readily be exploited. Transnational organized crime is a far greater threat to small and weak states with limited capacity and low levels of legitimacy than it is to strong, prosperous, well-functioning liberal democracies where it challenges law and order, but does not jeopardize the integrity and viability of the state. For most of the states of the EU, the US, Canada, Australia, New Zealand and Japan, organized crime – unless related directly to terrorism and the dangerous movements of hazardous goods discussed more fully below – is a nuisance, but not an existential security threat. For states in the developing world, however, organized crime poses a much greater threat, challenging the rule of law and their monopoly on violence. While variations in the impact of organized crime must be acknowledged, it is equally important to consider the levels at which threats have an impact. Accordingly, this chapter examines the ways in which organized crime challenges security at the global level, the national level and the individual level (human security). It focuses in large part on drug trafficking, which remains the most significant and lucrative of all transnational criminal activities; provides the major (although not the only) source for the concentration of illicit wealth and power in many societies; and is most closely associated with violence and corruption. In addition, the chapter looks at human trafficking, which is a direct threat to human security. The impact on security of other transnational criminal activities, as well as of criminal organizations that concentrate power and use corruption and violence to protect themselves and their activities, is also considered.

This suggests the need for a dual focus – on both organizations and activities. Indeed, the term 'transnational organized crime' can be understood in two different but complementary ways. The term can refer to transnational criminal enterprises, organizations, or networks. These entities are Clausewitzian in the sense that crime for them is simply a continuation of business by other means. Transnational organized crime can also refer to cross-border criminal activities that can be undertaken by a variety of non-state entities such as terrorists, warlords and militias. States – especially those that are both authoritarian and isolated – can also use criminal activities as ways of circumventing sanctions and obtaining foreign exchange. Sometimes, of course, there is a neat convergence between entities and activities. After all, transnational criminal organizations engage in transnational criminal activities; this is their essence. Such convergence is not necessary, however.

The rise and empowerment of transnational criminal enterprises is one of the by-products of globalization. The compression of time and space and the associated reductions in transaction costs have been as important to criminal enterprises as to licit businesses, and global expansion is a feature shared by both. At the same time, the rise of criminal organizations is part of a broader phenomenon involving the emergence of violent non-state actors that pose a fundamental, if long-term challenge to the viability of the Westphalian state. These actors have become particularly important in states that suffer from governance deficits and have a low legitimacy quotient. They typically appropriate transnational criminal activities, such as drug trafficking, as well as domestic criminal activities, such as extortion and kidnapping, to provide funding for their political and military agendas. The result is that while criminal organizations have become more powerful, criminal activities have become ubiquitous.

Threats to global security: global flows of dangerous commodities

At the global level, transnational criminal enterprises and activities pose several challenges to security and governance. The first stems from transnational criminal flows – the movement of illicit commodities across national borders. These products can be prohibited (illegal drugs), regulated (endangered species and cultural property), counterfeit (cigarettes and pharmaceuticals), or stolen (cars, art, nuclear and radioactive materials). In addition, people can be moved across borders illegally. One dimension of this is human smuggling – which circumvents immigration controls and is a crime against the state. Another is human trafficking for purposes of forced labour or commercial sex – a phenomenon discussed more fully below that is a crime against persons. In addition, the illegal proceeds of crime can be moved across borders as part of the money laundering cycle, in which funds derived from criminal activity are made to appear as legitimate. On some occasions, money is moved through multiple jurisdictions simply to complicate the task for law enforcement and to render it safe from seizure. Other global flows are digital – and while the vast majority of these are licit, the internet, for example, is also used for Nigerian '419 scams' or advance fee frauds (which are increasingly imitated by criminals elsewhere), child pornography, recruitment of terrorists, identity theft and extortion, financial fraud and money laundering. The global electronic space, while not wholly ungoverned, lacks effective regulation.

Of all these transnational criminal flows and movements, however, the smuggling of arms and nuclear material poses particularly serious challenges. Arms smuggling has traditionally undermined sanctions and embargoes imposed by the international community. The flow of arms to zones of ethnic conflict and civil wars has typically perpetuated and intensified these conflicts and encouraged the pillaging of natural resources to pay for the weaponry. The arrests of major arms traffickers such as Leonid Minin (arrested in a hotel near Milan in August 2000), Monzer al Kassar (arrested in Madrid in June 2007), and, perhaps most significantly, Viktor Bout (arrested in Bangkok in March 2008 in a sting operation by the US Drug Enforcement Administration) have removed some of the more prominent players in the illegal arms business, but done little to dent arms trafficking or to reduce the widespread availability of weapons not only in conflict zones but in many cities throughout the developed and developing world.

A dimension of arms trafficking that is often ignored, for example, is the way it contributes to the development of what Richard Norton has termed 'feral cities', that is, cities characterized by endemic violence and growing ungovernability (Norton 2003). Perhaps the most obvious feral city in the world is Mogadishu. Other cities that could move into this category include Cite Soleil in Haiti and even Rio de Janeiro, where armed gangs dominate the slums or favelas, trafficking in drugs and recruiting the Latin American urban equivalent of Africa's child soldiers. In effect, cities in many parts of the developing world are becoming 'fearscapes' (Canadian Consortium on Human Security and Department of Foreign Affairs and International Trade 2006).

Perhaps even more serious – in terms of potential impact, although not yet in terms of real damage done – is nuclear material trafficking. The International Atomic Energy Agency's (2008) Illicit Trafficking Database contains 1,340 confirmed incidents from 1993 to 2007. The majority of seizures and arrests, however, involve radioactive junk. Highly enriched uranium or plutonium was discovered in only 18 cases, and few of these involved significant amounts of weapons-grade material. Nevertheless, the IAEA acknowledges a 'persistent problem with the illicit trafficking in nuclear and other radioactive materials' and notes that such trafficking is 'a potential threat to the security of states and to international security. It could be a shortcut to nuclear proliferation and to nuclear or radiological terrorism' (International Atomic Energy Agency 2008). The conventional wisdom is that transnational criminal organizations are not involved in this business. A closer inspection reveals otherwise. If organized crime is narrowly defined in terms of traditional mafia organizations, then it has little involvement in nuclear material trafficking. In an analysis completed in 2002 for an IAEA Conference, however, two observers suggest that organized crime – encompassing local predatory criminal organizations; ethnically based smuggling groups and more diverse smuggling networks (both of which move seamlessly from one product to another); criminal controlled companies; crime-corruption networks; and sophisticated transnational criminal organizations – is extensively involved in nuclear material trafficking. Moreover, many of these organizations have the skill, resources, and ingenuity to carry out trafficking operations that are difficult to detect (Williams and Woessner 2001).

What makes all this even more disturbing is the possibility that such material will be sold to terrorists. Little evidence exists that nuclear material trafficking is designed to meet demand from terrorists (Russell 2006). Furthermore, the degree of cooperation between criminal and terrorist organizations is often exaggerated, not least by a failure to differentiate between insurgents such as FARC and terrorist organizations. Nevertheless, cooperation does not have to be close between criminals and terrorists for market transactions to take place. The possibility of al-Qaida acquiring the material for a radiological weapon, therefore, can certainly not be ruled out – particularly as criminals are unlikely to exercise due diligence in relations with their customers.

Some commentators also argue that transnational organized crime creates risks in the global financial system and has a damaging impact on global financial institutions. This can easily be exaggerated, however. Criminal proceeds are no more volatile than other forms of money, and in economies starved of foreign direct investment, they provide vital economic stimulation. Dirty money is no different from other money – it is equally liquid, equally mobile and equally fungible. Moreover, as the 2008 financial crisis reveals, governments and global financiers do not need organized crime to damage the system; they do a very good job of it themselves. At the national level, however, organized crime can do much more damage to institutions and the rule of law.

Threats to national security: drug traffickers, insurgents and spoilers

Threats to national security posed by transnational criminal organizations and activities are not uniform. States that are strong, effective and legitimate tend to be attractive markets for criminal organizations, but are able to limit the impact of criminal organizations and criminal activities on the state's ability to function. In contrast, weak states that become home or trans-shipment states for transnational criminal organizations are often seriously threatened by the power of these organizations and the strategies they adopt to protect their criminal activities. This is especially, but not uniquely the case for criminal organizations involved in drug trafficking. Three examples from the cocaine trade make this clear: they all show how major drug trafficking organizations directly and indirectly challenge national security and increase the level of violence in society.

During the 1980s, Colombia became the corporate headquarters of the burgeoning cocaine industry – surpassing both Peru and Bolivia, even though at that time the latter cultivated the vast majority of the coca grown in the Andes. Colombia had two comparative advantages: the relatively large Colombian population in the US, and the weakness of a state that – largely because of political divisions between left and right – had consistently failed to establish a high legitimacy quotient (Thoumi 2003). The resulting concentration of illicit power and wealth in the cities of Medellín and Cali challenged the Colombian state. Eventually, this challenge was beaten back, and the drug trafficking industry became more diffuse, with a small number of large organizations being succeeded by about 300 smaller groups. The drug business remained large and vibrant, but no longer seemed to threaten the state – at least for a few years.

The political divisions between left and right in society continued, however, and the Marxist insurgent group Revolutionary Armed Forces of Colombia (Fuerzas Armadas Revolucionarias de Colombia, FARC) became increasingly entangled in the drug business. Initially, FARC protected and taxed growers and traffickers; subsequently, some fronts in the organization became more directly involved in trafficking, providing cocaine to criminal organizations in Mexico and Brazil. Eventually, FARC members began trafficking cocaine directly into the US. Initially, the infusion of drug money appeared to strengthen FARC. The long-term effect, however, was less clear-cut, as FARC's emphasis on social justice was superseded by the desire for profit. FARC transformed itself from an ideological insurgency into a 'commercial insurgency' (Metz 1993: 13). As a result, it lost much of its appeal. By 2008, FARC was on the verge of defeat – as an insurgency. FARC groups remained active in the drug business, however. Ironically, many of the right-wing paramilitary groups that had been bitter enemies of FARC began to cooperate with their erstwhile enemy. Although the Uribe government had initiated a much-vaunted programme of disarmament, demobilization and reintegration (DDR), the process had many shortcomings (Porch and Rasmussen 2008). The result is the rise of 'new armed groups' in Colombia – some of which continue the fight against the FARC, while others have transcended former ideological differences and work with the FARC in the drug business (International Crisis Group 2007). Consequently Colombia is still bedevilled by high levels of organized violence, sustained by drug proceeds.

One reason the industry has remained so vibrant is the opening of new markets in Europe, markets made even more lucrative and attractive by the strength of the Euro currency. However, Colombian drug trafficking organizations have also had to contend with more effective interdiction of their transatlantic trade. One response has been the development of additional trans-shipment options. The target of choice as a trans-shipment state is Guinea-Bissau, one of the poorest countries in Africa. In the last few years, Guinea-Bissau has been taken over by Colombian drug trafficking organizations in a process of narco-colonization. Members of the government, the police and the military appear to be complicit in protecting cocaine loads flown or shipped across the Atlantic. The planes land on airstrips on islands off the coast of Guinea-Bissau, and there have even been reports that the traffickers have purchased one or two of these islands from the government. Indeed, for a poverty-stricken country dependent on cashew exports, the Colombian presence and the money it brings have been welcome. Yet, the overall result is a deterioration in governance and a decline of the rule of law. This is true throughout much of West Africa. As one report notes, 'drug money is perverting fragile economies and rotting society. Using threats and bribes, drug traffickers are infiltrating state structures and operating with impunity' (Costa 2007). In Guinea-Bissau, the climate of intimidation created by the collaboration between Colombian traffickers and high-ranking military and civilian officials is so deeply entrenched that the few critics brave enough to make allegations about official collusion have become targets for arrest and imprisonment. While Guinea-Bissau is an extreme case of state capture, it also reveals how powerful transnational criminal and drug trafficking organizations can undermine the security and integrity of weak states.

Mexico is an even more compelling example of how organized crime and drug traffickers threaten state security and public or citizen security (which is the dominant conception of security in Latin America and is an amalgam of notions of national and human security). Mexico has been involved in the drug business for several decades. Since 2000, however, the violence has spiked enormously This has coincided with increased competition as rival trafficking organizations battle for control of Mexican border cities that are used for strategic warehousing and as access points into the US, as well as with efforts by the state to control trafficking. The violence is characterized by:

- Increased professionalization. In the 1990s, the Gulf drug trafficking organization led by Osiel Cárdenas (now in a US prison) recruited former Mexican Special Forces members trained in the US as its enforcement arm. Known as the Zetas, these forces developed such a reputation for ruthlessness that their name is synonymous with violence – and sometimes used as a brand name for extra impact.
- Killing for effect. Torture and decapitation are increasingly common. On one occasion, five decapitated heads were thrown into a discotheque, and in September 2008, 12 decapitated bodies were discovered outside Merida in Yucatan, a city previously regarded as well away from the drug wars that had became so pervasive in the north of Mexico.
- Sophisticated weaponry. Mexican drug trafficking organizations are now so well armed that the police are vastly outgunned. Most of the weapons and ammunition used by the traffickers is of high quality and high calibre, smuggled in from the US. Indeed, military weaponry has become so widely distributed among the traffickers that even the Mexican army, which has been widely deployed by President Felipe Calderón, cannot count on the superiority of its firepower.
- Targeting of state officials. In one week in May 2008, five police chiefs (including the acting head of the Federal Police, the equivalent of the director of the Federal Bureau of Investigation in the US), were killed in what was a direct frontal assault on the Mexican state.
- The killing of innocent civilians. This trend became particularly evident in the latter half of 2008. In some cases, civilians were caught in the crossfire of violent clashes that had become increasingly blatant and uncontrolled. On 16 September 2008, two fragmentation grenades were thrown into a crowd in Morelia (the president's hometown) celebrating Mexico's Independence Day. The explosions killed eight people and hospitalized 75. Such acts are not entirely unprecedented. The Medellín trafficking organization of Pablo Escobar launched a terror campaign in Colombia, and in the early 1990s, the Sicilian mafia killed anti-mafia judges, bombed trains, and destroyed some of Italy's historic monuments.

In sum, the Mexican state is under siege, although whether out of desperation or boldness on the part of the trafficking organizations is uncertain. The state monopoly on the use of force has not simply been lost; it has been trampled underfoot. Although this is perhaps the most blatant example of the way in which organized crime can challenge security at the state level, it is far from the only case.

Sometimes the challenge is less brutal and more subtle, involving alternative forms of governance to the Westphalian state. Since 11 September 2001, the concept of 'ungoverned spaces' – which can all too easily be transformed into terrorist safe havens – has gained widespread currency among the US national security elite. In fact, most of these so-called ungoverned spaces are subject to alternative non-state forms of governance – some provided by organized crime. Paradoxically, organized crime is both predatory and paternalistic (Reno 2007). The 'dons' in the slums of Kingston, Jamaica, for example, are both criminals and community leaders (Gray 2004: 288). Alternative governance corrodes the legitimacy of the Westphalian state. Yet, it also reflects the failure of states throughout much of the developing world to provide good governance and meet the needs of their citizens. Unfortunately, in too many places, alternative governance is the only form of governance there is.

Organized crime also acts as a spoiler (Stedman 1997), seriously complicating efforts at post-conflict state building – as the US has discovered in both Iraq and Afghanistan. Although Stedman initially used the term 'spoiler' in relation to negotiations, it has much broader applicability in post-conflict situations. In Iraq, for example, criminal enterprises and criminal activities have contributed enormously to the instability. Kidnapping helped to create pervasive insecurity; the theft of copper from the electricity grid complicated reconstruction efforts; and oil smuggling and extortion funded the militias, insurgents and Al-Qaida in Iraq (AQI). The only consolation is that disputes over control of smuggling and other criminal activities between AQI and the Sunni tribes so provoked the latter that some of them defected from the insurgency and began working with the US against AQI.

In Afghanistan, too, organized crime and insurgency have effectively become fused: the Taliban as well as other local warlords allied with Western military forces are funded by profits from the opium and heroin trade. The real parallel here, however, is with the FARC in Colombia and its involvement in the cocaine business, although it is not clear that the Taliban will lose their religious zeal in the way that the FARC lost its revolutionary zeal. Taliban members barter heroin for weapons and ammunition supplied by Russian criminal organizations. They also tax the drug trade, with one estimate suggesting that the organization earned between US$200 and 400 million in 2007, between 5 and 10 per cent of a trade valued at around US$4 billion (Lynch 2008).

Threats to human security: extortion, kidnapping, and human trafficking

If drug trafficking and its associated violence, together with the concentration of illegal power, challenge the state monopoly of violence, the rule of law and the integrity of state institutions, and if illegal global movements of goods and people challenge control over national borders, other forms of transnational crime pose a more direct threat to human security. This is not always recognized, however. Some commentators on organized crime contend that the challenge to the state consists of no more than the provision of illegal goods and services and is simply a response to an existing demand. The notion that organized crime is victimless, however, is not persuasive. Organized crime is inherently violent or coercive. As suggested above, the violence associated with drug trafficking and the expansion or protection of markets is highly pernicious. Three other types of highly violent or coercive crimes stand out: extortion, kidnapping and trafficking in persons.

Extortion takes various forms, but typically involves pay-offs to criminal organizations by businesses. The payoffs are designed to ensure that criminal organizations do not engage in disruption of business activities, destruction of property, or harm to the directors or employees. From the criminal perspective, extortion is a low-cost means of ensuring a steady income flow. It depends on a credible threat of violence (a known reputation for violence is particularly useful) and is targeted against a variety of businesses. In some cases, reputation is sufficient to elicit payments without threats having to be carried out. In other instances, however, the threat has to be made credible by some demonstrative act of violence. Payments then become a means of avoiding further acts of violence against the business. The problem from the business perspective is that extortion, for the most part, is parasitical and diminishes profits (particularly damaging for small businesses operating on narrow margins) and reduces competitiveness. In some cases, extortion leads to the direct takeover of the business by organized crime. Indeed, during the 1990s in Russia, an important category of victims of contract killings consisted of businessmen who had resisted hostile takeovers of their companies by criminals (Volkov 2002). Although some of the killings were preceded by escalating violence designed to compel the target businessman to sell the business, when this failed to bring the desired result, the offending individual was simply eliminated in a very drastic form of hostile takeover. The other major category of victims of contract killings, apart from rivals in the criminal world, consists of those who pose a threat to organized crime – whether they be investigative journalists, reformist politicians or law enforcement personnel (police, customs, border guards) who do not succumb to the temptation of bribery and corruption.

Like extortion, kidnapping depends on force and coercion. Kidnapping for ransom is a specialist activity that has been adopted by criminal organizations in locations as diverse as the Philippines, Haiti, Colombia and Iraq. It is also used by insurgencies and terrorist organizations as it can instil a desired sense of fear while also providing income for the cause. Obtaining accurate figures on the scale of kidnapping is difficult. Nevertheless, it is clear that in some countries, kidnapping has become so pervasive that it contributes enormously to a climate of insecurity. Immediately after the occupation in Iraq, kidnappers targeted children, particularly of Assyrian Christians, and subsequently diversified their targets to include professors, doctors and businessmen. In spite of the publicity given to the kidnapping of foreigners – which led the French, German and Italian governments, among others, to pay multi-million dollar ransoms for the release of their citizens – Iraqis, rather than foreigners, were the primary targets. As many as 40 Iraqis a day were kidnapped for ransom in 2006 (Iraq Index). Although initial ransom demands were outlandish, kidnapping gangs were usually willing to negotiate, ultimately accepting what the family of the abducted person could pay. Sometimes this was as little as 10 per cent or even less of the initial ransom demands. An interesting variant on kidnapping has developed in Mexico City, where victims are kidnapped, forced to withdraw cash from ATMs, and then released.

Trafficking in people, especially women and children for commercial sex or forced labour (and even men for forced labour), also depends heavily on violence and intimidation. Although women are sometimes introduced to the commercial sex business through deception, trafficking in humans ultimately depends heavily on the fear of violence, both physical and sexual. In some cases, women are beaten into submission and so frightened that they do not even try to escape. Indeed, the business of trafficking in women would not be nearly as large, pervasive or lucrative without the central role of violence and the threat of violence. The business, which is global in scope, violates the human rights of the victims, who are often reduced to slavery. Although the 'businesses' vary considerably in size and scope and include individuals, small family establishments and small (often amateurish) criminal groups at the bottom end, efficient, large-scale transnational criminal organizations are also heavily involved. Russian, Ukrainian and Georgian criminal enterprises; Albanian clan-based groups; the Japanese Yakuza; Chinese Triads;

Nigerian groups; and Italian mafia organizations have all developed lucrative sources of income from trafficking women. Prostitution in Italy, for example, is dominated by Albanian traffickers who bring in women and girls from the former Soviet bloc and by Nigerians who bring in women from West Africa. Apart from the violence they have to endure, these women are also at risk of HIV/AIDS and other sexually transmitted diseases and obtain very little financial reward. For some, the only form of escape is promotion to management, which has personal benefits, but tends to have a self-perpetuating impact on the business. Many, and perhaps most

> women trafficked into prostitution report a never-ending cycle of debt – first they are charged exorbitant fees for the cost of transportation, but daily expenses are frequently added and mount up exponentially. Many women trafficked into prostitution receive no money from pimps or brothel owners. This becomes a cycle of entrapment.
>
> (State Department 2007: 26)

This cycle is buttressed by violence and the threat of violence. Apart from the killing of innocent people, this is perhaps the most serious threat to individual security, involving as it does fundamental violations of human rights and a contemporary form of slavery (Cameron and Newman 2007).

Conclusion

It is clear even from this brief survey that organized crime and drug trafficking have an impact on security at multiple levels. Moreover, states are often clumsy or inept in their efforts to counter transnational criminal networks, find it difficult to control criminal markets and have not fully appreciated the extent to which other non-state actors have appropriated the methodologies of organized crime as a funding mechanism. Indeed, since 2001, the efforts to combat transnational crime initiated by the UN and the Clinton administration have given way to a largely undifferentiated 'war on terror', a label that lumps together disparate phenomena in a way that does little to advance discriminating and effective strategies. Unfortunately, the problem of transnational organized crime is not going to go away. The long-term consequences of transnational organized crime, although subtle and insidious rather than dramatic and overt, will continue to challenge security at every level, from the global to the individual.

References

Adams, J. (1986) *The Financing of Terror*, New York: Simon and Schuster.
Cameron, S. and Newman, E. (eds) (2007) *Trafficking in Humans: Social, Cultural, and Political Dimensions*, Tokyo: United Nations University Press.
Canadian Consortium on Human Security and Department of Foreign Affairs and International Trade, (2006) *Human Security in Urban Spaces: Final Report*, Conference held by Canadian Consortium on Human Security and Department of Foreign Affairs and International Trade, Vancouver, 8–9 June.
Glenn, J. C., Gordon, T. J. and Florescu, E. (2008) *2008 State of the Future*, The Millennium Project, Washington, DC: World Federation of UN Associations.

Gray, O. (2004) *Demeaned but Empowered: The Social Power of the Urban Poor in Jamaica*, Jamaica: University of the West Indies Press.

Hobbs, R. (1998) 'Going down the glocal: The local context of organized crime', *The Howard Journal of Criminal Justice* 37, 4: 407–22.

International Atomic Energy Agency (2008) *International Atomic Energy Agency, Fact Sheet*. Available online at: www.iaea.org/NewsCenter/Features/RadSources/PDF/fact_figures2007.pdf (accessed 12 December 2008).

International Crisis Group (2007) *Colombia's New Armed Groups*, Latin America Report No. 20.

Iraq Index (2008) *Iraq Index: Tracking Variables of Reconstruction and Security in Post-Saddam Iraq*. Available online at: www.brookings.edu/saban/iraq-index.aspx (accessed 12 December 2008, continuously updated).

Lynch, C. (2008) 'Afghan opium production falls, UN reports', *Washington Post*, August 26.

Metz, S. (1993) *The Future of Insurgency*, Carlisle, PA: Strategic Studies Institute U.S. Army War College.

Naylor, R.T. (2005) *Wages of Crime: Black Markets, Illegal Finance, and the Underworld Economy*, Ithaca, NY: Cornell University Press.

Norton, R. (2003) 'Feral cities', *Naval War College Review*, Autumn. Available online at: www.nwc. navy.mil/press/Review/2003/Autumn/pdfs/art6-a03.pdf (accessed 12 December 2008).

OSC (2007) 'Analysis: West Africa's increased use as hub for drug trade', *West Africa – OSC Analysis*.

Porch, D. and Rasmussen, M.J. (2008) 'Demobilization of paramilitaries in Colombia: Transformation or transition?' *Studies in Conflict and Terrorism* 31, 6: 520–40.

Reno, W. (2007) 'Protectors and predators: Why is there a difference among West African militias?' in Andersen, L., Moller, B. and Stepputat, F. (eds) *Fragile States and Insecure People?: Violence, Security, and Statehood in the Twenty-First Century*, New York: Palgrave Macmillan, pp. 99–122.

Robinson, J. (1999) *The Merger*, New York: Simon and Schuster.

Russell, J. (2006) 'Peering into the abyss: Non-state actors and the 2016 proliferation environment', *Nonproliferation Review* 13, 3: 645–57.

Shultz, R.H., Farah, D. and Lochard, I.V. (2004) *Armed Groups: A Tier-One Security Priority*, Colorado: Institute for National Security Studies Occasional Paper 57.

State Department (2007) *Trafficking in Persons Report*, Washington, DC: US State Department.

Stedman, S.J. (1997) 'Spoiler problems in peace processes', *International Security* 22, 2: 5–53.

Sterling, C. (1994) *Thieves' World: The Threat of the New Global Network of Organized Crime*, New York: Simon and Schuster.

Thoumi, F. (2003) *Illegal Drugs, Economy and Society in the Andes*, Washington: Woodrow Wilson Center Press.

Volkov, V. (2002) *Violent Entrepreneurs: The Use of Force in the Making of Russian Capitalism*, Ithaca, NY: Cornell University Press.

Williams, P. and Woessner, P.N. (2001) 'Undercover operations and nuclear material trafficking', *International Atomic Energy Agency Proceedings of Conference on Nuclear Material Security*, Sweden.

Woodiwiss, M. (2001) *Organized Crime and American Power: A History*, Toronto: University of Toronto Press.

14

State failure and state building

Daniel Lambach and Tobias Debiel

For a few years, it has been *en vogue* to speak of failed and fragile states as threats to security (see, for example Mallaby 2002; Rotberg 2002). Western policymakers tend to emphasize the global-level dangers of state failure, while NGOs and representatives of developing countries highlight its impact at the regional, national, and local levels. Thus, it is imperative to ask 'whose security' (Baldwin 1997: 12) we are talking about.

For the purposes of this chapter, 'state failure' is defined as the inability of a state to provide security and public goods to its citizens; to collect taxes; and to formulate, implement and enforce policies and laws. It is acknowledged that the term 'state failure' can be somewhat misleading, since what is considered 'failure' can also be construed as an ongoing project of constructing patterns of political order that do not necessarily conform to Western notions of statehood. This semantic issue aside, state failure, however it is conceptualized, is a highly salient security issue on a number of levels.

In the following section, a definition of state failure and some theoretical background is provided. Subsequently, current trends of state failure and the results of research into its causes are presented. The third section details the security implications of state failure at the global, regional and national/local levels. The final section concludes by discussing the promises and shortcomings of state building as a strategy to overcome state fragility.

Old and new forms of statehood

Research on state failure requires a definition of statehood. Baker and Ausink provide a helpful definition that can serve as a stepping stone:

> We define state as a political entity that has legal jurisdiction and physical control over a defined territory, the authority to make collective decisions for a permanent population, a monopoly on the legitimate use of force, and a government that interacts or has the capacity to interact in formal relations with other such entities.
>
> (Baker and Ausink 1996: 4)

This definition represents an ideal-type understanding of consolidated statehood. However, it is quite clear that most states outside the industrialized countries of the OECD world (and even some of those countries) do not meet the above criteria. To describe this phenomenon, studies place states along a continuum of consolidated (strong), fragile (weak), failing, failed and collapsed statehood (or some variation thereof).

Research into state failure *sui generis* has only started fairly recently. When several fragile states, such as Liberia, Sierra Leone, Ethiopia, Cambodia or Haiti descended into long-lasting and brutal civil wars in the late 1980s and early 1990s, analysts were prompted to focus on the institutional settings that contributed to the outbreak of these conflicts. Quickly, the term 'failed state' (Helman and Ratner 1992) emerged to describe these polities. Since then, research into the topic has increased dramatically, fuelled not least by greater political interest since the terrorist attacks of 11 September 2001.

While the history of research into state failure is rather short, the history of state failure itself is anything but short. Even if one restricts oneself to post-colonial times, there are numerous instances of state failure that precede the end of the Cold War, from Congo-Kinshasa in the early 1960s to Uganda, Chad and Lebanon in the 1970s. The rather obvious point is that state failure was not an innovation of the 1990s. The less obvious point is that state failure has deep historical roots that have to be taken into account – the failure of Zaire in the 1990s cannot be understood without the collapse of the fledgling state in 1960. By viewing these crises in their historical context, it becomes possible not to portray them as 'breakdowns', but to focus on continuities and transformations. Thus, some authors even argue that what is seen as failure is in reality an ongoing process of state formation (Ayoob 1995).

There are other critiques of the concept that are worth mentioning. For instance, some authors have argued that the developmental state may to some degree be both weak and strong at the same time. Referring to Callaghy's (1987) concept of the 'lame leviathan', they juxtapose the state's substantial coercive apparatus with its general inability to provide public goods or to implement its policies. A situation in which the state is unable to extend its reach beyond urban core regions and to regulate social relations (Migdal 1988: 7) works rather well for the self-enrichment of politico-bureaucratic elites that have managed to 'capture' the state.

Another critique is that concepts of state failure and state formation inevitably share a more or less teleological outlook with the Weberian state as the 'natural' endpoint of post-colonial political development. This idea of the state is indeed very powerful among elites and ordinary citizens alike. Nevertheless, when this belief is used to inform policy, this results in a misguided attempt to recreate the Western state in a different environment and without regard to its historical roots. While state-building in Europe was a process spanning centuries, today's developing and transforming countries face the challenge of consolidating statehood within a much shorter period (Ayoob 1995). This pressure can easily lead to an overstretch of political, administrative and military capacities that frequently result in acute crises and an erosion of legitimacy. It also has to be acknowledged that modern statehood is based on a set of ideas about authority, such as the public–private distinction, that used to be quite specific to a handful of Western societies. While these ideas have begun to spread throughout the world, the fact is that political institutions, and the social and cultural foundations that they are built on, do not travel well (Fukuyama 2004). Hence, modernization-style approaches that attempt to 'build states' should be altered in favour of more agnostic ones that leave open the question of how societies provide order and governance. Only recently have analysts attempted to understand political order in 'failed states' not primarily in the sense of what is *not* there (the state), but of what actually *is* there (Clements et al. 2007).

Despite these theoretical shortcomings, state failure and state fragility are still useful concepts, because they direct attention to the role of political institutions. The next section shows how widespread this phenomenon is and looks at the causes of state failure.

Trends and correlates of state fragility

This section addresses two points. First it presents an overview of current datasets of state fragility. It then presents research into the causes of state failure.

Mapping state failure

Estimates on the number of fragile or failed states in the current international system vary widely. For instance, the *Economist* (2005) adopted a cautious approach, identifying just 20 'candidates for failure' based on World Bank data. The magazine highlighted the close correlation between state failure and conflict: fifteen of these 20 countries had experienced an armed conflict at some point since 1990. In contrast, the UK's Department for International Development produced a list of 46 countries that are home to 870 million people, i.e. 14 per cent of the world's population (DFID 2005, also Collier 2007).

A very recent and influential attempt to measure state failure and collapse is *The Failed States Index* (FSI), developed by the Fund for Peace, an independent research institute, together with the journal *Foreign Policy* (Fund for Peace 2005, 2008). The index is based on 12 social, economic, and political/military indicators relying on an analysis of events data gathered from media databases.[1] According to the FSI project, the problem of weak and failing states is far more serious than generally thought: the authors estimate that around two billion people live in insecure states, with varying degrees of vulnerability to widespread civil conflict.

This inconsistency in the classification of failed and fragile states has contributed to a dearth of knowledge about state failure. Since no one can agree on what a failed state is, very little is known about the similarities of these cases except for two things: (1) countries in sub-Saharan Africa are strongly over-represented in the sample, and (2) state failure and internal violence correlate closely. As to the first issue, state failure occurs in almost every region of the world. The 2008 ranking of the FSI includes such obvious candidates as Somalia, Sudan, Zimbabwe and Chad, but also countries such as Bangladesh (ranking 12th), Sri Lanka (20th) and Syria (35th). In spite of this geographical spread, sub-Saharan African countries dominate the list: among the ten countries most at risk, seven are located in Africa. Furthermore, most of the countries at the top of the ranking have experienced some form of large-scale internal violence in recent years. The University of Maryland's Peace and Conflict Project concludes: 'Seventy-seven percent of all international crises in the post-Cold War era (1990–2005) include one or more actors classified as unstable, fragile, or failed at the time of the crisis' (Hewitt et al. 2008: 17).

In addition to the characteristics of failed states, the lack of an agreed definition and solid data has also impeded the analysis of the causes of state failure. Nevertheless, there are findings that provide some insight into this question.

Correlates of and systemic perspectives on state failure

Due to the lack of a suitable dataset, there has been no large-N research into the causes of state failure. Thus, the current discussion frequently relies on results from what can be considered the next best thing: the work of the ill-named State Failure Task Force (SFTF). The SFTF was initiated in 1994 by then-US vice president Al Gore and is based at the University of Maryland. While the programme identified 136 events of state failure between 1955 and 1998, its concept of failure is far too broad: it defined state failure as 'serious political instability' including phenomena as diverse as genocides, disruptive regime changes, ethnic conflicts and revolutionary wars (State Failure Task Force Report 2003). Milliken and Krause rightly point out: 'This failure to distinguish conceptually the phenomena of state failure and collapse blurs the different processes that lead to functional failure or to institutional collapse, and obscures the relative rarity of full-blown state collapse' (Milliken and Krause 2002: 764f.).

However, due to the lack of better data, we may take the SFTF's results as a proxy for correlates of severe forms of state failure that are frequently accompanied by violence. In the Task Force's 'global model', regime type was the strongest predictor of imminent state failure. Strikingly, the authors found the odds of conflict and state failure to be seven times as high for partial democracies as they were for full democracies or autocracies. Other risk factors that roughly doubled the odds of state failure were low levels of material well-being, low trade openness and 'bad neighbourhood' effects such as the prevalence of armed conflicts in bordering countries.

Besides the global model, the SFTF also developed specific models, such as a regional model for sub-Saharan Africa. As with the global model, the strongest influence on the risk of state failure in Africa is regime type. Almost all the partial democracies failed within the first five years, and even in (apparently) full democracies, the probability of crisis was five times higher than it was for autocracies. This is particularly significant given that in sub-Saharan Africa, unlike other regions of the world, there has been a clear rise in the number of partial democracies over the past decade and a parallel decrease in the number of autocracies. Functioning democracies exist in some ten countries. In addition to the indicators identified in the global model, ethnic discrimination, unbalanced development (a high rate of urbanization with low per capita income) and leaders who are inexperienced or have remained too long in office are other risk factors in Africa. Finally, the adverse impact of 'bad neighbourhoods' is a powerful argument for including the international level in any analysis of the causes of conflict and state failure.

Collier (2007) has enumerated several possible causes for state failure that are, to a degree, self-reinforcing. Among his best-known concepts are the 'conflict trap' and the 'natural resource trap', but he also highlights the role of bad governance as well as geographical factors, such as access to the sea and the regional neighbourhood. He views these 'traps' as interlinked challenges and obstacles on the way to sustainable development.

Another argument is that internal conflicts contribute to state failure. This is in contrast to Tilly's well-known assertion about the European history of state formation, that 'war makes states' (Tilly 1985: 170). Since the mid-twentieth century, however, Tilly's claim does not seem to hold up any longer. In a radically changed international system, the internal wars waged in the global South from the 1950s to the 1990s have had the opposite effect, often contributing to state failure rather than to state-making. Herfried Münkler (2002: 18f.) considers these 'new wars', which he describes as depoliticized, brutal and complex, to be particularly destructive of state structures and as incomparable to Europe's 'state-making' wars of the late medieval and the modern period.

One key difference is that since 1945, the newly emerging states of the global South enjoyed a historically unprecedented level of protection (Jackson 1990). Thanks to the principles of self-determination and state sovereignty enshrined in international law, they were able to establish themselves as independent entities at the international level despite obvious deficits in their degree of state effectiveness. Once acquired, statehood was retained in perpetuity. During the Cold War, both sides were eager to shore up their respective clients via diplomatic, military and financial support. From this perspective, the brief surge in the number of civil wars and state failure events during the first half of the 1990s can be plausibly explained by the demise of the rivalry between the two super-powers. Without superpower support, repressive regimes in developing countries were abruptly confronted with massive demands for economic and political change and left without the resources to respond to these demands.

This discussion is important for this chapter in that some of the factors identified, such as the regional neighbourhood or internal conflicts, are intimately linked to security issues. As the next section shows, state failure per se is not as big a security threat as the various problems that arise out of it.

Security threats arising out of state fragility

State fragility causes different security threats at different levels. In the following, the global, regional and national levels will be addressed in turn.

The global level: failed states as the cause of transnational threats?

At the global level, the post-9/11 discourse links state failure to various kinds of immediate threats to international peace and stability. For instance, the 2002 National Security Strategy of the US posited that

> (t)he events of September 11, 2001, taught us that weak states, like Afghanistan, can pose as great a danger to our national interests as strong states. Poverty does not make poor people into terrorists and murderers. Yet poverty, weak institutions, and corruption can make weak states vulnerable to terrorist networks and drug cartels within their borders.
>
> (NSS 2002: Foreword)

In a similar manner, the European Security Strategy, adopted by the EU Heads of State in December 2003, identified state failure as one of five key threats to European security: 'Collapse of the State can be associated with obvious threats, such as organised crime or terrorism. State failure is an alarming phenomenon that undermines global governance and adds to regional instability' (Solana 2003: 4).

These statements betray an understanding of state fragility as a root cause or a facilitating condition for other, more immediate threats to Western/international security like terrorism, organized crime, refugee flows, migration and human trafficking. Even though all of these issues have by now entered the security discourse (see, e.g. Loescher and Milner 2004), terrorism is still the single most important issue, both at a discursive level as well as from the perspective of traditional concepts of national security.

At first glance, failed states seem to offer favourable conditions for the activities of transnational terrorist networks since the lack of state control opens up spaces where shadowy groups can operate undisturbed. However, recent research demonstrates that there is no generalizable impact of state failure on terrorism, regardless of whether terrorist incidents (Newman 2007), the presence of terrorist bases, or recruitment patterns (Simons and Tucker 2007) were used as the dependent variable. There are several reasons why the expected relationship cannot be confirmed empirically. First, most activities of terrorist groups are not made easier by state failure. For instance, communications, logistics and planning are much easier to conduct in places with the necessary infrastructure. Second, maintaining bases in failed states changes the internal logic of terrorist groups, necessitating the exercise of territorial control. Third, operating in 'ungoverned areas' means that terrorists have to become involved in local politics in order to guarantee their own security and their ability to operate.

However, while no general correlation between state failure and terrorism can be upheld, some researchers are approaching the problem in different ways. Korteweg and Ehrhardt (2006) take a very promising approach by looking at sub-national 'sanctuaries' rather than host states as a whole. They find that these sanctuaries (1) are characterized by a low level of governmental control and (2) offer comparative advantages to terrorist groups. Contributing factors to the latter condition include the presence of sympathetic ethnic/religious groups, a legacy of civil conflict, difficult geography, economic opportunities for the terrorist actors, economic grievances of the population and regional stimuli. Piazza (2007) takes a different approach by focusing his investigation on 19 Middle Eastern states between 1972 and 2003. While he retains a national-level perspective, his regression analysis shows that episodes of political instability contributed to terrorist activities in this area.

These studies move research into new directions and offer new insights into the relationship between statehood and terrorism, even though their results still have to be subjected to further empirical research. In addition to including sub-national and regional factors, a clearer focus on *transnational* terrorist actors would also be a useful modification to the research framework since these, with al-Qaida in particular, are of greatest interest to Western states.

Regional-level issues: escalation of conflict and refugees

The impact of failing states on the region can be generally divided into military, social and economic factors (Lambach 2007). In the military dimension, conflict can escalate by drawing in actors from neighbouring countries as well as by rebels seeking out sanctuary and constructing bases across the border, with or without the agreement of that country's government. Rarely can violent conflict that arises out of a state's failure be truly contained within its country of origin. On a social level, people, especially those living near the border, intensify their cross-border contacts when the state is weakening. When the state fails, refugees follow these links of solidarity to neighbouring countries. Refugee populations represent a tremendous social and economic burden for their host state, and in some cases, a security risk as well, by engaging in political or militant activity and by contributing to small arms proliferation. Finally, in the economic dimension, failing states often become hubs of a transnational shadow economy where drugs, guns and other illicit goods are traded. They also negatively affect neighbouring countries' growth rates by scaring away investors, disrupting trade routes and forcing neighbours to increase their military expenditures (Chauvet and Collier 2004).

While state failure is an internally driven process, it is embedded in its regional context. Where several neighbouring states are failing, their fates can become interlinked in a way that is comparable to what Rubin (2002) has called 'regional conflict formations'. Thus, the regional clustering of failing states, as seen in parts of West Africa during the 1990s, is neither the result of pure chance, nor is it specific to these particular countries. Instead, it is a systemic property emerging from the transnational interactions among processes of state failure.

Local/national-level issues: the human and economic costs of state failure

There are no specific estimates on the economic costs of state failure. However, using the quite similar World Bank concept of Low Income Countries Under Stress (LICUS), Collier and Hoeffler (2004) develop a model to gauge the social and economic costs incurred by a LICUS experiencing violent conflict. Their estimates are based on loss of economic growth, civilian opportunity costs of military expenditure and the impact of war on public health. For an average LICUS, the overall costs of armed conflict amount to US$29bn. Including the damage to neighbouring countries, the average overall cost of a single civil war adds up to US$64bn. Based on a comparable statistical model, Chauvet and Collier (2004: 3f.) found 'that LICUS status typically reduces the annual growth rate of peacetime economies by 2.3 percentage points relative to other developing economies'. This substantially diminishes the chance of beginning a sustainable turnaround, so that 'the typical LICUS is likely to stay in that state for decades'. Over the long-term, this amounts to a total loss of 4.6 times the initial GDP. This clearly shows that state fragility, armed conflict and poverty interact in complex and mutually reinforcing ways.

The negative impact of fragile statehood on development is unequivocal. But it is more than an economic burden on national economies. At a local level, vulnerable groups within fragile states will suffer from a decline of human security, defined here as the protection of 'people from critical (severe) and pervasive (widespread) threats and situations' (Commission on Human Security 2003: 4). Taking the core indicators of the Millennium Development Goals (MDGs) as a guideline, research has consistently shown that human insecurity is widespread within fragile states (Chauvet and Collier 2004). According to the DFID, child mortality is twice as high and maternal mortality actually is three times greater in fragile states than in other Low Income Countries with better institutional performance. Around one-third of the population is malnourished, and a higher proportion of the population suffers from malaria (DFID 2005: 9). De facto, the MDGs are unachievable for these countries.

Conclusion: state-building – the new panacea?

This chapter has sought to outline the various ways in which failed states can be considered a security threat. To this end, we first presented our understanding of state failure and presented some of the correlates and causes of this phenomenon. We then discussed the implications of state failure for various referents of security at the global, the regional and the national/local level. It should have become clear that failed states represent a different security threat for more remote countries than they do for neighbouring countries or for their own populations. Nevertheless, it is also obvious they are a security threat to all of these diverse referents. Hence, there should be a joint interest in developed and developing countries alike to prevent state failure or to alleviate its repercussions.

The main strategy that has been proposed as both a reactive and a preventive instrument is 'state-building' (Fukuyama 2004), which combines elements of security and development policy. This is underscored by the recent policy focus on the security–development nexus and a commitment by the international donor community to 'stay engaged, but differently' under conditions of state failure (Debiel and Ottaway 2007). For a long time, 'state-building' was understood as a historical process of state formation, exemplified by the development of the state as a distinctive mode of political organization in European history. In the 1950s and 1960s, modernization theory posited that post-colonial countries would undergo a similar process of state- and nation-building. However, the post-colonial state turned out to be plagued by weak institutions, and several newly independent countries succumbed to internal turmoil. In many others, democratic systems were supplanted by authoritarian ones.

Political actors have revitalized the state-building approach in recent years in light of experiences with state failure and internal war in Somalia, Rwanda, Cambodia, Bosnia-Herzegovina, Afghanistan and many other cases. However, the similarities between the old and the new approaches are limited. A major difference lies in the role that the strategies attribute to external actors. Whereas earlier concepts assumed that state-building was a 'natural' process that would simply run its course once the colonizing powers had withdrawn, 'state-building' as it is now understood virtually demands external intervention, although theorists differ as to whether outside actors can 'build states', or whether they can only support endogenous processes of state-building.

The particular appeal of the state-building framework is the possibility of integrating development measures with security and crisis prevention concerns (UK Prime Minister's Strategy Unit 2005). Development, security and crisis prevention experts agree that strengthening state institutions is an important goal when dealing with an unstable country. However, this potential has yet to be realized in practice. In post-conflict countries (where the international community is usually the most active), state-building too often still takes a back seat to holding elections, introducing free markets and providing social services. In countries like Afghanistan, 'fighting terrorists' is accorded a higher priority than putting the state on a stable footing.

Present efforts at post-conflict state-building are also hampered by overly ambitious reform agendas. Even in the best of circumstances, outside actors simply cannot transform a society to the degree that the architects of these missions envision. Marina Ottaway rightly points out the problems with such an activist approach: 'The model chosen by the international community is a short-cut to the Weberian state, an attempt to develop such an entity quickly and without the long, conflictual and often brutal evolution that historically underlies the formation of states' (Ottaway 2002: 1004). It is quite obvious that current state-building strategies have not yet shed the optimistic belief in social engineering they inherited from modernization theory.

These strategies also overlook the deeply political nature of the reforms they advocate. Political institutions cannot be easily transplanted from one country to another. Therefore, state-building has to consider how these institutions are embedded in society. Similar to Putzel's (1999) argument that lack of congruence between democratic, formal and informal institutions is an impediment to democratization, we argue that the institutions that make up the formal state have to be aligned with societal institutions if they are to be sustainable and effective.

Therefore, we would advocate an approach that takes the local context into account to a much greater degree, which we refer to as 'embedded state-building' (Debiel and Lambach

2008). This approach still focuses on increasing the institutional capacity of the state, yet it also emphasizes that reforms have to be aligned with local structures and resonate with local interests. Embedded state-building is informed by the view that sustainable state-building can only take place where there is congruence between formal and informal institutions and between external and domestic interests. In the end, this necessitates a more humble approach by outside actors: they cannot 'build' states in a purposive manner, but should instead try to find indigenous processes of state formation that they can support. A state that is developed in this way is more embedded in society, and thus much more sustainable.

Note

1 Most recently, the Brookings Institution has published an *Index of Weak States in the Developing World*, which works with a set of 20 indicators that are used as proxies for core aspects of state functions in four dimensions: economic, political, security and social welfare. For more detailed information, see Rice and Patrick (2008).

References

Ayoob, M. (1995) *The Third World Security Predicament: State Making, Regional Conflict, and the International System*, Boulder/London: Lynne Rienner.
Baker, P.H. and Ausink, J. (1996) 'State collapse and ethnic violence: Toward a predictive model', *Parameters* 26, 1: 19–31.
Baldwin, D.A. (1997) 'The concept of security', *Review of International Studies* 23, 1: 5–26.
Callaghy, T. (1987) 'The state as lame leviathan: The patrimonial administrative state in Africa', in Ergas, Z. (ed.) *The African State in Transition*, Houndmills: Macmillan, pp. 87–116.
Chauvet, L. and Collier, P. (2004) *Development Effectiveness in Fragile States: Spillovers and Turnarounds*, Oxford: Centre for the Study of African Economies, January 2004. Available online at: www.oecd.org/dataoecd/32/59/34255628.pdf (accessed 2 October 2008).
Clements, K.P., Boege, V., Brown, A., Foley, W. and Nolan, A. (2007) 'State building reconsidered: The role of hybridity in the formation of political order', *Political Science* 59, 1: 45–56.
Collier, P. (2007) *The Bottom Billion: Why the Poorest Countries are Failing and What Can Be Done About It*, Oxford: Oxford University Press.
Collier, P. and Hoeffler, A. (2004) *The Challenge of Reducing the Global Incidence of Civil War*, Oxford University: Centre for the Study of African Economies. Available online at: www.copenhagenconsensus.com/Files/Filer/CC/Papers/Conflicts_230404.pdf (accessed 2 October 2008).
Commission on Human Security (2003) *Human Security Now: Protecting and Empowering People*, New York, Oxford.
Debiel, T. and Lambach, D. (2008) 'From "Aid conditionality" to "engaging differently": How development policy tries to cope with fragile states', *Journal für Entwicklungspolitik/Journal for Development Policy* 23, 4: 80–99.
Debiel, T. and Ottaway, M. (2007) 'Stay engaged – Yes, but how? Summary of discussions', in InWEnt (ed.) *Stay Engaged! Fragile States and Weak Governance: A Development Policy Challenge*, Conference Report, InWEnt and BMZ (Federal Ministry for Economic Cooperation and Development), 30 November – 1 December 2006, Bonn, pp. 53–58.
Department for International Development (DFID) (2005) *Why We Need to Work More Effectively in Fragile States*, London: Department for International Development. Available online at: www.dfid.gov.uk/pubs/files/fragilestates-paper.pdf (accessed 2 October 2008).
Economist (2005) 'From chaos, order: Rebuilding failed states', *The Economist*, 3 March 2005.
——(2008) 'The failed states index 2008', *Foreign Policy*, Issue 197, pp. 64–68.

Fukuyama, F. (2004) *State-Building: Governance and World Order in the 21st Century*, Ithaca, NY: Cornell University Press.

Fund for Peace (2005) 'The state failure index 2005', *Foreign Policy* Issue 149, pp. 56–65.

Helman, G.B. and Ratner, S.B. (1992) 'Saving failed states', *Foreign Policy* 89: 3–20.

Hewitt, J.J., Wilkenfeld, J. and Gurr, T.R. (2008) 'Peace and conflict 2008: Executive summary'. College Park, MD: University of Maryland. Available online at: www.cidcm.umd.edu/projects/project.asp?id=32 (accessed 2 October 2008).

Jackson, R. (1990) *Quasi-States: Sovereignty, International Relations and the Third World*, Cambridge: Cambridge University Press.

Korteweg, R. and Ehrhardt, D. (2006) *Terrorist Black Holes: A Study into Terrorist Sanctuaries and Governmental Weakness*, 2nd edition, The Hague: Clingendael Institute for Strategic Studies.

Lambach, D. (2007) 'Close encounters in the third dimension: The regional effects of state failure', in Lambach, D. and Debiel, T. (eds) *State Failure Revisited I: Globalization of Security and Neighborhood Effects*, Duisburg: INEF-Report No. 87/2007, pp. 32–52.

Lambach, D. and Debiel, T. (eds) (2007) *State Failure Revisited I: Globalization of Security and Neighborhood Effects*, Duisburg: INEF-Report No. 87/2007.

Loescher, G. and Milner, J. (2004) 'Protracted refugee situations and state and regional insecurity', *Conflict, Security and Development* 4, 1: 3–20.

Mallaby, S. (2002) 'The reluctant imperialist: Terrorism, failed states, and the case for American empire', *Foreign Affairs* 81, 2: 2–7.

Migdal, J.S. (1988) *Strong Societies and Weak States: State-Society Relations and State Capabilities in the Third World*, Princeton, NJ: Princeton University Press.

Milliken, J. and Krause, K. (2002) 'State failure, state collapse, and state reconstruction: Concepts, lessons and strategies', *Development and Change* 33, 5: 753–74.

Münkler, H. (2002) *Die neuen Kriege* [The New Wars], Reinbek: Rowohlt.

NSS (2002) *National Security Strategy of the United States of America*, Washington, September 2002.

Newman, E. (2007) 'Weak states, state failure and terrorism', *Terrorism and Political Violence* 19, 4: 463–88.

Ottaway, M. (2002) 'Rebuilding state institutions in collapsed states', *Development and Change* 33, 5: 1001–23.

Piazza, J.A. (2007) 'Draining the swamp: Democracy promotion, state failure, and terrorism in 19 Middle Eastern countries', *Studies in Conflict and Terrorism* 30, 6: 521–39.

Putzel, J. (1999) 'Survival of an imperfect democracy in the Philippines', *Democratization* 6, 1: 198–223.

Rice, S.E. and Patrick, S. (2008) *Index of Weak States in the Developing World*, Brookings Institution. Washington: The Brookings Institution. Online. Available online at: www.brookings.edu/reports/2008/02_weak_states_index.aspx (accessed 2 October 2008).

Rotberg, R.I. (2002) 'Failed states in a world of terror', *Foreign Affairs* 81, 4: 127–40.

Rubin, B.R. (2002) *Blood on the Doorstep: The Politics of Preventive Action*, Washington, DC: Century Foundation Press.

Simons, A. and Tucker, D. (2007) 'The misleading problem of failed states: A "socio-geography" of terrorism in the post-9/11 era', *Third World Quarterly* 28, 2: 387–401.

Solana, J. (2003) *A Secure Europe in a Better World: European Security Strategy*, Document adopted by the Heads of State and Government at the European Council in Brussels on 12 December 2003, Paris: Institute for Security Studies.

State Failure Task Force (2003) *State Failure Task Force Report: Phase III Findings*, College Park, MD: University of Maryland, Center for International Development & Conflict Management. Available online at: www.cidcm.umd.edu/inscr/stfail/SFTF%20Phase%20III%20Report%20Final.pdf (accessed 2 October 2008).

Tilly, C. (1985) 'War-making and state-making as organized crime', in Evans, P.B., Rueschmeyer, D. and Skocpol, T. (eds) *Bringing the State Back in*, Cambridge: Cambridge University Press, pp. 169–91.

UK Prime Minister's Strategy Unit (2005) *Investing in Prevention: An International Strategy to Manage Risks of Instability and Improve Crisis Response*, London: Cabinet Office. Available online at: www.strategy.gov.uk/downloads/work_areas/countries_at_risk/cri_report.pdf (accessed 2 October 2008).

15

Migration and security

Jef Huysmans and Vicki Squire

Migration emerged as a security issue in a context marked both by the geopolitical dislocation associated with the end of the Cold War and also by wider social and political shifts associated with globalization. As such, current debates surrounding migration and security reflect changes both in the nature of migration and in the nature of thinking about migration. While it was previously considered to be a social and economic phenomenon belonging to the fields of socio-economic history, historical sociology and anthropology, migration is now pivotal in debates surrounding global politics (Castles and Davidson 2000; Castles and Miller 1993; Sassen 1996; Sayad 1999: 303–413; Soysal 1994). This is evident in its introduction to the expanding field of Security Studies, which has found in migration a means to develop an alternative narrative in a context where the fall of the Iron Curtain and the break up of the Soviet Union had destabilized its dominant script.[1]

As a sub-discipline of IR largely oriented towards the US and Europe, Security Studies fell into a crisis after 1989–91 (Bigo 1995), resulting in the introduction of various 'new' insecurities into the field of analysis. Indeed, the increasing use of the term 'security studies' was itself instrumental in opening up the military-focused bipolar security agenda to include new areas of study (Buzan 1984, 1991; Buzan et al. 1998; Haftendorn 1991; Tickner 1995). In this context, the cross-border movement of people was a key issue that moved into the sphere of Security Studies (e.g. Heisbourg 1991; International Institute for Strategic Studies 1991; Loescher 1992; Widgren 1990). However, migration opened up a contested terrain within Security Studies that this chapter explores further (Bigo 2002; Ceyhan and Tsoukala 1997; Guild and van Selm 2005; Huysmans 2002, 2006; Newman and van Selm 2003; Wæver et al. 1993). To what extent can migration be conceived of as security issue in the strategic sense that marks the conception of security prevalent in IR and among traditional Security Studies analysts? What kind of insecurities does migration raise, and for whom or what? What is the impact of framing migration in terms of security, and what alternative frames of reference might be used? How can a critical political analysis of mobility be developed out of the nexus of migration and security?

In charting the multitude of answers to such questions, this chapter draws attention to the complexity of current debates surrounding migration and security. The first section shows how the analysis of the migration–security nexus has been approached both from a traditional strategic perspective through a focus on the security of the state and from a human security perspective through a focus on the security of individual migrants. Drawing attention to the normative dilemmas posed by the framing of migration as a security issue, it concludes by drawing attention to the critical importance of conceptually re-framing the relation between migration and security. This feeds into the second section, which charts a diverse body of critical work in which security is conceived of as a knowledge, discourse, technology, or practice that mediates the relation between the social processes of human mobility and the search for governmental control and steering capacity over them. Considering how this body of work can be developed in terms that open up the migration–security nexus to a richer analysis of the relation between mobility and politics, the final section claims that security questions should not be allowed to dominate the terrain of migration, but should be examined in relation to a range of political and socio-economic questions.

Analysing the migration–security nexus

The migration–security nexus can be broadly viewed from two different directions: from a Security Studies perspective and from a Migration Studies perspective. This renders the field highly differentiated and contested, because it is structured according to divergent research agendas. Indeed, the fields of Security Studies and Migration Studies are themselves complex and multi-faceted. Within Security Studies, security can either be approached in strategic terms as a value or condition to be achieved, or it can be approached in critical terms as a knowledge, discourse, technology or practice. Within Migration Studies, migration can refer relatively narrowly to economic migration, or it can be approached more broadly to incorporate forced migration, thus bringing refugee studies and Labour Migration Studies into a broader field of research. This suggests that the very meaning of the concepts of migration and security are highly contested, and are used to identify various practices that articulate different rationales.

While we primarily approach the nexus of migration and security from a Security Studies angle in this chapter, we also draw attention to key developments in the broad field of Migration Studies that underscore this nexus. Specifically, we show how analysts from both Migration Studies and Security Studies tend to approach the migration–security nexus in traditional terms by conceptualizing security as a value to be achieved. The first part shows how this approach is developed in strategic terms through a focus on the security of the state, or in humanitarian terms through a focus on human security. Challenging these traditional approaches in terms of their failure to challenge exclusionary debates and practices in the global North, where migration is largely seen as 'threatening' if it is not carefully managed, the final part closes by making the case for a critical re-framing of migration and security.

Strategic and humanitarian approaches to the migration–security nexus

Many of the leading works introducing migration into the area of Security Studies have done so by defining migration as a central dimension of a rounded security agenda. Thus, it has been argued that migration needs to be factored into the calculations of national security strategy, and that national security needs to be factored into the calculations of migration policy (Koslowski 1998; Rudolph 2006). Such strategic approaches treat security as a value or condition that is affected by migration and, thus, by state policies to manage such movements of people. In this regard, they have been important in giving Migration Studies greater legitimacy within the US mainstream of IR and strategic studies (e.g. Choucri 2002; Weiner 1992/93).

These strategic analyses draw attention to the relevance of migration for Security Studies in two key ways. First, they calculate the extent to which migratory and demographic developments bear upon national security questions (Choucri 2002; Heisbourg 1991; Loescher 1992). Such considerations range from fears of refugees becoming violent political actors (Loescher 1992) to the effect of migration on social cohesion and the availability of a sufficient work force (Rudolph 2006). In this regard, scholars at the nexus of security and migration have opened up the area of Migration Studies beyond its classical economic focus on the state's selection of migrants (e.g. Constant and Zimmerman 2005). This has contributed to a wider process in which Migration Studies and refugee studies have begun to overlap.

Second, strategic analysts draw attention to the relevance of migration for Security Studies by showing how security concerns affect a state's migration policies (Loescher 1992; Rudolph 2006; Vernez 1996; Weiner 1995, 1992/93). In particular, such analyses focus on formulating general laws about how migration movements constrain or influence security policy, and vice versa. For example, it has been argued that: 'as geopolitical threats increase, policies regarding international labour mobility (migration) should become relatively more open in order to facilitate the production of wealth to support defense' (Rudolph 2006: 31). Although migration (or at least certain forms of migration) is often defined as 'threatening' national security, strategic analysts who approach security as a value or condition to aspire to have also made the case for less restrictive migration policies using security as a frame of reference.

In contrast to strategic analyses of migration and security, analysts of human security focus attention on the security of the individual rather than that of the state. This entails both a pragmatic and a normative or ethical dimension. In pragmatic terms, the emphasis on human security over state security can be understood as increasingly necessary in a context where political concerns regarding security and migration have shifted beyond the state to the transnational or global level. Such a shift is evident, for example, in the EU's commitment to a Global Approach to Migration (European Council 2005). In normative or ethical terms, a focus on human security signals a shift away from the state as the subject of security, and brings into view the security of humans who migrate. Such a focus largely entails a humanitarian approach, which has been re-affirmed in relation to refugees and asylum seekers (Nadig 2002), as well as in relation to the trafficking of (primarily women and children) migrants (Clark 2003).

Despite its widespread pragmatic and normative appeal, a focus on human security is of limited effect in radically re-framing migration. Human security is largely incorporated as a dimension that is internal to global migration management, and thus scholars from this school of thinking incur little risk beyond pragmatic intellectual exercises within the strategic frame of state security (Koser 2005). Even if we take the state out of the picture, human security remains caught within a framework that entails highly selective operations that effectively exclude those migrants that move between states within regions such as Europe, North America and Australasia. This is evident, for example, in the growing linkage between migration and development, which is largely oriented towards a security and migration control framework rather than a development framework (see Samers 2004; Lavenex and Kunz 2008). It can similarly be seen in relation to humanitarian intervention, which brings a commitment to human security in line with state security (Liotta 2002).

Notwithstanding these limitations, some analysts have made a pragmatic case for human security and humanitarianism in the attempt to ensure that liberal democratic states move 'closer to realizing the values they claim to live by now' (Gibney 2004: 260). A pragmatic humanitarianism may be critical as a normative or ethical approach that holds the liberal democratic state to account in the face of excessively restrictive migration controls. However, it is less critical as a political approach. Humanitarianism is essentially concerned with the protection of vulnerable populations and with redressing harmful practices, and in this regard, it tends to approach the migrant as a disempowered victim rather than as a political actor. In this regard, pragmatic humanitarians fail to move beyond a security frame in which 'undesirable' migrants are either politicized as 'threatening' subjects or de-politicized as 'vulnerable' subjects (see Aradau 2004a, 2008; Nyers 2005; Squire 2009).

Normative dilemmas and the migration–security nexus

Strategic and human security approaches to the migration–security nexus are problematic in terms of their potential reification of migration as a 'threat'. By approaching security as a value or a condition to aspire to, analysts from these approaches tend to assume that migration policy can be developed in terms that increase the security of states, in terms that increase the security of migrants, or in terms that increase the security of both states and migrants. In so doing, they bring free movement firmly into the field of security, thus consolidating the articulation of migration as a security 'threat' (Huysmans 1995). This clearly does not signal the definition of all migrants as 'threatening', but rather it legitimizes exclusionary distinctions that have become widespread across Europe, North America and Australasia in terms that identify 'undesirables' such as 'illegal immigrants' and 'asylum seekers' as necessitating intensified controls (Squire 2009). Both strategic and human security approaches thus potentially consolidate what Critical Security Studies scholars have defined as the securitization of migration or free movement (Bigo 2000, 2002, 2005; Huysmans 2006; van Munster 2009).

For this reason, strategic and human security approaches are limited in terms of their ability to open up the intellectual terrain at the nexus of security and migration in all its sociological, political and normative richness (Huysmans 2006). Strategic approaches not only eliminate from the security field the normative questions of how securitizing migration produces exclusion, violence and inequality; they also reduce the political and social complexity of migration to the strategic interaction between states. Migration becomes a factor in the calculation of power and national security of states (e.g. as an economic resource or as a cultural factor affecting social cohesion). Human security approaches open up normative questions and shift attention beyond the state, but do not go far enough in considering how framing migration in terms of two conflicting security claims – human versus national security – produces particular effects in terms of the assemblage of relations between people and in terms of the struggle for professional and political legitimacy. These questions require a critical and political analysis of the social processes that the linkage of migration and security entails.

Critical analyses of the migration–security nexus

One way in which a political sociological approach to the migration–security nexus can be developed is in the analysis of the effects that the political framing of migration as a threat has on public perception and opinion formation. Over recent years, public opinion regarding migration in many countries within the global North has become hostile toward 'asylum seekers' and 'illegal migrants'. An analysis of the discrepancy between perceptions of migration and the objective threat that migration poses, and an analysis of interrelation of threat perceptions of migration in the political elite and the wider public is of political interest in this regard (Lahav 2004). However, a cognitive approach underplays the social materiality of the securitizing processes – security seems to exist primarily in the mind. This requires a more critical analysis of the circulation of discourses; the application of technologies; the development of legal categories and questions of form-filling, professional routines and training that construct, sustain and constitute migration as a security 'threat'. A continuous and intensive circulation of discourses of immigration 'floods', for example, can change the dominant language through which migration is approached. Such changes usually go together with changes in institutional locations of migration policy. A language that employs metaphors such as 'floods' legitimates a stronger focus on border controls and a more crucial position of border police, as compared to employers interests for example. What matters here is not so much what people believe, but the nature and the available palette of languages that ordinary people, policymakers and professional organizations can draw upon when speaking about migration, as well as the skills and knowledge that border police bring to the management of migration as compared to the skills and knowledge of employer organizations and unions. It is here that Critical Security Studies opens up the analysis of the migration–security nexus to all its political and social richness, while at the same time maintaining a critical distance from objectivist accounts in which 'undesirable' migrants are identified as 'threatening'. Rather than a value or a fact, security becomes a language and/or an interest, knowledge, or professional skill linked to particular organizations, and is always shaped in relation to other languages, actors and practices that contest it.

Critical Security Studies scholars have developed various distinctly political analyses of the social processes that are constitutive of the migration–security nexus. Approaching security as a practice or frame of domination and/or exclusion, such analysts have examined various sites, agencies and technologies at the intersection of migration and security. Important sites in this regard are camps in which migrants are detained (Le Cour Grandmaison et al. 2007; Nyers and Moulins 2007; Perera 2002; Puggioni 2006) and border areas through which migrants pass, such as airports, embassies and customs (Bigo and Guild 2005; Bigo 1996b; Salter 2008; Muller 2005). In terms of agencies, critical analysts look at the increasing role of security professionals, including private agencies, in the regulation of movement (Bigo 1996a; Guiraudon 2000, 2003). They also examine various security technologies employed in the regulation of migration, such as visas, asylum procedures and surveillance (Bigo and Guild 2005; Lewis 2005; Lyon 2005; Salter 2003).

All of these approaches share the idea that security practice is a specific strategy or technique of (de-) politicizing and governing migration. In analysing the politics of insecurity, critical security analysts examine the struggles over the legitimacy of specific methods of governing the migration area (e.g. storing finger prints in police databases versus privacy rights) and the legitimizing effects that can be derived from using security language in politics (e.g. evoking terrorism and asylum abuse as political justification for unpopular security measures in airports). Such analysts focus on the precise nature and effects of using security instruments, knowledge and discourses in the area of migration (Aradau 2008; Huysmans 2006), as well as on the institutions sustaining the process (e.g.

Pilkington 1998). The presence of security policies in the migration area are thus explained both by the political use of security language in the migration field (Wæver et al. 1993) and by the use of references to migration-related issues in security debates like counter-terrorism (Huysmans and Buonfino 2008); as well as by the presence and relative power of security professionals and experts in a policy field (Bigo 1996a, 2002; Boswell 2007; Guiraudon 2000, 2003); and by the transfer of security practices between different policy areas, such as policing football hooligans and migration (Tsoukala 2004). In undertaking such analyses, critical scholars of the migration–security nexus highlight the exclusionary and violent effects of security practices on particular groups of migrants (Guild 2002, 2003; Le Cour Grandmaison et al. 2007; Walters 2002a, 2002b). In addition, they examine the political effects of profiling and surveillance techniques of mobile people, like finger-printing, data storage and mining, camps, visas, passports, etc. (Bigo 1996b; Bigo and Guild 2003, 2005; Bonditti 2004; Huysmans 2006; Walters 2002a, 2002b), while focusing attention on the exclusionary re-articulation of borders and identity (Epstein 2007).

Moving beyond the migration–security nexus

Critical Security Studies scholars have opened up a range of challenging questions that are important to the analysis of the migration–security nexus: What is the effect of framing social and political relations by means of security practice on the assembling of relations between people? What is the leverage of security discourse, technology, knowledge and practice in struggles for political and professional legitimacy? The focus on these questions signals a radically different conception of security (and insecurity) from that outlined in the first section, namely one in which security is conceived of less as a value to aspire to as it is conceived of as a *constitutive mediator* of the relation between mobility and politics. Rather than conceptualizing security in terms of an expression of the dangers that human mobility is perceived to pose, critical analysts thus conceive security as having various meanings and as constituting social and political techniques of governance that effectively shape human mobility. For example, framing female migrants as victims of human trafficking places their migration firmly in a criminalized context that reinforces exclusionary practices and underplays the impact of economic develop-ments, personal ambitions and family relations (Andrijasevic 2004, forthcoming). This brings to the fore the normative nature of writing security, where security knowledge easily slips into a securitizing knowledge. By borrowing the language of human traffick-ing, developing crime statistics that differentiate between immigrants and the native population, or presenting security as a choice between individual rights and national security, security knowledge sustains the idea that migration is a question of insecurity, which tends to radicalize exclusions and legitimize violence.

The issue of migration has brought to the fore questions as to whether or not, and how, an issue should be securitized. In this regard, one of the most important questions is whether it is possible to perform Security Studies without contributing to the process of securitization (Huysmans 2002). This has led to significant debates surrounding the de-securitization of issues such as migration (Wæver 1995; Huysmans 1998; Aradau 2004b). A critical way in which the reification of migration as a security 'threat' can be moder-ated, in this context, is to place the question of security practice within an agenda that researches the political nature of mobility. Security then becomes one of several issues that affects, shapes and constrains mobility, rather than being the central focus. This can be conceptualized as a critical political sociology or as critical political theory of the migration–security nexus.

There are various ways in which this critical approach can be developed. We will mention two of the many possibilities. First, it can be conceived of in terms of an analysis of the ways in which exclusionary techniques of governing remove the political agency of specific migrants (for example, by approaching migrants as victims requiring 'treatment' rather than as autonomous people making specific claims about their rights, ambitions and/or equal standing as human beings). Rather than focusing mainly on security, the question of how to reinsert political agency into the analysis becomes the key question, while security enters as a method of governing that affects the constitution, or more likely the destitution, of political agency (Nyers 2006; Aradau 2008; Neocleous 2008). This is more in line with a rights-based approach, which has been posed as an alternative to a security-oriented approach in relation to forced migration (Goodwin-Gill 2001); trafficking (Jordan 2002); and 'illegal immigration' (Cholenewski 2000). However, rather than focusing on the inherent rights of individuals, critical analysts have shown how mobility can serve as a mode of 'becoming political' in a context of global inequality (see Chimni 2000; Jordan and Duvell 2002). Analysts of migration and security have moved in this direction in recent years by considering how citizenship claims that are 'mis-placed' according to the exclusionary and de-politicizing frame of security entail a mobile form of political agency (Andrijasevic forthcoming; McNevin 2006; Nyers and Moulin 2007; Nyers 2008; Squire 2009).

A second example of how the migration–security nexus can be opened to a wider political analysis is to introduce the question of violence and its political legitimacy. Refugees fighting the government in their country of origin from abroad or the violence exercised upon the body of migrants would then not be reduced to a question of trading off human security against national security. Instead of security, the political nature of violence takes the foreground. For example, what does the exercise of violence against the body of refugees, i.e. in detention centres, and the resisting violence the latter impose upon their own bodies, i.e. by sewing lips and eyes or attempting suicide, tell us about the nature of the modern state and international politics and the political role of violence in it? (Edkins 2000; Edkins and Pin-Fat 2004, 2005; Le Cour Grandmaison et al. 2007; Nyers 2006: 97–122). What is important in each of these approaches is that security is not the central focus of analysis, but it is seen as one of the techniques at play in a larger setting. In this regard, security or securitization is not presumed to be central to the analysis of migration or mobility (see Boswell 2007). Rather, the central focus concerns the wider political questions that are articulated in relation to mobility and migration policies.

Conclusion

Addressing security in relation to conceptions of political agency, the legitimacy of violence, various technologies of inclusion and exclusion, and the struggle over conceptions of citizenship is an important move in ensuring that security does not do the unifying work in the analysis. Instead of focusing on security threats or the processes of securitization, the analysis places securitizing practices within a wider analysis of practices of citizenship, violence or political agencies. Security is a particular practice, concern and technique that always operates in relation to other political issues. Hence, political research on the migration–security nexus requires an understanding of how security practice operates within a political field where various approaches to human mobility are contested and how it bears upon struggles over the definition of (legitimate) political agency, the role of violence, competing conceptions of justice, etc. Such a reading of the migration–security nexus, undertaken in much of the critical work on migration and security, shifts the research away from simply refining our understanding of the security dimensions of migration and the nature of securitizing mobility. It embeds securitizing processes in social and societal negotiations of central political questions, which are rarely engaged exclusively in security terms. Instead of reaffirming assumptions regarding the 'threat' posed by migration to states or to individual migrants (section 1), and instead of remaining caught within the frame of security (section 2), a critical political theory or sociology of migration and security will therefore analyse security as a distinctly problematic mediator of the relationship between mobility and politics.

Note

1 Our presentation starts from developments in Security Studies in IR. Analysts from disciplines such as sociology, anthropology, criminology and social history have studied aspects of the nexus between migration and security, independent of the focus on migration that emerged in Security Studies towards the end of the twentieth century. The importance of this point is not that Security Studies in IR comes late to these issues, but rather to be clear on the disciplinary angle that informs our overview. Given its inherently multidisciplinary dimensions, migration remains one of these terrains in Security Studies that is particularly open, or at least has great potential, to be a productive meeting ground for various disciplinary foci.

References

Adamson, F. (2006) 'Crossing borders: International migration and national security', *International Security* 31, 1: 165–99.
Andrijasevic, R. (2004) 'Trafficking in women and the politics of mobility in Europe', PhD Thesis, Netherlands Research School of Women's Studies, Utrecht: Universiteit van Utrecht.
——(forthcoming 2010) *Sex Moves: Migration, Agency and Citizenship in Sex-Trafficking*, Palgrave.
Aradau, C. (2004a) 'The perverse politics of four letter words: Risk and pity in the securitisation of human trafficking', *Millenium: Journal of International Studies* 33, 2: 251–77.
——(2004b) 'Security and the democratic scene: Desecuritisation and emancipation', *Journal of International Relations and Development* 7, 3: 388–413.
——(2008) *Rethinking Trafficking in Women: Politics out of Security*, Hampshire: Palgrave.
Balzacq, T. (2007) 'The policy tools of securitization: Information, exchange, EU foreign and internal policies', *Journal of Common Market Studies* 46, 1: 75–100.
Bigo, D. (1995) 'Grands Débats Dans Un Petit Monde', *Cultures & Conflits* 19–20: 7–41.
——(1996a) *Polices En Réseaux: L'expérience Européenne*, Paris: Presses de Sciences Po.
——(ed.) (1996b) *Cultures Et Conflits No. 23: Circuler, Enfermer, Éloigner. Zones D'attentes Et Centres De Rétention Aux Frontières Des Démocraties Occidentales*, Paris: L'Harmattan.
——(2000) 'When two become one: Internal and external securitisations in Europe', in Kelstrup, M. and Williams, M.C. (eds) *International Relations Theory and the Politics of European Integration. Power, Security and Community*, London: Routledge, pp. 171–204.
——(2002) 'Security and immigration: Toward a critique of the governmentality of unease', *Alternatives* 27: 63–92.
Bigo, D. and Guild, E. (eds) (2003) 'La Mise à L'écart Des Étrangers: La Logique du Visa Schengen', *Cultures & Conflits* 49–50, Paris: L'Harmattan.

——(eds) (2005) *Controlling Frontiers: Free Movement into and within Europe*, Aldershot: Ashgate.

Bonditti, P. (2004) 'From territorial space to networks: A Foucaultian approach to the implementation of biopolitics', *Alternatives* 29: 465–82.

Boswell, C. (2007) 'Migration control in Europe after 9/11: Explaining the absence of securitization', *Journal of Common Market Studies* 45, 3: 589–611.

Buzan, B. (1984) 'Peace, power, and security: Contending concepts in the study of international relations', *Journal of Peace Research* 21, 2: 109–25.

——(1991) *People, States & Fear: An Agenda for International Security Studies in the Post-Cold War Era*, 2nd edn, London: Harvester Wheatsheaf.

Buzan, B., Wæver, O. and de Wilde, J. (1998) *Security: A New Framework for Analysis*, Boulder: Lynne Rienner.

Castles, S. (2003) 'Towards a sociology of forced migration an social transformation', *Sociology* 37, 1: 13–34.

Castles, S. and Davidson, A. (2000) *Citizenship and Migration: Globalization and the Politics of Belonging*, New York: Routledge.

Castles, S. and Miller, M J. (1993) *The Age of Migration: International Population Movements in the Modern World*, London: MacMillan.

Ceyhan, A. and Tsoukala, A. (eds) (1997) 'Contrôles: Frontières-Identités. Les Enjeux Autour De L'immigration Et De L'asile', *Cultures & Conflits* 26–27, Paris: L'Harmattan.

Chimni, B.S. (2000) 'Globalization, humanitarianism and the erosion of refugee protection', *Journal of Refugee Studies* 13, 3: 243–64.

Chiswick, B. (2000) 'Are immigrants favourably self-selected? An economic analysis', in Brettel, C. and Hollifield, J. (eds) *Migration Theory*, London: Routledge, pp. 61–76.

Cholenewski, R. (2000) 'The EU acquis on irregular migration: Reinforcing security at the expense of rights', *European Journal of Migration and Law* 2, 3–4: 361–405.

Choucri, N. (2002) 'Migration and security: Some key linkages', *Journal of International Affairs* 56, 1: 97–122.

Clark, M.A. (2003) 'Trafficking in persons: An issue of human security', *Journal of Human Development* 4, 2: 247–63.

Constant, A. and Zimmerman, K.F. (2005) 'Immigrant performance and selective immigration policy: A European perspective', *National Institute Economic Review* 194, 1: 94–105.

De Genova, N. (2007) 'The production of culprits: From deportability to detainability in the aftermath of "Homeland Security"', *Citizenship Studies* 11, 5: 421–48.

Doty, R.L. (2003) *Anti-Immigrantism in Western Democracies: Statecraft, Desire and the Politics of Exclusion*, London: Routledge.

Edkins, J. (2000) 'Sovereign power, zones of indistinction, and the camp', *Alternatives: Global, Local, Politica* 25: 3–25.

——(2005) 'Through the wire: Relations of power and relations of violence' *Millennium: Journal of International Studies* 34, 1: 1–24.

Edkins, J. and Pin Fat, V. (2004) 'Introduction: Life, power, resistance' in Edkins, J. and Pin-Fat, V. (eds) *Sovereign Lives: Power in Global Politics*, London: Routledge, pp. 1–22.

——(2005) 'Through the wire: Relations of power and relations of violence' *Millennium: Journal of International Studies* 34(1), 1–24.

Epstein, C. (2007) 'Guilty bodies, productive bodies, destructive bodies: Crossing the biometric borders', *International Political Sociology* 1, 2: 149–64.

European Council (2005) *Presidency Conclusions of the Brussels European Council*. Available online at: www.consilium.europa.eu/ueDocs/cms_Data/docs/pressData/en/ec/92202.pdf (accessed 3 October 2008).

Gibney, M. (2004) *The Ethics and Politics of Asylum*, Cambridge: Cambridge University Press.

Goodwin-Gill, G. (2001) 'After the Cold War: Asylum and the refugee concept move on', *Forced Migration Review* 10: 14–16.

Guild, E. (2002) 'Between persecution and protection. Refugees and the new European asylum policy', in Dashwood, A., Spencer, J., Ward, A. and Hillion, C. (eds) *Cambridge Yearbook of European Legal Studies, Volume Three 2000*, Oxford: Hart Publishing, pp. 169–97.

177

——(2003) 'International terrorism and EU immigration, asylum and borders policy: The unexpected victims of 11 September 2001', *European Foreign Affairs Review* 8, 3: 331–46.

Guild, E. and van Selm, J. (eds) (2005) *International Migration and Security: Opportunities and Challenges*, London: Routledge.

Guiraudon, V. (2003) 'The constitution of a European immigration policy domain: A political sociology approach', *Journal of European Public Policy* 10, 2: 263–82.

——(2000) 'European integration and migration policy: Vertical policy-making and venue shopping', *Journal of Common Market Studies* 38, 2: 251–71.

Haftendorn, H. (1991) 'The security puzzle: Theory-building and discipline-building in international security', *International Studies Quarterly* 35, 1: 3–17.

Heisbourg, F. (1991) 'Population movements in post-Cold War Europe', *Survival* 33, 1: 31–43.

Huysmans, J. (1995) 'Migrants as a security problem: Dangers of "securitizing' societal issues"', in Miles, R. and Thränhardt, D. (eds) *Migration and European Integration: The Dynamics of Inclusion and Exclusion*, London: Pinter, pp. 53–72.

——(1998) 'The question of the limit: Desecuritisation and the aesthetics of horror in political realism', *Millennium* 27, 3: 569–89.

——(2002) 'Defining social constructivism in security studies: The normative dilemma of writing security', *Alternatives* 27: 41–62.

——(2006) *The Politics of Insecurity: Fear, Migration and Asylum in the EU*, London: Routledge.

Huysmans, J. and Buonfino, A. (2008) 'Politics of exception and unease: Immigration, asylum and terrorism in parliamentary debates in the UK', *Political Studies* 56, 4: 766–88.

International Institute for Strategic Studies (1991) *Strategic Survey 1990–1991*, London: International Institute for Strategic Studies.

Jordan, A. (2002) 'Human rights or wrongs? The struggle for a right-based response to trafficking in human beings', *Gender and Development* 10, 1: 28–37.

Jordan, B. and Duvell, F. (2002) *Irregular Migration: The Dilemmas of Transnational Mobility*, Cheltenham: Edward Elgar.

Koser, K. (2005) 'Irregular migration, state security and human security', *Paper for the Global Commission on International Migration*. Available online at: www.gcim.org (accessed 10 August 2008).

Koslowski, R. (1998) 'International migration and European security in the context of EU enlargement', *Cambridge Review of International Relations* 12, 1: 30–48.

Lahav, G. (2004) *Immigration and Politics in the New Europe*. Cambridge: Cambridge University Press.

Lavenex, S. and Kunz, R. (2008) 'The migration-development nexus in EU external relations', *Journal of European Integration* 30, 3: 439–57.

Le Cour Grandmaison, O., Lhuilier, G. and Valluy, J. (eds) (2007) *Le Retour Des Camps? Sangatte, Lampedusa, Guantanamo … ,* Paris: Editions Autrement.

Lewis, N. (2005) 'Expanding surveillance: Connecting biometric information systems to international police cooperation', in Zureik E. and Salter, M.B. (eds) *Global Surveillance and Policing: Borders, Security, Identity*, Devon: Willan Publishing, pp. 97–112.

Liotta, P.H. (2002) 'Boomerang effect: The convergence of national and human security', *Security Dialogue* 33, 4: 473–88.

Loescher, G. (1992) 'Refugee movements and international security', *Adelphi Papers, 268*, London: International Institute for Strategic Studies.

Lyon, D. (2005) 'The border is everywhere: ID cards, surveillance and the other', in Zureik, E. and Salter, M.B. (eds), *Global Surveillance and Policing: Borders, Security, Identity*, Devon: Willan Publishing, pp. 66–82.

McNevin, A. (2006) 'Political belonging in a neo-liberal era: The struggle of the sans papiers', *Citizenship Studies 10, 2: 135–51.*

Muller, B. (2005) 'Borders, bodies and biometrics: Towards identity management', in Zureik, E. and Salter, M.B. (eds) *Global Surveillance and Policing: Borders, Security, Identity*, Devon: Willan Publishing, pp. 83–96.

van Munster, R. (2009) *Immigration, Security and the Politics of Risk in the EU*, Basingstoke: Palgrave.

Nadig, A. (2002) 'Human smuggling, national security, and refugee protection', *Journal of Refugee Studies* 15, 1: 1–25.

Neocleous, M. (2008) *Critique of Security*, Edinburgh: Edinburgh University Press.

Newman, E., and van Selm, J. (eds) (2003) *Refugees and Forced Displacement: International Security, Human Vulnerability, and the State*, Paris: United Nations University Press.

Nyers, P. (2003) 'Abject cosmopolitanism: The politics of protection in the anti-deportation movement', *Third World Quarterly* 24, 6: 1069–93.

——(2006) *Re-thinking Refugees*, London: Routledge.

——(2008) 'No one is illegal between city and nation', in Isin, E.F., *Acts of Citizenship*, London: Zed Books, pp. 160–81.

Nyers, P. and Moulins, C. (2007) '"We live in the country of UNHCR": Refugee protests and global political society', *International Political Sociology* 1, 4: 356–72.

Perera, S. (2002) 'What is a camp?' *Borderlands e-journal*, 1, 1. Available online at: www.borderlandsejournal. adelaide.edu.au (accessed 12 July 2007).

Pilkington, H. (1998) *Migration, Displacement and Identity in Post-Soviet Russia*, London: Routledge.

Puggioni, R. (2006) 'Resisting sovereign power: Camps in-between exception and dissent', in Huysmans, J. Dobson, A. and Prokhovnic, R. (eds) *The Politics of Protection: Sites of Insecurity and Political Agency*, London: Routledge, pp. 68–83.

Rudolph, C. (2006) *National Security and Immigration*, Stanford: Stanford University Press.

Salter, M.B. (2003) *Rights of Passage: The Passport in International Relations*, Boulder: Lynne Rienner.

——(2008) 'Imagining numbers: Risk, quantification and aviation security', *Security Dialogue* 39, 2: 243–66.

Samers, M. (2004) 'An emerging geopolitics of illegal immigration in the European Union', *European Journal of Migration and Law* 6, 1: 27–45.

Sassen, S. (1996) *Losing Control? Sovereignty in an Age of Globalization*, New York: Columbia University Press.

Sayad, A. (1999) *La Double Absence*, Paris: Seuil.

Soysal, Y.N. (1994) *Limits of Citizenship: Migrants and Postnational Membership in Europe*, Chicago: University of Chicago Press.

Squire, V. (2009) *The Exclusionary Politics of Asylum*, Basingstoke: Palgrave.

Tickner, J.A. (1995) 'Re-Visioning Security', in Booth, K. and Smith, S. (eds) *International Relations Theory Today*, Cambridge: Polity Press, pp. 175–97.

Tsoukala, A. (2004) 'Les Nouvelles Politiques de Contrôle du Hooliganisme en Europe: de la Fusion Sécuritaire au Multipositionnement de la Menace', *Cultures & Conflits* 51: 83–96.

Ullman, R. (1983) 'Redefining security', *International Security* 8, 1: 129–53.

Vernez, G. (1996) *National Security and Migration: How Strong the Link?*, Santa Monica, CA: RAND.

Wæver, O., Buzan, B., Kelstrup, M. and Lemaitre, P. (1993) *Identity, Migration and the New Security Agenda in Europe*, London: Pinter.

Wæver, O. (1995) 'Securitisation and desecuritisation', in Lipschutz, R. (ed.) *On security*, New York: Columbia University Press, pp. 46–86.

Walters, W. (2002a) 'Deportation, expulsion, and the international police of aliens', *Citizenship Studies* 6, 3: 265–92.

——(2002b) 'Mapping Schengenland: Denaturalizing the border', *Environment and Planning D: Society and Space* 20, 5: 561–80.

Weiner, M. (1992/93) 'Security, stability and international migration', *International Security* 17, 3: 91–126.

——(1995) *The Global Migration Crisis: The Challenge to States and to Human Rights*, New York: Harper Collins.

Widgren, J. (1990) 'International migration and regional stability', *International Affairs* 66, 4: 749–66.

16

Cyber-threats

Myriam Dunn Cavelty

Over the past decade, many public figures have portrayed attacks by means of computers – so called cyber-threats – as one of the gravest threats to national security today (cf. Poulsen 1999; Porteus 2001). What is remarkable about this threat representation is that while viruses, worms or cyber-crime are an undisputed and everyday reality, major disruptive cyber-attacks with grave impact, which would substantiate such reasoning, have remained mere chimeras. This raises at least two questions: first, why this threat representation has gained so much salience and continues to occupy such a prominent position among 'new threats' (as many of the post-Cold War threats are called); and second, to what extent the continued treatment of cyber-threats as a national security issue of highest priority is justified.

From a constructivist viewpoint, national security has always been about the social construction of specific issues as a threat, and about the definition of desirable responses to these issues. In the case of new threats, security professionals face an even greater need to establish a credible link to national security, because the national security dimension is less explicit when the environment, the society or the economy are concerned (Buzan et al. 1998). The necessity to make a convincing case for (national) security is even more pronounced as new threats are often framed as 'risks' (Daase et al. 2002; Rasmussen 2001): risks are indirect, unintended, uncertain and are, by definition, situated in the future, since they only materialize in reality when they are instantiated. Therefore, risks exist in a permanent state of virtuality and are only actualized through anticipation (van Loon 2002: 2). In the case of many new threats, threat images are thus characterized by reference to potential catastrophic occurrences in the future; and anticipation of these future disasters, rather than past experiences or solid justification for the current level of threat, is the main reason for action in the present.

Once this key characteristic has been recognized, the analysis of *threat representations* seems to become inevitable for understanding the politics surrounding new threats. This chapter therefore shows in a first section how the case for security is argued in three instances of cyber-threats – cyber-crime, cyber-terrorism and cyber-war – in particular, how the depiction of the threat is based on building 'threat clusters', in which traditional security issues are discursively interlinked with less typical ones, and which partly explain why these threat representations are so prominent. This chapter then looks at how justified these threat representations are, noting a high tendency for exaggeration due to the uncertainty surrounding the exact level of threat. It also addresses how a feasible 'security threshold' could be established, the need for which is well exemplified in the following quote: 'Setting the security trigger too low on the scale risks paranoia … setting it too high risks failure to prepare for major assaults until too late' (Buzan 1991: 115). In the third section, a glimpse into the future is provided: what can be said about the future potential for cyber-doom? The chapter ends by pointing out likely trends and action that should be taken by the international community to ensure that cyber-doom will never become a reality.

Types of cyber-threat representations

The cyber-threats debate originated in the US in the late 1980s, gained great momentum in the mid-1990s, and spread to other countries in the late 1990s. Both the threat perception and the envisaged countermeasures were shaped by the US over the years, with only little variation in other countries (Brunner and Suter 2008). On the one hand, the debate was decisively influenced by the larger post-Cold War strategic context, in which the notion of asymmetric vulnerabilities, epitomized by the multiplication of malicious actors (both state and non-state) and their increasing capabilities to do harm started to play a key role. On the other hand, discussions about cyber-threats always were and still are influenced by the ongoing information revolution, which is about the dynamical evolution and propagation of information and communication technologies into all aspects of life (Dunn and Brunner 2007). The US is also shaping the information revolution both technologically and intellectually, particularly by discussing its implications for International Relations and security (cf. Alberts and Papp 1997; Arquilla and Ronfeldt 1997; Henry and Peartree 1998) and acting on these assumptions. Against this backdrop, this chapter shows how cyber-threat clusters were formed over the years, looking in particular at cyber-crime, cyber-terrorism and cyber-war – all three of which coexist side by side today – and problematizes these characterizations.

Cyber-crime and the foreign intelligence threat

As the 1970s gave way to the 1980s, the merger of telecommunications with computers theoretically enabled everybody with a PC and a modem at home to exploit these emerging networks. Consequently, the amount of attention given to computer and communications security issues by political actors grew incrementally in response to well-publicized events such as politically motivated attacks, computer viruses and penetrations of networked computer systems for criminal purposes (cf. Bequai 1986; Parker 1983).

The distinct national-security dimension was established when computer intrusions were clustered together with the more traditional and well-established espionage discourse. More prominent hacking incidents – such as the numerous intrusions into government or other high-level computers perpetrated by the Milwaukee-based (mostly underage) '414s' (Covert 1983; Ross 1990) – led to a feeling in policy circles that there was a need for action: if teenagers were able to penetrate computer networks that easily, it was highly likely that better organized entities such as states would be even better equipped to do so. Other events, like the Cuckoo's Egg incident – an international KGB effort to connect to computers in the US and copy information from them that was only discovered by chance (Stoll 1989) – indeed made apparent that the threat was not just one

181

of criminals or juveniles playing games, but that classified or sensitive information could be acquired relatively easily by foreign nationals through hackers employed by foreign states.

However, at the time, cyber-threats did not receive much attention from the wider public, nor were they seen as a problem for society at large, as the threat pertained mainly to government networks and to the classified information residing in them. The technological substructure lacked the quality of a mass phenomenon that it would acquire once computer networks turned into a pivotal element of modern society – and which would also move the threat further into the limelight and to the forefront of the security discourse. Nonetheless, cyber-crime remains a driving factor in the discourse at large, as it is the threat representation with the closest link to reality.

Critical infrastructures and cyber-terrorism become an issue

In the mid-1990s, the issue of cyber-threats was truly catapulted onto the security political agendas of many countries when it was established by the strategic community that key sectors of modern society, including those vital to national security and to the essential functioning of industrialized economies, rely on a spectrum of highly interdependent national and international software-based control systems for their smooth, reliable, and continuous operation (PCCIP 1997). In this way, cyber-threats became to be seen as a threat to society's core values, and to the economic and social well-being of entire nations.

It was further established that because of the technological substructure, harmful attacks could be carried out in innumerable ways, potentially by anyone with a computer connected to the internet, and for purposes ranging from juvenile hacking to organized crime to political activism to strategic warfare. The new enemy was neither clearly identifiable nor associable to a particular state. Hacking tools could easily be downloaded and constantly became both more sophisticated and user-friendly. This diffuse threat-frame and the link to the fundament of society (critical infrastructures) opened the door for turning every small incident into a potential security issue of high urgency.

In particular, the image of cyber-terrorism emerged. Though a link between the cyber-domain and terrorism has been a theme in the US national security literature since the late 1980s (cf. National Academy of Sciences 1991), this cluster became far more convincing once critical infrastructures, the soft underbelly of liberal societies, were added. This threat cluster was pushed by US security officials who no longer only expressed concern about the security of classified data, but also about the possibility that terrorists might use cyber-attacks to counter the US's overwhelming military superiority, thus effectively mixing the asymmetry debate with the debate on vulnerability due to technological dependency. In this threat representation, the fear of random and violent victimization in the case of terrorism and the distrust or outright fear of computer technology, which both capitalize on the fear of the unknown, are combined (Pollitt 1997). The big problem with the use of the term 'cyber-terrorism' in this discourse is that the term has become totally bereft of meaning by its frequent evocation in the media for attacks of any kind with the help of computers, which is exacerbated by similar use of the term by government officials.

Cyber-war

The threat representation of cyber-war is strongly influenced by the increasing techno-logical sophistication of the US military and evolved in parallel with the one of cyber-terrorism. The Second Gulf War of 1990–91, in some circles called the first information war, was followed by a plethora of publications on the strategic use of information and information technology in conflicts (cf. Mahnken 1995; Molander et al. 1996; Campen *et al.* 1996). In its aftermath, the concept of cyber-war was coined (Arquilla and Ronfeldt 1997b) and various aspects of a military doctrine on the use of information in conflicts were developed, which acknowledged that one was striving to gain the 'information edge' (Nye and Owens 1996), while at the same time being disproportionately vulnerable due to high dependence on information technologies. Within the vast family of information warfare concepts, computer network attacks – 'actions taken through the use of computer networks to disrupt, deny, degrade, or destroy information resident in computers and computer networks, or the computers and networks themselves' (DoD Dictionary 2008) – are often equated with the initial idea of cyber-war.

This doctrinal development was driven by incidents in times of heightened tension or conflict, but it was also influenced by a global online community that started to acquire a voice of its own in times of conflict. NATO's 1999 intervention against Yugoslavia marked the first sustained use of the full-spectrum of information warfare components in combat. Much of this involved the use of propaganda and disinformation via the media (an important aspect of information warfare), but there were also extensive distributed denial-of-service (DDoS) attacks on various websites, as well as rumours that Yugoslav leader Slobodan Milosevic's bank accounts had been hacked by the US armed forces (Dunn 2002: 151). In addition, the increasing use of the internet during the conflict also gave it the distinction of being the 'first war fought in cyberspace' or the 'first war on the internet'.

However, the term 'cyber-war' is similarly plagued by vagueness as the term 'cyber-terror'. The popular usage of the word has come to refer to basically any phenomenon involving a deliberate disruptive or destructive use of computers (and is thus used interchangeably with 'cyber-terrorism'). For example, the cyber-confrontations between Chinese and US hackers in 2001 have been labelled the 'first Cyber World War'. The cause was a US reconnaissance and surveillance plane that was forced to land on Chinese territory after a collision with a Chinese jet fighter. Soon after, large-scale defacements of Chinese and US websites and waves of DDoS attacks began. Individuals from a variety of other nations joined in (Delio 2001) and the event was taken rather seriously by a variety of government officials on both sides – even though the actual effects of the cyber-attacks remained minimal. Recently, the issue of cyber-war gained renewed prominence when a three-week cyber-battle ensued and a wave of DDoS-attacks swamped and disabled various Estonian websites after the Estonian authorities removed a memorial to the Soviet forces of the Second World War. The attacks were readily attributed to the Russian government, and various officials claimed that this was the first known case of one state targeting another using cyber-warfare (Traynor 2007). Similar claims were made in the confrontation between Russia and Georgia of 2008. In all of these cases, it is still doubtful whether there was any direct government involvement and whether the term 'war' should really be invoked.

In search of a security threshold

It can be observed that in these threat representations, the security community – aided by the media – uses threat rhetoric evoking the image of imminent cyber-doom, even though nothing that happened ever came close to having a true and sustained society-threatening impact (the same is true for incidents that show the potential for grave society-wide impact – for example, a virus or worm affecting some critical services, or occasional intrusions into computers that contain classified and potentially harmful data). There always is a great reliance on hypotheses of what might happen and official reports and statements are full of 'could', 'would' and 'maybe' when describing the threat (Bendrath 2003). Even in political hearings, evidence is often anecdotal, and the uncertainty about the identity, actual capabilities and intentions of potential enemies appears very high (Dunn Cavelty 2008).

What remains is the *potential* for grave harm. It has become the norm today that every political tension or conflict is accompanied by heightened activity in cyberspace, and it is the norm that our societies are confronted daily with cyber-crime and all kinds of more or less disruptive cyber-incidents that cause minor and occasionally major inconvenience for private users, businesses and governmental organizations. The crucial question that needs to be asked is: when should these occurrences be treated as a matter of national security?

The danger of overly dramatizing the threat manifests itself in reactions that call for military retaliation (as happened in the Estonian case and in other instances) or other exceptional measures. This kind of threat rhetoric invokes enemy images even if there is no identifiable enemy, favours national solutions instead of international ones and centres on national-security measures instead of economic and business solutions. This is not to say that cyber-threats should under no circumstances be regarded as dangerous. But there needs to be clarity about which tools or measures are appropriate under which circumstances. This, so this chapter argues, can only be achieved with more knowledge about the actor and the intention behind an attack and the impact of the incident. Clearly, the terms as they are used in the discourse cannot serve as an analytical tool – they need to be clarified and sharpened to become useful for meaningful investigation of the issue of cyber-threats.

As previously noted, the spectrum of perpetrators that can engage in harmful cyber-activities ranges from teenagers to criminals to terrorist to nation-states. One useful way to approach the question of when something should be treated as a national security issue is to partition this wide range of actors into two groups: the first is called an 'unstructured' threat, while the latter is a 'structured' threat (National Academy of Sciences 1991; Minihan 1998). The unstructured threat consists of adversaries with limited funds and organization and short-term goals. The unstructured threat is not considered a danger to national security and is normally not of concern to the national security community. The structured threat, however, is considerably more methodical and better supported. Adversaries from this group have all-source intelligence support, extensive funding, organized professional support and long-term goals.

Another pragmatic and useful way to differentiate is to focus on the intention and the effect of the activities: Dorothy Denning, a US information security researcher, makes a distinction between three classes of politically motivated activity involving the internet – activism, hacktivism and cyber-terrorism (Denning 2001). Only the last of these is a structured effort and a case for national security. In her classification, (cyber-) activism is the normal, non-disruptive use of the internet in support of a (political) agenda or cause. Hacktivism is the marriage of hacking and activism, including operations that use hacking techniques against a target's internet site with the intention of disrupting normal operations. Cyber-terrorism, according to Denning, consists of unlawful attacks against computers, networks and the information stored therein, to intimidate or coerce a government or its people in furtherance of political or social objectives. Such an attack should result in violence against persons or property, or at least cause enough harm to generate the requisite fear level to be considered cyber-terrorism (cf. Conway 2008; Pollitt 1997; Devost *et al.* 1997).

184

In a similar vein, Bruce Schneier, a renowned security technologist and author, differentiates between cyber-vandalism, which includes the defacing of websites; cyber-crime, which includes theft of intellectual property and extortion based on the threat of DDoS attacks; cyber-terrorism, which refers to the hacking into a computer system to cause havoc by causing a nuclear power plant to melt down, floodgates to open, or two airplanes to collide; and cyber-war, which refers to the use of computers to disrupt the activities of an enemy country, especially deliberate attacks on communication systems (Schneier 2007). The first two represent an unstructured threat, while the second group would be considered a structured threat. The narrower and more precise the terms are defined and used, the better the phenomenon can be grasped. A narrow and precise definition also helps to circumvent other dangers inherent in the terms 'war' or 'terror-ism', like exculpating the victims of an attack from their own responsibility for the consequences of their negligence in terms of computer security, or creating pressure to forcefully retaliate against 'hackers', real or imagined (Libicki 1997: 38).

Both Denning's and Schneier's classifications construct a cyber-threat escalation ladder: from rung to rung, the potential effects are increasingly serious. The advantage of such a 'severity of effects' view is that it helps policymakers to prioritize. Only computer attacks whose effects are sufficiently destructive or disruptive should be regarded as a national security issue. Attacks that disrupt non-essential services, or that are mainly a costly nuisance, should not. At the same time, not every successful internet attack, no matter how deadly, is necessarily an act of cyber-war. The tools and tactics used by armies, terrorists and criminals in cyberspace are the same, but the ultimate goals of these groups are different. Schneier captures the distinction well when he writes that

> just as every shooting is not necessarily an act of war, every successful Internet attack, no matter how deadly, is not necessarily an act of cyberwar. A cyberattack that shuts down the power grid might be part of a cyberwar campaign, but it also might be an act of cyberterrorism, cybercrime, or even – if it's done by some fourteen-year-old who doesn't really understand what he's doing – cybervandalism. Which it is will depend on the motivations of the attacker and the circumstances surrounding the attack ... just as in the real world.
>
> (Schneier 2007)

Therefore, the only way to determine the source, nature and scope of an incident is to investigate. The authority to investigate and to obtain the necessary court orders or sub-poenas clearly resides with law enforcement. Other actors, namely the military, should be involved only when there is sufficient proof that an attack was targeted directly and deliberately at national security assets by another state, when its effects are widespread and not localized, or when special technical expertise is required that others do not have.

The future likelihood of cyber-doom

It was argued above that cyber-attacks resulting in deaths and injuries have remained fiction. But what about the future? Schneier states unequivocally that 'there should be no doubt that the smarter and better-funded militaries of the world are planning for cyber-war, both attack and defense' (Schneier 2007). There are various indications that this is indeed the case. The US, for example, is reportedly developing national-level guidance for determining when and how to launch cyber-attacks against enemy computer net-works (Bradley 2003). More recent reports discuss the founding of the US Air Force Cyber Command, which is tasked with both offensive and defensive cyber-activities (Kenyon 2007). US strategy experts assert that strategic rivals such as China and Russia have offensive information warfare programmes and are ready to use them (Thomas 2004; Mulvenon and Yang 1998; FitzGerald 1994).

It seems clear that until cyber-war is proven to be ineffective, states and non-state actors who have the ability to develop such 'weapons' will most likely try to do so, because they appear cost-effective, more stealthy and less risky than other forms of armed conflict. However, the mere existence of these capabilities does not necessarily mean that they will be used – or can be used. First of all, it is unclear whether such options are technologically feasible at all: many of the more tech-savvy political advisors and jour-nalists have written about the practical difficulties of a serious cyber-attack or the inability of bureaucracies like militaries or intelligence agencies as well as many terrorist groups to really acquire the skills needed to become successful hackers (Ingles-le Nobel 1999; Green 2002; Shea 2003). Others observe that, for any capability beyond annoying hacks, the barriers to entry are quite high (CSTIW 1999). Some experts would even say that cyber-terrorism remains a far-fetched prospect because technology is simply not essential to many of the objectives of terrorist groups and therefore does not generate enough interest to be employed as a weapon of choice (Barak 2004: 95). In addition, even though it is often claimed that hacking tools are simple to use, inexpensive and widely available on computer bulletin boards and various websites, sophisticated cyber-weapons would need to be a lot more powerful than that to be effective and to deliver 'effect' to a particular geographic conflict zone or enemy. We would need to see a qualitative leap in the ability to penetrate and manipulate ICT, but also to control aspects of the information infrastructure directly (Eriksson and Giacomello 2007).

But even if the technology existed and could be targeted specifically at enemy infra-structures, its use raises legal, ethical, but also strategic issues, especially as far as its use by state actors is concerned. Cyber-war experts Arquilla and Libicki believe that the Penta-gon actually did hack into Serbian computers to spy during the Kosovo conflict, but refrained from causing chaos principally for strategic reasons: widespread use of these new weapons and tools would probably have accelerated and focused foreign military research on them and threaten to deprive the US of its information warfare edge in a field where foes could catch up quickly and cheaply (Borger 1999).

Furthermore, nobody can be truly interested in allowing the unfettered proliferation and use of cyber-war tools, not even (or maybe least of all) the country with the offen-sive lead in this domain. Quite the contrary, very strong arguments can be made that the world's big powers have an overall strategic interest in developing and accepting inter-nationally agreed norms on the use and non-use of cyber-war, i.e. computer network attacks, and in creating agreements that might pertain to the development, distribution and deployment of cyber-weapons or to their use (Denning 2001). The most obvious reason is that the countries that are currently openly discussing the use of cyber-war tools are precisely the ones that are the most vulnerable to cyber-warfare attacks due to their high dependency on information infrastructure. A similar argument can be made for terror-ists: most terrorist organizations depend on the information infrastructure for conducting their 'daily business'.

In addition, the features of the emerging information environment make it extremely unlikely that any but the most limited and tactically oriented instances of computer attacks could be contained. More likely, computer attacks by the military could 'blow back' through the interdependencies that characterize the environment. Even relatively harmless viruses and worms would cause considerable random disruption to businesses, governments and consumers. Awareness that global information networks are routinely exploited by military actors would probably severely undermine the ongoing efforts to foster a reliable information society (Rathmell 2001), a key goal of many Western states. This loss would most likely weigh much heavier in the end than the uncertain benefits to be gained from cyber-war activities.

Conclusion

One of the main reasons why the issue of cyber-threats has gained so much attention in recent years is the fact that in the process of threat politics, US officials have convincingly argued that they threaten the very fabric of modern societies. It must be noted, however, that the defining characteristic of cyber-threats is their unsubstantiated nature: none of the worst-case scenarios have materialized, not even in part. The last few years suggest, instead, that computer network vulnerabilities are an increasingly serious business problem, but that their threat to national security has, in general, been overstated. At the heart of the issue lies the fact that we are dealing with a threat whose dimensions remain altogether uncertain – opening up a broad margin for political bargaining.

Does that mean that the cyber-dimension does not present a danger for national security at all? An answer in the affirmative would require knowledge of the future. But in light of the fact that the threat is frequently overstated and that this might result in detrimental countermeasures, a well-tempered approach as well as a careful estimation of a changing threat picture is in order. While it can be rightly argued that the future is unclear and the threat cannot be completely shrugged off, decision-makers and experts must be particularly careful not to foment unnecessary 'cyber-angst'. To forestall this, the level of threat should not be assessed by members of the strategic community alone, but by technical experts and infrastructure owners who have inside knowledge about exactly how vulnerable their assets are to a cyber-attack.

Probably the biggest issue that needs to be addressed, however, is the underlying tension between the desire of military establishments to exploit cyberspace for military advantages, and concerns about the dependency of governments, economies and societies on networked information systems. This contradiction needs to be addressed carefully before a conclusive international regime for the protection of cyber-space can be developed. Not only should international law enforcement agreements and capacities be strengthened, but a ban on the use of cyber-weapons by nation-states should also be given serious consideration, despite all the likely difficulties that such a regime would encounter, particularly in terms of enforcement. Cyberspace is too valuable an asset for the entire world to jeopardize it in the name of national security.

References

Alberts, D.S. and Papp, D.S. (eds) (1997) *The Information Age: An Anthology of Its Impacts and Consequences (Vol. I)*, Washington: National Defense University Press.
Arquilla, J. and Ronfeldt, D.F. (eds) (1997a) *In Athena's Camp: Preparing for Conflict in the Information Age*, Santa Monica: RAND.

——(1997b), 'Cyberwar is coming!', in Arquilla, J. and Ronfeldt, D.F. (eds) *In Athena's Camp: Preparing for Conflict in the Information Age*, Santa Monica: RAND, pp. 23–60.

Barak, S. (2004) 'Between violence and "e-jihad": Middle Eastern terror organizations in the information age', in Nicander, L. and Ranstorp, M. (eds) *Terrorism in the Information Age – New Frontiers?* Swedish National Defence College, pp. 83–96.

Bendrath, R. (2003) 'The American cyber-angst and the real world – Any link?' in Latham, R. (ed.) *Bombs and Bandwidth: The Emerging Relationship between IT and Security*, New York: The New Press, pp. 49–73.

Bequai, A. (1986) *Technocrimes: The Computerization of Crime and Terrorism*, Lexington: Lexington Books.

Borger, J. (1999) 'Pentagon kept the lid on cyberwar in Kosovo', *The Guardian*, 9 November. Available online at: www.guardian.co.uk/Kosovo/Story/0,2763,197391,00.html (accessed 9 January 2009).

Bradley, G. (2003) 'Bush orders guidelines for cyber-warfare: Rules for attacking enemy computers prepared as U.S. weighs Iraq options', *Washington Post*, 7 February, p. A01.

Brunner, E. and Suter, M. (2008) *The International CIIP Handbook 2008: An Inventory of Protection Policies in 25 Countries and 6 International Organizations*. Zurich: Center for Security Studies.

Buzan, B. (1991) *People, States and Fear: An Agenda for International Security Studies in the Post-Cold War Era*, 2nd edn, Brighton: Harvester Wheatsheaf.

Buzan, B., Wæver, O. and de Wilde, J. (1998) *Security: A New Framework for Analysis*, Boulder: Lynne Rienner.

Campen, A.D., Dearth, D.H. and Goodden, T. (eds) (1996) *Cyberwar: Security, Strategy and Conflict in the Information Age*, Fairfax, AFCEA International Press.

Conway, M. (2008) 'The media and cyberterrorism: A study in the construction of "reality"', in Dunn Cavelty, M. and Kristensen, K.S. (eds) *The Politics of Securing the Homeland: Critical Infrastructure, Risk and Securitisation*, London: Routledge, pp. 109–29.

Covert, C. (1983) 'Seven curious teenagers wreak havoc via computer', *Detroit Free Press*, 28 August, Section: WWL, p. 1F.

CSTIW, Center for the Study of Terrorism and Irregular Warfare (1999) *Cyberterror: Prospects and Implications*, White Paper.

Daase, C., Feske, S. and Peters, I. (eds) (2002) *Internationale Risikopolitik: Der Umgang mit neuen Gefahren in den internationalen Beziehungen*, Baden-Baden: Nomos Verlagsgesellschaft.

Delio, M. (2001) 'Is this World Cyber War I?' *Wired*, 1 May.

Denning, D. (2001) 'Activism, hacktivism, and cyberterrorism: The internet as a tool for influencing foreign policy', in Arquilla, J. and Ronfeldt, D. (eds) *Networks and Netwars: The Future of Terror, Crime, and Militancy*, Santa Monica: RAND, pp. 239–88.

DOD Dictionary of Military and Associated Terms (2008). Available online at: www.js.mil/doctrine/jel/doddict/data/c/01183.html (accessed 9 January 2009).

Devost, M.G., Houghton, B.K. and Pollard, N.A. (1997) 'Information terrorism: Political violence in the information age', *Terrorism and Political Violence* 9, 1: 72–83.

Dunn, M. (2002) *Information Age Conflicts: A Study on the Information Revolution and a Changing Operating Environment*. Zürcher Beiträge zur Sicherheitspolitik und Konfliktforschung, No. 64, Zurich: Center for Security Studies.

Dunn Cavelty, M. (2008) *Cyber-Security and Threat Politics: US Efforts to Secure the Information Age*, London: Routledge.

Dunn Cavelty, M. and Brunner, E. (2007) 'Information, power, and security: An outline of debates and implications', in Dunn Cavelty, M., Mauer, V. and Krishna-Hensel, S.-F. (eds) *Power and Security in the Information Age: Investigating the Role of the State in Cyberspace*, Aldershot: Ashgate, pp. 1–18.

Eriksson, J. and Giacomello, G. (2007) 'Conclusion: Digital-age security in theory and practice', in Eriksson, J. and Giacomello G. (eds) *International Relations and Security in the Digital Age*, London: Routledge, pp. 173–84.

FitzGerald, M.C. (1994) 'Russian views on electronic signals and information warfare', *American Intelligence Journal* 15, 1: 81–87.

Green, J. (2002) 'The myth of cyberterrorism', *Washington Monthly*, November 2002. Available online at: www.washingtonmonthly.com/features/2001/0211.green.html (accessed 9 January 2009).

Henry, R. and Peartree, E.C. (eds) (1998) *Information Revolution and International Security*, Washington: Center for Strategic and International Studies.

Ingles-le Nobel, J.J. (1999) 'Cyberterrorism hype', *Jane's Intelligence Review*, 21 October.

Kenyon, H.S. (2007) 'Cyberspace command logs in', *Signal* 61, 12: 35–38.

Libicki, M. (1997) *Defending Cyberspace*, Washington, DC: National Defense University.

van Loon, J. (2002) *Risk and Technological Culture: Towards a Sociology of Virulence*, London: Routledge.

Mahnken, T.G. (1995) 'War in the information age', *Joint Force Quarterly* 10: 39–43.

Minihan, K. (1998) *Statement of Lieutenant General Kenneth Minihan, USAF, Director, NSA to the Senate Governmental Affairs Committee Hearing on Vulnerabilities of the National Information Infrastructure*, 24 June 1998. Available online at: www.senate.gov/~govt-aff/62498minihan.htm (accessed 9 January 2009).

Molander, R.C., Riddle, A.S. and Wilson, P.A. (1996) *Strategic Information Warfare: A New Face of War*, Santa Monica: RAND.

Mulvenon, J.C. and Yang, R.H. (eds) (1998) *The People's Liberation Army in the Information Age*, Santa Monica: RAND.

National Academy of Sciences (1991) Computer Science and Telecommunications Board, *Computers at Risk: Safe Computing in the Information Age*, Washington, DC: National Academy Press.

Nye, J.S. Jr. and Owens, W.A. (1996) 'America's information edge', *Foreign Affairs* 75, 2: 20–36.

Parker, D.B. (1983) *Fighting Computer Crime*, New York: Charles Scribner's Sons.

PCCIP, President's Commission on Critical Infrastructure Protection (1997) *Critical Foundations: Protecting America's Infrastructures*, Washington, DC: US Government Printing Office.

Pollitt, M.M. (1997) 'Cyberterrorism – Fact or fancy?' *Proceedings of the 20th National Information Systems Security Conference*, pp. 285–89.

Porteus, L. (2001) 'Feds still need to define role in tackling cyberterror, panelists say', *GovExec.com*, 15 May 2001. Available online at: www.govexec.com/dailyfed/0501/051501td.htm (accessed 9 January 2009).

Poulsen, K. (1999) 'Info war or electronic sabre rattling?' *ZDNet*, 8 September. Available online at: http://news.zdnet.com/2100–9595_22–515631.html?legacy=zdnn (accessed 9 January 2009).

Rasmussen, M.V. (2001) 'Reflexive security: Nato and international risk society', *Millennium: Journal of International Studies* 30, 2: 285–309.

Rathmell, A. (2001) 'Controlling computer network operations', *Information & Security: An International Journal* 7, pp. 121–44.

Ross, A. (1990) 'Hacking away at the counterculture', in Penley, C. and Ross, A. (eds) *Technoculture*, Minneapolis: University of Minnesotta Press, pp. 107–34.

Schneier, B. (2007), 'Schneier on security: A blog covering security and security technology'. Available online at: www.schneier.com/blog/archives/2007/06/cyberwar.html (accessed 9 January 2009).

Shea, D.A. (2003) *Critical Infrastructure: Control Systems and the Terrorist Threat*, Congressional Research Report for Congress, RL31534, 21 February, Washington, DC: Congressional Research Service.

Stoll, C. (1989) *The Cuckoo's Egg: Tracking a Spy through the Maze of Computer Espionage*, New York: Doubleday.

Thomas, T.L. (2004) *Dragon Bytes: Chinese Information-War Theory and Practice*, Ft Leavenworth: Foreign Military Studies Office.

Traynor, I. (2007) 'Russia accused of unleashing cyberwar to disable Estonia', *The Guardian*, 17 May.

17

Old and new wars

Herfried Münkler

The end of the East–West conflict nurtured expectations that war and threats of war would from now on belong to the past. Mankind could finally realize its age-old dream of lasting, if not perpetual, peace, and thereby soon pocket a considerable peace dividend by reducing defence budgets. These expectations endorsed prognoses by numerous scholars, from Auguste Comte to Joseph Schumpeter, who regarded the penchant for war and military affairs as the disposition of an élite, which they thought would gradually disappear with the development of industrialization and capitalism. Immanuel Kant's essay *Perpetual Peace* was also based on the idea that the spirit of commerce, at least in the long run, is incompatible with that of war. After this development had been blocked by nationalism and totalitarianism, it was thought that with the end of the bloc confrontation, all of those dynamics and processes would resume and subsequently cause the disappearance of war. This, of course, was a delusion. What was coming to an end was the era of conventional interstate wars, of the *old wars*, but not war itself. This distinction between old and new wars – and the historic transition from the former to the latter – is the subject of this chapter. It is structured in three parts: first, the transition from old to new wars is traced in recent history. Second, some objections to the concept of new wars are discussed. The third part presents a conclusion and ventures an outlook on the future of warfare.

From old to new wars

The transition from old to new wars is a feature of twentieth-century history. In the course of this century, traditional interstate wars have become increasingly unlikely, mainly as a result of the technological developments – on the one hand due to the immense destructive power of nuclear weapons, on the other as a result of the dramatically increased vulnerability of modern industrial and service economies. Both factors together resulted in the costs of interstate wars exceeding their gains by a clear margin. This is the main reason why these wars lost their attractiveness, not only as gainful ways of forceful appropriation and territorial expansion, but also as a modus of political problem solving accelerated by means of military force. But this is not necessarily a new discovery: even at the end of the nineteenth century, a number of very different observers, among them Prussian chief of staff Helmuth von Moltke, Polish banker and publicist Johann von Bloch and the German-English industrialist and revolutionary Friedrich Engels, reached the conclusion that a war fought in Europe would lead to enormous social and political upheavals and fundamentally alter the continent's order (Münkler 2002: 116ff.). The First World War brought precisely this and, in some ways, Europe was working to clear away or at least deal with the consequences of this 'seminal catastrophe of the twentieth century' (Kennan 1979: 3) well into the 1990s. Today's European order – as originally conceived in the early 1950s – guarantees almost with certainty that war will no longer be an instrument of European cross-national politics. Indeed, at the beginning of the 1990s, European states, by reducing defence budgets, were able to receive considerable peace dividends. This is why Robert Cooper described the European constellation as a 'postmodern world', but also pointed out that the 'modern world' and especially the 'pre-modern world' continued to coexist with it (Cooper 2003).

This European trend, of course, could not be globalized, nor did it even spread throughout the whole of Europe, but left out its south-eastern flank, the Balkans. Along the European periphery too – in the Caucasus, the Middle East, and south-western Asia – wars continued to be waged. By the mid-1990s at the latest, hopes had vanished that the end of the East–West conflict would also bring about the end of war. Meanwhile, a number of conflicts had taken place, which, though not wars in the conventional sense, were all marked by a high degree of violence and had far-reaching consequences (Schreiber 2001). First, there are the two Gulf wars of 1990/91 and 2003 (Ismael and Ismael 1994; Freedman and Karsh 1993; Knights 2004). Second, there are the Yugoslav wars of disintegration (Bennett 1996; Ignatieff 2001). More than any other experience, the war in Bosnia quashed Europe's confidence in diplomatic negotiations and financial incentives as key means replacing the use of military force. Third, there were the wars in Somalia and Rwanda, and of course, these are only two examples for many others (Prunier 1995; Menkhaus 2004).

War had therefore not at all disappeared with the end of the East–West conflict, but had merely changed its appearance. In *On War*, Carl von Clausewitz described war as a chameleon that incessantly adapts itself to the existing conditions (von Clausewitz 1980: 212). The so-called de-statization of war is, in that sense, an adaptation of war to such altered conditions. Wars fought by regular armed forces that strove to defeat each other, thereby debilitating the political will of the enemy and forcing him to surrender, has been replaced by a diffuse amalgam of very different actors: from intervention forces mandated by international organizations and local warlords aiming to secure their reign within a limited territory, to private military companies taking action on behalf of governments and sometimes multinational corporations (Reno 1998; Thomas et al. 2005; Rich 1999; Bryden and Caparini 2006; Chesterman 2007; Jäger and Kümmel 2007; Kinsey 2006). These developments are of great consequence because conventional distinctions between wars among states and civil wars, between interstate wars and violent intra-societal conflicts, are blurred and both forms of warfare increasingly merge with each other.

What is more, the use of military force has become normatively justified in the deployment of multinational forces in wars of peace or peacekeeping missions, a development that has brought military and police action so close together that they often can hardly be differentiated. This 'constabularization' of the militaries, which was anticipated decades ago by Morris Janowitz (Janowitz 1966), is opposed by the deregulation of warfare in such way that war increasingly involves a type of actor who neither respects the 1907 Hague Regulations nor The Geneva Convention. On the contrary, these actors gain their ability to act precisely by using asymmetrical forms of warfare: they draw the civilian population into the conflict, either by using it for cover and as a logistic backbone or by making it the prime target of their attacks. Terrorism as global strategy is the current culmination of a development that has transformed war from confrontations between professionalized military machines into strategic massacres carried out among civilians by actors that can themselves no longer be distinguished from civilians (Münkler 2006: 221ff.; Hoffman 2006; Stepanova 2008; Richardson 2006). As a result, the most important achievement of international rules of war – the clear-cut distinction between combatants and non-combatants – has become obsolete.

For some observers, the above developments were sufficient evidence of altogether new forms of warfare and, accordingly, of *new wars* (van Creveld 1991; Kaldor 1999; Münkler 2005, 2007). In the history of war, as in military history, there has always been talk of military revolutions: innovations in weapons technology and the organizational structure of military forces during the sixteenth century have prompted scholars to conceptualize them as fundamental transformations of warfare. For example, the increasing use of heavy artillery in siege warfare, and soon thereafter also on the battlefield, transformed traditional fortification techniques and, later on, the order of battle almost completely (Parker 1988; Rogers 1995). The often cited *Revolution in Military Affairs* at the end of the twentieth century, in the wake of which the US gained military superiority – among other things, through the use of so-called smart bombs, the highly increased precision of long-range weapons and an incredibly accelerated flow of information in battle, which were all made possible by microelectronics (Gongora and von Riekhoff 2000; Halpin 2006; Hundley 1999; Coker 2004) – is at least comparable to the developmental thrust that took place at the beginning of the modern era. Generally, the concept of new wars captures more than just the transformation of military affairs and warfare. It also takes into account the social and political dimension, and the conditions and circumstances under which armies are raised and wars are waged.

In analysing old and new wars, it is in fact impossible to keep apart questions of warfare and of the socio-political order under which it takes place. The revolution in military affairs that occurred in the early modern era also transformed the political conditions that framed warfare in fundamental ways, and those conditions for their part only made possible the cost-intensive modernization of the European armies. The increasing use of heavy artillery rendered town walls and castles worthless and made the construction of effective defensive positions necessary. It also made it necessary to command all three forces – infantry, artillery and cavalry – to achieve effective collaboration among them on the battlefield, all of which caused the costs of military affairs to soar. As a result, the state, of course only the larger territorial state, rose to the position of a monopolist of war. The countless sub-state and quasi-private actors, feudal knights and capable war entrepreneurs (the condottieri) who had earlier filled the war zone now either disappeared from military affairs or were swallowed up by the state. It was precisely this separation of workers from their tools, to use Max Weber's expression (Weber 1995: 80ff.), that led to the statization of military affairs in the early modern era, thus creating one of the defining characteristics of the old wars. The new weapons were too expensive to be affordable by individuals who would follow their feudal lords into war with weapons of their own or be summoned for review and sell their services in exchange for lump sum or pay. In addition, troops had to be drilled to be useful in the new complex battle formations. They had to be maintained, disciplined and exercised, while their clothing and the weapons they carried were no longer their property, but that of the state. As a result of these innovations in weapons technology and organizational requirements, war became so expensive that it no longer provided a profitable field for private investment and thus needed to be brought under state control. The state became the master of war and, in its wake, these developments were cast into law.

In some respects, the new wars are a continuation of these developments; in others, they constitute a reversal and a regression. The revolution in military affairs mentioned above (giving rise to asymmetrical military superiority of the US), which also developed in the area of conventional warfare, imposes a limitation on a party's ability to engage in warfare due to increased costs of armaments. It therefore constitutes a continuation of the earlier development. In fact, the US is currently the only power capable of globally deploying forces in effective action.

However, since the 1980s there have been simultaneous, yet contrary developments. In countless wars along the borders of prosperity zones, the weapons used are not cost- and maintenance-intensive weapons systems whose deployment requires highly qualified specialists, but rather cheap weapons that can easily be operated by anyone: automatic rifles, landmines, multiple rocket launchers and, finally, pick-ups used as transport and fast combat vehicles. As a rule, even the troops deployed in those wars are not professional soldiers, but hastily recruited fighters – at times even children – for whom war has turned into a way of earning a living or a form of prestige. Wars of this kind are cheap to wage, and therefore the number of players able to engage in warfare has drastically increased. The threshold of war has thus been lowered to such a degree that it can be easily overcome by countless groups.

The last two decades have thus presented us with a confusing and deeply contradictory picture. On the one hand, the number of actors able to engage in warfare has been further reduced, in some respects leaving only the US capable of taking action, whereas on the other hand, their number dramatically increased. The progressive legal regulation of the war-related use of violence is in many wars contravened by the replacement of regular soldiers by fighters who neither feel bound by an ethos of chivalry nor by international rules of war. On the contrary, violence is used by those actors in whatever form is deemed functional or yields the desired results (Ignatieff 1998). Therefore, in certain political world regions a situation developed where war is no longer seriously considered an instrument of politics, as for example in Europe, while in other large regions, destabization has led to endemic war with no prospects of peace. The reasons are to be found in the multitude of players engaged in acts of war, their diffuse organizational structure and in the interconnection of economics of war and international organized crime. Many of the new wars therefore last not for months or years, but for decades.

In sum, the historic transition from old to new wars can be characterized by three basic features:

1   The development of insurmountable military asymmetry and, in reaction to it, the *asymmetricalization of war* by militarily inferior actors who are otherwise hardly capable of warfare (Münkler 2005: 25ff. and 66ff.). In order to understand this dimension well, it is necessary to take into account the history of both military and war. Such a survey clearly shows that not symmetry, but asymmetry is the standard

condition of war to be expected and against which a symmetrical order was set up by political means.

2 The gradual *privatization of war*, meaning that states are no longer the monopolists of war (Münkler 2005: 16ff.). In fact, this might never have been fully the case, but regarding international rules of war as well as international politics, this assumption proved very workable. However, this is no longer the case. Non- and sub-state actors have increasingly seized the initiative from states that, for the most part, have been reduced to reactive positions.

3 The *de-militarization of war*. Regular armed forces have lost both the control and monopoly of warfare (Münkler 2005: 81ff.). This can be seen in the diversity of players and their objectives. Dominant features are an increasingly colourful mix of combatants rather than regular armies; their targets are rarely genuinely military ones, but increasingly the civilian population and non-military infrastructure in general. The consequence is the dissolution of the clear distinction between combatants and non-combatants that had been one of the most important achievements of European rules of war.

Only when considered together can these features fully describe the new wars, as the concept of new wars is based on the assumption that all three characteristics are closely interlinked and that neither can be adequately understood and described without the others. Therefore, it is precisely the temporal coincidence of these three characteristics that constitutes the substantially new feature of the new wars. This fact, however, is often ignored, as recent debates over the term 'new wars' have shown.

Debates and criticism

Critics of the term 'new wars' have objected that what is labelled as 'new' is not new at all, but has in fact been a feature of warfare all along. Furthermore, the opposite concept of 'old wars' is criticized as being too Eurocentric and as passing over the question of European colonial warfare outside Europe. A final objection is that the concept of new wars also glosses over the continuing nuclear threat and overrates the importance of terrorism in world politics. In addition, it is feared that the concept of new wars smoothes the way for an anthropologizing of the general concept of war and thereby causes a regression far behind the idea of politically controlled warfare while narrowing the focus to some isolated phenomena of war only (Geis 2006).

These objections have a number of well-warranted points. However, they very rarely affect the concept of new wars as such, but only some of its advocates, while being unrelated to others. Overall, these objections miss the core of the problem. Furthermore, apart from endless enumerations of details and archiving of statistics, the critics too often fail to focus on the crucial question: has there been a change in the model of war on which the assessment of political rationality, strategic creativity, and finally, the legitimacy under international law of wars is based? Is it still possible to apply the admittedly Eurocentric model of war plausibly as an analytic framework to current wars – a model that, as a matter of principle, assumes symmetry between actors who, for their part, base the ethical and legal regulation of war on this symmetry? These questions need to be answered either in the positive or negative. Details and statistical studies can provide us with information about the variance of a model, but they cannot indicate shifts from one model to another.

However, is the question of what model of war to apply relevant at all? It certainly is; in fact, it is crucial, since it is decisive for the creativity, rationality and legitimacy of strategic actions undertaken by different actors. Only by reference to the assumptions inherent in a general model is it possible to judge an action creative or conventional; to label the use of force rational or irrational; and to designate a decision as legitimate or illegitimate, legal or illegal. Without such a framework, it is simply impossible to judge and adequately assess decisions made and actions taken – unless, of course, these are subjected to the kind of moral judgement that thinks itself incontestable by cultural and political diversity. Scientifically sound analysis, however, is only possible on the basis of conceptional assumptions governing the question of whether war is symmetrical or asymmetrical (Münkler 2006; Schröfl and Pankratz 2004; Schröfl et al. 2006), what kind of protagonists engage in it, what their ultimate goals or purposes are, etc. The concept of new wars assumes a fundamental shift in the model of war. Or, to use von Clausewitz's words: the *grammar* of war has changed in fundamental ways; current warfare follows different rules than it used to in the past.

This begs the question of whether these supposedly new rules did not govern non-European wars all along. This can hardly be denied. Nevertheless, the European model pre-determined political and military developments elsewhere, whether in America or Asia. Even those states that had won their independence in guerrilla wars followed the European example and raised regular armies. The admission into the circle of recognized states occurred on the basis of the requirement to demonstrate a capacity to wage war according to the European model. The transformation of guerrilla units into regular armed forces and the transformation of underground irregulars into soldiers both symbolize the intended concealment of the new state's asymmetrical origins when assenting to full sovereignty as well as the new state's claim to reciprocal recognition of its sovereignty by virtue of the ability to wage symmetrical war. Today, this mechanism of recognition has lost its formative power. Hardly any of the numerous warlords of the semi-privatized wars that occur in the periphery show any inclination to transform the temporal control that was gained over an area for the purpose of economic exploitation into a regular state order. Likewise, terrorist networks make no visible efforts to take on the shape of territorial statehood. For obvious reasons: they would, if they tried, be easily defeated by those hostile powers that they aim to damage severely by means of de-territorialized and non-state forms of violence. The occasionally voiced opinion that the new wars are state-building wars just as those in sixteenth- and seventeenth-century Europe therefore rests on shaky foundations. On the contrary, these wars are state-disintegrating wars. In any case, the spread of the new wars goes hand-in-hand with an increasing number of disintegrated states.

The decisively new feature of the new wars lies in the coincidence of all three of the characteristics mentioned above, while the classical model of war dramatically loses relevance and its capacity to provide orientation and guidance. This is not to say that the phasing-out of the model of classical interstate war is to be lamented. This type of war had released such enormous destructive force that it became impossible to wage for highly developed industrial nations, even before they reached deadlock with the development of nuclear arsenals. The classical interstate wars that occurred after 1945 were wars on the fringes of prosperity zones. The combatant states would not have been able to engage in warfare without supplies of weapons and equipment from industrial nations. This, in turn, was the reason why those states did not have the same high level of vulnerability as industrial nations did. Nor did these states possess a domestic industrial base

195

that could have been changed into a war economy. The devastating consequences of post-industrialization interstate wars were therefore only partly manifested in these cases. What remained nonetheless was a dent in the demographic structure of those societies caused by the large numbers of soldiers killed and wounded, and an enormous burden of debts. The last of these classical interstate wars were those between Iraq and Iran (1980–88); between Ethiopia and Eritrea; and between Russia and Georgia. Contrary to the guerrilla wars of the period of colonial liberation, symmetrical interstate wars of this kind had only a limited effect on international order: borders were moved or confirmed, but that was all. Leaving aside the First and Second World Wars, which can only be regarded as symmetrical wars to a limited degree, classical interstate wars were more likely have conservative effects on international order. By comparison, asymmetrical wars literally have revolutionary effects (Daase 1999). In asymmetrical wars, not only are entirely new kinds of actors involved, but the norms and rules of the existing order are also weakened or dissolved.

Conclusion

The era of classical interstate wars has most likely come to a close. But this by no means entails an end of the history of war. The concept of new wars attests to that. Most of the elements that were characteristic of European warfare after the Peace of Westphalia in 1648 had likewise existed long before. Only the combination of those elements, their formative power for every party involved, and the norms and rules they generated led to a new form of warfare. The Peace of Westphalia is, of course, only a symbolic encapsulation of this process of change that occurred over several decades. These historical changes often went unnoticed, and the process was imperceptible while it occurred. Nevertheless, at the end of this process, war had a different face. Much the same is true for the current changes in warfare. This is why criticism advanced against the concept of new wars is frequently based on the assumption that the changes are exaggerated. Nevertheless, this approach is precisely what is necessary to detect change at an early and, hence, politically timely stage. The goal of political theory, therefore, cannot lie in conceptually absorbing change only after it has happened and when everyone has already come to terms with it.

Does the concept of new wars then allow predictions regarding twenty-first-century warfare? There are probably three types of war that will play a decisive role in the new century's regimes of violence. First, there are *resource wars*, mostly on the periphery of prosperity zones, in which sub-state and semi-private players rival for control over local natural resources or raw materials as well as over the local population. This trend has been observed since the 1990s. The *purpose* of this type of war is to capitalize on natural resources that can be exploited at relatively little cost and effort, its *goal* is military control of a territory in which oil, diamonds, precious metals and tropical timber are found. The *means* to this end mainly consist in setting up a reign of terror over the local population, aiming not only to deprive them of their share of the natural resource dividend and, thereby, suppress any competition, but also to turn the population into a cheap labour force in order to rake in additional profits. In such wars, water can become a very important strategic resource, above all as a means of exerting control over and dominating the local population. Resource wars are financed by so-called open war economies, that is, through their economic links with the global economic flow of funds and commodities.

196

As a result, such wars do not end due to economic exhaustion or the fact that with growing physical exhaustion the belligerents develop a greater taste for peace; rather, *low-intensity war* itself is the economic flywheel for its own continuation. Therefore, the warring parties need the war to stay in business; and this is precisely the reason why this type of war goes on for such extended periods and is almost impossible to end through a peace settlement. For the time being, the Democratic Republic of the Congo remains the most apt example for this type of war.

Because wars of this kind are fuelled by many different links to the world economy, international organizations will always be tempted to dry them out by pursuing an embargo policy. Economic sanctions, however, will only have a limited effect. First, because the belligerents have long since established close ties with international organized crime and use the back channels of shadow globalization to transport raw materials, transfer assets and draw funds in ways that it is almost impossible to paralyse by implementing embargo policies. Secondly, where the flow of money and goods can be effectively cut off, warlords make sure that the effects of sanctions are above all felt by the local population, and that this fact gets full international media coverage. In this way, most embargo policies come under intense moral scrutiny and are later amended to include many exceptions that render them ineffective while resource wars continue uncurbed. In addition, regional warlords can gain political legitimacy by exploiting the ethnic, religious or cultural divisions that exist within the territory they control in order to justify their use of violence as part of a war of liberation or resistance.

This mechanism, by which resource wars become ideologically charged, is the reason why powers from the prosperity zones, first and foremost the US, interfere in, try time and again to end (or help one side to win) such wars, and even deploy their own troops to influence political outcomes. Of course, the involvement of those powers is sometimes due to their very own interests in the strategic control of resources. However, such interventions can also serve international disarmament regimes or aim to guarantee non-proliferation. In general, this type of war can be termed *wars of pacification*. Often geo-strategic, economic and humanitarian motives are intertwined to a degree where it becomes impossible to say which of these motives is the main factor in the decision to intervene. However, unless these interventions are only of short duration and do not entail heavy losses on the intervening side, they face inherent problems. The temporal discrepancy between prolonged resource wars and relatively short wars of pacification is one of the reasons why interventions are very rarely successful at all. In many cases, interventions are based not on the strategic considerations of the intervening powers but are instead a result of giving in to moral pressure exercised by NGOs and the media in the face of impending humanitarian catastrophes.

The regions of disintegrated statehood that emerged in the wake of such wars have seen the emergence and establishment of clandestine groups that possess a growing strategic capacity to attack the wealthy states of the OECD and are developing new forms of *wars of devastation* against the rich North. To this end, these groups often employ terrorism. Contrary to guerrilla wars as a conventional form of asymmetrical warfare, terrorist tactics can carry violence deep into the territory of the enemy. Whereas guerrilla wars are in principle a defensive variant of the asymmetricalization of war from a weaker position, terrorism as a political-military strategy is able to go back on to the offensive. Since terrorism has, in recent years, been very successful that way, it must be assumed that it will be continued with increased frequency in the future. Guerrilla war with its small and scattered combat units is dependent on the support of the local population, which takes over logistics and offers cover. Guerrilla wars are only possible if the guerrillas can rely on the support of the majority of the local population. Where support is lacking, war is lost. In the case of terrorism, however, the need for the support of the local population has been replaced by the use of the civil infrastructure of the country attacked. For terrorist operations, being completely clandestine is thus a vital pre-condition. Airlines, means of mass transport and communication, mass media and even holiday resorts have become both the means and the targets of terrorist attacks. The real target, however, is the unstable psychological infrastructure of above all the Western countries. By attacking this psychological infrastructure, the political will of the country attacked is to be exhausted. Terrorism aims to achieve the psychological effects of violence, that is, fear and – in the truest sense of the word – terror, both spread the more effectively the greater the density of media coverage in the attacked country. The goal of this strategic use of violence is the socio-economic damage caused by fear; it is not the actual material destruction that the attacks involve. The terrorists believe that those economic effects, when they reach an unbearable degree, will force the targeted state to give in. In this sense, even religiously motivated terrorism is a strategy of violence that will constitute one of the new forms of warfare in the twenty-first century.

References

Bennett, C. (1996) *Yugoslavia's Bloody Collapse: Causes, Course and Consequences*, New York: New York University Press.

Bryden, A. and Caparini, M. (eds) (2006) *Private Actors and Security Governance*, Zürich: Lit Verlag.

Chesterman, S. (ed.) (2007) *From Mercenaries to Market: The Rise and Regulation of Private Military Companies*, Oxford: Oxford University Press.

von Clausewitz, C. (1980) *Vom Kriege*, ed. by W. Hahlweg, 19th edn, Bonn: Ferdinand Dümmler.

Coker, C. (2004) *The Future of War: The Re-Enchantment of War in the Twenty-First Century*, Oxford: Blackwell.

Cooper, R. (2003) *The Breaking of Nations: Order and Chaos in the Twenty-first Century*, London: Atlantic Books.

van Creveld, M. (1991) *The Transformation of War*, New York: Free Press.

Daase, C. (1999) *Kleine Kriege – große Wirkung: Wie unkonventionelle Kriegführung die internationale Politik verändert*, Baden-Baden: Nomos.

Freedman, L. and Karsh, E. (1993) *The Gulf Conflict 1990–1991: Diplomacy and War in the New World Order*, London: Faber and Faber.

Geis, A. (ed.) (2006) *Den Krieg überdenken: Kriegsbegriffe und Kriegstheorien in der Kontroverse*, Baden-Baden: Nomos.

Gongora, T. and von Riekhoff, H. (eds) (2000) *Toward a Revolution in Military Affairs? Defense and Security at the Dawn of the Twenty-first Century*, Westport, Conn.: Greenwood Press.

Halpin, E. (2006) *Cyberwar, Netwar, and the Revolution in Military Affairs*, Basingstoke, Hampshire: Palgrave Macmillan.

Hoffman, B. (2006) *Inside Terrorism: Revised and Enlarged Edition*, New York: Columbia University Press.

Hundley, R.O. (1999) *Past Revolutions, Future Transformations: What Can the History of Revolutions in Military Affairs Tell us about Transforming the U.S. Military?*, Santa Monica, CA: Rand.

Ignatieff, M. (1998) *The Warrior's Honor: Ethnic War and the Modern Conscience*, London: Chatto and Windus.

——(2001) *Virtual War: Kosovo and Beyond*, New York: Picador.

Ismael, T.Y. and Ismael, J.S. (eds) (1994) *The Gulf War and the New World Order: International Relations of the Middle East*, Gainesville: University of California Press.

Jäger, T. and Kümmel, G. (eds) (2007) *Private Military and Security Companies: Chances, Problems, Pitfalls and Prospects*, Wiesbaden: VS Verlag für Sozialwissenschaften.

Janowitz, M. (1966) *The Professional Soldier: A Social and Political Portrait*, New York: The Free Press.

Kaldor, M. (1999) *New and Old Wars: Organized Violence in a Global Era*, Stanford, CA: Stanford University Press.

Kennan, G.F. (1979) T*he Decline of Bismarck's European Order: Franco-Russian Relations, 1875–1890*, Princeton, NJ: Princeton University Press.

Kinsey, C. (2006) *Corporate Soldiers and International Security: The Rise of Private Military Companies*, Abingdon: Routledge.

Knights, M. (ed.) (2004) *Operation Iraqi Freedom and the New Iraq: Insights and Forecasts*, Washington, DC: Washington Institute for Near East Policy.

Menkhaus, K. (2004) *Somalia: State Collapse and the Threat of Terrorism*, Oxford: Oxford University Press.

Münkler, H. (2002) *Über den Krieg: Stationen der Kriegsgeschichte im Spiegel ihrer theoretischen Reflexion*, Weilerswist: Verlag Velbrück.

——(2005) *The New Wars*, Cambridge: Polity Press.

——(2006) *Der Wandel des Krieges: Von der Symmetrie zur Asymmetrie*, Weilerswist: Verlag Velbrück.

——(2007) 'What is really new about the new wars?' in Olsen, J.A. (ed.) *On New Wars*, Oslo Files On Defence and Security 4/2007, pp. 67–82.

Parker, G. (1988) *The Military Revolution: Military Innovation and the Rise of the West, 1500–1800*, Cambridge: Cambridge University Press.

Prunier, G. (1995) *The Rwanda Crisis: History of a Genocide*, New York: Columbia University Press.

Reno, W. (1998) *Warlord Politics and African States*, Boulder: Rienner.

Rich, P. (ed.) (1999) *Warlords in International Relations*, Basingstoke, Hampshire: Macmillan.

Richardson, L. (2006) *What Terrorists Want: Understanding the Terrorist Threat*, London: Murray.

Rogers, C.B. (ed.) (1995) *The Military Revolution Debate. Readings on the Military Transformations of Early Modern Europe*, Boulder: Westview Press.

Schreiber, W. (2001) 'Die Kriege in der zweiten Hälfte des 20. Jahrhunderts und danach', in T. Rabehl and W. Schreiber (eds) *Das Kriegsgeschehen 2000*, Opladen: Verlag Leske und Budrich, pp. 11–46.

Schröfl, J. and Pankratz, T. (eds) (2004) *Asymmetrische Kriegführung – ein neues Phänomen der internationalen Politik?* Baden-Baden: Nomos.

Schröfl, J., Pankratz, T. and Micewski, E. (eds) (2006) *Aspekte der Asymmetrie: Reflexionen über ein gesellschafts-und sicherheitspolitisches Phänomen*, Baden-Baden: Nomos.

Stepanova, E. (2008) *Terrorism in Asymmetrical Conflict: Ideological and Structural Aspects*, Oxford: Oxford University Press.

Thomas, T.S., Kiser, S.D. and Casebeer, W.D. (2005) *Warlords Rising: Confronting Violent Non-State Actors*, Lanham: Lexington Books.

Weber, M. (1995) *Der Sozialismus*, with an introduction by H. Münkler, Weinheim: Beltz Athenäum Verlag.

18

The privatization of international security

Anna Leander

The concept of the privatization of international security can refer to a wide range of phenomena, reflecting the growing role of non-state actors in international security. This Handbook's entries on New Wars, Terrorism, State Failure, Migration, Organized Crime or Energy Security can be read as reflections on 'the privatization of international security'. This chapter does not replicate their arguments or try to cover privatization in this broad sense. Rather, it explores privatization in the more specific sense of the word, namely as referring to the incidence or process of transferring ownership, control or competencies from the public sector (state) to the private sector (business); in this case, within the realm of international security. In other words, it discusses how the development of a market for force and the private military and security companies (PMSCs) operating in it have become part of the academic literature in Security Studies.

PMSCs are companies that buy and sell military and security services internationally. Their activities encompass logistics, intelligence, consultancy, training and protection services. What they have in common is that they take on tasks that armed forces can also or do take on and that this directly ties them to the use of force. Since many contemporary conflicts are not international, this use of force might not be strictly speaking 'military' but may fall within the 'security' realm, hence the importance of referring to PMSCs rather than just PMCs. In fact, companies (particularly those providing protection services, such as Blackwater, recently renamed 'Xe') insist on defining their activities as falling in the security realm to avoid association with mercenarism. Like many other markets, the market for force is highly segmented, with companies specializing in different activities, catering for specific demands and (hence) having varied relations to clients and following different formal (laws, regulations) and informal (codes of conduct, norms) rules.[1]

Estimates (more akin to wild guesses) have conveyed the rapid and recent expansion and growth of the market. The private military sector reportedly doubled in size between 1990 and 1999 (growing from US$55 to US$100 bn) and is expected to double again by 2010 (reaching US$200 bn). Another indicator often used is the increased ratio of contractors to US soldiers, which is said to have been 1:60 in the 1991 Gulf War, increasing to 1.3:1 in Iraq in 2007. At the same time, a growing number of incidences (extensively covered in the media) involving PMSCs have come to epitomize their presence in public discussions. Few will have remained unaware, for example, of the shootings of 17 Iraqi civilians by Blackwater employees in Baghdad in 2007; the 'trophy' video showing Aegis employees randomly shooting at civilian vehicles while 'driving in Iraq' in 2004; the involvement of Titan and CACI employees in the abuse of Abu Ghraib inmates in 2003–4; the lynching of four Blackwater employees in Fallujah in 2004; or the role of Executive Outcomes in the Sierra Leonean civil war 1995–96.

The integration of private international security into Security Studies reflects this relatively recent nature of the market. The literature on the topic revolves around the themes of placing private international security on the agenda (the first section of this chapter); explaining and understanding the market; and problematizing its relationship to central questions in international security. The current trend (the second section of this article) in the field is to face the – still largely open – challenge of taking research further, both by completing, refining and updating current research efforts and by expanding and enriching the research agenda to more fully explore the politics of market development. Paradoxically, as this entry concludes, this is leading scholars to abandon the focus on 'privatization' and instead pushing them to formulate research agenda in new terms such as commercialization, commodification, governance or governmentality.

Key themes

Work on the privatization of security expresses the recent nature of the phenomenon. It evolves around the basic need of attracting attention to the significant developments that have taken place since the end of the Cold War, to affirm its general political salience and, of course, to show that it is a topic worthy of scholarly attention. Much of this work is not strictly academic. Practitioners have had strong reasons to push for more engagement with private international security. This section sketches out the key themes in the resulting literature.

Discovering/documenting/denouncing private international security

If this Handbook had been written 10 years ago, this entry would almost certainly not have been included. This is partly because the market expanded radically only after the end of the Cold War. But it is also because conventional scholarship in Security Studies and International Relations refused (and in many camps still refuse) to acknowledge its significance, reducing firms to prolongations of states and denying the existence of markets. As a consequence, a recurrent issue in the literature about private international security has been establishing its existence and relevance.

Non-academic work by journalists, think tanks, advocacy NGOs and security professionals (including members of armed forces and the private security sector) has played a key role in documenting the significance of the market. Their closeness to the practice of security makes them acutely aware of the changing role of markets and PMSCs. It also directly implicates them in the various problems and prospects inherent in market development. Business professionals and their professional associations have documented the part played by private security companies in a number of conflicts and suggested ways of using it more constructively (Spicer 1999; Barlow 2008; London 2008; Shepherd 2008; BAPSC 2009; IPOA 2009). All major companies have their own websites and often engage in the debate on the utility of their work. Some companies even provide links to the broader discussion on the theme. Lawyers from the armed forces have documented the role of 'contractors on the battlefield' and pressed for clarifications of what can be demanded of them and what responsibility the armed forces have towards them (Zamparelli 1999; Guillory 2001; Heaton 2005). Political activists have raised concerns about the issues of political and legal accountability when war becomes business (Musah and Fayemi 2000; ICIJ 2009). Public accountants have scrutinized the existing systems of economic accountability (GAO 2005; Rasor and Bauman 2007). Human rights activists and lawyers have debated the degree to which markets raise human rights concerns and how these might be dealt with (War on Want 2006; Human Rights First 2008; ICRC 2008; UN 2009). Finally, journalists working in conflict areas and/or with international security have pushed for greater awareness of the roles of the market and market actors (Silverstein 2000; Young Pelton 2006) as well as studied specific firms (Scahill 2007), specific sub-sectors (Shorrok 2008) or the specific conflicts (Fainaru 2008).

The result is an extensive body of work on private international security driven by the concerns of those engaged in its practice. It is difficult to overstate the significance of this work for the development of the scholarly field. It has diffused information and details about a sector that can be difficult to access. It has done so in dialogue with think tanks (including DCAF 2009; IPI 2009; ISS 2009; PMO 2009) and the academic world, providing 'facts' and ideas about key issues and processes. This practice-driven engagement with private security has been a crucial part of public debate on the issue. Public awareness, in turn, has triggered a demand for scholarly work on the subject and has generated funding for projects and legitimacy for research in the field. The consequence is that, to a degree that is rather uncommon in scholarly Security Studies – possibly reflecting more general transformations of knowledge production – work on private international security is 'problem driven' and is formulated in dialogue with those engaged in the practice who discover, document and denounce the sector.

Explaining and understanding private international security

The academic pendant of the need to discover, document and denounce is to explain and understand. As academia has become increasingly engaged with private international security, a second focus therefore emerges: explaining and understanding private international security, including its origins, its workings and its government.

What made the development of private international security possible in the first place is an intriguing and interesting question. Why would states loosen their control over the sensitive security sector and why professionals both in the formerly protected, heavily state-subsidized military/security business and in the armed forces have welcomed and often encouraged its development are questions that figure prominently in the current academic literature on private international security. Arguments that recur in the answers include changing political conditions, and particularly the end of the Cold War, which drove states to reduce their defence budgets and hence pushed security firms and professionals (unemployed professionals) to provide for themselves, effectively creating a market (CRIA 1998; Shearer 1998; Kinsey 2006). More than this, region-specific changes are often invoked as explanations. In Africa, for example, the end of apartheid left a large professional security force in search of alternative occupations. At the same time, revisions in international development aid strategies and internal political alliance strategies made African states adopt market-based security solutions (Musah 2002; Abrahamsen and Williams 2007). Finally, changes in arms technology and the organization of armed forces; the revolution in military affairs; and the associated use of 'dual-use' and 'off the shelf' technology as well as shifts in overarching governance patterns – Post-Fordism and new public management – have been proposed as factors making inevitable the intro-duction of less statist and more market-oriented strategies, including in the security sector (Kaldor et al. 1998; Susman and O'Keefe 1998; Markusen et al. 2003).

A second, equally intriguing and difficult question that almost automatically follows from the previous one is how private international security works and particularly whe-ther or not it is efficient. Is the market merely a shift in the way states do things and not really a private market at all, with firms functioning as instruments of war in the hands of states? Or are the firms genuinely private actors, working in a private market with its own, admittedly idiosyncratic, norms and rules? Whether they are private or not, are these markets effective or – perhaps more adequately in view of the unravelling eco-nomic scandals – can they be made effective? What kind of institutions would it actually take to ensure that the markets proved capable of doing more than merely diverting the post-Cold War peace dividend towards those who were supposed to pay it? These questions are not minor or narrowly economic ones. They are of intense political rele-vance since efficiency and cost savings have been pivotal in legitimizing outsourcing and privatization strategies everywhere (Markusen 2003; Minow 2003). They also have ramifications for theoretical literature on organizational and governance structures in other areas, and they very explicitly raise the question of how private international security is and should be governed.

To explain and understand the government of private international security is indeed a final central theme in existing scholarly work on private international security (Chester-man and Lehnardt 2007). This should hardly come as a surprise, since clarifying the relationship between markets and regulatory institutions is fundamental to understanding which firms can be held accountable and where regulatory change is required – and politically feasible – to bring them under control (Sapone 1999; Coleman 2004). This is the area where the interests of academics and those engaged in security practices overlap most directly and where the line between the two is decidedly blurred. In the 'mad scramble' (Kierpaul 2008) to bring companies to justice, a great number of publications in scholarly journals, in the form of commissioned reports and advocacy papers, have appeared to clarify, explain and improve the possibilities of holding market actors accountable to civilians, their own employees, the states, armed forces, business and institutions that contract them. Conversely, some publications have demanded that the companies should have ways of demanding accountability in return. These discussions have resulted not only in momentous progress in understanding the regulatory options, but also in growing clarity about where core disagreements and positions lie on how these can/should be used (de Wolf 2007; Leander 2009b). Work explaining and under-standing private international security has contributed far more to the clarification of disagreements than to the production of consensus knowledge.

Debating the consequences of private international security

A final key theme in the study of private international security has been the substantive implication of privatization for international security. The development of a private international security market poses real questions about the way security is organized, distributed and understood.

The state monopoly on the legitimate use of force (SMLF) is arguably at the heart of the organization of international security. It certainly underpins conventional thinking about international security where states are the main actors and are assumed to have such a monopoly. Altering (e.g. by making more legitimate) or bolstering (e.g. by tightening control) the state monopoly on legitimate force are therefore also options that figure largely in debates about how to deal with international security problems. How privatization affects this monopoly on the use of force – and hence the organization of international security – consequently figures largely in the study of private international security. Is one of the fundamental institutions of international society undergoing far-reaching change or not? Have we seen a revision of the longstanding strong norm/weak law banning mercenarism in international relations (Milliard 2003; Percy 2007)? The answers span the full spectrum of possibilities. Some scholars depict a world where private international security has fundamentally undermined the SMLF by creating a world of legitimate security activities beyond the state; a 'new-medievalism' or coming anarchy where companies compete with states. However, most scholars prefer to discuss transformations (Avant 2005; Verkuil 2007) and many suggest that state authority might in fact be rather untouched by the development of private international security since the centrality of sovereignty is not affected by it (Thomson 1994). Private international security might solidify the conventional organization of international security by rendering sovereignty and the SMLF even more central to international security relations. The market sharpens the divide between states who can bolster private international security to their own advantage and those that cannot not (Leander 2009c).

This evokes questions about what the development of private international security entails for the distribution of international security. *Cui bono?* The classical question has also been a key cause of disagreement in the discussions surrounding private international security. This question can of course be posed at the level of hierarchies among states as just indicated. Whose states security interests are served by the development of private international security and whose are not? For some, private international security is, above all, the enabling condition of aggressive US/Western unilateralism (Tiefer 2007) or of a form of corporate neo-imperialism allowing companies to govern economic activities and the territory necessary to that end (Francis 1999; Musah 2002). Either way, private international security exacerbates inequalities among states in the international system. For others, private international security is the condition which makes it possible for (some) weak and crumbling states to upgrade their armed forces and defend themselves against the spill-overs from regional conflicts (Brooks 2000; Howe 2001). In this account, private international security bolsters weak states and hence diminishes inequality in the relations between states.

Moving beyond the question of hierarchies among states to the matter of whose security needs are served by the development of private international security, we again find sharply contrasting positions. Some scholars see private international security as the only alternative that individuals, companies, NGOs and public institutions can avail themselves of when they operate in areas where public security has broken down. They hence point out that this might balance out the obvious moral dilemma of embracing a system where only those in possession of the necessary financial means receive protection. Other scholars suggest that although this might be true at the individual level, it has the overall broader effect of further militarizing and securitizing social relations by increasing the presence, use and centrality of armed security. It hence leads to a deterioration of public security, not to its restoration (for discussions on this issue, see Leander 2005a; Abrahamsen and Williams 2006; Cockayne 2006; Spearin 2008).

This leads straight to a final central theme in the study of private international security, namely its significance for security understandings, for the 'construction' of threats, and for the formulation of security strategies and politics. Does it matter for our conception of threats that security is partly provided through markets? The (often implicit) answer to this question, given particularly by those who advocate privatization, but also by many other contributors to the discussions surrounding private international security, is that companies respond to a given demand. They are 'agents' of 'principals'; when the military is involved, the principal is usually a state, while security services may be sold also to business, journalists and NGOs. The companies offer services to respond to pre-defined needs and threats; e.g. a state that contracts a private airlift to transport soldiers or an NGO needing convoy protection in Afghanistan. The market does not define the threats. However, from a critical vantage point, it has been suggested that the companies actually re-shape security understandings as a part of their perfectly normal and legal activities, for example through their consultancy services, trainings, advertisements, routine practices and participation in public discussions: due to the very basic fact that they promote security products, they heighten awareness of insecurity and hence alter security perceptions (Der Derian 2001; Leander 2005b). This raises the more general question about whether or not there is a need to think about private security as a 'contested commodity' on a par with the trade in organs or prostitution, where the strong moral and ethical stakes would warrant serious thinking about regulations on lobbying, public engagement, marketing and information about the sector (Sapone 1999; Krahmann 2007).

Trends and challenges ahead

Just as the key themes in the study of private international security bear the mark of the recent history of the field, so do the current research trends and challenges ahead. The basic needs of discovering, explaining and understanding basic aspects of private international security continue to play an important role and will do so for the foreseeable future. In addition to this, as the study of private international security is becoming more established, the trend and challenge ahead is to refine and enrich the questions asked about it. Paradoxically (perhaps), this seems to be leading scholars away from the study of privatization.

Filling the gaps

Publications about private international security are mushrooming in all academic fields, including in Security Studies. However, and in spite of this, there are major gaps in the basic knowledge and understanding of it. One trend at present is to close these gaps by both looking at the many still under-researched aspects of private international security and by integrating the constant evolution into the study area.

Writing about private international security has been rather narrow in its focus. It has been built largely around two empirical areas of study. The first is the role of private international security in the developing world. The reason is the central and much-debated role of large private companies in key conflicts, including, for example, the role of Executive Outcomes in Sierra Leone and Angola; of Sandline in Sierra Leone and Papua New Guinea (neither company exists today); of DynCorp in Colombia; and of

MPRI in Bosnia. The second is the role of large contractors to the US armed forces in Iraq and Afghanistan. This means that large swaths of private international security remain under-studied. This is true of private international security outside the geographic areas just mentioned, including private international security in Europe (an exception being, e.g. Krahmann 2005), but also in the developing world beyond the 1990s and beyond Iraq and Afghanistan. More than this, the focus on the large firms has meant that the role of smaller firms or firms working outside the conflicts that have been extensively covered in the media has been largely left off the radar screens. The implication is that the vast subcontracting sector, the global employment practices and the ramifications of the global market remain ill understood, as the UN working group insists in all its reports (UN 2009). One of the current trends is therefore to expand the understanding of private international security in these directions.

Second, private international security is not a fixed entity. On the contrary, the size-able public debate and reflexivity about it makes it a dynamic and evolving area with constantly shifting and contested boundaries. The regulation and international standards governing private international security are developing rapidly, as illustrated by changes in national and international regulations, including the 2007 expansion of the US Uniform Code of Military Justice; the adoption of the ICRC Montreux Document; the changes occurring in the UN working group on mercenaries; or the shifting fates of the codes of conducted published, e.g. by the DCAF, IPOA and BASCP. More than this, governance is changing shape, particularly because of the steady growth of private-sector involvement. Private security actors are implicated to a growing extent in various forms of private–public partnerships and hybrid institutions governing private international security, but also increasingly in other realms, including, for example, training policies or efforts to establish standards (Dorn and Levi 2007; Leander 2009a). Finally, the over-arching logic for governing conducts (governmentality) in the security field, as in other areas, is increasingly 'neo-liberal' (in the Foucauldian understanding);[2] a trend that is both shaped by and shaping the privatization of security. Analysing the meaning, implications and causes of these changes is a trend in the scholarly literature (e.g. Salter 2008; Leander 2009b).

Finally, scholars are expanding the kinds of questions asked of private international security. Projects are emerging on a wide range of central issues that have remained under-explored. One example is the relation of private international security to gender inside the market, among security professionals, but also in society more broadly, including both the home context of the companies and the places where they operate (Schultz and Yeung 2008). This is but one example intended to highlight the trend not only to fill in the gaps in knowledge, but to open the field of private international security toward the study of a range of interesting issues.

Acknowledging the limitations of private international security

Perhaps the most interesting trend – and future challenge – is the critical evaluation of the limits inherent in a research agenda formulated around *private* international security.

One of the many established truths about private international security has been that the boundaries between states and markets are 'blurred' and that there are many revolving doors at all levels. For all practical purposes, the two spheres are partly enmeshed. The practical implication has been that privatization understood as shifting ownerships, control and authority is difficult to establish. But perhaps even more significantly, the extent of overlap or enmeshment means that substantial political changes may take place without necessarily involving shifts in the formal private–public divide. For example, shifts in public discourses shaped by private international security advertising and lobbying, shifts in routine intelligence practices, or shifts in the hierarchies among security professionals linked to the growth of private international security may be of substantial political salience, but entail no shifts in public–private authority. A discourse focusing on that divide may hence not only miss key political developments, but even obscure them. The focus on the public–private divide distracts attention from critical inquiry and (thereby) bolsters the impression that private international security may have developed without significant political implications.

Scholars working on private international security have increasingly become (more or less articulately) aware of these drawbacks that are linked to a research agenda framed in terms of privatization. The consequence has been a trend to steer away from privatization and instead formulate research in terms that do not direct attention to the public or private status of actors, but rather to the effects of creating security markets. Commodification, commercialization, governance and governmentality have come to figure more centrally on the research agenda. This move links studies of private international security more tightly to the broader 'new' or 'critical' security agenda. Questions surrounding the commercial production of new insecurities, the commercial refashioning of security spaces and the everyday commercial security practices figure prominently on this new research agenda (as elaborated in Leander 2009a). The irony is that in their effort to gain a foothold in understanding the politics of private international security, researchers have had to confront the inherent limitations of an agenda focused on privatization: they have moved from studying the privatization of international security to the study of commercial insecurity. The bibliography below is designed to give anyone interested in this rapidly evolving field and its change plenty of entry points for judging whether or not they agree with this depiction of the field and the many other claims advanced above.

Notes

1 For in-depth definitions and descriptions of this sector, see the relevant overview chapters in Singer (2003), Avant (2005), Leander (2006) or Isenberg (2008).
2 The term 'neo-liberal' here refers to decentralized forms of government through quasi markets and the empowerment and responsibilization of individuals that Foucault identifies as a specific historical form of government (or governmentality) differing from other historical forms such as liberal, bureaucratic and sovereign.

References

Abrahamsen, R. and Williams, M.C. (2006) *The Globalization of Private Security: Country Report Nigeria*, Aberystwyth: University of Wales.
——(2007) 'Special issue: The privatization and globalisation of security in Africa', *International Relations* 21, 2.
Avant, D. (2005) *The Market for Force: The Consequences of Privatizing Security*, Cambridge: Cambridge University Press.
BAPSC (2009) 'The British Association of Private Security Companies'. Available online at: www.bapsc.org.uk/ (accessed 24 February 2009).

Barlow, E. (2008) *Executive Outcomes: Against All Odds*, Alberton, South Africa: Galago Publishing.

Brooks, D. (2000) 'Write a cheque, end a war: Using private military companies to end African conflicts', *Conflict Trends* 1: 33–35.

Chesterman, S. and Lehnardt, C. (eds) (2007) *From Mercenaries to Markets: The Rise and Regulation of Private Military Companies*, Oxford: Oxford University Press.

Cockayne, J. (2006) 'Commercial security in the humanitarian space: Towards best practice', New York: International Peace Academy. Available online at: www.ipacademy.org/pdfs/COMMERCIAL_SECURITY_FINAL.pdf (accessed 28 February 2009).

Coleman, J.R. (2004) 'Constraining modern mercenarism', *Hastings Law Journal* 55: 1493–1537.

CRIA (1998) 'Special issue on private military companies', *Cambridge Review of International Affairs* 13, 1.

DCAF (2009) 'The Geneva Centre for the Democratic Control of Armed Forces programme on the Privatization of Security'. Available online at: www.privatesecurityregulation.net/introduction (accessed 24 February 2009).

de Wolf, A. H. (2007) 'Privatizing war from the perspective of international and human rights law', *Indiana Journal of Global Legal Studies* 13: 315–35.

Der Derian, J. (2001) *Virtuous War: Mapping the Military-Industrial-Media-Entertainment Network*, Boulder CO: Westview Press.

Dorn, N. and Levi, M. (2007) 'European private security, corporate investigation and military services: Collective security, market regulation and structuring the public sphere', *Policing and Society* 17, 3: 213–38.

Fainaru, S. (2008) *Big Boy Rules: In the Company of America's Mercenaries Fighting in Iraq*, Cambridge: Da Capo Press.

Francis, D.J. (1999) 'Mercenary intervention in Sierra Leone: Providing national security or international exploitation?' *Third World Quarterly* 20, 2: 319–38.

GAO (2005) Government Accountability Office, *Rebuilding Iraq: Actions Needed to Improve Use of Private Security Providers*, GAO-05-737, Washington: Government Accountability Office.

Guillory, M.M.E. (2001) 'Civilianizing the force: Is the United States crossing the rubicon?' *The Air Force Law Review* 51: 111–42.

Heaton, J.R. (2005) 'Civilians at war: Reexamining the status of civilians accompanying the armed forces', *Air Force Law Review* 57: 157–208.

Howe, H.M. (2001) *Ambiguous Order: Military Forces in African States*, Boulder, CO: Lynne Rienner.

Human Rights First (2008) *Private Security Contractors at War: Ending the Culture of Impunity*. Available online at: www.humanrightsfirst.org (accessed 28 February 2009).

ICIJ (2009) 'The International Consortium of Investigative Journalists project on the business of war'. Available online at: http://projects.publicintegrity.org/bow/ (accessed 24 February 2009).

ICRC (2008), 'International Committee of the Red Cross and Swiss Government: Montreux document on pertinent international legal obligations and good practices for states related to operations of private military and security companies during armed conflict'. Geneva. Available online at: www.icrc.org/web/eng/siteeng0.nsf/htmlall/montreux-document-170908 (accessed 28 February 2009).

IPI (2009) 'The International Peace Institute database over researchers on international private security'. Available online at: www.ipinst.org/our-work/coping-with-crisis/grips/ (accessed 24 February 2009).

IPOA (2009) 'International Peace Operations Association'. Available online at: http://ipoaworld.org/eng/ (accessed 24 February 2009).

Isenberg, D. (2008) *Shadow Force: Private Security Contractors in Iraq*, New York: Praeger.

ISS (2009) 'The Institute for Security Studies (Pretoria ZA) privatization project'. Available online at: www.issafrica.org/index.php?link_id=30&link_type = 12&tmpl_id = 2 (accessed 24 February 2009).

Kaldor, M., Albrecht, U. and Schméder, G. (eds) (1998) *Restructuring the Global Military Sector. The End of Military Fordism*, London: Pinter.

Kierpaul, I. (2008) 'The rush to bring private military contractors to justice: The mad scramble of congress, lawyers, and law students after Abu Ghraib', *The University of Toledo Law Review* 39: 407–35.

Kinsey, C. (2006) *Corporate Soldiers and International Security: The Rise of Private Military Companies*, London: Routledge.

Krahmann, E. (2005) 'Controlling private military companies in the UK and Germany: Between partnership and regulation', *European Security* 13, 2: 277–95.

——(2007) 'Security: Collective good or commodity?' *European Journal of International Relations* 14, 3: 379–405.

Leander, A. (2005a) 'The market for force and public security: The destabilizing consequences of private military companies', *Journal of Peace Research* 42, 5: 605–22.

——(2005b) 'The power to construct international security: On the significance of private military companies', *Millennium* 33, 3: 803–26.

——(2006) *Eroding State Authority? Private Military Companies and the Legitimate Use of Force*, Rome: Centro Militare di Studi Strategici.

——(2009a) 'Commercial security practices', in Burgess, P.J. (ed.) *Handbook of New Security Studies*, London and New York: Routledge.

——(2009b) 'New roles for external actors? Disagreements about international regulation of private armies', in Aggestam, K. and Björkdal, A. (eds.) *War and Peace in Transition: Changing Roles for External Actors*, Lund: Nordic Academic Press, pp. 32–52.

——(2009c) 'Securing sovereignty by governing security through markets', in Adler-Nissen, R. and Gammeltoft-Hansen, T. (eds) *Sovereignty Games: Instrumentalising State Sovereignty in Europe and Beyond*, London: Palgrave.

——(WP) 'working papers on civil military relations, the impunity of contractors, international legal instruments of regulation and industry self images'. Available online at: www.cbs.dk/content/view/pub/38570 (accessed 24 February 2009).

London, J. (2008) *Our Good Name: A Company's Fight to Defend its Honour and Get the Truth told About Abu Ghraib*, Washington, DC: Regenery Publishing.

Markusen, A.R. (2003) 'The case against privatizing national security', *Governance: An International Journal of Policy, Administration, and Institutions* 16, 4: 471–501.

Markusen, A.R., DiGiovanna, S. and Leary, M.C. (eds) (2003) *From Defense to Development? International Perspectives on Realizing the Peace Dividend*, London and New York: Routledge.

Milliard, M.T.S. (2003) 'Overcoming post-colonial myopia: A call to recognize and regulate private military companies', *Military Law Review* 176: 1–95.

Minow, M. (2003) 'Public and private partnerships: Accounting for the new religion', *Harvard Law Review* 116: 1229–70.

Musah, A.-F. (2002) 'Privatization of security: Arms proliferation and the process of state collapse in Africa', *Development and Change* 33, 5: 911–33.

Musah, A.-F. and Fayemi, K.J. (eds) (2000) *Mercenaries: An African Security Dilemma*, London: Pluto Press.

Percy, S. (2007) 'Mercenaries: Strong norm, weak law', *International Organization* 61, 2: 367–97.

PMO (2009) 'privatemilitary.org company and literature links'. Available online at: www.privatemilitary.org (accessed 24 February 2009).

Rasor, D. and Bauman, R. (2007) *Betraying Our Troops: The Destructive Results of Privatizing War*, New York: Palgrave.

Salter, M. (2008) 'Imagining numbers: Risk, quantification, and aviation security', *Security Dialogue* 39, 2–3: 243–66.

Sapone, M. (1999) 'I have rifle with scope, will travel: The global economy of mercenary violence', *California Western International Law Journal* 30: 1–43.

Scahill, J. (2007) *Blackwater: The Rise of the World's Most Powerful Mercenary Army*, Washington: Nation Books.

Schultz, S. and Yeung, C. (2008) 'Private military and security companies and gender Washington', UNINSTRAW, United Nations International Research and Training Instiute for the Advancement of Women.

Shearer, D. (1998) 'Private armies and military intervention'. *Adelphi Paper* 316.

Shepherd, B. (2008) *The Circuit: An Ex-SAS Soldier's True Account of One of the Most Powerful and Secretive Industries Spawned by the War on Terror*, London: Macmillan.

Shorrok, T. (2008) *Spies for Hire: The Secret World of Intelligence Outsourcing*, New York: Simon and Schuster.

Silverstein, K. (2000) *Private Warriors*, New York and London: Verso.

Singer, P.W. (2003) *Corporate Warriors: The Rise of the Privatized Military Industry*, Ithaca, NY and London: Cornell University Press.

Spearin, C. (2008) 'Private, armed and humanitarian? States, NGOs, international private security companies and shifting humanitarianism', *Security Dialogue* 39, 3: 363–82.

Spicer, T.L.C. (1999) *An Unorthodox Soldier: Peace and War and the Sandline Affair*, Edinburgh: Mainstream.

Susman, G. and O'Keefe, S. (eds) (1998) *The Defense Industry in the Post-Cold War Era: Corporate Strategies and Public Policy Perspectives*, Oxford: Pergamon.

Thomson, J. (1994) *Mercenaries, Pirates, and Sovereigns: State-building and Extraterritorial Violence in Early Modern Europe*, Princeton: Princeton University Press.

Tiefer, C. (2007) 'The Iraq debacle: The rise and fall of procurement-aided unilateralism as a paradigm of foreign war', *University of Pennsylvania Journal of International Economic Law* 29: 1–56.

UN (2009) 'The UN working group on the use of mercenaries as a means of violating human rights and impending the exercise of the right of peoples to self-determination'. Available online at: www2.ohchr.org/english/issues/mercenaries/wgstandards.htm (accessed 24 February 2009).

Verkuil, P. (2007) *Outsourcing Sovereignty: Why Privatization of Government Functions Threatens Democracy and What We Can Do about It*, Cambridge: Cambridge University Press.

War on Want (2006) *Corporate Mercenaries*. Available online at: www.waronwant.org/Corporate%20Mercenaries%2013275.twl (accessed 28 February 2009).

Young Pelton, R. (2006) *Licensed to Kill: Hired Guns in the War on Terror*, New York: Crown Publishers.

Zamparelli, C.S.J. (1999) 'Competitive sourcing and privatization: Contractors on the battlefield', *Air Force Journal of Logistics*, XXIII: 1–17.

19

Energy security

Robert W. Orttung and Jeronim Perovic

Oil price volatility, fears of instability in the Middle East and other energy-producing regions, anxiety about a looming 'peak oil' and concerns about global warming have moved energy security to the top of the international political agenda. Oil in particular has evolved from being the world's most important traded commodity to a powerful tool in the political and economic relations among countries: whether a country produces oil and gas for the global market or must rely on fuel imports, energy helps define its position in international politics.[1]

Energy is redefining the international security structure as the high revenues generated by oil sales since 2002 transfer more wealth from consumers, mainly in the West, to producers largely located in other regions. The rise of new energy consumers, such as China and India, is exacerbating the competition for dwindling resources and creating a new source of demand outside the West. State-controlled companies in resource-rich countries have replaced Western international private companies as the owners of the shrinking supply of energy resources. Accordingly, they are becoming much more assertive and powerful actors on the international stage and frequently challenge Western interests.

While the combination of rising powers and shrinking energy resources contains the potential for conflict, we argue that the current situation may also present opportunities for global cooperation. Both energy exporters and consumers are essentially interested in a stable energy system with functioning market mechanisms. In addition, as new technologies and alternative energies develop, the relative importance of traditional sources of energy will change and again transform international power relations.

This chapter first examines the various definitions of energy security. Second, it provides a brief overview of the history of energy security. Third, it examines the many sources of change currently affecting the international energy system. Fourth, it analyses the impact of energy on international politics, showing how the search for energy security can alternatively foster conflict and cooperation. The final section looks at challenges for the future.

Differing definitions and strategies

Countries have different perspectives on energy security depending on whether they import or export energy (SIPRI 1974: 17–20). Importing countries emphasize reliable supplies of ample energy, affordable prices, a diversity of producers and adequate infrastructure to transport oil and gas (Kalicki and Goldwyn 2005: 9f.). Traditional energy consumers include the US, Europe and Japan. These countries have recently been joined by rising new powers, such as China and India. Although the US has extensive sources of domestic energy, it has relied on imported oil since the 1960s to meet its growing demand (Heinberg 2005: 75). European import dependence varies from country to country, but the continent as a whole relies heavily on oil from the Middle East and natural gas from Russia. China and India began importing energy in the 1990s, much later than the West, but now their enormous need for all kinds of energy is transforming the market. China and India together will account for 45 per cent of the total increase in world primary energy consumption by 2030 (IEA 2007: 42).

Energy exporting countries stress other aspects when defining energy security (Yergin 2006). They prefer high prices and stable demand, typically provided by a diversity of customers; maintaining maximum control over their energy industries, while obtaining sufficient domestic or foreign investment to maintain or increase output; and ensuring that their economies are sufficiently diversified so that they are not reliant on fluctuating energy commodity prices. The Middle East, Venezuela and Russia control the world's largest oil reserves, and Canada joins these ranks if tar sands, an unconventional form of oil, are included. Russia and Saudi Arabia are the biggest oil producers, while the Organization of Petroleum Exporting Countries (OPEC) controls three-quarters of the world's oil deposits. Russia, Iran and Qatar have the largest natural gas reserves, though Russia, the US and Canada are currently the largest producers (US Department of Energy 2007; British Petroleum 2007).

Definitions of energy security are largely driven by national interests, particularly by the question of whether a country depends on foreign energy imports or on the income it derives from exports. Importers have sought to keep energy prices relatively low through the development of a highly competitive market for energy resources. This approach favours open access to oil and gas fields, free-flowing investment by private corporations to develop resources and the use of military force to ensure that supply lines remain open. Exporters seek to maximize the return they receive from selling their energy assets on the market. Accordingly, they have resorted to strategies of asserting state control over assets, blocking foreign companies from exploiting their resources and even reducing energy supplies if that will increase their profitability.

The strategies of consumers and producers differ in their reliance on market or statist solutions, and the result is increased friction. While consumers favour competitive markets to ensure low-priced, reliable supplies, producers are increasingly asserting control through state-owned companies to maximize their profits. Western companies are more frequently being squeezed out of countries that want to take control of their own resources. At the same time, petro-states find that they now have more money, which makes them important players on the world stage and allows them to assert their interests. Another difference between consumers and producers is that importing states are constantly seeking to reduce their demand for foreign energy, either through domestic sources, increased efficiency or the development of alternative sources (though with little success so far). If consumers actually succeed in reducing demand, it will undermine the position of the exporters.

Despite these differences, producers and consumers share an interest in maintaining the stability of the current international energy system. If prices rise too high or supplies become too scarce, energy costs could undermine economic growth, thereby hurting the economic interests of all countries. The fact that the producers and consumers share similar interests is important because it makes possible a web of interconnecting trade ties among countries that helps to preserve international stability. Both producers and consumers have an interest in insuring that the energy pipelines and transportation routes are secure from terrorist attack, extreme weather such as hurricanes and excessive costs imposed by transit country governments (Deutch and Schlesinger 2006: 9).

Historical background

In the twentieth century, oil fuelled Western economic growth and sustained armies worldwide. The control of oil became a key question of national military strategy when First Lord of the Admiralty Winston Churchill, on the eve of the First World War, decided to shift the British navy from domestic sources of coal to foreign sources of oil (Yergin 2006). Oil also played an extremely important role in the Allied defeat of the Axis powers in the Second World War, as Germany ran short of fuel for its offensives in Russia and Africa, and Japan lacked the energy to keep its military machine running (Singer 2008). In the aftermath of the Second World War, the direct influence of oil on military affairs declined, but the control of oil has remained a strategic goal ever since.

The most prominent use of energy as an economic weapon was the Arab oil embargo of the US and several European countries. The Arab countries sought to end US support for Israel after the 1973 Yom Kippur War by slashing energy shipments to the US. This led to a fourfold increase in oil prices and ultimately imposed some pain not only on the US, but Western consumers in general. Ultimately, however, the US did not change its foreign policy, and the embargo did not achieve its goal. Higher prices drove down US oil consumption, causing prices to fall and leading to overproduction and a glut on the market. The subsequent era of relatively cheap oil (under US$30 per barrel) lasted through to the end of the 1990s. The oil embargo had a powerful, but short-term, impact on thinking about energy security. Until that crisis, politicians and analysts had assumed that energy supplies would remain relatively cheap and accessible. In the years after the crisis, Western countries began making plans for dealing with future energy crises. However, the return of cheap energy in the early 1980s took away the impetus for this kind of action, and the topic received little attention until the dramatic rise in prices that began in 2002.

Immediately following the 1973 embargo, the major powers set up international institutions to coordinate their energy policies better. The embargo was possible because the oil-producing countries were organized through the Organization of Petroleum Exporting Countries (OPEC), which was established in 1960 and brought together many of the key oil producers. In 1974, the Western countries set up the International Energy Agency (IEA) to coordinate Western energy policies, prevent oil supply disruptions, advocate alternative energy solutions and provide information about the energy situation. A major limitation on the IEA is that countries must be members of the Organization for Economic Co-operation and Development (OECD) to join, and therefore the new consuming countries like China and India are not members. The only energy-focused organization that includes all major producers and consumers is the International Energy Forum (IEF), which was established in 2003 in an effort to promote dialogue between producers and consumers at the ministerial level. Despite its inclusive character, this organization has had little practical impact.

Beyond the reformed institutional structure, the West also set up strategic reserves of oil and began to diversify its sources of energy away from the Middle East. At the same time, the US entered into a bargain with Saudi Arabia in which the US offered protection from Iraqi or Iranian aggression, while Saudi Arabia provided spare capacity, which it used to maintain sufficient supplies during crises, such as the Iraqi invasion of Kuwait in 1990, followed by the US-led effort to repel the threat.

Key trends and themes in energy security today

Today, it is widely accepted that the existing energy system is no longer sustainable and that extensive changes are inevitable. First, and most importantly, oil prices are now extremely volatile, rising rapidly following decades of stability from around US$30 in 2002 to a record high over US$140 in the middle of 2008, but then falling again well below US$50 by the end of the year as the global recession drove down expectations for energy demand. While it is difficult to say how long the economic difficulties will last and what the impact will be on energy prices, several trends are exerting upward pressure on prices. Global demand for energy will continue to grow as China and India modernize their economies and expand access to cars, appliances and larger homes for their citizens. Likewise, many of the energy-producing countries in the Middle East and Russia are increasing domestic consumption, leaving less energy for export. Overall global oil consumption rose from 68.9 million barrels a day (mbd) in 1994 to an estimated 86.4 mbd in 2008 (Mufson 2008a). Other causes pointing to rising prices include: fewer investment opportunities for international oil companies as governments take over fields in many of the key producing countries; insufficient investment in developing new fields as old ones begin to run dry; little excess production capacity; production obstacles in countries like Iraq, Iran, Nigeria and Russia; and uncertain prospects for the US dollar, the currency in which oil sales are denominated.

Second, with price volatility as a defining feature, both consumers and producers now realize that they are vulnerable to the market. Over the last 40 years, power seesawed between the two sides. Western consumers benefited after the failure of the Arab oil embargo left Saudi Arabia with excess capacity and Western countries as the only customer, leading to an era of cheap energy. The advantage shifted to the producers between 2002 and the summer of 2008, when growing demand in Asia erased the excess capacity and the rise of new customers meant that producers could sell to consumers outside the West. Although energy producers have always benefited financially from their sales, the enormous influx of energy money due to higher prices meant that producing countries, such as Russia and Venezuela, felt that they could play a more assertive role in international politics. With the sudden drop in energy prices in the fall of 2008, the producers no longer look as powerful, while consumers benefit from low energy prices even as the rest of their economies face great difficulties.

Third, the Western-based international oil companies (IOCs) that once controlled most of the world's energy reserves have lost much of their past power to national oil companies (NOCs). Until the Arabs started privatizing their oil industries in the 1960s, privately owned Western oil companies, once defined as the 'Seven Sisters', controlled 85 per cent of oil and gas reserves. These companies were the dominant players until the rise of OPEC (Sampson 1975). Currently, the NOCs control 77 per cent of the world's oil reserves, while the IOCs control 10 per cent, IOCs and NOCs jointly control 7 per cent, and Russian oil companies control 6 per cent (Jaffe 2007). The rise of the NOCs means that producer countries now have much greater control over how their reserves are used and gain a greater share of the profits than in the past.

A fourth change is the type of fuel dominant in the international system. Traditionally, oil has been the most important fuel, particularly in the US. While oil is a finite resource, it will remain an important fuel source for many decades to come (Vaitheeswaran 2007: 24). Nevertheless, there are signs that the reign of oil is coming to an end. The US reached peak production of domestic oil in 1970, and output has declined since then. Likewise, oil production is now declining in key non-OPEC producers such as Britain, Norway and Mexico, and is static in Russia. Many questions remain unanswered about when, and if, oil will reach a global peak and what the consequences will be. The peak oil theory suggests that once oil production hits its peak, output will drop off sharply (Hubbert 1956), with potentially catastrophic economic consequences for oil-consuming countries if they do not take proper preventive action (Hirsch et al. 2005). Pessimists argue that the world has passed or will soon pass peak production (Deffeyes 2006). According to International Energy Agency Chief Economist Fatih Birol, non-OPEC oil production will peak by 2010 (Pagnamenta 2008), meaning that the Western countries will become increasingly reliant on OPEC producers. Other analysts suggest that peak oil will not occur soon, and that the current literature that makes predictions to this effect is based on incorrect assumptions. More optimistic analyses claim that, if non-conventional sources of oil are included, current global reserves are much greater than the peak oil literature claims (3.74 trillion barrels instead of 1.2) (Cambridge Energy Research Associates 2006). Saudi Minister of Petroleum and Mineral Resources, Ali al-Naimi, claims that technology will make it possible to find much more oil than is currently known and extractable (Mufson 2008b). Others argue that the question really is not so much the looming peak, but an issue of investment and access to new frontier regions such as the Arctic, which the US Geological Survey believes could contain up to 22 per cent of the world's undiscovered oil and gas resources.

Fifth, with concerns about high oil prices and the size of the world's reserves, consumer countries are looking for new types of energy. In the near future, natural gas will become increasingly important, particularly with the extension of the liquefied natural gas infrastructure. Nuclear power now supplies 16 per cent of the world's electricity production, and countries such as France have invested heavily in this technology (Struck 2007). Many countries are interested in building new nuclear facilities as an alternative to fossil fuels. Several countries have invested in alternative sources like solar energy, wind power and cellulosic ethanol, but it remains unclear when these technologies will be price competitive with conventional sources on a large scale.

Finally, a growing awareness of global warming provides another source of change in the international energy system (Solomon et al. 2007). Fears that continued use of hydrocarbon-based energy at current or accelerating rates would lead to catastrophic environmental changes have altered the way that many individuals view their energy habits. Many people in the West have stated that they are ready to pay a higher price for energy if such consumption will have a smaller impact on the environment.

Impact of energy on international security

Energy became a matter of national security when countries began to depend on imports to secure the continued operation of their economies. Since energy is now essential to most aspects of civilized life, it has become a central issue in politics at both the international and national levels (Proninska 2007). If managed poorly, energy resources can provide the basis for tensions and potentially even violent conflict within and among states. If managed wisely, however, energy can stimulate international cooperation and the development of a conflict-inhibiting environment.

Pessimistic scenarios suggest that competition over increasingly scarce energy supplies will inevitably lead to more frequent international conflicts (Klare 2001). In the most straightforward example of such a 'resource war', Saddam Hussein invaded Kuwait in 1990 to gain control of its oil. Because of the size of its population and resulting energy needs, China is frequently portrayed as potentially fomenting conflict over resources in part because it is willing to invest in areas of the world shunned by the West, such as Sudan, Iran and Zimbabwe, to secure the energy it needs to fuel its rapid growth. Additionally, disputes over energy exist in a variety of areas, such as the Caspian, Central Asia, the Middle East, Africa and Latin America (Heinberg 2005: 210–20).

Given energy's centrality to economic life, the most extreme theorists of resource wars expect struggles over energy to override all other considerations (Klare 2008: 7). They argue that states will increasingly use their powers to ensure that they have sufficient supplies of energy. Oil will no longer be a commodity to be bought and sold on the international market, but will be an object of armed confrontation. Likewise, energy-deficient countries will seek to ensure their energy supplies by building alliances with energy producers through massive arms transfers, particularly to unstable regions in Africa, the Middle East and the Caspian basin (Klare 2008: 239). A more nuanced version of the resource wars thesis argues that resource stress is an indirect cause of violence that interacts within a complex web of factors by causing social dislocations that include widening gaps between rich and poor, increased rent seeking by elites, weakening of states and ethnic cleavages (Homer-Dixon 2008).

In addition to contributing to international conflict, energy supplies are a source of instability in the countries that produce them. According to an extensive literature on the 'resource curse', the presence of natural resources has a negative impact on a country's growth rate (Sachs and Warner 1995), level of democracy (Ross 2001: 356), debt level and unemployment rate, and greatly stimulates the prevalence of corruption (Kang 1999: 46). One specific consequence of the resource curse is that oil-producing countries are much more prone to civil wars and internal conflict than countries without such resources (Ross 2008: 2). In addition to disrupting a county's economics and politics, oil makes it easier for insurgents to fund their uprisings and intensifies ethnic grievances. In places like Iraq and Nigeria, insurgents have sold oil on the black market to continue their war-fighting efforts.

Such predictions of resource wars are not universally accepted, however (Victor 2007; Tompson 2006; Hamilton 2003). The resource wars literature basically argues that energy consumers are fighting over a shrinking supply of energy in what amounts to a zero-sum game. However, if countries view energy as just another commodity, then the problem becomes how best to build efficient markets to deliver this commodity regardless of its physical location. In that sense, the zero-sum game is transformed into a mutually advantageous task where energy-consuming countries have a common interest in managing markets effectively (Victor 2007).

Cooperation could be facilitated by recognizing common interests on the part of energy consumers. The US and China, the world's two largest energy consumers, could work together on alternative sources of energy that are environmentally friendly and reduce oil dependence (Zha and Hu 2007: 111). The two countries could also develop new ways of saving energy in industrial and residential applications.

Such cooperative efforts need not be limited to energy consumers. Net energy producers such as Saudi Arabia and Russia are consuming increasing amounts of energy and have a strong interest in increasing their energy efficiency to prolong existing supplies of fossil fuels and develop alternative sources when those limited supplies run out. Therefore, both consumers and producers share an interest in developing new technologies for solar and wind energy, efficient building design, electric cars and a host of other technologies. The problem is that these common interests first need to be articulated on a political level to facilitate cooperation among consumers and producers.

Challenges for the future

The quest for energy security in the future faces a number of challenges. First, a key challenge for the West will be addressing potential threats posed by the newly powerful energy exporters. As a result of high energy prices, Western countries transferred a significant amount of wealth to countries that do not support Western foreign policy interests, such as Iran, Russia and Venezuela. Several of the countries that have accumulated large oil profits have diverted this money into state-controlled sovereign wealth funds (SWF) that they can use to invest in foreign stock markets and purchase stakes in Western financial institutions and companies. On one hand, the SWFs are generally seeking high return for their investment, as would any other investor. On the other, the enormous transfer of wealth from energy-consuming to producing countries is creating a new situation where states can play a much larger role on international financial markets than they ever did in the past, potentially using their growing leverage for political purposes (Teslik 2008). In another challenge, Russia is using its energy wealth as a way to assert its interests in Europe, which is heavily dependent on Russian oil and gas supplies (Perovic et al. 2009). Russia is seeking to purchase retail energy distribution systems in wealthy European countries, which could give it even greater influence in the continent. The Europeans are divided in their approach toward Russia and are therefore not able to respond with a unified policy (Lucas 2008).

Second, in order to address these challenges from the energy producers, energy consumers will have to reorganize their societies over the coming decades to deal with the dual challenges of increasingly expensive and scarce conventional energy supplies and global warming. Such change will require increasing energy efficiency and finding new sources of energy to gradually transform the existing energy system into one that is sustainable over the long term. While increased energy efficiency will reduce the rate of consumption growth and hopefully reduce absolute demand, it will require extensive investment to produce more efficient cars and construct greener buildings. Encouraging individuals to make such decisions will require the implementation of innovative policies that provide incentives to adopt sustainable and energy-conscious behaviour patterns (McKinsey 2007: 40f.).

The Western public debate on energy is often unrealistic and does not allow for subtle policy variation (Lee et al. 2008). Politicians and scientists in energy-importing countries can gain great popularity by touting schemes to achieve 'energy independence' for their country, which would end the need for future oil imports (Sandalow 2008). For the foreseeable future, an interdependent energy market is a fact of life and probably a stabilizing influence in the world. Until a few years ago, the international energy market supplied importers with stable supplies of relatively cheap energy (Verrastro and Ladislaw 2007: 99). It also set constraints on the amount of violence in the system. Even at the height of the Cold War, the Soviet Union reliably supplied energy to Europe, and Venezuela still supplies oil to the US despite strong anti-US rhetoric on the part of Venezuelan leader Hugo Chavez. Likewise, for all of its upheavals, the Middle East has been a generally reliable energy supplier to the West (Fattouh 2007).

Third and finally, future research should focus on addressing the key technological and policy challenges that must be overcome to transform existing energy usage patterns into more sustainable practices that will serve the security interests of current energy producers and consumers. There are several key technological challenges facing energy scientists today. One example is the development of cheap photovoltaic cells along with distribution and storage systems that can efficiently convert sunlight into electricity, move the voltage from where it is produced to where it is needed and store it until the final customer wants to consume it (Woods 2008). There are similarly important technical challenges in the field of wind energy and biofuels.

In addition to addressing the technical issues, researchers also need to define energy policies that will encourage greater energy efficiency and the use of alternatives to fossil fuels. Many innovators advocate a cap-and-trade system as a way to increase the economic incentives for each individual consumer to take action to improve energy efficiency and lower greenhouse gas emissions (Krupp and Horn 2008). Such policies are not perfect, however, and there is much work to be done. Researchers particularly need to define how governments can best intervene, through tax incentives, mandates and other measures, to encourage more sustainable energy usage when markets do not provide these kinds of incentives.

To be sustainable over the long term, any new policies must meet the differing needs of countries that import energy and those that export it. While policies that improve efficiency and promote alternative sources have obvious applications for today's energy importers, they also benefit energy exporters. Many of the exporters are trying to diversify their economies away from a reliance on energy and therefore are beginning to consume more energy as they develop other industries. Since energy-rich countries are among the most inefficient energy users in the world, they too will benefit from the development of new technologies. A gradual evolution away from fossil fuels has the potential to preserve the cooperative aspects of the current energy system, while moving it in an environmentally sustainable direction.

Note

1 Oil is the most important source of energy, providing 37 per cent of overall consumption in 2006, followed by coal (27 per cent) and natural gas (24 per cent) (BP 2007).

References

Aslund, A. (2007) 'The truth about sovereign wealth funds', *Foreign Policy*, Web Exclusive, December. Available online at: www.foreignpolicy.com/story/cms.php?story_id=4056 (accessed 16 December 2008).

British Petroleum (2007) *BP Statistical Review of World Energy*, June. Available online at: www.bp.com/sectiongenericarticle.do?categoryId=9023753&contentId = 7044109 (accessed 16 December 2008).

Cambridge Energy Research Associates (2006) 'Peak oil theory – "World running out of oil soon" – Is faulty; could distort policy and energy debate', November 14. Available online at: www.cera.com/aspx/cda/public1/news/pressReleases/pressReleaseDetails.aspx?CID=8444 (accessed 16 December 2008).

Deffeyes, K.S. (2006) *Beyond Oil: The View from Hubbert's Peak*, New York: Hill and Wang.

Deutch, J. and Schlesinger, J.R. (2006) *National Security Consequences of U.S. Oil Dependency*, New York: Council on Foreign Relations.

Energy Information Administration (2007) *Country Analysis Briefs: Iran*, October. Available online at: www.eia.doe.gov/emeu/cabs/Iran/pdf.pdf (accessed 16 December 2008).

Fattouh, B. (2007) 'How secure are Middle East oil supplies?', Oxford Institute for Energy Studies, WPM 33, Oxford: Oxford Institute for Energy Studies. Available online at: www.oxfordenergy.org/pdfs/WPM33.pdf (accessed 16 December 2008).

Hamilton, A. (2003) 'Resource wars and the politics of scarcity and abundance', *Dialogue* 1, 3: 27–38.

Heinberg, R. (2005) *The Party's Over: Oil, War and the Fate of Industrial Societies*, 2nd revised and updated edn, Gabriola Island, Canada: New Society Publishers.

Hirsch, R.L., Bezdek, R. and Wendling, R. (2005) 'Peaking of world oil production: Impacts, mitigation, and risk management', Washington, DC: Department of Energy. Available online at: www.netl.doe.gov/publications/others/pdf/Oil_Peaking_NETL.pdf (accessed 16 December 2008).

Homer-Dixon, T. (2008) 'Straw man in the wind', *The National Interest online*, January 2. Available online at: www.nationalinterest.org/PrinterFriendly.aspx?id=16522 (accessed 16 December 2008).

Hubbert, M.K. (1956) 'Nuclear energy and the fossil fuels', paper presented at Spring Meeting of the Southern District, Division of Production, American Petroleum Institute, San Antonio, TX, March 7–9. Available online at: www.hubbertpeak.com/hubbert/1956/1956.pdf (accessed 16 December 2008).

International Energy Agency (IEA) (2007) *World Energy Outlook 2007: China and India Insights*, Paris: International Energy Agency.

Jaffe, A.M. (2007) 'The changing role of national oil companies in international energy markets', presentation at the James A. Baker III Institute for Public Policy, Rice University, March 1. Available online at: www.rice.edu/energy/publications/docs/NOCs/Presentations/Hou-Jaffe-KeyFindings.pdf (accessed 16 December 2008).

Kalicki, J.H., and Goldwyn, D.L. (2005) *Energy and Security: Toward a New Foreign Policy Strategy*, Baltimore: Johns Hopkins University Press.

Kang, D. (1999) *Crony Capitalism*, New York: Cambridge University Press.

Klare, M.T. (2001) *Resource Wars: The New Landscape of Global Conflict*, New York: Henry Holt and Company.

——(2008) *Rising Powers, Shrinking Planet: The New Geopolitics of Energy*, New York: Metropolitan Books.

Krupp, F. and Horn, M. (2008) *Earth, The Sequel: The Race to Reinvent Energy and Stop Global Warming*, New York: W. W. Norton & Company.

Lee, H., Clark, W. C. and Devereaux, C. (2008) 'Biofuels and sustainable development', Harvard Kennedy School of Government. Available online at: http://belfercenter.ksg.harvard.edu/files/biofuels%20and%20sustainable%20development.pdf (accessed 16 December 2008).

Lucas, E. (2008) *The New Cold War: Putin's Russia and the Threat to the West*, New York: Palgrave Macmillan.

McKinsey & Co. and the Conference Board (2007) *Reducing U.S. Greenhouse Gas Emissions: How Much at What Cost?* December. Available online at: www.mckinsey.com/clientservice/ccsi/pdf/US_ghg_final_report.pdf (accessed 16 December 2008).

Mufson, S. (2008a) 'This time, it's different', *The Washington Post*, 27 July.

——(2008b) 'Calif. field goes from rush to reflection of global limits', *The Washington Post*, 29 July.

Pagnamenta, Robin (2008) 'IEA warns non-OPEC oil could peak in two years', *The Times* (London), 21 July. Available online at: http://business.timesonline.co.uk/tol/business/industry_sectors/natural_resources/article4368523.ece (accessed 16 December 2008).

Perovic, J., Orttung, R.W. and Wenger, A. (2009) *Russian Energy Power and Foreign Relations: Implications for Conflict and Cooperation*, London: Routledge.

Proninska, K.(2007) 'Energy and security: Regional and global dimensions', SIPRI Yearbook. Available online at: http://yearbook2007.sipri.org/chap6 (accessed 16 December 2008).

Ross, M.L. (2001) 'Does oil hinder democracy?', *World Politics* 53, 3: 325–61.

——(2008) 'Blood barrels: Why oil wealth fuels conflict', *Foreign Affairs* 87, 3: 2–9.

Sachs, J.D. and Warner, A.M. (1995) 'Natural resource abundance and economic growth', *NBER Working Paper 5398.*

Sampson, A. (1975) *The Seven Sisters: The Great Oil Companies & the World They Shaped*, New York: Viking.

Sandalow, D. (2008) *Freedom from Oil: How the Next President Can End the United States' Oil Addiction*, New York: McGraw Hill.

Singer, C. (2008) *Oil and Security*, Stanley Foundation Political Analysis Brief, January.

Stockholm International Peace Research Institute (SIPRI) (1974) *Oil and Security*, New York: Humanities Press.

Solomon, S., Qin, D., Manning, M., Chen, Z., Marquis, M., Averyt, K.B., Tignor, M. and Miller, H.L. (eds) (2007) *Climate Change 2007: The Physical Science Basis – Contribution of Working Group I to the Fourth Assessment Report of the Intergovernmental Panel on Climate Change*, New York: Cambridge University Press.

Struck, D. (2007) 'In the global energy rush, nuclear gets a resurgence', *The Washington Post*, 6 January.

Teslik, L.H. (2008) 'Backgrounder: Sovereign wealth funds', Washington, DC: Council on Foreign Relations, 18 January. Available online at: www.cfr.org/publication/15251 (accessed 16 December 2008).

Tompson, W. (2006) 'A frozen Venezuela? The "resource curse" and Russian politics', in Ellman, M. (ed.), *Russia's Oil: Bonanza or Curse?* London: Anthem.

US Department of Energy (2007) Energy Information Administration, *Annual Energy Review 2006*, Washington, DC, June. Available online at: www.eia.doe.gov/aer (accessed 16 December 2008).

Vaitheeswaran, V.V. (2007) 'Think again: Oil', *Foreign Policy* 163, November–December: 24–30.

Verrastro, F. and Ladislaw, S. (2007) 'Providing energy security in an interdependent world', *The Washington Quarterly* 30, 4: 95–104.

Victor, D.G. (2007) 'What resource wars?' *National Interest online*, November 12. Available online at: www.nationalinterest.org/PrinterFriendly.aspx?id=16020 (accessed 16 December 2008).

Woods, R. (2008) 'How China's thirst for oil can save the planet', London: *The Sunday Times*, 6 July.

Yergin, D. (2006) 'Ensuring energy security', *Foreign Affairs* 85, 2: 69–82.

Zha, D. and Hu, W. (2007) 'Promoting energy partnership in Beijing and Washington', *The Washington Quarterly* 30, 4: 105–15.

20

Resources, the environment and conflict[1]

Nils Petter Gleditsch and Ole Magnus Theisen

Since the Second World War, around 235 armed conflicts in 120 countries have claimed some 10 million lives in battle-related violence.[2] The number of ongoing, armed conflicts has declined markedly since the early 1990s, levelling out in the last few years. The number of annual battle-deaths has seen a long-term decline since the Second World War. However, the 30+ armed conflicts that are currently ongoing remain a crucial component of human insecurity. In addition to the direct loss of life in battle, armed conflict claims high human costs through disease, refugee flows and the destruction of infrastructure. Reducing armed conflict makes a major contribution to improving human security. Although the work summarized in this chapter deals mostly with direct violence between organized parties within and between states, it is likely to have implications for other forms of violent human insecurity as well.

Armed conflict is a product of identity, motivation and opportunity (Gurr 1970; Ellingsen 2000). Both parties to an armed conflict need some kind of identity (regional, cultural, economic or ideological) to organize for armed struggle. They need the motivation to fight, whether it is to redress a grievance, to capture an economic advantage or to defend the status quo. Finally, they need the opportunity to fight, in geographical (proximity and terrain) as well as financial terms (to pay the troops).

One set of hypotheses sees scarce natural resources as a motive for insurrection. Increasing concern with the state of the world's environment in the 1970s led many to believe that environmental degradation might become sufficiently serious to lead to violence. Many saw the role of resources as filling the explanatory gap as wars continued even after the decline of conflict along ideological lines at the end of the Cold War. This chapter focuses on the debate between neo-Malthusians, who see the growing scarcity of renewable resources as detrimental to human security, and technological optimists or cornucopians. We deal more briefly with political ecology and liberalism, which have also contributed to the debate, but leave out any discussion of 'the resource curse' hypothesis, which focuses on local abundance of globally scarce resources (de Soysa 2002). We critique the theoretical and empirical literature on armed conflict generally, with a focus on internal conflict. We find the more dramatic version of neo-Malthusian thought to have little empirical foundation, particularly if scarcity in and by itself is expected to produce conflict. Scarcity seems more likely to increase the risk of conflict when interacting with governance or level of development.

Schools of thought

The neo-Malthusians

The original model of Malthus (1798/1993) assumed that any human population would grow at an exponential rate, while food production could only grow linearly. Thus, the amount of food produced per capita must decline, with drastic consequences. Important elements of this model can be found in current conflict theory. The general argument is that natural resources are limited on 'spaceship Earth' and that human rationality under stressful conditions is limited. Population growth, increasing consumption of resources and harmful methods of extraction combine to deplete or depreciate these resources. The resulting scarcity can lead to competition and eventually armed conflict. Moderate neo-Malthusians argue that this generally happens through increased grievances (Homer-Dixon 1999), but also through lower labour costs of rebel soldiers (Ohlsson 2003). This line of thinking is found in the Club of Rome's *The Limits to Growth* (Meadows et al. 1972), in the report by the Brundtland Commission (1987) on the environment and development, and in several scholarly works (e.g. Homer-Dixon 1999; Gleick 1993; Kahl 2006; Myers 1993). It is also reflected in the literature of most environmental pressure groups, many environment ministries, and other official bodies, as well as in the justification for awarding the Nobel Peace Prize for 2004 to Wangari Maathai and for 2007 to Al Gore and the IPCC. Scarce resources considered important enough to fight for include land, freshwater and food; these resources are thought to become even scarcer due to population growth and, more recently, climate change. A great deal of public attention has also been given to the prospects of 'water wars', where upstream countries would use up river water and provoke downstream countries to go to war (McLoughlin 2004). Focusing on developing countries, neo-Malthusians emphasize the consequences of resource scarcity for food production.

The cornucopians

The cornucopians, labelled after the Horn of Plenty,[3] recognize that natural resources are theoretically limited, but stress that they are more abundant than realized by the neo-Malthusians. They argue that resources can be substituted and recycled when necessary and that technological development may make it possible to consume less. Cornucopians argue that the relative importance of renewable resources decreases as technology is advancing mainly due to human ingenuity and demands from the market economy. If resources are scarce to the point where people will fight for them, it is because politics has interfered. To avoid waste, inefficiency and local scarcity, resources must be properly priced and trading allowed.

Moderate neo-Malthusians counter these points by stating that markets and institutions are frequently dysfunctional in developing states, and they thus fail to alleviate scarcities; that new technology (such as the Green Revolution) is too expensive for poor farmers and leads to further degradation; that some resources, such as water, are non-substitutable; and that environmental degradation often follows a non-linear pattern, making preventive measures hard to apply (Homer-Dixon 1999; Kahl 2006).

Regarding the demographic component of the neo-Malthusian case, cornucopian responses are divided into two groups. Boserup (1965) argues that population growth is frequently conducive to rural economic growth.[4] Simon (1989, 1996) argues that human ingenuity is the only scarce resource and that continued population growth will provide an advantage in the indefinite future. Most cornucopians, however, would follow the argument by Lomborg (2001), who argues that the second demographic transition (lower fertility) is cancelling out the effects of the first (lower mortality) and that global population is levelling out at 9 billion (UN 2004). The 'population explosion' feared by early neo-Malthusians is no longer likely to be global, although some countries still have high population growth. In recognition of this, some moderate neo-Malthusians argue that renewable resource scarcity will only be a *temporary* security issue (Cincotta et al. 2003: 40). At the global level, food production should be able to handle the projected 9 billion humans by a comfortable margin. Figure 20.1 shows the trend in food prices for the period 1960–2007. The long-term development lends support to the cornucopian position, despite the increase in food prices from 2000.

Most cornucopian arguments concern environmental degradation or economic development rather than conflict, but they have clear implications for conflict. If resources are globally abundant and can be priced, substituted and traded to avoid serious scarcities, and if the increase in population can be held in check, there is no obvious reason why groups or countries should fight over natural resources.

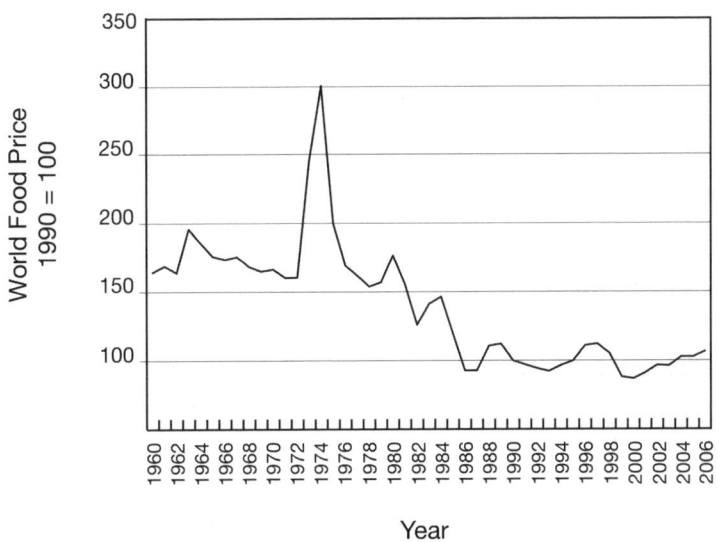

Figure 20.1 World food prices 1960–2007.
Note: World Bank, various sources, based on personal communication with Betty Dow, commodities information analyst, Development Prospects Group, World Bank, 11 March 2008. The price is weighted by the Manufactures Unit Values Index and is given in constant 1990 US$, thus reflecting real prices. For the trend to reflect real food availability, all markets have to be open (to make the price mechanisms work properly). If this caveat holds, there seems to be a marked decline in global food prices up to the mid-1980s, when it stabilizes, and a possible increase since 2000. The peak in 1974 is due to increased production costs (and perhaps increased hoarding) due to the 1973 oil crisis. The current rise is variously attributed to increased productions of bio-fuel, economic growth in China and India, and market distortion by subsidized agriculture in rich countries.

The role of institutions: liberals and political ecologists

Liberals share with many cornucopians a belief in the beneficial effects of the market. With political ecologists, they share a focus on institutions, which they see as more important than the physical state of the environment. While liberals tend to focus on liberal principles such as democracy and cooperation, political ecologists usually emphasize questions of distribution. Therefore, the views of these two schools on the effects of trade liberalization on local scarcity differ considerably.

Liberal conflict theory rests primarily on the role of cooperation and the role of democracy. It argues that an emerging resource scarcity may stimulate cooperation as well as violent conflict. Fighting over a shared resource may be more costly than working out ways to share it (Wallensteen 1992). Low-level conflict may serve as a warning signal that prompts states or groups into cooperation (Lonergan 2001; Wolf 1999).

Democracy is relevant to resource conflict in two ways. First, some liberal theorists argue that democracy is likely to promote resource conservation (Payne 1995; Gleditsch and Sverdrup 2002, but see also Midlarsky 1998) or at least environmental commitment (Neumayer 2002). Sen (1989) points out that famines rarely, if ever, occur in democracies, because press freedom and other features of democracy provide warning signals and mobilize countermeasures. Secondly, democracies are very unlikely to fight each other (Gleditsch and Hegre 1997) or to suffer serious internal violence (Hegre et al. 2001). If democracies do not fight internally or among themselves for any other reason, then they are not likely to do so because of resource scarcity.

Political ecology, the fourth general strand of thought, denies any strong *direct* linkage between renewable resource scarcity and conflict (Hildyard 1999; Hartmann 2001). If scarcity seems to bring about conflict, it is most likely a third factor that causes both kinds of misery. Issues of distribution, access and policy are therefore seen as more important than resource scarcity itself. While political ecologists do not generally side with cornucopian optimists, they are frequently found to criticize neo-Malthusians (see Fairhead 2001; Hartmann 2001; Hildyard 1999; Peluso and Watts 2001).

The state of research

Theoretical shortcomings

The argument between the different schools of thought has generated much heat, as evidenced by the polemics by Lomborg (2001) against 'the litany' and the scalding tone of his critics.[5] Can we adjudicate this debate by means of systematic empirical evidence? The existing empirical literature suffers from several methodological problems (Gleditsch 1998). Prime among them is selection bias. Homer-Dixon (1999) and his associates have made general arguments based on armed conflict cases only, a design that deprives them of the possibility of comparing cases with and without conflict. They are therefore unable to say whether countries in conflict suffer from more severe scarcities than countries at peace. Case studies are frequently defended because they allow more detailed knowledge of each conflict and 'process tracing' of causal mechanisms (Schwarz et al. 2001). However, most of the case studies in question use relatively shallow sources, not including archival research, detailed field research or opinion surveys. Thus, decisive contextual factors for the occurrence or non-occurrence of conflict can be ignored. A better research design was used by Bächler (1999), who studied 21 conflict and 21 non-conflict cases, concluding that resource scarcity per se does not suffice to bring about conflict. However, when it occurs in interaction with severe discrimination and when the prerequisites for the mobilization of a rebel army are apparent, violence is much more likely to follow.[6]

A second issue is how to measure scarcity. The concept of environmental scarcity (Homer-Dixon 1999: 49ff.) includes *supply-induced scarcity*, referring to the absolute supply of a resource, the ways of extracting it, and its vulnerability; *demand-induced scarcity*, which is driven by increasing consumption per capita; and *structural scarcity*, the distribution of a resource. Fairhead disputes the usefulness of lumping the three together since scarcity of farmland (i.e. demand-induced scarcity) is frequently a motivation for more intensive crop methods and economic diversification, while severe pollution or degradation (i.e. supply-induced scarcity) is much less likely to produce the same outcome (Fairhead 2001: 219).[7]

Finally, there is a tendency to refer to future wars as evidence. The pronouncement by Ehrlich (1968: 11) that the battle to feed humanity has been lost, is one example, the many references to 'water wars' another. While there may well be a potential for future conflict, pessimistic predictions must be accompanied by a solid theoretical argument for why the future will be different from the past.

Large-n studies of the scarcity–conflict nexus

There are a number of large-n studies of scarcity and conflict. To the extent that the relationships they uncover are strong and robust, such studies may allow us to generalize to other, similar situations. If scarcities increase in the future, it can also be plausibly argued that we should expect more scarcity-based conflict. An early study (Hauge and Ellingsen 1998) found that population density, deforestation, land degradation and water scarcity were associated with a higher risk of internal conflict at the end of the Cold War period. However, their results cannot be replicated (Theisen 2008). Esty et al. (1998) did not find *any* direct relationship between indicators of environmental scarcity and state failure. Urdal (2005) finds that population density, when it coincides with population growth, increases the risk of conflict, but only for the 1970s, while for the whole period 1945–2001, high pressure on cropland is negatively correlated to civil conflict, implying more support for the cornucopian than the neo-Malthusian view. De Soysa (2002) finds that countries with a high population density have a higher risk of armed conflict, but the effect is much weaker than economic and governance factors. Collier and Hoeffler (1998), however, do not find it significant in explaining civil war. De Soysa (2002) also finds that, contrary to neo-Malthusian expectations, rural population density and renewable resource *wealth* in conjunction increase the risk of civil conflict. Miguel et al. (2004) use measures of deviations in rainfall as an instrument for economic shocks in sub-Saharan economies, and find that they increase the risk of conflict considerably. Hendrix and Glaser (2007) find that the lagged percentage change in rainfall, relative to the previous year, increases the risk of conflict onset in Sub-Saharan Africa. Binningsbø et al. (2006) find that a society's current consumption of eco-services relative to capacity, *lowers* the risk of civil conflict. Testing six indicators of resource scarcity, Theisen (2008) finds only weak support for neo-Malthusian arguments. Overall, there is only scant evidence for the scarcity–conflict nexus within nation-level studies on resource scarcity and civil conflict.

More than half of today's on-going civil conflicts concern a sub-national territory rather than the integrity of the national government. For example, in the conflict in Aceh, the motivating force might be the occurrence of oil in that province and nowhere else in Indonesia (Buhaug and Lujala 2005). A second generation of studies has used data on sub-national units to overcome this challenge. Raleigh and Urdal (2007) find a significant relationship between freshwater availability, population growth, soil degradation and conflict measured sub-nationally for the world as a whole. However, several of the indicators have a more pronounced effect in developed rather developing countries, contrary to neo-Malthusian expectations. Urdal (2008) finds some support for neo-Malthusian concerns in a study of India, as states with low agricultural output combined with land scarcity, and more densely populated states run a higher risk of experiencing conflict. In addition to the studies on civil conflicts, some recent work has examined conflicts in which the state is not a warring party. Meier et al. (2007) find that scarcity of water and forage do not lead to an increased frequency of inter-tribal conflict behaviour, but that the most severe incidents take place in times of scarcity (ibid.: 22). André and Platteu (1998) studied resource scarcity and distribution, and communal violence in North-Eastern Rwanda and found that a decreasing land per person ratio, in interaction with rising inequalities and low off-farm employment opportunities, increases tensions considerably, including violence. Thus, some of the more geographically sophisticated analyses show a clearer link between resource scarcity and armed conflict, although economic and political factors normally dominate these in importance.

There also are a few large-n studies of the international implications of scarcity. Tir and Diehl (1998) found that population growth has a moderate, yet positive impact on interstate conflict. Stalley (2003) replicated this finding and found a significant and positive relationship between soil erosion[8] and conflict.

Most empirical studies on interstate conflict and renewable natural resources investigate the argument that cross-border river basins involve a higher risk of conflict, particularly when an upstream country appropriates water that is needed downstream (Bächler 1999; Homer-Dixon 1999; Klare 2001). A series of studies (most recently Gleditsch et al. 2006) have found that shared rivers increase the risk of low-level interstate conflict substantially over and beyond the inherent conflict potential between neighbours, although water scarcity does not appear to be very important. Brochmann and Gleditsch (2007) found that states that share a river basin generally have more cooperation as well as conflict. Sowers (2002) found shared water resources to be related to the intensity of dyadic disputes. Hensel et al. (2006) analysed specific river claims and found that water scarcity in the challenger state increases the risk of the militarization of a river claim, while specific river institutions decrease the risk of a militarized outcome. Wolf (1999) found a very strong record of cooperative behaviour over water issues between states, and only four violent skirmishes in modern times. Summing up, there does seem to be a higher risk of a military interstate dispute when two or more countries share a basin, but these disputes are likely to be of low intensity and cooperation is a more likely outcome. For internal conflicts, there seems to be a relationship between temporary water scarcity and conflict, at least for sub-Saharan Africa. Geographically disaggregated analyses also give a more realistic assessment than national-level studies, reflected by Raleigh and Urdal (2007) who found systematic support for a link between resource scarcity and armed conflict. Other consequences of an allegedly growing resource scarcity lend little support to the neo-Malthusian conflict scenario.

Is there a 'coming anarchy'?

The more drastic apocalyptic scenarios forecasting global scarcities, mass deprivation and major interstate and intrastate violence should be viewed with scepticism – at least in the absence of major unpredictable shifts. However, local and regional scarcities are still possible and in some cases even plausible. A major war over shared water resources seems very unlikely, while local and smaller armed clashes and military posturing cannot be ruled out. Resource scarcity is also likely to interact with factors such as economic development and political institutions in increasing the risk of conflict.

What possible drastic shifts might change this picture? Human-induced climate change is often presented as the ultimate neo-Malthusian scenario. However, we know even less about the consequences of global warming than about how it is generated. Even if we accept the generally accepted scenario of a human-induced rise in global average temperature of several degrees centigrade in the twenty-first century, we are far from being able to account reliably for the negative and positive effects on human affairs. While the Maldives and substantial parts of Bangladesh may be flooded by sea-level rise, Siberia may bloom from a rising temperature. Drastic climatic change will require adaptation, which, while costly, may also lead to innovation. The climate change literature that specifically relates to conflict is, so far, extremely sparse and largely speculative.[9]

Figure 20.2 below shows the Northern Hemisphere temperature patterns for the last 1000 years, the famous 'hockey stick', where the rise in temperatures for the twentieth century forms the blade of the stick.[10] If the dominant factor influencing the increment in temperature for the twentieth century is indeed greenhouse gas emissions, it is likely

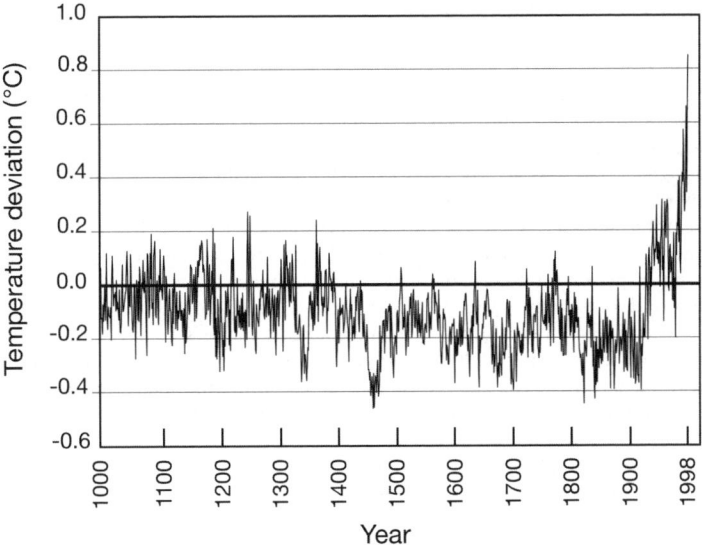

Figure 20.2 Temperature deviations 1000–1998 for the Northern Hemisphere.
Note: The graph, calculated from Mann *et al.* (1999), shows temperature deviations from the 1902–80 mean in degrees Celsius for the Northern Hemisphere for the years 1000–1998. Estimates prior to 1400 are considerably less reliable than the latter period, due to fewer available proxies. From 1902 onwards, the data shows the trend in the measured data; for 1000–1901, the trend is reconstructed by using proxies.

that the rise will continue. This rise in temperatures *can* lead to scenarios in which *some* neo-Malthusians (Gleick 1989; Homer-Dixon 1999; Myers 1993) claim will bring some parts of the world more prone to violent conflict than they are today (for a rebuttal see Bächler 1999). However, if nations act in unison to combat climate change and its adverse consequences, it could also have a rallying effect and lead to more cooperation and less conflict.

While climate change may be the most important link between the environment and conflict, it does not yet provide a very feasible avenue for investigating this link until better arguments, data and improved models are developed. Environmental and resource factors in conflict certainly warrant our attention; but our knowledge is limited. Although the human impact on the physical environment is increasing, the relative importance compared to the effects of natural processes is far from established. Only by mobilizing considerable hubris can we take for granted that man's domination of his environment is as benevolent as envisaged by the cornucopians or as malevolent as outlined in neo-Malthusian scenarios.

Notes

1 We thank the Research Council of Norway for their support; Naima Mouhleb for her assistance; Helga Malmin Binningsbø, Halvard Buhaug, Steen Nordstrøm, Indra de Soysa, Arild Blekesaune and Ragnhild Nordås for their comments; and Michael E. Mann and Betty Dow for sharing data. Some of the research summarized in this chapter is discussed more fully in Gleditsch (2001a, 2001b, 2003) and Theisen (2008). Replication data for the two graphs can be found at www.prio.no/cscw/datasets. Gleditsch was a member of the Scientific Steering Committee of the Global Environmental Change and Human Security (GECHS) project until 2005 and would like to acknowledge the prompting of GECHS colleagues in starting the work of this chapter.
2 Based on the UCDP/PRIO conflict data, which include all armed conflicts with more than 25 battle-related deaths in a given year (Gleditsch et al. 2002; Harbom et al. 2008). For battle-death figures, see Lacina and Gleditsch (2005). The figures for battle deaths include military and civilians.
3 They are also variously called Prometheans or technological optimists.
4 In the Machakos District in Kenya both the area's population and development level increased, resulting in higher yields per hectare and labour shortage (Tiffen et al. 1994).
5 For a review of the debate about Lomborg's work, see Gleditsch (2003, Section 26.5).
6 Investigating three conflict and three non-conflict cases, Hauge (2003) concludes that increased resource scarcity is only of secondary importance to the onset of conflict. Thus, her conclusions are even less resource pessimistic than those of Bächler.
7 Commenting on Homer-Dixon's study of the Chiapas insurgency, Bobrow-Strain (2001) attributes the conflict to unemployment rather than increasing resource scarcity. The liberalization of the Mexican economy in the early 1990s favoured cattle herding rather than agriculture, leading to a process that *on the surface* looked like increasing scarcity, as the number of unemployed surged.
8 This GLASOD-measure, which was also used by Hauge and Ellingsen (1998), has been criticized by Niemeijer and Mazzucato (2002).
9 See Nordås and Gleditsch (2007). For a well-publicized crisis scenario, see Schwarz and Randall (2003).
10 For a critique of the hockey stick, see Lomborg (2007: 68f.).

References

André, C. and Platteu, J.-P. (1998) 'Land relations under unbearable stress: Rwanda caught in the Malthusian trap', *Journal of Economic Behaviour and Organization* 34, 1: 1–47.
Bächler, G. (1999) *Violence through Environmental Discrimination*, Dordrecht: Kluwer Academic.

Binningsbø, H.M., de Soysa, I. and Gleditsch, N.P. (2006) 'Green giant, or straw man?', *Population and Environment* 28, 6: 337–55.

Bobrow-Strain, A. (2001) 'Between a ranch and a hard place: Violence, scarcity, and meaning in Chiapas, Mexico', in Peluso, N.L. and Watts, M. (eds) *Violent Environments*, Ithaca, NY and London: Cornell University Press: pp. 155–85.

Boserup, E. (1965) *The Conditions of Agricultural Growth: The Economics of Agrarian Change under Population Pressure*, London: Allen and Unwin.

Brochmann, M. and Gleditsch, N.P. (2007) 'Shared rivers and international cooperation', revised version of a paper presented at the 47th Annual Convention of the International Studies Association, San Diego, CA, 22–25 March.

Brundtland Commission (1987) *Our Common Future*, Oxford: Oxford University Press, for the World Commission on Environment and Development.

Buhaug, H. and Lujala, P. (2005) 'Accounting for scale: Measuring Geography in quantitative studies of civil war', *Political Geography* 24, 4: 399–418.

Cincotta, R.P., Engelmann, R. and Anastasion, D. (2003) *The Security Demographic: Population and Civil Conflict after the Cold War*, Washington, DC: Population Action International.

Collier, P. and Hoeffler, A. (1998) 'On the Economic causes of civil war', *Oxford Economic Papers* 50, 4: 563–73.

de Soysa, I. (2002) 'Ecoviolence: Shrinking pie or honey pot?', *Global Environmental Politics* 2, 4: 1–34.

Ehrlich, P.R. (1968) *The Population Bomb*, New York: Ballantine.

Ellingsen, T. (2000) 'Colorful community or ethnic witches' brew? Multiethnicity and domestic conflict during and after the Cold War', *Journal of Conflict Resolution* 44, 2: 228–49.

Esty, D., Goldstone, J.A., Gurr, T.R., Harff, B., Levy, M., Dabelko, G.D., Surko, P. and Unger, A.N. (1998) *State Failure Task Force Report: Phase II Findings*, McLean, VA: Science Applications International, for State Failure Task Force.

Fairhead, J. (2001) 'International dimensions of conflict over natural and environmental resources', in Peluso, N.L. and Watts, M. (eds) *Violent Environments*, Ithaca, NY and London: Cornell University Press, pp. 213–36.

Furlong, K., Gleditsch, N.P. and Hegre, H. (2006) 'Geographic opportunity and neomalthusian willingness: Boundaries, shared rivers, and conflict', *International Interactions* 32, 1: 79–108.

Gleditsch, N.P. (1998) 'Armed conflict and the environment: A critique of the literature', *Journal of Peace Research* 35, 4: 363–80. Revised version in Diehl, P.F. and Gleditsch, N.P. (eds) *Environmental Conflict*, Boulder, CO: Westview, 2001, pp. 251–72.

——(2001a) 'Environmental change, security, and conflict', in Crocker, C., Hampson, F.O. and Aall, P. (eds) *Turbulent Peace: The Challenges of Managing International Conflict*, Washington, DC: United States Institute of Peace Press, pp. 53–68.

——(2001b) 'Resource and environmental conflict: The-state-of-the-art', in Petzold-Bradley, E., Carius, A. and Vincze, A. (eds) *Responding to Environmental Conflicts: Implications for Theory and Practice*, NATO Science Series vol. 2. Environmental Security, 78, Dordrecht: Kluwer, pp. 53–66.

——(2003) 'Environmental conflict: Neomalthusians vs. Cornucopians', in Brauch, H. G., Liotta, P.H. and Marquina, A. (eds) *Security and the Environment in the Mediterranean: Conceptualising Security and Environmental Conflicts*, Berlin: Springer, pp. 477–85.

Gleditsch, N.P. and Hegre, H. (1997) 'Peace and democracy: Three levels of analysis', *Journal of Conflict Resolution* 41, 2: 283–310.

Gleditsch, N.P. and Sverdrup, B.O. (2002) 'Democracy and the environment', in Redclift, M. and Page, E.A. (eds) *Human Security and the Environment*, Cheltenham: Edward Elgar, pp. 45–70.

Gleditsch, N.P., Furlong, K., Hegre, H., Lacina, B. and Owen, T. (2006) 'Conflicts over shared rivers: Resource scarcity or fuzzy boundaries?' *Political Geography* 25, 4: 361–82.

Gleditsch, N.P., Wallensteen, P., Eriksson, M., Sollenberg, M. and Strand, H. (2002) 'Armed conflict 1946–2001: A new dataset', *Journal of Peace Research* 39, 5: 615–37. Available online at: www.prio.no/cscw/datasets (accessed November 2008).

Gleick, P.H. (1989) 'Climate change and international politics: Problems facing developing countries', *Ambio* 18, 6: 333–39.

——(1993) 'Water in the 21st century' in Gleick, P.H. (ed.) *Water in Crisis: A Quick Guide to the World's Fresh Water Resources*, Oxford and New York: Oxford University Press: pp. 10–12.

Gurr, T.R. (1970) *Why Men Rebel*, Princeton, NJ: Princeton University Press.

Harbom, L., Melander, E. and Wallensteen, P. (2008) 'Armed conflict and its dyadic dimensions, 1946–2007', *Journal of Peace Research* 45, 5: 617–31.

Hartmann, B. (2001) 'Will the circle be unbroken: A critique of the project on environment, population, and security', in Peluso, N.L. and Watts, M. (eds) *Violent Environments*, Cornell University Press, pp. 39–62.

Hauge, W. (2003) *Causes and Dynamics of Conflict Escalation: The Role of Economic Development and Environmental Change: A Comparative Study of Bangladesh, Guatemala, Haiti, Madagascar, Senegal and Tunisia*, PhD dissertation, University of Oslo.

Hauge, W. and Ellingsen, T. (1998) 'Beyond environmental scarcity: Causal pathways to conflict', *Journal of Peace Research* 35, 3: 299–317.

Hegre, H., Ellingsen, T., Gates, S. and Gleditsch, N.P. (2001) 'Towards a democratic civil peace? Democracy, political change, and civil war, 1816–1992', *American Political Science Review* 95, 1: 17–33.

Hendrix, C.S. and Glaser, S.M. (2007) 'Trends and triggers: Climate change and civil conflict in sub-Saharan Africa', *Political Geography* 26, 6: 695–715.

Hensel, P., Mitchell, S. McLaughlin and Sowers II, T.E. (2006) 'Conflict management of riparian disputes', *Political Geography* 25, 4: 383–411.

Hildyard, N. (1999) 'Blood, babies and the social roots of conflict', in Suliman, M. (ed.) *Ecology, Politics and Violent Conflict*, London: Zed, pp. 3–24.

Homer-Dixon, T. (1999) *Environment, Scarcity, and Conflict*, Princeton, NJ: Princeton University Press.

Kahl, C. (2006) *States, Scarcity, and Civil Strife in the Developing World*, Princeton, NJ: Princeton University Press.

Klare, M.T. (2001) *Resource Wars: The New Landscape of Global Conflict*, New York: Metropolitan.

Lacina, B. and Gleditsch, N.P. (2005) 'Monitoring trends in global combat: A new dataset of battle deaths', *European Journal of Population*, 21, 2–3: 145–66. Available online at: www.prio.no/cscw/cross/battledeaths (accessed November 2008).

Lomborg, B. (2001) *The Skeptical Environmentalist: Measuring the Real State of the World*, Cambridge: Cambridge University Press.

——(2007) *Cool It: The Skeptical Environmentaliusts Guide to Global Warming*, London: Marshall Cavendish and Cyan.

Lonergan, S.C. (2001) 'Water and conflict: Rhetoric and reality', in Diehl, P.F. and Gleditsch, N.P. (eds) *Environmental Conflict*, Boulder, CO: Westview, pp.109–24.

Lujala, P., Gleditsch, N.P. and Gilmore, E. (2005) 'A diamond curse? Civil war and a lootable resource', *Journal of Conflict Resolution* 49, 4: 1–25.

McLoughlin, P. (2004) 'Scientists say risk of water wars is rising', *Environmental News Network*, in Reuters, 24 August. Available online at: www.enn.com/top_stories/article/11097/print (accessed 10 February 2009).

Malthus, T. [1798] (1993) *An Essay in the Principle of Population*, Reprinted, Oxford: Oxford University Press.

Mann, M.E., Bradley, R.S. and Hughes, M.K. (1999) 'Northern hemisphere temperatures during the past millennium: Inferences, uncertainties, and limitations', *Geophysical Research Letters* 26, 6: 759–62.

Meadows, D.H., Meadows, D.L., Randers, J. and Behrens, W. (1972) *The Limits to Growth: A Report for the Club of Rome on the Predicament of Mankind*, New York: Universe.

Meier, P., Bond, D. and Bond, J. (2007) 'Environmental influences on pastoral conflict in the Horn of Africa', *Political Geography* 26, 6: 716–35.

Midlarsky, M.I. (1998) 'Democracy and the environment: An empirical assessment', *Journal of Peace Research* 35, 3: 341–61.

Miguel, E., Satyanath, S. and Sergenti, E. (2004) 'Economic shocks and civil conflict: An instrumental variable approach', *Journal of Political Economy* 112, 4: 725–53.

Myers, N. (1993) *Ultimate Security: The Environmental Basis of Political Stability*, New York: Norton.

230

Niemeijer, D. and Mazzucato, V. (2002) 'Soil degradation in the West African Sahel: How serious is it?', *Environment* 44, 2: 20–31.

Neumayer, E. (2002) 'Do democracies exhibit stronger environmental commitment? A cross-country analysis', *Journal of Peace Research* 39, 2: 139–64.

Nordås, R. and Gleditsch, N.P. (guest eds) (2007) 'Climate change and conflict', special issue of *Political Geography* 26, 6: 627–38.

Ohlsson, L. (2003) 'The risk of livelihood conflicts and the nature of policy measures required', in Kittrie, N., Mancham, J.R. and Carazo-Odio, R. (eds) *Seeds of True Peace: Responding to the Discontents of a Global Community*, Washington, DC: Carolina Academic Press.

Payne, R.A. (1995) 'Freedom and the environment', *Journal of Democracy* 6, 3: 41–55.

Peluso, N.L. and Watts, M. (2001) 'Violent environments', in Peluso, N.L. and Watts, M. (eds) *Violent Environments*, Ithaca, NY and London: Cornell University Press, pp. 3–38.

Raleigh, C. and Urdal, H. (2007) 'Climate change, environmental degradation, and armed conflict', *Political Geography* 26, 6: 674–94.

Schwarz, D.M., Deligiannis, T. and Homer-Dixon, T. (2001) 'The environment and violent conflict', in Diehl, P.F. and Gleditsch, N.P. (eds) *Environmental Conflict*, Boulder, CO: Westview, pp. 273–94.

Schwartz, P. and Randall, D. (2003) *An Abrupt Climate Change Scenario and its Implications for United States National Security*, Washington, DC: Environmental Media Services. Available online at: www.edf.org/documents/3566_AbruptClimateChange.pdf (accessed 10 February 2009).

Sen, A. (1989) 'Food and freedom', *World Development* 17, 6: 769–81.

Simon, J. (1989) 'Lebensraum: Paradoxically, population growth may eventually end wars', *Journal of Conflict Resolution* 33, 1: 164–80.

——(1996) *The Ultimate Resource 2*, Princeton, NJ: Princeton University Press.

Sowers, T.E. II (2002) *The Politics of Freshwater Resources*, PhD dissertation, Florida State University.

Stalley, P. (2003) 'Environmental scarcity and international conflict', *Conflict Management and Peace Science* 20, 2: 33–58.

Starr, J.R. (1991) 'Water wars', *Foreign Policy* 82: 17–36.

Theisen, O.M. (2008) 'Blood and soil? Renewable resource scarcity and internal armed conflict', *Journal of Peace Research* 45, 6: 801–18.

Tiffen, M., Mortimore, M. and Gichuki, F. (1994) *More People, Less Erosion Environmental Recovery in Kenya*, Chichester: Wiley.

Tir, J. and Diehl, P.F. (1998) 'Demographic pressure and interstate conflict: Linking population growth and density to militarized disputes and wars, 1930–89', *Journal of Peace Research* 35, 3: 319–99.

Toset, H., Petter, W., Gleditsch, N.P. and Hegre, H. (2000) 'Shared rivers and interstate conflict', *Political Geography* 19, 8: 971–96.

United Nations (2004) *World Population to 2300*. New York: United Nations, Department of Economic and Social Affairs, Population Division. Available online at: www.un.org/esa/population/publications/longrange2/2004worldpop2300reportfinalc.pdf (accessed 10 February 2009).

Urdal, H. (2005) 'People vs Malthus: Population pressure, environmental degradation and armed conflict revisited', *Journal of Peace Research* 42, 4: 417–34.

——(2008) 'Population, resources and political violence: A sub-national study of India 1956–2002', *Journal of Conflict Resolution* 52, 4: pp. 590–617.

Wallensteen, P. (1992) 'Environmental destruction and serious social conflict: Developing a research design' in Lodgaard, Sverre and af Ornäs, A.H. (eds) *The Environment and International Security*, PRIO report No.3 Oslo: International Peace Research Institute, pp. 47–54.

Wolf, A.T., (1999) '"Water wars" and water reality: Conflict and cooperation along international waterways', in Lonergan, S. (ed.) *Environmental Change, Adaptation, and Human Security*, Dordrecht: Kluwer Academic, pp. 251–65.

World Bank (2001) *World Bank Commodity Price Data*. Washington, DC: World Bank.

21

Emerging dangers of biological weapons

Barry Kellman

Biological weapons are devices for the malevolent infliction of disease. Using biological weapons, a small group of haters can spread illness, perhaps at catastrophic levels, perhaps on a global scale. Moreover, these weapons mutate due to the accelerating pace of scientific advance; tomorrow it will be slightly easier to use biological weapons than it is today. The notion that no one will ever use such capabilities is simply untenable. At the root of the matter is an existential challenge: scientific progress is intertwined with escalating malevolence threatening human security. Progressing capabilities improve our lives and yet, inextricably, enable the development of weapons that are truly harmful weapons to humanity.

While it is difficult to judge when this danger will strike, there should be no doubt that we are vulnerable to an attack. Attackers can choose from many disease agents and many dispersal modes, and they can hit targets anywhere in the world. Preparing and executing the attack can be done anonymously; the outbreak might initially be seen as natural. An attack with a contagious agent can spread through time and space; potentially imperilling everyone. These dangers of biological weapons do not argue for slowing scientific progress, but they undercut notions that new challenges can be effectively addressed with yesterday's policies.

This chapter briefly introduces the background for biological weapons security policy. It is followed by an overview of the likely agents and methods of use as weapons. The third section discusses the states and groups that have developed biological weapons and considers who might pose future threats and why. The fourth and fifth sections are devoted to a discussion of security strategies for reducing biological weapons dangers focusing on a critique of the existing policy framework and offering a summary of policy pillars that can augment security.

The evolution of biological weapons policy

In the aftermath of the horrific use of chemical weapons in the First World War, the League of Nations adopted the Geneva Protocol of 1925 banning the use of such weapons. Although there had been no widespread use of biological weapons, the Protocol also banned use of *bacteriological weapons* both because such weapons were viewed as inhumane and because such weapons were uncontrollable and thus would likely harm non-combatants. The Geneva Protocol, however, did not ban the production or deployment of banned weapons – only their use. Even the ban was only against their first use – a nation that had been attacked with such weapons could legally retaliate in kind. Most important, the Geneva Protocol had absolutely no enforcement mechanism whatsoever.

The impotence of the Geneva Protocol was demonstrated, as recounted below, by the Japanese use of biological weapons in the Second World War and the elaborate biological weapons programmes of the mid-twentieth century. During the Cold War, biological weapons, nuclear weapons and chemical weapons came under the heading of 'weapons of mass destruction', which meant that the UN was committed, at least rhetorically, to their prohibition and eventual elimination.

In 1972, the Biological Weapons Convention (BWC) was signed, enshrining a prohibition against bioweapons in international law. In contrast to the Geneva Protocol, the BWC prohibits the production, acquisition or retention of biological weapons. – ensconcing a prohibition against bioweapons into international law. Its entry into force was a non-proliferation landmark. For the first time, a treaty outlawed an entire class of weapons and compelled destruction of weapons stockpiles. This normative prohibition against bioweapons has become more profoundly entrenched during the intervening decades. Most legal experts agree that the BWC's normative prohibition against bioweapons extends to all states, a position long avowed by the US (Bureau of Verification, Compliance and Implementation 2005).

Yet, most diplomats and experts believe that the BWC is far too weak, and efforts to strengthen it have been notably controversial. For nearly two decades, the BWC has been mired in a contentious debate about how to verify state compliance. In sharp contrast to analogous agreements to control nuclear or chemical weapons, the BWC has no mechanism to verify state compliance. In this context, *verification* includes: (1) state declaration of facilities that could constitute a prohibited weapons capability; (2) regular reports about each facility's activities to enable monitoring that critical items are not wrongfully produced or diverted; and (3) on-site inspections of those facilities to verify the reports' accuracy.

As the BWC contains no verification system that is comparable to those for chemical and nuclear weapons, the regime for preventing bioweapons proliferation is asserted to be uniquely deficient. However, bioweapons do not neatly fit the nuclear or chemical non-proliferation paradigm where only a select number of uniquely specialized facilities have materials or equipment that, if diverted, could readily foster the development of illegal weapons. A near-infinite number of biological facilities lacking distinctive features could readily produce offensive weapons. Few experts take seriously, therefore, the idea that states or non-state actors will produce bioweapons at select declared sites. It is more likely that, if bioweapons emerge, their source will be any of the indistinguishable locales that are never declared or inspected. Therefore, verification modalities – declaration of critical facilities that must report on their activities and be inspected – would provide copious data about sites where bioweapons risks are negligible but would provide scant information about where bioweapons are being developed.

More centrally, the BWC – as a typical arms control treaty – embodies a set of techniques that are designed to limit state weapons programmes. It does not meaningfully address the two critical aspects of biological weapons: (1) biological weapons are by far the most powerful means of destruction and terror available to non-state actors; and (2) anti-biological weapons policies must focus on prevention, not just on accountability.

The BWC Article IV requires states parties to enact domestic measures to prohibit persons within their jurisdiction from developing or acquiring biological weapons, but there is no substance to this requirement. Does it mean that national laws must restrict possession of pathogens or equipment that can be used to make biological weapons? Must access to sophisticated biolabs be curtailed? Must these laws prohibit certain types of advanced experimentation that might facilitate the preparation of a biological weapon? Must the trade of pathogens or equipment, domestically and internationally, be restricted? All of these questions, among many others, remain unanswered within the BWC context.

In operational terms, the BWC can at most require states to punish biological weapons perpetrators after the fact. That is, if there is an attack with biological weapons and if the perpetrators can be identified, then a state party will be obligated to hold those perpetrators to account for their crime. This requirement is not insignificant, but it pales against the implications of a biological catastrophe. In the wake of an attack that could inflict thousands or even millions of casualties, billions of US dollars in losses and global panic, the prosecution of perpetrators (who are likely to either have died in the attack or escaped to an unfriendly locale) is an insufficient policy goal.

None of this is intended to undervalue the power of the norm embodied in the BWC, nor to diminish the prohibition of state bioweapons programmes. States have unparalleled capacities for making bioweapons, and these capacities can be the source (wittingly or not) for non-state biological weapons. In addition, state use of bioweapons is likely to be of a size and scale that exceeds what terrorists or fanatics can accomplish. No policy against biological weapons could be effective unless there is unequivocal denunciation of any state that develops or assists others in developing bioweapons, and any state that puts bioweapons to hostile use must know that it will suffer the harshest consequences permissible under international law.

Yet, in the last three decades as the international community has discovered illegal biological weapons programmes in the former Soviet Union, Iraq and elsewhere, unsuccessful efforts have been made to strengthen the unenforceable BWC, calling into question whether the mechanisms of arms control and international humanitarian law are appropriate for addressing the unique policy challenges posed by biological weapons. Put simply, application of arms control mechanisms against biological weapons is absolutely necessary but substantially insufficient.

Biological weapons – An existential danger

Making biological weapons is technically more difficult than producing some conventional weapons but certainly far easier than making a nuclear weapon. Refined seed stocks of pathogens that can potentially be used to create weapons are found widely in laboratories around the world. Acquiring weapons-grade nuclear material is, by contrast, extraordinarily difficult and far more expensive. The equipment necessary to produce nuclear weapons is far more tightly regulated than that required for developing biological weapons. Biological weapons can be made in facilities that are difficult to detect, and a single individual can transport bioweapons across borders by land, sea or air and through airports and customs controls.

There are countless ways to commit a biological attack. There are many types of bio-weapons that can be used to various effect. Potential perpetrators can choose from a wide array of pathogens and even more methods of dissemination to create many combinations; each method faces different obstacles and has different consequences. No single pathogen is perfect for all objectives. Some are harmful to humans; some attack livestock or crops. A few are contagious. Some are easy to acquire but need to be highly refined for weapons use; some are difficult to acquire but, if obtained, can be readily deployed. Vaccines exist against some pathogens; some pathogens are susceptible to environmental stress; some have long incubation periods; some cause diseases that are difficult to distinguish from a natural outbreak.

Smallpox, *Variola major*, is exceptionally lethal (up to 30 per cent of otherwise healthy victims die) and contagious. Although eradicated from nature over thirty years ago, there is a possibility that scientists might re-create the virus using modern genetic engineering techniques. There are other contagious viruses that are far more available than smallpox. The genome of the 1918 *Spanish Flu* pandemic (that killed upwards of 40 million people) has been deciphered, published on the internet and reconstituted in laboratories. Experts are concerned that hostile perpetrators could abuse these widely understood techniques to reproduce the disease or to manipulate the avian flu virus to augment its contagiousness (Webby and Webster 2003). Hemorrhagic fever viruses such as Ebola and Marburg are extremely lethal; no cure now exists. They are difficult to disseminate and kill too quickly to ignite a global pandemic, but emerging genetic manipulation techniques could be used to make the Ebola virus kill more slowly, allowing it to be spread farther before its debilitating effects altogether consume its carrier.

Anthrax, the agent used in the 2001 bio-terror attacks against members of the US Congress and the media is remarkably lethal (though not contagious); the fatality rate for untreated inhalational anthrax is close to 100 per cent. The WHO estimates that 50 kilograms of anthrax disseminated over an urban population of five million would cause 250,000 casualties (Inglesby et al. 1999). Obtaining natural anthrax is easy (it is endemic to grazing animals), but the preparation of anthrax for a mass catastrophe is challenging. Only certain strains can be aerosolized – a process that requires meticulous refining, separation from the growth medium and milling. The hardest technical challenge of anthrax biological weapons is to match the agent's characteristics with appropriate dissemination technology. It is most likely to be used in a confined space such as crowded stadiums, office buildings or subway systems.

The contamination of livestock or food supplies is a relatively easy way to trigger widespread disruption and crippling economic costs. Getting a sample of agro-pathogens is easy, and a few milligrams could initiate multiple outbreaks in widely dispersed locales. Pathogens could also be introduced to the food supply. Toxins can be spread by hand; indeed, a cult in Oregon spread salmonella on salad bars. An attack causing mass casualties is thought to be harder, but a recent report suggests that terrorists could kill or injure hundreds of thousands of people by putting botulinum toxin in the milk supply (Wein and Liu 2005).

Techniques that were only available on the cutting edge of science a decade or two ago are rapidly mutating as progress in the biological sciences enables new ways to produce a lethal catastrophe. Emerging scientific disciplines – notably genomics, nanotechnology and other microsciences – could alter pathogens for use as weapons. These scientific disciplines offer profound benefits for humanity, yet there is an ominous security challenge in minimizing the danger of their hostile application. For example, highly dangerous agents can be made resistant to vaccines or antibiotics. In Australia, scientists introduced a gene into mousepox (a cousin of smallpox) to reduce pest populations – it worked so well that it wiped out 100 per cent of affected mice, even mice who had immunity against the disease. Experts are concerned that the publication of these results might enable terrorists to create a super-disease that can overcome immunization (Jackson et al. 2001).

Various bacterial agents such as plague or tularemia (rabbit fever) could be altered to increase their lethality or to evade antibiotic treatment. Diseases once thought to be eradicated can now be re-synthesized, enabling them to spread in regions where there is no natural immunity. The poliovirus has been synthesized from scratch; its creators called it an 'animate chemical'. Soon, it may be re-synthesized into a form that is contagious even among vaccinated populations. The re-creation of long-eradicated livestock diseases could ravage herds severely lacking in genetic diversity, damage food supplies and cause devastating economic losses.

Advanced drug delivery systems can be used to disseminate lethal agents to broad populations. Bio-regulators, small organic compounds that modify body systems, could enhance targeted delivery technologies. Some experts are concerned that new weapons could be aimed at the immune, neurological and neuroendocrine systems. Nanotechnology that lends itself to mechanisms for advanced disease detection and drug delivery – such as gold nanotubes that can administer drugs directly into a tumour – could also deliver biological weapon agents deep into the body, substantially raising the weapon's effectiveness.

Today, these techniques are on the horizon. Within a decade, they will be pedestrian. According to the National Academies of Science: 'The threat spectrum is broad and evolving – in some ways predictably, in other ways unexpectedly. In the future, genetic engineering and other technologies may lead to the development of pathogenic organisms with unique, unpredictable characteristics' (National Research Council of the National Academies 2006).

Who has developed biological weapons, and who intends to do so?

Ever since mankind discovered how to isolate pathogens, people have developed hostile applications of biological agents.

National bioweapons programmes

Japan used bioweapons (plague, cholera and epidemic hemorrhagic fever) in China in the Second World War, causing perhaps a quarter of a million casualties. Soon thereafter, the US developed its own biological weapons programme including large-scale production facilities for human and agricultural pathogens; mass production of anthrax and virulent brucellosis for filling bombs; and cluster bombs for biological munitions. In 1969, however, President Richard Nixon, concerned that biological weapons offered little value to the US arsenals but their proliferation might undermine nuclear deterrence, unilaterally cancelled the US offensive programme. Shortly thereafter, the US Army officially ceased developing bioweapons and began developing vaccines (Guillemin 2005).

The largest military bioweapons programme belonged to the Soviet Union, which produced weapons versions of typhus, tularemia and Q fever. Even after the Soviet Union ratified the Biological Weapons Convention in the early 1970s, the Soviet biological warfare agency, *Biopreparat* produced and stockpiled hundreds of tons of plague,

236

tularemia, glanders, anthrax and smallpox agents at 52 biotechnology sites employing over 50,000 scientists and technicians. A high priority was to mass produce exceptionally viable agents with short incubation periods that could resist vaccines. In order to deploy these agents, the Soviet army had specially equipped crop duster planes, medium-range bombers, intercontinental ballistic missiles and cruise missiles capable of delivering agents to multiple cities. Notably, smallpox was produced in liquid form and loaded into sub-munitions that SS-18 ICBMs could deliver against enemy cities. In 1992, President Boris Yeltsin officially announced the end of the offensive bioweapons programme, but worrisome stockpiles remain, and there are reports that former Soviet scientists are working abroad, possibly for Iran and North Korea (Post 2002).

Other substantial bioweapons programmes were maintained by Iraq and South Africa. The Iraqi offensive bioweapons programme, discovered by UN inspectors in the mid-1990s, produced nearly 20,000 litres of concentrated botulinum toxin, nearly 10,000 litres of concentrated anthrax, and lesser quantities of other toxins, tularemia, plague, brucellosis and camelpox. The programme also produced missile warheads and aerial bombs that could deploy biological agents. Prior to the US-led invasion of Iraq in 2003, the Bush Administration cited discrepancies in Iraq's reports of its bioweapons destruction efforts as proof that it was concealing a still active programme. However, no evidence of a continuing bioweapons programme has yet appeared. The South African *Project Coast* produced plague, salmonella and botulinum as well as genetically modified anthrax that was allegedly incurable by conventional treatments The programme was dismantled in 1993, and the post-apartheid government unsuccessfully prosecuted its head, Dr. Wouter Basson ('Dr. Death'). Today, not a single state admits to having a bioweapons programme, but US intelligence officials assert that as many as ten states might have active programmes, including North Korea, Iran and Syria (Goss 2005).

Terrorists

Even the most fanatical terrorists must realize that conventional attacks are not bringing modern society to its knees. The September 2001 attacks, the bombing of the Madrid and London subways, and numerous smaller attacks have dramatically increased fear of terrorism but have not fundamentally transformed government structures or policies. From the terrorists' perspective, the stakes must be raised. Indeed, many terrorist organizations have expressed interest in acquiring biological weapons (Deputy Director of National Intelligence for Analysis 2004).

Whatever weight the taboo against inflicting disease might have for nation states, it is obviously irrelevant to terrorists, criminals and lunatics. Deterrence by threat of retaliation is essentially meaningless for groups with suicidal inclinations who are likely to intermingle with innocent civilians. Al Qaida and affiliated fundamentalist organizations have overtly proclaimed their intention to develop and use bioweapons. The 11th volume of al-Qaida's *Encyclopedia of Jihad* is devoted to chemical and biological weapons. Indeed, al-Qaida has acknowledged that 'biological weapons are considered the least complicated and easiest to manufacture of all weapons of mass destruction' (Salama and Hansell 2005).

Al-Qaida is widely reported to have acquired legal pathogens via publicly available scientific sources (Allen-Mills and Mahnaimi 2005). Before 2001, al-Qaida operatives reportedly purchased anthrax and plague from arms dealers in Kazakhstan, and the group has repeatedly urged followers to recruit microbiology and biotechnology experts.

Following the Taliban's fall, five al-Qaida biological weapons labs in Afghanistan tested positive for anthrax. Documents calculating aerial dispersal methods of anthrax via balloon were discovered in Kabul along with anthrax spore concentrate at a nearby vaccine laboratory.

According to a lengthy fatwa commissioned by Osama bin Laden, jihadists are entitled to use weapons of mass destruction against the infidels, even if it means killing innocent women, children and Muslims. No matter that these weapons cannot be specifically targeted: 'nothing is a greater duty, after faith itself, than repelling an enemy attacker who sows corruption to religion and the world'. According to the fatwa 'No conditions limit this: one repels the enemy however one can' (Al-Fahd 2003). The sentiment might be reprehensible, but it is certainly not irrational. Biological weapons are perhaps the most dire and easiest to execute existential danger.

Consequences and implications

In comparison to use of conventional or chemical weapons, the potential death toll of a biological weapons attack could be huge. Although the number of victims would depend on where an attack takes place, the type of pathogen and the sophistication of the weapons maker, there is widespread consensus among experts that a high-end attack would inflict casualties in number that would only be surpassed by all-out nuclear war. Various types of biological weapons attacks could result in more than 100,000 casualties, perhaps far more.

Even more than the death toll, the truly unique characteristic of some biological weapons that distinguishes them from every other type of weapon is contagion. No other type of weapon can replicate itself and spread. Any other type of attack, no matter how severe, occurs at a certain moment in time at an identifiable place. Anyone far away will not be physically injured by the attack. An attack with a contagious agent can spread, potentially imperilling target populations far from where the agents are released. A bio-offender could infect his accomplices with a disease and send them across borders before symptoms are obvious. Carriers will then spread it to other unsuspecting victims who would themselves become extended bioweapons, carrying the disease indiscriminately.

All this leads to the most important characteristic of biological weapons: a biological attack creates incomparable levels of panic. For people who seek to rattle the pillars of modern civilization and perhaps cause it to collapse, the effective use of disease would set in motion political, economic and health consequences so severe that they call into question the ability of existing governments to maintain their citizens' security.

Defining the security agenda

There are security policies that can substantially reduce the dangers of biological weapons if they are pursued in ways that promote the advance of bioscience and that elevate global attention to public health. One principle is paramount: anti-biological weapons policies must be global. Perpetrators from anywhere can obtain pathogens from virtually everywhere. Bioresearch labs are widely proliferating, expanding the risks that lethal agents could be diverted and misused. Transnational criminal networks can easily prepare an attack; terrorists can slide across borders and release disease anonymously. A contagious agent would spread without regard for boundaries, race, religion or nationality. Public health responses would have to be internationally coordinated. New modes of international legal cooperation would be needed to investigate the crime.

The essence of a biological weapons prevention strategy can be expressed as follows:

Prevention = Complication + Preparation + Non-proliferation

Each of these dimensions of a prevention strategy captures or erases some risks of biological weapons, and together they are likely to deter malevolent actors from pursuing such capabilities.

Complication

Denial measures should make it hard for actors to acquire biological weapons, and if they try to do so, *interdiction measures* should make it more likely they will be discovered and stopped. It will be harder for a perpetrator to acquire critical pathogens and equipment if only legitimate scientists are allowed to have access to such items. Cutting off or limiting wrongful access to refined agents, equipment or laboratories would create obstacles for producing biological weapons. These denial measures should be linked to observable warnings that can alert law enforcers who are authorized, trained and equipped to look for such indicative behaviour.

However, the police forces of most nations are insufficiently authorized, equipped and trained for this purpose. Moreover, international cooperation with respect to the arrest, extradition and criminal prosecution of individuals involved in biological weapons is inadequate. Every nation's laws should criminalize unauthorized possession of pathogens and access to laboratories. Police training should be promoted in developing countries, including enhancing forensic capabilities for attributing responsibility for wrongful use/ release of pathogens. Accordingly, international policies should be direct toward strengthening law enforcement capabilities for the prevention, response and punishment of biological crimes. These efforts should include enhanced capabilities and training for the detection and forensic analysis of illicit biological activities.

Information is critical. Systematic collection, analysis and sharing of relevant information could reveal patterns that arouse suspicion of illicit bio-preparations and could enable intelligence and law enforcement authorities to disrupt those preparations. However, too much of the critical information about the location of particularly dangerous pathogen strains is unknown, and there is no systematic capability to track movements of such strains. Neither is there any uniform, worldwide census of biological facilities. It is imperative, therefore, to develop an interlinked global database on the location of pathogens of concern, laboratories that stock such pathogens, transfers of pathogens and equipment, and incidents of concern.

Preparation

If appropriate vaccines and antidotes could be stockpiled in sufficient quantities and if efficient emergency distribution capabilities could be established, then authorities would be better able to contain the consequences of an attack with biological weapons. These vaccines and medicines have to be produced in sufficient quantities, distributed globally and allocated with respect for adverse side effects. However, there are substantial disincentives against the discovery and production of such medicines. Moreover, stockpiling of medications is not cheap, and unaddressed difficulties of distributing vaccines globally undermine confidence in the fairness of allocation plans. These considerations are compounded by legal constraints on the mass dissemination of medications in an emergency.

Preparedness measures also include establishing lines of communication between public health authorities and law enforcers so that an attack using biological weapons can be quickly identified, victims can be treated and the spread of contagion can be contained. The challenge is how to advance systems where more secure bioscience and better law enforcement capabilities are integrated with and complementary to promoting global public health preparedness. What is needed is a global system that is capable of producing and distributing appropriate medications rapidly upon diagnosis of an attack. The international community should develop an efficient multilateral distribution system that would work through and resolve the many legal constraints and planning considerations on a systemic basis, substantially reducing the transaction costs associated with ad hoc negotiations. In this context, there are important lessons to be learned from the experience of the US and other developed countries concerning programmes for disease surveillance, early attack warning and attack response. A biological weapons prevention strategy should highlight effective preparedness, detection and response mechanisms that could be usefully adapted for other nations, regional organizations or the global community generally.

Non-proliferation

Combined complication and resilience measures are the most effective way to address threats of terrorists and criminals. There remains, however, the rare but very serious threat of state military programmes because states have unique capabilities for committing violence and making covert preparations. As previously mentioned, the Biological Weapons Convention (BWC) has become mired in diplomatic friction that undermines its ability to prevent the production and proliferation of biological weapons. Four key issues need to be addressed.

1 By what process should biological weapons be defined; most especially, how should so-called non-lethal biological agents be considered?
2 How can states be confident of their mutual compliance and be assured that burgeoning national bio-defence programmes are not covers for offensive programmes?
3 How can the BWC process encourage and oversee the dismantlement of existing bioweapons stockpiles particularly in the former Soviet Union?
4 How can an international investigative capability be established to assess allegations of bioweapons production and use, and how should the UN Secretary General's mechanisms to investigate alleged use of WMD and the BWC's Article V consultation and cooperation process be enhanced?

International governance architecture

In view of the inherently international character of biological weapons, the governance architecture must be global. Moreover, it should integrate disparate functions: some policies must engage law enforcement; some must engage public health; some must engage science and development. One idea is to centralize governance in Interpol, which has the world's largest programme exclusively devoted to reducing bio-threats. Strengthening law enforcement is pivotal, but Interpol is ill suited to oversee the public health aspects of biological weapons prevention. Conversely, the World Health Organization (WHO) should oversee bio-surveillance and medical response in the context of biological attacks, but it is wholly inappropriate to ask the WHO to investigate and interdict illicit activities. Actually, about three dozen international organizations and professional associations have specialized expertise; each can contribute to preventing biological weapons. However, biological weapons prevention is not the responsibility of only scientists or only police or only medical responders. There is no need to re-invent these centres of relevant expertise, but there is a need to coordinate their many beneficial activities into a coherent strategy.

This coordination role must be assumed by the UN. Endowing the UN with additional responsibilities must be done warily with due recognition of the institution's inefficiency and spotty record in addressing strategic dangers. However, the UN has been admirably successful in addressing global issues pertaining to science – e.g. satellite placement, meteorology and geological monitoring. Moreover, its programmes that coordinate specialized functions – e.g. UNAIDS – have effectively taken advantage of smaller bodies' otherwise disaggregated initiatives. In the final analysis, if the governance architecture for addressing this threat is not vested in the UN, then a new body will have to be created, and that body is likely to have flaws every bit as serious as the UN. There is really no other choice: biological weapons are a threat to international peace and security that requires multilateral and multi-disciplinary action.

Conclusion

This chapter's fundamental thesis is that it is counter-productive to try to squeeze security policies for reducing biological threats into policy constructs for other security challenges. A security strategy for dealing with biological weapons must grapple with the potential dangers emerging from bioscience, fully recognizing that biological weapons prevention should be conceived of as a facet of a broad international commitment to: (1) prevent the spread of disease (e.g. public health); (2) enhance protection against and cures for disease (e.g. vaccination and drug therapies); (3) supervise the conduct of biological science and; (4) criminalize unauthorized or improper use of pathogens.

Such effort could form the basis of a policy commitment to the growth of bioscience as a global public good, and policies to encourage its worldwide spread must be supported. All states must strive to prevent biological weapons even as bioscience is promoted as a fundamental pillar of humanity's progress. Responsibilities should be common to all, even as the burdens associated with those responsibilities are differentiated according to wealth and capability.

In summary, the dangers of biological weapons are the dark side of globalization, calling for global implementation of prevention and response strategies. Thus, preventing the use of biological weapons portends a new chapter in the human species' most basic and most long-lasting struggle against lethal microbes and offers a new vision of how to organize global security under law.

References

Al-Fahd, Nasir Bin Hamd (2003) *A Treatise on the Legal Status of Using Weapons of Mass Destruction Against Infidels*, Rabi I 1424 (May 2003). Available online at: www.carnegieendowment.org/static/npp/fatwa.pdf.

Allen-Mills, T. and Mahnaimi, U. (2005) 'Al-Qaeda seeks toxins for biowarfare attack', *Sunday Times*, January 2. Available online at: www.timesonline.co.uk/tol/news/world/article407762.ece (accessed 14 February 2009).

Bureau of Verification, Compliance and Implementation (2005) *Case Study: Yellow Rain*, Fact Sheet, October 1. Available online at: www.state.gov/documents/organization/57428.pdf (accessed 14 February 2009).

Deputy Director of National Intelligence for Analysis (2004) 'Unclassified report to Congress on the acquisition of technology relating to weapons of mass destruction and advanced conventional munitions, 1 January – 31 December 2004'. Available online at: www.globalsecurity.org/wmd/library/report/2006/wmd-acq_cia_2004.htm (accessed 14 February 2009).

Goss, P.J. (2005) 'Testimony of Director of Central Intelligence Porter J. Goss, global intelligence challenges 2005: meeting long-term challenges with a long-term strategy, before the Senate Select Committee on Intelligence', February 16. Available online at: www.globalsecurity.org/intell/library/congress/2005_hr/050317-goss.htm (accessed 14 February 2009).

Guillemin, J. (2005) *Biological Weapons: From the Invention of State-Sponsored Programs to Contemporary Bioterrorism*, New York: Columbia University Press.

Inglesby, T.V. et al. (1999) 'Anthrax as a biological weapon: Medical and public health management', *Journal of the American Medical Association* 281, 18: 1735–45.

Jackson, R.J., Ramsay, A.J., Christensen, C.D., Beaton, S., Hall, D.F. and Ramshaw, I.A. (2001) 'Expression of mouse interleukin-4 by a recombinant ectromelia virus suppresses cytolytic lymphocyte responses and overcomes genetic resistance to mousepox', *Journal of Virology*, 75, 3: 1205–10.

Nasr, B. (2003) 'A treatise on the legal status of using weapons of mass destruction against infidels'. Available online at: www.carnegieendowment.org/static/npp/fatwa.pdf (accessed 14 February 2009).

National Research Council of the National Academies (2006) *Globalization, Biosecurity, and the Future of the Life Sciences*, Committee on Advances in Technology and the Prevention of their Application to Next Generation Biowarfare Threats, Washington, DC: National Academies Press.

Post, G. (2002) 'Biotechnology and terrorism', *Prospect Magazine*, 74: 48–52.

Salama, S. and Hansell, L. (2005) 'Does intent equal capability? Al-Qaeda and weapons of mass destruction', *Nonproliferation Review* 12, 3: 615–53.

Webby, R.J. and Webster, R.G. (2003) 'Are we ready for pandemic influenza?' *Science* 302, 3650: 1519–22.

Wein, L.M. and Liu, Y. (2005) 'Analyzing a bioterror attack on the food supply: The case of botulinum toxin in milk', in *Proceedings of the National Academy of Sciences of the United States of America* 102, 28: 9984–89.

22

Security and health in the twenty-first century

Colleen O'Manique and Pieter Fourie

Certain transmissible pathogens have become increasingly securitized in the contemporary global context. Within a single decade, there have been two UN Security Council special sessions devoted to the threat of AIDS; and the global response to Severe Acute Respiratory Syndrome (SARS) and H5N1 (avian influenza) were effective and well-coordinated operations executed with military precision and urgency – and accompanied by a military discourse: the language within which particular viruses have been couched has become increasingly militarized, with 'enemies' to be 'combated' and 'wars' to be won. For instance, instead of 'medical interventions to counter the HI virus', it is common to refer to the 'war on AIDS' – or cancer or drugs. In the short term, this response has been effective: both SARS and H5N1 have (for now) been contained.

But within this political and discursive trajectory, there is evidence of tension between health as a human security issue, linked to a broader developmental and human rights agenda, and health as a national security issue manifested in the form of a few diseases that seem to directly threaten the industrialized world. This tension has implications for the policy responses that governments implement; for instance, a 'national security' response would enable much more invasive prescriptions such as shutting down airports, detaining the carriers of certain viruses and even waiving some international legislation in the name of the national interest. A developmental response to health issues implies less invasive, more human rights-centred approaches and policy prescriptions.

Just over 30 years ago, member states of the World Health Organization (WHO) adopted the Alma Ata Declaration, 'Health for All by the Year 2000', which called for 'the attainment by all citizens of the world by the year 2000 of a level of health that will permit them to lead a socially and economically productive life' through the implementation of a broad primary healthcare vision. The neoliberal economic and political restructuring of states through World Bank and IMF conditionalities was introduced soon after, beginning in the 1980s and, with the introduction of Structural Adjustment Programs (SAPs), vertical interventions focused on single diseases became more fashionable, while the understanding of public health became increasingly disengaged from health's social determinants. This transformation has occurred within the context of a mostly discreet, yet influential battle between individual state sovereignty and its concomitant prescriptions on how to respond to new epidemics on the one hand, and the multilateralization and globalization of diseases on the other. One of the ways in which this tension has manifested itself has been through appeals to the dangers that certain diseases imply for state survival, or an agenda that appeals more directly to a softer human-security approach that underlines the nefarious implications both of the erosion of the social determinants of health and of epidemic disease for individual human rights related to health. But there is also evidence of the convergence of these discourses of hard and soft security. In Alan Ingram's words (2007: 514), 'continuing domestic and international campaigns on development and health have offered an opportunity ... to show a human face as well as an iron fist in ... foreign policy'.

This chapter examines how the relationship between global health and security has been historically constructed, and looks at the effects of the securitization of certain diseases on the global architecture of health governance. The first section is a brief overview of the state of global health. The second section places 'health security' within the broader security polemic that has evolved over the past few decades, presenting an account of the contemporary evolution of the 'mainstream' securitization of emerging pandemics, drawing on the specific cases of avian influenza, SARS and AIDS. The third section focuses on the role of the UN over the years as a securitizing actor, the G8 countries and the US in particular. Finally, the consequences of the contemporary securitization of disease and emergent policy responses for global public health and the challenges shaping the future of global health in the contemporary global context are sketched.

The global health context

Figure 22.1 sizes territories in proportion to the absolute number of people who died from infectious and parasitic conditions in 2002. Of the deaths recorded here, 27 per cent of

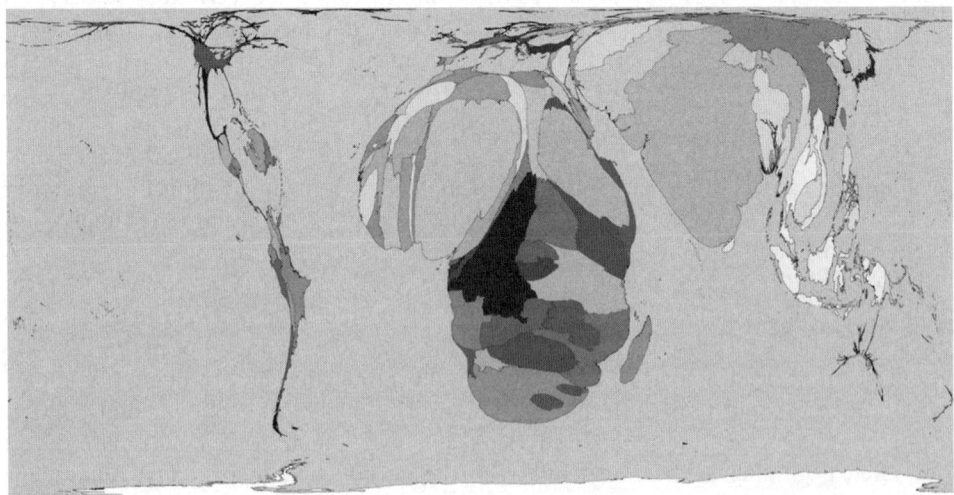

Figure 22.1 Infectious and parasitic disease deaths.
Source: www.worldmapper.org, © Copyright 2006 SASI Group (University of Sheffield) and Mark Newman (University of Michigan).

deaths were caused by AIDS, 17 per cent by diarrhoeal diseases, 14 per cent by tuberculosis (TB), eight per cent by malaria and, within the childhood-cluster diseases, six per cent by measles, three per cent whooping cough and two per cent by tetanus. Also causing two per cent of these deaths each were sexually transmitted diseases (STDs) and meningitis. All other categories were under two per cent each. These infectious and parasitic diseases caused 19 per cent of all deaths worldwide in 2002, for an average of 1,766 deaths per million people. In the territory with the highest rate of deaths, Botswana, with 19,642 deaths per million people, 95 per cent were caused by AIDS. This disease also caused about 85 per cent of deaths in the next three highest territories, Lesotho, Swaziland and Zimbabwe.

The map illustrates that the world has a dramatically unequal disease burden, with a class of countries set apart by vastly disproportionate levels of disease-related morbidity and mortality. The unequal disease burden corresponds to a global context within which disease surveillance systems and basic healthcare systems are poorly funded and staffed, and where the social determinants of health are scarce. The 2005 WHO World Health Report estimated that the number of children under five years to die that year would be 11 million; more than half of these were expected to be related to hunger, the rest from preventable and treatable infectious diseases and HIV infection. A total of 850 million people suffer from chronic hunger (FAO 2005); almost half of the population in the global South are suffering from one or more of the main diseases associated with inadequate provision of water and sanitation services (Becker et al. 2006: 22). Clearly, the world is an unsafe and lethal place for many people in the global South in particular.

Some in the global South posit that such a worldwide health apartheid is the consequence of political actions or inactions, such as colonialism and its contemporary exponents, which exacerbate long-established patterns of poverty. Conversely, others argue that bad health follows bad governance, and that 'good' governance (and neoliberal democracy in particular) can and should be used as a political vaccine or prescription against poverty and related health pathologies. In this way, global disease burdens have come to be seen as a *political* problem rather than as an issue that belongs exclusively to the field of clinical health management; these days, politicians and statesmen 'do' health as much as medical personnel. Moreover, some diseases such as TB, AIDS, SARS and bird flu are seen as such threats to the well-being of peoples and states that they have come to be viewed as threats to the national interest or national security.

The securitization of health issues

Until the Industrial Revolution of the nineteenth century, state-centred interventions to limit the spread and impact of disease focused mostly on isolated epidemic outbreaks, as was the case with the quarantining of people and goods suspected of harbouring infectious disease (a practice that originated in the Port of Venice during the plague epidemics of the fourteenth century) (King 2002: 764). According to Zacher (2007: 15–29), global health collaboration has evolved through three historical regime periods.

First, from the mid-nineteenth century to the early twentieth century, a treaty to control the international spread of epidemic disease was negotiated, mostly by European states. This happened in parallel with the Industrial Revolution, as colonial masters interacted more frequently with and were more exposed to the diseases of other parts of the world. The negotiations followed on a conference held in Paris in 1851 to address cholera, and culminated in the acceptance of the International Sanitary Regulations of

1903, which were later renamed the International Health Regulations (IHR). The second major development in the search for an international health regime was the establishment of the World Health Organization (WHO) in 1948 under the aegis of the UN. The WHO championed and approved revised versions of the IHR in 1951, 1969, 1973 and 1981. Lastly, since 1990, there has been a dramatic expansion in multilateral efforts at global health cooperation. After the SARS scare of 2003, the IHR was again amended; the revised version was formally adopted in May 2005 and came into force in June 2007. A key thrust of this evolving health regime is health surveillance (Davies 2008: 308–13), along with emergency interventions to control epidemic outbreaks. Fidler and Gostin (2006: 86) argue that the new IHR is a paradigm shift compared to the old version, to the extent that it will transform and expand 'the scope of the IHR's application, incorporate international human rights principles, contain more demanding obligations for states parties to conduct surveillance and response, and establish important new powers for WHO' (Fidler and Gostin 2006: 86).

Fidler (2007: 41–66) points out that this regime is noted for its embrace of health problems as security issues. In fact, he postulates that we now operate in a 'post-securitization phase', in which '[v]iewing public health through the lens of security has become an integral aspect of public health governance in the 21st century' (Fidler 2007: 41). He goes on to argue that the contemporary securitization of health is the result of post-Cold War fears regarding the proliferation of bioweapons, and the global spread of communicable diseases in particular (especially HIV/AIDS, but also the SARS and H5N1 scares of the last few years), as well as mounting sensitivities regarding the vulnerability of populations in both rich and poor countries in the context of rapid globalization. Zacher contends that there is no simple explanation for the change in the international health regime, but that a contributing factor has been the emergence of new and more virulent pandemic diseases; a greater understanding of the costs of disease to economies and societies that are more deeply linked through processes of globalization; the expansion of the participation of civil society and private actors (many via public-private partnerships (PPPs)) in global health governance; and the improvement of disease detection and surveillance via the internet (Zacher 2007: 21ff.).

Health has thus come to be viewed as exemplar of humanity's 'new collective insecurity' (Shaw et al. 2006: 5). According to Pirages (2007: 625), such 'growing complexity requires more sophisticated forms of governance', as well as the move from a state-centric to a supranational level of global public health governance to address what are, in essence, health issues that transcend national borders. Emerging from these new realities is the tension between the broader human-centric perspective on health, which views health as a basic individual human right linked to broader rights of citizenship and health's social determinants, and the understanding of health that links health to securitization. Securitization was introduced into political science discourse in the 1990s, when Ole Wæver, Barry Buzan and other members of the so-called 'Copenhagen School of security' coined it to advance discourse regarding security 'beyond a focus on the nation-state and on the provision or analysis of military security issues only' (Kelle 2007: 218). The securitization process is summarized by Buzan and Wæver (and quoted in Cook 2008) as follows:

> A security issue is posited (by a securitizing actor) as a threat to the survival of some referent object (nation, state, the liberal economic order, the rain forests), which is claimed to have a right to survive. Since a question of survival necessarily involves a

point of no return at which it will be too late to act, it is not defensible to leave this issue to normal politics. The securitizing actor therefore claims a right to use extraordinary means or break normal rules, for the reasons of security.

(Cook 2008: 6)

In the time since 11/9 (9 November 1989: the fall of the Berlin Wall) and 9/11 (the terrorist attacks on the US in 2001), we have seen UN agencies in particular as well as the nations of the G8 in the throes of what could potentially be an interesting marriage between a traditional, militaristic way of thinking about security, and the more contemporary, human security perspective alluded to above. The war on terror and 'the war on HIV/AIDS' for example, are seen as two sides of the same coin: both have been constructed by the US State Department, for example, as risks requiring the rapid mobilization of resources, and have become a central subject of foreign policy requiring US leadership and international collaboration.

Key securitizing actors

After the Second World War, a new system of multilateral governance was entrenched institutionally through the creation of the UN, which was couched in the context of an evolving global legal system based broadly on guarantees of state sovereignty, collective state security and individual human rights. The ideal became a rather interesting hybrid of state-centric and human-centric discourses applied within the multilateral organization, with members of especially the new Second and Third Worlds emphasizing (discursively at least) notions of greater global class equity and fairness. After 1989, the UN began to reconsider its conception of security: The world was no longer subject to conventional notions of conflict; new threats started to permeate the orthodox description of *realpolitik*. The global context had moved on from narrow notions regarding an ideological battle between the First and the Second Worlds played out through proxy wars in mainly the Third World. After 1989, nationalism reasserted itself, from intra-state conflicts in the Balkans and in Africa to the appearance of a new kind of terrorism largely understood to be rooted in fundamentalist or politicized religion. As the traditional, military notions of security threats started to recede in the early 1990s, the United Nations Development Programme (UNDP) released its World Development Report in 1994, coining the concept 'human security', taken to refer to any threat (military or other) that threatens the well-being of humans (rather than the well-being of states only).

In 1990, the US Central Intelligence Agency (CIA) for the first time added HIV/AIDS as one variable that might cause greater state fragility and eventual failure, particularly in the developing world (Fourie and Schönteich 2002: 8). But it was not until a decade later that the UN Security Council (UNSC) was critical in securitizing HIV/AIDS, '*constructing* the disease as something extraordinary which demanded international attention and action' (McInnes 2006: 315; emphasis added). In the short term, the securitization of AIDS in particular achieved exactly what many said it needed to: a sense of urgency to respond, and increased funding and position on the political agenda of individual states as well as of multilateral organizations. The formal securitization of AIDS was enacted after a visit by the US ambassador to the UN, Richard Holbrooke, to Africa in December 1999 to witness personally the impact of the growing AIDS epidemic. On 10 January 2000, the UN Security Council (UNSC) for the first time in its history

247

debated what was ostensibly a health issue in terms of security (Behrman 2004: 158–65). This meeting was followed in July 2000 by UN Resolution 1308, which formalized the securitization of HIV/AIDS by referring to it explicitly as a national security crisis. It is important that these developments took place within the UNSC: in the days of the Cold War this was the UN body where global powers could engage in posturing; the UNSC is a state-centric vehicle par excellence. However, in terms of how Resolution 1308 formally securitized the pandemic, the language of human security was evoked to a large extent, and UNAIDS was charged with the responsibility of responding to this challenge. In the same year, the Millennium Development Goals (MDGs) were also adopted as a programme of action by the UN, with goal six of the MDGs referring specifically to the imperative to 'combat AIDS, malaria and other diseases' (Poku et al. 2007: 1162).

One year after Resolution 1308, in mid-2001, the UN General Assembly held a special session on HIV/AIDS (UNGASS), which went even further in putting the pandemic on the multilateral agenda – during the special session, the former chairman of the US Joint Chiefs of Staff and then-secretary of state, General Colin Powell, declared that 'there is no enemy in war more insidious than AIDS' (Behrman 2004: 266). In May 2002, the Clinton administration designated the global spread of AIDS as a threat to national security (O'Manique 2006: 170).

Gray argues that the UN seems to be working towards resolving the ostensible tension between state sovereignty and post-Second World War multilateralism by unequivocally accepting the state as the global unit of analysis in terms of security (Gray 2005: 212), while drawing special attention to the obligation that states also have to protect individuals' rights to health and safety from epidemics. The revised International Health Regulations are guided by a WHO strategic plan to 2012 to ramp up, in all countries, the core surveillance, detection, outbreak alert and response capacities to diseases that are particularly epidemic-prone, with the global community assisting countries with low capacity (WHO 2008). Disease affects people, but as the director general of the WHO stated in the 2007 WHO report aptly titled *A Safer Future: Global Public Health Security in the 21st Century*: 'Shocks to health reverberate as shocks to economies and business continuity in areas well beyond the affected area. Vulnerability is universal' (ibid.: vi).

The UN has also recently produced other influential reports that explicitly frame the multilateral response to health threats, thus reaffirming the contemporary global health regime. The first is the *Report of the Secretary-General's High-Level Panel on Threats, Challenges and Change* (UN 2004), in which paragraph 66 explicitly refers to global health threats. Significantly, UN Secretary-General Kofi Annan used the foreword to the High-Level Panel Report to reiterate the central role of states in combating today's security threats, thus emphasizing the realist underpinnings of the modern global state system, and the concomitant implications for the definition and locus of security that this invokes: 'the front line in today's combat must be manned by capable and responsible *States*' (UN 2004: vii). However, in the two following paragraphs, Annan qualifies such realism by reflecting on the human security obligations that such a role implies for sovereign states – in relation to what he refers to as both 'development' and 'biological security'. The High-Level Panel Report is thus quite explicit in its advocacy of a new security consensus that does not state the conceptualization of 'security' in either/or, 'hard' vs. 'soft'/ 'human' security terms (UN 2004: 1f.).

John Kirton and Jenevieve Mannell (2007) argue that the G8 has also been instrumental in mobilizing resources and shaping institutions of governance for global health over the past decade, which they attribute to 'the increasingly equal vulnerability of each

G8 member to a new generation of infectious diseases' (ibid.: 134). According to Kirton and Mannell, the rising panic over HIV/AIDS and the apparent threat that it posed to the US and Europe first drove the G8's concern. Other health concerns subsequently came onto the G8's agenda over public panic over infectious diseases, such as SARS and avian influenza, or possible instances of biological terrorism. In addition, the G8 has been active in the mobilization of resources for boosting research and health systems more generally. The authors point to the G8's central role in eliminating polio, strengthening UNAIDS and in establishing the Global Fund to Fight AIDS, Tuberculosis and Malaria, which since 2002 has disbursed over US$11 billion. Global health has been added as a main item on the agenda at the G8 annual summits, and since 1999, there have been annual ministerial meetings on health security and biological terrorism: 'Since the onset of rapid globalization in 1996, the G8 has emerged through several stages as an effective, high performing centre of global health governance across the board' (Kirton and Mannell 2007: 133).

The consequences of the securitization of health

The securitization of an issue is useful as it forces states to put issues such as bird flu, SARS or AIDS on the public agenda. By applying the language of war or imminent threat, a polemic is presupposed, and states respond to crises by mobilizing resources. As McInnes puts it, 'there is more than a suspicion that the securitizing move [within the UN] was part of an attempt to gain greater political attention' (McInnes 2006: 326).

Some scholars (e.g. Anand et al. 2006; Daniels 2008; Hilts 2005) have responded to the way that health has been understood as a security issue by pointing to the silence within the dominant polemic about the structural inequalities emerging from the contemporary governance of the global economy, and their role in shaping both people's access to the social determinants of health and access to healthcare and medicines. The literature on the global political economy of health has provided ample evidence that health sector reforms that have been part of the past three decades of neoliberal economic restructuring have been largely detrimental to the health conditions of the poorest, and have instigated a significant drain of skills from South to North, from greatest to least need (Yong et al. 2000; Labonte et al. 2004). The chronic diseases of poverty are not transmissible pathogens with the potential to disrupt the state and material interests of Northern countries dramatically; nor do they pose a threat to the lives of the rich; while new pathogens that will continue to develop with increasing frequency and speed will have different consequences for different people. Mike Davis (2005) points out that a future influenza pandemic will have the most catastrophic effects in places marked by poverty, malnutrition, chronic illness, other co-infections, poor sanitation, overcrowding and limited access to health services.

Prioritizing diseases and/or health systems in countries that are understood as critical to Northern economic and geopolitical interests is seen as another potential consequence. The foreign policies of nation-states (particularly of the global North) tilt towards addressing selective global public health issues, not in the sense of traditional development (or 'soft security') concerns, but as threats to economies, public sectors, militaries and vital geopolitical and strategic interests. Mark Duffield describes the present as a new biopolitical era in which '[i]nternational danger now equates with unsecured circulatory flows and networked interconnections associated with the social, economic and political life of global population' (Duffield 2005: 143). While the subjects of 'health security' are human bodies, the objects to be secured through increased attention to global health threats are economies, militaries and ecosystems – in short, the current global order. Today's global health governance exposes the contradictions of a global order in which health is increasingly shaped by global forces, while the responsibility to protect health is still principally nested within the nation-state (O'Manique 2007).

SARS is a case in point. Health risks are socially constructed; if populations that are unaccustomed to risk believe that they are at risk, governments with the capacity to do so will be more inclined to act. McInnes (2005: 15) identifies factors that contribute to a collective sense of risk: the likelihood and outcome of infection and especially the chance of death; the adequacy of extant preventative and protective measures; the rate and nature of the number of cases; uncertainty over how the pathogen is spread; people's confidence in statements made by authorities; and whether there is a suspicion that risks are downplayed. SARS was constructed in the Canadian and the global media as a major threat, nurturing what amounted to minor panic among the citizens of Toronto, through testimonials from nurses and relatives of the 'victims' and reports of the impact measured not only in terms of morbidity and mortality, but also lost tourism dollars, lower productivity, negative effects on the local economy and interference with travel. SARS claimed 43 lives and infected 251 people in total. For a relatively well-insulated population largely ignorant of the human toll of the diseases of the poor, SARS was a minor crisis, yet instilled fear and a bunker mentality.

In contrast, the diseases of the poor have always been with us; they pose no immediate threat or danger to citizens living in the global North. The exception is HIV/AIDS, which has been securitized despite its concentration in Sub-Saharan Africa. The security polemic on AIDS has focused on a number of interrelated issues, the key 'threats' emerging from HIV morbidity and mortality: economic and state collapse; increased violence; migration and population movements with a focus on soldiers, peacekeepers and migrant labourers; low-intensity war and HIV spread; livelihood and food security; and broader geo-strategic 'threats' resulting from high levels of HIV in already unstable parts of the global South (Fourie 2007; O'Manique 2006). But there are few indications that the 'threat' of such a long-wave event is real; given that the AIDS epidemiological cycle might be up to 120 years, it is now becoming clear that few definite conclusions regarding the socio-political impacts can be stated with great certainty (Fourie 2007). In short, the phase of hard securitization and the push for a concomitant polemicization of AIDS that we saw in the first half of this decade has passed – for now. The securitization project seems to have been driven by ideological or strategic considerations related to funding and the AIDS industry, rather than by fact.

Some analysts (O'Manique 2006; Tiessen 2006; Ingram 2007) point out that both the gendered and the structural analysis of the spread and the impact of HIV are hidden or obscured in the security discourse. Policies emerging from the securitization of AIDS skew responses toward the armed forces and countries of vital interest, and away from the real security crisis of AIDS, namely the crisis at the household level that is experienced largely (although not exclusively) by women who shoulder the main burden of care, and the multiple impacts. This is where many people die quietly and invisibly. Other analysts have warned that securitization might actually have a counter-productive affect: by 'othering' and stigmatizing selective aspects of epidemics, one might create a space where individuals are seen as the enemy rather than the pathogens that affect them (cf. Elbe 2006; Sontag 2002). For instance, during the early years of the AIDS pandemic, homosexuals, intravenous drug users, sex workers and foreigners were all (and in some communities still are) seen as the carriers of a condition that they have 'brought on themselves' due to their 'immoral behaviour'. This mindset sometimes exacerbated the criminalization of individuals, such as gays, intravenous drug users, prostitutes and foreigners, rather than eliciting a response driven by the imperative to make these communities less vulnerable to the HI virus.

Conclusion

Some see the convergence of health and security as a 'compelling lens for viewing how major international health issues are being framed in terms of a security agenda' (Patel et al. 2004: 59), while others see the dark side of the securitization discourse as shoring up the hegemonic global health governance agenda, which today pays little attention to the root causes or structural determinants of health and disease. Susan Strange, in her last completed article in 1999, wrote:

> The discrepant and divergent figures on infant mortality, on children without enough to eat, on the spread of AIDS in Africa and Asia, and on every other socio-economic indicator tell the story. The gap between rich countries and poor countries and very poor ones is widening, and so is the gap between rich and poor in the poor countries and the rich and poor in the rich countries.
>
> (Strange 2002: 248)

We have seen and are bound to witness a dramatic increase in the appearance and global impact of diseases and other maladies. As political complexities, modalities and choices increase, the global management/governance of these conditions will turn into a game of even higher stakes. Within this context, it is imperative that analysts and global health watchers remain vigilant regarding the norms, ideologies and other vested interests that determine which conditions and diseases are framed as threats, and how this informs responses. Political vaccines are neither innocent nor spontaneous.

References

Anand, S., Peter, F. and Sen, A. (2006) *Public Health, Ethics, and Equity*, Oxford: Oxford University Press.

Becker, L., Levine, R. and Wolf, J. (2006) *Measuring Commitment to Health*, Global Health Indicators Working Group Consultation Report: Centre for Global Development.

Behrman, G. (2004) *The Invisible People: How the US has Slept through the Global AIDS Pandemic, the greatest Humanitarian Catastrophe of our Time*, New York and London: Free Press.

Cook, A. (2008) 'Securitization of disease in the US: Globalisation, public policy, and pandemics', unpublished thesis, East Carolina University.

Daniels, N. (2008) *Just Health: Meeting Health Needs Fairly*, Cambridge: Cambridge University Press.

Davies, S. (2008) 'Securitizing infectious disease', *International Affairs* 84, 2: 295–313.

Davis, M. (2005) *The Monster at our Door: The Global Threat of Avian Flu*, New York: New Press.

Duffield, M. (2005) 'Getting savages to fight barbarians: Development, security and the colonial present', *Conflict, Security and Development* 5, 2: 141–59.

Elbe, S. (2006) 'Should HIV/AIDS be securitized? The ethical dilemmas of linking HIV/AIDS and security', *International Studies Quarterly* 50, 1: 119–44.

FAO (2005) *State of Food Insecurity in the World*. Available online at: ftp//ftp.fao.org/docrep/fao/008/a0200e/a0200e00pdf (accessed 18 June 2008).

Fidler, D. (2007) 'A pathology of public health securitism: Approaching pandemics as security threats', in Cooper, A., Kirton, J. and Schrecker, T. (eds) *Governing Global Health – Challenge, Response, Innovation*, Aldershot: Ashgate Publishing, pp. 41–64.

Fidler, D. and Gostin, L. (2006) 'The New International Health Regulations: An historic development for international law and public health', *Journal of Law, Medicine and Ethics* 34, 1: 85–94.

Fourie, P. (2007) 'The relationship between the AIDS pandemic and state fragility', *Global Change, Peace and Security* 19, 3: 281–300.

Fourie, P. and Schönteich, M. (2002) 'Africa's new security threat', *African Security Review* 10, 4: 29–44.

Gray, C. (2005) 'Peacekeeping and enforcement action in Africa: The role of Europe and the obligations of multilateralism', *Review of International Studies* 31: 207–23.

Hilts, P. (2005) *Rx for Survival: Why we must Rise to the Global Health Challenge*, London: The Penguin Press.

Ingram, A. (2007) 'HIV/AIDS, security and the geopolitics of US–Nigerian relations', *Review of International Political Economy* 14, 3: 510–34.

Kelle, A. (2007) 'Securitization of international public health: Implications for global health governance and the biological weapons prohibition regime', *Global Governance* 13, 2: 217–35.

King, N.B. (2002) 'Security, disease, commerce: Ideologies of postcolonial global health', *Social Studies of Science* 32, 5/6: 763–89.

Kirton, J. and Mannell, J. (2007) 'The G8 and global health governance', in Cooper, A., Kirton, J. and Schrecker, T. (eds) *Governing Global Health – Challenge, Response, Innovation*, Aldershot: Ashgate Publishing, pp. 115–46.

Labonte, R., Sanders, D. and Schrecker, T. (2004) *Fatal Indifference: The G8, Africa and Global Health*, Cape Town: University of Capetown Press/IDRC.

McInnes, C. (2005) *Health, Security and the Risk Society*, London: Nuffield Trust.

——(2006) 'HIV/AIDS and security', *International Affairs* 82, 2: 125–41.

O'Manique, C. (2006) 'The securitization of HIV/AIDS in Sub-Saharan Africa: A critical feminist lens', in MacLean, S., Black, D. and Shaw, T. (eds) *A Decade of Human Security: Global Governance and the New Multilateralisms*. Aldershot: Ashgate Publishing, pp. 161–76.

——(2007) 'Global health and universal human rights: A case for G8 accountability' in Cooper, A., Kirton, J. and Schrecker, T. (eds) *Governing Global Health – Challenge, Response, Innovation*, Aldershot: Ashgate Publishing, pp. 207–26.

Patel, P., Lee, K. and Williams, O. (2004) 'Health, development and security', in Ingram, A. (ed.) *Health, Foreign Policy and Security: Towards a Conceptual Framework for Research and Policy*, Nuffield Trust/Nuffield Health and Social Services Fund, pp. 59–72.

Pirages, D.C. (2007) 'Nature, disease, and globalization: An evolutionary perspective', *International Studies Review* 9, 4: 616–28.

Poku, N., Renwick, N. and Porto, J. (2007) 'Human security and development in Africa', *International Affairs* 83, 6: 1155–70.

Shaw, T., Maclean, S. and Black, D. (2006) 'Introduction: A decade of human security: what prospects for global governance and new multilateralisms?', in Maclean, S., Black, D. and Shaw, T. (eds) *A Decade of Human Security: Global Governance and New Mulitlateralisms*, Aldershot: Ashgate Publishing, pp. 3–18.

Sontag, S. (2002) *Illness as Metaphor and AIDS and its Metaphors*, London: Penguin Classics.

Strange, S. (2002) 'The Westfailure system 1999', in Tooze, R. and May, C. (eds) *Authority and Markets: Susan Strange's Writings on International Political Economy*, Basingstoke: Palgrave Macmillan, pp. 241–50.

Tiessen, R. (2006) 'A silent killer: HIV/AIDS metaphors and human (in)security in Southern Africa', in Maclean, S., Black, D.R. and Shaw, T.M. (eds) *A Decade of Human Security: Global Governance and the New Multilateralisms*, Aldershot: Ashgate, pp. 145–60.

United Nations (2004) *A More Secure World: Our Shared Responsibility*, Report of the Secretary-General's High-Level Panel on Threats, Challenges and Change, UN A/59/565, December.

World Health Organization (2003) *World Health Report*, Geneva.

——(2006) *World Health Report 2006: Working Together for Health*, Geneva: WHO.

——(2008) *World Health Report 2007: A Safer Future: Global Public Health Security in the 21st Century*, Geneva: WHO.

Yong, J., Millen, J.V., Irwin, A. and Gershaman, J. (2000) *Dying for Growth: Global Inequality and the Health of the Poor*, Monroe: Common Courage Press.

Zacher, M. (2007) 'The transformation in global health collaboration since the 1990s', in Cooper, A., Kirton, J., and Schrecker, T. (eds) *Governing Global Health – Challenge, Response, Innovation*, Aldershot: Ashgate Publishing, pp. 16–27.

Part III

Regional security challenges

23

China's rise

Intentions, power and evidence

David C. Kang

Since the introduction of market reforms in 1978, China has rapidly emerged as a major regional and even global power, averaging over nine per cent economic growth over the past 30 years. Although China's economy in 1980 was less than 10 per cent of the size of the US economy, by 2006 it had grown to almost half that of the US when measured by consumption (Figure 23.1). Foreign businesses have flocked to invest in China, while Chinese exports have begun to flood world markets. China is modernizing its military, has joined numerous regional and international institutions, and is increasingly visible in international politics.

The world has reacted in two ways to China's rise. On the one hand, policymakers, business executives and the popular press have marvelled at China's successes and scrambled to participate in the tremendous economic opportunities that have arisen in

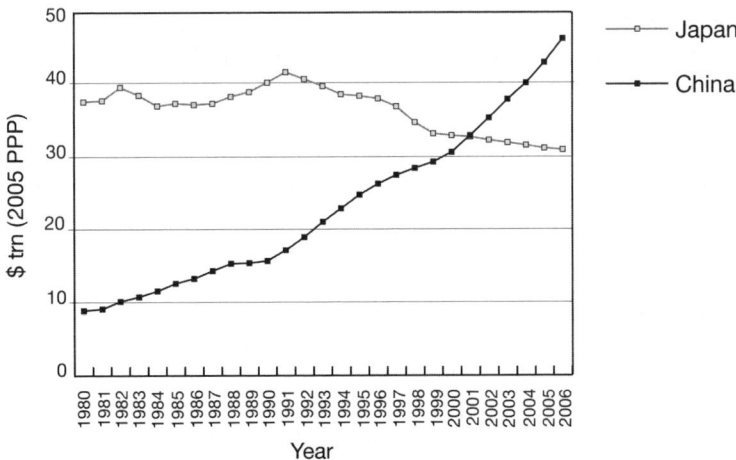

Figure 23.1 GDP as a per cent of US GDP (constant 2005 PPP).
Source: World Bank, World Development Indicators Online.

257

the past few decades. Indeed, seven consecutive US presidents have encouraged China's integration into the global system, from Richard Nixon's belief that 'dealing with Red China … means pulling China back into the world community' (Nixon 1967: 123) to President George W. Bush welcoming 'the emergence of a China that is peaceful and prosperous, and that supports international institutions' (*Washington Post* 2006).

On the other hand, there is increasing concern that the arrival of a new superpower may challenge the US politically and perhaps even lead to military conflict. The Pentagon's 2008 assessment of China's military power concludes that 'much uncertainty surrounds China's future course, in particular in the area of its expanding military power and how that power might be used' (US Department of Defense 2008). Whether China can rise peacefully, or whether it can even continue that rise, is thus one of the major policy and scholarly issues of our time.

Within the scholarly literature on International Relations, there are theoretical arguments for both optimistic and pessimistic expectations regarding China's rise. This chapter surveys those theoretical arguments, contrasting the variety of material and ideational hypotheses. It then explores two central issues related to China's rise. First, how great is China's power, and what are the potential challenges that China faces that could derail growth and make this question moot? Second, what is the evidence to date about how states are responding to China's emergence? The chapter concludes by looking to the future and identifying the variables most likely to affect how China will rise and whether or not it can be peaceful.

Power and institutions

Scholars who emphasize material power – both military and economic – have long predicted that other states would fear China and balance against it. Offensive realism, with its emphasis on balance-of-power politics and the maximization of power, has had the most consistently pessimistic expectations for East Asia (Friedberg 1993/1994; Waltz 1993; Roy 1994; Layne 1993). The offensive realist logic is fairly straightforward: because states can never be sure about the intentions or even the capabilities of other states, they must constantly guard their own interests, which usually requires military power. As states become more powerful, they inevitably wish to control more of their own fate and to defend their interests, thus leading them to become increasingly interventionist. Furthermore, International Relations theorists have traditionally associated the rise and fall of great powers with war and instability (Kennedy 1987; Chan 2008; Kugler 2006). Robert Gilpin (1981: 187) reflects the conventional wisdom when he writes that, 'as its relative power increases, a rising state attempts to change the rules governing the system'.

Thus, even if states do not fear China today, they worry about how China will act tomorrow, when it may be even more powerful than it is today. For example, as Richard Betts (1993/94: 55) asked: 'Should we want China to get rich or not? For realists, the answer should be no, since a rich China would overturn any balance of power.' Similarly, John Mearsheimer (Brzezinski and Mearsheimer 2005: 47) confidently argues that, 'China cannot rise peacefully … Most of China's neighbors, including India, Japan, Singapore, South Korea, Russia, and Vietnam, will likely join with the United States to contain China's power.'

Yet in contrast to offensive realists, other realists are more sanguine about the potential threat that China may pose. These 'defensive realists' tend to argue that both nuclear weapons and geography militate against an inevitable showdown between China and the

US (Goldstein 2005). Both these factors make territorial conquest much more difficult now, in contrast to the nineteenth century, when imperial expansion was an input to power. Nuclear weapons in particular are seen to stabilize deterrence among great powers, in what has become known as the 'nuclear peace' (Waltz 1990). Geography also plays a role, since there is an ocean between the US and China, and because China is a continental power, while the US a maritime power, this may mitigate the influence of the security dilemma (Ross 1999).

Liberals, with their focus on economic interdependence and the constraining effect of international institutions and the potential pacifying effect of democratic states, tend to see China's rapid and deep economic integration with the rest of the world as a positive aspect to its rise (Grieco 2002; Papayounou and Kastner 1999; Wan 2003). These scholars see deep and multiple economic relations between two states as creating ties that increase the benefits of stable relations between the two sides, and decreasing the benefits of going to war. Thus, as China continues to grow, and because that growth relies heavily on deep interactions with world markets and investment, China and other states have much to gain from stable relations and much to lose from conflict (Brzezinski and Mearsheimer 2005).

Two other strands of liberalism hold that global and domestic institutions can mitigate conflict and promote cooperation. The more China becomes involved with international institutions, the more it both adjusts its own grand strategy to accommodate the needs of other countries, and also sends signals about its intentions and willingness to work with the broader international community (Keohane 1998). Furthermore, many scholars argue that democracies are less prone to fight each other than authoritarian regimes, and thus if China does become a democracy, they would expect it to be less destabilizing than if it remains an authoritarian regime run by the Communist Party (Gilley 2004).

Yet liberal arguments are not entirely optimistic, and some of those who argue that China's increased economic interdependence with the world will constrain its behaviour are sceptical that this by itself can solve the security fears of East Asian states (Ikenberry 2004). Furthermore, although China may one day become a democracy, it certainly remains a repressive authoritarian regime today, and the prospects for its democratization appear to be far in the future at best.

Ideas and interests

The foregoing arguments, whether optimistic or pessimistic, tend to emphasize material and structural factors, such as military power, economic interdependence or domestic and international institutions. However, an alternative theoretical approach sees ideas as being independent of power, and as Robert Powell writes,

> Although some structural theories seem to suggest that one can explain at least the outline of state behavior without reference to states' goals or preferences ... in order to specify a game theoretic model, the actor's preferences and benefits must be defined.
>
> (Powell 2002: 17)

Material capabilities do not necessarily lead directly to intentions, and while stronger states can do more than weaker states, their intentions may vary quite widely (Fearon 1997). Thus, what China wants may be more important for stability than how powerful it becomes, and other states are constantly engaged in the process of interpreting and updating Chinese goals, values and intentions (Legro 2007). Here, too, ideational theories provide both optimistic and pessimistic hypotheses.

One common way in which International Relations theories incorporate identity and intentions into theories of threat in the context of a rising power lies in the distinction between those states that embrace the status quo and revisionist ones. Definitions of status quo and revisionist powers vary, but they tend to centre on whether a state is satisfied with the current international order (Johnston 2008; Organski and Kugler 1980; Schweller 1994). That is, the main driver of instability is the difference between the situation that a state desires and the status quo: the greater the difference between the two, the greater the likelihood that a state will use force to redress the difference. A powerful, revisionist China seething with resentment would prompt different responses from East Asian states than would a powerful China that advocates preserving the status quo and desires peace and stability.

How the Communist Party evolves, and whether it even survives, will be a key element determining how China's foreign policy develops. However, a key lesson that the Chinese leadership has learned over the past century is the importance of Westphalian norms, chief among them, sovereignty (Carlson 2005). This has combined with a traditional Chinese concern with territorial integrity, and the more recent struggles that China faced in the nineteenth century to preserve that territory against the numerous incursions from outside powers. As Chinese rulers adjusted to the changing nature of the international system, they came to identify sovereignty as a key aspect of International Relations. Samuel Kim (1994: 428) observes that 'China has remained compulsively sovereignty-bound on most basic global issues and problems'.

While the question of how the Chinese Communist Party evolves will be an important factor in determining China's goals and intentions, just as important will be the views of the Chinese people themselves. How Chinese nationalism and national identity develop will have a key impact on China's behaviour in the future. China's outlook on the world could be cooperative or competitive, and the future course of Chinese nationalism is not yet clear. There are numerous strands to Chinese national identity, and multiple traditions in Chinese history and experience that inform its current views. Scholars have tended to emphasize a preoccupation with a 'century of shame', and a virtual obsession with attaining sufficient state power to compete with the US, Japan and Russia (Karl 2002; Nathan and Ross 1997; Leifer 1996). Conversely, China is also becoming more globalized, its people travel widely around the globe and, while nationalist sentiment appears to be on the rise in China, the direction that such nationalism may take is not yet clear.

In sum, the theoretical literature contains a number of competing hypotheses, both optimistic and pessimistic, about China's rise. Power-based offensive realists are most pessimistic, while defensive realists are somewhat more optimistic, as are those who emphasize economic interdependence and the constraining influence of international institutions. Those who focus on ideas believe that China's rise depends on how Chinese goals and identity evolve, and they think that what China wants may be more important than how powerful it becomes.

How powerful is China today, and can it continue?

A key factor often overlooked in the debate about China is an actual assessment of how influential and powerful it actually is. Close examination reveals that China is unlikely to replace the US as the largest, most technologically advanced and militarily dominant country in the world within the foreseeable future. However, this does not mean that China is weak. China is already very strong and very big, and it is centrally situated in East Asia. By virtue of its population, geography, economic growth and military power, China is already a major regional power in East Asia and, by some measures, it is already a global power.

Measuring China's importance is a difficult exercise, and estimates vary widely. From 1978 to 2003, China averaged 9.7 per cent growth. The World Bank (2008b) estimates that from 1978 to 2005, Chinese economic growth lifted 402 million people out of poverty (defined as living on US$1 a day) – the largest poverty eradication in history. The CIA uses a purchasing power parity estimate (PPP), which produces a 2005 Chinese GDP of US$8.85 trillion, versus US$4.01 trillion for Japan.[1] Measured by exchange rates, China's GDP in 2005 was US$2.22 trillion, compared to US$4.50 trillion for Japan (CIA 2008). Indeed, China has been under intense pressure by the US to revalue the *renminbi*, and most economists believe that it may be undervalued by between 15 and 40 per cent. If so, the corresponding measure of China's GDP is also undervalued by a similar amount.

By other measures, however, China remains a developing country. In terms of per capita income, China remains a third-world country. Even when measured at PPP, Chinese per capita income is far smaller than that of Japan: US$5,000 versus US$28,000 (CIA 2008). Using market rates, the World Bank (2008a) estimates Chinese per capita income in 2002 at US$944, compared to almost US$45,000 in Japan. Technologically, China is a developing country, and although it is rapidly increasing its technological and scientific prowess, for the most part it is a low-cost, low-value manufacturer, far behind the advanced countries. However, China does not have to catch up with the rest of the great powers in order to project influence. Richard Betts (1993/94: 52) makes this argument clearly: 'If [China] ever achieved a per-capita GNP just one-fourth that of the United States, it would have a total GNP *greater* than that of the United States ... it would be an epochal change in the distribution of world power'.

China continues to modernize its military, yet it spends about one-fifth of what the US spends on defence every year, and for the past fifteen years, its defence spending has been stable at 8 per cent of its total government spending (Scobell et al. 2007). As Taylor Fravel (2008: 137) notes, 'even using the highest estimate from the Pentagon, China's total defense spending in 2007 ($139 billion) was slightly less than just the budget for the US Navy ($147 billion)'. At present, increasing power projection capabilities does not appear to be a priority (Shambaugh 2004/05). Currently, China's nuclear arsenal comprises about 150 nuclear warheads, and China has approximately 20 nuclear-capable DF-5 ICBMs with an estimated range of 13,000 kilometres. China has also deployed 600 short-range ballistic missiles around the Taiwan Strait. However, China has not increased its arsenal beyond this small nuclear deterrent force for some years, although there are concerns that this may change in the future (Uruyama 2000; Christensen 2000).

Thus, China is not yet a true peer-competitor with the US, and there is good reason to be sceptical that China can actually continue to grow as quickly and consistently in the future as it has in the past. China faces a slew of political, economic and social problems. Politically, there are the issues of regional separatism, a tenuous balance of power between the central and local governments, the erosion of state capacity, extensive government corruption and a host of other issues (Pei 2006; Shirk 2007). Economically, major issues include how to raise the standard of living of China's vast rural population;

labour unrest; inefficient state-owned enterprises that still comprise about 30 per cent of China's economy; a backward, corrupt and heavily regulated banking and financial system; a weak and ineffective legal system; and a dearth of trained technical and managerial talent (Economy 2004). Socially, China faces problems with rising nationalism, the impact of a one-child policy and minority resentment in some provinces (Pei 2006).

China also faces environmental and energy supply problems on a staggering scale, both of which threaten to derail any long-term growth. China doubled its coal consumption between 2000 and 2007, yet it requires six times as many resources as in the US to produce a similar quantity of goods (Economy 2007). Rapid deforestation, water pollution and urbanization have polluted not only China, but have also affected surrounding countries. In 1985, China was Asia's largest oil exporter, but by 2005, it had become the region's second-largest oil importer, after Japan. China now uses upwards of 25 per cent of the total global consumption of basic resources such as aluminium, copper and iron (Zweig and Bi 2005).

In sum, although China is not yet a mature, advanced economy, on a number of criteria that are important for International Relations, it is increasingly clear that China is already a significant, and soon perhaps will even be the dominant, East Asian state. China is already a large presence in economic markets around the globe. Its population and landmass make it an important demographic power no matter the level of development. Its nuclear arsenal and military are among the largest (although not most advanced) in the world, and exceed those of any other East Asian state. Still, by many measures, China is still a developing country and faces numerous problems, many of which are getting worse and lack any clear solution. The range of long-term predictions about China's growth is thus extremely wide – from continued rise to crashing failure.

What does the evidence show?

China is in the middle of a long ascent, and thus any conclusions at this point about the ultimate course of China's rise are partial at best. Yet China's rise is not a new phenomenon – the country's influence has been growing rapidly for three decades – and it is possible to draw some initial conclusions. Overall, it appears that globally and within East Asia, states are cautiously welcoming China's emergence as a great power. In East Asia, the Chinese economic opportunity and military threat towards its regional neighbours are both potentially huge. However, East Asian states see substantially more economic opportunity than military threat associated with China's rise. Furthermore, East Asian states prefer China to be strong rather than weak, because a strong China stabilizes the region, while a weak China invites chaos as other states attempt to control it (Kang 2007). Indeed, as a region, East Asia has become more peaceful and more stable over the past 30 years – not less.

Perhaps the most careful study of China's recent behaviour is by Iain Johnston. He writes that,

> It is hard to conclude that China is a clearly revisionist state operating outside, or barely inside, the boundaries of a so-called international community ... the PRC has become more integrated into and more cooperative within international institutions than ever before.
>
> (Johnston 2003: 49)

Indeed, as recently as the mid-1980s, observers of Chinese foreign policy were sceptical that China would involve itself in international institutions, noting China's preference for bilateral relations and its disdain for multilateral or cooperative institutions (Levine 1984). However, as China has grown more powerful, it has become more, not less involved in international institutions (Carlson 2003). China has joined a range of institutions, from the WTO to the ASEAN Regional Forum to the ASEAN Plus Three's negotiations with China over a free trade area. China's more active diplomacy includes growing and increasing trade relations with East Asia; the signing of numerous cooperative agreements; joining and proposing multilateral, bilateral and informal ('Track II') institutions and forums; resolving its border disputes; and increased high-level military and diplomatic visits to numerous countries (Medeiros and Fravel 2003; Economy 2005).

For East Asia, East Asian states have moved to increase their economic, diplomatic and even military relations with China. Taiwan is the only East Asian state that fears the Chinese use of force, and no other East Asian state is arming itself against China, nor seeking military alliances with which to contain China. Overall, East Asian states see substantially more economic opportunity than military threat associated with China's rise. South Korea and China share similar interests in dealing with the North Korean nuclear issue, and both countries vociferously dispute Japanese territorial claims. Southeast Asian states have rapidly increased their trade and investment in China, and although no state is bandwagoning with China, none is actively pursuing a balance against China, either (Goh 2007). Japan remains the most sceptical East Asian country regarding China. Japan will not lightly cede economic leadership to China, and it also remains unsure of Chinese motives. Nevertheless, even Japan has not yet embarked on a course of outright containment policy towards China, and economic relations between the countries continue to deepen (Samuels 2007).

Europe and Russia have also grown closer to China. European states have generally welcomed China's economic emergence and attempted to incorporate China into a wide-ranging set of international institutions that give China a stake in the status quo (Shambaugh 2005). As for Russia, its relations with China are more stable now than they were during the height of the Cold War. Both countries are actively engaged in organizations such as the Shanghai Cooperation Organization; they have institutionalized an annual bilateral security dialogue; and have even engaged in occasional joint military exercises (Shambaugh 2004/05). China's need for raw materials has also led it to expand economic and military ties rapidly in both Africa and Latin America, prompting some speculation about whether China is attempting to replicate the old European colonial relations with these regions (Gill et al. 2007). Still, for all the concern about Sino-African relations, those ties do little to tip the balance of power, and all states – not just China – are actively exploring ways to meet increased energy demands and to deal with environmental issues such as climate change.

However, despite these positive trends, there are also worrying trends. Uncertainty remains over the ultimate trajectory of Chinese nationalism, which in recent years has become more pronounced, as evidenced by such mass demonstrations that broke out to protest the 1999 US bombing of the Chinese embassy in Belgrade, and those that protested against the Japanese soccer team at the 2004 Asian soccer championships held in Beijing. However, there has also been increasingly public discussion in China about how to move beyond the long-held victim mentality (*shouhaizhe xintai*) that emphasizes 150 years of humiliation, and discussion of China's 'great power mentality' (*daguo xintai*) is increasingly prevalent. Thus, Evan Medeiros and Taylor Fravel (2003: 32) note that,

'Chinese officials now talk explicitly about the need to "share global responsibilities"', while Peter Gries (1999: 63) notes that Chinese nationalism is not inevitably dangerous, arguing that 'Chinese nationalism will evolve in dynamic relationship with the West'.

China's military moves have also provoked scepticism, and the US military tends to be more suspicious of Chinese motives than is the US business sector. For example, the Pentagon's *Quadrennial Defense Review* (QDR) noted that China has the 'greatest potential to compete militarily with America', and said that Chinese military modernization 'already puts regional balances at risk'. In response, the QDR recommends deploying six aircraft carriers and 60 per cent of US submarines to the Pacific to 'support engagement, presence, and deterrence' (US Department of Defense 2006: 47). Despite these concerns, the US itself still views China as more an opportunity than a threat, and official US policy is to encourage China to become a 'responsible stakeholder' in international affairs (US Department of State 2005). As Thomas Christensen notes,

> Especially if one uses the United States' containment policies toward the Soviet Union as a basis of comparison, the [argument] that the United States has been dedicated to a grand strategy of containment of China as a general policy to maintain U.S. hegemony – is, for the most part, divorced from reality.
>
> (Christensen 2006: 108)

In sum, while China may be a future threat, states in the region and the US have not yet decided that China poses an imminent threat, and indeed seem to be focused more on the possible benefits that an increasingly rich China might provide.

Conclusion: the future

China is in the middle of a long transition, and at this point the future place of China in the world is still unclear. Indeed, at this point, prediction is mere speculation. How Chinese identity and power will develop is unknowable, and speculation is not a very satisfying scholarly exercise. But it is possible to delineate – however roughly – some of the important variables that will affect China's rise.

Chinese – and other states' – goals, intentions, power and identities, and how they evolve, will be central to determining whether states adjust to and accept China, or whether they increasingly compete with and fear China. Indeed, Chinese goals and identities are still in the process of being determined. Little is fixed, and there is no immutable 'Chinese mindset'. Whether Chinese nationalism remains brittle, chauvinist and insecure, or whether it becomes more moderate, globalized and responsible, is still unclear. How the Communist Party will evolve, and whether it will still exist 30 years from now, is also unclear. These are the key questions and the answers will determine much of whether the future of East Asia is increasingly stable or increasingly unstable. According to Richard Samuels,

> the challenge for China is how to become socialized into a world order with rules and norms valuing democracy and human rights ... For the rest of us ... the challenge is to socialize ourselves to an emerging new order that makes room ... for Chinese power – even in terms of moral authority.
>
> (Samuels 2007: 208)

Furthermore, the actions that other states take toward China today will have an effect on how China develops and reacts in the future. As Avery Goldstein writes,

> The future will depend on the policies China and others choose to embrace once its current strategy has run its course, the transition is complete, and China has risen to the ranks of the great powers. At that time, different leaders in Beijing will make choices that reflect their country's new capabilities and transformed international constraints that cannot be confidently foreseen ... speculation is premature at best and unwisely provocative at worst.
>
> (Goldstein 2005: 39)

As the twenty-first century begins, we would be wise to remain appropriately cautious in our predictions about the future.

Note

1 PPP reflects the price of a commodity (or a bundle of commodities) that is the same between countries, as expressed in a common currency. The exchange rate used in converting the GDP of one country to another for the purpose of inter-country comparison does not normally reflect the purchasing power parity (PPP), because many commodities are not traded internationally.

References

Betts, R.K. (1993/94) 'Wealth, power, and instability: East Asia and the United States after the Cold War', *International Security* 18, 3: 34–77.

Brzezinski, Z. and Mearsheimer, J. (2005) 'Clash of the titans', *Foreign Policy* 146: 46–49.

Carlson, A. (2003) 'Constructing the dragon's scales: China's approach to territorial and border relations in the 1980s and 1990s', *Journal of Contemporary China* 12, 37: 677–98.

——(2005) *Unifying China, Integrating with the World: Securing Chinese Sovereignty in the Reform Era*, Stanford, CA: Stanford University Press.

Central Intelligence Agency (2008) *World Factbook*, CIA. Available online at: www.cia.gov/cia/publications/factbook/index.html (accessed 4 June 2008).

Chan, S. (2008) *China, the U.S., and the Power-Transition Theory: A Critique*, London: Routledge.

Christensen, T. (2000) 'Theater missile defense and Taiwan's security', *Orbis* 44, 1: 79–90.

——(2006) 'Fostering stability or creating a monster?' *International Security* 31, 1: 81–126.

Economy, E. (2004) *The River Runs Black: The Environmental Challenge to China's Future*, Ithaca, NY: Cornell University Press.

——(2005) 'China's rise in Southeast Asia: Implications for the United States', *Journal of Contemporary China* 14, 44: 409–25.

——(2007) 'The great leap backward? The costs of China's environmental crisis', *Foreign Affairs* 86, 5: 38–47.

Fearon, J.D. (1997) 'Signaling foreign policy interests: Tying hands versus sinking costs', *Journal of Conflict Resolution* 41, 1: 68–90.

Fravel, M.T. (2008) 'China's search for military power', *The Washington Quarterly* 31, 3: 125–41.

Friedberg, A. (1993/94) 'Ripe for rivalry', *International Security* 18, 3: 5–33.

Gill, B., Huang, C. and Morrison, S. (2007) 'Assessing China's growing influence in Africa', *China Security* 3, 3: 3–21.

Gilley, B. (2004) *China's Democratic Future: How it will Happen and Where it will Lead*, New York: Columbia University Press.

Gilpin, R. (1981) *War and Change in World Politics*, Cambridge: Cambridge University Press.

Goh, E. (2007) 'Great powers and hierarchical order in Southeast Asia: Analyzing regional security strategies', *International Security* 32, 3: 113–57.

Goldstein, A. (2005) *Rising to the Challenge*, Stanford, CA: Stanford University Press.

Grieco, J. (2002) 'China and America in the world polity', in Pumphrey C.W. (ed.) *The Rise of China in Asia: Security Implications*, Carlisle: Strategic Studies Institute.

Gries, P.H. (1999) 'A "China threat"? Power and passion in Chinese "face nationalism"' *World Affairs* 162, 2: 63–75.

Ikenberry, G.J. (2004) 'American hegemony and East Asian order', *Australian Journal of International Affairs* 58, 3: 353–67.

Jisi, W. (1994) 'International relations theory and the study of Chinese foreign policy: A Chinese perspective', in Robinson, T. and Shambaugh, D. (eds) *Chinese Foreign Policy: Theory and Practice*, Oxford: Clarendon Press, pp. 481–505.

Johnston, A.I. (2003) 'Is China a status quo power?' *International Security* 27, 4: 5–56.

——(2008) *Social States: China in International Institutions, 1980–2000*, Princeton, NJ: Princeton University Press.

Kang, D.C. (2007) *China Rising: Peace, Power, and Order in East Asia*, New York: Columbia University Press.

Karl, R. (2002) *Staging the World: Chinese Nationalism at the Turn of the 20th Century*, Durham, NC: Duke University Press.

Kennedy, P. (1987) *The Rise and Fall of the Great Powers: Economic Change and Military Conflict From 1500 to 2000*, New York: Random House.

Keohane, R. (1998) 'International institutions: Can interdependence work?' *Foreign Policy* 110: 82–96.

Kim, S. (1994) 'Sovereignty in the Chinese image of world order', in Macdonald, R.S.J. (ed.) *Essays in Honor of Wang Tieya*, London: Martinus Mijhoff.

Kugler, J. (2006) 'The Asian ascent: Opportunity for peace or precondition for war?' *International Studies Perspectives* 7, 1: 36–42.

Layne, C. (1993) 'The unipolar illusion: Why new great powers will rise', *International Security* 17, 4: 5–51.

Legro, J. (2007) 'What China will want: The future intentions of a rising power', *Perspectives on Politics* 5, 3: 515–34.

Leifer, M. (1996) *The ASEAN Regional Forum*, London: IISS.

Levine, S. (1984) 'China in Asia: The PRC as a regional power', in Harding, H. (ed.) *China's Foreign Relations in the 1980s*, New Haven: Yale University, pp. 107–45.

Medeiros, E. and Fravel, M.T. (2003) 'China's new diplomacy', *Foreign Affairs* 82, 6: 22–35.

Nathan, A. and Ross, R. (1997) *The Great Wall and the Empty Fortress: China's Search for Security*, New York: W.W. Norton.

Nixon, R.M. (1967/68) 'Asia after Viet Nam', *Foreign Affairs* 46, 1: 111–33.

Organski, A.F.K. and Kugler, J. (1980) *The War Ledger*, Chicago: The University of Chicago Press.

Papayounou, P. and Kastner, S. (1999) 'Sleeping with the potential enemy: Assessing the U.S. policy of engagement with China', *Security Studies* 9, 1/2: 164–95.

Pei, M. (2006) *China's Trapped Transition: The Limits of Developmental Autocracy*, Cambridge, MA: Harvard University Press.

Powell, R. (2002) 'Bargaining theory and international conflict', *Annual Review of Political Science* 5: 1–30.

Ross, R. (1999) 'The geography of the peace: East Asia in the twenty-first century', *International Security* 23, 4: 81–118.

Roy, D. (1994) 'Hegemon on the horizon? China's threat to East Asian security', *International Security* 19, 1: 149–68.

Samuels, R.J. (2007) 'How Japan balances strategy and constraint', *Asia Policy* 4: 204–8.

Schweller, R. (1994) 'Bandwagoning for profit: Bringing the revisionist state back in', *International Security* 19, 1: 72–108.

Scobell, A. et al., (2007) 'Roundtable: Sizing the Chinese military', *Asia Policy* 4: 53–105.

Shambaugh, D. (2004/05) 'China engages Asia: Reshaping the regional order', *International Security* 29, 3: 64–99.

——(2005) 'The new strategic triangle: US and European reactions to China's rise', *Washington Quarterly* 28, 3: 7–25.

Shirk, S. (2007) *China: Fragile Superpower: How China's Internal Politics Could Derail its Peaceful Rise*, Oxford: Oxford University Press.

U.S. Department of Defense, annual report to Congress (2006) *Quadrennial Defense Review 2006*. Available online at: www.comw.org/qdr/qdr2006.pdf (accessed 28 June 2008).

——(2008) 'Military power of the People's Republic of China, 2008'. Available online at: www. globalsecurity.org/military/library/report/2008/2008-prc-military-power.htm (accessed 15 May 2008).

U.S. Department of State (2005) 'Deputy Secretary Zoellick statement on conclusion of the second US–China senior dialogue'. Available online at: www.state.gov/r/pa/prs/ps/2005/57822.htm (accessed 7 April 2008).

Uruyama, K. (2000) 'Chinese perspectives on theater missile defense: Policy implications for Japan', *Asian Survey*, 40: 599–621.

Waltz, K.A. (1990) 'Nuclear myths and political realities', *American Political Science Review* 84, 3: 731–45.

——(1993) 'The emerging structure of international politics', *International Security* 18, 2: 44–79.

Wan, M. (2003) 'Economic interdependence and economic cooperation: Mitigating conflict and transforming security order in Asia', in Alagappa, M. (ed.) *Asian Security Order*, Stanford, CA: Stanford University Press, pp. 280–310.

Washington Post (2006) 'U.S. President George W. Bush and Chinese President Hu Jintao', April 20. Available online at: www.washingtonpost.com/wp-dyn/content/article/2006/04/20/AR2006042000694.html (accessed 28 June 2008).

World Bank (2008a) *World Development Indicators*. Available online at: http://devdata.worldbank.org/dataonline/ (accessed 17 June 2008).

——(2008b) 'China's 8–7 poverty reduction program', *Shanghai Poverty Conference: Case Study Summary*. Available online at: info.worldbank.org/etools/docs/reducingpoverty/case/33/summary/China-8-7PovertyReduction%20Summary.pdf (accessed 14 July 2008).

Zweig, D. and Bi, J. (2005) 'China's global hunt for energy', *Foreign Affairs* 84, 5: 25–34.

24

The Korean peninsula

On the brink?

Scott Snyder

The stand-off on the Korean peninsula has long been considered a holdover from the Cold War that has held Northeast Asia back from entering head-long into the post-Cold War era. A generation after the end of the Cold War, it is fair to ask why and how conflict on the Korean peninsula persists; whether the region has already adjusted to a post-Cold War security framework even if it does not live up to the ideal representations that some analysts had hoped would be achieved; whether the nature of the conflict has either transmuted itself or been subsumed by new, equally intractable concerns regarding the possession and proliferation of nuclear arms; or whether the economic and political imbalance between the two Koreas has grown so great that reunification is only a matter of time. Following a background summary of the history of the division of the Korean peninsula, this chapter assesses the peninsular, regional, functional and international sources of conflict on the Korean peninsula and analyses the likely future course of Korea's division and implications for peninsular and regional security in Northeast Asia.

Korea divided

The accidental division of the Korean peninsula at the hands of Gen. Charles Bonesteel and Lt. Col. Dean Rusk in the bowels of the Pentagon in the waning days of the Second World War was meant to mark a temporary division of responsibility between US and Soviet troops that had advanced to secure territory occupied by imperial Japan following Emperor Hirohito's surrender announcement on 15 August 1945. Based on conversations held at Yalta in the closing days of the war, the conquering powers did not foresee a Korea able to autonomously participate in elections or to select a government following decades of Japanese occupation without a period of trusteeship to be administered by the international community (Oberdorfer 1997: 5ff.).

In the early days following the end of the Second World War, however, the Korean peninsula was one of the early regions of Cold-War competition, fuelled by the intensification of an ideologically based power struggle among pre-existing Korean factions-in-exile that had led an anti-colonial struggle against imperial Japan. The Soviet-backed

North Korean leader Kim Il Sung and the US-backed Southern leader Syngman Rhee sought not only to consolidate their rule on either side of the peninsula with backing from their respective external patrons, but also to lead a unified Korea. Rising tensions between separately administered territories in North and South Korea hardened and led to the outbreak of the Korean War and to interventions by the UN (largely led by US political and military efforts) and the People's Republic of China (under the auspices of 'volunteer' forces), respectively. There has been an active debate among historians over the relationship between the international and domestic origins of the Korean War. Some historians have emphasized the international origins of the Korean War, viewing the conflict through the lens of a great power conflict between Washington and Moscow (Gaddis 1972; Stueck 1995), while others have emphasized the domestic origins of the war and the pre-existing ideological conflicts between leaders dedicated to achieving Korean unification on their own terms (Cumings 1994; Merrill 1989). Following the negotiation of an armistice that remains in place to this day, the two Korean states continued their competition for legitimacy on the international stage through the 1980s.

South Korea's economic rise, a political transition from military authoritarianism to democratic government and Seoul's hosting of the 1988 Olympics gradually illustrated that South Korea was outpacing the North. In the wake of the Olympic Games, South Korea pursued a policy of *Nordpolitik*. This led to South Korea's diplomatic normalization with Eastern Europe, the Soviet Union and the PRC, and opened the way for the opening of an inter-Korean dialogue and the signing of a 1991 landmark Agreement on Reconciliation, Nonaggression, Exchanges and Cooperation (also known as the Basic Agreement). The agreement envisaged a series of practical confidence-building measures designed to bring about mutual understanding and peaceful coexistence between the two Koreas in the security, political and socio-cultural spheres. Chinese efforts to promote a cross-recognition formula whereby the US and South Korea would normalize relations with an increasingly isolated and economically needy North Korea in concert with South Korea's rapprochement with the former Communist world came to naught. Given North Korea's diplomatic isolation and the collapse or economic reform path of its closest patrons, many analysts expected that Korean reunification might follow the model of absorption set in Germany; however, South and North Korean leaders took opposing lessons from the collapse of Communism in Eastern Europe and from German reunification.

Faced with an increasing gap in conventional military capabilities, North Korean nuclear weapons pursuits in the early 1990s provided new grist for an extended series of confrontations with the US as nuclear proliferation emerged as the top US concern in international security. The first crisis in the early 1990s ended with a bilateral US–DPRK negotiation that resulted in the Agreed Framework of 1994. This promised two 1000-MW light water reactors (LWRs) and annual deliveries of 500,000 tons of heavy fuel oil in return for North Korea's freeze and eventual resumption of the full range of safeguards under the Nuclear Non-Proliferation Treaty (NPT) (*Agreed Framework* 1994). However, there were delays in providing the light water reactors and problems with heavy fuel oil deliveries, while North Korea decided to covertly explore uranium-enrichment as a means to nuclear weapons development. The DPRK established links with the Pakistan military and the A.Q. Khan network in the late 1990s in an apparent exchange of Scud missile technology from North Korea that would help Pakistan to augment the range of its missile delivery capacity in return for nuclear expertise, including centrifuges, aluminium tubes and other components that could be used by North Korea to set up its own uranium-enrichment capacity.

A second crisis over North Korea's nuclear weapons developments broke out in 2002 under the administration of George W. Bush over suspicions regarding North Korea's covert uranium enrichment efforts. Following terrorist attacks in the US in 2001, anti-terrorism efforts led to a special focus on counter-proliferation and the determination not to 'allow the world's most dangerous regimes to threaten us with the world's most dangerous weapons' (Bush 2002). Although North Korea had no significant contact with terrorism efforts led by al-Qaida, it was included along with Iraq and Iran in the 'Axis of Evil' as part of Bush's 2002 State of the Union Address. Later that year, Bush administration Special Envoy James Kelly confronted North Korea over its covert efforts to develop a uranium-based path to nuclear weapons. That confrontation resulted in a decision by the Bush administration to end heavy fuel oil deliveries and eventually to shut down the light water reactor project while North Korea kicked out IAEA nuclear inspectors, resumed operation of its 5-MW reactor and reprocessed fuel rods that had been stored in the country but not removed during the 1994 crisis.

In response to these developments, the Bush administration pursued a regional solution to the North Korean nuclear crisis through the establishment of the Six-Party Talks (including the US, China, Japan, Russia, South Korea and North Korea), a dialogue hosted in Beijing that emphasized regional roles and responsibilities for addressing the crisis. Following several initial rounds that were hampered by a US unwillingness to pursue bilateral talks with North Korea, the Six-Party Talks produced a Joint Statement on 19 September 2005 that recognized a regional consensus in favour of preserving a non-nuclear Korean peninsula; the economic development of North Korea; normalization of diplomatic relations among all parties in Northeast Asia, including between North Korea and the US and Japan, respectively; and the need to replace the Korean armistice with a permanent peace regime (*Joint Statement of the Fourth Round of the Six-Party Talks* 2005). This document provided general guidelines for the pursuit of a 'diplomatic normalization for denuclearization' grand bargain between the US and North Korea while laying the foundations for a potential multilateral peace and security mechanism in Northeast Asia.

North Korea's 4 July 2006 missile tests and the 9 October 2006 test of a nuclear device galvanized the passage of UN Security Council resolutions 1695 and 1718 condemning North Korea's actions and authorizing international economic sanctions against North Korea (United Nations 2006). But the tests also catalyzed renewed Six-Party dialogue and US–DPRK bilateral negotiations, resulting in a 13 February 2007 agreement marking the first tangible steps towards the implementation of the 19 September 2005 Joint Statement (*North Korea – Denuclearization Action Plan* 2007). These events illustrate the extent to which inter-Korean confrontation and division has been complicated and has become inextricably intertwined with regional security factors, nuclear non-proliferation concerns and issues stemming from the continued US–DPRK political confrontation. While it is necessary to consider each strand of the conflict on the Korean peninsula individually, all of these issues must be addressed in tandem with each other to achieve a final resolution of conflict on the Korean peninsula.

Inter-Korean relations

Following decades of competition on the international stage in pursuit of 'war by other means', the first opening for inter-Korean dialogue occurred in the early 1970s in the context of US President Richard M. Nixon's overtures towards China. This shift in global geopolitics made a deep impression on both Kim Il Sung and Park Chunghee, to the extent that secret talks were arranged that led to a landmark 4 July 1972 Joint Declaration that emphasized the importance of Korea's independent efforts in pursuit of Korean unification (*South–North Joint Communique* 1972); however, the opening for dialogue proved to be short-lived. Two decades of intermittent contacts followed, usually in the context of tactical manoeuvring by either Korea to gain the upper hand in the eyes of the international community. South Korea's economic growth, political transition to democracy and the end of the Cold War converged in the late 1980s to create a situation in which South Korea had the clear upper hand. High-level inter-Korean talks resumed in 1990 at the prime minister-level and resulted by December of 1991 in the aforementioned landmark Agreement on Reconciliation, Nonaggression, Exchanges, and Cooperation. However, the concrete implementation of exchanges and confidence-building measures came to a halt in 1992–93 in the context of the first North Korean nuclear crisis and the passing of North Korea's founder, Kim Il Sung, on 8 July 1994 (Oberdorfer 1997).

Following a period of political transition and the outbreak of a major famine in North Korea in the mid-1990s, Kim Il Sung's son and appointed successor Kim Jong Il consolidated his rule at the same time that South Korea's most famous democracy activist, Kim Dae Jung, came to office. Kim Dae Jung's Sunshine Policy abandoned competition with the North in favour of pro-active efforts to promote exchanges and reconciliation through the 'separation of economics and politics'. South Korea's generous provision of assistance to the North and the promotion of inter-Korean economic cooperation projects through tourism at Mount Kumgang opened the way for a landmark inter-Korean summit held in Pyongyang on 13–15 June 2000, which further catalyzed opportunities for economic exchanges and cooperation, albeit on terms that were economically generous to the North.

An inter-Korean Joint Declaration signed by the two leaders on 15 June 2000, underscored five principles:

1 independent efforts by the two Koreas to achieve Korean reunification on their own;
2 to work toward reunification on the basis of common elements of respective proposals by the two sides;
3 cooperation on humanitarian issues including meetings for divided families;
4 'balanced development of the national economy' through economic cooperation and enhanced cultural exchanges; and
5 ongoing dialogue between the authorities of the two Koreas (*North–South Joint Declaration* 2000).

The summit succeeded in promoting inter-Korean economic and cultural exchanges and gave rise to political divisions in South Korea over whether the approach to the North was excessively one-sided or lacking in reciprocity. For instance, the establishment of the Kaesong Industrial Zone located in North Korea in a region adjacent to the Demilitarized Zone (DMZ) allowed South Korean firms access to low-cost North Korean labour, but required South Korea to provide all the necessary financial and physical infrastructure to support the project (Moon and Steinberg 1999). The inter-Korean summit resulted in increasing South Korean flows of money, goods and people to North Korea, but only a small number of trusted cadres were allowed to visit the

South; and the mix of inter-Korean economic exchange remained primarily aid- rather than trade-focused.

The North Korean leadership showed a willingness to engage in inter-Korean exchange, but for a price. As exchanges went on it became clear that the goal of the top leadership was to extract economic benefits from the relationship, while South Korean leaders seemed satisfied to make a down payment to the North to enhance South Korean security while also believing that South Korea's economic influence would translate into other types of influence in Pyongyang. Despite these exchanges, however, there was virtually no inter-Korean progress on confidence-building measures in the security field. The continuation of North Korea's missile and nuclear programme developments led to criticisms among South Korean conservatives that the North was financing these programmes with funds raised through inter-Korean exchanges. It became clear that the North Korean leadership was focused on ensuring the survival of its own system, not on pursuing economic reforms that might threaten North Korea's autarkic system of political control in which the first rule was the dominance of the leader.

The overhang of the North Korean nuclear crisis and nagging South Korean frustrations with the one-sided nature of the inter-Korean relationship became a major drag on momentum for improved inter-Korean relations under Kim Dae Jung's successor, Roh Moo-hyun (2003–8). Although Roh and Kim Jong Il held a summit in the waning months of his presidency, which fleshed out far-reaching and expensive plans for expanded economic cooperation contained in a 4 October 2007 inter-Korean joint declaration (*Declaration for Advancing Inter-Korean Relations and Peace and Prosperity* 2007), the summit appeared to be more a North Korean attempt to expand the flow of South Korean economic support to Pyongyang while attempting to influence South Korea's presidential election to bolster prospects for continued progressive policies in inter-Korean relations.

However, South Korean public disillusionment with the lack of change in North Korea following ten years of progressive policies toward North Korea have been reflected in the 2007 election of Lee Myung-bak, who advocated a 'Denuclearization, Opening, 3000' policy during his election campaign that placed greater emphasis on North Korean actions to resolve the North Korean nuclear stand-off as a prerequisite for a potentially far-reaching programme of development assistance to Pyongyang. However, the inter-Korean relationship foundered in the early days of the Lee Myung-bak administration, as the DPRK responded poorly to South Korea's change in rhetoric and to a more conditional approach to provision of economic assistance to North Korea. South Korean public sentiment continues to support engagement with North Korea, but desires a more responsive and grateful attitude, and more serious evidence of self-reform efforts on the part of the North Korean leadership (Hwang 2008).

By any measure, the balance of power on the Korean peninsula itself has shifted to the South. South Korea's per capita GDP is 17 times that of the North and its external trade is 248 times greater than that of the North, while North Korea's leaders are economically dependent for their survival on trade and aid primarily from Beijing and Seoul (Kim 2008). However, South Korea clearly does not desire North Korea's collapse, which would bring about immediate and enormous political, economic and social burdens. Lee Myung-bak seems much more anxious to promote a 'global Korea' by taking measures to enhance South Korea's profile in the international community through the expansion of South Korean contributions to peacekeeping operations; an enlarged South Korean programme of overseas development assistance; and continued expansion of South Korean cultural diplomacy, than to solve the longstanding division of the Korean peninsula (Lee 2008). However, North Korea's nuclear pursuits continue to pose a security threat and its systemic failures pose serious moral hazard and humanitarian problems that South Koreans cannot afford to ignore. Increasingly, there is a recognition that the inter-Korean relationship must move in tandem with efforts to solve the nuclear issue, and those efforts will require enhanced regional cooperation in Northeast Asia. A Korean peninsula on the brink of reunification would involve massive political, economic and structural changes and would entail significant economic costs that are likely to fall disproportionately on South Korea's efforts to consolidate its standing as a capable regional player.

Korean peninsula and the regional context

Efforts by the Bush administration to promote a regional framework for addressing the North Korean nuclear issue through the establishment of the Six-Party Talks underscore the regional dimension of the Korean peninsula conflict. Such a framework both illustrates the necessity of regional dialogue and cooperation in pursuit of the denuclearization of the Korean peninsula and the sensitive nature of the Korean peninsula as a historical strategic flashpoint for rivalry and military conflict in the context of regional power transitions: Sino-Japanese conflict (1890s), Russo-Japanese War (1904–5) and Korean War (1950–53). Given the geo-strategic location of the Korean peninsula at the nexus of four regional powers, Korean reunification has the potential to once again spark strategic anxiety or to spur security dilemmas among Korea's neighbours.

In one sense, North Korea – serving as a flashpoint and catalyst for crisis – has been the focal point for the practical development of Northeast Asian multilateralism during the past two decades. No other issue has motivated successive ad hoc efforts at multilateral cooperation so consistently as the dilemma posed by North Korea's nuclear development. From the establishment of the Korean Peninsula Energy Development Organization (KEDO) – including participation by the US, Japan, Korea and the European Union – as the vehicle for building light water reactors (LWRs) in North Korea in accordance with the 1994 US–DPRK Geneva agreed framework to the establishment of the Trilateral Cooperation and Oversight Group (including the US, Japan and South Korea) and Four Party Talks (including the US, China and the two Koreas) in the late 1990s to the launch of the Six-Party Talks in response to the latest North Korean crisis, each successive effort has built on prior experience and has come closer to the establishment of a regional multilateral framework. The Six-Party Talks format itself has created a working group on Northeast Asia peace and security that is anticipated to outlast the Six-Party process itself by institutionalizing a multilateral mechanism for promoting stability in Northeast Asia.

It remains to be seen whether the establishment of such a mechanism will be able to overcome fully the remaining security dilemmas that Japan, China and others might feel in the context of pondering real progress toward Korean reunification. The international diplomatic orientation of a unified Korea would influence security perceptions of each of Korea's neighbours, to the extent that it becomes difficult to imagine that the Korean unification process might be successful without the consensual endorsement of Korea's neighbours.

Former ROK President Roh Moo-hyun announced a controversial 'balancer' doctrine in early 2005 as tensions rose between China and Japan. This concept envisioned that South Korea would somehow mediate to reduce friction between Asia's major powers and was also informed by Roh's concern that excessive trilateral cooperation among the US, South Korea and Japan might incite a second Cold War in Asia. But the concept encountered criticism, especially from those who felt that South Korea would not be effective in playing any such role without standing firmly on the platform provided by a strong US–ROK alliance (Snyder 2007).

Within South Korea, two sets of debates have provided insight into South Korean thinking regarding its future security orientation. The first debate has been over the extent to which South Korea might pursue 'self-reliant national defence' as a means by which to reduce dependence on the US–ROK alliance. The Roh Moo-hyun administration envisioned greater reliance on South Korean forces to provide South Korea's security and pursued the end of joint operational command arrangements with the US, which would have the effect of returning sole operational control of Korean military forces to the Republic of Korea.

Second, South Korean specialists have debated prospects for a power transition in East Asia and the implications of China's rise for the future of the US–ROK alliance. Some specialists have sought greater flexibility and diplomatic independence from the US, while others believe the long-term interests of a unified Korea would best be protected by continuing an alliance with the US (Hamm 2006; Chung Jae Ho 2006). Some US specialists presume that in the context of China's rise, it will be inevitable for the US–ROK alliance to end and for South Korea to return to its historical role of dependence within a China-centred regional order (Kang 2007).

South Korea has traditionally been one of the most active promoters of enhanced multi-lateralism in Northeast Asia. As early as the late 1980s, then-president Roh Tae Woo advanced the idea of a Northeast Asia cooperation grouping in his speech at the UN (Lewis 1988). Successive South Korean administrations have continued to embrace this idea in various forms, with Kim Dae Jung as an active advocate of Asia-wide community building, while Roh Moo-hyun actively promoted Northeast Asia cooperation arrange-ments, including the idea that South Korea could play a regional financial and logistics 'hub' role in Northeast Asia. The Lee Myung-bak administration has thus far been cooler to the idea of such arrangements. However, from a South Korean perspective, regional cooperation is attractive because it gives South Korea an 'equal' seat at the table with its great-power neighbours, whereas regional arrangements based on hegemony or concert tend to force South Korea (or a future reunified Korean peninsula) into a subordinate role.

Korean reunification remains the most significant potential development on the Korean peninsula that might exacerbate the security dilemmas of neighbours to the Korean peninsula. In this respect, both China and Japan still have concerns about the prospect of a unified Korean peninsula under the influence or control of a hostile leadership as a potential threat to their respective core security interests. Chinese analysts worry that a unified democratic Korea friendly to the US might be another step in an effort to encircle or contain China, while Japan has traditionally viewed Korea as critical to its own security. Reunification of the Korean peninsula would have a less direct impact on Russian or US security interests, although both countries have had historical security interests in the diplomatic orientation of a reunified Korea (Snyder 2008).

North Korea's non-proliferation challenge and US–DPRK relations

Although the nuclear element of the Korean security crisis is arguably a symptom of underlying changes in the peninsular and the regional security balance, the primary driver for international diplomatic attention to these issues in recent decades has been the specific challenge to the international community posed by North Korea's nuclear weapons development efforts. That challenge is complicated further by the fact that North Korea's strategic objective in nuclear negotiations has traditionally been to engage with the US (not the international community), while the US must view the ramifications of and precedents that might be set by North Korean nuclear negotiations for the international non-proliferation regime. This pairing of asymmetrical objectives has continued to bedevil both the negotiation and the implementation of agreements addressing the North Korean nuclear issue.

During the first nuclear crisis of 1992–94, the IAEA pressed for an intrusive inspections regime in North Korea, based on evidence collected during inspections in North Korea and the organization's humiliating experience of having failed to detect Iraqi nuclear development efforts in the aftermath of the first Persian Gulf War. In March of 1993, the DPRK announced that it would take the unprecedented step of leaving the Nuclear Non-Proliferation Treaty. The IAEA referred the issue to the UN Security Council, which issued a statement in April of 1993 welcoming 'all efforts aimed at resolving the situation' (Chung Oknim 1995). The US initiated negotiations with North Korea designed to halt its nuclear programme; in the process it marginalized the IAEA and limited its role to a rubber-stamp affirmation that North Korea's nuclear fuel rods were being stored with the assistance of the US Department of Energy. Moreover, the US–DPRK agreed framework tied the improvement of bilateral political relations to North Korea's return to full-scope safeguards, but the main focus of implementation shifted to political and technical difficulties surrounding the construction of light water reactors in North Korea. The role of the IAEA has barely been mentioned during the course of six-party negotiations, although it is likely to play a limited role in verifying North Korea's denuclearization commitments as part of the process.

The North Korean use of the 'nuclear card' as an instrument for attracting the attention of the US has been even more obvious during the second nuclear crisis that began in 2003. The Bush administration initially attempted to take a different approach from that chosen by the Clinton administration by insisting that the North Korean nuclear issue was a 'regional problem' to be addressed through the Six-Party Talks. It then refused to hold bilateral talks with North Korea during the first several rounds of talks in 2003–4 (North Korea likewise has fended off persistent attempts by South Korea to discuss the nuclear issue in inter-Korean talks, but North Korea has firmly insisted that the nuclear issue can only be discussed with the US). North Korea upped the ante in early 2005 by declaring itself a nuclear weapons state and insisting on arms control talks. Within a few months, the second Bush administration had adopted a different approach, led by Assistant Secretary of State Christopher Hill, that included intensive bilateral US–DPRK meetings in the context of the Six-Party format and resulted in the 19 September 2005 Joint Statement by the six parties. A second stalemate ensued over DPRK funds that had been frozen in a Macao-based bank that was suspected of enabling North Korean money-laundering activities, but that stalemate was broken following North Korean missile and nuclear tests in July and October of 2006. Once again, the DPRK attempted to shift the focal point of the action away from the Six-Party Talks and onto bilateral US–DPRK negotiations, with the Six-Party agreement on 13 February 2007 essentially serving as a fig-leaf and rubber-stamp for prior understandings regarding the disabling and declaration of North Korea's nuclear facilities that had been reached between the US and North Korea in Berlin the previous month (Funabashi 2007; Chinoy 2008).

Opposition to US-led negotiations on North Korean nuclear issues have revolved around four primary arguments:

1 North Korea cannot be trusted to live up to its agreements;
2 negotiation with North Korea involves forms of recognition that enhance the legitimacy of an odious regime that has defied the international community;
3 any provision of rewards or benefits to North Korea as a violator of the international regime involves a moral hazard and sets a negative precedent for other nuclear aspirants; and
4 North Korean tactical use of extortion through crisis escalation should not be rewarded.

However, in the absence of effective coercive instruments to compel North Korea to give up its nuclear development efforts, diplomatic negotiations involving a combination of pressure and inducements have thus far been the only reasonable means by which to address this issue. North Korean tactics by which to pursue attention and respect from the US have been simultaneously effective and self-defeating, reinforcing a broader debate even while negotiations over the viability and likely longevity of the current regime continue. One result is that the prospect of a normalized relationship with North Korea remains politically controversial in Washington, and it is hard to imagine that such a relationship would be meaningful or even possible without a dramatic transformation in the approach (and in the nature) of the North Korean regime to the outside world.

However, the prospect of North Korea's collapse carries with it heavy burdens for neighbouring states and uncertain implications for proliferation. The question of how to recover North Korea's loose nukes in the event of political instability mixes nuclear proliferation concerns with regional and peninsular security dilemmas in a particularly unstable brew. Several of North Korea's neighbours have developed contingency plans for dealing North Korea as a 'failed state', but a lack of effective coordination raises the prospect that conflicting responses to North Korean instability could lead to broader conflict among regional parties (Finnegan 2008; Glaser et al. 2008).

Korean peninsula on the brink: implications for international security

The peninsular, regional and nuclear proliferation-related strands of the Korean peninsula crisis often come into conflict with each other, adding to the intractability of the Korean conflict. Increasingly, the core challenges derive from North Korea's political weakness and the nuclear countermeasures that North Korea's political leadership have taken to enhance their domestic, regional and international standing. Inter-Korean and international exchanges may serve to forestall the prospect of North Korea's collapse, but have thus far failed to effectively promote North Korea's economic and political integration into the international community since that prospect may pose an existential threat to North Korea's unique – and failed – domestic political leadership. The moral hazards of dealing with North Korea and the desired policy outcomes come into direct conflict, while North Korea's leadership manoeuvres to take advantage of security dilemmas as a means to create space for its own survival.

North Korea's nuclear programme has served Pyongyang well in several respects. First, the use of an asymmetric threat has served to deter the combined conventional military threat represented by the US and South Korea, providing space for North Korea's regime survival. Second, the North Korean leadership has used its nuclear and missile programmes as a symbol of power for the purposes of domestic political legitimation and the reinforcement of domestic political control. Third, the nuclear programme has proved successful as a bargaining chip to extract the economic resources necessary to ensure North Korea's political survival. Fourth, the nuclear issue has diverted the diplomatic agenda of international cooperation away from the future of the Korean peninsula and towards the nuclear issue, providing the North Korean leadership with a proxy issue on which they can manoeuvre to exploit the respective security dilemmas of the key stakeholders interested in the stability and security of the peninsula. As a result, the North Korean nuclear issue is a symptom that has thus far prevented all parties from dealing collectively with the core problem of the future of a North Korean regime that is increasingly anachronistic and unsustainable.

The inter-Korean competition for legitimacy is over, but the prospect of moving to a new era in Northeast Asia has thus far posed uncertainties for each party so daunting that it has been easier to hold on to the new status quo than to embrace the uncertainties of a new order. A critical question is whether a transformed North Korea will continue to have a role in that new order or whether the long-awaited prospect of Korean reunification might bring with it new and more volatile challenges for stability in Northeast Asia. Although some features of a new order have begun to take shape, it is still difficult to determine whether the Korean peninsula and Northeast Asia are on the brink of a new form of stability or the renewal of historical security dilemmas. Only time will tell.

References

Agreed Framework between the United States of America and the Democratic People's Republic of Korea (1994) Geneva, 21 October. Available online at: www.nti.org/db/China/engdocs/agfrm.htm (accessed 10 February 2009).

Agreement on Reconciliation, Nonaggression, and Exchanges and Cooperation between South and North Korea (1991) 13 December. Available online at: www.international.ucla.edu/eas/documents/korea-agreement.htm (accessed 10 February 2009).

Bush, G.W. (2002) *Transcript of remarks to students of the Virginia Military Institute*, 17 April, Federal News Service, Washington, DC.

Chinoy, M. (2008) *Meltdown: The Inside Story of the North Korean Nuclear Crisis*, New York, NY: St. Martin's Press.

Chung, J.H. (2006) *Between Ally and Partner: Korea-China Relations and the United States*, New York, NY: Columbia University Press.

Chung, O. (1995) *588 Days of North Korean Nuclear Crisis!* [in Korean] UN Security Council Statement S/25562, 8 April, 1993, Seoul Press, p. 279.

Cumings, B. (1994) *Origins of the Korean War, Vol. II*, Ithaca, NY: Cornell University Press.

Declaration for Advancing Inter-Korean Relations and Peace and Prosperity (2007) 4 October. Available online at: www.koreatimes.co.kr/www/news/nation/2008/12/120_11295.html (accessed 10 February 2009).

Finnegan, M.J. (2008) 'What now? The case for U.S.–ROK–PRC coordination on North Korea', *PacNet #48*, 11 September, Honolulu, HI: Pacific Forum CSIS.

Funabashi, Y. (2007) *The Peninsula Question: A Chronicle of the Second North Korean Nuclear Crisis*, Washington, DC: Brookings Institution Press.

Gaddis, J.L. (1972) *The United States and the Origins of the Cold War, 1941–1947*, New York: Columbia University Press.

Glaser, B., Snyder, S. and Park, J. (2008) 'Keeping an eye on an unruly neighbor: Chinese views of economic reform and stability in North Korea', *U.S. Institute of Peace Special Report*, Washington, DC.

Hamm, T.Y. (2006) 'The self-reliant national defense of South Korea and the future of the U.S.–ROK alliance', Nautilus Institute Policy Forum Online 06-49A, 20 June. Available online at: www.nautilus. org/fora/security/0649Hamm.html (accessed 10 February 2009).

Hwang, J.J. (2008) 'Lee announces N.K. policy shift', *The Korea Herald*, 12 July.

Jae-kyoung, K. (2008) 'N. Koreans earn 1/17 of Southerners' income', *Korea Times*, 18 June.

Joint Statement of the Fourth Round of the Six-Party Talks (2005) Beijing, 19 September. Available online at: www.state.gov/r/pa/prs/ps/2005/53490.htm (accessed 10 February 2009).

Kang, D.C. (2007) *China Rising: Peace, Power, and Order in East Asia*, New York: Columbia University Press.

Kim, J.K. (2008) 'N. Koreans earn 1/17 of Southerners' income', *Korea Times*, 18 June.

Lee, M.B. (2008) 'Together we shall open a road to advancement', Seoul, Republic of Korea, 25 February.

Lewis, P. (1988) 'South Korean chief, at U.N., calls for world talks and unification', *New York Times*, 19 October.

Merrill, J. (1989) *Korea: The Peninsular Origins of the War*, Wilmington, DE: University of Delaware Press.

Moon, C.I. and Steinberg, D. (1999) *Kim Dae Jung Government and Sunshine Policy: Promise and Challenges*, Asian Studies, Program, Georgetown University, Washington, DC.

North Korea – Denuclearization Action Plan (2007) 13 February. Available online at: www.state.gov/r/pa/prs/ps/2007/february/80479.htm (accessed 10 February 2009).

North–South Joint Declaration (2000) 15 June. Available online at: www1.korea-np.co.jp/pk/142th_issue/2000061501.htm (accessed 10 February 2009).

Oberdorfer, D. (1997) *The Two Koreas*, Reading, MA: Addison-Wesley Press.

Sigal, L.V. (1997) *Disarming Strangers: Nuclear Diplomacy with North Korea*, Princeton, NJ: Princeton University Press.

Snyder, S. (2007) 'The China–Japan rivalry: Korea's pivotal position?' in Gi-wook, S. and Sneider, D. (eds) *Cross Currents: Regionalism and Nationalism in Northeast Asia*, Palo Alto, CA: Shorenstein Asia Pacific Research Center, Stanford University, pp. 241–58.

——(2008) 'The Korean Peninsula and Northeast Asian stability', in Shambaugh, D. and Yahuda, M. (eds) *International Relations of Asia*, Lanham, MD: Rowman and Littlefield, pp. 258–76.

South–North Joint Communique (1972) 4 July. Available online at: http://15cwd.pa.go.kr/english/diplomacy/sn_kr_2000/bg_m_6.php (accessed 10 February 2009).

Stueck, W. (1995) *The Korean War: An International History*, Princeton, NJ: Princeton University Press.

United Nations (2006) 'Security Council condemns nuclear test by Democratic People's Republic of Korea, unanimously adopting resolution 1718', 14 October. Available online at: www.un.org/News/Press/docs/2006/sc8853.doc.htm (accessed 10 February 2009).

Wit, J., Poneman, D. and Gallucci, R.L. (2004) *Going Critical: The First North Korean Nuclear Crisis*, Washington, DC: Brookings Institution Press.

Yang, S.C. (1994) *The North and South Korean Political Systems: A Comparative Analysis*, Boulder, CO: Westview Press.

25

Indian security policy

Sumit Ganguly[1]

India's security policy is in a state of transition as the country attempts to secure its position as an emergent power in Asia and beyond. The willingness on the part of Indian policymakers to accept the use of force as a critical element of national power represents a profound shift from the ideational outlook that had influenced Indian policymaking in the immediate post-independence era. The task before them now involves making judicious choices about military commitments, deployments and accordingly appropriate levels of defence spending.

The scholarship on India's security policy is limited and mostly dated (Kavic 1967; Thomas 1978; Gordon 1995). Such a lacuna in the literature is a puzzle because of India's overt acquisition of nuclear weapons in 1998, its abandonment of its commitment to nonalignment after the Cold War and its growing significance as an Asian power (Ganguly 2003–4). Despite these profound changes, scholarship on Indian security policy continues to be dogged by a lack of attention.

This chapter traces the origins, evolution, current state and future directions of the country's security policy since its emergence as an independent state following the collapse of the British Indian Empire in 1947. It looks at the impact of critical political choices on the part of the country's leadership, the role of regional security threats and India's relative lack of importance to the global rivalry during much of the Cold War era. The chapter deals with the intellectual rationale for India's initial security policies, their re-evaluation and transformation in the aftermath of the 1962 Sino-Indian border war, its conflicts with Pakistan, its quest for nuclear weapons, its responses to internal uprisings and its attempts to extend its reach beyond the confines of the subcontinent.

Post-independence concerns

In the immediate aftermath of India's emergence as an independent state in 1947 following the end of the British colonial empire in South Asia, Indian policymakers adopted an ideational foreign policy which sought to de-emphasize military preparedness. A number of factors shaped India's defence policies in the post-independence era. Most importantly, Prime Minister Jawaharlal Nehru, the principal architect of India's foreign and security policies, was acutely concerned about the significant opportunity costs of defence spending (Cohen 1971). Simultaneously, he feared that a large military establishment could also encourage Bonapartist ambitions and undermine India's nascent democracy (Ganguly 1991). Finally, he also hoped to contribute to a world order where the use of force was proscribed in international politics.

Nehru's wishes notwithstanding, almost immediately after its independence, India found itself embroiled in a war with Pakistan over the status of the state of Jammu and Kashmir (Ganguly 2001). The war ensued because of Pakistan's attempts to exploit a tribal rebellion in the western reaches of this state (Hodson 1969; Khan 1975). In keeping with their faith in multilateral institutions and acting on the advice of Lord Louis Mountbatten, the last viceroy, India's political leadership referred the Kashmir dispute to the United Nations Security Council (Gupta 1966). The war ended on 1 January 1949, when the Security Council imposed a ceasefire as multilateral negotiations to resolve the dispute began.

The Indian military possessed sufficient military capabilities to cope with the threat from Pakistan. However, it was fundamentally ill-equipped to deal with the threat that arose from the People's Republic of China (PRC) over a disputed border along much of India's Himalayan frontier (Hoffmann 1990). Prime Minister Nehru and his Defense Minister, V.K. Krishna Menon, believed that the threat from the PRC could be contained through diplomacy and conciliation. To that end, India made significant concessions to the PRC. It resorted to the mildest criticism of the Chinese invasion and occupation of Tibet in 1950, even though China's move meant the end of a strategic buffer (Sen 1960). Specifically, at the behest of the PRC, the Indian government eschewed all extra-territorial rights in Tibet that it had inherited as holdovers from the British colonial period.

More to the point, Nehru was convinced that the great powers would not remain passive in the event of a Sino-Indian conflict and thereby moved to promptly contain the tensions. As it turned out, this assumption proved to be completely flawed. Negotiations aimed at resolving the border dispute broke down in 1960. Worse still, India, despite its inadequate military capabilities, embarked upon a strategy of compellence. This strategy involved sending in lightly armed Indian troops in 'penny packets' to display India's resolve to hold territory that the Chinese had claimed. When the PRC chose to attack these Indian pickets, they proved no match for the battle-hardened People's Liberation Army (PLA). The Indian troops lacked adequate clothing, firepower and logistical support. Worse still, the Indian military reinforcements that were abruptly moved from the plains were not acclimatized to high-altitude warfare and, consequently, faced multiple and crippling health hazards. This short but brutal war proved to be a military and diplomatic debacle for India. Militarily, the Indian armed forces suffered a stinging defeat and diplomatically India found itself bereft of support apart from some limited assistance from the US and the UK.

The aftermath of 1962

In the wake of this conflict, India's policymakers were forced to re-evaluate India's military preparedness to cope with on-going threats from both Pakistan and, more importantly, the PRC. Since India had acquitted itself adequately against Pakistan in the 1947–48 war, the principal threat it had to contend with involved the PRC. To that end, Indian policymakers chose to embark on the creation of a 45-squadron air force equipped with supersonic aircraft; a million-man army with ten new mountain divisions trained in high-altitude warfare; and a modest programme of naval modernization (Thomas 1978).

The Indian fixation on countering the potential security threat from the PRC and the concomitant rearmament programme provoked Pakistani anxieties. From the Pakistani standpoint, India's increased military capabilities could make a crucial difference in a future Indo-Pakistani conflict. Fearing that a window of opportunity might be closing to reclaim the disputed territory of India's Jammu and Kashmir state through the use of force, the Pakistani politico-military elite fashioned an elaborate strategy to seize Kashmir militarily (Ganguly 1989). The plan had two distinct phases. In the first phase, code-named 'Operation Gibraltar', Pakistani troops disguised as locals would infiltrate the Kashmir Valley and seek to sow discord among the population. Exploiting these dis-turbances that they had successfully stirred, Pakistan would launch a full-scale invasion of Kashmir ('Operation Grand Slam') and seize it in a short war.

To the dismay of the Pakistani war planners, none of their assumptions proved ten-able. Though some Kashmiris were discontented with Indian rule, they nevertheless evinced little interest in assisting the Pakistani infiltrators. Instead, they alerted Indian authorities who promptly moved to seal the Cease-Fire Line. Despite the loss of strategic surprise, the Pakistani leadership went ahead with its war plans and launched an assault on Kashmir in early September 1965. The Indian forces were prepared for this attack and succeeded in blunting the Pakistani onslaught. The war lasted for about three weeks and was brought to a close through a United Nations Security Council resolution. Since the US demonstrated little interest in promoting a post-war accord, the Soviet Union step-ped into the breach. Moscow persuaded the adversaries to return to the status quo ante and to abjure from the use of force to settle the Kashmir dispute (Brines 1968).

Despite this commitment to refrain from the use of force to settle bilateral disputes, India and Pakistan became involved in a third war in 1971. This conflict stemmed from the exigencies of Pakistani domestic politics and the emergence of Bengali sub-nationalism in East Pakistan (Jahan 1972; Zaheer 1994). However, after negotiations in the wake of Pakistan's first free and fair national elections broke down, the Punjabi-dominated Pakistani military resorted to a brutal crackdown in East Pakistan. In the face of widespread repression, close to ten million Bengalis fled to India. Burdened with this significant refugee influx, Indian policymakers, having exhausted the diplomatic alternatives, fash-ioned a politico-military strategy designed to break up Pakistan (Jackson 1975; Jacob 1997). Indian military planners trained, armed and provided sanctuaries to an indigenous guerrilla movement, the 'Mukti Bahini' (literally 'liberation force'), and ultimately pro-voked the Pakistani regime to launch a military assault on India in early December 1971. Indian forces, which had been carefully arrayed to respond with a 'blitzkrieg strategy', managed to bring the war to a successful close within three weeks (for a discussion of the Indian blitzkrieg strategy, see Mearsheimer 1983). The war led to the break-up of Paki-stan and the creation of the independent state of Bangladesh. Following this war, India emerged as the pre-eminent military power in the subcontinent. In addition, given India's military preponderance, a long peace ensued on the subcontinent until the out-break of an indigenous insurgency in India's disputed state of Jammu and Kashmir in 1989.

The nuclear conundrum

Contrary to many analyses,[2] the origins of the Indian nuclear weapons programme can be traced quite clearly to the country's perception of threat emanating from the PRC.

Within two years of India's disastrous defeat at the hands of the PRC, the Chinese had tested their first nuclear weapon at Lop Nor. The Chinese nuclear test set off a firestorm of controversy in the Indian parliament (Mirchandani 1968). Segments of the Indian right wing wanted the country to abandon nonalignment and seek a nuclear guarantee against the PRC from the Western world. Others wanted India to develop its own nuclear weapons capabilities to cope with this emergent threat from the PRC. After considerable debate, the leadership chose neither to dispense with nonalignment nor to pursue a nuclear weapons programme. Instead, it made a feeble effort to seek a nuclear guarantee from the great powers, notably the UK, the Soviet Union and the US. In the event, all three states rebuffed India (Noorani 1967).

In the wake of this failure to obtain a nuclear guarantee, India embarked upon the Subterranean Nuclear Explosions Project (SNEP). Simultaneously, at the international level, it maintained its spirited opposition to the drafting of the Nuclear Nonproliferation Treaty (NPT) in the Eighteen Nation Disarmament Committee (ENDC) in Geneva. India's opposition was straightforward: it contended that the treaty was inherently inequitable. It sought to prevent the *horizontal* spread of nuclear weapons while urging good-faith efforts to curb *vertical* proliferation (Kapur 1976).

Not surprisingly, India chose not to accede to the NPT when it was passed and entered into force on 1 January 1970. As a consequence of its refusal to join the NPT regime, India found itself isolated from global nuclear commerce. Despite its inability to participate in international nuclear activities, India went ahead with both its peaceful and its military nuclear programmes. In May 1974, it tested its first nuclear weapon in the Rajasthan desert and promptly faced a series of bilateral and multilateral sanctions (Ganguly 1983). Given the country's parlous economic conditions, its leaders chose not to carry out further tests, but work on the nuclear weapons programme proceeded apace, even though individual Indian governments chose to either retard or accelerate the program (Tellis 2000).

Crossing the nuclear Rubicon

In the late 1990s, because of developments at the global, regional and national levels, India chose to dispense with its policy of nuclear ambiguity and crossed the nuclear Rubicon in May 1998. Specifically, four factors influenced the Indian decision to end its nuclear restraint. The first two factors were located at the global level. First, at the NPT Review Conference in May 1995, the US managed to persuade the vast majority of UN members to extend the NPT indefinitely and unconditionally. Second, it sought to pass the Comprehensive Test Ban Treaty in 1998, despite vigorous objections from India and a handful of other states to one particular clause in the CTBT that required 44 states with on-going nuclear power programmes to ratify the treaty before September 1998 to enable it to enter into force.

The significance of the indefinite and unconditional extension of the NPT and the requirement that a sub-set of states ratify the CTBT to enable its entry into force was not lost on Indian policymakers. They correctly concluded that the widespread global support for the NPT in the wake of the 1995 Review Conference placed India in an extremely isolated position and thereby subjected it to potentially acute pressures to accede to this global regime. Additionally, they also realized that inexorable pressure would mount on them to sign and ratify the CTBT before September 1998.

Apart from these two global considerations, two other factors played critical roles in compelling India's policymakers to depart from their commitment to nuclear abstinence. First, with the end of the Cold War and the Soviet collapse, India's policymakers realized that they could no longer count on the Soviet security guarantee that was embedded in the 20-year Indo-Soviet treaty of 'peace, friendship, and cooperation', even if it were to be renewed (Horn 1982; Racioppi 1994). Consequently, India could no longer expect Russia to act as a brake on possible Chinese revanchism. Second, they also concluded that in the late 1980s and early 1990s, the PRC had made Pakistan its virtual strategic surrogate in South Asia through the transfer of nuclear weapons and ballistic missile technology (Nuclear Threat Initiative 2008).

Given these global and regional considerations, India's policymakers determined that they could not afford to abandon the nuclear weapons option. With the seemingly inexorable movement toward the conclusion of a Comprehensive Test Ban Treaty (CTBT), Indian policymakers feared that their ability to carry out nuclear tests would be foreclosed, leaving India in a strategically vulnerable position. In the aftermath of the nuclear tests, India faced widespread international condemnation and a new raft of US-initiated sanctions. However, through patient and deft diplomacy, it managed to get the bulk of them lifted within about two years (Talbott 2004). Despite its failure to persuade India (and Pakistan) to foreswear their nascent nuclear weapons capabilities, the Clinton administration left office convinced that nuclear weapons in the region were a deeply destabilizing force.

A seismic policy shift

A significant policy shift occurred under the administration of George W. Bush. Initially, it was concerned about Pakistan's nuclear weapons programme. However, in the aftermath of the terrorist attacks of 11 September 2001, the US needed to engage Pakistan. Apart from its interest in ensuring the security and safety of the Pakistani nuclear weapons infrastructure, the Bush administration evinced little interest in rolling back Pakistan's capabilities. Simultaneously, it did little to pressure or persuade India to abandon its nuclear weapons programme. On the contrary, in 2005, the Bush administration started negotiations with India on a comprehensive civilian nuclear agreement that would enable India to maintain its nuclear arsenal and also participate in global nuclear commerce (Ganguly and Mistry 2006). Protracted and difficult negotiations ensued over the next three years. In October of 2008, after considerable spirited debate in both the US and India, a deal was finally agreed. Under the terms of this agreement, India can now engage in normal nuclear commerce without being subjected to the bilateral and multilateral sanctions that had been imposed on it in the aftermath of its first nuclear test in 1974.

Is the region more stable as a consequence of the acquisition of nuclear weapons by India and Pakistan? There is a growing and vigorous debate on this subject (for arguments for nuclear stability, see: Ganguly and Hagerty 2005; for an alternative view, see: Kapur 2007). The proponents of stability contend that the mutual possession of nuclear weapons has all but eliminated the prospect of full-scale war in the region as both sides understand the consequences of the nuclear revolution (on the significance of the nuclear revolution, see Jervis 1989). Others contend that given Pakistan's revisionist ambitions, the region has actually become more war-prone. They contend that Pakistani decision-makers are more likely to provoke India, secure in the knowledge that India has no viable conventional military options because of Pakistan's possession of nuclear weapons and the concomitant fears of escalation to the nuclear level. Given their fundamentally divergent premises about the effects of nuclear weapons on the likelihood of war, the two sides drew vastly different inferences from the Kargil conflict of 1999. The proponents of nuclear deterrence argue that the looming presence of nuclear weapons prevented the horizontal escalation of the conflict. Their critics, however, contend that Pakistan felt emboldened to make an intrusion into Kargil because of its acquisition of a nuclear weapons capability.

The Kargil war and after

In 1999, India and Pakistan became involved in the third war over Kashmir. Pakistan initiated this conflict. The precise origins of the war remain controversial, but there is little question that it stemmed from the successful infiltration of Pakistani forces across the Line of Control in the Kargil region in the spring of 1999 (for various discussions of the Kargil conflict, see Chari and Mehta 2001; Malik 2006; Bajpai et al. 2001; Singh 2001; Swami 1999).

What prompted Pakistan to undertake this 'limited probe'?[3] There is no clear-cut answer to this question. However, it appears that the Pakistani military leadership was keen on jump-starting the insurgency in Kashmir, which had started to flag thanks to the success of India's sustained counter-insurgency campaign. To that end, Pakistani military planners undertook a probing action designed to test the extent of India's commitment. At another level, they were no doubt aware that if they succeeded in breaching the Indian defences in the region, they would be able to interdict India's principal link from the Kashmir Valley to the northern region of Kashmir, Ladakh. The initial Pakistani intrusion into this sector was extremely successful for a number of reasons. The most notable of these was the Indian conviction that in the aftermath of the peace process that had been initiated in February 1999, any offensive Pakistani operations in Kashmir were unlikely. Consequently, both Indian civil and military intelligence organizations had lowered the level of vigilance along the Kashmir border (*Kargil Committee Report* 2000).

Despite the initial failure to detect the Pakistani intrusions, the Indian military acted with alacrity and vigour to stem them. To that end, India brought considerable firepower to bear in a concentrated fashion. It also utilized its air force, but placed significant constraints on the use of air power. Specifically, the air force was explicitly forbidden from crossing the Line of Control for fear of provoking a wider war. The reasons for Indian restraint were straightforward. This was the first Indo-Pakistani conflict since the two countries had acquired nuclear weapons. Indian decision-makers were acutely aware of the dangers of nuclear escalation (Ganguly 2008a; for an alternative view, see Kapur 2008).

Shortly after the Kargil war, Indian defence planners sought to formulate a military doctrine and strategy that would enable them to respond to Pakistani probing actions without risking full-scale war. To that end, various Indian military officials – most notably General Ved Prakash Malik, a former chief of staff of the Indian Army – called for a doctrine of 'limited war under the nuclear umbrella' (Malik 2006). Details about this strategy, however, are mostly lacking in the public domain. Most of the discussions and criticisms of the strategy have focused on its feasibility and the dangers of escalation (Raghavan 2001). These concerns were further reinforced due to the lack of any militarily viable options when India faced another crisis with Pakistan in the wake of a terrorist attack on the Indian parliament on 13 December 2001. In an attempt to induce a change in Pakistani behaviour, India mobilized its substantial conventional forces and embarked upon a massive and prolonged exercise of coercive diplomacy, but to little effect (Ganguly and Kraig 2005).

In the aftermath of these two episodes, Indian military planners focused on developing a doctrine of swift mobilization and calibrated response to limited Pakistani-sponsored terrorist attacks. This doctrine, dubbed 'Cold Start', envisages responding with speed and vigour against a future Pakistani terrorist provocation. However, some scholars who have examined the premises of the doctrine and India's capabilities question its strategic assumptions and operational features (Ladwig 2007).

Coping with internal conflicts

In addition to the two major external security threats from Pakistan and the PRC, the Indian state's security policies have also included a series of domestic counter-insurgency operations (Chadha 2005). The vast majority of these insurgencies are due to Indian domestic politics. Several of them stem from ethnic and religious tensions, although one particular insurgency, the Naxalite Rebellion, is due to class conflict (Chakravarti 2008). However, external involvement in these insurgencies has expanded their scope, increased their intensity and prolonged their duration. In a number of cases, Pakistan and the PRC played vital roles in sustaining these insurgencies.

The Indian state has successfully, albeit at considerable cost, defeated every insurgency barring one. The Kashmir insurgency, which erupted in 1989, has been contained but has yet to be suppressed (Ganguly 1997). There are compelling reasons for India's failure to end the Kashmir insurgency. Kashmir, unlike the other cases, involves a significant territorial dispute. Also, since Kashmir is contiguous to Pakistan, the Pakistani state has been able to provide the Kashmiri insurgents with weaponry, training, logistics and, above all, sanctuaries. It has also organized, trained and directed a series of insurgent groups to enter and wreak havoc in Indian-controlled Kashmir (Swami 2007; Byman 2005). In addition to Pakistan's involvement, unlike in the vast majority of the other insurgencies where disaffection with the Indian state was limited, the Kashmir conflict is fuelled by alienation from India on the part of many Kashmiris. Consequently, the Indian state has had considerable difficulty in suppressing this insurgency.

Apart from these insurgencies that have wracked the country, India has faced a renewed spate of ethno–religious violence in recent years. The sources of this discord are complex, but have much to do with growing levels of political mobilization, the decline of political institutions and the exploitation of internal grievances by external actors (Ganguly 2008b).

A recent episode underscored the seriousness of the threat. On 26 November 2008, a group of ten terrorists attacked two prominent hotels, a major railway station and several other crowded venues in the city of Bombay (Mumbai). Over the next two days, they battled local police and national commandos. After a two-day siege they were finally overpowered but after considerable loss of life. Based upon electronic intelligence inter-cepts Indian officials asserted that the terrorists belonged to a notionally banned Pakistani terrorist group, the Lashkar-e-Taiba. Despite widespread public anger, the government of India chose to exert concerted diplomatic pressure on Pakistan to end its involvement with terrorist organizations and chose not to use military force. Whether or not this strategy will yield the desired results remains an open question.

Current and future directions

All three branches of the Indian armed forces are now in the midst of a major modernization drive. Thanks to a growing economy, India is able to devote a greater share of its resources to defence spending and military modernization. Expanded defence spending is determined by a number of factors. First, the shelf life of various weapons systems that the Indian armed forces had acquired in the 1980s and earlier is now expiring. Consequently, a new generation of weapons systems is required. The replacement of major weapons systems is most urgent in the Indian Air Force, which still relies on the obsolescent MiG-21 fighter. Second, despite cosmetic improvements, the Indo-Pakistani relationship remains fraught despite some limited and fitful progress in the waning days of the Musharraf presidency. More to the point, as argued earlier, since the 2001–2 crisis, India has been seeking a new military doctrine designed to deal with Pakistani provocations short of provoking a full-scale war. Third, Indian military planners are still faced with growing and improved Chinese military capabilities. In the absence of a settlement of the border dispute, the military considers it prudent to invest in the maintenance of an effective conventional deterrent force along the Himalayan border. Fourth and finally, India's defence modernization is also a product of its desire to protect its littoral regions and particularly sea-lanes that lead to the Persian Gulf. The protection of these sea-lanes is of critical importance to India because 70 per cent of India's oil is imported from the Persian Gulf region (Ganguly and Pardesi 2008).

Conclusions

Indian security policy is driven by certain constant factors, including the standoff with Pakistan over Kashmir and the disputed border with the PRC. Beyond these factors, however, India is now also involved in a wider competitive relationship with the PRC. Indian policymakers, fearful of provoking the PRC, are usually loath to admit publicly to the existence of such a competition. Nevertheless, India's force acquisitions clearly suggest that a revanchist PRC remains the country's principal long-term security concern. Such concerns have been exacerbated with increased Chinese naval activity in the Indian Ocean littoral and its growing presence in Myanmar (Burma) (for a discussion of Indian concerns about Chinese naval activity in the Indian Ocean, see International Institute of Strategic Studies 2008). India's continued attempts to acquire and upgrade the former Russian carrier *Admiral Gorshkov* at prohibitive cost, to replace one of its aging aircraft carriers, is emblematic of the country's quest to maintain a significant naval presence in the Indian Ocean. The Indian Navy has also started to hold a series of routine naval exercises with the naval forces of Australia, Japan and the US (Holmes and Yoshihara 2008).

Apart from these bilateral security concerns, given India's recent spurt in economic growth, its policymakers now visualize a larger role for India in Asia (on India's economic prospects, see Panagariya 2008). India has already demonstrated its capability as a regional actor when its naval forces acted in concert with those of the US, Japan, Singapore and Australia to provide relief to Sri Lanka, Thailand and Indonesia after the tsunami in December 2004.

Finally, India will continue to make modest investments in its incipient nuclear capabilities to pursue a secure, but robust nuclear deterrent (Basrur 2006). Despite bureaucratic and scientific pressures, it is unlikely that Indian policymakers will pursue a substantial nuclear arsenal. Such an arsenal would provoke regional adversaries and place an undue burden on the Indian exchequer. This argument can be asserted with some authority based upon India's propensity for fiscal prudence in matters of defence spending and its orientation toward incremental decision-making.

Notes

1 The author wishes to acknowledge the substantial research assistance of Scott Nissen.
2 E.g. Sagan (1996) traces the origins of the nuclear programme to what he terms the 'domestic politics model'.
3 On the concept of a 'limited probe' see, George and Smoke (1974).

References

Bajpai, K., Karim, A. and Mattoo, A. (2001) *Kargil and After*, New Delhi: Har-Anand.
Basrur, R. (2006) *Minimum Deterrence and India's Nuclear Security*, Stanford: Stanford University Press.
Brines, R. (1968) *The Indo-Pakistani Conflict*, New York: Pall Mall.
Byman, D. (2005) *Deadly Connections: States that Sponsor Terrorism*, Cambridge: Cambridge University Press.
Chadha, V. (2005) *Low Intensity Conflicts in India: An Analysis*, New Delhi: Sage.
Chakravarti, S. (2008) *Red Sun: Travels in Naxalite Country*, New Delhi: Penguin.
Chari, P.R. and Mehta, A.K. 2001, *Kargil: The Tables Turned*, New Delhi: Manohar.
Cohen, S.P. 1971, *The Indian Army: Its Contribution to the Development of a Nation*, Berkeley: University of California Press.
Ganguly, S. (1983) 'Why India joined the nuclear club', *Bulletin of the Atomic Scientists* 39, 4: 30–33.
——(1989) 'Deterrence failure revisited: The India–Pakistani war of 1965', *Journal of Strategic Studies* 13, 4: 77–93.
——(1991) 'From aid to the civil to the defense of the nation: The army in contemporary India', *Journal of Asian and African Affairs* 26, 1: 1–12.
——(1997) *The Crisis in Kashmir: Portents of War, Hopes of Peace*, Cambridge: Cambridge University Press.
——(2001) *Conflict Unending: India–Pakistan Tensions Since 1947*, New York: Columbia University Press.
——(2003–4) 'India's foreign policy grows up', *World Policy Journal* 20, 4: 41–47.
——(2008a) 'Nuclear stability in South Asia', *International Security* 33, 2: 45–70.
——(2008b) 'India held back?' *Current History* 107, 712: 369–74.
Ganguly, S. and Hagerty, D. (2005) *Fearful Symmetry: India and Pakistan in the Shadow of Nuclear Weapons*, Seattle: University of Washington Press.
Ganguly, S. and Kraig, M. (2005) 'The 2001–2 Indo-Pakistani crisis: Exposing the limits of coercive diplomacy', *Security Studies* 14, 2: 290–324.
Ganguly, S. and Mistry, D. (2006) 'The case for the US–India nuclear agreement', *World Policy Journal* 23, 2: 11–20.
Ganguly, S. and Pardesi, M. (2008) 'India and energy security: A foreign policy priority,' in Pant, H.V. (ed.) *Indian Foreign Policy in a Unipolar World*, London: Routledge, pp. 99–127.
George, A. and Smoke, R. (1974) *Deterrence in American Foreign Policy*, New York: Columbia University Press.
Gordon, S. (1995) *India's Rise to Power in the Twentieth Century and Beyond*, New York: St. Martin's Press.
Gupta, S. (1966) *Kashmir: A Study in India–Pakistan Relations*, Bombay: Asia Publishing House.
Hodson, H.V. (1969) *The Great Divide: Britain, India, Pakistan*, London: Hutchinson.
Hoffmann, S. (1990) *India and the China Crisis*, Berkeley: University of California Press.
Holmes, J.R. and Yoshihara, T. (2008) 'China and the United States in the Indian Ocean: An emerging strategic triangle?', *Naval War College Review* 61, 3: 40–60.

Horn, R. (1982) *Soviet–Indian Relations: Issues and Influence*, New York: Praeger.

International Institute of Strategic Studies (2008) *Strategic Survey*, New York: Routledge.

Jackson, R. (1975) *South Asian Crisis: India, Pakistan, Bangla Desh*, London: Chatto and Windus for the International Institute for Strategic Studies.

Jacob, J.F.R. (1997) *Surrender at Dhaka: Birth of a Nation*, New Delhi: Manohar Publishers & Distributors.

Jahan, R. (1972) *Pakistan: Failure in National Integration*, New York: Columbia University Press.

Jervis, R. (1989) *The Meaning of the Nuclear Revolution: Statecraft and the Prospects of Armageddon*, Ithaca, NY: Cornell University Press.

Kapur, A. (1976) *India's Nuclear Option: Atomic Diplomacy and Decision Making*, New York: Praeger.

Kapur, S.P. (2007) *Dangerous Deterrent: Nuclear Weapons Proliferation and Conflict in South Asia*, Stanford: Stanford University Press.

——(2008) 'Ten years of instability in a nuclear South Asia', *International Security* 33, 2: 71–94.

Kargil Committee Report: From Surprise to Reckoning (2000) Available online at: www.fas.org/news/india/2000/25indi1.htm (accessed 13 October 2008).

Kavic, L.J. 1967, *India's Quest for Security, Defense Policies, 1947–1965*, Berkeley: University of California Press.

Khan, A. (1975) *Raiders in Kashmir*, Islamabad: National Book Foundation.

Ladwig, W. (2007) 'A cold start for hot wars? The Indian army's new limited war doctrine', *International Security* 23, 3: 158–90.

Malik, V.P. (2006) *Kargil: From Surprise to Victory*, New Delhi: HarperColllins.

Mearsheimer, J. (1983) *Conventional Deterrence*, Ithaca, NY: Cornell University Press.

Mirchandani, G.G. (1968) *India's Nuclear Dilemma*, New Delhi: Popular Book Services.

Nuclear Threat Initiative. (2008) *China's Missile Exports and Assistance to Pakistan*. Available online at: www.nti.org/db/China/mpakpos.htm (accessed 8 October 2008).

Noorani, A.G. (1967) 'India's quest for a nuclear guarantee', *Asian Survey* 7, 7: 490–502.

Panagariya, A. (2008) *India: Emerging Giant*, Oxford: Oxford University Press.

Racioppi, L. (1994) *Soviet Policy Towards South Asia Since 1970*, Cambridge: Cambridge University Press.

Raghavan, V.R. (2001) 'Limited war and nuclear escalation in South Asia', *Nonproliferation Review* 8, 3: 82–98.

Sagan, S.D. (1996) 'Why do states build nuclear weapons? Three models in search of a bomb', *International Security* 21, 3: 54–86.

Sen, C. (1960) *Tibet Disappears: A Documentary History of Tibet's International Status, the Great Rebellion and its Aftermath*, London: Asia Publishing House.

Singh, A. (2001) *A Ridge Too Far: War in the Kargil Heights, 1999*, Patiala: Motibagh Palace.

Swami, P. (1999) *The Kargil War*, New Delhi: LeftWord.

——(2007) *India, Pakistan and the Secret Jihad: the Covert War in Kashmir, 1947–2004*, London: Routledge.

Talbott, S. (2004) *Engaging India: Diplomacy, Democracy and the Bomb*, Washington, DC: The Brookings Institution.

Tellis, A. (2000) *India's Emerging Nuclear Posture: Between Recessed Deterrence and Ready Arsenal*, Santa Monica: The Rand Corporation.

Thomas, R.G.C. (1978) *The Defense of India: A Budgetary Perspective of Strategy and Politics*, Delhi: MacMillan.

——(1986) *Indian Security Policy*, Princeton: Princeton University Press.

Zaheer, H. (1994) *The Separation of East Pakistan: The Rise and Realization of Bengali Muslim Nationalism*, New York: Oxford University Press.

26

Pakistan's security predicament

Religion, economics or geopolitics?

Masooda Bano

Faced with the choice of standing 'with or against' the US in the autumn of 2001, then-president General Pervez Musharraf announced a u-turn on Pakistan's two-decades old policy of training and supporting the *mujahideen* – a process in which Pakistani intelligence agencies have been actively involved since the Soviet–Afghanistan war. But despite active cooperation with the US through the provision of extensive logistical support, intelligence-sharing and the implementation of numerous counter-insurgency measures within the country (Cohen and Chollet 2007), seven years later, Pakistan was ranked as 'the world's most dangerous place' (*The Economist* 2008; Moreau and Hirsh 2008). Its tribal belt, and increasingly the whole of the North West Frontier Province (NWFP), is reportedly slipping out of state control and becoming a focal point for the gathering of Muslim militants from across the globe. Pakistan today therefore has the unique status of being criticized as a rogue state and praised for being on the front line of the 'war on terror' at the same time (Cohen 2004). The US policy towards Pakistan remained an important electoral concern in the 2008 US presidential elections (Rafique 2008). On the one hand, it is feared that the country's nuclear weapons might fall in the hands of Islamic militants, who could use them for potentially devastating acts of political violence; on the other, the rise in militancy arguably threatens the survival of the Pakistani state.

The Bush administration has used both carrot and stick policies to persuade the Pakistani government to support counter-insurgency programmes. General Musharraf was pressured to launch military operations starting from 2003 – which continue to date, despite the transfer of power to the Pakistan Peoples Party after the 2008 elections – to flush out militants from the tribal belts; in addition, the US has on occasion carried out aerial strikes in the tribal belt (HoC 2007). At the same time, the Western governments have increased aid to Pakistan to sustain Islamabad's cooperation in the 'war on terror' and to help improve the state of human development. The British Department for International Development (DFID), for instance, increased its development aid to Pakistan from £97 million in 2000 to £236 million for the period 2005–8 and then doubled it to £480 million for the period 2008–11 (DFID 2008). The failure of these hard and soft measures to check militancy in Pakistan highlights the need to reassess the presumed causes of Muslim radicalism in Pakistan as well as the feasibility of the existing counter-terrorism strategies.

After briefly introducing some basic facts about Pakistan, this chapter explores two central questions: first, how legitimate are the concerns about Pakistan having become, or moving towards becoming, the focal point for gathering and training of Muslim militants to plot serious attacks on Western targets? Here, the chapter discusses the evidence of insecurity. Second, what explains the heightened Muslim militancy in Pakistan despite the implementation of 'war on terror' strategies? The chapter thus traces the causes of insecurity before it concludes by exploring the nature of domestic and international interventions required to address the security concerns in Pakistan.

Pakistan: some basic facts

Knowledge of a few basic facts about the country is important in interpreting its current security concerns. Created as a result of Indian Muslims' demand for a separate homeland at the time of the British exit from the Indian sub-continent in 1947, Pakistan is one of the few countries to be established in the name of religion (Cohen 2004). With a population of 150 million, which is expected to double in 20 years, Pakistan is the sixth most populous country in the world and hosts the largest number of Muslims after Indonesia – one-half of whom are under the age of 15. Located at the juncture of South Asia, West Asia and Central Asia, its location has added to its geo-strategic importance. Sharing borders with four important countries, namely India, China, Afghanistan and Iran, Pakistan has been important to US strategic plans for the region since its very inception (Cohen 2004; Cohen and Chollet 2007; Grare 2007). Furthermore, the country's borders cut through ethnic groups, with the result that Pashtun tribes reside on both sides of the Durand Line, which marks the Afghanistan–Pakistan border; and Baluch-Brahui tribal ties persist across the Iran–Pakistan border. In addition, the Muslim identity marking Pakistan's very inception has nurtured a strong sense of affiliation with the Middle East (Haqqani 2005). Pakistan's location and history thus have an important bearing on its current security concerns.

Evidence of insecurity

Fears about Pakistan's stability, though at times exaggerated, are not unfounded when set against the evidence of growing signs of religious militancy in Pakistan. The seeds of the country's current association with jihad were sown in the early 1980s (Roy 1990; Yousaf and Adkin 1992; Rashid 2000), but since 11 September 2001, Muslim militancy in Pakistan has acquired new characteristics. While in the 1980s and 1990s, Pakistan's engagement in jihad was aimed at cross-border activities, where the jihadis trained in Pakistan found targets in Kashmir and Afghanistan (Roy 1990; Rashid 2000), in recent years, Pakistan has witnessed increased militancy within its own territory. At the heart of the problem is the fact that the Federally Administered Tribal Areas (FATA) on the Pakistan and Afghanistan border, where al-Qaida and Taliban leaders are believed to have found a safe refuge when forced to retreat from Afghanistan by the US and allied forces, remain outside the jurisdiction of Pakistani courts (ICG 2006).

Shared ethnicity and a strong presence of Islam in the tribal belt led to the formation of strong ties between the locals and the *mujahideen* during the Soviet–Afghanistan war of the 1980s, when the area served as the main transit route for fighters entering Afghanistan

(Yousaf and Adkin 1992; Rashid 2000). These ties, forged over two decades, remained active when the Pakistani government decided to support the US military intervention in 2001. Despite sustained military operations in the area and the deployment of 70,000 troops, the Pakistani military has failed to check recruitment by extremist groups operating in the area. The heavy losses faced by the military during these operations thrice made the government enter a peace pact with the militant leaders between 2004–7 and forced it to make major concessions to the militants. In the September 2006 peace pact between the Pakistani government and local tribesmen in North Waziristan, for instance, the Pakistani Army agreed to dismantle checkpoints it had set up recently inside North Waziristan, release tribesmen it had arrested and return weapons it had confiscated, in return for a promise that tribesmen would stop attacking the military and cease cross-border infiltration into Afghanistan. The strength of these militant groups had to be recognized when Baitullah Mehsud, a local Taliban leader, held 250 Pakistani soldiers hostage in the autumn of 2007. In addition, three other factors point towards the increasing complexity of religious militancy in Pakistan.

First, the presence of militants has now spread out of the tribal belt to the rest of the country. This became clear in the Red Mosque standoff, where between January and July 2007, the clerics of the central mosque of Islamabad, with support from over 6,000 male and female students, were involved in bloody fighting with the state organs besieging their compound, demanding an end to military operations in the tribal belt and imposition of Sharia law. The military operation that ended their resistance in July 2007 resulted in the deaths of 100 students, but did not deter another cleric in Swat (a settled area in the NWFP), who had for some time been running a local FM radio channel on Islam, to take up arms for the imposition of Sharia. Since 2008, the Pakistani military has routinely carried out operations against alleged militant hideouts in settled areas of the NWFP.

Second, there is further blurring of an already vague enemy. After seven years of the military operations and intelligence gathering, the government of Pakistan still cannot identify these militants beyond superficial labels. The already blurred distinction between Afghan Taliban and Pakistani Taliban has been further diluted by a continuously increasing number of splinter organizations claiming to represent the latter – for example, *Fidayeen-e-Islam*, a radical group which claimed responsibility for the suicide attack that razed the multi-story Marriott building in Islamabad in September 2008, had no prior history. There is little understanding within the public or the state officials of the differences in the membership base, motives or strategies of these groups. What is clear, however, is that these groups are no longer purely fighting for the assertion of the Muslim faith, which was the stated mission of the Talibans who formed the government of Afghanistan between 1996 and 2001 (Rashid 2000); instead, Pashtun ethnicity, with its emphasis on revenge and honour (Ahmed 1980, 1986), plays an important role in the organization and recruitment of these groups. As things stand today, it is very difficult to differentiate between religiously and ethnically motivated fighters.

Third, the method of attack used by these militant groups has moved towards the extreme option, namely suicide attacks, which were unknown in Pakistan prior to the 11 September 2001 attacks in the US. These suicide attacks have primarily been targeted at military and police personnel. Despite the military operations and intelligence sharing between Pakistan and Western intelligence agencies, the persistence of these militant groups has in recent months led to concerns in Western circles about continued support for militant groups within elements of the Pakistani military and intelligence agencies

(Grare 2007). Such speculations have, in turn, prompted Pakistani government officials to accuse external forces of financially and militarily supporting these groups in their efforts to destabilize Pakistan.

The threat posed by these groups to the stability of the Pakistani state becomes more pronounced when analysed against the existing ethnic tensions marking the relations of three smaller provinces with the federal government, which is seen as being dominated by Punjab province – the most populated province of the country, which thus has the largest representation in the parliament. The three smaller provinces of Pakistan, namely Sindh, the NWFP and Balochistan, nurture strong nationalist movements (Jaffrelot 2002); the situation is most tense in Balochistan, which is the poorest province, but rich in mineral resources. Balochistan is estimated to receive only 12.4 per cent of the total royalty it is rightfully due from the national government for utilization of its natural gas reserves (Grare 2006). Weakening of the state at the centre can also reinvigorate the Sindhi and Pashtun nationalist movements; the country already suffered at the hands of the Bengali resistance movement in 1971, when the East Pakistan province of Bengal became the independent state of Bangladesh (Sisson and Rose 1992). A destabilized Pakistan, whether resulting from such internal frictions or external interference, will create a major regional disaster, leaving its population of 150 million people free to wreak chaos on the already porous and fragile borders with the states of India, Afghanistan and Iran. Neither is an instable Pakistan in the interests of the world community, as Pakistan is also a nuclear power. There are already serious concerns about the role of Dr. Abdul Qadeer Khan, known as the father of the Pakistani bomb (Zahid 1992), in nuclear proliferation. He is accused of having sold nuclear technology to Iran, Libya and North Korea. Due to such concerns, as well as the unclear control and command structure (Gregory 2007) – the former prime ministers of Pakistan, Nawaz Sharif and Benazir Bhutto, have said that the military command refused to give them information about basic facts (such as the current status of the nuclear arsenal, plans for future acquisitions) on the country's nuclear weapons – as well as fears of an Islamist lobby within the Pakistani intelligence, made a recent panel of US Congress conclude: 'Were one to map terrorism and weapons of mass destruction today, all roads would intersect in Pakistan' (Smith 2008).

Causes of insecurity

There is a dearth of serious academic analysis on the causes of militancy in Pakistan; the few reports produced by US and Western think tanks, which draw on anecdotal evidence rather than rigorous analysis of data, place emphasis on both the ideological and structural factors (Stern 2000; Singer 2001; ICG 2002). The most widely argued position is that the primary source of militancy in Pakistan is the religious indoctrination of children from poor families within the madrassas (Islamic seminaries). These children, lacking options for making a decent living, are easily swayed by jihadi ideology with its promises of otherworldly rewards. Studies of religious militancy in the Middle Eastern context, however, provide more nuanced analysis of the role of ideology and structural deprivations in harbouring Muslim extremism. While initial scholarship placed the onus of responsibility on the hegemonic aspirations within Muslim theology, an increasing number of scholars argue for noting the importance of structural factors, namely economic deprivation, disenchantment with unrepresentative political leaders and the failure of Muslim states to deliver the promises of modernity (Esposito 1992; Eickelman and Piscatori 1996). Euben (1999), conversely, argues for taking into account the moral appeal of the Islamic ideals, which arguably provide equally appealing, though alternative notions of modernity. Studies of Muslim militancy in different contexts also identify secular colleges and universities rather than madrassas as the primary conduit for recruiting militants (Esposito 1992; Eickelman and Piscatori 1996; Lapidus 1997; Ricolfi 2005). The educational biographies of 300 known members of violent Islamist groups from 30 countries show that the vast majority – 69 percent – had attended college, and of those with clear areas of study, nearly half had gone into engineering (Gambetta and Hertog 2006). Though this literature remains yet to be developed in the context of Pakistan, the recognition of the role of ideology and socio-economic deprivation, the failure of governance, regional dynamics and the relationship with the US provide useful pointers to understanding the causes of militancy in Pakistan.

Ideology and economics

The purely ideological explanations prove inadequate to explain the current strands of Islamic militancy in Pakistan, given the insufficient evidence of links between madrassas and jihadis. What is evident, however, is a genuine appreciation for Islam in society and a deep sense of affiliation with the Muslim ummah. In a country that emerged in response to a demand for a separate homeland for the Muslims, Islam remains an important mobilizing force (Nasr 1994; Haqqani 2005). The religious parties, such as Jamiat Ulema-e-Pakistan (Barelvi), Jamiat Ulema-e-Islam-F (JUI-F) and Jamaat-e-Islami, continue to exert pressure for the imposition of Sharia law (Cohen 2004). Furthermore, though claims linking madrassas to jihad remain unsubstantiated, the presence of 16,000 registered madrassas and many times more unregistered Quranic schools reflects the high value placed on Quranic education in Pakistani society. One study shows that 98 per cent of parents want some Muslim education for their child in addition to the secular education (Nelson 2006). Zulfiqar Ali Bhutto, the prime minister who laid the foundation of Pakistan's nuclear programme, advertised it as an 'Islamic bomb' to Middle Eastern allies (Cohen 2004). This strong preference for Islam leads to the harbouring of a sense of injustice against the West, especially the US, for what many within the Pakistani public perceive to be the latter's unwavering support for Israel. The US failure to develop a long-term strategy towards Pakistan, as elaborated in a later section, has not helped overcome this distrust, either.

The theories linking socio-economic deprivation with the rise of radical Islam also find support in Pakistan: thirty-three per cent of the population live below the poverty line and 60 per cent are illiterate, while an equal number have no access to basic health or sanitation facilities (MHHDC 2008). Pakistan, along with Nigeria, will account for one-third of the world's out-of-school children by 2015 (UNESCO 2008). Nevertheless, the Pakistani state prefers to spend 3.4 per cent of its GDP on the military, compared to 1.2 per cent for the social sector (Nawaz 2008). Pakistan's defence budget is only one-fifth of India's, but it consumes a higher percentage of Pakistan's GDP and supports 619,000 personnel (HoC 2007). Such extreme deprivation increases the probability of young men embarking on jihad out of a sense of frustration; it also makes them vulnerable to joining radical elements for promises of financial compensation. Thus, while economic vulnerability does not account for the planners of the militant groups, it does help provide a potential pool of foot soldiers.

Failure of governance: civil–military dynamics

The causes of this failure of human development rest in the failure of governance. The political power has been concentrated in a handful of feudal and business elites, who have been reluctant to establish representative democratic institutions (Noman 1990; Zaidi 1999). In addition, repeated military interventions (Pakistan has been ruled by four generals for more than 40 out of its 62 years of existence) have further checked progress towards the establishment of representative political institutions (Jalal 1990). Even the devolution plan launched in 2000 by General Musharraf's regime aimed to weaken the provinces *vis-à-vis* the federal government by devolving many of their powers to the lower tier of government, but failed to delegate any of the powers from the centre to the provinces (ICG 2004). The result of such concentration of power in the hands of a few has been widespread corruption and bad governance: in 2006, the US Fund for Peace's Failed States Index ranked Pakistan in ninth place, one place worse than Afghanistan (HoC 2007). Thus, an absence of representative institutions has led to the socio-economic deprivation that has, in turn, facilitated the mobilization of young people to radical groups.

Since 11 September 2001, military rule in Pakistan has also contributed to increasing militancy in Pakistan in an indirect manner. The support that the US government provided to General Musharraf in return for the latter's role as an ally in the 'war on terror' created perverse incentives for the Musharraf regime to sustain Islamic militancy in the country (Bennett-Jones 2002; Grare 2007). With only weak domestic legitimacy, which over time eroded further as the government failed to improve the living conditions for ordinary Pakistanis, General Musharraf's regime relied largely on the financial and diplomatic support of its Western allies (Cohen and Chollet 2007; ICG 2004). General Musharraf was repeatedly accused in the domestic press of deliberately projecting a militant image of Pakistan, especially when on foreign tours, to retain Western backing for his regime. At the peak of the Red Mosque standoff, a major segment of the population believed that the government itself had engineered the confrontation to threaten the West with radical alternatives if support for Musharraf's government was withdrawn.

Role of regional dynamics

In addition to the role of ideology and economics and the failure of governance in shaping Islamic militancy in Pakistan, regional dynamics have played a major role in mobilizing Pakistani youth for jihad. The unresolved issue of Kashmir (a territory that has remained disputed between India and Pakistan since the time of the partition, and two-thirds of which remains under Indian control, though being inhabited by a largely Muslim population) has helped the Pakistani military mobilize the *mujahideen* to fight for the 'Muslim Kashmiri brother' (Ganguly 1986; Schofield 2000). This has had two negative consequences for Pakistan: the Kashmir issue has helped mobilize jihadi sentiment in Pakistan; and, more importantly, this tension has helped the Pakistani military claim a higher share of the government annual budget and as a result has strengthened the military *vis-à-vis* the civilian governments. The fear of a bigger hostile neighbour has enhanced the prestige of the Pakistani army, giving the chief of army staff (COAS), i.e. the highest-ranking general in the Pakistani army, greater legitimacy to stage repeated coups (Jalal 1990; Cohen 1998; Siddiqa-Agha 2007), which, as noted above, has been a major cause of human insecurity in Pakistan.

While state involvement with jihadis began sporadically around Kashmir, it was Pakistan's proximity with Afghanistan that created an opportunity for the state to make serious efforts to establish jihadi organizations (Yousaf and Adkin 1992). The links between the Pakistani state and jihadi organizations were formalized in the 1980s, when the Pakistani state and intelligence agencies, in particular the Inter-Services Intelligence (ISI), supported by the US and Saudi Arabia, played a critical role in training the *mujahideen* to fight against the Soviets in the Soviet–Afghanistan war (Rashid 2000; Cohen and Chollet 2007). This association between elements within the ISI and Islamic militants was further strengthened under the Taliban rule in Afghanistan (Rashid 2000). The Western governments to date remain suspicious of links between elements in the ISI and Muslim militants (Grare 2007) – a concern repeatedly voiced by the Indian and US governments in the aftermath of the 2008 Mumbai attacks. Thus, regional dynamics have played a critical role in developing a close bond between the Pakistani military and the militant groups. China, however, remains a longstanding ally of Pakistan and has assisted in the development of its nuclear weapons and ballistic programmes (Bennett-Jones 2002).

The relationship with the US

A close ally of the US since its inception in 1947, where it supported the US in the Cold War and later in the Soviet–Afghan war, Pakistan has repeatedly been ignored by the US and even labelled a rogue state soon after the US attained its objectives. Pakistan has made many efforts to work with the US. In the late 1950s, Pakistan allowed the construction of a then secret air base in Peshawar from which U-2 intelligence aircraft made reconnaissance flights over the Soviet Union; in the 1980s, it helped the US efforts to push back against the Soviets in Afghanistan; and, since 2001, it has been an active ally in the 'war on terror'. However, US policy towards Pakistan has been shaped by short-term concerns advanced through supporting military generals in Pakistan rather than developing a long-term strategy of engagement with the Pakistani public (Cohen and Chollet 2007).

As a result, Pakistanis view the US as an untrustworthy ally that befriends the country's leadership when it suits its geo-political interests and is quick to sever the links once those objectives are met; it is increasingly seen as a more natural ally of India, whose expanding market is arguably more attractive for US commercial interests. The 'quid pro quo' nature of this engagement with Pakistan, where successive US governments have financially compensated the respective military governments in Pakistan for delivering the required results rather than investing in a long-term engagement with the Pakistani public (Cohen and Chollet 2007), has on the one hand reinforced the anti-Muslim image of the US among the conservatives, and on the other has alienated the Pakistani liberals who find the US an unreliable partner in their fight for democracy. The strong sense of belonging to the Muslim Ummah and a sense of injustice concerning US policies towards the Middle East and its support for military regimes in Pakistan have thus helped foster militant sentiment within the Pakistani public.

Interactions between the US and Pakistani officials since 2001 have followed the same pattern: the US has preferred to fight the entire 'war on terror' by providing very personalized incentives to General Musharraf's regime rather than by investing in long-term institutional reforms in Pakistan. The public was never brought on board to support the 'war on terror'. The greatest part (around 57 per cent) of the US$10 billion that the US has provided to Pakistan since 11 September 2001 has gone towards Coalition Support

Funds, money intended to reimburse US partners for their assistance in the 'war on terror' (Cohen and Chollet 2007; Grare 2007), and less than 10 per cent has gone towards development and humanitarian assistance. Pakistan's education sector, which the 9/11 Commission report argued should be central to US engagement in Pakistan, 'received only $64 million per year for more than 55 million school-aged children, or $1.16 per child per year' (Cohen and Chollet 2007). The reliance on the military option over a development or diplomatic one has strengthened the reactionary sentiment in the local population, especially in the NWFP region. Furthermore, the strategy of compensating Pakistani military and intelligence officials for handing over Pakistani suspects to US authorities (Musharraf 2006), without giving them a trial in the country and without informing their families has made the 'war on terror' lose all legitimacy in the public perception.

Conclusion

The increased scale of Muslim militancy within Pakistan since 11 September 2001, where the militant groups operating within the country are no longer focused exclusively on cross-border targets, but rather are increasingly fighting the Pakistani state, raises serious threats to the country's stability. The case of Pakistan illustrates how the different dimensions of security, such as a lack of investment in human capital, regional tensions, territorial insecurity, weak civil–military relations and the geo-strategic importance of a country, feed into each other and contribute to the rise of militancy. It is clear that there is no one source of militancy, such as religious indoctrination in Islamic schools; nor is there a single solution to the problem. Instead, there is a need for a multi-pronged strategy that addresses some of the core causes of insecurity.

First, the push for reform has to come from the Pakistani government rather than being dictated from the outside. The Pakistani government is best placed to assess the domestic situation; it is also more likely to convince the local population that fighting religious militancy is in Pakistan's own interest. If the counter-militancy measures continue to be viewed as being imposed by the US, the 'war on terror' will not win the support of the Pakistani public.

Second, regional dynamics will be critical in shaping the future of Islamic militancy in Pakistan. As long as the Kashmir dispute remains unresolved, Pakistan will have a strong incentive to stay engaged with the religious extremist insurgents there. This is the one area where the international community needs to help reach a solution – given the internal politics of this issue, India and Pakistan are unlikely to reach a compromise on their own. The success of US and allied troops in checking militant groups in Afghanistan and better regulating the Pakistan–Afghanistan border will be another important factor.

Third, civil–military dynamics will also play a role in determining the future of Islamic militancy. The military governments might be more willing to push the Western policies within the country, but they are not good at winning popular support for them. Most importantly, reliance on military regimes to fight Islamic militancy is a dangerous strategy because it creates vested incentives for these regimes to actually support militancy. Strengthening democracy is vital for finding long-term solutions to the challenge of Muslim militancy in Pakistan.

Fourth, serious financial investments in the social sector are required, especially in the field of education. Better education opportunities will not only reduce the demand for madrassas, but will also provide a route out of poverty that makes young men vulnerable to joining jihadi groups. This requires that the institutions disbursing aid to Pakistan put in place better accountability mechanisms so that development funds are used more effectively.

Finally, it is important to note that, while these internal reforms are critical for checking religious militancy in Pakistan, eradicating extremism altogether will remain a challenging task for as long as international disputes over issues such as Palestine, Iraq, Afghanistan and Kashmir remain unresolved. The sense of belonging to the Ummah does play a role in mobilizing the *mujahideen*. This requires a review of the effectiveness of the 'war on terror' strategies as implemented not just in Pakistan, but also across the globe.

References

Ahmed, A.S. (1980) *Pukhtun Economy & Society: Traditional Structure and Economic Development in Tribal Society*, London: Routledge.

——(1986) *Pakistan Society: Islam, Ethnicity and Leadership in South Asia*, Karachi: Oxford University Press.

Ahmed, S. and Cortright, D. (eds) (1998) *Pakistan and the Bomb: Public Opinion and Nuclear Options*, Notre Dame, IN: University of Notre Dame Press.

Ali, T. (1983) *Can Pakistan Survive*, Middlesex: Penguin Books.

Ali, Z. (2007) *Pakistan's Nuclear Assets and Threats of Terrorism: How Grave is the Danger?*, Washington, DC: The Henry L. Stimson Center.

Amin, S.M. (2000) *Pakistan's Foreign Policy: A Reappraisal*, Karachi: Oxford University Press.

BBC (2008) 'Militants claim Marriott attack', *BBC News*, 22 September. Available online at: http://news.bbc.co.uk/1/hi/world/south_asia/7630024.stm (accessed 10 February 2009).

Bennett-Jones, O. (2002) *Pakistan: Eye of the Storm*, New Haven and London: Yale University Press.

Brookes, P. (2007) 'Peril in Pakistan', *Armed Forces Journal*, June. Available online at: www.armedforces journal.com/2007/06/2732023 (accessed 12 March 2009).

Burki, S.M. and Ziring, L. (1990) *Pakistan's Foreign Policy: An Historical Analysis*, Karachi: Oxford University Press.

Cohen, C. and Chollet, D. (2007) 'When $10 billion is not enough: Rethinking U.S. strategy towards Pakistan', *The Washington Quarterly* 30, 2: 7–20.

Cohen, S.P.C. (1998) *The Pakistan Army*, Karachi: Oxford University Press.

——(2004) *The Idea of Pakistan*, Washington, DC: Brookings Institution Press.

Curtis, L. (2007) *Pakistan: Defense and Security Challenges*, Heritage Lectures. Washington, DC: The Heritage Foundation.

Department for International Development (DFID) (2008) *Pakistan: Country Profile*. Available online at: www.dfid.gov.uk/countries/asia/Pakistan.asp (accessed 10 February 2009).

Eickelman, D.F. and Piscatori, J. (1996) *Muslim Politics*, Princeton, NJ: Princeton University Press.

Esposito, J. (1992) *The Islamic Threat: Myth or Reality*, New York: Oxford University Press.

Euben, R. (1999) *Enemy in the Mirror: Islamic Fundamentalism and the Limits of Modern Rationalism – A Work of Comparative Political Theory*, Princeton, NJ: Princeton University Press.

Gambetta, D. and Hertog, S. (2006) 'Engineers of jihad', *Sociology Working Papers: Paper No. 2007–10*, Department of Sociology: University of Oxford.

Ganguly, S. (1986) *The Origins of War in South Asia: Indo-Pakistan Conflicts since 1947*, Boulder, CO and London: Westview Press.

Grare, F. (2006) *Pakistan: The Resurgence of Baluch Nationalism*, Carnegie Endowment Papers, No. 65, Washington, DC: Carnegie Endowment for International Peace.

——(2007) *Rethinking Western Strategies Towards Pakistan: An Action Agenda for the United States and Europe*, Carnegie Endowment Report, Washington, DC: Carnegie Endowment for International Peace.

Gregory, S. (2007) *The Security of Nuclear Weapons in Pakistan*, Pakistan Security Research Unit, University of Bradford, Brief Number 22.

Haqqani, H. (2005) *Pakistan: Between Mosque and Military*, Lahore: Vanguard Books.

297

House of Commons (HoC) Library (2007). *Pakistan's Political and Security Challenges*, Research Papers 07/68, 13 September.

International Crisis Group (ICG), Pakistan (2002) 'Madrasas, extremism, and the military', *Asia Report 36*, Islamabad: ICG.

——(2004) 'Devolution in Pakistan: Reform or regression?' *Asia Report* 77, Islamabad: International Crisis Group.

——(2006) 'Pakistan's tribal areas: Appeasing the militants', *Asia Report 125*, Islamabad: International Crisis Group.

Jaffrelot, C. (2002) 'Nationalism without a nation: Pakistan searching for its identity', in Christophe, J. (ed.) *Pakistan; Nationalism without a Nation?* New Delhi: Zed Books.

Jalal, A. (1990) *The State of Martial Rule: The Origins of Pakistan's Policy Economy of Defence*, Cambridge: Cambridge University Press.

Lapidus, I. (1997) 'Islamic revival and modernity: The contemporary movements and historical paradigms', *Journal or Economic and Social History of the Orient* 40, 4: 444–60.

Mahbub ul Haq Human Development Centre (MHHDC) (2008) *Human Development in South Asia 2007*, Islamabad: Pakistan.

Markey, D. (2007) 'False choice in Pakistan', *Foreign Affairs* 86, 4: 85–102.

Moreau, R. and Hirsh, M. (2007) 'Where the jihad lives now', *Newsweek*, 29 October. Available online at: www.newsweek.com/id/57485 (accessed 10 February 2009).

Musharraf, P. (2006) *In the Line of Fire: A Memoir*, New York: Free Press.

Nasr, S.V.R. (1994) *The Vanguard of the Islamic Revolution: The Jamaat-i Islami of Pakistan*, Berkeley: University of California Press.

Nawaz, S. (2008) *Crossed Swords: Pakistan, its Army, and the Wars Within*, Karachi: Oxford University Press.

Nelson, M.J. (2006) 'Muslims, markets and the meaning of a "good" education in Pakistan', *Asian Survey* 46, 5: 699–720.

Noman, O. (1990) *Pakistan: A Political and Economic History since 1947*, London: Kegan Paul International.

Piscatori, J. (1988) *Islam in a World of Nation-States*, Cambridge: Cambridge University Press.

Rafique, N. (2008) *US Presidential Debates 2008 – Foreign Policy Concerns and Perspectives*. Situational Paper. Islamabad: Institutes of Strategic Studies Islamabad. Available online at: www.issi.org.pk/situational_paper/2008_files/Debate_Table.pdf (accessed 10 February 2009).

Rashid, A. (2000) *Talibans*, London: I.B. Tauris.

Ricolfi, L. (2005) 'Palestinians, 1981–2003', in Gambetta, D. (ed.) *Making Sense of Suicide Missions*, Oxford: Oxford University Press, pp. 77–129.

Rizvi, H.A. (2000) *Military, State and Society in Pakistan*, London: Macmillan Press.

Roy, O. (1990) *Islam and Resistance in Afghanistan*, Cambridge: Cambridge University Press.

Schofield, V. (2000) *Kashmir in Conflict*, London: I.B. Tauris.

Siddiqa-Agha, A. (2007) *Military Inc.: Inside Pakistan's Military Economy*, London: Pluto.

Singer, P.W. (2001) *Pakistan's Madrasahs: Ensuring a System of Education not Jihad*, Brooking Institute Analysis Paper No. 21.

Sisson, R. and Rose, L. (1992) *War and Secession: Pakistan, India and the Creation of Bangladesh*, Oxford: Oxford University Press.

Smith, E. (2008) 'Panel foresees unconventional terror threat', *International Herald Tribune*. 1 December 2008. Available online at: www.iht.com/articles/2008/12/01/america/terror.php (accessed 10 February 2009).

Stern, J. (2000) 'Pakistan's jihad culture', *Foreign Affairs* 79, 6: 115–26.

The Economist (2008) 'Pakistan: The world's most dangerous place', *The Economist* Available online at: www.economist.com/opinion/displaystory.cfm?story_id=10430237 (accessed 10 February 2009).

United Nations Educational, Scientific and Cultural Organization (UNESCO) (2008) *Overcoming Inequality: Why Governance Matters*, Paris: UNESCO.

Yousaf, M. and Adkin, M. (1992) *The Bear Trap: Afghanistan's Untold Story*, London: Leo Cooper.

Zahid, M. (1992) *Dr. Abdul Qadeer Khan and the Islamic Bomb*, Islamabad: Hurmat.

Zaidi, A.S. (1999) *Issues in Pakistan's Economy*, Karachi: Oxford University Press.

27

Afghanistan

A state in crisis

Amin Saikal

Afghanistan has historically been characterized by weak state power in dynamic tension with a strong society. Its population is composed of various ethnic, tribal, linguistic, cultural and religious groups forming distinct micro-societies, with most of them having extensive cross-border ties with Afghanistan's neighbours. These social and cultural divisions have traditionally played a critical role in attempts to create national unity and institutionalized processes of state building in the country. Although the turbulence of the past 30 years has profoundly affected Afghanistan, the country's micro-societies have remained salient in shaping Afghan politics and society. However, since the attacks in the US on 11 September 2001 and Washington's immediate response to them, three additional factors, partly grounded in these social divisions, have come to undermine quite seriously the process of stabilization and reconstruction of Afghanistan: the fragmentation and corruption of the governing elite, the flawed strategy of the US and its NATO allies in dealing with Afghanistan's problems and the strengthening of counter-systemic actors. These are the key issues on which this chapter focuses.

Background

Afghanistan has been a seriously disrupted country ever since the pro-Soviet communist coup of 27 April 1978, which brought to power a cluster of Marxist–Leninists within the People's Democratic Party of Afghanistan (PDPA). This cluster had no internal cohesion, historical legitimacy, administrative experience or popular base of support to achieve its publicly professed goal of transforming Afghanistan – a traditional, multifaceted Muslim country – into a modern Socialist state. As the PDPA disintegrated into factionalism and faced growing popular resistance from religious groups, the Soviet Union finally invaded Afghanistan in late December 1979 to save the rule of the PDPA and to protect its own long-standing political, economic and military investment in Afghanistan, where it had been engaged in the context of the Cold War since the mid-1950s.

However, three factors prevented the Soviets from accomplishing their mission. First, they could not unite the PDPA's rival factions to create an effective government in

Kabul. Second, they could not convince either the Afghan people or the international community that the invasion was justified. Third, the US and its allies found a unique opportunity to inflict a mortal blow on the USSR by backing various Afghan Muslim resistance groups (the *mujahideen*) to mount a jihad ('holy war') against the Soviet occupation. In the process, they helped to mobilize a large number of volunteers from the Muslim world, especially from Arab countries, to assist the *mujahideen*, and used the neighbouring Muslim country of Pakistan as the main conduit for financial, logistical and military support.

The Soviet defeat and withdrawal from Afghanistan by May 1989 opened the way for the *mujahideen* to institute a conservative religious government for the first time in Afghan history. Meanwhile, the US dramatically scaled down its involvement in Afghanistan, leaving the post-conflict management of the country to its predatory and rival neighbours, particularly Pakistan. The *mujahideen* consisted of a number of disparate groups divided along ethnic, tribal, linguistic, sectarian and personality lines, reflecting the socially divided nature of the Afghan society. As they turned their guns on one another, Afghanistan was plunged into an internecine conflict.

To advance its regional interests, which largely coincided with those of the US and several pro-Western conservative Arab states (led by Saudi Arabia), particularly against the Iranian Islamic regime, Pakistan, or more specifically its powerful Inter-Services Intelligence (ISI) military intelligence service, found it expedient to raise a new extremist Islamic force – the Taliban – to take power in Afghanistan. The Taliban took over Kabul in September 1996, and within two years were in control of 80 per cent of Afghanistan. Commander Ahmed Shah Massoud, who had previously served as the defence minister in the government of the *mujahideen* leader Burhanuddin Rabbani, retreated to north-eastern Afghanistan, now to fight what was widely perceived as Pakistan's 'creeping invasion'. At the same time, a prominent Saudi veteran of the Afghan jihad, Osama bin Laden, accompanied by many of his al-Qaida operatives, returned (via Pakistan) to Afghanistan to help the Taliban in return for safe sanctuaries. In 1997, bin Laden was joined by the leader of the Egyptian Islamic Jihad, Ayman al-Zawahiri and many of his supporters, strengthening the al-Qaida network.

It was from Afghanistan that the al-Qaida leadership masterminded a number of terrorist operations against US targets. The most significant of these were the 11 September 2001 attacks on New York and Washington, which prompted the US to retaliate with military operations against the Taliban and al-Qaida in Afghanistan, as well as a broader so-called 'global war on terrorism'. By November 2001, the Taliban government had been toppled. A month later, the internationally backed government of Hamid Karzai was installed to transform Afghanistan into a secure, viable and democratic state. However, neither the Karzai government nor its international backers, particularly the US, have been able to achieve their objectives so far. The reasons for this failure are embedded in the following.

Elite fragmentation

The fragmentation of the governing elite has proved to be highly damaging to Afghanistan's transition. Although all elite elements have expressed public allegiance to Islam as the common thread running through Afghan micro-societies, they are in general divided into two informal clusters. One is made up of those who have taken over the reins of power primarily on the basis of an alliance with the US and signed up to American-induced processes of secular change, democratization and the so-called 'war on terror-ism'. The other is composed of those who have entered a nominal partnership with the first cluster, but have grown highly sceptical of the US approach and agenda.

The first cluster is essentially led by the US-backed President Hamid Karzai. It has included many figures who have come from the ranks of the Afghan diaspora, primarily from the US and Europe, and currently occupy most of the important cabinet posts, specifically the Ministries of Defence, Finance, the Interior, the Economy and Foreign Affairs. Lacking popular constituencies of their own in Afghanistan, they have generally grown dependent on the US and therefore vulnerable to the ideological and policy preferences of the administration of President George W. Bush (2001–9). Initially, the overall goal was not only to marginalize the defiant anti-US radical forces of political Islam, most importantly al-Qaida and its supporters, but also to cement the position of the US as the only superpower in the twenty-first century.

Zalmay Khalilzad, an Afghan-born American neoconservative and US presidential envoy to Afghanistan from late 2001 to late 2003 and then ambassador to the country from 2003–5, played a determining part in managing Afghanistan's transition according to the new US foreign-policy agenda. He acted so vigorously that he gained a reputation as being the real ruler of Afghanistan. Despite serving as US ambassador to Iraq (2005–7) and then to the UN (2007–9), he continued an intimate involvement in the conduct of US Afghanistan policy, especially through a close relationship with Karzai and some of the high-ranking members of his entourage, in whose appointment he had a critical hand.

From the start, President Karzai and many of his cohorts actively worked towards a strong presidential system of government, which was enshrined in a new constitution adopted by a Loya Jirga (the traditional Afghan assembly) in January 2004. In the process, they ignored warnings that such a system was unlikely to work in a war-torn country like Afghanistan with its myriad tribal, ethnic, linguistic and sectarian divisions, and that it would typically produce one winner and many disgruntled but powerful losers with the capability to challenge or undermine the victor. A more suitable alternative proposal was to create a parliamentary system of government, with the executive power resting with a prime minister and his/her cabinet to be drawn from the parliament (see Saikal and Maley 2008). There were two important reasons. First, it would provide for a range of actors to be locked in a framework of national obligations and responsibilities, giving them involvement in national affairs. On the one hand, it would give micro-societies the necessary degree of autonomy in the exercise of their local affairs; while on the other hand, it would embed them in the overall political system through their local representative bodies and the national parliament. Second, it would not place too much burden on one individual, who could easily become the focus of public discontent if things went wrong. In the meantime, it would prevent the winner from using the powers of his office to build up a system of patronage and from acting as a delegative leader between elections, particularly in the absence of a firm separation of powers, of the rule of law, established systems of checks and balances, and of effective mechanisms of public scrutiny.

Under the 2004 constitution, Afghanistan also elected a two-chamber parliament in 2005. Only individuals were allowed to stand for election, while political parties were banned under electoral legislation. This parliament has been far from perfect: it is a fragmented body, reflecting partly the fragmented nature of the Afghan society and partly Karzai's original opposition to party politics. Its members have operated within informal groupings and ad hoc alliances, based mostly on tribal, religious, factional and ethnic allegiances. It includes many strong local power holders or warlords, many of whom have records of human rights violations and are determined to do whatever it takes to protect themselves against any public scrutiny and prosecution. In many ways, the assembly is reminiscent of the highly fragmented and ineffective parliaments that existed under the monarchy of King Mohammad Zahir during the period of 'New Democracy' (1964–73), when governments often had to resort to bribery, nepotism and temporary alliances and counter-alliances to ensure the passage of their bills or to secure a vote of confidence for ministers (for a detailed discussion, see Saikal 2006, chapter 6).

Even so, the present parliament has proved to be far more representative than any before it. It was elected on the basis of universal suffrage, through a process endorsed by a number of credible international observers as largely fair and free. It has provided a venue for a range of voices to be heard, and has the potential to act more effectively than it has so far in fulfilling its constitutional duties. However, the executive branch has vigorously sought to marginalize the role of parliament in the processes of governance.

The growing lack of trust between the executive and legislative branches has seriously undermined the processes of building inter-institutional cooperation and institutionalized rather than personalized politics in Afghanistan. One of Afghanistan's deep-seated problems has historically been that power and political culture in the country have revolved around political personalities rather than political institutions as the foundation for stability and continuity. Political institutions have risen and fallen with personalities, rather than the former governing and regulating the behaviour of the latter. When the Taliban were ousted, Karzai, who enjoyed more international support than any of his predecessors, had a unique opportunity to turn a new page in Afghan history in this respect. However, his actions have perpetuated dysfunctional Afghan political traditions.

Karzai has behaved more or less like any other Pashtun *khan* or tribal leader. He has used his powers and international support to fill important governmental positions on the basis of family, tribal, ethnic and factional connections and to build patronage networks based on a system of favour and disfavour (Risen 2008). While Karzai has largely been bottled up in the presidential palace, some of his ministers have turned various ministries into disconnected fiefdoms, often operating independently of the president. There has been little effort to institute reforms and to create a unified, viable administration equipped with a well-trained and effective bureaucracy.

Despite his initial promise to downplay the role of ethnicity in the interest of national unity, Karzai has increasingly found it expedient to pander to his own ethnic group, the Pashtuns. Populating mainly southern and eastern Afghanistan along the border with Pakistan, the Pashtuns have historically been made up of rival tribes (most importantly the Durranis, to which Karzai and most of his cohorts belong, and the Ghilzais, who make up the bulk of the Taliban and their supporters). The Pashtuns have traditionally formed the single largest cluster, but not the majority of the Afghan population. By leaning towards the Pashtuns, Karzai in effect has promoted a policy of ethnic imbalance, which has caused growing concern among the non-Pashtun segments of the population. The latter suffered enormously under the highly discriminatory theocratic rule of the Taliban rule (1996–2001) and waged an armed opposition to it (for details, see Rashid 2000).

The second cluster within the governing elite has generally been composed of those who have felt increasingly uncomfortable with Afghanistan's pro-Western transformation and Washington's decisive role in the process. They have advocated a more indigenously based, pro-Islamic mode of change and one that is ostensibly more in tune with the social and cultural milieu of Afghanistan, as well as a more independent foreign policy posture. This cluster includes many Afghans who remained in Afghanistan during the long years of turmoil preceding the US-led intervention; have had their own power bases in Afghanistan; and come from a strong traditional religious background, but have found it expedient to join the governing elite as the best way to advance their personal ambitions and protect the interests of their constituencies. They include many former *mujahideen* leaders and local strongmen who have emerged since the fall of the Taliban. A number of them hold formal government positions.

Although these two clusters have not been cohesive and have involved a degree of inter-cluster fluidity, some elements within the second cluster have acted from time to time as a counter-elite. They have sought, either through string pulling within the government or through direct civil society activities, to influence government policies according to their preferences. In this, they have resorted to various civilian and military organs of the state (most importantly the cabinet and parliament); private print and electronic media outlets; and even peaceful public agitation, as well as pandering to the armed opposition whenever appropriate, to maximize pressure on the Karzai-led cluster.

Such elite fragmentation (Saikal 2006) has resulted not only in highly damaging political intrigues and rivalries, but also in a lack of clear ideological direction within the government. From the start, the government has been unclear on what it precisely stands for: is it a pro-Western secular democracy, with a pro-capitalist mode of development? Such an approach would be in line with the preferences of the US and its allies, with which a great majority of the Afghan people have not traditionally been able to identify. Or is it a blend of Western and Afghan values and practices, amalgamated with traditions of religious authoritarianism?

The problems at the elite level are echoed within the population at large, particularly in the major urban centres. The years since the pro-Soviet Communist coup of April 1978 have been marked by turbulence, bloodshed, uncertainty and unpredictability. During this time, at least four different ideological groups have seized power in Afghanistan. Many ordinary citizens have had to deal with deceitful and corrupt practices in order to survive.

At the same time, the external involvement of too many state and non-state actors in Afghanistan's transition has created a culture of dependency and complacency. As many of these actors have not been driven by altruistic aims, their activities have enhanced rather than diminished the culture of corruption and bribery among the Afghans. Society at large has become in many ways as dysfunctional and corrupt as the state bureaucracy.

US and NATO strategy

From the inception, the US as the driving power in Afghanistan failed to map out a strategy to integrate Afghanistan's security building with the country's political and economic reconstruction. The US initially deployed only 10,000 troops, toppling – but not defeating – the Taliban and their al-Qaida supporters. Other NATO countries contributed 5,000 troops to the International Security Assistance Force (ISAF) in Kabul. ISAF came under a separate command from the US forces, and there was little coordination between the two contingents. While ISAF was initially only tasked with securing Kabul in support of the Karzai government, the US troops, who formed the bulk of the international military presence as part of 'Operation Enduring Freedom', were focused on hunting down al-Qaida and Taliban leaders. This level of troop deployment soon proved to be inadequate in a country that had been seriously disrupted by 24 years of warfare and bloodshed. It left the field wide open for the Taliban, their supporters and a range of other sub-national actors – from local warlords and poppy farmers to drug traffickers and criminal gangs – to regroup and start making a comeback within a year of the US-led intervention (for failures of US and NATO strategy, see Jones 2006; Rubin and Rashid 2008).

Although it became clear as early as mid-2003 that more troops and resources were needed to expand the operations of ISAF and other foreign troops, neither the US nor its allies were willing to meet this requirement, especially because the US focus had already shifted away from Afghanistan to Iraq. However, for many NATO members, involvement in security building and reconstruction in Afghanistan was from the start a short-term commitment, undertaken largely as a way of avoiding sending troops to Iraq, for which there was little domestic support.

Even so, when, in 2004, the US and its partners finally found it necessary to boost their troop deployment and expand their operations, they opted for a safe and incremental troop build-up. By the end of 2008, there were 40,000 ISAF troops (including 10,000 US soldiers) operating under NATO's command and 20,000 under the US command. But several European members of NATO still remained unwilling to deploy their troops in danger zones in the south. Repeated NATO requests for additional troops and better strategic coordination have so far produced little result. The US has kept reassuring the world that its efforts and those of its allies in building the Afghan National Army (ANA), police force and border guard are effective in allowing them to take on increasing security responsibilities. However, the ANA, which consists of 70,000 troops, has the capacity to participate in some operations, but is far from being able to engage in any major military engagement without the full support of foreign forces. This is expected to remain the case for some years to come. As for the police force and border guard, the first is corrupt and unreliable, and the second remains underdeveloped and poorly equipped to make any meaningful contribution towards securing Afghanistan's borders, particularly the long and treacherous frontier with Pakistan (see Rashid 2008: chapter 10; Saikal 2008). The only security apparatus that has performed with any degree of effectiveness is the domestic intelligence agency, the National Directorate for Security. But even this agency, like other branches of state power and the government as a whole, is suspected of being penetrated extensively by opposition forces (for an example, see Schmitt 2008).

The US and many of its allies have failed to focus on the significant linkage between military security and human development. US policymakers in particular have demonstrated a poor understanding of Afghanistan's history and its social, cultural and regional complexity. Washington initially shunned the idea of a 'Marshall Plan for Afghanistan' because, in its view, a small amount of money could go a long way in the country. According to a major report by the Agency Coordinating Body for Afghan Relief (ACBAR), of the more than US$20 billion promised by the international donors between January 2002 and January 2008, some US$9 billion was still outstanding. Of the amount distributed, 40 per cent went back to the donor countries in consultant fees and expatriates' pay, with most of the remaining funds being spent on the operations of the UN and non-governmental organizations as well as foreign contractors and sub-contractors.

The same report makes it clear that 'while the US military spends $100 million a day, the average amount of aid spent by all donors combined has been just $7 (million) a day since 2001' (Leithead 2008). The result has been far less investment in the reconstruction of Afghanistan per head of the population than has been the case with three concurrently disrupted states: Bosnia, Kosovo and East Timor. This has meant that a majority of the Afghans have not benefited from the post-Taliban reconstruction and have not experienced a positive change in their living conditions. They have therefore had little reason to remain supportive of the Karzai government and its foreign backers.

From the start, the US regarded Afghanistan's transformation as being conditional on the success of the 'war on terror' and Pakistan's partnership in achieving this success. However, concerned about possible developments that could result in the isolation of nuclear-armed Pakistan, Washington did not insist upon structural adjustment in Islamabad's approach to Afghanistan. The regime of General Pervez Musharraf, who was forced out of office on 18 August 2008 after nine years of military dictatorship, made the most of Washington's approach to help promoting his regime's interests rather than those of the US in the region (Hussain 2005: chapter 6). While he received massive US economic and military assistance, amounting to more than US$10 billion by 2007, Musharraf neither denied the Taliban sanctuaries in Pakistan nor withheld logistic support.

Musharraf's policies contributed to the 'Talibanization' of Pakistan's border areas with Afghanistan, undermining the US and NATO's stabilization efforts in Afghanistan on the one hand, and generating a serious threat to Pakistan's stability and security on the other. Musharraf's successor, Asif Ali Zardari, is a highly controversial, polarizing and unpopular figure and has little influence with Pakistan's powerful military and intelligence agency (ISI), which has acted as the driving force in Pakistani politics for a long time. Zardari cannot be expected to be able to weaken the Pakistani and Afghan Taliban for as long as they are supported by elements within the military and more specifically the ISI.

NATO members continue to have serious disagreements over their approach to both Afghanistan and Pakistan. They remain divided over the depth and length of their involvement and the degree of coordination with the Afghan government and among themselves. They have been confused over not only how to differentiate between 'core Taliban' and 'non-core Taliban' as well as between the 'old Taliban' and the 'new Taliban', but also how to stem the tide of opium production in Afghanistan, which made the country the largest producer in the world in 2007.

For all practical purposes, Afghanistan has become a narco-state, which will continue to be the case even if the Taliban are eliminated (see Rubin and Sherman 2008). Proceeds from the drug trade have become a main source not only for funding the operations of the Taliban and other private militias, but also for enriching many government officials who have been heavily involved in the industry. The Afghan government and outside actors have not come up with a common approach to tackle the problem. Even at the Bucharest summit of NATO and non-NATO countries in April 2008, the participants remained as divided as ever before on the issue.

Counter-systemic actors

The factors of elite fragmentation, poor and corrupt governance, societal decline and a flawed approach by external actors (mainly the US) to Afghanistan's transformation have interacted unfavourably to generate the space and opportunities for a number of counter-systemic actors. Chief among these are the Taliban, with two noted spoilers on their tail: the *Hizb-e Islami* (Islamic Party) of the former *mujahideen* leader Gulbuddin Hekmatyar and al-Qaida. The Taliban are not the best-trained, equipped or led force. The movement is largely made up of poorly trained, fed and clothed fighters, who lack support from external global powers, unlike the *mujahideen* in the 1980s, who were backed by the US. It has become formidable largely because of the political and security vacuum that the failures of the Karzai government and its foreign allies have generated. The Taliban have skilfully drawn on these failures at both the strategic and the operational levels to mount a serious challenge from outside the system. The Taliban's projection of themselves as defenders of the faith, country and honour as well as providers of better security and living conditions has resonated historically and culturally among the Afghan people. This has been nowhere more evident than among the ethnic Pashtuns.

The Afghans are now caught between three forces. One seeks to lead them down a path of secular political change, which is very much dictated by outside interests. Another would like to see them move down the lane of an indigenous-based moderate religious transformation. The third wants them to embrace radical political Islam as the only viable ideology of salvation. The last of these groups – comprising the Taliban and their allies – has grown convinced that despite their public rhetoric, the US and its allies will not and cannot afford to endure the burdens of Afghanistan indefinitely. The latest world financial crisis and the degradation of US economic power have simply strengthened their conviction.

The major challenge now is how to build effective bridges between the first two forces, co-opt the third one and to generate the right conditions for stability, security and viability in Afghanistan. There is a need for a new approach, a new strategy and possibly a new compact between Afghanistan and the international community.

The way forward

To move forward, it is imperative to start the process with a focus on four main areas. The first is to change the Afghan political system to a strong, diversified parliamentary system of governance, headed by a prime minister who would come from the parliament with a parliamentary majority under a figurehead president, elected by the parliament and a majority of provincial assemblies. Such a system can provide more accountability, transparency, efficiency and popular connection to the political system than has been the case under the strong presidential model. To achieve this, the new Afghan constitution should be substantially modified. For this purpose, a new Loya Jirga similar to the one that ratified the present constitution should be convened to legitimize the constitutional changes.

In all this, the emphasis should not be on democracy, but rather on creating a workable political system, with a united governing elite and culturally relevant national political manifesto that could help generate good governance and civil society as a precursor to democracy. Elections are too often equated with democracy. It is important to remember that in a country like Afghanistan, which has never had a tradition of democracy, elections can only produce a minimalist or procedural form of democracy. To progress from this state to substantive democracy, a society will have to transform itself not only on the political, but also on the economic and social fronts. However, this can only be achieved if more emphasis is placed on civil society and liberty as foundations for something more than procedural democracy.

The second important aspect is that, given its geopolitical complexities, Afghanistan's traditional status as a neutral state in world politics needs to be formally reaffirmed. Such a position, which is incompatible with the Afghan–US Strategic Partnership of 2005, would reassure Afghanistan's neighbours that a neutral, but rebuilt and stable Afghanistan would not become a source of a threat to them by way of a third party using its territory. At present, Iran is deeply concerned about the prospect of a long-term US presence in Afghanistan and the possibility of Pakistan – a major non-NATO ally of the US – reasserting its influence in the country, as was the case under the rule of the Taliban. While the Iranian concern is shared by Russia and some of the Central Asian republics, India wants to see Pakistan's regional ambitions curtailed. However, Islamabad too is likely to remain vigilant of any development in Afghanistan that could work against Pakistan's interests. Meanwhile, a majority of the Afghan people would appreciate a status of neutrality, symbolizing their sense of sovereignty and independence as was the case from 1919 up to the Soviet invasion of Afghanistan in late 1979.

The third is that the non-ethnic Pashtun population of Afghanistan should be discouraged from going down the same path toward the Karzai government and its international backers as has been trodden by many of their Pashtun counterparts. While the Pashtun-dominated provinces are hotbeds of insurgency, the predominantly non-Pashtun areas in northern, central and western Afghanistan have been relatively peaceful, but many in these areas feel that they have not been rewarded for their cooperation. More international reconstruction investment is needed in health, education, administration and infrastructural building to prevent them from becoming further disillusioned with the central government and foreign involvement.

The fourth area of concern is the need for the international community to adopt an integrative approach to Afghanistan's transition, with a collective resolve not only to engage the irreconcilable counter-systemic actors by military means, but also to address the political and economic sources of insecurity as equally important. This should be accompanied by the establishment of a firm and realistic withdrawal timetable for foreign forces to spur the Afghan people to shake off their culture of dependency and to delegitimize the claim by the counter-systemic actors that Afghanistan is subject to permanent military occupation.

Such changes can foster the conditions for better governance, more reconstruction and security, putting the Taliban and their allies on the defensive and opening the way for the government to seek negotiation with these counter-systemic actors from a position of strength. The Karzai government and its international backers have now reached a consensus on the need for negotiation with the Taliban. But if they negotiate a power-sharing arrangement with them from their current position, they will not be able to bargain for a settlement that would receive widespread support from a cross-section of the Afghan micro-societies. The Taliban suppressed not only women, but also the non-Pashtun and non-Sunni elements of the Afghan society when they were in power. These elements are already well armed and can expect support from Afghanistan's neighbours other than Pakistan to fight any Taliban-dominated government. This can only plunge the country into wider fighting and bloodshed, and return it to the state in which it found itself before the US-led intervention.

References

De Young, K. (2008) 'Only a two-page "note" governs U.S. military in Afghanistan', *Washington Post*, August 28.
Hussain, R. (2005) *Pakistan and the Emergence of the Islamic Militancy in Afghanistan*, London: Ashgate.
Jones, S.G. (2006) 'Averting failure in Afghanistan', *Survival* 48, 1: 111–27.

Leithead, A. (2008) 'Donors accused of failing Afghans', *BBC News*, 25 March. Available online at: http://news.bbc.co.uk/2/hi/south_asia/7311972.stm (accessed 10 February 2009).

Rashid, A. (2000) *Taliban, Militant Islam, Oil and Fundamentalism in Central Asia*, New Haven: Yale University Press.

——(2008) *Descent into Chaos: The United States and the Failure of Nation Building in Pakistan, Afghanistan, and Central Asia*, New York: Viking.

Risen, J. (2008) 'Reports link Karzai's brother to heroin trade', *The New York Times*, 4 October.

Rubin, B.R. and Rashid, A. (2008) 'From the great game to grand bargain', *Foreign Affairs* 87, 6: 30–44.

Rubin, B.R. and Sherman, J. (2008) *Counter-Narcotics to Stabilise Afghanistan: The False Promise of Crop Eradication*, New York: Center on International Cooperation.

Saikal, A. (2006) *Modern Afghanistan: A History of Struggle and Survival*, London: I.B. Tauris.

——(2008) 'Securing Afghanistan's border', *Survival* 48, 2: 129–41.

Saikal, A. and Maley, W. (2008) 'The president who would be king', *The New York Times*, 6 February.

Schmitt, E. (2008) 'Afghan officials aided an attack on US soldiers', *The New York Times*, 4 November.

28

The Middle East as a crisis region

Martin Beck

Since the 1970s, the Middle East[1] region has failed to keep pace with major global processes that have helped to promote dynamic developments in many other world regions. Among the most striking factors are a political, an economic and a security-related one. Firstly, the Arab World and Iran did not participate in the 'third wave of democratisation' (Huntington 1991): with the exception of Israel, within the boundaries of 1949, no democracy exists in the Middle East. Freedom House (2008) does not list any single Arab country as 'free'. This finding is particularly intriguing because at the beginning of the twenty-first century – in contrast to the period before the third wave – quite a few democracies existed in Africa, Asia, Latin America and Eastern Europe. Thus, there is strong evidence that the supposedly Western model of democracy works outside the West – yet in the Arab Middle East and Iran, it has not yet gained ground.

Secondly, apart from being a major supplier of world energy, the Middle East's degree of participation in the globalization process is very limited (Beck 2003): as a part of the world that has failed to transform its systems from resource-dependent to knowledge-based economies, the Arab Middle East and Iran lack attractiveness as an investment location beyond the oil and gas sectors. By attracting less than five per cent of global foreign direct investment, the Arab Middle East lags even behind sub-Saharan Africa (Brach 2008: 7). Moreover, the degree to which the Middle East participates in global communication is comparatively low: internet accessibility in most Middle East countries is lower than in other world regions and is often restricted by state censorship (ONI 2007).

Thirdly, the Middle East as a 'regional security complex' (Buzan and Wæver 2003: 187–218) is characterized by a high degree of political violence involving all kinds of different levels and actors: The Middle East is the centre of international terrorism. Islamist violence is not only 'exported' to the US, Europe and other places, rather, most targets are situated in the Middle East itself. For the same reason, the region is the global centre of violent counter-terrorism. Moreover, the Middle East is among the very few world regions in which classic interstate wars still play a major role, most recently in 2003, when the US-led 'Coalition of the Willing' invaded Iraq. Finally, the Middle East is home to decades-old regional violent conflicts, particularly those over Palestine and Kurdistan.

This chapter discusses three major factors that contribute to a deeper comprehension – and may actually build the basis for an explanation – of the situation in the Middle East as described above. Firstly, it argues that basic development problems are related to the regional system of petrolism: rent income has proven to be a major burden for the region. Secondly, it discusses how Islamism as the dominant oppositional ideology – as well as the ways the ruling regimes deal with it – shapes Middle Eastern politics, particularly in terms of its contribution to authoritarianism and political violence. Finally, it addresses the role of Western, particularly US, influence. In the course of this discussion, an aspect is emphasized that is often overlooked as a result of the Gulf wars of 1991 and 2003: US oil policy towards the region has been shaped by cooperation with regional actors. Still, due to the authoritarianism of the regional cooperation partners, such cooperation has contributed to the Middle Eastern crisis situation in terms of authoritarianism, underdevelopment and violent conflict.

Rent, rentier states and rentierism

The key feature of developmental regression in the Middle East is the prevalence of rentier states. The state budgets of oil-exporting countries depend on rent income – that is, an earning that is not derived from investment or labour, but is based on oil deposits, the production costs of which are comparatively low. Contrary to entrepreneurs, rentiers do not need to reinvest the bulk of their income to accrue earnings in the future. Thus, a rent is at the free disposal of its owner. State bureaucrats, as the main recipients of rents, tend to invest in maintaining their privileges rather than in democratization and economic development.

As a result of the oil bonanza of the 1970s, the oil rentier states of the Gulf region aimed to achieve regional stabilization and established the Middle Eastern system of 'petrolism' (Korany 1986). Thereby, major non-oil producing Arab countries received political rents, that is, budget transfers from oil-rich countries. Although the rent income of the political rentiers was significantly lower than that accrued by oil rentiers, it shaped similar features. On the one hand, petrolism contributed to regional stability, as will be discussed in the first subsection. On the other hand, after the 1990s, the explosive potential of petrolism became more obvious, especially with the wars in Algeria and Iraq, as will be discussed in the second subsection.

The making of stable rentier states

As an outcome of the debate on the 'resource curse', the mainstream opinion holds that dependence on natural resources results in an increased likelihood of violence (see Collier and Hoeffler 2002). Since resources tend to trigger material covetousness and/or create financial opportunities to combat drawbacks, they are believed to increase the danger of violent conflict behaviour as a consequence of 'greed' and 'grievances', respectively. Initially, however, oil in the Middle East contributed to regional stability rather than violence.

In many cases, especially in the Gulf monarchies, the transition to a rentier state system was fairly smooth. In the 1950s in Saudi Arabia and Kuwait, for instance, oil royalties revolutionized the state budget, which had previously been dependent on marginal sources such as pilgrimage and pearl diving. At the same time, the traditional social fabric remained largely intact, which is why the ruling state bureaucracies enjoyed favourable conditions for using the petrodollars to establish stable state-dominated orders.

However, in some cases the ruling elite proved to be overwhelmed by the influx of external rents. When Iraq[2] became an oil rentier state in the 1950s, it was governed by a monarchy that had become dependent on a small class of big landowners (Batatu 1978: 106f.). Instead of using its externally generated income to establish a balance between divergent social actors, the monarchy allowed the bulk of the rent to flow into the agrarian sector, thereby exacerbating social tensions (Pawelka 1993: 83). The failure of the Iraqi monarchy to use oil rents in an efficient way was sealed in 1958 with the takeover of power by the 'free officers'.

Yet, in the end, revolutions in the Middle East did not lead to dynamic socio-economic and political developments. Rather, the newly established state bureaucracies used the petrodollars according to the rationality of rentier states: based on complex distributional and oppressive policies, they depoliticized their societies. Thus, revolutionary as well as non-revolutionary states in the Middle East formed stable state-centred regimes. In light of the significant differences in contemporary historical developments in Middle Eastern politics, the recent similarities between former revolutionary and non-revolutionary Middle Eastern rentier states are striking. For instance, in 'modern' Syria, even the recruitment pattern for the ruler's succession mimicked the monarchical system when Bashir al-Assad inherited the president's office from his father in 2000.

Oil has proved to be conducive to a stable political order in the Middle East insofar as the rent income generated by energy exports is accrued by the central state. Rebel groups lack the capital, the expertise and the infrastructure necessary to exploit oil deposits, unlike alluvial diamonds, which are comparatively easy to extract. Oil-exporting countries in the Middle East have formed rentier states whose budget is primarily com-posed of external income. In resource-poor, but aid-receiving Middle Eastern countries such as Egypt, the state has also enjoyed a prominent role, since its capacities for absorbing external aid have by far outweighed those of non-governmental actors. Thus, not only oil-exporting nations, but also aid-receiving states in the Middle East are – in comparison to most other world regions – strong *vis-à-vis* their own societies (Beblawi and Luciani 1987).

Thus, all other things being equal, oil rentier states develop stable authoritarian regimes because society lacks the economic means to challenge the ruling state bureaucracy. Rather than being financed by society through taxes, the state tends to subsidize social groups – be it by promoting state-dependent enterprises, handing out monopolies and licenses, offering jobs or subsidizing bread prices – thereby depoliticizing them (Najma-badi 1987a). An additional strategy used by the state bureaucracy to preserve its political privilege is the 'investment' in internal security, which is very often a repression appara-tus. Most rentier states have developed a complex mixture of carrots and sticks, but the ratio varies: Iraq as governed by Saddam Hussein was an extremely repressive state, whereas Oman has focused on pacifying strategies. Although differences in the degree of repression are less extreme where political rentiers are concerned, differences are obser-vable in these countries as well. For instance, Jordan is 'softer' on its own society than Egypt (see Beck 2007).

There are only two major exceptions to the pattern of stability described above: first, the Iranian revolution of 1979, when the regime of Shah Mohammad Reza Pahlavi collapsed; second, the annulment of the Algerian elections of 1991/92, which resulted in a major civil war. The Iranian case is a major exception because – in contrast to the overthrows of the Iraqi and Libyan monarchies – the revolution toppled a state bureau-cracy that was experienced in managing a rentier state. However, despite its revolutionary Islamist rhetoric, the regime created by Ayatollah Ruhollah Khomeini joined the ranks of rentier states. The government in Tehran failed to decrease dependence on the West: the dominance of oil in the economic system could not be reduced and petrodollars continued to be used to support a stabilizing distributional policy whose primary aim was to preserve the prerogatives of the ruling authoritarian elite (Karshenas and Hakimian 2008).

In contrast to the Iranian revolution, the crisis of the Algerian regime was a result of shrinking rent income. When oil prices fell in the 1980s, the regime reacted with a policy of borrowing and economic liberalization. When, due to its mixed blessings, this policy became increasingly disputed in the ruling state bureaucracy, President Chedli Benjedid expanded liberalization to the political level. However, the regime underestimated the capabilities of the Islamist opposition and unleashed by default a democratization of the political system, which peaked with the electoral defeat of the ruling National Liberation Front in the national elections of 1991/92. To avoid a takeover by the challenging Islamic Salvation Front, the regime annulled the election results and the country ended up in a brutal civil war (Quandt 1998: 42–80).

With declining oil prices in the 1990s, liberalization policies became common in the Middle East. Thus, hopes rose that liberalization could open out into democratization processes – with more positive results than in Algeria. Yet, generally, rather than initiating democratization, liberalization processes in the Middle East mainly strengthened the authoritarian regime by expanding its social basis. Very often, periods of liberalization alternated with phases of repression (Kienle 1998). In addition, resource-poor political rentiers turned out to be effective in recruiting additional rent donors. When Middle Eastern rent sources happened to dry up – for example, in the case of Egypt in the late 1970s and the Palestinian Liberation Organization (PLO) in the early 1990s, as a result of their agreements with Israel – Western actors sometimes stepped into the breach. Therefore, the rent web of the Middle East is much more closely meshed than that in any other world area.

Rentierism and regional (de-)stabilization

The Algerian case mentioned above shows in a dramatic way the potential security challenges faced by a rentier state as the result of failed domestic crisis management. The crisis of a rentier state can also lead to regional turmoil, as has been the case in the Gulf as a result of Iranian and, above all, Iraqi regional policies.

After the oil bonanza of the 1970s, Iraq faced a severe rent income crisis in the late 1980s and was heavily indebted. To a certain degree, Iraq's troubles were due to the same cause as the Algerian crisis: shrinking oil prices. However, an even more important explanatory factor for the Iraqi misery is its war with Iran (1980–88): firstly, Iraq suffered war damages to its oil-exploration infrastructure and, secondly, the regime had to resort to external financing to support the war.

Iraq's main donors had been the neighbouring oil monarchies. Why? Although these countries also felt menaced by Iraq, Iran seemed even more dangerous to them. Although material politics in Iran did not exceed the limits of a rentier state, the Islamist ideology was threatening to its neighbours. The regime in Tehran always underlined the transnational, 'Islamic' character of the revolution and aspired to export it to its neighbours. The Gulf monarchies suspected that Khomeini's ideology might appeal to the Shi'ite segments of the Arabian Peninsula and to Islamists in general. Actually, the transnational ambitions of the Iranian revolutionary movement corresponded with the frustrations of many representatives of the Arab middle and lower classes in terms of economic stagnation and political standstill (Nahas 1985).

From the perspective of the Gulf monarchies, as long as the two potential regional hegemons of the Gulf were entangled in war, they mutually absorbed their own threatening power. Yet, when the US and the Soviet Union brokered a ceasefire, the monarchies, particularly Kuwait, clashed with Iraq. The main issue was Iraq's indebtedness to the monarchies, which wanted to use this debt as a tool to tame Iraqi ambitions of regional domination after those of Iran had been contained as a result of the gruelling war. However, Hussein revoked debt service, instead demanding that Kuwait adjust its oil policy to Iraqi needs. Due to war damage to its oil infrastructure, Iraq lacked the capability to increase production and therefore condemned Kuwait's strategy of raising income by expanding production rather than reducing it to boost prices. Moreover, Iraq accused Kuwait of slant drilling in the cross-border Rumaila oil field during the Iraq–Iran War.

By invading Kuwait, Hussein attempted to solve the problem his way: if successful, he would not only have conquered additional rent sources, he would also have 'convinced' neighbouring oil-producing countries of his leadership in international oil politics (Claes 2001: 95–130).

On the one hand, the strategy chosen by Iraq fits within the logic of rentierism: Hussein attempted to solve the country's rent crisis by usurping new rent sources abroad. On the other hand, if Iraq had succeeded, it would have destroyed the foundation of autonomous rent policies in the Gulf States, with incalculable repercussions on domestic and regional stability. However, a well-functioning alliance between the US and Saudi Arabia proved to provide effective crisis management: by increasing its oil production, Saudi Arabia kept oil prices stable despite the production shortfall that resulted from Iraq's aggression towards Kuwait. The US for its part restored Kuwaiti sovereignty and then effectively contained Iraqi regional ambitions by imposing a crippling sanctions regime on Baghdad (Niblock 2001: 97–195).

Islamism

Notwithstanding the Islamist claim to represent genuine Islam, most social scientists are sceptical that an 'essentialist' analysis of Islamism is fruitful: popular claims that Islamism (as an ideology) can be traced back to a resistance to democracy and/or an affinity to violence rooted in Islam (as a religion) are afflicted with major theoretical and methodological problems (see Anderson 1997; de Juan 2008). For instance, is there *one* Islam, and even if there is, can its scriptures be interpreted in one authoritative manner, and how does one differentiate between Islam as an *explanans* and an *explanandum*? Still, factors related to Islamism are of major importance in understanding the social reality of the contemporary Middle East. In terms of the prolonged crisis of the Middle East, three factors shall be taken into account.

Firstly, although many scholars doubt the philosophical validity of Islamism, it has proven to play a fairly strong role in the Middle East for decades. The success of Islamism as the dominant ideology of opposition movements is related to the fact that it is efficiently adapted to the political conditions in the Middle East. From an institutionalist perspective, the network of mosques turned out to be an efficient basis for Islamism: while 'modern' political opposition parties can be monitored and their headquarters ultimately shut down, authoritarian regimes have faced difficulties in maintaining efficient control over nationwide networks of mosques, which are protected by the aura of sanctity. Moreover, the idea of justice, which plays a major role in Islam, is perfectly suited as an oppositional ideology in a rentier state and is therefore widely employed by the Islamist opposition: since the rentier state has financial means at its disposal that most citizens are keen, if not dependent on receiving, the latter will not primarily demand freedom (from state influence) but rather 'justice', that is, the redistribution of state funds to their own advantage (Najmabadi 1987b).

Secondly, Islamism is both a reflex of and an exacerbating factor of the Middle Eastern crisis situation. Although it was established as a modern political ideology and movement as early as the 1920s, its major breakthrough in the Middle East came with the failure of (Pan-)Arabism, which became apparent with the stagnating modernization processes 'from above' in Egypt and Syria in the 1960s and the two countries' disastrous defeats in the June 1967 War against Israel. However, the main reason for Islamism's lasting role as the main oppositional ideology in the Arab world has long been its capability of mobilizing mass support. Its rise is due to appeals to traditional values; the organization of social services for needy people neglected by elitist regimes; and the presentation of apparently trustworthy leaders as alternatives to corrupt state bureaucrats. Thus, the ruling regimes inadvertently provided a favourable framework for the flourishing of Islamism. Moreover, the very existence of 'secular' and 'Western' institutions and ideologies, which were used by authoritarian regimes to preserve their own prerogatives, became an issue of identity that could not be dealt with in pragmatic bargaining processes. Thus, on the side of both terrorist as well as counter-terrorist actors, the use of violence – which often ignores the basic human rights of civilians – was legitimized by the necessity of each side's 'survival'.

Thirdly, due to the dominance of Islamism in contemporary political affairs, the Middle East plays an 'exotic' or even deviant role in world politics. Actually, the prominence of Islamism as the leading ideology of the opposition in the Middle East and the governments' authoritative manner of dealing with it has shaped both the institutional settings and political discourses in the Middle East in an unproductive manner. For instance, on the one hand, Islamist groups have a vested interest in democratizing the political systems of the Middle East. This is the case simply because an abolition of authoritarian measures and the introduction of fair elections would empower Islamist groups and their role in the formal political system. Still, although many Islamists actually demand reforms, they very often reject democracy as an allegedly Western concept. At the same time, the ruling regimes that have for decades been demonstrating their unwillingness to democratize often pay lip service to democratization. Moreover, they take advantage of Western scepticism towards anti-Western Islamism and sidestep international demands for democratization by arguing that doing so would abet religiously legitimized extremism rather than a liberalization of society (see Brumberg and Diamond 2003).

In general, many challenges that are dealt with in a more pragmatic way in other world regions easily become issues of major ideological significance in the Middle East. For example, issues such as whether and how to participate in globalization, to adapt ideas and concepts developed in the US to one's own needs, or to liberalize the political and economic systems are often debated as matters that touch the basic values of the 'Muslim world' as opposed to the US or the West in general. That the ideological focus on 'Islam' often creates a dynamic of its own can also be observed in the growing rivalry between Shi'a and Sunna, as well as in the competing relations of other Islamist ideologies with the two major communities of Islam. For instance, what initially appeared as a classic conflict over power distribution in post-Hussein Iraq became increasingly poisoned by its portrayal as a matter of religious orthodoxy (see Nasr 2006). The Arab–Israeli conflict, which both parties regarded for much of the twentieth century as a conflict over governance, has also recently tended to be perceived as a conflict over identities that cannot be compromised.

Western interference

As early as the nineteenth century, the Middle East became one of the world regions most intensively penetrated by external actors (Brown 1984) – and it continued to be so in the twentieth and early twenty-first centuries. There can be no doubt that the initiative was taken by Western actors within the framework of imperialism and colonialism. However, many local elites quickly discovered that external powers could be instrumental in allowing them to prevail in local or regional rivalries. Thus, local elites frequently encouraged the involvement of external actors, thereby exploiting rivalries among them. The complexity of relations between local and external actors, both in the Gulf and the Mashriq, resulted in conflicts that were often resolved through violence – but also frequently in a cooperative, albeit asymmetrical, way.

The positions of external and internal actors in the Gulf region after the Second World War created opportunities for asymmetrical cooperation between local and external actors. The US was the unchallenged hegemonic power of Western capitalism whose dynamic worldwide expansion after the war had to be stabilized through major international regimes. In addition to currency and trade management (Bretton Woods, GATT), a third supporting pillar of US hegemony was an international oil regime, with the Gulf monarchies as the core production units. The main actors were the seven major transnational oil companies – headed by Exxon, British Petroleum and Shell – and the Gulf States. However, the US administration itself also played a decisive role: guided by the long-term aim of establishing a stable world energy system, it pushed the companies to agree to provide payments to the ruling elites in the Gulf that were significantly higher than what the weak local states could have secured in regular bargaining processes against some of the strongest companies worldwide (Schneider 1983: Chap. 1; Tétreault 1985: Chap. 2). Despite some revolutionary interludes – particularly the reign of Mohammed Mosaddeq in Iran (1951–53) – the main result of the international oil regime was political stability in the Gulf.

In the immediate post-war era, rather than becoming directly involved in the intensifying Arab–Israeli conflict that dominated interstate relations in the Mashriq, the US resorted to a manoeuvring policy aimed at securing good relations with both Israel and Egypt. Only after the showdown of the June 1967 War did the US take sides and begin to establish a firm alliance with Israel, which had proven to be by far the most powerful actor in the Middle East. Ever since, the US has strongly supported Israel, be it in periods of peace processes, such as the 1990s, or in periods of war, as in the summer of 2006. Moreover, the US has also contributed to the strengthening of regional rentierism in the Mashriq. In addition to Egypt, the US also boosted Jordan financially, thereby providing Israel with a secure border whose stability was not even seriously threatened after Israel's conquest of the West Bank in the war of June 1967.

At first glance, regional developments since the 1970s, especially in the Gulf region, create the impression that relations between the US and the Middle East have been driven by confrontation rather than cooperation. There can be hardly any doubt that there is some truth in this assessment. The US has developed hostile relations with two major regimes: first, the former major US ally Iran, which turned hostile after the fall of the Shah's regime in 1979, and then, as of the early 1990s, Iraq. Then, on 11 September 2001, al-Qaida attacked the US and, in 2003, the US invaded Iraq.

However, these aspects of confrontation should not blind us to significant cooperative policies. The oil crisis of 1973–74 was a major clash between the transnational oil companies, which had previously been in a commanding position, and the oil states which finally prevailed in enforcing the principle of state autonomy over national resources. However, the oil revolution was also the starting point for intensified financial and economic cooperation between Western actors, particularly the US, and the Gulf States. The Gulf States reinvested the bulk of their additional income by establishing the system of petrodollar recycling. Thus, they expanded their imports from the West on several different levels to include food, luxury goods and turnkey factories. Moreover, they put savings into the Western financial system, particularly that of the US (Spiro 1999: iv–xv, 103–26).

Above all, good relations between the West and the Gulf in general and the close alliance between the US and Saudi Arabia in particular created a solid foundation for protecting Western oil-supply security. The Arab Gulf states that had come under pressure from nationalist regimes since the 1950s were now in a position to promote regional stability by converting the influx of economic rents into political rents at the regional level in the interests of the conservative ruling segments in the Middle East. At the same time, despite the founding of the Gulf Cooperation Council (GCC) in 1981, which was meant to balance Iraqi and Iranian threats, the Gulf States remained dependent on US military protection, as became evident when Iraq invaded Kuwait in 1990.

The terrorist attacks in New York and Washington in 2001 came as a shock to the US and triggered a debate over the fundamental direction of the country's Middle East policy. Since the Second World War, the governing interest of US policy in the Middle East had been to promote stability based on the oil trade and on close ties with financially privileged allies such as Egypt. At the same time, apart from some short-lived experiments with multilateralism, such as the Baghdad Pact in the mid-1950s, the US had preferred to nurture bilateral relations in the region. It had experienced the limits of this approach several times: some closely allied regimes such as Iran fell victim to the lack of legitimacy of authoritarian rulers. In other cases, such as Syria and Iraq, the US had to face another disadvantage of having non-democratic allies: their rulers may easily decide to change allegiance. At the end of the twentieth century, it had already become obvious to the US that Israel was its only fully reliable partner in the Middle East. But it was only when the US was attacked in September 2001 by terrorists who were citizens of long-term allies, particularly Saudi Arabia, that cooperation with Middle Eastern authoritarian regimes became subject to contentious discussion.

By launching the Greater Middle East Initiative in 2004, which after coordination with the EU became known as the Broader Middle East Initiative, the US and the West in general discovered a doctrine of International Relations that had so far been confined to fairly limited academic circles: the theorem of democratic peace, which stipulates that democracies refrain from waging war against one another. If the logic of this assumption is applied to the Middle East, the possible implications are quite impressive. If all Middle Eastern states were democracies, a breeding ground for terrorists could be removed, and conflicts between Middle Eastern and Western states would be dealt with peacefully.

However, the postulate of democratic peace applies to consolidated democracies only, whereas political entities still undergoing a process of democratization sometimes even trigger internal and external violence, since the increase in participation as a consequence of democratization is not balanced by the moderating effect of institutions such as a powerful supreme court that is characteristic of fully-fledged democracies (Mansfield and Snyder 1995). Moreover, the main opposition groups in the Middle East are Islamists who either openly declare that they do not subscribe to democratic values or may do so only for tactical reasons, and who are hostile to the West, especially the US. Thus, although the West actually has incentives for promoting democratization in the Middle East, there are, at the same time, contradictory stability interests. Thus, the Middle East policies of Western countries, and particularly of the US, in the early twenty-first century have appeared to be guided by a desire for democracy, but fear of democratization. It remains to be seen whether Barack Obama will bring change in this respect.

Conclusion

The Middle East has been in permanent, comprehensive crisis since the 1970s and lags behind the achievements made in many other world regions, including in developing areas. The main explanatory factor for Middle Eastern stagnation is the abundance of rent income, with its complex implications for Middle Eastern security affairs. Although it has triggered socio-economic and political stagnation, rent income prevents the regional system from collapsing. Instead, both oil and political rents have enabled elites to stabilize political systems and regional relations.

Western influence has played a decisive role. The foundations of the Middle East as a region shaped by rent income were laid by US actors after the Second World War. To date, the US has been a major player in the Middle East. Although West–East cooperation is far from smooth, common interests between the elites in the US and major Middle Eastern countries have contributed to the general outcome of 'stable stagnation'.

With oil prices skyrocketing up to mid-2008 and a growing market share in internationally traded oil, the leeway for implementing distributional policies in the oil-exporting countries increased once again. High oil prices tend to lead to stabilized rentierism and authoritarian rule rather than liberalization and democratization, whereas the downward trend of oil prices triggered by the global financial crisis indicates that new dynamics could be ahead.

Notes

1 That is, the Arab world plus Iran and Israel. However, since Israel is an exceptional case in many respects, it cannot be covered in more detail in the present short article.
2 Another pertinent case study is Muammar Gaddafi's revolution in Libya in 1969.

References

Anderson, L. (1997) 'Fulfilling prophecies. State policy and Islamist radicalism', in: Esposito, J.L. (ed.) *Political Islam. Revolution, Radicalism, or Reform?*, Boulder, CO: Lynne Rienner, pp. 17–31.
Batatu, H. (1978) *The Old Social Classes and the Revolutionary Movements of Iraq: A Study of Iraq's Old Landed and Commercial Classes and of its Communists, Ba'thists, and Free Officers*, Princeton, NJ: Princeton University Press.

Beblawi, H. and Luciani, G. (eds) (1987) *The Rentier State*, London: Croom Helm.

Beck, M. (2003) 'Resistance to globalization and limited liberalization in the Middle East', in: Barrios, H., Beck, M., Boeckh, A. and Segbers, K. (eds) *Resistance to Globalization. Political Struggle and Cultural Resilience in the Middle East, Russia, and Latin America*, New Brunswick, NJ: Transaction Publishers, pp. 14–33.

——(2007) 'Der Rentierstaats-Ansatz und das Problem abweichender Fälle', *Zeitschrift für Internationale Beziehungen* 14, 1: 43–70.

Brach, J. (2008) *Constraints to Economic Development and Growth in the Middle East and North Africa*, GIGA Working Paper No. 85. Available online at: www.giga-hamburg.de/dl/download.php?d=/content/publikationen/pdf/wp85_brach.pdf (accessed 22 December 2008).

Brown, L.C. (1984) *International Politics and the Middle East: Old Rules, Dangerous Game*, Princeton, NJ: Princeton University Press.

Brumberg, D. and Diamond, L. (2003) 'Introduction', in Diamond, L., Plattner, M.F. and Brumberg, D. (eds) *Islam and Democracy in the Middle East*, Baltimore, MD: John Hopkins University Press, pp. ix–xxvi.

Buzan, B. and Wæver, O. (2003) *Regions and Powers: The Structure of International Security*, Cambridge: Cambridge University Press.

Claes, D.H. (2001) *The Politics of Oil-Producer Cooperation*, Boulder, CO: Westview.

Collier, P. and Hoeffler, A. (2002) *Greed and Grievance in Civil War*, CSAE Working Papers 2002–01. Available online at: www.csae.ox.ac.uk/workingpapers/pdfs/2002–01text.pdf (accessed 3 October 2008).

Freedom House (2008) *Freedom in the World: Comparative Scores for all Countries from 1973 to 2008*. Available online at: www.freedomhouse.org/uploads/FIWAllScores.xls (accessed 19 July 2008).

Huntington, S.P. (1991) *The Third Wave of Democratization in the Late Twentieth Century*, Norman: University of Oklahoma Press.

de Juan, A. (2008) 'Kriegsreligion oder Opfer der Umstände? Die Rolle des Islam in innerstaatlichen Konflikten', in Albrecht, H. and Köhler, K. (eds) *Politischer Islam im Vorderen Orient: Zwischen Sozialbewegung, Opposition und Widerstand*, Baden-Baden: Nomos, pp. 51–71.

Karshenas, M. and Hakimian, H. (2008) 'Managing oil resources and economic diversification in Iran', in Katouzian, H. and Shahidi, H. (eds) *Iran in the 21st Century. Politics, Economics and Conflict*, London: Routledge, pp. 194–216.

Kienle, E. (1998) 'More than a response to Islamism: The political deliberalization of Egypt in the 1990s', *Middle East Journal* 52, 2: 219–35.

Korany, B. (1986) 'Political petrolism and contemporary Arab politics, 1967–83', *Journal of Asian and African Studies* 21, 1–2: 66–80.

Mansfield, E.D. and Snyder, J. (1995) 'Democratization and the danger of war', *International Security* 20, 1: 5–38.

Nahas, M. (1985) 'State-systems and revolutionary challenge: Nasser, Khomeini, and the Middle East', *International Journal of Middle East Studies* 17: 507–27.

Najmabadi, A. (1987a) 'Depoliticisation of a rentier state: The case of Pahlavi Iran', in Beblawi, H. and Luciani, G. (eds) (1987) *The Rentier State*, London: Croom Helm, pp. 211–27.

——(1987b) 'Iran's turn to Islam: From modernism to moral order', *Middle East Journal* 41, 2: 202–17.

Nasr, V. (2006) 'When the Shiites rise', *Foreign Affairs* 85, 4: 58–74.

Niblock, T. (2001) *'Pariah States' and Sanctions in the Middle East: Iraq, Libya, Sudan*, London: Lynne Rienner.

ONI (Opennet Initiative) (2007) *Middle East and North Africa (MENA)*. Available online at: http://opennet.net/research/regions/mena (accessed 22 December 2008).

Pawelka, P. (1993) *Der Vordere Orient und die Internationale Politik*, Stuttgart: Kohlhammer.

Quandt, W.B. (1998) *Between Ballots and Bullets: Algeria's Transition from Authoritarianism*, Washington, DC: Brookings.

Schneider, S.A. (1983) *The Oil Price Revolution*, Baltimore, MD: Johns Hopkins University Press.

Spiro, D.E. (1999) *The Hidden Hand of American Hegemony: Petrodollar Recycling and International Markets*, Ithaca, NY: Cornell University Press.

Tétreault, M.A. (1985) *Revolution in the World Petroleum Market*, Westport, CT: Quorum.

29

Iran's nuclear challenge[1]

Mark Fitzpatrick

Iran launched its uranium-enrichment programme in the mid-1980s in the middle of the war with Iraq, after it was attacked with chemical weapons. This decision was a reversal of the leadership's original opposition to the Shah's nuclear programme, which was based on moral grounds. Iranians argue that Saddam Hussein would not have dared to start the war or use chemical weapons if Iran had possessed a nuclear capability. It is also often remarked that Iran inhabits a dangerous region, with four close neighbours (Israel, Russia, Pakistan and India) that possess nuclear weapons, and a domineering superpower with troops positioned to its east in Afghanistan and to its west in Iraq, and with naval forces off its coast to the south. Pronouncements by the Bush administration assigning Iran to the 'axis of evil', a policy of 'preventive deterrence', and loose talk of regime change on the part of the US have undoubtedly motivated the Iranian leadership to develop the ability to resist coercive measures.

The exposure in August 2002 of Iran's uranium enrichment and plutonium-production programmes prompted intense scrutiny, diplomatic enticements and financial coercion on the part of the major powers to persuade Iran to stop work that is giving it a latent nuclear weapons capability. Although technical difficulties and limited components still may restrict the size and effectiveness of its programmes, Iran's ability to produce enriched uranium has become a fait accompli. By early 2009, Iran had produced enough low-enriched uranium to supply the feed material for an atomic bomb if further enriched and put to weapons use.

Time would appear to be on Iran's side as it advances its weapons capabilities. There are no good options for dealing with Iran's nuclear challenge. As Harvard scholar Matthew Bunn (2007) puts it, the choice is between the 'least-bad' options.

This chapter describes Iran's pursuit of uranium enrichment and plutonium production facilities and the reasons many in the West conclude that its purpose is to acquire a weapons capability. It also assesses Western strategy to date, starting with the denial of supply policy tools employed for two decades and the more recent 'demand-side' strategies focused on both sanctions and incentives. The conclusion addresses the key question of whether Iran's latent capability can be kept from crossing the line of being used for a weapon.

The pursuit of fissile material: a security challenge

More than three decades ago, US strategist Albert Wohlstetter (1976–77) warned of the proliferation risk posed by countries that were coming close to possessing nuclear weapons by developing sensitive technologies not restricted by the Nuclear Non-Proliferation Treaty (NPT). Uranium enrichment and plutonium reprocessing are considered sensitive technologies because in addition to their civilian purposes, they can be put to weapons use. Uranium enrichment is the process of increasing the concentration of radioactive U-235 isotopes from the average of 0.7 per cent found in uranium in nature either to 3.5–5 per cent to make fuel for reactors or to above 90 per cent for nuclear weapons. Uranium enrichment is the dual-use nuclear technology of greatest current concern with regard to Iran because it is Tehran's preferred path. However, the heavy-water-production facility and heavy-water-moderated research reactor under construction at Arak could give Iran an alternative plutonium path to nuclear weapons, if it also acquired a facility to separate, or reprocess, the plutonium from the reactor's spent fuel.

Iranian officials insist that their country does not seek nuclear weapons. They point out that possession of nuclear weapons would undermine Iran's security by making it a sure target for US and Israeli attack and a worldwide economic boycott, with the loss of the protection currently offered by Russia and China. Overt development of nuclear weapons could also stimulate similar efforts on the part of Iran's Arab Sunni neighbours, thereby negating its conventional strategic advantage (Evans 2007; Parsi 2007: 269). In addition, in August 2005, Supreme Leader Ayatollah Sayyid Ali Khamenei issued a fatwa against the development, production, stockpiling and use of nuclear weapons. Fatwas may be changed on the grounds of new circumstances, but, given the pervasive religiosity of the regime, it is unlikely that Iran's supreme leader would be secretly endorsing military activity in explicit contradiction of his own religious edict.

However, there are compelling reasons as to why Iran would pursue a weapons capability. In addition to the deterrence motivation noted in the Introduction, Iran seeks nuclear technology for the prestige that the possession of such advanced technologies bestows. The pursuit of sensitive technologies is an emotive assertion of sovereignty for a nation with still-vibrant memories of national humiliation and dependence on major powers. An advanced nuclear capability is seen as conferring the major-power status that Iran seeks, thus aiding its aspirations for regional leadership. Iran regards its enrichment programme as a fundamental national right, central to its sovereignty and nationhood. Consequently, with widespread domestic backing, the programme partly functions to legitimize a regime that has otherwise lost popular support.

Viewed from the outside, therefore, Iranian intentions are unclear. In any case, Iran's leaders do not yet need to make a decision about whether to produce nuclear weapons. They can wait until after the fissile material is produced to decide if and when to develop the physics package needed for a weapon. There can be no doubt, however, that Iran has decided to acquire the technical capability to produce fissile material. Its nuclear hedging strategy is designed to bring the country right up to the threshold of a breakout capability while remaining within the legal limits of the NPT. This goal commands strong support within Iran's political elite and the country at large. However, while 'pragmatic conservatives' are willing to negotiate on the timeframe for developing a weapons capability, President Mahmoud Ahmadinejad and other hardliners will brook no delay (Chubin 2006: 28–36).

The November 2007 US National Intelligence Estimate (NIE) concluded that Iran had stopped explicit development of nuclear weapons four years earlier. The NIE also concluded that Iran's uranium-enrichment programme gives it the option of developing nuclear weapons in the future. Producing fissile material – either highly enriched uranium (HEU) or weapons-usable plutonium – is the hardest part of developing a nuclear bomb. Work is also proceeding apace on the third main ingredient: a range of missile systems that could also serve as delivery vehicles for nuclear warheads.

The secrecy surrounding Iran's enrichment activities indicates the potential military purpose of the programme and has caused friction with the international community. According to statements made to the International Atomic Energy Agency (IAEA), shortly after Iran launched its uranium-enrichment programme in the mid-1980s, it contacted the nuclear black market network led by Pakistani metallurgist Abdul Qadeer Khan for the basic technology and a starter set for gas-centrifuge enrichment. Iran kept the Natanz enrichment plant and the reactor construction site at Arak hidden until August 2002, when they were revealed by an exile group. Iran rationalizes that under its safeguards agreement with the IAEA, it was not required to report either facility to the agency until six months before the introduction of nuclear material into those plants. Nevertheless, it did have a legal obligation to report the import and use of nuclear material in general. When IAEA officials were finally able to visit facilities and to investigate Iran's programme in 2003, they documented 14 different ways in which Iran had systematically violated its safeguards agreement over an 18-year period (IAEA 2003a). It was because of these violations that, in September 2005, the IAEA Board of Governors found Iran to be in non-compliance with its safeguards obligations (IAEA 2005a). A non-compliance finding had been put off for as long as Iran suspended its enrichment activity, which it did, partially and fitfully, until August 2005. Several months later, the Board reported the issue to the Security Council.

Would transparency be enough?

IAEA Director General Mohamed ElBaradei has repeatedly emphasized that the IAEA will not be able to give Iran a clean bill of health unless it addresses outstanding questions about weapons development work[2] and implements the Additional Protocol giving the IAEA expanded rights to access and information. The question remains, however, whether even a fully compliant, fully transparent Iran could be trusted with enrichment. Given the apparent military purpose of its programme, there is reason to fear that Iran might break out of the NPT and use a stockpile of low-enriched uranium (LEU) to quickly produce HEU for weapons purposes. This concern is not diminished by the fact that the IAEA has never found any evidence of diversion. IAEA safeguards protect against diversion, but it is far more difficult to guard against the clandestine replication of facilities, and IAEA inspections are no defence at all against breakout. The Western countries maintain that the only guaranteed way of preventing such a scenario is for there to be no enrichment activity at all.

No enrichment: a consistent transatlantic objective

The insistence that Iran refrain from enriching uranium has been a constant central theme of transatlantic policy towards Iran. In an August 2003 letter to their Iranian counterpart, the Foreign Ministers of Britain, France and Germany (E3) urged Iran to 'cease its development of facilities which would give it the capability to produce fissile material, including any enrichment or reprocessing capability'. In order to forestall any IAEA Board moves to send the issue to the Security Council, Iran voluntarily agreed, in a joint statement at the end of the E3 foreign ministers' visit to Tehran in October of that year, to suspend all uranium enrichment and reprocessing activities 'as agreed by the IAEA' (IAEA 2003b).

Disagreements over the scope of the suspension continued until November 2004, when Iran agreed to a new deal with the E3 spelling out the suspension conditions in detail. Signed in Paris, this agreement said that suspension would continue while nego-tiations on a long-term agreement were under way, and that the long-term arrangements that would come out of those negotiations would 'provide objective guarantees that Iran's nuclear program [was] exclusively for peaceful purposes' (IAEA 2004).

The E3 negotiations with Iran centred – and eventually foundered – on the meaning of 'objective guarantees'. Iran pressed for solutions that would guarantee the peaceful nature through IAEA inspections, but allow enrichment to continue. It was the European view, however, strongly reinforced by Washington, that the only real objective guaran-tee would be the total cessation of the enrichment programme and any reprocessing activities, without which Iran could not produce fissile material for a nuclear weapon.

Later in 2005, the Europeans, with US support, did move conclusively away from the demand for permanent cessation. The E3 proposal for a long-term agreement made to Iran in August 2005, which included a long list of economic, political, nuclear-energy and other incentives, called on Tehran to make a 'binding commitment' not to pursue fuel-cycle activities other than nuclear reactors moderated by light water (which are less proliferation-sensitive than heavy-water reactors), but proposed that this commitment be reviewed every ten years (IAEA 2005a). However, Iran had by this time already resumed enrichment activity, and showed no interest in the proposal.

Iran insists that it will not give up enrichment

Since talks on the issue began in 2003, Iran has never given any serious indication that it would be willing to give up the aim of acquiring enrichment technology, whatever inducements or disincentives the West might put forward. From 2003 to 2005, the gov-ernment of President Mohammad Khatami was willing to suspend parts of the enrich-ment programme in exchange for the issue not being reported to the Security Council. In the summer of 2005, after the E3 had rejected a proposal for limits on centrifuge numbers with a phased expansion up to 50,000 machines and Ahmadinejad won a sur-prise victory in the presidential election, the outgoing Khatami government decided to end the suspension. Ever since, Iranian officials have insisted that suspension is non-negotiable because enrichment is the 'national will'.

Western strategy to date

For many years, the US-led strategy for impeding Iran's nuclear project was strictly supply-side, based on denying Iran the wherewithal to produce nuclear weapons. For nearly two decades, bilateral diplomacy to discourage potential suppliers coupled with multinational export controls effectively closed many of Iran's avenues to dual-use equipment of pro-liferation concern. Concerns about Iran's nuclear intentions grew in the 1990s, in the face of mounting evidence of the country's interest in acquiring experimental uranium-isotope-separation equipment and heavy-water-moderated research reactors that appeared to be mainly intended to produce weapons-grade plutonium. Iran also sought to procure equipment that would help its nuclear engineers learn how to process irradiated fuel to separate out the plutonium. But throughout the 1990s, the US was able to persuade Argentina, China, Kazakhstan and other countries not to sell Iran facilities or material that could be used for uranium enrichment or plutonium production (Fitzpatrick 2006: 534). The US also used its leadership in the Nuclear Suppliers Group (NSG) to deny sensitive nuclear technology to Iran. The denial strategy gained a higher public profile in May 2003 upon the inauguration of the US-led Proliferation Security Initiative, which built on national maritime interdiction efforts and the ad hoc multinational cooperation that had been developing for several years to stop the illicit transfer of nuclear and chemical goods suitable for weapons and missile production.

To complement the supply-side denial tactics, European nations have led a strategy aimed at changing Iran's demand for sensitive nuclear technologies. Originally, this was focused on inducements by holding out the prospect of greater European trade and investment. Since 2001, negotiations on an EU–Iran Trade and Cooperation Agreement have been tied to changes to Iran's nuclear posture as well as to progress on human rights, terrorism and Iran's approach towards the Middle East peace process. The trade links between Iran and the West were strengthened in the November 2004 Paris Agreement.

Meanwhile, from 2003, the US sought to add negative incentives to the demand-side strategy. Convinced that the European engagement approach was doomed to failure, the Bush administration stood apart from the process for four years, until 2005. The US instead pushed for Security Council sanctions from the moment in June 2003 when IAEA inspectors first documented Iran's failure to comply with its safeguards agreement. In 2005, the US accepted the European argument that sanctions needed to go hand-in-hand with inducements. In exchange, the E3 agreed to bring Iran's case to the Security Council if inducements failed to halt enrichment activities.

In May 2006, the US agreed to a new package of incentives offered to Iran, this time by the E3 joined by China, Russia and the US. The inducements included direct US engagement in the negotiations and offers of state-of-the-art nuclear technology, as well as refinements of the economic and political incentives that the E3 had – unsuccessfully – put forward in August 2005. Offering to join negotiations and, implicitly, to lift sanctions in any final accord with Iran was a major policy shift for the Bush administration, even if the promised benefits to Iran were not immediately tangible.

Iranian leaders did not find the offer of US engagement as enticing as the Europeans had expected. It is possible that no US incentive would be sufficient to persuade Iran to give up its weapons option. In any case, Iran probably did not believe that Washington would in fact lift US sanctions. This would not have been an unreasonable assessment, given the antagonism towards Iran that prevails in the US Congress, which would have to approve any termination of sanctions. Iran also noted that the US had baulked at including in the 2006 offer the prospect of security assurances to Iran and guarantees of its territorial integrity, which the previous E3 offer had contained. Above all, the Iranians were unwilling to accept the precondition of a uranium-enrichment suspension, seeing it as a trap. They feared that suspension would only encourage Washington to make additional demands on missiles, terrorism, human rights, recognition of Israel and other contentious issues. The general perception in Tehran was that the proposals contained few guaranteed benefits (Chubin 2006: 75f.; Sadjadpur 2008: 16; Redaelli 2008).

The demand-side strategy is geared towards changing Iran's strategic analysis. In concluding that Iran had halted its nuclear-weapons programme in 2003, the November

2007 NIE judged that Iran's leaders were operating rationally, guided by a cost-benefit approach rather than an insistence on developing weapons at any cost, and that the decision to halt had been made in response to international scrutiny and pressure. This, the report said, suggests that some combination of threats and pressure, along with credible inducements, might prompt Iran to extend the halt, which the NIE judged 'with moderate confidence' had held at least up to mid-2007. The NIE also assessed, however, that it would be difficult to convince the Iranian leadership to forgo the eventual development of nuclear weapons altogether (National Intelligence Council 2007: 7).

Sanctions and pressure

The US push for UN sanctions did not succeed until three and a half years after Iran's safeguards violations were first documented, and then only after a series of other diplomatic efforts reached a dead end. The delay in adopting the first sanctions resolution reflected the European view that the threat of sanctions was more powerful than their actual imposition. Indeed, the sanctions threat had persuaded Iran to accept the first suspension agreement in October 2003 and the strengthened suspension agreement of November 2004. However, once the issue was sent to the UN, Iran began to attribute less significance to the threat, realizing that it could easily cope with the limited sanctions that the Security Council was able to muster.

UN Security Council Resolution (UNSCR) 1737 passed unanimously on 23 December 2006, banned technical and financial assistance to Iran's enrichment, reprocessing, heavy water and ballistic-missile programmes and froze the foreign-held assets of 12 Iranian individuals and ten Iranian organizations involved in those programmes. The resolution also restricted the IAEA's technical cooperation with Iran.

UNSCR 1747 passed unanimously on 24 March 2007, barred arms exports to Iran and doubled the number of Iranian entities subject to an asset freeze because of their involvement in Iran's nuclear and missile work. The resolution also called on UN members not to enter into new commitments for grants or concessional loans to Iran. Although this was not mandatory, it provided a legal basis for states to apply financial pressure.

UNSCR 1803 was adopted 3 March 2008 by a 14–0 vote (Indonesia abstaining) after the US had submitted to the IAEA additional documents detailing studies on the development of weapons and the IAEA had reported Iran's refusal to answer questions about the alleged studies and its work on advanced centrifuge designs. In addition to adding names to the asset freeze and travel ban, UNSCR 1803 authorized the inspection of shipments suspected of containing banned items carried by an Iranian airline firm and a shipping company, and called for vigilant monitoring of the activities of certain Iranian financial institutions.

UNSCR 1835 adopted unanimously on 27 September 2008, repeated the previous demands that Iran suspend enrichment and reprocessing and cooperate with the IAEA, but added no new sanctions or any new deadline. Intended to demonstrate that the Security Council remained unified, the resolution was quickly adopted once Russia had made clear that it would not accept anything harsher.

Separate from the Security Council sanctions route, the US has engaged in a determined campaign to impose costs on Iran by limiting its access to the international business sector. This campaign of financial isolation involves legal action taken to bar Iranian entities officially from operating in the US financial system, as well as informal pressure on foreign firms not to conduct business with Iran.

Is the strategy working?

However much Iran's nuclear programme was impeded in the past, Western strategies have failed to prevent Iran from acquiring a uranium-enrichment capability. By the end of January 2009, Iran was producing 100 kg of LEU a month and had stockpiled 1010 kg. If it is further enriched, the uranium content of that much LEU is sufficient in principle to provide the fissile material for one nuclear weapon. Iran thus had achieved a (very limited) latent breakout capability.

The accumulation of this much LEU makes the Iran challenge more acute. However, several caveats are in order; in particular, one should bear in mind the range of uncertainty in the variables that feed into the equation of how much is enough for a weapon. Because the LEU is under IAEA surveillance, it could not be further enriched without inspectors being aware. The basic truth that having a stockpile of enriched uranium is not the same as having a bomb also bears repeating.

For a weapon, the low-enriched uranium first would have to be further enriched to 90 per cent or more. More than half of the effort required to produce weapons-grade uranium has already been expended by the time it is enriched to just 3.5 per cent. Nevertheless, the further enrichment to weapons-grade would still take several weeks. Based on public information, it is impossible to say how long it would then take Iran to reconvert the gaseous highly enriched uranium to metal and fashion a weapon from it, but a very rough estimate might assign at least six months or more to this task.

Having just enough enriched uranium for one weapon cannot be said to confer nuclear weapons status, even once it has been enriched to weapons-grade quality. A real deterrent capability would require more. Most countries also feel the need for a test to ensure reliability, although this perhaps would not be necessary if Iran received a proven weapons design through the black market. Khan sold a design for a nuclear weapon to Libya at the beginning of the decade, and other members of his network made digital copies of the blueprints. There is no publicly available evidence that Iran obtained a weapons design as well.

The West's failure thus far to stop Iran does not mean that Iran is 'winning'. Although many Iranians would claim that successful defiance of the West is victory enough, defiance comes at the high cost of political and economic isolation. The outcome so far can best be characterized as 'lose-lose'. For the rest of the world, the costs include a loss of transparency in Iran's nuclear programme, with Tehran responding to sanctions with sharply reduced cooperation with the IAEA. Overall, Britain, France and the US contend that it is too early to conclude that Western policy has failed, because it has not yet been fully implemented, especially as regards the more painful sanctions.

Immediate and future challenges

Because Iran's intentions are suspect, its capabilities tend to be judged according to worst-case assumptions. In Iran's case, the line between a nuclear programme for civilian purposes and a military nuclear programme is thin to the point where it is perceived by many to be non-existent. There are some things that would be clear indicators of a weapons decision, including the discovery of clandestine enrichment, HEU production or weaponization work, a declaration of weapons status or the unveiling by intelligence of such a status and testing. However, the common wisdom in the West remains that Iranian possession of nuclear weapons will not be known until after the fact (Federation of American Scientists 1998). The 2007 NIE draws a distinction between Iran's 'declared civil work' on uranium enrichment and 'nuclear weapon design and weaponization work' (National Intelligence Council 2007: 6). The issue is how to build confidence that the line between civilian and military capability would hold, and whether it can be built at all while Iran continues its enrichment activity.

Military options

Some commentators maintain that the only viable fallback option is military action aimed at disabling Iran's sensitive nuclear facilities. An increasing number of officials and analysts conclude, however, that bombing Iran would be both ineffective and counterproductive. Given the extent to which Iran has dispersed its nuclear activities; buried and hardened its facilities; and kept many components out of sight of inspectors, air strikes would set back the enrichment programme for too short a period. Even if the underground enrichment plant at Natanz could be destroyed, it could probably be rebuilt within a few years, if not sooner and, in all probability, it would no longer be subject to inspection. Iran could be expected to withdraw from the NPT and engage the full resources of a unified nation in a determined nuclear weapons-development programme. Bombing Iran's nuclear facilities would probably do more to spur the country's acquisition of nuclear weapons than to delay it. Any gains that might be had from a bombing campaign would hardly be worth the risk of unintended consequences, including asymmetrical responses by Iran and its surrogates. Whether or not US forces participated in an attack on Iran, the US would be perceived to be involved. In the absence of a broadly recognized casus belli, the human suffering and economic losses stemming from such an attack would further erode the moral standing of the US and the solidarity of its alliances. The hard-line Iranian government would garner more domestic and international support, severely weakening the international pressure on Iran's programme. An overstretched US military would become even harder pressed to meet its goals in Afghanistan.

Fallback proposals

A number of proposals have been made for reducing the risk of Iran crossing the proliferation line. It is widely acknowledged that zero enrichment would be best, but many observers believe that this has become an impossible goal. Since early 2006, Mohamed ElBaradei has argued that the policy focus should be on transparency and Iran not enriching on an industrial scale, rather than on the suspension of enrichment activity, on the grounds that the latter goal has been superseded by events and that Iran does not present an imminent threat.

Lack of confidence in Iran's intentions is the central problem. Given the evidence that the principal purpose of Iran's enrichment programme is to create a nuclear weapons capability, it is argued that no technical solution will work, because Iran will not accept any condition that would prevent it from attaining this objective (Samore 2008). The history of the October 2003 Tehran Agreement on suspension, the terms of which Iran repeatedly redefined and renegotiated, is offered as evidence in this regard. Sceptics also recall the justification of the agreement that was offered to a domestic audience by former chief negotiator Hassan Rowhani – that Iran had agreed to suspend activities only in areas in which it did not have technical problems, and that in the calm diplomatic environment of the suspension, Iran would be able to complete work on the uranium-conversion process (Rowhani 2005).

Notwithstanding the evidence of some debate within Iran, the country's willingness to compromise or even negotiate has decreased even as external pressure on it to do so has increased. The enrichment programme has become ingrained in Iranian national consciousness as a 'right' that cannot be circumscribed. The country's negotiating flexibility is also constrained by Ayatollah Khamenei's entrenched view that any compromise with the US will only be met with demands for additional compromises (Sadjadpour 2008: 15f.).

The intelligence assessment that Iran made a choice in 2003 to suspend enrichment activity and work on developing weapons gives reason to believe that the suspension called for in the Security Council resolutions may still be possible, despite Iran's rejection of this demand to date. The Western nations are intent on maintaining the binary choice put to Iran since 2005: international integration, with foreign cooperation on state-of-the-art nuclear-power projects and guaranteed supply of sensitive fuel-cycle services; or political and economic isolation as the price of persisting with indigenous enrichment and plutonium production. The various French and US nuclear-cooperation agreements with Arab countries that accept fuel-cycle services from abroad indicate an alternative pathway that is open to Iran.

If future Iranian leaders show a willingness to negotiate, the incentives package could be strengthened. The US has many potential incentive cards to play in future negotiations, such as the release of impounded Iranian funds (amounting to around US$10bn) and the lifting of sanctions imposed since 1979. Alone, however, tangible incentives such as these do not appear to affect the motivations behind Iran's enrichment programme. If Iran is ever to be persuaded to forgo sensitive fuel-cycle technologies, some substitute will be needed for the prestige and security benefits that Iranian leaders believe they derive from the enrichment programme.

If Iran is not willing to negotiate on the central issue of its enrichment capability, containment and deterrence strategies will be critical to keeping it from crossing the line to weapons production. Deterrence policies were employed effectively during the Cold War against far more powerful opponents, and there is reason to believe that such policies would be effective in forestalling the emergence of a nuclear-armed Iran. A dual policy of engagement and sanctions, with containment strategies targeted at limiting Iranian access to sensitive technologies and materials, is one way for the major powers to test possibilities for Iranian cooperation while maintaining vigilance and controls to limit the threat of nuclear proliferation.

Notes

1 This chapter draws from the author's Adelphi Paper, *The Iranian Nuclear Crisis: Avoiding Worst-case Outcomes* (Fitzpatrick 2008).
2 The IAEA says the evidence of weapons development work came from several sources. The main source was the set of thousands of documents stored on the hard drive of a laptop computer that

reportedly was turned over to a US embassy in 2004 by a walk-in defector. The documents alleg-edly included designs for a ballistic-missile re-entry vehicle to carry an object that had all the attri-butes of a nuclear weapon and scientific notes highly suggestive of triggers to compress HEU spheres into a critical mass for an atomic explosion, as well as sophisticated drawings for a 400 m-deep shaft that appeared designed for an underground nuclear test. Iran claims that the documents are forgeries.

References

Bunn, M. (2007) *Constraining Iran's Nuclear Program: Assessing Options and Risks*, Presentation at Oak Ridge National Laboratory, Tennessee. Available online at: http://belfercenter.ksg.harvard.edu/publication/17694/constraining_irans_nuclear_programme.html (accessed 9 March 2009).

Chubin, S. (2006) *Iran's Nuclear Ambitions*, Washington, DC: Carnegie Endowment for International Peace.

Evans, G. (2007) 'The right nuclear red line', *Washington Post*, 5 December.

Federation of American Scientists (1998) 'Executive Summary', in *Report of the Commission to Assess the Ballistic Missile Threat to the United States*. Available online at: www.fas.org/irp/threat/missile/rumsfeld/execsum.htm (accessed 9 March 2009).

Fitzpatrick, M. (2006) 'Lessons learned from Iran's pursuit of nuclear weapons', *The Nonproliferation Review* 13, 3: 527–37.

——(2008) *The Iranian Nuclear Crisis: Avoiding Worst-Case Outcomes*, London: Routledge.

International Atomic Energy Agency (2003a) 'Implementation of the NPT safeguards agreement in the Islamic Republic of Iran', GOV/2003/75, Report by the Director General, 10 November 2003. Available online at: www.iaea.org/Publications/Documents/Board/2003/gov2003–75.pdf (accessed 9 March 2009).

——(2003b), 'Statement by the Iranian Government and visiting EU Foreign Ministers', Available online at: www.iaea.org/NewsCenter/Focus/IaeaIran/statement_iran21102003.shtml (accessed 9 March 2009).

——(2004) 'Communication dated 26 November 2004 received from the permanent representatives of France, Germany, the Islamic Republic of Iran and the United Kingdom concerning the agreement signed in Paris on 15 November 2004', INFCIRC/637.

——(2005a) 'Communication dated 8 August 2005 received from the resident representatives of France, Germany and the United Kingdom to the agency', INFCIRC/651.

——(2005b) 'Implementation of the NPT safeguards agreement in the Islamic Republic of Iran: Resolution adopted on 24 September 2005', GOV/2005/77. Available online at: www.iaea.org/Publications/Documents/Board/2005/gov2005–77.pdf (accessed 9 March 2009).

National Intelligence Council (2007) *National Intelligence Estimate; Iran: Nuclear Intentions and Capabilities*. Available online at: http://www.dni.gov/press_releases/20071203_release.pdf (accessed 9 March 2009).

Parsi, T. (2007) *Treacherous Triangle: The Secret Dealings of Israel, Iran and the United States*, New Haven, CT: Yale University Press.

Redaelli, R. (2008) 'Why selective engagement? Iranian and Western interests are closer than you think', Stanley Foundation Policy Analysis Brief, June. Available online at: www.stanleyfoundation.org/publications/pab/RedaelliPAB608.pdf (accessed 9 March 2009).

Rowhani, H. (2005) 'Beyond the challenges facing Iran and the IAEA concerning the nuclear dossier', *Rahbord* [in Persian], trans. Foreign Broadcast Information Service (2006). Available online at: www.armscontrolwonk.com/file_download/30 (accessed 9 March 2009).

Sadjadpour, K. (2008) *Reading Khamenei: The World View of Iran's Most Powerful Leader*, Washington, DC: Carnegie Endowment for International Peace.

Samore, G. (2008) 'Policy options paper: Iran', unpublished draft report, Council on Foreign Relations.

Wohlstetter, A. (1976–77) 'Spreading the bomb without quite breaking the rules', *Foreign Policy* 25: 88–94 and 145–79.

30

Intervention in Iraq

Regime change and the dialectics of state-building

Gareth Stansfield

Six years after the US-led invasion, the situation in Iraq remains precarious. While some improvements in security could be seen following the 'surge' of US troops that started in 2007, Iraq's future stability cannot be taken for granted. The US-led intervention in Iraq has been profoundly transformative. At the national, regional and international levels alike, the invasion of Iraq and its subsequent post-war experience caused a transformation of security at these inter-related levels that has not, as yet, stabilized.

The situation in Iraq is often considered through the intellectual prism of security. This is understandable considering Iraq's geopolitical significance. With proven petroleum reserves of 113 billion barrels, second only to Saudi Arabia, Iraq has inherent strategic value for the world's economy (Alnaswari 1994; Alkadiri 2001; Energy Information Administration 2007). Nevertheless, its geographic position has tended to overshadow even its immense natural wealth when considering the regional security dimension. Iraq has proven to be a vital component of the Middle East security infrastructure particularly since the 1970s, with Arab states and Western powers alike viewing the country as a strategic bulwark against the Islamic Republic of Iran, only for Iraq itself to be viewed as an equal, if not greater threat following the end of the First Gulf War with Iran, when Baghdad's attention turned toward Kuwait in 1990.

It is to Iraq's invasion of Kuwait in 1990 that the immediate causes of the current security problems can be traced. Though Saddam Hussein's regime survived the routing of Iraqi forces from Kuwait in 1991 by a US-led coalition, Iraq was not rehabilitated within the international system. Instead, the Ba'ath regime of Iraq was considered to be a pariah in the international community (Niblock 2002) and later identified as an agent of insecurity. In the aftermath of the al-Qaida attacks of 11 September 2001, US policymakers promoted the idea of regime change and the reconstruction of the Iraqi state as a 'beacon' of neoliberal democracy at the heart of the Middle East (Anderson and Stansfield 2005).

This chapter focuses on the breakdown of security in Iraq following the invasion of 2003, considering the interplay of indigenous Iraqi political forces and external US policies. The emergence of communal-based politics in Iraq is discussed together with the impact of these changes upon the regional security architecture of the Middle East. The chapter

concludes with an assessment of the situation from the perspective of early 2009, identifying the variables that may influence Iraq's development in the future and the role of
the US. In order to make sense of the situation in Iraq, the spatial layering of security
concerns has some utility as an analytical framework operating across three discrete but
overlapping spheres – domestic, regional and international.

Spatial spheres of security

When considering the post-2003 period, the debate on security and Iraq has been as
varied as it has been vigorous. It has also been confusing because concerns that have at
times been seen as local issues, such as the presence of militias or the approach taken to
governance, often have ties to wider motivating and mobilizing factors, such as religious
authorities, tribal allegiances, Arab nationalist sentiment, or even the economic investment of regional powers. While it is only one of several possible approaches to discussing
security in Iraq, considering the interaction across different spheres of security allows us
to at least understand the complexity of the situation.

The domestic sphere

The debate among academics has been at its most intense when the domestic level of
Iraq's security has been considered, with the scholarly literature focusing upon the nature
of Iraqi society and US strategies for reconfiguring the state (Herring and Rangwala 2006;
Stansfield 2007a; Visser 2008a). Most commonly, this literature focused upon the construct of the Iraqi state since its inception following the demise of the Ottoman Empire.
Scholars who presented a vision of Iraqi society as being largely secular and imbued with
notions of civic nationalism were countered by those who suggested that communal
identities of ethnicity and religion were dynamics that could not be easily dismissed.

The regional sphere

These local security considerations linked automatically into wider regional perspectives.
Reports documenting the rise of Shi'ite Islam in the Middle East became increasingly
common, with notions of a 'Shi'a crescent' spreading from Iran through the Gulf States
and Iraq and culminating in Lebanon receiving widespread attention (Nasr 2004, 2006;
Nakash 2006; Pelham 2008). To the north, the consolidation of the Kurdistan region of
Iraq and the influence – at least as an example – that the Iraqi Kurds could have on their
brethren living in Turkey, prompted Turkey's military establishment to move forcefully
to counter any possible threat posed to the territorial integrity of Turkey from groups
such as the Kurdistan Workers' Party (PKK) (Gunter and Yavuz 2005; Lundgren 2007).
Across the rest of the region, the deterioration of security in Iraq was viewed with alarm,
particularly as it became clear that al-Qaida elements were attempting to establish
themselves in what appeared to be a heavily weakened state.

The international sphere

These security problems, which are widespread in Iraq, originated from three inter-
related dynamics driven largely by complexes of decisions made at the international level.

The first of these complexes was the failure of US policymakers to understand the nature of the Iraqi state in the years prior to 2003. The second of these dynamics was driven by the policies taken to reconstruct Iraq, and these mistakes then created a third dynamic of new realities that needed to be addressed five years later.

With so much political, financial and human capital invested in the Iraq project, failure in Iraq would have a profound impact on future perceptions of the US in the Middle East (Kahl et al. 2008).[1] Military defeat or the failure of the state-building project, or both, would embolden those opposed to the US in general, but also undermine US domestic support for such actions in the future (Korb et al. 2008). The Iraq experience was not only deeply transformative for the US. It also suggested to other actors that a unipolar world dominated by the US might be more fiction than fact.

This chapter refers to dynamics within the international sphere that affected Iraq – and particularly those pertaining to US involvement. Indeed, it is impossible to ignore the impact of the 'US' dimension on security issues relating to Iraq since 2003. However, the substantive focus will be upon developments inside Iraq itself – which were of course heavily influenced by international actors – and on the way in which these developments affected the wider region.

The localization of security

One of the most contentiously debated issues was the deterioration of security inside Iraq. This dynamic was tied closely to the failure to resurrect state institutions capable of administering and controlling society. There were various attempts to apportion blame for these failures.

For some analysts, the fault lay squarely on the shoulders of US policy planners whose conceptualization of Iraq was wrong. Believing Iraqi identity to be fractured, it is argued, the US based its plans on a 'historically illiterate' model (Visser 2008b). This model – which identified communal identities as the principle organizing blocks of Iraqi politics – then determined how the US reconstructed the state. It is easy to attack the US for doing this, particularly if one considers the scale of the problems that now afflict Iraq. However, how fair is it to do this, and how logically coherent are the arguments used by those who contend that a different approach would have been better? While it might have theoretically been advantageous, for example, to build a political system in Iraq upon notions of civic nationalism and individual rights, the fact remained that Iraqi actors themselves had become organized into communal blocks. Just as imposing a communal view of Iraqi political life upon the country can be seen as simplistic, to impose a political system that ignored these blocks would have been perhaps more morally repugnant.

The paucity of options

While the US has been complicit in building a political structure that is at best cumbersome, at worst unworkable, the critics of US actions did not propose suggestions that were any more workable. The accepted view of Iraqi political mobilization was that a cohesive nationalist project existed that would ultimately harden either in support of the US, or against it. These analysts were largely wrong. Instead, it is more persuasive theoretically and empirically to argue that the endemic insecurity had Iraqi origins.[2] A more nuanced argument is that US decisions acted as a catalyst in allowing inherent communal-based divisions to emerge and deepen in a political environment freed from the strictures of dictatorship. However, rather than a singular nationalist project emerging, multiple Iraqi nationalisms appeared. Religiously minded Shi'ites merged the language of nationalism with their own communal worldview, as did Sunnis and even some Kurds. Certainly, each of these groups had its own concept of how a future Iraq might be shaped, but rarely was there space in their visions for the views of the other groups. The result of this development was predictable, as the competition between groups became increasingly fractious.

Before the invasion of Iraq, the question of how Iraqi society would be altered by removing the incumbent regime was not sufficiently pondered. The US planners did not consider questions of state building, let alone the matter of how Middle East security would be configured in the absence of a strong Iraqi state. The pre-eminent security concern focused on the threat posed by Iraq's presumed WMDs and aspirations toward the region. In comparison, the post-invasion scenario planning received less attention. By the time of the invasion, the Bush administration had clearly accepted the arguments promoted by neo-conservative policy advisers that after the overthrow of Hussein, US strategies to democratize the state according to a US-orientated worldview and apply the economic neoliberal rules of the Washington Consensus would be embraced (Burgos 2008; Dunne and Stansfield 2008; Schmidt and Williams 2008).

This did not prove to be the case. By 2005, the empowerment of political parties organized along lines of communal identity was complete, and in areas dominated by a particularly community, security was provided by the most powerful parties of that region. In the north, security was managed by the indigenous Kurdish 'peshmerga' fighters. In the south, the militias of the Supreme Council for the Islamic Revolution in Iraq (SCIRI, later known as the Supreme Islamic Iraqi Council, or SIIC) and other smaller parties such as *Fadilah* meted out security and justice.[3] In the centre and the north, vast swathes of territory fell under the changeable control of Sunni tribes, remnant Ba'athist organizations, or prominent groupings linked to al-Qaida (Stansfield 2007b; Long 2008).[4]

The situation was such that the smallest spark would have the potential to ignite inter-communal conflict. With sectarian tensions increasing from 2005 following the boycotting of elections by Sunni Arabs and the subsequent dominance of the state by Shi'ite and Kurdish parties, Sunni-Shi'ite violence spread across central and south Iraq. This violence erupted in February 2006 with the destruction of the Shi'ite Askariyya shrine in Samarra. The sectarian war that followed resulted in ethnic cleansing of mixed towns and the effective partitioning of Baghdad, with the city effectively being taken over by Shi'ites by the end of 2007.

A further, ethnic fault-line opened up from late 2007. Kurdish aspirations to maintain the autonomy within Iraq that they had enjoyed since 1991 and to expand their control to other disputed territories (and particularly the province of Kirkuk) brought them into direct confrontation with both Sunni and Shi'ite Arabs, Turkmens and Christians (Stansfield 2003; Romano 2007; Gunter 2008; International Crisis Group 2008; Anderson and Stansfield 2009).

This situation was arguably even more serious than the sectarian conflict of 2006–7. Even though during the earlier phase, the bloodshed was far more significant and the spectacle of violence more grotesque, the conflict never threatened the integrity of the state. Of course, swathes of territory fell out of the control of the state and became the preserve of insurgents and militias, but the political process in Baghdad continued in a reasonably unaffected manner. The conflict between the Kurdistan Regional Government

(KRG) and the Iraqi government, however, not only threatened to turn violent on several occasions, most notably in Khanaqin in August 2008 (Peterson 2008), but destabilized the political alliance underpinning the government. The Kurds demanded the implementation of Article 140 of the Constitution, which would almost certainly see the province of Kirkuk merge with the Kurdistan Region, while the government of Nouri al-Maliki and Arab parliamentarians were resolutely opposed to this. Thus, the scene was set for a serious political and military confrontation.

US responses – the 'surge' and the localization of security

For the embattled US government, which was desperate to show that Iraq was stabilizing and would not need a sizeable US troop presence there in the future, the collapse into civil war was problematic. The US responded with a multi-faceted approach based upon increasing the military presence in Baghdad, and also by seeking to bring into the security structure Sunni Arabs previously attracted to the neo-Ba'athists and al-Qaida. The strategy was built upon the notion of 'local solutions for local problems' and appeared to be successful. The numbers of fatal attacks in Baghdad dropped spectacularly, as did the targeting of Multi-National Forces.

Two questions suggest themselves when considering this development. The first is whether the surge was responsible for the decline in violence, or whether other factors, including the ceasefire called by Muqtada al-Sadr, a religious and militia leader, were decisive. Did the surge prevent violence, or was the impetus behind sectarian conflict particularly in Baghdad diluted because the communities had largely separated themselves into distinct ghettos by the end of 2007?

The second question focuses more on the implications of the 'surge'. Put simply, while the increase of US forces and the participation of Sunnis in the security system may have been successful, do these short-term gains have long-term consequences? Did the localization and communalization of security come at the price of the building of a cross-communal Iraqi identity?

In the north, the *peshmerga* were re-badged as the Kurdish contingent of the Iraqi Security Forces (ISF). A similar strategy was followed with regard to the militia of the SIIC – the Badr Army. Recruited en masse into the ISF, the intelligence service and the police force, the prominence of Badr members in the ISF led to accusations that the institutions of state security were infiltrated by Shi'ite militias. In Sunni areas, the US set about promoting local 'councils' or groups to take security matters into their own hands. Often referred to as the 'Awakening' movement, this strategy succeeded in empowering tribes and local neighbourhoods against groups claiming association with al-Qaida, yet they remained opposed to the dominance of the state by Shi'ites and Kurds. The animosity was shared by those in government, particularly as the US expected the Iraqi government to incorporate the 'Awakening' groups into the formal security services from mid-2008 onwards. There was little enthusiasm within a Shi'a-dominated Iraqi government at the prospect of not only accepting, but also funding what was seen as an extra-legal Sunni militia diametrically opposed to those in power.[5]

The chaotic devolution of political power proved to be semi-permanent and not a transient feature of the post-2003 political landscape. The problem of localized power was not only felt in Iraq. The fragmentation of authority was viewed with concern in regional capitals. Not only was Iraq important as a major state with immense oil wealth and a leading force in the Arab world, it was also seen by its neighbours as a useful asset due to its ability to limit the influence of Shi'ites in the affairs of Arab states and the rise of Kurdish nationalism.

The regional dimension

The current weakened state of Iraq is particularly worrisome to many observers because it has enhanced the influence of neighbouring powers, and particularly that of Iran. However, just as Iraq has a pivotal role in the regional security complex of the Middle East due to the internal characteristics of the country and the domestic conditions of neighbours, so too do these countries have influence inside Iraq.

The threat of Shi'a Islam

The first of these characteristics concerns the nature of Iraq as home to the sacred sites of veneration for Shi'ites and home to a majority Shi'ite population. Worries about the potential of Shi'a Islam to destabilize the Gulf can largely be reduced to two issues. The first is concern about the potential 'rise of the Shi'a crescent' starting in Iran and ending in Lebanon, and the possibility that Shi'ite communities in Gulf states could regard the rise of their co-religionists in Iraq as a model to emulate. Their behaviour can be influenced by Iran to a considerable degree, and this Sword of Damocles hanging over the Gulf States has served to focus minds about the intentions of Tehran.

Considerable attention has been paid to what some analysts have described as the Shi'ites' 'reaching for power' (Nakash 2006; Nasr 2006). For these observers, the terrible events in Iraq cannot be considered in isolation, but are part of a wider regional context. Vali Nasr noted that 'Iraq's sectarian pains are all the more complex because reverberations of Shi'a empowerment will inevitably extend beyond Iraq's borders, involving the broader region from Lebanon to Pakistan' (Nasr 2004).

The second issue is that of a proxy war against the US being fought in Iraq that could spill over into a wider confrontation between the US and Iran. Tehran has no chance of defeating the US military in a conventional conflict. But Iran has managed to successfully 'fight' the US inside Iraq, through supporting Shi'ite proxies in particular, in a manner that undoubtedly influenced US decisions as to whether it could attack Iran more openly over Tehran's WMD programme. Any plans for an attack against Iran must factor into the military equation the certainty that Iran can exact a terrible revenge upon the US in Iraq. It can also further destabilize Lebanon, heighten the problems faced by NATO in Afghanistan and even influence events in Palestine. A proxy war against the US in the Middle East is a struggle that Iran can carry out, and perhaps even win.

The rise of the Kurds

The second of these internal characteristics relates to ethnicity. Since its inception, Iraq has been seen as a bulwark of Arab nationalism, and successive regimes sought to position Iraq as the leading power among Arab nations (see Dodge 2003; Stansfield 2007a). While the regional competition created problems with Arab neighbours, the appeal to Arab nationalism also created internal problems with those Iraqis who are not ethnic Arabs. Since their incorporation into Iraq in 1926, the Kurds remained discontented subjects under the monarchy. However, even the Kurds were able to accept an Iraq where Iraqi nationalism was the basis of the state's historical memory and narrative. They could not, however, accept a state whose raison d'être was based on Arab nationalism. Faced with an increasingly Arab nationalist regime in the form of the Ba'ath Party, the Kurds engaged in a violent rebellion against Iraqi government forces, with the Ba'ath regime committing ever more grievous atrocities to quell them, culminating in the use of chemical weapons in the now infamous Anfal Campaign of the 1980s.

Nevertheless, the Kurdish insurgency survived and, taking advantage of Hussein's tactical miscalculations that led him into defeat in 1991, carved out an autonomous region in the north of Iraq. Neighbouring countries that also had a significant Kurdish population – especially Turkey and Iran, and to a lesser extent Syria – regarded this development as a threat to their national security. Keen to ensure that the Kurds of Iraq would neither be independent and thereby threaten their own integrity through irredentist demands, nor act as an example to the often fractious Kurds in their own countries, Turkey and Iran have sought through various means to manipulate the situation in the north of Iraq. These means have usually been by coercion, but increasingly also by other less obvious means – including economic investment and political negotiations. However, especially in the post-2003 environment, the newfound status of the Kurds of Iraq, now with a constitutionally recognized KRG and significant financial resources, remains a key security concern for all neighbouring states and the US.[6]

Conclusion: the past as prologue

The invasion of Iraq in 2003 was a watershed in the history of the country. By removing the Ba'ath regime from power, the US-led coalition effectively brought to an end political dominance by Arab Sunnis, which had lasted nearly a century. The period since 2003 has been a time of exceptionally complex political dynamics, with reactions against an occupying force, the emergence of vigorous communal politics and the extensive involvement of external powers in Iraq's affairs. At the core of this complexity was a change in the domestic political rules of the game. In this respect, the US intervention was of formative political importance.

By invading Iraq, crushing the military and finally capturing the most important regime personalities, the US not only achieved its first goal of regime change (the second being regime replacement). It also fundamentally altered the nature of politics in Iraq by removing the structures of the authoritarian Ba'athist state and destroying the psychological hold of dictatorship. Following this, it was all but impossible to restore the Iraqi state to its former state by undertaking some sort of 'lightweight' regime replacement, as was initially intended. Instead, new leaders from previously suppressed communities came forward, while new ideas emerged concerning the future governance of the country, both of which dynamics have had profound implications for Iraq since 2003. Not only did new leaders emerge, but also the very idea of Iraq is now subject to re-interpretation. The state is no longer legitimized by notions of secularism, Arabism or notions of unspoken Sunni dominance. Instead, the victors in the new Iraq can now impose their own notions of Iraqi identity on the state. The Shi'ites and Kurds, in particular, are now well placed to pursue their own agendas without fear of retribution, while Iraqi nationalism is fed by understandable negative sentiments brought about by the US occupation.

Whatever the starting point of the deterioration of security in Iraq, however, two facts can be highlighted. The first is that, by 2008, identity politics had largely taken hold of

335

Iraq. It was no longer possible to understand Iraqi politics without referring to 'Shi'ite', 'Kurdish' or 'Sunni/Arab' parties. As Iraq approaches its sixth year since the US invasion, its future remains as doubtful as at any time since 2003. Indeed, the problems facing the country are perhaps even more serious than at any time before. In the coming years, important and indeed existential decisions will be required that go to the very core of the debate over Iraq's identity and the future structure of the state. These decisions have, to a large extent, been glossed over in previous years and are now coming to a head.

At the top of these problems is the relationship between Iraq and the US. The UN Security Council mandate that legitimizes the presence of the Multi-National Force in Iraq expired at the end of 2008. In the run-up to this date, Iraqi and US negotiators embarked upon a series of tough meetings to hammer out the details of a 'Status of Forces Agreement' (SOFA) that would outline the parameters of US military operations in Iraq from 1 January 2009. The negotiations over the SOFA proved to be very pro-blematic. The US, perhaps for the first time since 2003, faced an Iraqi government that was not willing to simply accept whatever the US embassy staff presented. Rather, Prime Minister Maliki's negotiating team proved its skill at brinkmanship and compromise, ultimately accepting a SOFA arrangement with terms far more acceptable to Iraq than what the US had originally envisaged. The SOFA sets a three-year timetable for the withdrawal of US forces and reduces the freedom of operation they enjoyed before 2009. Nevertheless, the relationship between the Iraqi government and the US will still be critical for Iraq's future. As a balancing act for any Iraqi leader, it is particularly diffi-cult. While Iraq's domestic security remains so fragile, the US presence is deemed favourable, at least from the perspective of the government. However, the US presence is deeply unpopular among the Arab Iraqi electorate. Considering that the negotiations for a follow-up agreement to the Anglo-Iraqi Treaty with the UK broke down half a century ago due to a vibrant Iraqi nationalist anti-imperialist movement, an even stronger opposition to the US can be expected to develop in future months and years.

Other issues of course remain, not least the relationship between Iraq's communities and the state. Several problems have to be addressed, including not only the reincor-poration of Sunnis into the political process, but also the acceptance of a powerful Sunni Arab voice in the government of Iraq, which will almost certainly happen. How this will be achieved remains to be seen, but the coalition of Arab parliamentarians in Baghdad is distinctly delicate, and it is a mistake to assume that the days of sectarian conflict in Iraq are over. Perhaps even more pressing is the need to find, once and for all, a political solution to Kurdish demands in Iraq. Throughout 2007 and 2008, disagreements between the now powerful Kurds and the Iraqi government have brought the Iraqi governmental system to a standstill. It is critically important that the status of Kirkuk be resolved and the KRG's federal rights as defined in the Constitution be recognized.

Looking to the future from a different perspective, the Iraq War has undoubtedly had a profound effect upon how the US will conduct itself in future foreign interventions (see Dodge 2008). Clearly, the US and its allies have had the opportunity to learn valu-able lessons about the utility of military intervention, and the practice of it. This failure to arrive at what is referred to increasingly in the UK as an accurate 'cultural estimate' has caused governments on both sides of the Atlantic to assess the mistakes made in Iraq and Afghanistan and to consider how to prevent them from happening again in the future – presuming that military intervention as a tool of statecraft is not totally off the menu of possible strategies in future years.

Notes

1 In economic terms alone, Joseph Stiglitz (a Nobel Prize-winning economist) estimated that the Iraq War would cost the US taxpayer some US$3 trillion. With macroeconomic costs and interest included, the sum rose by another 50 per cent (Stiglitz 2008).

2 Both sets of analyses tended to use the same source materials, but in very different ways. Hanna Batatu's very detailed book was frequently referred to and used to illustrate not only the development of civic Iraqi nationalism, but also the existence of a society highly variegated by ethnicity, religion and class. Other works by Iraqis, including Ali Wardi, were often cited to illustrate the complexity of Iraqi society and Western analysts' inadequate understanding of it (cf. Batatu 1978 and Wardi 1991–92).

3 See Jabar 2003 for an overview of Shi'ite parties in Iraq.

4 To make matters even more complicated, in the Sunni areas of Iraq, groups often changed their allegiance. For example, some tribes that had been members of insurgent or religious militias when it proved to be in their interests later took part in the US-sponsored *sahwa* (Awakening) movement when it was deemed beneficial to change sides.

5 Problems between the *sahwa* leaders and the Iraqi government became apparent almost as soon as the US stopped funding them directly from October 2008. Though the militias had previously been paid US$300 per person by the US military, the Iraqi government immediately announced that it would only guarantee reduced salaries of US$250 for 20,000 soldiers out of the 100,000-strong force. The response of *sahwa* leaders was to warn that their people could rejoin insurgent groups or criminal gangs. See Liz Sly, 'Iraq plans to cut Sunni fighters' salaries', *Chicago Tribune*, 2 November 2008.

6 At the top of the list of concerns is the status of territories disputed by the KRG and the Iraqi government, and especially the oil-rich province of Kirkuk. See International Crisis Group 2008; Anderson and Stansfield 2009 for analyses of the problem of disputed territories.

References

Alkadiri, R. (2001) 'The Iraqi Klondike: Oil and regional trade', *Middle East Report* Fall, 220: 30–35.

Alnaswari, A. (1994) *The Economy of Iraq: Oil, Wars, Destruction of Development and Prospects, 1950–2010*, London: Greenwood Publishers.

Anderson, L. and Stansfield, G. (2005) *The Future of Iraq: Dictatorship, Democracy, or Division?* 2nd edn, New York: Palgrave Macmillan.

——(2009) *Crisis in Kirkuk: The Ethnopolitics of Conflict and Compromise*, Philadelphia, PA: University of Pennsylvania Press.

Batatu, H. (1978) *The Old Social Classes and Revolutionary Movements of Iraq: A Study of Iraq's Old Landed and Commercial Classes and of its Communists, Ba'thists and Free Officers*, Princeton, NJ: Princeton University Press.

Burgos, R.A. (2008) 'Origins of regime change: "Ideapolitik" on the long road to Baghdad, 1993–2000', *Security Studies* 17, 2: 221–56.

Cordesman, A. (2008) 'Conditions-based US withdrawal from Iraq', *CSIS Commentary*, Washington, DC: Center for Strategic and International Studies.

Dodge, T. (2003) *Inventing Iraq: The Failure of Nation-Building and a History Denied*, London: Hurst & Co.

——(2008) 'Iraq and the next American President', *Survival* 50, 5: 27–60.

Dunne, T. and Stansfield, G. (2008) 'International relations and the "War on Terror": Realist and reflectivist perspectives', in Owens, J. and Dumbrell, J. (eds) *America's War on Terrorism and Contemporary US Foreign Policy*, Lexington, MA: Lexington Press, pp. 139–58.

Energy Information Administration (2007) *Iraq*, Washington, DC: EIA.

Gunter, M. (2008) *The Kurds Ascending: The Evolving Solution to the Kurdish Problem in Iraq and Turkey*, New York: Palgrave Macmillan.

Gunter, M. and Yavuz, H. (2005) 'The continuing crisis in Iraqi Kurdistan', *Middle East Policy* 12, 1: 122–33.

Herring, E. and Rangwala, G. (2006) *Iraq in Fragments: The Occupation and its Legacy*, London: Hurst & Co.

International Crisis Group (2008) *Oil for Soil: Toward a Grand Bargain on Iraq and the Kurds*, Middle East Report No. 80 (28 October), Washington, DC: International Crisis Group.

Jabar, F.A. (2003) *The Shi'ite Movement in Iraq*, London: Saqi Books.

Kahl, C., Flournoy, M. and Brimley, S. (2008) *Shaping the Iraq Inheritance*, Washington, DC: Center for a New American Security.

Korb, L., Katulis, B., Duggan, S. and Juul, P. (2008) *How Does This End? Strategic Failures Overshadow Tactical Gains in Iraq*. Washington, DC: Center for American Progress.

Long, A. (2008) 'The Anbar awakening', *Survival* 50, 2: 67–94.

Lundgren, Å. (2007) *The Unwelcome Neighbour: Turkey's Kurdish Policy*, London: I. B. Tauris.

Marr, P. (2004) *The Modern History of Iraq*, 2nd edn, Boulder, CO: Westview Press.

Nakash, Y. (2006) *Reaching for Power: The Shi'a in the Modern Arab World*, Princeton, NJ: Princeton University Press.

Nasr, V. (2004) 'Regional implications of Shi'a revival in Iraq', *The Washington Quarterly* 27, 3: 7–24.

——(2006) *The Shi'a Revival: How Conflicts Within Islam will Shape the Future*, New York: Norton.

Niblock, T. (2002) *'Pariah States' and Sanctions in the Middle East: Iraq, Libya, Sudan*, Boulder, CO: Lynne Rienner.

Pelham, N. (2008) *A New Muslim Order: The Shi'a and the Middle East Sectarian Crisis*, London: I. B. Tauris.

Peterson, S. (2008) 'US referees Iraq's troubled Kurdish-Arab faultine', *Christian Science Monitor*, 21 October.

Romano, D. (2007) 'The future of Kirkuk', *Ethnopolitics* 6, 2: 265–83.

Rosen, N. (2007) 'The death of Iraq', *Current History*, December: 409–15.

Schmidt, B. and Williams, M. (2008) 'The Bush doctrine and the Iraq war: Neoconservatives versus realists', *Security Studies* 17, 2: 191–200.

Stansfield, G. (2003) *Iraqi Kurdistan: Political Development and Emergent Democracy*, London: Routledge.

——(2007a) *Iraq: People, History, Politics*, Cambridge: Polity Press.

——(2007b) *Accepting Realities in Iraq*, London: Chatham House.

Stiglitz, J. (2008) *The Three Trillion Dollar War: The True Cost of the Iraq Conflict*, New York: Norton.

The Task Force for a Responsible Withdrawal from Iraq (2008) *The Necessary Steps for a Responsible Withdrawal from Iraq*, Cambridge, MA: Commonwealth Institute.

Visser, R. (2008a) 'The United States and Iraq: Still getting it wrong', *OpenDemocracy*, 3 October.

——(2008b) 'Historical myths of a divided Iraq', *Survival* 50, 2: 95–106.

Wardi, A. (1991–92) *Lamahat Ijtima'iyah min Ta'rikh al-'Iraq al-Hadith*, London: Kufaan Publishing.

31

The Israeli–Palestinian conflict

Mark A. Heller[1]

The Israeli–Palestinian conflict is one of several unregulated legacies of the Ottoman Empire that continue to vex the international order. At first glance, this might seem counterintuitive. After all, this conflict has not been fought out over large swathes of strategically vital territory; has not directly involved the military forces of major powers since the end of the British Mandate in 1948; and has not produced massive disruption or casualties on the scale to which the world in the twentieth century became accustomed. It is true that the territory variously called Palestine, the Land of Israel or the Holy Land has a unique religious-historical resonance, and the cultural affinities between the protagonists and other populations outside the region have guaranteed that it would generate not just interest, but passion. Still, the most persuasive explanation for this phenomenon is that the conflict between Jews and Arabs has often seemed to be important, even critical, to the overall alignment of the Middle East and perhaps even of the whole Arab or Muslim world. The latter, in turn, has always had strategic significance. Even before the discovery of oil, the region's location at the crossroads of Europe, Asia and Africa made it an object of interest for almost every imperial power. And since the Second World War, the Middle East's position as the repository of the world's largest known oil reserves has added a major geo-economic dimension to its traditional geopolitical role.

Conflation of the Israeli–Palestinian conflict with the destiny of the Middle East as a whole distorts reality and does not stand up to rigorous scrutiny. Nevertheless, the link has been asserted so insistently and so often by Middle Eastern interlocutors that extra-regional actors have been persuaded that the Israeli–Palestinian conflict demands their attention, not just for its own sake, but also as a determinant of larger strategic outcomes. The 'international community' has therefore committed huge resources and political capital to its resolution or at least its management and containment, and the conflict, barring an unlikely peaceful resolution, is likely to stay at or near the top of the international political-security agenda for the foreseeable future.

This chapter first traces the contemporary history of the conflict and delineate its recurrent themes. It then analyses the current state of affairs and prospects for conflict management and resolution. Finally, the chapter discusses the implications of the conflict for broader regional and international security.

Historical background

Any periodization of protracted conflicts risks setting arbitrary boundaries on dynamics that have earlier roots and later consequences. Nevertheless, there have been some discrete events over the course of this conflict that signalled changes in the relationships and even identities of the main protagonists and/or in the issues apparently at stake. By these criteria, the history of the conflict can be divided into four main stages:

- 1917–48: zero-sum communal conflict between Jews and Arabs in Palestine in the context of foreign (British) rule;
- 1948–67: subordination of the communal (Jewish-Palestinian/Arab-Palestinian) dimension to the dictates of Arab–Israeli interstate conflict;
- 1967–93: revival of the zero-sum communal conflict following Israel's occupation of those parts of the British mandatory territory that came under Jordanian and Egyptian rule after 1948;
- 1993–: transformation of the communal conflict into a 'mixed-sum' game following the public commitment by the leaderships of both parties to a negotiated settlement of the conflict, i.e. to engage in what has come to be known as 'the peace process'.

1917–48: the Ottoman legacy and British rule

The territory over which the Israeli–Palestinian conflict has been waged did not exist as a distinct political entity for almost 2,000 years until after the Ottoman defeat in the First World War. The first stage of the conflict, however, predated the British overthrow of Turkish rule in 1917–18 in the sense that the land had already become the focus of competing Jewish and Arab aspirations. During the course of the war, the British government undertook seemingly contradictory, albeit ambiguous, commitments to Jews and Arabs. To the Zionist Federation, it declared in the so-called Balfour Declaration that it viewed 'with favour the establishment in Palestine of a national home for the Jewish people'; to Sharif Hussein of Mecca, the leader of the Arab revolt against the Ottomans, it expressed its willingness to 'recognise and support the independence of the Arabs', though with exceptions that arguably applied to the territory later demarcated as Palestine.[2]

When Britain received a League of Nations mandate for the territory after the war, it assumed not only the de jure authority for governing but also the de facto responsibility for mediating or arbitrating Jewish and Arab claims. Unable to reconcile those claims and faced with increasingly violent Arab opposition in the 1930s to Jewish immigration and land purchases, in 1937 the British proposed to partition the territory between Jews and Arabs. The leadership of the Jewish community accepted the proposal, albeit unenthusiastically, but the Palestinian Arab leadership rejected it categorically in the conviction that the entire land belonged rightfully to the Arab side and that the Jews had no collective rights to any part of it, only individual rights that would ostensibly be respected in a unitary state. This was the first iteration of the 'one-state vs. two-state' dichotomy that would become a recurring theme in subsequent decades.

Its first reiteration came a decade later when Britain returned the 'Palestine file' to the international community, now reconstituted as the United Nations. Like its British predecessor, a UN commission of inquiry recommended partition, which was endorsed in General Assembly Resolution 1810. As before, the principle of partition was accepted by the Jewish side and rejected by the Palestinian Arab side (and all the independent Arab states). This time, however, there was no status quo on which to fall back in case of diplomatic deadlock, since the British had already announced their intention to withdraw by 15 May 1948. Instead, the outcome would be decided by a clash of arms, first, between Palestinian Arabs and Jews and then, after 15 May, between the armies of neighbouring Arab states and that of the nascent State of Israel.

The result of this confrontation was the partition of Palestine that the Arabs had rejected, though on territorial terms more favourable to the Jewish side than those proposed in the UN report. However, the State of Israel's 'partners' in this partition were not the Palestinian Arabs. Instead, the armistice agreements that ended the fighting in 1949 formalized a de facto division between Israel, Transjordan and Egypt of the territory designated for Palestinian statehood. Israel immediately incorporated its part into the new state, Transjordan did the same to its part – the West Bank – within a year (and renamed itself the Hashemite Kingdom of Jordan) and Egypt placed its part – the Gaza Strip – under military government. That situation prevailed for the next 18 years.

1948–67: defining and defending borders and identities

The 1949 agreements stipulated, at Arab insistence, that the armistice lines were not permanent borders; those would be negotiated in final peace agreements. Peace, however, did not follow war. Since Israel was unable either to pose a credible threat to resume hostilities or to offer sufficiently appealing concessions, the Arabs had little incentive to abandon their principled rejection of any Jewish state in Palestine. Instead, they preferred to bide their time, insisting that conditions would eventually permit a 'second round'. However, the conflict did not simply persist; it became more complex because the disruptive effects of its consequences were added to its original unresolved cause. In particular the fate of hundreds of thousands of Arab refugees, whose status the host countries (except for Jordan) and the Palestinians themselves refused to regularize, lest that be interpreted as tacit endorsement of the new reality. At the same time, Palestinians themselves ceased to be the main actor in the confrontation with Israel. Indeed, for most of this period, they ceased to be a coherent political factor at all.

The war in 1947–49 had had a devastating effect on Palestinian political institutions and social formations. Even the distinct national consciousness of the Palestinians – always problematic because what had distinguished them from the Jews in Palestine before 1948 had been their Arab identity rather than their Palestinian identity – began to atrophy. As a result, while Palestine remained the primal issue in Israeli–Arab relations, the Palestinians were replaced as central protagonists by Arab states, which pursued particularistic state and/or regime concerns that sometimes overshadowed and obscured the Palestine issue. Arab states' confrontations with Israel were still garbed in the rhetoric of 'liberation', but more often than not they were centred on land and/or water disputes in border areas.

If the prominence of the Palestinian dimension in the conflict diminished, the engagement of outside powers intensified. As the Cold War cast its shadow over regional politics and strategic gains and losses came to be defined by the alignment of regional actors, the Soviets abandoned their initial support for Israel's 'objectively' anti-imperialist struggle against Britain and its Arab allies and began to provide rhetorical and material support for Arab regimes inclined to accept it, particularly the radical nationalist forces whose driving force was Egyptian President Gamal Abdel Nasser of Egypt. As long as Arab nationalist

341

ire was directed primarily against Britain and France, the US sought to block the Soviet presence and influence not through frontal confrontation, but rather through competition for the loyalty of other Arab states. As a result, US–Israeli relations remained correct, but cool, well into the 1960s.[3] However, all these considerations, by both regional and extra-regional actors, were only indirectly connected to the original issue of Palestine.

1967–93: the re-emergence of communal conflict

This began to change after 1967, when the conflict reverted to its original dimensions. The shift was not immediate; several uniquely Palestinian organizations, including the Palestinian Liberation Organization, had been formed as before the war in 1967 (some by Arab regimes bent on destabilizing or discrediting other Arab regimes) and had even contributed to the chain of events that culminated in the outbreak of that war. Nor was it ever total; much of the post-1967 Arab–Israeli agenda was taken up with efforts by Egypt and Syria to deal with the consequences of the 1967 war, i.e. to recover the territory they had lost in the fighting, and the largest and most costly military conflict since then – the war of 1973 – was precisely about that, rather than about the Palestinian issue per se.

Nevertheless, 1967 marks a signal change in two important respects. The first is that it represented a high-water mark in the tide of pan-Arab nationalism; the military defeat of Nasir weakened the primacy of the Arab cause, even in Egypt, and led most states to refocus on narrower local concerns. The second, no less significant, was the enhancement of Palestinian particularism, partly because the Palestinians, too, began to lose faith in the ability/willingness of the other Arabs to confront Israel on their behalf, mostly because the Israeli victory undid the effective partition of Palestine in 1948–49 and sharpened the socio-cultural contradiction between the Arab residents of the West Bank and Gaza and the controlling power in those areas. That development might have been arrested had circumstances enabled Jordan and Egypt to regain the whole of the West Bank and Gaza in a fairly short time, by political or military means. But the Arab Summit Conference of September 1967, which resolved that there would be 'no peace with Israel, no recognition of Israel, no negotiations with it', precluded that first possibility, and the military balance precluded the second.

Over time, the Palestinian issue grew increasingly salient on the regional and international agenda, as did the understanding that the Palestinians, themselves, would provide the Arab interlocutor on this issue. That interlocutor was the PLO, whose position as the 'sole legitimate representative of the Palestinian people' was confirmed by the October 1974 Rabat Arab summit conference. However, the PLO was committed to the establishment of an Arab state in all of Mandate Palestine by military means and was initially no more amenable to compromise than the pre-1948 Palestinian leadership had been. Moreover, most of its constituency consisted of exiles living 'outside'; their main focus was on Israel per se, and the refugee issue was at least as salient in their eyes as the territorial issue. Israel, for its part, was willing to return some of the West Bank to Jordan in exchange for peace, but it categorically rejected proposals to engage with the PLO (which anyway showed no inclination to engage with Israel). In addition, after the Likud came to power in 1977, Israeli governments rejected the idea of any territorial concessions at all. In effect, the conflict had reverted to its pre-1948 dimensions, including its 'zero-sum' character. Although attempts were made, especially after the Egyptian–Israeli peace treaty in 1979, to mobilize alternative Palestinian interlocutors or to propose alternatives to the 'one-state, two-state' dichotomy (e.g. autonomy), that situation persisted until 1993.

1993–present: the peace process

In September 1993, Israel and the PLO signed a Declaration of Principles on Interim Self-Government Arrangements. That agreement seemed to signal a fundamental transformation. Like most seemingly transformational changes, this one was not an abrupt, isolated event, but rather the culmination of a series of developments – the outbreak of civil disobedience and violence in the West Bank and Gaza in 1987 (the so-called *intifada*); the emergence of challenges to the PLO's primacy in the form of an increasingly outspoken local nationalist leadership as well as an energized Islamist alternative (Hamas); the PLO's endorsement of Resolution 242 and renunciation of terrorism in 1988; the PLO's ill-advised support of Saddam Hussein after the Iraqi invasion of Kuwait in 1991 (which prompted the Gulf oil producers to expel several hundred thousand Palestinian residents and cut off all funding to the PLO); and the return to power of the Labor Party following Israeli elections in 1992. Nor was the 'Oslo Agreement' a true peace. Rather, it was an agreement to pursue peace by non-violent means. Still, though the substance of a final status agreement was not specified, the spirit of the accord as well as the stipulated transfer of Gaza and parts of the West Bank to PLO control during a transitional period clearly implied that the parties had come to terms, however reluctantly, with the idea of peace based on partition and the existence of two states.

Given the history of the conflict, this was a truly significant development. It made possible what had never existed before – an Israeli–Palestinian peace process – and it also paved the way for a peace agreement between Israel and Jordan and for official relations between Israel and several other Arab states. But even those momentous changes could not overcome the obstacles that stood between process and actual peace – especially the huge substantive gaps on what came to be known as 'final-status' issues: Jerusalem, refugees, settlements, security arrangements and borders. In anticipation of negotiations on these issues, each side tried to improve its bargaining position while enhancing its ability to blame the other in case negotiations broke down. That approach inevitably destroyed mutual confidence rather than building it.

Moreover, doubts persisted on each side about the sincerity of the other's ultimate intentions. Finally, substantial elements in the body politic of both sides remained overtly hostile to the very idea of peace based on two states – on the Palestinian side, unreconstructed nationalists, even in Arafat's own Fatah party, as well as a growing Islamist camp; on the Israeli side, the Jewish settlers in the West Bank and Gaza and their religious-nationalist hinterland inside Israel, along with a large number of doubters who might admit the principle of peace based on two states, but were not persuaded that abstract concessions from the Palestinian side justified the concrete concessions that Israel would have to make.

As a result, the peace process made little material progress during the 1990s. In 1994, Israel handed over Gaza and Jericho to the PLO, which established a National Authority – a government with limited powers – and transferred control of other West Bank cities in 1995 despite growing Palestinian violence, including suicide bombs inside Israel that had augmented domestic Israeli opposition to the process, culminating in the assassination of Prime Minister Yitzhak Rabin in late 1995. The following year, elections brought the anti-Oslo Likud to power in Israel and confirmed the leading role of Yasser Arafat and Fatah in the Palestinian Authority. However, Arafat's victory was marred by the refusal of Hamas to participate in and thus legitimize what it termed an 'Oslo-inspired' process, thereby obscuring growing discontent with his rule. For the next three years, there was virtually no movement at all apart from a localized agreement to transfer most of Hebron, the last major city in the West Bank, to the Palestinian Authority. Whatever hopes for renewed momentum had been raised following the return of the Israeli Labor Party to power in 1999 were dashed soon after, when long-deferred final-status negotiations were held. In 2000, a summit-level meeting at Camp David under the auspices of US President Bill Clinton broached all the final-status issues, including Jerusalem (hitherto an Israeli taboo). But despite Clinton's active mediation, eventually amounting to a proposal with fairly detailed guidelines, no peace agreement was reached, and by the time follow-on discussions were convened, the atmosphere had been poisoned by the outbreak of a second *intifada*, this one far more violent than its predecessor. The result was the election of Ariel Sharon as Israeli prime minister, with a mandate to pursue security, not peace; and the perpetuation of an increasingly dysfunctional Palestinian leadership unable to pursue any coherent policy at all.

After two to three years of intensive military efforts and the construction of a security barrier (partly wall, partly fence) that blocked access to Israel and Israeli settlements in about six to eight per cent of the West Bank, Israel managed to reduce the levels of violence. Nevertheless, it had little confidence that reliance on military means alone was a viable long-term policy. At the same time, Camp David and its aftermath also caused large numbers of Israelis to lose faith in the prospects for peace with the Palestinians. What emerged as a default option was 'unilateral disengagement' (code words for partial withdrawal) in order to contain damage and minimize costs. Ironically, this option was promoted by Sharon, hitherto the champion of the settler movement and a stalwart opponent of any territorial concessions, and he persisted in it even after Arafat died in 2004 and was succeeded by Mahmoud Abbas, someone ostensibly far more committed to a two-state peace agreement and opposed to the use of violence to promote it.

Thus, when Israel actually dismantled settlements in Gaza and a small part of the northern West Bank and withdrew its military forces from the former in August 2005, Hamas was able to claim that Israel's actions were not part of a peace process advocated by Abbas, but rather constituted surrender to the kind of violent confrontation waged by Hamas. Not only did unilateral disengagement not enhance Israeli security – Israeli towns bordering Gaza were subjected to intensified rocket fire following the withdrawal – but Hamas's domestic popularity improved to the point where it won the 2006 parliamentary elections and formed the new government of the Palestinian Authority. Moreover, a year later, when the Fatah-dominated security forces refused to subordinate themselves to the new government, Hamas launched what it claimed was a pre-emptive counter-coup and took complete control of Gaza, prompting Abbas to appoint a separate emergency government in the West Bank. By 2007, the Palestinians therefore had two separate governments and two pseudo-states, and the peace process was close to being clinically dead.

Current status and future prospects

In every practical sense, the Israeli–Palestinian conflict is stalemated. Majorities on both sides are still prepared, in principle, to accept peace based on the partition of Mandate Palestine, and the mainstream leadership on both sides has become progressively more explicit in defining the 'two-state' peace as its ultimate objective. That position also enjoys a widespread international consensus. In fact, the US has even elaborated a set of fairly concrete guidelines, sometimes referred to as the 'Clinton parameters' of 2000, which has been implicitly endorsed by the Bush administration and other major international actors. These provide for a Palestinian state that would include the Gaza Strip and 'the vast majority of the West Bank'; a solution for the Palestinian refugees that would allow them to return to a Palestinian State or find new homes in their current locations or in third countries and receive compensation; 'a non-militarized Palestine', with border security and monitoring to be provided by an 'international presence'; and 'fair and logical propositions' for Jerusalem that would encompass its international recognition as the capital of two states while ensuring that it remain 'open and undivided'.[4]

However, major camps on both sides continue to reject the very idea of two states. Moreover, even between the so-called 'peace camps' on each side, the substantive gap on the permanent-status issues, especially Jerusalem and the refugees, appears to be too wide to be bridged by either persuasion or coercion. Israel will not offer even what the Palestinian 'peace camp' seems prepared to accept and the Palestinians cannot force it to; the Palestinians will not accept even what the Israeli 'peace camp' seems prepared to offer and Israel cannot force them to. In these circumstances, even some adherents of the Palestinian 'peace camp' have begun to advocate abandoning the 'two-state' formula in favour of one state in all of Mandate Palestine. That idea, in one variant or another, had long been the only acceptable outcome for almost all Palestinians, and it remains so for a significant number of them.[5] But Israelis are no more amenable to such a formula than they have been over the past century and Palestinians and their supporters are no more capable of imposing it. The 'one-state' solution therefore does not offer a viable alternative to 'two states,' and absent any agreement on the terms of partition, the most likely prospect is continuation of the status quo.

Implications for international security

Visible efforts to resolve or manage the Israeli–Palestinian conflict have become a staple on the agenda of almost every major international actor. The conflict is at the centre of UN activities; many countries have appointed special peace process representatives or monitors; the EU has devoted considerable attention and financial resources to it; and all US administrations in the last four decades have included the issue on their 'to-do' list, some with genuine enthusiasm, others because they were enjoined to do so as part of a superpower's responsibility. An example of the latter is the Bush administration, which apparently concluded from the experience of previous administrations that the dubious prospects of success did not warrant intensive investment of time and effort. Nevertheless, it continued to show sporadic involvement and eventually organized a high-level conference at Annapolis, Maryland in late 2007. Annapolis produced a joint commitment to work toward a comprehensive peace agreement before the end of Bush's term of office, but there were few indications at the time that this effort might be crowned with success, and though Israeli Prime Minister Ehud Olmert and Abbas filled the following year with what were portrayed as serious negotiations, nothing transpired to confound the sceptical assessments of what Annapolis had actually accomplished.

Given the dismal historical record of peacemaking, it is not altogether obvious why appearing to be dealing with this conflict remains on every aspiring statesman's job description. During the Cold War, the seamless web of competitive superpower interests might have sustained the argument that regional conflicts involving local actors could

345

transmogrify into superpower confrontation and that resolution or at least containment of the Israeli–Palestinian conflict was therefore urgent to reduce the risk of horizontal (into the rest of the region) and vertical (up to the global level) escalation. Whatever merit that logic may have had before the collapse of the Soviet Union, it is far less compelling now. No power other than the US has the global ambitions (backed up by a universal ideological message) to underwrite security commitments to geographically distant partners or protégés. Furthermore, the evolving web of regional relations means that Israeli–Palestinian confrontation is far less likely to spark a broader conflagration or jeopardize the unimpeded flow of oil – unlike, say, widespread instability and violence in the Persian Gulf.

Only two reasons would seem to justify proactive third-party involvement. One is humanitarian. The prolonging of the conflict inflicts direct costs on the belligerents themselves. These may be alleviated by palliatives (lulls in violence and other conflict-management techniques), but the effect will almost certainly be transitory as long as the underlying conflict is unresolved. That, alone, should be a sufficient incentive for intervention, but it is normally not. The other reason is the ostensible link between a festering Israeli–Palestinian conflict and the empowerment of radical forces with hegemonic aspirations – Islamist terrorism in the Sunni world and the Iranian-led camp of 'resistance' in the Shi'ite world. The Palestinian cause undoubtedly provides a lever of mobilization and recruitment for both forces and may even constitute a bridge between the two (e.g. Hizbollah's focus on Israel in its fight for power in Lebanon; and Iran's direct support to Hamas in its efforts to appeal to Sunni Arab publics over the heads of their governments). It is, of course, not the only and perhaps not even the primary explanation for whatever popularity these forces enjoy; other contributory factors include Muslim opposition to Indian control in Kashmir; the traditional hegemonial aspirations of Iran that far predate the Islamic Revolution of 1979; widespread disaffection with the incompetence and/or corruption of authoritarian Arab governments; the alienation of Shi'ites in Sunni Arab countries and of Muslims in Europe (and Russia and China); and generalized resentment towards economic and cultural globalization. These will continue to fuel movements that threaten regional and international security, whatever the course of the Israeli–Palestinian conflict. Indeed, their existence in many cases actually complicates the search for peace, that is, they are as much causes as consequences of protracted conflict.

Nevertheless, even the marginal amelioration of the conditions nourishing these forces would justify a continued effort to promote a resolution of the conflict. But since no amount of third-party encouragement, persuasion, mediation and 'good offices' has succeeded in producing agreement, promotion of conflict resolution appears to be reduced to two other options: coerced agreement or imposition of a solution. Neither is really a solution unless coercion/imposition is merely a pretext to overwhelm domestic opposition to terms that are largely acceptable anyway to the critical mass on both sides. Except in those circumstances, however, coercion implies irresistible pressure on one side or the other (or both) to agree to otherwise unacceptable terms. This approach would require the 'international community' to agree on the precise terms. Even in the unlikely event that that could be secured, third parties – especially the US – would then have to exert the kind of brute pressure on Israel that Western political systems would find difficult to tolerate, and that might not work anyway because the imbalance of power might well be neutralized by the imbalance of interests (it would be more vital for Israel to resist than for the international community to continue to press). The same is true on the Palestinian side. The 'international community' – especially the Arab states – would have to exert the kind of pressure on the Palestinians that Arab political systems would probably not tolerate and that might also very well fail for exactly the same reason: mutually neutralizing imbalances of power and interest. The imposition of a solution confronts the same obstacle of achieving consensus on ends among interveners and the additional disadvantage of requiring the interveners to continue committing resources and perhaps lives until the imposed solution becomes self-sustaining. These drawbacks have thus far outweighed the potential benefits of the types of coercion or imposition proposed in the past, and they are likely to continue to do so in the future.

Overall, then, there seems little near-term prospect for a breakthrough either through bilateral agreement or third-party intervention. However, that does not argue in favour of neglect. Apart from those eager to exploit opportunities the conflict presents, all parties directly and indirectly involved have an interest in the appearance of a viable process while simultaneously acting to minimize the adverse consequences of failure to consummate that process. For mainstream Israelis and Palestinians, this means containing the violence and improving day-to-day conditions on the ground. For the rest of the international community, it means ongoing diplomacy coupled with determined efforts to reduce exposure to the dysfunctions of the Middle East, of which the Israeli–Palestinian conflict is a prominent symptom, cause, and consequence.

Notes

1 The author would like to thank Eliza Gheorghe for her invaluable assistance in preparing this chapter for publication.
2 See Europa Publications, *A Survey of Arab-Israeli Relations*, 2nd edn, London and New York: Europa Publications, 2004, p. 316, for the text of Balfour Declaration; the 15 October 1915 communication of British High Commissioner Sir Henry McMahon (part of the so-called Hussein–McMahon correspondence) is reproduced on pp. 313f.
3 For more on the dynamics of Cold War rivalries in the region, see Spiegel et al. 1988.
4 No official text of the Clinton Parameters was issued. Clinton delivered them orally to Israeli and Palestinian negotiators at a meeting in the White House on 23 December 2000 and they were transcribed by those present and checked by Clinton's aides. A copy of the transcription is reproduced in Rabinovich and Reinharz 2008: 518–21.
5 For a fuller elaboration of the argument that the 'one-state' option is a reversion to the traditional, deep-seated Palestinian position that denies the legitimacy of Jewish sovereignty in any part of Palestine, see Jonathan Spyer 2008.

References

Ajami, F. (1981) *Arab Political Thought and Practice Since 1967*, Cambridge: Cambridge University Press.
Antonius, G. (1965) *The Arab Awakening: The Story of the Arab National Movement*, New York: Capricorn Books.
Doran, M. (1999) *Pan-Arabism Before Nasser: Egyptian Power Politics and the Palestine Question*, New York: Oxford University Press.
El-Sadat, A. (1977) *In Search of Identity: An Autobiography*, New York: Harper & Row.
Heller, M.A. (1983) *A Palestinian State: The Implications for Israel*, Cambridge, MA: Harvard University Press.
Heller, M.A. and Hollis, R. (2005) *Israel and the Palestinians: Israeli Policy Options*, London: Royal Institute of International Affairs.
Hurewitz, J.C. (1976) *The Struggle for Palestine*, New York: Schocken Books.
Johnson, N. (1982) *Islam and the Politics of Palestinian Nationalism*, London: Kegan Paul International.

Lea, D. (ed.) (2004) *A Survey of Arab–Israeli Relations*, 2nd edn, London & New York: Europa Publications.

Miller, A.D. (2008) *The Much Too Promised Land: America's Elusive Search for Arab-Israeli Peace*, New York: Basic Books.

Rabinovich, I. and Reinharz, Y. (eds) (2008) *Israel in the Middle East: Documents and Readings on Society, Politics, and Foreign Relations, pre-1948 to the Present*, 2nd edn, Waltham: Brandeis University Press.

Ross, D. (2004) *The Missing Peace: The Inside Story of the Fight for Middle East Peace*, New York: Farrar, Straus, and Giroux.

Rubin, B. (1981) *The Arab States and the Palestine Conflict*, Syracuse: Syracuse University Press.

Sahliyeh, E. (1988) *In Search of Leadership: West Bank Politics since 1967*, Washington, DC: The Brookings Institution.

Sayigh, Y. (1997) *Armed Struggle and the Search for State: The Palestinian National Movement, 1949–1993*. Oxford: Oxford University Press.

Segev, T. (2001) *One Palestine, Complete: Jews and Arabs Under the British Mandate*, London: Abacus.

Spiegel, S.L., Heller, M.A., and Goldberg, J. (eds) (1988) *The Soviet–American Competition in the Middle East*, Lexington, MA: Lexington Books.

Spyer, J. (2008) 'Forward to the past: The fall and rise of the "one-state" solution', *MERIA*, 12, no. 3, September. Available online at: www.meriajournal.com/en/asp/journal/2008/september/spyer/index.asp.

32

Russia's revival

Jeffrey Mankoff

The past decade has witnessed a revival in Russia's international role that few could have expected in the chaotic 1990s. The Russia that has emerged in the early twenty-first century is a sometimes uncomfortable amalgam of Soviet nostalgia, nationalist insecurity and the aspiration to be accepted as a fully fledged member of a new Great Powers club (albeit one where economic rather than military power is the most important foundation of a state's position in the world). Its recent presidents – Vladimir Putin (2000–2008) and Dmitry Medvedev (2008–) have emphasized the need for their country to return to its historic role as a major power, with its priorities dictated solely by its own sense of national interest.

Today's newly confident Russia is keen to portray itself as an independent pole in a multi-polar international system, manoeuvring between the West and other centres of power to maximize its flexibility and influence, while bucking the assumption that the natural progression of its post-Communist development would lead it to join the camp of Western liberal democracies (*Izvestiya* 2007b). In freeing itself from Western tutelage, Russia has increasingly clashed with both the United States and Europe, while often seeking better relations with China, Iran and other major non-Western powers.

This chapter starts with an overview of Russia's stark political and economic decline after the end of the Cold War. It continues with an analysis of the restoration of political stability in the following decade under Vladimir Putin, which has led to an increasingly assertive, self-confident Russian foreign policy, and goes on to describe the potentially profound consequences of Russia's revival for the rest of the world. It argues that the main challenges for the West in dealing with Moscow lie in convincing it that binding itself to the existing liberal international order would be in Russia's interest. It concludes with an outlook on Medvedev's presidency, and finally questions the strength of the foundations of Russia's revival.

Decline: the 1990s

Russia's political and economic decline after the fall of the Soviet Union was stark. The Soviet command economy was dismantled almost immediately. Former officials, however, manoeuvred to seize control of many of the most lucrative assets for themselves. In the process, they created a new class of oligarchs whose reach extended from business into politics. Oligarchic capitalism bred corruption on a massive scale, which, along with mounting unemployment, high inflation and pervasive gangland violence, led many Russians to look back nostalgically to the stability of the Soviet Union. Economic upheaval also did much to undermine the legitimacy of President Boris Yeltsin's government.

During the early 1990s, inflation – unleashed by the freeing of prices and exacerbated by the Central Bank's decision to print more money – reached over 2,400 per cent per year. This hyperinflation eventually abated, but not before wiping out most people's savings. Another bout of high inflation following the 1998 financial crisis crippled the nascent middle class that had begun to emerge from the wreckage. According to the State Statistics Committee (*Goskomstat*), unemployment during Yeltsin's final year in power was at 13.3 per cent, though the real figure may have been nearly twice as high (Rosenfielde 2000: 1437f.). Meanwhile, the incomplete privatization of many large firms (which remained a drag on the state budget), coupled with the drying up of markets for Russia's uncompetitive exports, left the country badly indebted. Servicing large loans from both the International Monetary Fund (IMF) and sovereign creditors – extended to aid Russia's transition – only exacerbated the debt problem, while foreign reserves totalled only US$14 billion in mid-1998 (O'Donnell 2006).

The impression of decline such economic difficulties conveyed was made worse by Russia's geopolitical retreat. With the end of the Cold War, Russia lost the empire it had controlled within the Soviet Union, as well as the informal empire of the Warsaw Pact and the international Communist bloc. The Soviet Union itself fragmented into 15 independent states. With the loss of the other 14 Soviet republics, Russia was reduced to its smallest territorial extent since before the conquest of Kazan and Astrakhan by Ivan the Terrible in the mid-sixteenth century. Eastern Europe, which had served the USSR as a strategic glacis against the West, threw off its Communist leadership and clamoured, successfully, for admission to NATO. Moscow's most important satellite – East Germany – vanished from the map entirely, swallowed up by capitalist West Germany. Soviet proxies around the globe either vanished (South Yemen) or made their peace with the triumph of capitalism (Vietnam).

Even the integrity of the rump Russian Federation was threatened during the 1990s. The two wars in Chechnya (1994–96 and 1999–2006) exposed not only the Russian military's decline, but also the strong centrifugal tendencies at work in a country with a weak central government and a wide range of ethnic groups inhabiting its territory.[1] While Chechnya, whose mercurial strongman Dzhokhar Dudaev declared his republic's independence from Russia in 1993, represented the most extreme manifestation of Russia's fragmentation, other regional governments asserted extensive autonomy from the Kremlin, encouraged by the 1992 Federal Treaty that declared Russia's ethnically-based regions 'sovereign republics within the Russian Federation' (Erlanger 1992). Ethnic enclaves, such as Dagestan, Tatarstan and Bashkortostan, competed to see how far they could push the principle of sovereignty, while even ethnically Russian areas such as Primorskii Krai on the Pacific coast often functioned outside of Moscow's reach (Teague 1994).

Powerful economic actors, including state-owned companies like gas monopoly Gazprom, also operated largely independently of Kremlin control. Gazprom placed its own people in important positions in the upper reaches of the Russian government, including the long-serving prime minister, Viktor Chernomyrdin, who had been chairman of Gazprom before Yeltsin appointed him to run the government in late 1992. Gazprom also maintained the effective right to control access to Russia's network of gas export pipelines and blocked Kremlin attempts to impose restructuring on the company, despite the fact that the state remained its largest shareholder (Stulberg 2007: 68f.). Other 'oligarchs', including the notorious Boris Berezovsky, who served as deputy head of the Russian Security Council, used their connections to Yeltsin and their domination of the media to promote their own economic interests.

Revival: the 2000s

The beginning of Russia's global resurgence largely coincided with the start of Vladimir Putin's first term in the Kremlin. If the 1990s in Russia were a time of upheaval and decline, the subsequent decade saw the restoration of political stability and an increasingly assertive, self-confident foreign policy. As president, Putin presented a stark contrast to the erratic and often seriously ill Yeltsin. By re-establishing Kremlin control over the bureaucracy, the Duma, the media, local elites and big business, Putin reversed much of Russia's Yeltsin-era fragmentation. This consolidation of power allowed the Kremlin to pursue a more ambitious role on the world stage.

One of Putin's major initiatives was to reassert Kremlin authority over both regional elites and powerful economic actors. This process, which Putin termed 'restoring the power vertical', led to the appointment of powerful presidential envoys to seven newly created 'super-regions' as early as 2000. Agreements between Moscow and the regions were renegotiated, limiting the ability of local officials to conduct their own foreign policy (*Izvestiya* 2005). Another part of the Kremlin's centralization strategy was the installation of Putin loyalists (many of them *siloviki*, figures with backgrounds in the security services) in important positions throughout both the administrative apparatus of the state and on the boards of major companies (Bremmer and Charap 2006–7: 84ff.; Orekhin and Samedova 2005). Though he is not a *silovik*, Medvedev, who worked closely with Putin in the St Petersburg mayor's office in the early 1990s and later was chairman of Gazprom before becoming president, is the most prominent example.

Apart from the centralization of power, Russia's revival has had much to do with events beyond the Kremlin's control. The most obvious reason for Russia's revival as a major power was the dramatic increase in world energy prices, which allowed it to recover from the collapse that followed the 1998 financial crisis. Russia is the world's second-largest oil producer, after Saudi Arabia, and the largest producer of natural gas (British Petroleum 2007).[2] Since the oil shocks of the 1970s, the Soviet/Russian economy has depended heavily on sales of oil and gas, particularly to Europe. When Putin came to power at the beginning of 2000, oil prices hovered around US$10 per barrel. Eight years later, when Medvedev replaced Putin, oil was trading at over US$120 per barrel, before collapsing, along with the Russian economy, in late 2008. Thanks to the resulting influx of wealth, Moscow had paid off its debts to the IMF and the Paris Club of sovereign creditors by 2003, and amassed the third-largest foreign currency reserves in the world (a total of US$476 billion) by 2008. Growing energy revenues also spawned a US$151 billion fund to cushion the economy against future declines and provide a source of capital for investment abroad (Pascual 2008: 7).

Not only do oil and gas help to fill the Russian treasury, but Moscow's control of the infrastructure to move energy from Russia and Central Asia to Europe and, in the future, East Asia gives it significant influence over both producers and consumers through its ability to manipulate prices and supplies. The Kremlin has converted its control of energy into geopolitical influence by withholding deliveries to recalcitrant customers; buying up distribution networks; muscling aside foreign investors from big energy projects; and moving aggressively to block the construction of pipelines it does not control. Alongside such 'sticks', Russia has dangled 'carrots', holding out lucrative bilateral deals to favoured partners such as Germany, Italy and, potentially, China.

While Russia has actively sought to maintain its control over the pipelines that link producer states like Turkmenistan to world markets, the role of energy in Russia's revival has been most visible in Moscow's approach to downstream states whose economies depend on Russian energy (Stulberg 2007: 110–15). Following the 2004 Orange Revolution and Ukraine's expression of interest in joining NATO, the Kremlin attempted to pressure Kyiv into abandoning its pro-Western course, ratcheting up the pressure over a long-standing payment dispute, which culminated in the decision to stop gas deliveries to Ukraine on the first day of 2006 in a bid for higher prices (Adams 2002: 18f.).[3] When Kyiv began siphoning gas flowing through Ukraine to Europe, it was EU consumers who felt the brunt of Gazprom's actions, and EU leaders came to see energy supplies as Russia's most potent foreign policy tool.

Towards an independent foreign policy

In the US and the West more broadly, the 1990s are remembered fondly as a time of peace, prosperity and unrivalled international influence. The Soviet collapse had left the US as the world's sole superpower, a position enhanced by the general prosperity of the Clinton era. This 'unipolar moment' after Communism and before the emergence of radical Islamism as a direct threat was the apex of US (and Western) power and influence (Krauthammer 1990–91). Over the course of the following two decades, the emergence of new power centres, particularly in East Asia, coupled with the US's own economic and political difficulties, contributed to the replacement of unipolarity by a world that the Russian elite sees as increasingly multipolar, with a handful of major countries inheriting responsibility for upholding global order (Mankoff 2009: 12–16).

In contrast to the West, Russians largely perceive the 1990s as a time of chaos and instability, which many Russians have since come to associate with the concept of democracy itself. Russia's re-emergence over the past decade has therefore entailed a conscious repudiation of the legacy of the 1990s, of the turmoil as well as the halting steps towards democratization. In part because the most chaotic period of Russia's post-Communist transition (roughly 1991–94) coincided with the period of greatest optimism about the possibility of integration into the geopolitical and ideological amalgam of 'the West', repudiating the legacy of the 1990s has also entailed rejecting the notion that Russia is fundamentally part of the West. Rather, Russia's leaders and populace largely agree in thinking that Russia must look out for itself in a dangerous, self-interested world.

Within the new international balance of power, Russia has often sought to manoeuvre among other major states in a way that resembles the behaviour of the nineteenth-century great powers comprising the Concert of Europe. The conviction that the unipolar moment in modern history is over has played a substantial role in persuading Moscow to adopt a more independent foreign policy course, one that mixes bandwagoning with balancing, and that often treats Asia as at least a potential counterweight to the liberal powers of the US and Europe (Russian Ministry of Foreign Affairs 2007; *Izvestiya* 2007b). Russian elites have long sought such an autonomous foreign policy for their country, but it is only with these systemic changes that Russia has actually been able to act on the preferences of its elites.

Russia's vision of the global order emphasizes the interaction of sovereign states as the basis for International Relations. For this reason, Moscow has consistently opposed what it sees as interference in other states' internal affairs, whether in Sudan, Burma or elsewhere. Moscow strongly supports the role of the UN Security Council (where it holds a veto) as a forum for Great Power decision making, in contrast to the unilateral approach that it accuses Washington of favouring (Kozunin 2006). Medvedev, like Putin, has called such US unilateralism a threat to international stability (Medvedev 2008a). Its partiality to the Security Council is generally couched in terms of respect for international law – even if Russia's own behaviour in the area of the former USSR often contravenes international legal norms.

Russia's revival has in particular complicated its relationship with the major Western powers. The tone of relations between Moscow and Washington slipped to a post–Cold War low during Putin's second term as president. In part, the downturn in relations was the result of unfulfilled expectations on both sides. After Putin declared in 2001 that Russia would be a partner to the US in the unfolding 'war on terror', Washington expected Russia to make a fundamental decision that its historical destiny lay in integration with the West (Nichols 2002–3: 13f.). For the Russian leadership, though, cooperation with the US and its allies in Afghanistan was both in Russia's own immediate interest (given Russia's struggles with Islamist militants in the context of the Chechen war), and a way to carve out a role as the West's indispensable partner and bridge to the East. Instead of being treated as an indispensable ally, though, Russia found itself shunted aside on major issues including the invasion of Iraq and the further expansion of NATO (*Izvestiya* 2007a). Many Russian leaders, as well as the public at large, came to feel that the strategy of seeking a privileged partnership with the West to enhance Russia's international standing had been a mistake (Simes 2007).

As on the question of NATO expansion, Russia's revival has been felt most directly by its neighbours in the former Soviet Union, which Moscow continues to view as its own sphere of influence. While Moscow never fully renounced its intention of exerting a predominant influence in the 'Near Abroad', Russian attention to the region increased dramatically as a result of political upheaval in several post-Soviet states, above all the 2004 Orange Revolution in Ukraine. The Orange Revolution, along with similar 'coloured revolutions' in Georgia and Kyrgyzstan, and serious unrest that shook the government in Uzbekistan, demonstrated that the rule of post-Soviet strongmen faced a crisis of legitimacy. Russian elites feared that similar discontent could threaten their own rule.

They also saw Russian influence over its former empire slipping away, since the new regimes in Tbilisi and Kyiv were strongly pro-Western and advocated eventually joining NATO (Trenin 2005). The Kremlin thus came to see pro-democracy movements as a kind of stalking horse for the expansion of Western influence. Consequently, Russian foreign policy in the former Soviet bloc has focused on preserving the post-Soviet status quo, where secular, largely Russian-speaking elites continue to dominate business and politics – as well as stopping or slowing the drift of former Soviet republics into Western-dominated institutions like NATO. In part, this strategy has entailed supporting pro-Russian politicians, such as the former Ukrainian prime minister Viktor Yanukovich, as well as separatist movements in places like Abkhazia, South Ossetia, Transdniester and

Crimea – regardless of the fact that doing so violates the principle of state sovereignty that the Kremlin defends elsewhere.

In resisting the West's perceived attempts to dictate the functioning of the post-Cold War world unilaterally, Russia has also increasingly sought backing from China, both bilaterally and through institutions like the Shanghai Cooperation Organization (SCO). Thanks to its rapid modernization, its massive size and its resistance to Western notions of liberalism, China has found itself backing Russia on a range of contentious international issues, from the war in Iraq to opposing US democracy promotion efforts. Russian analysts of all political stripes have called for embracing China, in part as an alternative to seeking a privileged partnership with the West (Lukin 2001).

Yet using China as a counterweight to the West remains problematic. China's economy is much more dynamic than Russia's, and many Russians fear being relegated to the status of junior partner. Already, China's booming population is spilling into Russia's sparsely inhabited Far East, feeding Russian fears that in the long term, Beijing intends to displace Moscow as the dominant power in the region (Latynina 2007).

Moreover, despite the rhetoric of partnership, Russo-Chinese competition is increasing, particularly over energy resources in Central Asia. Nor can partnership with China aid Russia's quest to be accepted as a responsible global player or member in key international organizations. While Moscow needs good relations with Beijing, most Russian statesmen recognize that relations with the West will continue to be the central consideration for Russian foreign policy.

The challenge for the West

After more than a decade of decline, Russia's revival at the start of the twenty-first century is beginning to have an effect on the international security architecture. Increasingly, Russia's leaders see the world order forged at the end of the Cold War as one that excludes them from any meaningful role (Simes 2007). Ensuring Moscow's acceptance of the liberal world order, whose origins date to the end of the Second World War, will be the pre-eminent challenge for the West's Russia policy over the next decade.

Western policy needs to aim at anchoring Russia in the web of institutions and rules that comprise the modern international system. That means giving Moscow a stake in upholding stability and discouraging it from seeking to form – with China, Iran or others – a bloc of major powers that reject the current system's legitimacy. The West should be willing to tolerate Russia's ambition to play a larger international role, but in return demand that Moscow abide by the rules of the system into which it is being welcomed.

This process is most straightforward in the economic sphere. The Western powers should push hard to complete negotiations on Russia's ascension to the World Trade Organization (WTO), which would aid Russia's integration into the world economy and provide a forum for resolving trade disputes (though following the collapse of the Doha Round of trade talks, finding the political will may prove difficult). Likewise, the Europeans ought to be more proactive in constructing a framework for resolving energy disputes.

Western officials, especially in the US, also need to end counterproductive discussions about expelling Russia from the G-8. They should also take seriously Russian objections to using force without UN Security Council approval; give greater substance to clubs where Russia already has a voice, such as the NATO–Russia Council; and encourage

Russia to play an active (and constructive) role on issues where it has real leverage, such as the Iranian nuclear problem.

However, the West has a right to demand that Russia abide by the same international rules that it invokes in defence of Robert Mugabe's Zimbabwe and others. Defending the sovereignty of Russia's post-Soviet neighbours should be a top priority and NATO expansion provides the most auspicious framework for doing so. The West should make the process of NATO expansion more transparent, emphasizing to Moscow that potential members (including Ukraine and Georgia) have a right to decide for themselves whether or not to join the alliance, but only after meeting a series of objectively measured steps toward political and military reform.

Meanwhile, Europe in particular needs to work harder to address the complications stemming from its dependence on Russia for oil and gas supplies. Fear mongering about Russia's alleged energy imperialism is not particularly helpful. In any case, Russia needs the income it derives from selling gas to Europe to finance its own political and economic recovery, while Europe's dependence on Russian energy will only grow in the coming years. This interdependence makes Russia's 'energy weapon' less potent than many Europeans fear. The real threat lies in the possibility of supply shortfalls resulting from chronic underinvestment in Russia's energy sector and growing domestic demand (Hill 2005).

The EU and its member states need to work on building an integrated gas market for the entire continent to limit the opportunities to play individual consumers off against one another, to encourage joint ventures, and to continue working on a set of rules to govern cross-border investment in energy and other strategic industries. Russian investment should be encouraged, as long as recipient countries can be confident that its aims are purely commercial and that their companies will have similar opportunities to invest in the rapidly developing Russian market. The West also needs to enhance the sovereignty and viability of weak post-Soviet states in the Caucasus and Central Asia by boosting foreign investment in their energy sectors and encouraging economic diversification.

Conclusion and outlook

With the inauguration of Dmitry Medvedev as president in May 2008, the Russian Federation entered its third decade in a position of apparent strength. A lawyer by training, Medvedev has emphasized the need to build a law-based state and enhance Russia's economic competitiveness. The Russia he inherited is wealthier and more confident than at any previous moment in its post-Soviet history, and largely remains so even after the onset of a severe financial crisis just months later. Of course, Medvedev has not been in office long enough to say with any degree of certainty what effect he will ultimately have on Russian foreign policy. His rhetoric about the West has been rather less confrontational than Putin's second-term harangues about plots to dismember and humiliate Russia. While Putin often spoke of the danger to Russia from the West's hard military power, Medvedev listed global financial instability, terrorism, crime and corruption as the greatest threats to Russian national security (Medvedev 2008b). On economics, the new president's instincts are clearly more liberal than those of his predecessor. If successful, Medvedev's calls to promote the rule of law and reduce the state's role in business will do much to reduce Russia's reliance on oil and gas sales to power its economy.

However, despite hints of a more liberal outlook, Medvedev has given no indication he intends to alter Russia's basic foreign policy orientation or ambitions (Medvedev 2008c). And, whatever his ultimate preferences, Medvedev's path remains rocky because of uncertainties about his power. Putin remains onstage as prime minister and the *siloviki* still lurk behind him; indeed, it was Putin, not Medvedev, who seemed in command during the opening stages of Russia's war with Georgia in mid-2008. Medvedev may want to ease the *siloviki* out of their lucrative posts on corporate boards, but it is a fair bet that they will not all go quietly. Confrontation with the West only strengthens the hand of these hardliners, since it allows them to assume the mantle of Russia's defenders. If the West wants to weaken these illiberal, nationalist elements, it should engage the new Russian president and lay out a clear roadmap for rapprochement that respects Russia's desire to play a more prominent international role, but insists that Russia cease fostering instability in neighbouring states such as Georgia and Ukraine.

Whatever Medvedev's aims, the long-term durability of Russia's resurgence remains open to question. As remarkable as Russia's revival as a major international actor over the last decade has been, the foundations of that revival are uncertain, and it remains to be seen whether Russia will be able to fulfil its increasingly global ambitions in the coming years. Much of Russia's increased strength remains tied to energy prices that have fallen by over 70 per cent since mid-2008. Nevertheless, the unpredictability of global energy markets, as well as Russia's own chronic underinvestment in its energy sector, makes the economic foundation of the country's revival somewhat precarious.

In a century where power will be increasingly tied to economic rather than military strength, Russia has not adapted as quickly or effectively as rivals such as China. It has been unable to use its vast mineral wealth to promote the development of other, more sustainable sources of economic growth. State interference in the economy and the pervasive culture of corruption that has ensued continue to stifle innovation, leaving Russian growth lagging behind that of the more dynamic economies of East Asia. The energy sector, which has been central to Russia's revival, is undercapitalized and based on outdated technology (Saivetz 2007). Furthermore, Russia suffers from a range of other chronic problems, including political rigidity, a rapidly diminishing population (Ambrosio 2006; Eberstadt 2004: 7) and military dysfunction (Miller 2004). An increasingly centralized political system that lacks outlets for popular disaffection seems ill suited for addressing Russia's underlying social and economic problems.

Today's Russia is no doubt a major, if troubled, power with interests spanning much of the world. It continues to seek a larger role commensurate with its newfound power. Its size and strength entitle it to a seat at the table, but it also has to show that it accepts the rules of the game. To succeed, Russia needs the cooperation of the major Western powers; in exchange, the West needs to demand that Russia uses its power and status responsibly.

Notes

1 While no agreement officially ending the Second Chechen War has been signed as of mid-2008, major combat operations ended after the fall of Grozny and other major population centres in late 2000, while large-scale guerrilla operations have declined substantially since the death of Chechen field commander Shamil Basayev in July 2006. Smaller clashes remain frequent in Chechnya and the surrounding republics of the North Caucasus.

2 In 2007, Russia produced 9.98 million barrels per day of crude oil (behind only Saudi Arabia's 10.4 million) and 607.4 billion cubic metres (bcm) of natural gas, ahead of the second place United States with 545.9 bcm.

3 When Kyiv stalled Moscow's demand that it accept a price increase from US$50 to US$160 per thousand cubic metres of gas in late 2005, the Russian leadership responded by threatening to cut off gas deliveries to Ukraine altogether – and demanding that Kyiv now pay US$230 per thousand cubic metres. Kyiv refused, and Gazprom stopped deliveries on the first day of January 2006 (Sokov 2006). In this case, Russian pressure backfired, as Ukraine began siphoning gas bound for Europe for its own use and the EU accused the Kremlin of both blackmailing Ukraine and jeopardizing European economic security. In the end, Moscow and Kyiv were forced to compromise, as the Kremlin realized that its energy weapon could be double-edged. At the same time, the unintended consequences of the Russo-Ukrainian gas crisis lent greater urgency to Russian plans for the construction of new undersea pipelines to the EU that bypass neighbouring states with which Russia has had difficult relations, including Ukraine, Poland and Lithuania.

References

Adams, J.S. (2002) 'Russia's gas diplomacy', *Problems of Post-Communism* 49, 3: 14–22.

Ambrosio, T. (2006) 'The geopolitics of demographic decay: HIV/AIDS and Russia's great-power status', *Post-Soviet Affairs* 22, 1: 1–23.

Asmus, R.D. (2008) 'A war the West must stop', *The Washington Post*, 15 July.

Bremmer, I. and Charap, S. (2006/07) 'The *siloviki* in Putin's Russia: Who they are and what they want', *The Washington Quarterly* 30, 1: 83–92.

British Petroleum (2007) 'Statistical review of world energy 2007'. Available online at: www.bp.com/productlanding.do?categoryId=6848&contentId = 7033471 (accessed 6 May 2008).

Bunn, G. et al. (1997) *Open Letter to President Bill Clinton*. Available online at: www.armscontrol.org/act/1997_06–07/natolet.asp (accessed 12 May 2008).

Eberstadt, N. (2004) 'The Russian federation at the dawn of the twenty-first century: Trapped in a demographic straightjacket', *National Bureau of Asian Research (NBR) Analysis*, 15.

Erlanger, S. (1992) 'Most pieces of Russia agree to coalesce, for now', *The New York Times*, 1 April.

Hill, F. (2005) *Beyond Co-Dependency: European Reliance on Russian Energy*, Brookings Institution U.S.-Europe Analysis Series.

Izvestiya (2005) 'Tatarstan vzial stol'ko suvereniteta, skol'ko pozvolila Moskva', 31 October.

——(2007a) 'Gosdep SShA prosit Rossiiu ne obol'shat'sia svoei voennoimoshch'iu', 16 April.

——(2007b) 'Lavrov prokommentiroval otnosheniia Rossii s SShA', 21 May.

Kozunin, A.V. (2006) 'Sil'naia OON—osnova zdorovykh mezhdunarodnykh otnoshenii' *Mezhdunarodnaya zhizn'*, 11.

Krauthammer, C. (1990/91) 'The unipolar moment', *Foreign Affairs* 70, 1: 23–33.

Latynina, Y. (2007) 'Liubov k Dal'nemu', *Novaia Gazeta*, 11 January.

Lukin, A. (2001) *Russia's Image of China and Russian-Chinese Relations*, Brookings Institution CNAPS Working Paper. Available online at: www.brookings.edu/fp/cnaps/papers/lukinwp_01.pdf (accessed 19 May 2008).

Mankoff, J.A. (2009) *Russian Foreign Policy: The Return of Great Power Politics*, Lanham, MD: Rowman & Littlefield.

Medvedev, D.A. (2008a) 'Vystuplenie na Voennom parade v chest' 63-i godovshchiny Pobedy v Velikoi Otechestvennoi Voine, Kremlin. Available online at: www.kremlin.ru/appears/2008/05/09/1111_type82634type122346_200412.shtml (accessed 19 May 2008).

——(2008b) 'Interview with Reuters'. Available online at: www.reuters.com/article/topNews/idUSL2555064220080625 (accessed 16 July 2008).

——(2008c) 'Vystuplenie Dmitriia Medvedeva na II Obshcherossiiskom grazhdanskom forume', Russian Government. Available online at: www.government.ru/government/rfgovernment/rfgovernmentvicechairman/chronicle_mda/arc.hive/2008/01/22/9747889.htm (accessed 18 May 2008).

Miller, S.E. (2004) 'Moscow's military power: Russia's search for security in an age of transition', in Miller, S.E. and Trenin, D.V. (eds) *The Russian Military: Power and Policy*, Cambridge, MA: American Academy of Arts and Sciences, pp. 1–41.

Nichols, T. (2002–3) 'Russia's turn West', *World Policy Journal* 19, 4: 13–22.

O'Donnell, S. (2006) 'S&P raises Russia currency debt ratings: Balance sheet seen as strengthening', *The International Herald Tribune*, 5 September.

Orekhin, P. and Samedova, E. (2005) 'Korporatsiia "Kreml" uspeshno porabotala', *Nezavisimaia Gazeta*, 26 July.

Pascual, C. (2008) *The Geopolitics of Energy: From Security to Survival*, Brookings Institution Analytic Report. Available online at: www.brookings.edu/~/media/Files/rc/papers/2008/01_energy_pascual/01_energypascual.pdf (accessed 5 May 2008).

Rosenfielde, S. (2000) 'The civilian labor force and unemployment in the Russian Federation', *Europe-Asia Studies* 52, 8: 1433–57.

Russian Ministry of Foreign Affairs (2007) 'Obzor vneshnei politiki Rossiiskoi Federatsii'. Available online at: www.mid.ru/brp_4nsf/sps (accessed 6 May 2008).

Saivetz, C. (2007) 'Russia: An energy superpower?', MIT Center for International Studies. Available online at: http://web.mit.edu/CIS/images/audit_12_07_saivetz.pdf (accessed 15 May 2008).

Simes, D.K. (2007), 'Losing Russia', *Foreign Affairs* 86, 6: 36–52.

Sokov, N. (2006) 'Alternative interpretations of the Russian–Ukrainian gas crisis', PONARS Policy Memo, 404, Center for Strategic and International Studies.

Stulberg, A.N. (2007) *Well-Oiled Diplomacy: Strategic Manipulation and Energy Statecraft in Eurasia*, Albany, NY: SUNY Press.

Teague, E. (8 Apr 1994) 'Russia and Tatarstan sign power-sharing treaty', RFE/RL Research Report.

Trenin, D. (2005) 'Vneshnee vmeshatel'stvo v sobytiia na Ukraine i rossiisko-zapadnye otnosheniia', Carnegie Moscow Center Briefing Paper.

33

The Western Balkans

On the path to stability

Richard Caplan

The Western Balkans has been one of the most unstable regions in Europe since the end of the Cold War. All of the countries in the region – Slovenia, Croatia, Bosnia and Herzegovina (BiH), Serbia, Montenegro, Kosovo, Macedonia and Albania – have experienced major unrest, if not violent conflict, since the collapse of the Communist regimes that governed them for more than four decades.[1] Concerted third-party efforts, working both with and against domestic tendencies, have helped to put the Western Balkans on the path to stability, although there has been considerable regional variation. Some states are now flourishing; others are extremely fragile. The region as a whole, however, appears to be moving gradually towards a secure peace and the consolidation of democratic rule.

This chapter examines the turbulence that has buffeted the region and some of the strategies that have been employed to promote recovery and transformation. The first part discusses the problems that gave rise to unrest and violence in the early 1990s. The second section examines the challenges to stability in the region and shows how these challenges have been or are being met. The third and final part looks at the prospects for the future. As will be seen, the Western Balkans has benefited from considerable international, especially European, intervention at all levels – military, political, economic and administrative – that has helped to bolster the region's stability. European 'soft power' – the allure of membership in the family of European institutions – has reinforced these efforts. There has been and continues to be opposition to reform, especially among hardline nationalists, but significant resistance has largely been overcome. While the future of the Western Balkans remains uncertain, the prospects for peace and stability are promising – provided that the European Union (EU) maintains its commitment to a European perspective for the region.

Western Balkan implosions

The turbulence that engulfed the Western Balkans in the early 1990s had its origins in a number of long-standing problems, notably chronic economic crises; declining regime legitimacy; growing political conflict; and weak governmental norms and institutions that were unable to cope with the combined stresses. These problems were not unique to the Western Balkans. However, while most Communist states elsewhere in East and Central Europe embarked on reasonably successful paths of liberal democratic reform and market-oriented economic restructuring after the Cold War, the Socialist Federal Republic of Yugoslavia (SFRY) and, to a lesser extent, Albania in effect imploded beneath the weight of their respective difficulties.

The violent break-up of Yugoslavia was not inevitable. Indeed, to many observers in the late 1980s, Yugoslavia seemed poised, together with the other newly democratizing states of East and Central Europe, to benefit from closer relations with the European Community (EC) as the international system began to thaw after the end of the Cold War (Edwards 1992: 168). However, sharp economic decline aggravated strains between the constituent republics, which, since the death of Tito in 1980, had been coexisting in an increasingly delicate equilibrium. Slovenia and Croatia – the more prosperous northern republics – sought greater autonomy and a looser confederal structure, while Serbia, under Slobodan Milošević, sought to establish greater central control over the country (Cohen 2001; Woodward 1995). These tensions, and the crises that lay beneath them, provided fertile ground for a rise in nationalist politics in all of the republics, facilitated by political liberalization that ended the dominance of the League of Communists of Yugoslavia (LCY). When the tensions proved to be irreconcilable, Slovenia and Croatia declared their independence in June 1991, thus precipitating a conflict that would engulf much of the region in a maelstrom of violence as Milošević and his supporters employed force in failed attempts first to maintain the unity of the SFRY and then to fashion a 'Greater Serbia' that united Serb-majority populations while brutally displacing or annihilating non-Serbs (Daalder 1996; Gow 2003). This pattern of behaviour, which introduced the term 'ethnic cleansing' to the diplomatic lexicon, inspired militant nationalists elsewhere in the region as violence begat revenge and counter-revenge. By early 2008, seven new states had emerged from the wreckage of the former Yugoslavia, two of them (BiH and Kosovo) under some form of international administration.

In Albania, largely a mono-ethnic state, there were no significant national divisions (although there were some tensions with the Greek population in the south). Political competition was instead regional and clan-based. Even more than the former Yugoslavia, however, Albania suffered from a democratic deficit and severe economic weaknesses, made worse by years of international isolation and economic backwardness. With the collapse of Communist rule in 1991, armed gangs gained ascendance – a direct challenge to legitimate governmental authority, which was already very weak. Meanwhile, money manipulators promoted pyramid schemes that, at their height, attracted the savings of nearly two-thirds of the population. When the schemes collapsed in 1997, thousands took to the streets to vent their anger, leading to fighting between the supporters of President Sali Berisha and his rival, Fatos Nano, and culminating in the collapse of public order as army conscripts deserted and protesters marched on all major population centres (Pond 2006: Ch. 8). While order was restored with the help of an Italian-led multinational force (Operation Alba), Albania continues to face enormous political and economic problems.

Stabilizing the Western Balkans

The states that make up the Western Balkans have suffered and continue to suffer from a number of challenges to their stability, understood here in the two-fold sense as threats to security and threats to democratic political order. Only one state from the region, Slovenia, can be said to have managed the post-Communist, post-conflict transition successfully. It achieved its independence relatively painlessly: ethnic geography, among other factors, favoured the republic (the vast majority of the population consists of ethnic Slovenes), which Belgrade relinquished after a ten-day war. Slovenia has faced no threats to its stability subsequently. It enjoys secure borders and a stable democratic system and has benefited from a sound and prosperous economy that many regard as the most successful of all post-Communist transition states in Europe. As a testament to its strong and rapid progress, Slovenia was the first Western Balkan country to accede to membership in the Council of Europe in 1993; the North Atlantic Treaty Organization (NATO) and the EU in 2004; and the Eurozone in 2007.

The other states of the Western Balkan region, following Anastasakis and Koppa (forthcoming 2009), fall into three broad and overlapping categories: slowly transforming, post-Communist transition states (Albania); nationalist, post-authoritarian states (Croatia, Serbia and Montenegro); and post-conflict states (BiH, Kosovo and Macedonia). The principal challenges to stability arising from the conditions found in these states and the international policy responses they have elicited – ranging from external assistance to direct governance – have been military challenges, political challenges, and economic and governance challenges. All three are discussed below.

Military challenges

The most potentially damaging threat to stability in the region has been the resumption of armed conflict. The actual risk of renewed fighting, however, has been slight in recent years, even if there has been considerable dissatisfaction in some quarters with the strategic status quo. In Slovenia, the war ended with the defeat or acquiescence of the Yugoslav People's Army (JNA). Similarly, the defeat of Serbian forces in Croatia in 1995 and Kosovo in 1999 brought a decisive end to the fighting in those two territories, although Kosovo has experienced periodic unrest subsequently. Elsewhere, the peace has been more tenuous – in BiH, a stalemate prevailed among the Bosniak (Muslim), Croat and Serb forces in 1995; while in Serbia and Macedonia, ethnic Albanian militants have sporadically taken up arms in defiance of the national authorities since 1999.

This containment of risk has been achieved through various military and non-military means. In the case of Croatia, the military defeat of Serbian forces was accomplished in part because of US-backed train-and-equip efforts: with US encouragement, the Croatian government contracted with MPRI, a private US security firm, to help Croatia prepare a series of blitzkrieg offensive operations to re-take Serbian-held Croatian territories in 1995 (Burg and Shoup 1999: 339). Direct train-and-equip efforts were employed by the US in BiH after the war to strengthen the Bosniak forces in relation to the militarily superior Bosnian Croat and Serb forces (Van Metre and Akan 1997), while arms reductions mandated by the Dayton peace agreement also helped to achieve parity among the three warring parties (General Framework Agreement 1995: Annex 1B). Arms reduction was also achieved through a UN weapons buy-back programme in Croatia (Boothby 1998) and NATO-led demilitarization programmes in Kosovo and Macedonia (Pond 2006: 247, 176). The gradual integration of the three rival ethnic military forces in BiH under a unified command has also contributed significantly to the reduction of risk in that country.

Perhaps the most critical factor in containing risk has been the deployment of outside military forces to the region. In the first few years of the Yugoslav wars of succession, states were unwilling to intervene militarily in an effort to stop the fighting. Instead, UN forces (UNPROFOR) were deployed to help keep the peace when, in fact, there was often no peace to keep – especially in BiH (Cohen and Stamkoski 1995). After thousands of deaths and the forcible displacement of several hundred thousand more people, patience wore thin, and in 1995 NATO forces, interpreting their UN Security Council mandate more broadly, used air power in support of Bosnian Croat and Muslim ground offensives to bring the Bosnian war to an end (Holbrooke 1998: Chs 10 and 11). Then, in 1999, as Serbian forces in Kosovo stepped up their campaign of violence against the civilian population, NATO responded with air power to compel Belgrade to withdraw (Daalder and O'Hanlon 2000). NATO-led forces have also played an important role in helping to stabilize post-war BiH (from 1996 to 2005), Kosovo (from 1999) and Macedonia (from 2001 to 2003) – a responsibility that the EU has been assuming progressively with the deployment of Operation Concordia in Macedonia in 2003 and Operation Althea in BiH in 2004. Other significant deployments of force include the 7,000-strong Italian-led multinational force (Operation Alba) sent to Albania from April to August 1997 to restore order, enable democratic elections to take place and facilitate the resumption of control by governmental institutions (Greco 1998). And in the first, and to date only, preventive deployment in the region, UN peacekeepers (UNPREDEP) were dispatched to Macedonia in 1995 (until 1999) to prevent the spill-over of conflict from elsewhere in the former Yugoslavia. UNPREDEP arguably also functioned as an important stabilizing factor within the state.

The use of outside military forces in the Western Balkans has been controversial for a number of reasons. First, UN peacekeeping efforts in the former Yugoslavia, and BiH in particular, tarnished the reputation of the institution for many years, as critics castigated the UN for its 'collective spinelessness' (Weiss 1996). Had the same robust forces been available to the UN as were available to NATO, many have argued, UN peacekeepers might have been able to prevent some of the worst atrocities that Europe has witnessed on its soil since the Second World War. Second, NATO's use of force in the former Yugoslavia constituted the first out-of-area deployment of NATO troops in the history of the alliance. These interventions have raised questions about the purpose of the organization in the post-Cold War era (Chandler 1999: 188). They have also raised questions about Europe's willingness and capacity to manage conflicts on its own continent more effectively (France 1999: 7–12). Third, because NATO's military actions against Serbia over Kosovo were not authorized by the UN Security Council, they weakened international legal prohibitions against the use of force. However, these actions arguably have also facilitated the emergence of a new doctrine – the 'responsibility to protect' – that for many states legitimizes the use of force to prevent or mitigate the most severe humanitarian crises (UN General Assembly 2005; see also the chapter by Bellamy in this volume). These and other issues relating to military deployments in the Western Balkans continue to be topics of controversy within International Relations.

Political challenges

There have been several significant political challenges to stability in the region. The most fundamental has arisen from the break-up of the Socialist Federal Republic of Yugoslavia in 1991 and the associated self-determination claims. Although the bids for independence by Slovenia and Croatia in 1991 were treated initially by many states as acts of attempted secession, in time, most states came to accept the view that the SFRY had dissolved involuntarily into its six constituent (republic) units (Crawford 2006: 707–14). The subsequent recognition of the republics as sovereign states was a bold move that was thought by Germany and other EU member states to have the potential to mitigate the conflict, in part by internationalizing it (Caplan 2005a: Ch. 1). While the independence claim of Kosovo, an autonomous province of Serbia, was rejected in 1991 (along with the self-determination claims of other non-constituent units within the SFRY, notably the Serb-majority areas of Croatia and BiH), Kosovo would achieve independence in 2008 after nine years of direct governance by the United Nations (UNMIK) following NATO's 1999 military campaign against Serbia. Diplomats have been at pains to stress the uniqueness of the Kosovo case, but there is concern that, however unprecedented, the development has reinforced the separatist aspirations of Kosovo Serbs, Bosnian Serbs, Macedonian Albanians and other national minorities in the region who observe that the principle of territorial integrity may not be so sacrosanct after all.

Other political challenges have arisen from continuing ethnic tensions in the region, which, if they have not yet threatened the integrity of any of the states, have nonetheless impeded their functioning. Serbian opposition, first to the UN administration of Kosovo from 1999 and then to Kosovo's 'supervised independence' since 2008, has resulted in little or no Serbian participation in the organs of government and an unwillingness to accept the writ of the Kosovo government in the northern municipalities where Serbs are a majority. In BiH, which has been under international supervision since the end of the war in 1995, similar tensions among Bosniaks, Croats and Serbs have for a long time jeopardized the viability of the state. Although there has at times been willingness among the three ethnic groups to cooperate and, with international prodding, to support the establishment of state-level institutions that are necessary if BiH is ever to accede to membership in the EU, in recent years, political differences among the groups have become more acute: the Bosnian Serb leadership has been seeking to weaken the state institutions, while the Bosniak leadership has been seeking to strengthen them at the expense of the federal structure that offers protection to all three ethnic groups (Ashdown and Holbrooke 2008).

The fundamental problem is that many of the arrangements that helped to win the peace in 1995 – the various 'ethnic security' provisions of the Dayton peace agreement – are the very same arrangements that prevent BiH from functioning efficiently today. For instance, in an effort to accommodate the three principal ethnic groups, the country was divided into two highly autonomous entities, the Serbian Republic and the Bosniak–Croat Federation, the latter of which was divided further into ten (mostly Bosniak- or Croat-majority) cantons. The price for this decentralization has been fragmentation and enormous public administration costs – especially for the Bosniak–Croat Federation – in large part due to excessive governmental bureaucracy. Bosniak efforts to abolish the entities to create a (Bosniak-majority) non-federal state have only fuelled Bosnian Serb insecurities.

Ethnic insecurity in the region more generally has been addressed in a number of ways – including through the promotion of human and minority rights; power-sharing arrangements; proportional and over-representation of minorities at all levels of government; co-decision or veto mechanisms; security-sector reform; executive interventions by the international community (notably in the international administrations of Eastern Slavonia (Croatia), BiH and Kosovo); and the prosecution of individuals implicated in genocide, war crimes and crimes against humanity. The latter effort has seen the establishment of the International Criminal Tribunal for the Former Yugoslavia (ICTY), the first international tribunal to be established under Chapter VII of the UN Charter as a measure to maintain peace and security (Kerr 2004). Stability has not been the only objective of the international community in the region, of course; the pursuit of justice has been a parallel and even competing objective. But while efforts, for instance, to reverse 'ethnic cleansing' – through property restitution and the return of refugees and displaced persons – have sometimes heightened ethnic tensions, the regular contact achieved through reintegration has also had the effect of eroding ethnic hostility. In Modrica, a town in Republika Srpska where horrible atrocities were committed during the war and extremist violence continued after the war, half of the pre-war Bosniak population has now returned, and the two communities have been re-establishing harmonious relations (Cox 2008: 257).

As with the measures employed in response to the military challenges to stability in the region, some of the policies used to address the political challenges have also generated controversy and debate. The controversy surrounding the recognition of new states has already been noted above. Another debate concerns the appropriate use of international executive authority. In the cases of Eastern Slavonia (Croatia), BiH and Kosovo, the international authorities have had unparalleled power to administer these war-torn and contested territories. Critics have argued that the UN and other bodies have wielded their authority too frequently and too indiscriminately, thus inhibiting the development of local capacity and the assumption of political responsibility by local parties who, instead, have tended to defer to the international authorities to make the hard decisions that they would rather avoid (Knaus and Martin 2003; Caplan 2005b: Ch. 8). Moreover, international authority has often suffered from an accountability deficit evident in the widespread lack of transparency, the broad immunities that international personnel enjoy and the absence (with rare exception) of local checks on the use of international power.

A third debate relates to militant nationalism and how best to deal with political elites who have inspired the commission of serious violations of international humanitarian law. Some have argued in favour of extirpating militant nationalists, an approach reflected in 'de-Nazification' efforts in Germany after 1945 (Denitch 1996: 8). Others have maintained that nationalists should be offered a stake in the political system where their survival will depend on their being more responsive to popular demands and the financial support of the international community (European Stability Initiative 2001). Both approaches have been employed in the region, with the ICTY, for instance, serving to remove alleged war criminals from the political arena (e.g. Radovan Karadšić in BiH, Slobodan Milošević in Serbia and Ramush Haradinaj in Kosovo) and with internationally regulated political processes, notably free and fair elections, creating incentives for nationalists to compete for power non-violently within the political arena.

A fourth debate concerns the capacity of a criminal tribunal to function in the context of an ongoing conflict without either politicizing the judicial process or undermining the peace process (McDonald 2004). Criticism was levelled against the US, for instance, for failing to furnish evidence to the ICTY that might have assisted the tribunal in its investigation into war crimes allegedly committed by Milošević and Franjo Tudjman, the late president of Croatia. US and European politicians were evidently reluctant initially to prosecute Milošević and Tudjman out of concern that both were key to achieving a negotiated peace in the region (Williams and Scharf 2002). However, both leaders arguably also helped to sustain the conflict in the region until their arrest and death, respectively. There have also been questions about whether the tribunal has exacerbated nationalist tensions rather than promoted ethnic reconciliation and/or the coming to terms with the past. Serbian perceptions of an anti-Serb bias on the part of the ICTY, for instance, have made it difficult for the tribunal to achieve one of its objectives, notably the establishment of a historical record that resonates with all of the national communities in the region.

Economic and governance challenges

Economic anaemia and weak state capacity have been problems generally for many of the states in the Western Balkans. Weak state capacity has consequences for all aspects of recovery and transformation, but it has a particularly strong bearing on economic development. States that lack adequate governance capacity are unable to make effective use of donor aid; establish and maintain the institutional infrastructure necessary to attract foreign investment (e.g. properly functioning judiciaries); legislate and implement reforms required to satisfy the conditions that will allow them to accede to membership in the EU and other organizations; and keep corruption and tax evasion at bay. States whose economies are weak, in turn, suffer high levels of unemployment and the loss of skilled labour; encourage the proliferation of informal and illicit economic activities; and, in post-conflict states, threaten to undermine peace-building efforts, all of which can put stability at risk (*International Peacekeeping* 2008).

Numerous multilateral organizations and agencies, some of them specially created for the Western Balkans, have been engaged in efforts to promote economic development and to strengthen governance capacity in the region. These include the World Bank, the International Monetary Fund, the United Nations Development Program, the EU, the Stability Pact for South Eastern Europe (and its successor, the Regional Cooperation Council) and the European Agency for Reconstruction, among others. Since the Kosovo war, the EU has been assuming principal responsibility for these activities with an eye towards the 'integration [of the Western Balkan states] into European structures and ultimate membership into the European Union', in the words of the final communiqué of the European Council's June 2003 Thessaloniki summit (European Council 2003). The two main frameworks to achieve integration have been the Stabilization and Association Process (SAP), which helps to prepare countries for eventual membership, and the Instrument for Pre-Accession (IPA),[2] through which financial assistance is provided to candidate countries (Croatia and Macedonia in 2008) and potential candidate countries (Albania, BiH, Montenegro, Serbia and Kosovo in 2008).

There have been several characteristics of the EU's promotion of economic development and governance enhancement in the region. The first is the EU's multilateral approach. While many member states of the EU have established bilateral aid relations with states in the Western Balkans, the EU has sought to achieve greater policy coherence by channelling or coordinating financial aid and technical assistance through the European Commission and its subsidiary bodies. Another characteristic has been the EU's emphasis on regional cooperation. Recognizing the value of cross-border projects for building better relations and the fact that many problems in the region require a common approach, the EU has insisted on regional cooperation among the recipients of aid, much like the US did with the Marshall Aid programme after the Second World War. A third characteristic has been the EU's broadly technocratic approach to reform that is aimed principally at strengthening effective governance and creating the conditions for full integration of Western Balkan states into the EU's economic, political and security structures. As a consequence of this approach, however, the EU Commission has tended to be very prescriptive, telling countries precisely what they have to do and often leaving little scope for public deliberation and choice (Bechev and Andreev 2005).

Prospects for the future

While stability in the Western Balkans cannot be taken for granted, the prospects for continued progress are reasonably strong. The allure of membership in the EU and other European institutions, notably NATO, has been a particularly significant factor in helping governments in the region to maintain their commitment to a reform agenda that, if adopted, can only entrench stability further (Vachudova 2005; Gheciu 2005). That the government of Serbia – an implacable opponent of integration with Europe for years – should, in 2008, ratify a Stabilization and Association Agreement (SAA) with the EU; sign a Partnership for Peace (PfP) agreement with NATO; and surrender one of the most notorious war criminals, Radovan Karadšić, to the ICTY is evidence of a determination to join Europe that represents a significant turning point for the entire region.

Further progress towards regional stabilization could be slowed or even derailed, however, for a number of reasons, the most serious being the risk of enlargement fatigue and the so-called integration capacity of the EU. Although the EU has committed itself in principle to continued enlargement that will embrace the Western Balkans, actual enlargement will depend on the willingness of member states to accept new candidates when they have satisfied the conditions for membership. If the process is too protracted, candidates may lose patience with the EU, and more parochial nationalist politics may begin to prevail locally.

There is the related risk associated with the EU moving the goal posts. Candidate states are required to meet the so-called Copenhagen criteria. These are:

> stability of institutions guaranteeing democracy, the rule of law, human rights and respect for and protection of minorities; the existence of a functioning market economy as well as the capacity to cope with competitive pressure and market forces within the Union [and] ability to take on the obligations of membership including adherence to the aims of political, economic, and monetary union
>
> (European Council 1993: 13)

However, specific criteria, such as those established for the SAP, could also introduce delays that frustrate candidates by appearing to raise the threshold for EU membership.

Finally, there is the risk that individual countries, in particular Albania and Kosovo (which to date is only a partially recognized state), may find it difficult to overcome the structural barriers to economic development and governance enhancement that condemn them to continued deprivation, thus raising the spectre of instability as criminal elements exploit these weaknesses. In contrast with the early 1990s, however, there is now broad recognition within the EU of the shared strategic interest among member states in the stabilization of the region (Yannis 2005: 2). As a consequence, it is hard to imagine that the EU will allow a 'black hole' – and the attendant security problems it threatens to bring – to persist for long in its own backyard. Eventually the EU will bring the entire region into its fold. Until then, and even after, there will probably be the need for continued assistance, monitoring and crisis management – by the EU and other third parties – to ensure a stable peace.

Notes

1 'Western Balkans' is a term devised by the European Union in the context of its enlargement policy and refers to all of the states cited with the exception of Slovenia, which is included here for analytical purposes.
2 Formerly Community Assistance for Reconstruction, Development and Stabilisation (CARDS).

References

Anastasakis, O. and Koppa, M. (forthcoming 2009) *Democratisation in the Postcommunist Balkans*, Basingstoke: Palgrave Macmillan.

Ashdown, P. and Holbrooke, R. (2008) 'A Bosnian powder keg', *The Guardian*, 22 October.

Bechev, D. and Andreev, S. (2005) 'Top-down vs bottom-up aspects of the EU institution-building strategies in the Western Balkans', *SEESOX Occasional Paper*, No. 3/05, St Antony's College, University of Oxford.

Boothby, D. (1998) 'The UNTAES experience: Weapons buy-back in Eastern Slavonia, Baranja and Western Sirmium (Croatia)', *ICC Brief*, 12, Bonn: Bonn International Center for Conversion.

Burg, S.L. and Shoup, P.S. (1999) *The War in Bosnia-Herzegovina: Ethnic Conflict and International Intervention*, Armonk, NY: M.E. Sharpe.

Caplan, R. (2005a) *Europe and the Recognition of New States in Yugoslavia*, Cambridge: Cambridge University Press.

——(2005b) *International Governance of War-Torn Territories: Rule and Reconstruction*, Oxford: Oxford University Press.

Chandler, D. (1999) *Bosnia: Faking Democracy After Dayton*, London: Pluto Press.

Cohen, L.J. (2001) *Broken Bonds: Yugoslavia's Disintegration and Balkan Politics in Transition*, 3rd edn, Boulder, CO: Westview Press.

Cohen, B. and Stamkoski, G. (eds) (1995) *With No Peace to Keep: United Nations Peacekeeping and the War in the Former Yugoslavia*, London: Grainpress.

Cox, M. (2008) 'Bosnia and Herzegovina: The limits of liberal imperialism' in Call, C.T. and Wyeth, V. (eds) *Building States to Build Peace*, Boulder, CO: Lynne Rienner, pp. 249–70.

Crawford, J. (2006) *The Creation of States in International Law*, 2nd edn, Oxford: Clarendon Press.

Daalder, I.H. (1996) 'Fear and loathing in the former Yugoslavia', in Brown, M.E. (ed.) *The International Dimensions of Internal Conflict*, Cambridge, MA: MIT Press, pp. 35–67.

Daalder, I.H. and O'Hanlon, M.E. (2000) *Winning Ugly: NATO's War to Save Kosovo*, Washington, DC: Brookings Institution Press.

Denitch, B. (1996) *Ethnic Nationalism: The Tragic Death of Yugoslavia*, Minneapolis: University of Minnesota Press.

Edwards, G. (1992) 'European responses to the Yugoslav Crisis: An interim assessment' in Rummel, R. (ed.) *Toward Political Union: Planning a Common Foreign and Security Policy in the European Community*, Boulder, CO: Westview Press, pp. 165–87.

European Council (1993) 'Conclusions of the Presidency – Copenhagen, 21–22 June 1993', Doc No. SN 180/1/93 REV 1.

——(2003) 'EU–Western Balkans Summit Declaration', Thessaloniki, 21 June.

European Stability Initiative (2001) 'Reshaping international priorities in Bosnia and Herzegovina, Part III: The end of the nationalist regimes and the future of the Bosnian State'.

France (1999) *Les enseignements du Kosovo*, Paris: Ministry of Defence.

General Framework Agreement for Peace in Bosnia and Herzegovina ('Dayton Agreement') (1995).

Gheciu, A. (2005) *NATO in the 'New Europe': The Politics of International Socialization after the Cold War*, Stanford, CA: Stanford University Press.

Gow, J. (2003) *The Serbian Project and its Adversaries: A Strategy of War Crimes*, London: Hurst & Co.

Greco, E. (1998) 'Delegated peacekeeping: The case of Operation Alba', *Working Paper*, Rome: Istituto Affari Internazionali (IAI).

Holbrooke, R. (1998) *To End a War*, New York: Random House.

International Peacekeeping (2008), special issue on 'Post-Conflict peacebuilding and corruption', 15, 3.

Kerr, R. (2004) *The International Criminal Tribunal for the Former Yugoslavia: An Exercise in Law, Politics and Diplomacy*, Oxford: Oxford University Press.

Knaus, G. and Martin, F. (2003) 'Travails of the European Raj', *Journal of Democracy* 14, 3: 60–74.

McDonald, G.K. (2004) 'Problems, obstacles and achievements of the ICTY', *Journal of International Criminal Justice* 2, 2: 558–71.

Pond, E. (2006) *Endgame in the Balkans: Regime Change, European Style*, Washington, DC: Brookings Institution Press.

United Nations General Assembly (2005) '2005 World outcome summit', UN Doc. A/60/L.1, 20 September.

Vachudova, M.A. (2005) *Europe Undivided: Democracy, Leverage and Integration after Communism*, Oxford: Oxford University Press.

Van Metre, L. and Akan, B. (1997) 'Dayton implementation: The train and equip program', *USIP Special Report No. 25*, Washington, DC: United States Institute of Peace (USIP).

Weiss, T.G. (1996) 'Collective spinelessness: U.N. actions in the former Yugoslavia', in Ullman, R.H. (ed.) *The World and Yugoslavia's Wars*, New York: Council on Foreign Relations, pp. 59–96.

Williams, P.R. and Scharf, M.P. (2002) *Peace with Justice? War Crimes and Accountability in the former Yugoslavia*, Lanham, MD: Rowman & Littlefield.

Woodward, S.L. (1995) *Balkan Tragedy: Chaos and Dissolution after the Cold War*, Washington, DC: The Brookings Institution.

Yannis, A. (2005) 'EU foreign policy in the Balkans: A credibility test', *FORNET CFSP Forum* 3, 2: 1–3.

Part IV
Confronting security challenges

Computing security challenge

34

The European Union

From security community towards security actor

Victor Mauer

When, under the leadership of President Jacques Chirac and Prime Minister Tony Blair at the Franco-British summit held in St. Malo on 4 December 1998, the European Union's two pre-eminent military powers agreed to launch a joint initiative that was to be turned into a common European project of the then 15 EU member states six months later at the Cologne European Council, and eventually enshrined in the 2001 Treaty of Nice, a more than 40-year deadlock over a genuine and autonomous European role in security and defence was broken. Even though the path towards a common European Security and Defence Policy (ESDP) was an evolutionary, if arduous, highly contested and deeply controversial process, scholars and policymakers alike were quick to label the EU's embrace of security and defence as a separate policy area 'Europe's military revolution' (Andréani, Bertram and Grant 2001; Howorth 2007: 36).

Since its inception, ESDP has indeed developed into one of the most dynamic policy fields of the EU: a whole array of new institutions was added to the existing complex institutional framework. Catalogues and headline goals for military and civilian capabilities were adopted and – due to both a lack of implementation and the rapidly changing nature of the international system – constantly refined. A European Defence Agency (EDA) was set up to support the improvement of the military capability. The Brussels European Council of December 2003 approved the EU's first European Security Strategy (European Council 2003; Biscop 2005). In addition, from January 2003 to March 2009, the EU launched no fewer than 23 operations. While the overall range of ESDP missions underlines the global nature of EU interventions, the majority of them were not military, were small in scope and – with the exception of Operation Althea in Bosnia and Herzegovina – were limited in size (Messervy-Whiting 2006; Howorth 2007: 207–41; Menon 2009). While it would be wrong to claim that the EU has emerged as a major new strategic actor in world politics, the positive impact of EU interventions seems undisputed.

For many years, the scholarly literature concentrated on the diverse aspects of the EU's international relations (Hill and Smith 2005; Rees and Smith 2008). Since 1999, a lively academic debate has contributed to an ever-growing body of literature on the EU's role in security and defence. Those more concerned with empirical studies suggested that ESDP had ended the age of 'innocence' of Europe as a *civilian power* (Deighton 2002:

728). They also cautioned against the militarization of EU policies (Lagendijk 2002; Manners 2006); warned that the ESDP was 'misguided and dangerous for the [Atlantic] Alliance' (Menon 2003: 203; Eilstrup-Sangiovanni 2003); or, on the contrary, emphasized the positive consequences for the EU itself and its relations both with NATO and with the US (Howorth 2003; Kupchan 1998, 2000, 2004–5; Sloan 2000).

Echoing some of these sentiments, the various schools of International Relations theory and of European Integration theory, while (still) struggling to explain the existence of ESDP, have either, in the structural realist tradition, referred to a supposedly (soft) balancing behaviour of the EU *vis-à-vis* US power (Posen 2004, 2006; Art 2005: 180–83; Walt 2005: 121, 129; Jones 2006, 2007); some, although contradicting neo-functionalist (Sandholtz and Sweet 1998) as well as (liberal) intergovernmentalist (Hoffmann 1966; Moravcsik 1998) predictions for the high politics of security and foreign policy, have suggested that the implementation of ESDP could be understood as the result of spillover effects driven not least by external events, of pressures from outside actors leading to the decision to pool resources in order to maximize efficacy (Smith 2004a: 241; Andreata 2005: 22; Ojanen 2006), or of a process of both the internationalization of European armed forces since the end of the Second World War and the Europeanization of foreign policy since the beginnings of the EU (Mérand 2008: 14f.); while others again, in line with constructivist explanations, have focused on the development of a genuine European strategic culture based on common beliefs, norms, values, ideas and patterns of behaviour (Cornish and Edwards 2001, 2005; Meyer 2005, 2006; Giegerich 2006). Although the respective arguments remain powerful in themselves, one school alone cannot explain the emergence of the EU as an, albeit limited, security actor in its own right with a range of instruments at its disposal.

This chapter consists of three main sections. By looking at early efforts – and failures – to anchor security and defence in the European integration process, the first section suggests that, although dependent on US protection for their external security and defence, the EEC was established and perceived as a nested security community. The second section focuses on the emergence and development of the EU's Common Foreign and Security Policy (CFSP) between national preferences and the institutionalization of cooperation. The third part highlights the driving forces that led to the creation of ESDP; it looks, however briefly, at some of the challenges inherent in the EU's transformation from a 'mere' security community to a security actor; and it describes the slow emergence of a distinct EU strategic culture and security governance.

Nested security community

Since its inception in the early 1950s, the European integration process has been driven by recourse to the past as a negative mirror image of the realities of the immediate postwar years. For those determined to break with a system that, according to their reading, had not only left Europe devastated and devoid of major influence in international affairs after 1945, but had above all contributed to two world wars, security and defence were of paramount importance. The Franco-British Treaty of Dunkirk of March 1947 was more reminiscent of classical defence agreements of the past, even if it reflected a convergence of short-term interests – the alleviation of French security concerns *vis-à-vis* Germany – and long-term calculations – which anticipated the treaty serving as a stepping-stone towards broader West European cooperation (Young 1993: 12). Its successor, the

Brussels Pact of March 1948 between the UK, France, Italy and the Benelux countries, was the brainchild of UK foreign secretary Ernest Bevin's initiative to form a 'Western Union'; it indicated two future trajectories that, under the circumstances of the rapidly evolving Cold War security system, ultimately proved to be mutually exclusive: on the one hand, the West European ambition to establish Europe (i.e. for the time being, the Western part of the continent) as, in Jean Monnet's words, a *force d'équilibre*; and on the other hand, due to its lack of political power and military might, the anything but reluctant Western European reliance on, and indeed embrace of, the US nuclear umbrella.

Before the bipolar system was firmly established in 1955, enshrining the demise of an independent European Third Force between capitalism and communism, the quest for European security was as ambitious and bold as it was revolutionary. Conceived in 1950 as a way to complement the federalist approach of the European Coal and Steel Community (ECSC); to protect the West against the Soviet threat; to make war between Germany and France impossible; and to give Europe an autonomous voice in international affairs, the European Defence Community (EDC) would have been overseen by a supranational authority, chaired by a European defence minister and composed of multinational military forces from France, West Germany, Italy, Belgium, the Netherlands and Luxembourg. The EDC – in Winston Churchill's words a 'sludgy amalgam' (James 1986: 347) – failed in August 1954 not only because of French domestic political concerns (Fursdon 1980; Parsons 2004), but also because of its revolutionary top-down character.

The failure of the EDC dealt a lasting blow to the federalists' notion that only the complete abolition of national independence could cure the ills of the international system, while at the same time, the bottom–up approach emphasized by neofunctionalists gained ground (Haas 1958). Though predominantly concerned with low politics, they would not rule out the prospect that eventually a new central authority could also emerge in the field of security and defence as an unintended consequence of incremental earlier steps, with 'loyalties, expectations, and political activities [being shifted] toward a new and larger center, whose institutions possess or demand jurisdiction over the pre-existing national states' (Haas 1961: 367).

Successive attempts to revive the quest for European security, however, remained elusive until the late 1990s (Duke 2000). These efforts ranged from the establishment, and immediate fall into oblivion, of the Western European Union (WEU) in October 1954 (Deighton 1997; Rees 1998), via the Fouchet Plans of 1961/2; European Political Cooperation (EPC) (Nuttall 1992; Möckli 2009), which was not brought into the remit of the EC until 1987; and the failed revival of the WEU in 1987, to their culmination in the EU's CFSP as enshrined in the Maastricht Treaty of 1993. As a consequence, for more than four decades, the US served both as a 'reluctant sheriff' (Haass 1997) *and* as a willing backstop taking on European security issues.

Nevertheless, the EU, which remained 'in some way insulated from the hurly-burly of normal international relations' (Rees and Smith 2008: xxi) while still being conscious of the broader demands of world order, has played a role in security affairs *sui generis* ever since its inception. The integration of individual policy sectors beyond the high politics of security and defence and the concomitant transfer of state sovereignty to a supranational level not only raised the degree of mutual dependency, but also enhanced the sovereignty of all, while at the same time discarding the prevalent anarchical system among the states of Western Europe, eliminating the traditional security dilemma between them and ultimately making internecine war among them materially impossible.

Thus, while being protected by the US-led Atlantic Alliance and failing to serve as a security provider beyond its borders, the EEC/EC of the Cold War was a nested security community in the *Deutschian* sense (Deutsch et al. 1957), where member states share values, norms and symbols 'that provide a social identity, and engage in various interactions in myriad spheres that reflect long-term interest, diffuse reciprocity, and trust [...], and, conversely, anticipate that security cooperation will deepen those shared values and transnational linkages' (Adler and Barnett 1998: 3f.). While member states ceased to concern themselves with military threats from others within the community, they identified economic and social welfare concerns as security issues.

Taking issue with the popularized notion of Western Europe as a 'civilian power' and the proposed assumption that the 'inwardly-preoccupied communities of the West [were] likely to become more amilitary rather than less so' (Duchêne 1972: 39), Hedley Bull argued that in order to become an actor in international affairs, Western Europe should seek to develop its own sources of military power (Bull 1982: 153). While this sentiment was echoed by the WEU Platform on European Security Interests in October 1987, which stated that 'the construction of an integrated Europe will remain incomplete as long as it does not include security and defence' (*Platform on European Security Interests* 1987), the high-sounding language of the Treaty on European Union (TEU) according to which 'a common foreign and security policy is hereby established' (*Treaty on European Union* 1992), seemed to indicate a major policy shift as the member states' political ambitions came to the fore.

Between national preferences and the institutionalization of cooperation

The question of a European foreign policy had been raised since the early 1960s and had, in the form of the European Political Cooperation (EPC), led to a better understanding of the respective foreign policy positions among member states throughout the 1970s and 1980s, without however resulting in a coordinated, institutionally-anchored European foreign policy approach. Indeed, the successes of the EPC were short-lived and highly dependent on the respective state of East–West relations during the Cold War. In other words, while the détente of the early 1970s increased the EC's scope of action, e.g. during the process leading to the Helsinki Final Act of the Conference on Security and Cooperation (CSCE), the rapid deterioration of East–West relations in the late 1970s and early 1980s relegated the EC to its role of subordinate partner dependent on US leadership.

It is therefore not surprising that the establishment of the CFSP was the result more of external than of internal events, i.e. of the fundamental changes in the international system in 1989/91. The collapse of the Soviet Union; Eastern Europe's desire to rejoin the West politically and economically (Schimmelfennig 2004); the unification of Germany; and the US's foreign and security policy shift away from a seemingly pacified European continent, as well as (the perception of) new security challenges, led to a commitment to reinforce the EU's international position (Hoffmann 2000: 191) and to address the relationship between the internal integration process and the wider world.

However, the CFSP – constructed on the basis of intergovernmental cooperation – also reflected the long-term struggle between European states with 'some ... pressing on towards communautarization and others at least as much concerned with national independence or special relationships'. This dichotomy, in turn, resulted in a considerable 'capability-expectations gap' (Hill 1993: 325, 305f.), with the EU lacking the necessary decision-making procedures, instruments and resources to address the new security challenges, as became blatantly obvious during the Balkan wars during the first half of the 1990s.

Lacking both sources of military power of its own and, as many lamented, the more important element of self-sufficiency in providing for its defence, the politics of war and peace beyond its borders seemed to be off the EU agenda. However, the EU enlargement process of the 1990s – initially a policy of security projection through stabilization and association – which resulted in the inclusion of 12 new member states in 2004 and 2007, can itself be considered a security-policy response to the profound transformations that followed the collapse of the Soviet empire. First, this move dispelled the dual security concerns of the majority of Central and Eastern European states concerning Russia and Germany. Secondly, it made it possible to extend support to the political, economic and cultural transformation processes based on a policy of strict conditionality (Grabbe 2006). In this way, former neighbours become integrated partners who join efforts with the old EU members as part of a regional power for peace in order to stabilize the new neighbourhood. Following the 1990s blueprint, the new neighbours are offered close cooperation in return for political and economic reforms, in order to foster the emergence of a zone of stability and prosperity beyond the EU's borders as well.

The EU's most successful instrument for creating stability in its immediate vicinity, the prospect of membership, is approaching the limits of its applicability. The European Neighbourhood Policy (ENP) is a response to the key question of how to deal with future neighbouring states that have a special relationship with the Union, but have no prospect of membership for the foreseeable future or do not aspire to accession. In this respect, the EU's actions are based on the same principle as its enlargement strategy: they are aimed at establishing a ring of stability around the EU. The goal is to achieve an expansion without institutional enlargement, or in other words: a hegemonial strategy aiming to influence the domestic development of the ENP countries through tailored, differentiated integration (Smith 2005).

Debates about the implications of a European foreign and security policy became central to the study of European integration. However, the TEU also caused renewed scholarly interest in theoretical explanations of the EU's foreign and security policy. Since the EU lacks an overarching federal centre, the federalists' approach remained largely ignored. Neorealists, in turn, have, in the first instance, struggled to explain closer European cooperation on foreign and security policy – given that the collapse of the bipolar order should, according to their logic, have reinforced inner European competition rather than led to closer cooperation. The alternative explanation, according to which the CFSP, and later the ESDP, reflect a balancing behaviour on behalf of the EU vis-à-vis the US, is not supported by the evidence at hand (Brooks and Wohlforth 2008: 80–83). 'Such considerations are [potential] outcomes … of the project, rather than drivers. They are hypothetical consequences rather than motivating forces or intentions.' (Howorth 2007: 51).

Regardless of closer cooperation efforts in the context of the CFSP, intergovernmentalists have consistently emphasized the theoretical limits of European integration, thereby echoing Stanley Hoffmann's catchphrase according to which in matters of diplomacy, security and defence, the state remains 'more obstinate than obsolete' (Hoffmann 1966). According to this school, member states would share their sovereignty only when, first, the perceived gains of common action would outweigh the potential costs of lost sovereignty; when, secondly, government preferences or perceived national interests had converged sufficiently; and when, thirdly, the particular interests of large states remained protected (Gordon 1997–98: 80; Moravcsik 1998: 428).

While there is no doubt that the agenda-setting in European foreign and security policy has, more often than not, been the result of grand bargains among member states, such an approach tends to underestimate the importance of greater institutionalization, coordination and, indeed, Europeanization of EU foreign and – to a limited extent – security policy that has taken place over the past decades. This has resulted in a multi-level governance where authority is shared across an 'institutionalized, hierarchically structured set of actors with varying degrees of unity/coherence, commitment to EU norms, and power resources', which in turn makes it difficult to devise national policies without reference to EU activities (Smith 2004b: 743; Smith 2001; Tonra 2003).

In sum, security through integration was the guiding principle during the Cold War years, whereas in the 1990s, the EU relied on a policy of security projection through stabilization and association of its Eastern neighbourhood, without questioning its basic principles or fundamentally adapting its range of security policy instruments. At the end of the 1990s, the experience of failure in the Balkan wars gave rise to a determination that the EU as an intergovernmentally organized 'superpower' (Blair 2000), supported by a comprehensive civilian and military arsenal of foreign and security policy instruments, should act as a reg-ulative force beyond the European continent by leveraging its member states' political, economic and military potential across multiple pillars, thus gaining the power to shape the course of events on the global stage and fundamentally transforming the occasionally insular character of the EU in strategic matters. Today, these three very different approaches to security policy continue to coexist and are sometimes mutually dependent.

Towards autonomy, strategic culture and security governance

While the establishment of the CFSP in the early 1990s reflected a major shift on the part of EU member states towards the aspiration of building a common foreign policy and even moving towards a common defence policy, complemented by the develop-ment of a third justice and home affairs pillar to deal with internal security matters, the EU member states' intention of June 1999 to acquire 'the capacity for autonomous action, backed up by credible military forces, the means to decide to use them, and a readiness to do so, in order to respond to international crises' (European Council 1999) signalled the emergence of an unprecedented political project that did not, however, in any way take recourse to the historical EDC project with its supranational, top-down approach. For the first time since the failure of the EDC in 1954, security and defence were firmly on the agenda of the EU. And, for the first time since the beginnings of the transatlantic bargain in the late 1940s, it was believed that, despite initial and continuing tensions, a genuine European security policy could exist alongside transatlantic security.

The launch of the ESDP project was the result of a Franco-British bargain. For decades, the antagonism between their respective positions had prevented the EU from assuming a role in security and defence. While both countries maintained a considerable degree of 'constructive ambiguity' (Heisbourg 2000), Prime Minister Tony Blair's commitment to a policy of constructive engagement within European institutions and France's, though at times reluctant, acknowledgement of NATO's role in European security matters served as major catalysts. Though they did not entail the same sense of urgency at the time, some of the factors that had already been fundamental drivers behind the birth of the CFSP in the early 1990s considerably influenced the respective policy shift in London and Paris: the emergence of new security challenges; the reappearance of military conflict on the European continent; Europe's diminishing political and military significance in the eyes of the US; a general determination to serve as a force for good in international affairs; internal EU dynamics; and the forging of a European defence industry (Howorth 2007: 51–57).

New decision-making bodies reflecting the institutionalization of European security policy and the development of civilian and military capabilities have given the ESDP real meaning (Howorth 2007: 61–134). At the same time, serious challenges remain. First, two institutional issues are at stake: one concerns the interaction between national capitals and the EU institutions in Brussels; the other concerns coherence across the EU's institutional pillars. Secondly, the gap between declared ambition and capabilities remains considerable (Witney 2008; Giegerich 2008; Menon 2009). Third, the EU's security ambitions have given rise to transatlantic debates since the launch of the CFSP, that is, long before the decision was made to create the ESDP. The US still sees the ESDP primarily as a means of increasing European military capabilities and regards the EU's role as a security actor *sui generis* as a secondary aspect. In addition, the relationship between the EU and NATO needs to be clarified. And fourth, the unresolved issue of the Treaty of Lisbon prevents important institutional changes from taking effect.

Another potential impediment to collective European security efforts relates to the contested concept of a European strategic culture, which has been aptly defined as

> comprising the socially transmitted, identity-derived norms, ideas and patterns of behaviour that are shared among a broad majority of actors and social groups within a given security community, which help to shape a ranked set of options for a community's pursuit of security and defence goals
>
> (Meyer 2005: 528)

Despite the absence of an EU-wide identity and despite limited empirical evidence, one can detect a cautious convergence of attitudes on humanitarian intervention abroad, on the thresholds for international authorization and on the EU's role as an actor in security and defence matters (Meyer 2005: 543–46). Adaptation pressures, however, especially when they are high, can have the reverse effect on the Europeanization of strategic culture.

These considerations relating to the emergence of a strategic culture also indicate the creation of a multi-layered structure of European defence policy, which can no longer be adequately described by the term 'intergovernmentalism', but instead indicates the incremental formation of an EU Security Governance (Webber et al. 2004), to which researchers should devote increasing attention in the coming years. In any case, the development of the ESDP in the past decade has intensified the pace of integration between foreign and security policy issues and areas of activities within the EU, with special emphasis being devoted to decision-making processes that preserve the principle of sovereignty as well as incentives towards common action and stronger collaboration with international organizations (Diedrichs 2008: 342).

Conclusion

If the extent of the gap between expectations, on the one hand, and capabilities in terms of institutions, instruments and resources, on the other, is to be regarded as the benchmark for measuring the incremental change of European foreign and security policy (Hill 1998; cf. Ginsberg 1999), then it is fair to state – considering the 50-year European integration process and irrespective of the EU's utter inability to act in the face of the Iraq crisis – that even though it continues to be marked by fragmentation and cooperation, institutional untidiness, a limited range of instruments and disputes over resources, the EU has become an actor *sui generis* in foreign and security policy affairs. In the past years, the EU has increasingly taken on responsibility for regional and, to a still limited extent, global security – initially through its successful enlargement rounds, which continued the EU's founding principles of security through integration and have consolidated the EU's position as a hegemonial force for peace on its own continent, and then through a policy of limited security projection into its immediate neighbourhood. Subsequently, it held out the prospect of EU accession, which exerts a magnetic force that has decisively boosted the process of political, economic and social transformation in the bordering countries. Finally, the EU shouldered the burden of providing security through numerous civilian, military and civil–military missions in the Balkans, Africa, the Near and Middle East, and into Asia. While the scope of these missions is closely circumscribed, they nevertheless aim at a comprehensive approach to crisis management; at the same time, the indispensable absorption of lessons learned will not only help to optimize decision-making processes, but will also foster the emerging development of a strategic culture. The EU's impact on foreign and security policy in global affairs has increased in recent years. However, not least due to its specific character as a community of states aiming for an ever-closer union, the EU will not take on the role of a traditional great power or that of a balancer between various power blocs. Its security policy orientation will be increasingly aligned towards regional affairs (Maull 2005).

The 'method of gaining sovereignty by ceding sovereignty' (Haftendorn 2001: 436) was originally practised in a vastly different context, but its usefulness is now widely appreciated among EU member states. However, it occasionally clashes with the defiant desire of the European great powers to engage in unilateral action, which ultimately leads to a policy of readjustment of the integrative equilibrium within the community of an enlarged EU. This dialectic has given the modern-day EU a foreign and security policy that exists in parallel with the national foreign and security policies of its member states and in fact exerts a centripetal force. It allows the member states to make use of the common foreign and security policy both to conceal and to promote their national interests, to enhance the legitimacy of their policies by acting collectively, or to reduce risks and costs, while at the same time being more than a zero-sum game (Mauer 2006). European foreign and security policy does not feature a single overriding authority at its core, but while the EU remains a fragmented and incomplete actor in international and security affairs, its foreign and security policy does provide an umbrella for bringing together the national member states and the EU's institutions, instruments and resources, thereby contributing to the emergence of a distinct EU security governance.

References

Adler, E. and Barnett, M. (1998) 'Security communities in theoretical perspective', in Adler, E. and Barnett, M. (eds) *Security Communities*, Cambridge: Cambridge University Press, pp. 3–28.
Andréani, G., Bertram, C. and Grant, C. (2001) *Europe's Military Revolution*, London: Centre for European Reform.

Andreata, F. (2005) 'Theory and the European Union's international relations', in Hill, C. and Smith, M. (eds) *International Relations and the European Union*, Oxford: Oxford University Press, pp. 18–38.

Art, R.J. (2004) 'Europe hedges its security bets', in Paul, T.V., Wirtz, J.J. and Fortmann, M. (eds) *Balance of Power: Theory and Practice in the 21st Century*, Stanford, CA: Stanford University Press, pp. 179–214.

——(2005) 'Striking the balance', *International Security* 30, 3: 177–85.

Biscop, S. (2005) *The European Security Strategy: A Global Agenda for Positive Power*, London: Ashgate.

Blair, T. (2000) 'Europe's political future', Speech to the Polish Stock Exchange, 6 October. Available online at: www.number-10.gov.uk/output/Page3384.asp (accessed 14 September 2008).

Brooks, S.G. and Wohlforth, W.C. (2008) *World Out of Balance: International Relations and the Challenge of American Primacy*, Princeton, NJ: Princeton University Press.

Bull, H. (1982) 'Civilian power Europe: A contradiction in terms?', *Journal of Common Market Studies* 21, 2: 149–70.

Cornish, P. and Edwards, G. (2001) 'Beyond the EU/NATO dichotomy: The beginnings of a European strategic culture', *International Affairs* 77, 3: 587–603.

——(2005) 'The strategic culture of the European Union: A progress report', *International Affairs* 81, 4: 801–20.

Deighton, A. (ed.) (1997) *Western European Union 1954–1997: Defence, Security, Integration*, Oxford: European Interdependence Research Unit.

——(2002) 'The European security and defence policy', *Journal of Common Market Studies* 40, 4: 719–41.

Deutsch, K.W. et al. (1957) *Political Community and the North Atlantic Area: International Organization in the Light of Historical Experience*, Princeton, NJ: Princeton University Press.

Diedrichs, U. (2008) 'Neue Dynamik in der Europäischen Außen-und Sicherheitspolitik: auf dem Weg zu einer Security Governance', in Tömmel, I. (ed.) *Die Europäische Union: Governance und Policy-Making*, Wiesbaden: VS Verlag für Sozialwissenschaften, pp. 343–64.

Duchêne, F. (1972) 'Europe's role in world peace', in Mayne, R. (ed.) *Europe Tomorrow: Sixteen Europeans Look Ahead*, London: Fontana, pp. 32–47.

Duke, S. (2000) *The Elusive Quest for European Security: From EDC to CSFP*, Houndmills, Basingstoke: Macmillan.

Eilstrup-Sangiovanni, M. (2003) 'Why a common security and defence policy is bad for Europe', *Survival* 45, 3: 193–206.

European Council (1999) *Presidency Conclusions*. Cologne European Council, 3 and 4 June 1999.

——(2003) *A Secure Europe in a Better World: European Security Strategy*.

Fursdon, E. (1980) *The European Defence Community: A History*, London: Macmillan.

Giegerich, B. (2006) *European Security and Strategic Culture: National Response to the EU's Security and Defence Policy*, Baden-Baden: Nomos.

——(2008) *European Military Crisis Management: Connecting Ambition and Reality* (Adelphi Papers), London: Routledge.

Ginsberg, R.H. (1999) 'Conceptualizing the European Union as an international actor: Narrowing the theoretical capability-expectations gap', *Journal of Common Market Studies* 37, 3: 429–54.

Gordon, P.H. (1997–98) 'Europe's uncommon foreign policy', *International Security* 22, 3: 74–100.

Grabbe, H. (2006) *The EU's Transformative Power: Europeanization Through Conditionality in Central and Eastern Europe*, Houndmills, Basingstoke: Palgrave Macmillan.

Haas, E.B. (1958) *The Uniting of Europe: Political, Social, and Economic Forces, 1950–1957*, Stanford, CA: Stanford University Press.

——(1961) 'International integration: The European and universal process', *International Organization* 15, 3: 366–92.

Haass, R.N. (1997) *The Reluctant Sheriff. The United States after the Cold War*, Washington, DC: Brookings Institution.

Haftendorn, H. (2001) *Deutsche Außenpolitik zwischen Selbstbeschränkung und Selbstbehauptung 1945–2000*, Stuttgart/München: Deutsche Verlags-Anstalt.

Heisbourg, F. (2000) 'Europe's strategic ambitions: The limits of ambiguity', *Survival* 42, 2: 5–15.

379

Hill, C. (1993) 'The capability-expectations gap, or conceptualizing Europe's international role', *Journal of Common Market Studies* 31, 3: 305–28.

——(1998) 'Closing the capabilities-expectations gap?' in Peterson, J. and Sjursen, H. (eds) *A Common Foreign Policy for Europe? Competing Visions of the CFSP*, London: Routledge, pp. 18–38.

Hill, C. and Smith, M. (eds) (2005) *International Relations and the European Union*, Oxford: Oxford University Press.

Hoffmann, S. (1966) 'Obstinate or obsolete: The fate of the nation state and the case of Western Europe', *Daedalus* 95, 2: 862–915.

——(2000) 'Towards a common European foreign and security policy?' *Journal of Common Market Studies* 38, 2: 189–98.

Howorth, J. (2003) 'Why ESDP is necessary and beneficial for the alliance', in Howorth, J. and Keeler, J.T.S. (eds) *Defending Europe: The EU, NATO and the Quest for European Autonomy*, New York: Palgrave Macmillan, pp. 219–38.

——(2007) *Security and Defence Policy in the European Union*, London: Palgrave Macmillan.

James, R.R. (1986) *Anthony Eden*, London: Weidenfeld & Nicolson.

Jones, S.G. (2006) 'The rise of a European defense', *Political Science Quarterly* 121, 2: 241–67.

——(2007) *The Rise of European Security Cooperation*, Cambridge: Cambridge University Press.

Kupchan, C. (1998) 'After Pax Americana: Benign power, regional integration, and the sources of a stable multipolarity', *International Security* 23, 2: 40–79.

——(2000) 'In defence of European defence: An American perspective', *Survival* 42, 2: 16–32.

——(2004–5) 'The travails of union: The American experience and its implications for Europe', *Survival* 46, 4: 103–20.

Lagendijk, J. (2002) 'Green views on the European Security And Defence Policy (ESDP)', in Hoyer, W. and Kaldrack, G.F. (eds) *Europäische Sicherheits-und Verteidigungspolitik. Der Weg zu integrierten europäischen Streitkräften?*, Baden-Baden: Nomos, pp. 145–55.

Manners, I. (2006) 'Normative power Europe reconsidered: Beyond the crossroads', *Journal of European Public Policy* 13, 2: 182–99.

Mauer, V. (2006) 'Die Sicherheitspolitik der Europäischen Union', *Aus Politik und Zeitgeschichte* 43: 10–16.

Maull, H.W. (2005) 'Europe and the new balance of global order', *International Affairs* 81, 4: 775–99.

Menon, A. (2003) 'Why ESDP is misguided and dangerous for the alliance', in Howorth, J. and Keeler, J.T.S. (eds) *Defending Europe: The EU, NATO and the Quest for European Autonomy*, New York: Palgrave Macmillan, pp. 203–17.

——(2009) 'Empowering paradise? The ESDP at ten', *International Affairs* 85, 2: 227–46.

Mérand, F. (2008) *European Defence Policy. Beyond the Nation State*, Oxford: Oxford University Press.

Messervy-Whiting, G. (2006) 'ESDP deployments and the European security strategy', in Deighton, A. and Mauer, V. (eds) *Securing Europe? Implementing the European Security Strategy*, Zurich: ETH Zurich, pp. 31–41.

Meyer, C.O. (2005) 'Convergence towards a European strategic culture? A constructivist framework for explaining changing norms', *European Journal of International Relations* 11, 4: 523–49.

——(2006) *The Quest for a European Strategic Culture: Changing Norms on Security and Defence in the European Union*, Houndmills, Basingstoke: Palgrave.

Möckli, D. (2009) *European Foreign Policy during the Cold War: Heath, Brandt, Pompidou and the Dream of Political Unity*, London: I.B. Tauris.

Moravcsik, A. (1998) *The Choice for Europe: Social Purpose and State Power From Messina to Maastricht*, Ithaca, NY: Cornell University Press.

Nuttall, S.J. (1992) *European Political Cooperation*, Oxford: Oxford University Press.

Ojanen, H. (2006) 'The EU and NATO: Two competing models for a common defence policy', *Journal of Common Market Studies* 44, 1: 57–76.

Parsons, C. (2004) *A Certain Idea of Europe*, Ithaca, NY: Cornell University Press.

Platform on European Security Interests, The Hague, 27 October 1987. Available online at: www.weu.int/documents/871027en.pdf.

Posen, B. (2004) 'ESDP and the structure of world power', *The International Spectator* XXXIV, 1: 5–17.

——(2006) 'European Union security and defense policy: Response to unipolarity?', *Security Studies* 15, 2: 149–86.

Rees, W. (1998) *The Western European Union at the Crossroads: Between Transatlantic Solidarity and European Integration*, Boulder, CO: Westview.

Rees, W. and Smith, M. (eds) (2008) *International Relations of the European Union*, 4 vols., London: SAGE Publications.

Sandholtz, W. and Sweet, A.S. (eds) (1998) *European Integration and Supranational Governance*, Oxford: Oxford University Press.

Schimmelfennig, F. (2004) *The EU, NATO, and the Integration of Europe: Rules and Rhetoric*, Cambridge: Cambridge University Press.

Sloan, S.R. (2000) *The United States and European Defence*, Paris: WEU Institute (Chaillot Paper 39).

Smith, K. (2005) 'The outsiders: The European neighbourhood policy', *International Affairs* 81, 4: 757–73.

Smith, M.E. (2001) 'Diplomacy by decree: The legalization of EU foreign policy', *Journal of Common Market Studies* 39, 1: 79–104.

——(2004a) *Europe's Foreign and Security Policy: The Institutionalization of Cooperation*, Cambridge: Cambridge University Press.

——(2004b) 'Toward a theory of EU foreign policy-making: Multi-level governance, domestic politics, and national adaptation to Europe's common foreign and security policy', *Journal of European Public Policy* 11, 4: 740–58.

Tonra, B. (2003) 'Constructing the common foreign and security policy: The utility of a cognitive approach', *Journal of Common Market Studies* 41, 4: 731–56.

Treaty on European Union, 7 February 1992. Available online at: http://eur-lex.europa.eu/en/treaties/dat/11992M/htm/11992M.html.

Walt, S.M. (2005) *Taming American Power: The Global Response to U.S. Primacy*, New York: W.W. Norton & Company.

Webber, M., Croft, S., Howorth, J., Terriff, T. and Krahmann, E. (2004) 'The governance of European security', *Review of International Studies* 30, 1: 3–26.

Witney, N. (2008) *Re-energising Europe's Security and Defence Policy*, London: European Council on Foreign Relations.

Young, J.W. (1993) *Britain and European Unity, 1945–1992*, Houndmills, Basingstoke: Macmillan.

35

Alliances

Carlo Masala[1]

Alliances have been an important element of security policy since long before the rise of the modern nation-state. Tribes, princedoms and later nation-states have always sought out allies with whom they could pool their resources in the pursuit of common goals. Therefore, the history of alliances is as long as the history of relations between cohesive units of human coexistence.

In this chapter, an alliance is regarded – in accordance with the definition of Stephen Walt (1987: 1) – as a 'formal or informal relationship of security cooperation between at least two sovereign states'. Therefore, alliances can take the shape of either formal or informal international institutions (Duffield 2007). Furthermore, their structure can correspond to one of two ideal types (Weber 1997: 33) – hierarchical or egalitarian.[2] The former type is characterized by significant imbalances of capabilities between alliance members, whilst in the latter type, power is distributed more or less evenly among most members.

Hierarchically structured alliances can be further differentiated into hegemonic and imperial alliances. This distinction refers to the way the strongest power in the alliance exerts its leadership. If the strong state leads with the consent of the smaller powers, their relationship is considered a hegemonic one (cf. Triepel 1938). Arrangements under which the relationship between the strongest state and the other alliance members is based on coercion (as was the case, e.g. in the Warsaw Pact) are considered imperial alliances.

Although alliances are a core element in the history of International Relations and the concept itself is a 'key term' (Modelski 1962: 773) in academic discourse, alliances are at the same time 'understudied' (Snyder 1997: 1). There are plenty of studies on alliance management, but research is lacking on why alliances are formed and when they dissolve, which is astonishing given the fact that 'alliances are apparently a universal component of relations between political units, irrespective of time and place' (Holsti et al. 1973: 2).

One of the reasons for this puzzle is that the specific issue of alliances is difficult to separate from other fields in the discipline of International Relations. It is impossible to discuss alliances without referring to more general theories of International Relations, e.g. realism (Morgenthau 1948), neorealism (Waltz 1979), neoliberal institutionalism (Keohane 1984) or constructivism (Wendt 1999), or touching upon so-called 'substantive issues' (Carlsnaes et al. 2002: iv), e.g. conflict theory (Zartman 1985) or deterrence (Freedman 2004). Because the topic of alliances is inextricably intertwined with other fields of the discipline, theorists have either focused on a particular alliance (mostly on NATO) or developed partial theories focusing on particular aspects of alliances.

So far, there have been only three attempts to create anything close to a comprehensive theory of alliances. The first attempt was George Liska's (1962) 'Nations in Alliance', followed 25 years later by the seminal work of Stephen Walt (1987) on 'The Origins of Alliances' and, another decade later, Glenn Snyder's (1997) work on 'Alliance Politics'. All three studies have their limitations. Liska's attempt to elaborate a theory of alliances, although it gives some useful insights on the creation of alliances and patterns of cooperation among its members, clearly suffers from its anecdotal character. Walt's work is limited, as the title indicates, to the origins of alliances, and Snyder's book on alliances in multipolar systems focuses on the management of member relations.

The lack of a discrete body of knowledge about alliances became very much apparent during the 1990s, when the question of NATO's survival after the end of the Cold War led to an academic battle between various schools of thought[3] without any tangible results in terms of cumulative knowledge (Lakatos and Musgrave 1970) or paradigm shift (Kuhn 1962). Much of the debate seemed to be self-referential and focused on the affirmation of the different research programmes, rather than striving for the enhancement of our knowledge about alliances.

This chapter tries to cut through the current confusion about alliances by providing an overview of different, occasionally competing, explanations. The following addresses three issues that are fundamental for our understanding of alliance politics. Firstly, why do alliances exist? Secondly, how do they function? And thirdly, when do alliances dissolve, and under which conditions do they survive?

The origins of alliances

There is a widespread agreement among the neorealist, neoliberal institutionalist and constructivist schools of thought that states do act and interact in the absence of a centralized authority capable of providing protection and the 'redress of grievances' (Grieco 2002: 65). Each of these approaches to understanding alliance formation is discussed in more detail below.

Balancing and bandwagoning

For neorealists, alliances are tools for balancing where states are unable to establish equilibrium by relying on their own means.[4] Therefore, states use alliances as an instrument to maintain or improve their relative power position globally or regionally. Neorealists believe that states decide to form or to join alliances based on exogenous, not endogenous motivations, because '[a]lliances are against, and only derivatively for, someone or something' (Liska 1962: 12). Alliances therefore can be regarded as a particular outcome of a conflict. By building alliances, states try to maximize their capabilities to counterbalance the overwhelming power of another individual state or group of states.

Stephen Walt has modified this neorealist account of alliance formation somewhat. By including perceptual and behavioural variables in the body of neorealist theory, he argues that states do not aim to counterbalance power per se, but the power of actors they perceive as threatening (Walt 1987: 21–28). However, seeking to establish equilibrium is only one option available to states. If states that feel threatened are unable to pursue a balance-of-power strategy on the strength of their own capabilities and have no potential allies, they may be forced to 'accommodate the most imminent threat' (Walt 1987: 30) to their security. From this point of view, bandwagoning is a strategy to avoid becoming the victim of a threatening state or to enjoy the anticipated spoils of victory. But, in general, Walt (1987: 33) concludes, states are inclined to balance rather than to band-wagon, since bandwagoning always involves an unequal exchange where one state (the weaker one) accepts a subordinate role.

While Walt considers bandwagoning to be a kind of anomaly within the neorealist research framework on alliances, Randall Schweller (1994) regards it as being compatible with realist assumptions about state behaviour, if the motivation of a state that joins the stronger rather than the weaker side is revisionist, meaning that the state in question is primarily concerned with destroying the current order and securing additional gains. 'Many, therefore, choose to bandwagon with revisionist great powers bent on constructing a new international system; they are "power-maximizing states"' (Zongyou 2006: 196).

From a neorealist perspective, alliances are a form of 'regression' in conflict regulation behaviour (Singer 1949). Such regression (which refers to an elimination of tensions through reduction of complexity in the relations between alliance members and the threatening power[s]) among conflict parties goes hand in hand with integration, or strengthening of the alliance's overall fabric as a result of intensified relations among its members. Therefore, members of an alliance face an additional constraining effect on their action and interaction, because, from a neorealist perspective, an alliance does not abolish the constraining effects emanating from the anarchical structure of the international system on state behaviour, but merely modifies them.

Cooperation as reward

While neoliberal institutionalists do not deny that states are acting and interacting under conditions of system-wide anarchy, they do not attribute the same effects of anarchy to state behaviour that realists/neorealist do (Masala 2005: 92; Keohane 1984). Anarchy, therefore, is not an obstacle to lasting cooperation among states. States engage in alliances because, as self-interested actors, they anticipate a mutually rewarding exchange among the members of an alliance (Stein 1990: 7). But what exactly are those rewards that states expect to reap?

Firstly, states create alliances in the expectation that the alliance members can achieve a certain degree of cooperation. As long as the costs for the creation of alliances do not outweigh the perceived benefits from cooperation, states are eager to cooperate (Wallander 2000: 706). From this point of view, an external threat can trigger alliance formation, but there are further advantages beyond the mere engagement in a counterbalancing effort that make alliance membership an attractive proposition for states. From a neo-liberal institutionalist viewpoint, alliances provide reciprocity, make members accountable for their actions, and contribute to the creation and maintenance of cooperative security strategies. They also reduce uncertainty by providing credible information on the behaviour of member states and make state behaviour among members of the alliance more predictable by developing norms and rules that regulate it (Wallander et al. 1999: 3f.). Although there is a price to pay for joining such institutions, as they impose constraints upon state strategies and have an influence on state preferences, it is a price that states may consider commensurate with the expected benefits. In fact, it is precisely because institutions and actions undertaken by them are costly (politically and economically) that they are credible and therefore can be valuable to self-interested states (Wallander and Keohane 1999: 30). To summarize: from an institutionalist perspective, alliances offer their member states many advantages, which guarantee that alliances persist beyond the conditions in which they were created.

The domestic factor

A third and relatively new account of how and why alliances are created is offered by the liberal school. Liberalism in general 'seeks the roots and causes of external behaviour in domestic structure and process' (Müller 2002: 376). In general, liberals share the belief that states engage in alliances when there is a convergence of national preferences created by domestic coalitions (Risse-Kappen 1991; Moravcsik 1998). Risse-Kappen believes that the creation of NATO was not dependent on a real or perceived threat, or even a constructed one. However, Risse-Kappen and Moravcsik both focus on democracies only, leaving aside the possibility of preference conversion amongst non-democratic states. Thus, liberals are able to explain why NATO was created, but have difficulties explaining the foundation of the Warsaw Pact Organization, which was formed under Soviet leadership amongst Socialist or Communist countries.

Common identity and ideas, values and norms

So far, not much work has been done by constructivists with regard to alliances. The most elaborate and sophisticated constructivist-inspired analysis on the question of why alliances (specifically NATO) are created is offered by Thomas Risse-Kappen (1996).

According to Risse-Kappen, NATO was not created as an effort to counterbalance the Soviet material threat. Rather, NATO represents the institutionalized form of common ideas and worldviews about the coming international order after the Second World War shared by the founding states of the alliance (ibid.: 387). Those with similar worldviews and fundamental beliefs founded an alliance whose guiding principles were consistent with their values and norms. In this respect, NATO is an alliance of identity that is not threat-based, but reflects a relationship between states based on a common understanding of their shared traits.

With his emphasis on shared beliefs, Risse-Kappen paved the way for others to apply the same concept to other alliances. Michael Barnett (2002) in his article on alliance formation in the Middle East challenges directly Stephen Walt's assertion that ideologies have played an 'important but ultimately limited role' (Walt 1987: 203). Barnett argues instead that identity, and thus ideology, is a key element to social and political interactions, that has to be examined closely to understand why states form an alliance. 'A starting point for the study of identity is a belief that social groups need to establish a positively valued distinctness from other groups in order to provide members with a positive identity' (McCalla 1996).

How do alliances work? Alliance management

While our knowledge on why and how alliances are created is limited, the literature on the management of relations among alliance members is manifold. There are a number of partial theories focusing on different aspects of alliance management.

The distinction between different types of internal alliance structures is important for the analysis of alliance management. Depending on their internal structure, alliances may face different management challenges. This section touches on three central aspects of alliance management: (a) hegemonic stability; (b) the alliance internal security dilemma; and (c) alliance cohesion. While the last two aspects are important for understanding alliance management within hegemonic/imperial as well as egalitarian alliances, the first occurs only in hegemonic alliances.

Hegemonic stability

The internal structure of an alliance has implications for the management of intra-alliance relations. In a hegemonic alliance, smaller states are only willing to subordinate themselves to the leadership of a bigger state, thereby constraining their sovereignty, if the hegemon provides a public good that the smaller states are unable to produce sufficiently by themselves. This is the core of the hegemonic stability theory (Kindleberger 1986). There are, however, differences in explaining why hegemons provide public goods. Neorealists emphasize that it is in the interest of hegemonial powers to create alliances, to shape them and to exert their influence upon other states through forms of institutionalized cooperation (Gilpin 1981). Neoliberal institutionalists on the other hand, emphasize that the hegemon's behaviour is driven by enlightened self-interest. The hegemonial power provides the public good and lets others participate because it is in the interest of all member states of an alliance (Keohane 1984). The difference between the neorealist and the neoliberal institutionalist reasoning is that neorealists would always highlight the fact that the hegemon gains a political advantage from the provision of a public good for free, and only provides this good for as long as it is in the interest of the leading power and it is able to use the other alliance members for its own purposes. From a neorealist perspective, public goods are provided because the hegemon is interested in relative gains. Neoliberals instead would argue that the provision of a public good by a hegemon is not linked to the political exploitation of other alliance members. From a neoliberal perspective, the hegemon is interested in absolute gains and will therefore refrain from exploiting the fact that its relations with the other alliance members are asymmetric in nature.

Both schools of thought would agree, however, that the type of relationship between the hegemon and its followers as outlined above entails the risk of free riding. If the hegemon provides a collective good, smaller states do not see the need to increase their efforts to contribute to the production of this public good. In the long term, this creates tension within the alliances. The difference between both schools of thought is, however, that realists argue that tensions only occur in the absence of a commonly faced threat, while neoliberal institutionalists see tensions as a permanent feature of relations between alliance members.

The internal security dilemma

A feature that is common to both the hegemonic and the egalitarian alliance is what Glenn Snyder – using Robert Jervis's (1976: 63) concept – has described as the alliance internal security dilemma (Snyder 1997: 180–83). In an alliance, as in the international system in general, the absence of a supranational authority leads to a situation where many of the steps pursued by states to bolster their security have the effect – often unintended – of making other states less secure. Since alliance members can never be certain of other alliance members' future or present intentions, they embark on policies *vis-à-vis* their alliance partners aimed at enhancing security.

Snyder's starting assumption is that the interests of alliance members never fully converge. Since alliance members have committed themselves in a more or less binding way to certain goals, every alliance member faces two potential dilemmas. The first is the risk of entrapment (Snyder 1997: 1981). Entrapment refers to a situation where an alliance member (A) faces the choice of supporting another alliance member (B) as a result of treaty obligations, although A has no particular interest in supporting B, or staying out of a conflict. Country A fears involvement in a conflict that does not involve its vital interests. However, if A, despite its commitments, stays out of the conflict, it may risk defection by its ally.

The second risk Snyder describes is the fear of abandonment. Abandonment characterizes a situation from the perception of state A, which has a particular interest in a conflict with a non-alliance member, but cannot be sure of the active support of other allies.

To attenuate both dilemmas by avoiding entrapment as well as abandonment is one of the biggest tasks in the management of an alliance. Both the management of the alliance internal security dilemma as well as the structural problems inherent to hegemonic stability theory point to a much larger problem that alliance members face in the management of their relations, namely how to ensure alliance cohesion.

Alliance cohesion

From the neorealist point of view, alliance cohesion, whether in a hegemonic or an egalitarian alliance, depends on the degree of the external challenge. The bigger the threat alliance members face (or perceive), the greater alliance cohesion will be (Mearsheimer 1990). There is disagreement, however, as to the role that the hegemon plays in maintaining alliance cohesion. While some authors regard it as crucial (Gowa 1999), others are sceptical, particularly concerning the phase when the commonly perceived threat decreases (Masala 2003). When the threat decreases, smaller alliance members are less and less willing to subordinate themselves to a hegemon. The simple causality of neorealist reasoning is as follows: high levels of threat perception lead to high alliance cohesion, while conversely, low threat perception levels result in low alliance cohesion.

From a (liberal) institutional perspective, alliance cohesion is guaranteed by the multiple advantages that alliances provide for their member states. The reduction of transaction costs; the ability to control other alliance members; the access to information about the intentions and behaviour of alliance partners; and the iterated games that are played within the cooperative framework of an alliance – all of these advantages outweigh the potential costs and frictions emanating from different national preferences (Keohane and Nye 1993).

Constructivists (similar to neoliberal institutionalists) argue that alliances have cohesion because of the 'republican liberalism linking domestic polities systematically to the foreign policy of states' (Risse-Kappen 1996: 358). Among liberal democracies, coherence is guaranteed because liberal democracies are more inclined to cooperate closely with other liberal democracies. This is because liberal democracies do not regard other liberal democracies as a potential threat. Among liberal democracies, there is no fear that cooperation will be exploited by allies in the future; therefore, the problem of relative gain distribution (Grieco 1990) does not exist. Additionally, constructivists point to the fact that democracies are characterized by transparency; high audience costs; consistent policy behaviour; civilian control of the armed forces (which is important for military alliances between democracies); and the capacity to make enduring commitments (Lai and Reiter 2000) – all of which are factors that facilitate closer cooperation between such regimes. To summarize: the more similar the regimes are that cooperate, and the more their values converge, the more cohesive the alliance they form will be.

As with the question of why alliances are formed, there is no clear-cut answer to the question of how they are managed.

Why do alliances end, why do they survive and how?

The issue of how alliances survive and why they end was hotly debated among scholars of International Relations during the first half of the 1990s. It should not come as a surprise that the results were, at best, mixed.

The linchpin for this debate was, of course, the question of whether NATO would survive the end of the Cold War. Unsurprisingly, neorealists were very sceptical concerning the future of alliances after the disappearance of the cohesive force that holds them together; namely, the commonly perceived threat. Scholars like Waltz and Mearsheimer were quite outspoken about the future of alliances, especially of NATO, after the demise of the Warsaw Pact and particularly after the collapse of the Soviet Union. They believed NATO had become an anachronism (Waltz 1990: 21, 2000: 18; Mearsheimer 1990). Waltz believed that the reason why NATO still existed, even ten years after the fall of the Berlin Wall, was the fact that the US had an interest in maintaining its 'grip' (Waltz 2000: 19) on developments in Europe. Stephen Walt joined his former Ph.D. supervisor in this rationale by pointing out that US hegemony could well explain why NATO remained one of the main relevant political institutions in transatlantic affairs (Walt 1997: 171). But even the continuation of US hegemonic policy, according to Waltz, would not prevent NATO from becoming an irrelevant institution, because other alliance members would be less and less willing to accept US supremacy within the institution.

On the other side, neoliberal institutionalists have been extremely optimistic with regard to the possibility of cooperation within alliances even without an external threat or a hegemon (Haftendorn et al. 1999). Besides the already mentioned positive effects that alliance members enjoy by virtue of their alliance membership, institutional inertia contributes to the prolongation of cooperation within an alliance.[5] Furthermore, as long as alliance members have an interest in keeping their cooperation alive (Keohane 1984: 31), the chance that alliances may survive and even adapt to a new environment – even in the absence of an overwhelming threat – are quite high.

An argument as to why NATO survived the end of the East–West conflict that is fully in line with the basic tenets of neoliberal institutionalism has been developed by Celleste Wallander (2000). Institutions with general assets,[6] she argues, will be adaptable to new problems. Because the assets are not specific to a given relationship, location or purpose, using them for new purposes will be low-cost and broadly effective (Wallander 2000: 709). NATO, she concludes in her empirical analysis, has been successful in adapting its assets to a new security environment (ibid: 732) that is not characterized by a unifying threat.

According to the constructivist point of view, the survival of an alliance depends on the continuation of the underlying reason for the alliance's existence, which, as discussed above, is not a common threat, but the perception of having a common destiny. Therefore, alliances can survive major changes in their environment if their members still feel that they belong together and share the same norms and values. From a constructivist perspective, the end of the East–West conflict does not mark the end of NATO, since it did not terminate the community of values. Frank Schimmelfennig (1999) argued that after the fall of the Berlin Wall, the Western value community extended into the newly democratic countries of Eastern Europe, and NATO played (and still plays, according to this view) a crucial role in socializing these states. As long as alliance members build a security community (Deutsch et al. 1957)[7] and have a sense of belonging to it, security cooperation will continue.

Conclusion and outlook

This chapter has attempted to remove some of the confusion surrounding the study of alliances by systematically structuring the existing literature into various categories along three important questions.

We are left with the insight that, although alliances are important in structuring relations between states, we still do not know much about them. The lack of knowledge about alliances also has policy implications. One important question concerns the purpose of alliances (from an alliance member perspective). Do they serve as an instrument for (counter-) balancing real or perceived threats and risks? Are they instruments for the management of relations between member states? Or are the ties that bind members of an alliance together based on the notion that the states in question belong to a community of a shared identity? The answer is that each of the competing perspectives sketched above captures important aspects of alliances, and it would be misleading if policymakers confined their thinking about the role of alliances to only one perspective. Heads of state and diplomats should be aware of the role that neorealists allocate to power, but also take into account the domestic and institutional aspects as well as the ideational foundations that scholars from the neoliberal institutionalist, liberal and constructivist camps assign to alliances. A syncretistic conception of alliances might result in a better understanding of the 'real-world developments' of alliances than the one resulting from a continuous battle for supremacy between various schools of thought.

Secondly, all three major schools of IR theory focus on the question of whether or not alliances ultimately wither away. As far as this issue is concerned, neorealism, neoliberal institutionalism and constructivism offer relatively static explanations.

What is lacking is a dynamic approach focusing not on the question of why NATO still exists, but on how NATO is developing. All three of the approaches outlined above shed some light on important issues, but none manages to explain comprehensively the developments and dynamics that have taken place, especially in NATO since 1990. The central hypothesis of a theory focusing on change in alliances is borrowed from neofunctionalist theory, according to which the form of an institution follows its function (Mitrany 1976). There is a direct relation between the external environment and the degree of institutionalization within an alliance. If substantial changes in the environment are taking place, a high degree of institutionalization within an institution may give rise to conflicts among its members (Simmel [1918] 1984: 38) if the commonly perceived threat has withered away. If member states of an alliance have an interest in keeping the alliance alive, institutional engineering is required to adapt the alliance to its new environment.

In this process of institutional re-adaptation, the internal security dilemma poses a major challenge to alliance members. At the theoretical level, there are two ways of attenuating this dilemma: either through a higher degree of institutionalization or through a weakening of institutional ties among member states. The first option, which entails the strengthening of commitments among alliance member states, can be successful where there is an increase in threat perception. If the new alliance environment is characterized by a commonly perceived threat, an integrative strategy (reinforcing institutional ties) might be an appropriate way to ensure that fears of entrapment or abandonment are assuaged.

The second strategy seems to be adequate if member states cooperate in an environment that is characterized by 'risk-diffusion' (Masala 2003: 13) and an interest on the part of member states in maintaining institutionalized cooperative relations. In such a situation, a lessening of institutional constraints might give member states a higher degree of freedom of action while at the same time minimizing any fears of abandonment or entrapment that might exist.

Such a flexible alliance (Masala 2003: 32–36) could – from a member-state perspective – constitute an appropriate response to the changed environment and thereby guarantee the continuation of institutionalized security cooperation in the form of alliances even in the future. This approach to studying changes in alliances has two distinct advantages:

Firstly, it borrows important insights from most of the theories dealing with alliances (or at least some important aspects of them) and tries to combine them into a line of inquiry that is not only relevant from a political-science point of view, but also from a political point of view.

Secondly, it leaves open the question of whether an alliance will survive or not. Both trajectories are possible, and the answer depends on real-world developments within alliances and among their members.

Notes

1 I would like to thank Myriam Dunn Cavelty and Victor Mauer for their comments on an earlier draft of this chapter.
2 Holsti et al. (1973: 166) distinguish between monolithic and pluralistic alliances.
3 For an overview, see Hellmann 2008.
4 On the distinction between internal and external balancing, see Waltz 1979: 116–28.
5 For an elaborate argument that NATO's continued existence after the end of the East-West conflict can be explained by institutional inertia, see McCalla 1996.
6 Wallander (2000: 731) distinguishes between general assets (e.g. transparency, procedures and interoperability) and specific assets (e.g. Article 5 of the North Atlantic Treaty).
7 See also Adler and Barnett 1998.

References

Adler, E. and Barnett, M. (eds) (1998) *Security Communities*, Cambridge: Cambridge University Press.
Barnett, M. (2002) 'Alliances, balances of threats, and neo-realism: The accidental coup', in Elman, C. and Vasquez, J. (eds), *Realism and the Balancing of Power: A New Debate?*, New York: St. Martin's Press, pp. 222–49.
Carlsnaes, W., Risse, T. and Simmons, B. (eds) (2002) *Handbook of International Relations*, London: Sage.
Deutsch, K.W., Burrell, S.A., Kann, R.A. and Lee, M. Jr. (1957) *Political Community and the North Atlantic Area: International Organization in the Light of Historical Experience*, Princeton: Princeton University Press.

Duffield, J. (2007) 'What are international institutions?', *International Studies Review* 9, 1: 1–22.

Freedman, L. (2004) *Deterrence*, Cambridge: Polity Press.

Gilpin, R.G. (1981) *War and Change in World Politics*, Cambridge: Cambridge University Press.

Gowa, J. (1999) *Ballots and Bullets: The Elusive Democratic Peace*, Princeton: Princeton University Press.

Grieco, J.M. (1990) *Cooperation among Nations: Europe America and Non-Tariff Barriers to Trade*, Ithaca, NY: Cornell University Press.

——(2002) 'Modern realist theory and the study of international politics in the 21st century', in Brecher, M. and Harvey, F.P. (eds) *Millennial Reflections on International Studies*, Ann Arbor: University of Michigan Press, pp. 65–78.

Haftendorn, H., Keohane, R.O. and Wallander, C.A. (eds) (1999) *Imperfect Unions: Security Institutions over Time and Space*, Oxford: Oxford University Press.

Hellmann, G. (2008) 'Inevitable decline versus predestined stability: Disciplinary explanations of the evolving transatlantic order', in Anderson, J.J., Ikenberry, G.J. and Risse, T. (eds) *The End of the West? Crisis and Change in the Atlantic Order*, Ithaca, NY: Cornell University Press, pp. 28–52.

Holsti, O.R., Hopmann, P.T. and Sullivan, J.D. (1973) *Unity and Disintegration in International Alliances*, New York: Wiley.

Jervis, R. (1976) *Perception and Misperception in International Politics*, Princeton: Princeton University Press.

Keohane, R.O. (1984) *After Hegemony*, Princeton: Princeton University Press.

Keohane, R.O. and Nye, J.S. (1993) 'Introduction: The end of the Cold War in Europe', in Keohane, R.O., Nye, J.S. and Hoffmann, S. (eds) *After the Cold War: International Institutions and State Strategies in Europe 1989–1991*, Cambridge, MA/London: Harvard University Press, pp. 1–19.

Kindleberger, C. (1986) *The World in Depression 1929–1938*, Berkeley: University of California Press.

Kuhn, T. (1962) *The Structure of Scientific Revolutions*, Chicago: University of Chicago Press.

Lai, B. and Reiter, D. (2000) 'Democracy, political similarity, and international alliances 1816–1992', *Journal of Conflict Resolution* 44, 2: 203–27.

Lakatos, I. and Musgrave, A. (1970) (eds) *Criticism and the Growth of Knowledge*, New York: Cambridge University Press.

Liska, G. (1962) *Nations in Alliance*, Baltimore: Johns Hopkins Press.

McCalla, R.B. (1996) 'NATO's persistence after the Cold War', *International Organization* 50, 3: 445–75.

Masala, C. (2003) *Den Blick nach Süden? Die NATO im Mittelmeerraum (1990–2003). Fallstudie zur Anpassung militärischer Allianzen an neue sicherheitspolitische Rahmenbedingungen*, Baden-Baden: Nomos.

——(2005) *Kenneth N. Waltz*, Baden-Baden: Nomos.

Mitrany, D. (1976) *The Functional Theory of Politics*, New York: St. Martin's Press.

Mearsheimer, J.J. (1990) 'Back to the Future: Instability in Europe After the Cold War', *International Security* 15, 4: 5–56.

Modelski, G. (1962) *A Theory of Foreign Policy*, New York: Praeger.

Moravcsik, A. (1998) *The Choice for Europe*, Ithaca, NY: Cornell University Press.

Morgenthau, H.J. (1948) *Politics among Nations*, New York: Knopf.

Müller, H. (2002) 'Security cooperation', in Carlsnaes, W., Risse, T. and Simmons, B. (eds) *Handbook of International Relations*, London: Sage, pp. 369–92.

Risse-Kappen, T. (1991) 'Public opinion, domestic structure, and foreign policy in liberal democracies', *World Politics* 43, 4: 479–512.

——(1996) 'Collective identity in a democratic community: The case of NATO', in: Katzenstein, P. (ed.) *The Culture of National Security: Norms and Identity in World Politics*, New York, Chichester: Columbia University Press, pp. 357–99.

Schimmelfennig, F. (1999) 'NATO's enlargement: A constructivist explanation', *Security Studies* 8, 2–3: 198–234.

Schweller, R.L. (1994) 'Bandwagoning for profit: Bringing the revisionist state back in', *International Security* 19, 1: 72–107.

Simmel, G. [1918] (1984) *Der Konflikt der modernen Kultur*, Berlin: Wagenbach.

Singer, K. (1949) *The Idea of Conflict*, Melbourne: Melbourne University Press.

Snyder, G.H. (1997) *Alliance Politics*, Ithaca, NY: Cornell University Press.

Stein, A.A. (1990) *Why Nations Cooperate? Circumstance and Choice in International Relations*, Ithaca, NY: Cornell University Press.

Triepel, H. (1938) *Die Hegemonie. Ein Buch von führenden Staaten*, Stuttgart: Kohlhammer.

Wallander, C.A. (2000) 'Institutional assets and adaptability: NATO after the Cold War', *International Organization* 54, 4: 705–36.

Wallander, C.A. and Keohane, R.O. (1999) 'Risk, threat, and security institutions', in: Wallander, C.A., Haftendorn, H. and Keohane, R.O. (eds) *Imperfect Unions: Security Institutions over Time and Space*, Oxford: Oxford University Press, pp. 21–47.

Wallander, C.A., Haftendorn, H. and Keohane, R.O. (eds) (1999) *Imperfect Unions: Security Institutions over Time and Space*, Oxford: Oxford University Press.

Walt, S. (1987) *The Origins of Alliances*, Ithaca, NY: Cornell University Press.

——(1997) 'Why alliances endure or collapse', *Survival* 39, 1: 156–79.

Waltz, K.N. (1979) *Theory of International Politics*, Reading: Addison-Wesley.

——(1990) 'Realist thought and neorealist theory', *Journal of International Affairs* 44, 1: 21–37.

——(2000) 'Structural realism after the Cold War', *International Security* 25, 1: 5–41.

Weber, M. (1997) *Gesammelte Aufsätze zur Wissenschaftslehre*, Tübingen: Mohr.

Wendt, A. (1999) *Social Theory of International Politics*, Cambridge: Cambridge University Press.

Zartman, I.W. (1985) *Ripe for Resolution*, New York: Oxford Univ. Press.

Zongyou, W. (2006) 'In the shadow of hegemony: Strategic choices', *Chinese Journal of International Politics* 1, 2: 195–229.

36

Deterrence

Richard Ned Lebow

Threat-based strategies have always been central to International Relations. Deterrence and compellence represent efforts to conceptualize these strategies to make them more understandable in theory and more effective in practice. These efforts, which have been underway since the end of the Second World War, remain highly controversial. There is no consensus among scholars or policymakers about the efficacy of these strategies or the conditions in which they are most appropriate.

Deterrence is both a theory in International Relations and a strategy of conflict management. It can be defined as an attempt to influence other actors' assessment of their interests. It seeks to prevent an undesired behaviour by convincing the party who may be contemplating such an action that its cost will exceed any possible gain (Lebow 1981: 83). Deterrence presupposes that decisions are made in response to some kind of rational cost-benefit calculus, that this calculus can be successfully manipulated from the outside, and that the best way to do so is to increase the cost side of the ledger. Compellence, a sister strategy, uses the same tactics to attempt to convince another party to carry out some action it otherwise would not. Although they have not always been called 'deterrence', threat-based strategies that attempt to manipulate the cost-calculus of other actors have long been practised: there is ample evidence of their use by all the ancient empires.

The advent of nuclear weapons made it imperative for policymakers to find ways of preventing catastrophically destructive wars while exploiting any strategic nuclear advantage for political gain. This chapter describes early theoretical approaches to deterrence, their application in practice and the subsequent critique of them. Drawing on works that made use of Soviet, US, Chinese and Israeli archives, and interviews with officials from these countries and Egypt, the following discussion provides an overall assessment of the consequences of deterrence during the Cold War. The chapter concludes with a brief discussion of post-Cold War deterrence and promising areas for research.

The golden age of deterrence theory

In analytical terms, theories of deterrence must be distinguished from the strategy of deterrence. The former address the logical postulates of deterrence and the political and psychological assumptions on which they are based, the latter the application of the theory in practice. The theory of deterrence developed as an intended guide for the strategy of deterrence.

Scholars and policymakers became interested in deterrence following the development of the atom bomb. The first wave of theorists wrote from the late 1940s through the mid-1960s. Early publications on the subject (Brodie 1947) recognize that a war between states armed with atomic weapons could be so destructive as to negate Carl von Clausewitz's (1976: 75–89) classic description of war as a continuation of politics by other means. In 1949, the problem of deterrence gained a new urgency as the Cold War was well underway and the Soviet Union, in defiance of all US expectations, detonated its first nuclear device in October of that year. In the 1950s, often referred to as the Golden Age of deterrence, Bernard William Kaufmann (1954), Henry Kissinger (1957) and Bernard Brodie (1959), among others, developed a general approach to nuclear deterrence that stressed the necessity but difficulty of imparting credibility to threats likely to constitute national suicide. The 1960s witnessed an impressive theoretical treatment by Thomas Schelling (1966) that analysed deterrence in terms of bargaining theory, drawn from microeconomics, and elaborated a set of bargaining tactics based on tacit signals.

The early literature (Kaufmann 1954; Brodie 1959; Schelling 1966) began with the assumption of fully rational actors and was largely deductive in nature. It stressed the importance of defining commitments, communicating them to adversaries, developing the capability to defend them and imparting credibility to these commitments. It explored various tactics that leaders could exploit towards this end, concentrating on the problem of credibility. This was recognized as the core problem when deterrence was practised against another nuclear adversary – and the implementation of the threats in question could entail national suicide (Jervis 1979). Thomas Schelling (1966) went so far as to suggest that it was rational for a leader to develop a reputation for being irrational so his threats might be believed. Richard Nixon indicates that he took this advice to heart in his dealings with both the Soviet Union and North Vietnam (Kimball 1998: 76–86).

All of the so-called Golden Age literature focuses almost entirely on the tactics of deterrence, as do Kaufmann and Brodie, or, like Kissinger, on the force structures most likely to make deterrence credible. Thomas Schelling fits in the former category, but unlike other students of deterrence in the 1950s and 1960s, he attempts to situate his understanding of tactics in a broader theory of bargaining that draws on economics and psychology. His *Strategy of Deterrence* (1960) and *Arms and Influence* (1966) are the only works on deterrence from this era that are widely cited and continue to be read.

As a practising economist, Schelling might have been expected to privilege material capabilities in his analysis. In *Arms and Influence*, he makes a ritual genuflection in this direction on the opening page when he observes that with enough military force, a country may not need to bargain. His narrative soon makes clear that military capability is decisive in only the most asymmetrical relationships, and even then only when the more powerful party has little or nothing to lose from the failure to reach an accommodation. When the power balance is not so lopsided, or when both sides would lose from non-settlement, it is necessary to bargain. Bargaining outcomes do not necessarily reflect a balance of interests or military capabilities. Three other influences are important.

The first is *context*, which for Schelling consists of the stakes, the range of possible outcomes, the salience of those outcomes and the ability of bargainers to commit to those outcomes. In straightforward commercial bargaining, contextual considerations may not play a decisive role. In bargaining about price, there will be a range of intervals between the opening bids of buyer and seller. If there is no established market price for the commodity, no particular outcome will have special salience. Either side can try to gain an advantage by committing itself to its preferred outcomes. Strategic bargaining between states is frequently characterized by sharp discontinuities in context. There may be a small number of possible outcomes, and the canons of international practice, recognized boundaries, prominent terrain features or the simplicity of all-or-nothing distinctions can make one solution more salient than others. Salient solutions are easier to communicate and commit to, especially when the bargaining is tacit (Schelling 1966: 6–16).

The second consideration is *skill*. Threats to use force lack credibility if they are costly to carry out. To circumvent this difficulty, clever leaders can feign madness, develop a reputation for heartlessness or put themselves into a position from which they cannot retreat. Other tactics can be used to discredit adversarial commitments or minimize the cost of backing away from one's own (Schelling 1960).

The third, and arguably most important, determinant of outcome is *willingness to suffer*. Paraphrasing Carl von Clausewitz, Schelling describes war as a contest of wills. Until the mid-twentieth century, force was used to bend or break an adversary's will by defeating his army and holding his population and territory hostage. Air power and nuclear weapons revolutionized warfare by allowing states to treat one another's territory, economic resources and population as hostages from the outset of any dispute. War is no longer a contest of strength, but a contest of nerve and risk-taking, of pain and endurance. For the purposes of bargaining, the ability to absorb pain counts just as much as the capability to inflict it (von Clausewitz 1976: Book 6, ch. 26).

Schelling does not say so, but it follows from his formulation that the capacity to absorb suffering varies just as much as the capacity to deliver it. Clausewitz recognized this variation. Increases in both capabilities, he argued, made possible the nation in arms and the revolutionary character of the Napoleonic Wars (von Clausewitz 1976: 585–94). By convincing peoples that they had a stake in the outcome of the wars, first the French and then their adversaries were able to field large armies, extract the resources necessary to arm and maintain them, and elicit the extraordinary level of personal sacrifice necessary to sustain the struggle.

The Clausewitz–Schelling emphasis on pain has wider implications for bargaining. The ability to suffer physical, economic, moral or any other loss is an important source of bargaining power and can sometimes negate an adversary's power to punish. Realist approaches to bargaining tend to neglect this dimension of power and focus instead on the power to hurt and how it can be transformed into credible threats. Schelling also ignores the pain absorption side of the power–pain equation when analysing compellence in Vietnam, an oversight that led to his misplaced optimism that Hanoi could be coerced into doing what Washington wanted. The power to punish derives only in part from material capabilities. Leaders must also have the will and freedom to use their power. Schelling observes that Genghis Khan was effective because he was not inhibited by the usual mercies. Modern civilization has generated expectations and norms that severely constrain the power to punish. The US bombing campaign in Vietnam, in many people's judgement the very antithesis of civilized behaviour, paradoxically demonstrates this truth.

Deterrence strategy

Deterrence played a central role in the US strategy in Indochina during the Johnson and Nixon administrations. Deployment of forces, the character of the engagements they sought and the level and choice of targets for bombing were never intended to defeat the National Liberation Front of South Vietnam (Viet Cong) or North Vietnam, but to compel them to end the war and accept the independence of South Vietnam. The Indochina intervention ended in disaster and helped to spawn a series of critiques of the theory and strategy of deterrence in the 1970s.

As mentioned, Vietnam paradoxically demonstrates the truth that modern civilization has generated expectations and norms that severely constrain the power to punish. The air and ground war aroused enormous opposition at home, in large part because of its barbarity, and public opinion ultimately compelled a halt to the bombing and withdrawal of US forces from Indochina. The bombing exceeded the Second World War in total tonnage, but was also more restricted. The US refrained from indiscriminate bombing of civilians and made no effort to destroy North Vietnam's elaborate system of dikes. The use of nuclear weapons was not even considered. Restraint was a response to ethical and domestic political imperatives. Similar constraints limited US firepower in Iraq in the Gulf War of 1990–91, and enabled the Republican Guard and Saddam Hussein to escape destruction.

The ability to absorb punishment derives even less from material capabilities, and may even be inversely related to them. One of the reasons why Vietnam was less vulnerable to bombing than Schelling and Pentagon planners supposed was its underdeveloped economy. There were fewer high-value targets to destroy or hold hostage. With fewer factories, highways and railroads, the economy was more difficult to disrupt, and the population was less dependent on existing distribution networks for its sustenance and material support. According to North Vietnamese strategic analyst Colonel Quach Hai Luong: 'The more you bombed, the more the people wanted to fight you' (McNamara et al. 1999: 194). Department of Defense studies confirm that bombing 'strengthened, rather than weakened, the will of the Hanoi government and its people' (McNamara et al. 1999: 191, 341f.). It is apparent in retrospect that the gap between the protagonists in material and military capabilities counted for less than their differential ability to absorb punishment. The US won every battle, but lost the war because its citizens would not pay the moral, economic and human cost of victory. Washington withdrew from Indochina after losing 58,000 American lives, a fraction of Viet Cong and North Vietnamese deaths even at conservative estimates. As Clausewitz understood, political and moral cohesion based on common interests is more important than material capabilities.

A comparison between South and North Vietnam is even more revealing. The Army of the Republic of South Vietnam (ARVN) was larger and better equipped and trained than the Viet Cong or the North Vietnamese, and had all the advantages of US air power, communications and logistics. The Republic of South Vietnam crumbled because its forces had no stomach for a fight. The Viet Cong and North Vietnamese sustained horrendous losses whenever they came up against superior US firepower, but maintained their morale and cohesion throughout the long conflict. Unlike ARVN officers and recruits, who regularly melted away under fire, more Viet Cong and North Vietnamese internalized their cause and gave their lives for it. At the most fundamental level, the Communist victory demonstrated the power of ideas and commitment.

Critiques

From the beginning, deterrence theory and strategy has spawned critiques. The most interesting are those that evaluate deterrence strategy in the light of empirical evidence from historical cases. The work of Milburn (1959), George and Smoke (1974), Lebow (1981) and Jervis et al. (1984) is representative. George and Smoke recognized that challenges short of full-scale attacks – what they called 'probes' – were difficult to deter and might be instituted by adversaries to test a state's resolve. They and Milburn attempted to put deterrence into a broader context and argued that it might be made a more efficacious strategy if threats of punishment were accompanied by promises of rewards for acceptable behaviour.

An important distinction must further be made between general and immediate deterrence (Morgan 1983). *General deterrence* is based on the existing power relationship and attempts to prevent an adversary from seriously considering any kind of military challenge because of its expected adverse consequences. *Immediate deterrence* is specific; it attempts to forestall an anticipated challenge to a well-defined and publicized commitment. Immediate deterrence is practised when general deterrence is thought to be failing. It is almost impossible to know when general deterrence succeeds because non-action by a target state can be the result of many reasons, including any lack of intention to use force. Because cases of the success or failure of immediate deterrence are somewhat easier to identify, most research has sought to explain their outcomes. Analyses of immediate deterrence that ignore its relationship to general deterrence offer a biased assessment of its success rate and an incomplete picture of the conditions and processes that account for its outcome.

For many years, however, empirical research on deterrence, whether qualitative or quantitative, drew primarily on cases of immediate, conventional deterrence. Empirical studies of immediate deterrence are surrounded by considerable controversy in the absence of compelling evidence about the intentions and calculations of the leaders of target states (Huth and Russett 1984, 1988; Lebow and Stein 1990). Beginning in the late 1980s, evidence on Soviet and Chinese foreign policy began to become available, and it became possible for the first time to reconstruct critical Soviet–US and Sino–US deterrence encounters and to make some observations about the role of general deterrence in these relationships. It transpired that there had been striking differences among leaders on opposing sides about who was practising deterrence and who was deterred. In many so-called deterrence encounters (Garthoff 1989; Lebow and Stein 1990), both sides considered themselves the deterrer. This is often due to different interpretations of the status quo. In the Cuban missile crisis (Lebow and Stein 1994), Khrushchev understood the secret Soviet missile deployment in Cuba to be part and parcel of his attempt to deter a US invasion of Cuba. Kennedy and his advisors interpreted the deployment as a radical and underhanded effort to upset the strategic status quo.

Immediate deterrence

From cases such as these, Janice Gross Stein and Richard Ned Lebow (Lebow 1981; Jervis et al. 1984; Lebow and Stein 1987) developed an extensive critique of immediate deterrence with three interlocking components: political, psychological and operational. The political component concerns the motivation behind foreign policy challenges. Deterrence is unabashedly a theory of 'opportunity'. Adversaries are assumed to seek

397

opportunities to make gains and pounce when they find them. Case studies of historical conflicts point to an alternative explanation for challenges, including resorts to force, which Lebow and Stein term a theory of 'need'. Strategic vulnerabilities and domestic political needs can push leaders into acting aggressively. Khrushchev's Cuban missile deployment, to cite one instance, was motivated by his perceived need to protect Cuba and offset US strategic superiority, and his anger at Kennedy for deploying missiles in Turkey – making him look weak in the eyes of hardliners (Lebow and Stein 1994: 19–66). When leaders become desperate, they may resort to force even when the military balance is unfavourable and there are no grounds for doubting adversarial resolve. Deterrence may be an inappropriate and provocative strategy in these circumstances.

The psychological component is also related to the motivation behind deterrence challenges. To the extent that policymakers believe in the necessity of challenging the commitments of their adversaries, they become predisposed to see their objectives as attainable. When this happens, motivated bias can be pronounced and take the form of distorted threat assessments and insensitivity to warnings that the policies to which our leaders are committed are likely to end in disaster. Policymakers can convince themselves, despite evidence to the contrary, that they can challenge an important adversarial commitment without provoking war. Because they know the extent to which they are powerless to back down, they expect their adversaries to accommodate them by doing so. To continue with our Cuban missile crisis example, Khrushchev brushed aside the advice of top political and diplomatic advisors who warned him that the missiles would be discovered before they were operational and would provoke a serious crisis with the US. He sought refuge instead in promises of marginal military officials with little knowledge of Cuba or US intelligence capabilities (Lebow and Stein 1994: 67–93).

The practical component highlights the distorting effects of cognitive biases and heuristics, political and cultural barriers to empathy, and the differing cognitive contexts that the deterrer and would-be challengers are apt to use to frame and interpret signals. Problems of this kind are not unique to deterrence; they are embedded in the very structure of International Relations. They nevertheless constitute particularly severe impediments to deterrence because of a deterrer's need to understand the world as it appears to the leaders of a would-be challenger in order to manipulate effectively its cost-benefit calculus. Failure to do this in the desired direction can make the proscribed behaviour more attractive to a challenger. In the case of Cuba, Kennedy's deployment of Jupiter missiles in Turkey and his warnings that under some circumstances the US would not hesitate to strike first, given its strategic nuclear advantage, were intended to moderate Khrushchev, but instead they convinced him of the even greater costs to the Soviet Union of remaining passive in the face of these US threats. Kennedy, in turn, had made these threats because of Khrushchev's browbeating of him at the Vienna summit and threats to the Western position in Berlin (Lebow and Stein 1994: 19–50). The missile crisis was, in effect, the product of a series of escalating threats and actions by both sides, each attempting unsuccessfully to deter the other.

General nuclear deterrence

Research on the Cuban missile crisis, the Soviet–US crisis arising out of the 1973 Middle East War, and the two Taiwan Straits crises of 1954 and 1958 tend to confirm the findings of critics of conventional deterrence. So does research on general nuclear deterrence. Based on the study of Soviet–US relations in the Khrushchev and Brezhnev eras, Lebow and Stein offer the following conclusions about the role of general nuclear deterrence:

1   leaders who try to exploit real or imagined nuclear advantages for political gain are not likely to succeed;
2   credible nuclear threats are very difficult to make;
3   nuclear threats are fraught with risk;
4   strategic build-ups are more likely to provoke than to restrain adversaries because of their impact on the domestic balance of political power in the target state;
5   nuclear deterrence is robust when leaders on both sides fear war and are aware of each other's fears.

We must distinguish between the reality and the strategy of nuclear deterrence. The former, at least in the case of the Cold War, led to self-deterrence, as leaders on both sides were horrified by the prospects of a nuclear conflict. Not knowing of each other's fears, or refusing to acknowledge them, both superpowers practised the strategy of deterrence with a vengeance. This entailed arms build-ups, forward deployments and threatening rhetoric, often in combination. Practised this way, the strategy of deterrence was responsible for the series of crises that escalated to the Cuban missile crisis, where both sides stepped down from the brink and sought to reassure their adversary (Lebow and Stein 1994: 348–68).

Zhang (1992), Hopf (1994) and Lebow and Stein (1994) further find that deterrers do worry about their reputations and the credibility of commitments, but that the targets of deterrence rarely question their adversary's resolve. For this reason, efforts to communicate resolve were often perceived as gratuitously aggressive behaviour and sometimes provoked the kind of challenges they were designed to prevent. In doing so, the strategy of deterrence helped to provoke the Cuban missile and Taiwan Straits crises and to prolong the Soviet–US and Sino–US conflicts.

End of the Cold War

The end of the Cold War, accompanied by the opening of the archives of the participants, brought another wave of reassessment. No consensus has emerged, but the issues have been clarified and enriched by much new evidence. The debate about deterrence has also extended beyond conflict management to conflict resolution. Supporters of former US president Ronald Reagan, and conservatives more generally, credit Reagan's arms build-up and the Strategic Defense Initiative (Star Wars) with ending the Cold War. They are alleged to have brought the Soviet Union to its senses and provided strong incentives for it to seek an accommodation with the US (Matlock 1995). According to this thinking, Gorbachev and his advisors became convinced that they could not compete with the US and ought to negotiate the best deal they could before Soviet power declined even further (Davis and Wohlforth 2004). Western liberals, former Soviet policymakers and many scholars attribute the end of the Cold War to 'New Thinking' and the political transformation it brought about within the Soviet leadership. Gorbachev, they contend, considered the Cold War dangerous and a waste of resources and sought to end it to bring the Soviet back into Europe, facilitate political reform at home and free resources for domestic development (Brown 1996; English 2000; Levesque 1997; Herrmann 2004).

These contending interpretations base their respective arguments on very different kinds of arguments. Those who credit Reagan's arms build-up with ending the Cold War build their case entirely on inference. The arms build-up is supposed to have signalled resolve to Moscow and convinced rational Soviet leaders to make the concessions necessary to end the Cold War. No evidence is offered to indicate that Gorbachev and his advisors were influenced by this logic. Those who attribute Gorbachev's eagerness to end the Cold War and to make some important one-sided concessions toward that end, offer considerable evidence in support of their contentions based on records of discussions among Soviet leaders, including notes of Politburo meetings; interviews with Gorbachev and his principal advisors from 1986–92; and interviews with former Eastern European officials reporting their discussions with the Soviet leadership. In any court, evidence trumps inference, so for the moment at least, the liberal claims that changing ideas were the catalyst for the Cold War's end is more credible than the conservative assertion that it was a growing differential in power between the superpowers.

Contemporary deterrence strategy

The contemporary debate is far more international than it was during the Cold War, in part because there are more nuclear powers. Studies of deterrence by Indian, Pakistani and Chinese scholars and military think tanks have supplemented those of the US, the UK and Israel.

The big question for scholars may not be whether deterrence helped to prevent World War III, but why and how leaders and lesser officials in both superpowers and so many scholars convinced themselves that it was necessary to the point that, until the advent of Gorbachev, they repeatedly confirmed this belief tautologically. Such behaviour has not stopped with the end of the Cold War. Reputable scholars routinely claim that nuclear weapons have kept the peace between India and China, and that the US invasion of Iraq brought about an about-face in Libyan foreign policy. With the possible exceptions of Israel and conservative British defence analysts, the US appears to stand alone in the faith it places in deterrence and the credit it gives it for preventing war. What theorists say about deterrence may tell us more about their ideological assumptions and their country's strategic culture than it does about the nature and efficacy of threat-based strategies.

During the Cold War, the theory and practice of deterrence and compellence focused on making credible threats on the assumption that they were necessary to moderate adversaries. Self-deterrence – the unwillingness of actors to assume the risks and costs of using force independently of efforts by others to deter them – received little attention or credence. One of the more interesting characteristics of post-Cold War deterrence and compellence is the extent to which self-deterrence has become a major phenomenon for the US and European powers. In Somalia, the US withdrew its forces after losing 18 US Army Rangers. In Rwanda, genocidal Hutus deterred Western intervention by killing ten Belgian soldiers. In Bosnia, compellence clearly failed against Milošević, who continued his policy of ethnic cleansing of Albanians in Bosnia despite Western threats. Pushed by Western public opinion, NATO finally screwed up its courage to intervene, but then failed to go after known war criminals because of the vulnerability of its lightly armed forces, whose primary mission was the distribution of aid (Freedman 2004: 124f.). There is an important lesson here, and one that has been consistently ignored by theorists of threat-based strategies. As in the Indochina War, it has to do with the ability to inflict pain versus the willingness to suffer it. As we observed, Schelling and US policymakers ignored the latter in Indochina, concentrating only on how much damage they could inflict on North Vietnam and the Viet Cong. The US lost the war because its Vietnamese opponents were willing to accept far more suffering than the American people were. This phenomenon is equally pronounced today. Self-deterrence, in effect, prevented intervention in Rwanda and stalled it for a long time in the former Yugoslavia. It did not have this effect in Afghanistan and Iraq, where the Bush administration grossly underestimated its costs and duration.

In the West, the focus of deterrence has turned away from restraining large state actors with nuclear weapons to smaller, so-called 'rogue' states thought to be trying to acquire such weapons. Since 11 September 2001, there has also been a debate about the applicability of deterrence to the problem of terrorism. Libya, North Korea and Iran have been the major targets of US pressure because of their support of terrorism and pursuit or funding of nuclear weapons programmes. Libya radically altered its foreign policy, and supporters of compellence assert that US pressure and an unsuccessful attempt to take out the country's leader in an air attack were responsible. If true, a failed assassination attempt does not qualify as compellence, which aims to use the threat of force to achieve political ends. If force is used, compellence has failed, even if it succeeds in its goals. Libya's leader, Colonel Muammar Ghaddafi, is by all accounts an enigmatic figure whose authoritarian rule has provided little information on which to base serious analyses of his policies. Until such information becomes available, all one can do is speculate about Ghaddafi's motive for his about-face, or indeed about most of his major policy initiatives.

North Korea resembles Libya in this respect. Its father and son leaders have run what is arguably the most reclusive regime in the world. Foreign experts are exasperated by the lack of information available to them and freely admit that their analyses entail considerable amounts of pure speculation (Harrison 2002). North Korea has been the target of US compellent threats and rhetoric and also of reassurance. At the time of writing, North Korea has agreed to dismantle a principal nuclear facility and to provide documents to the West about its nuclear programme in return for security guarantees and economic aid (Arms Control Association 2008). Once again, experts debate the extent to which the carrot or the stick, respectively, was primarily responsible for this result and whether the result is meaningful (Ihlwan 2008). Iran is a different case, as it is a more open society with many democratic features. Like North Korea, it appears to have an active nuclear programme, and one that the US has sought to deter through compellent threats, sanctions and its invasion of Iraq. The latter, among other goals, was expected to make Iran more compliant to US demands, but appears to have made it more truculent. Once again, proponents of carrots and sticks draw different conclusions (Shaw 2008).

Conclusion and promising areas of research

Two concluding observations are in order. The first grows out of the record of deterrence and compellence during the Cold War and its aftermath. These conflicts suggest that the political and psychological dynamics governing cost estimates and the relative willingness to bear the costs of military action remain the critical consideration for leaders contemplating the use of threat-based strategies and their probability of success or failure. Much important research can be done in this connection, especially in conflicts that pit highly developed industrial powers, with a low tolerance for loss of life, against weaker, less developed, more traditional countries where honour remains important and death in combat or by suicide missions is more acceptable.

The second concerns the general efficacy of deterrence as a strategy. Its many drawbacks do not mean that it should be discarded. Rather, scholars and statesmen must recognize the limits and inherent unpredictability of deterrence and make greater use of other strategies of conflict prevention and management.

There are many important theory and policy questions that need careful empirical research. Foremost among these is the role of nuclear weapons in conflict management. The contrasting views about the role nuclear weapons played in the resolution of the Cold War have been noted. Are these lessons transferable to other cases? Do other cases help us reflect back on the Cold War and discriminate more effectively among its competing sets of lessons? What about the lessons drawn by policymakers in other nuclear powers (i.e. France, China, Israel, India and Pakistan) about nuclear weapons and the Cold War, and nuclear weapons and the conflict in which they are involved? How similar and different is such 'learning', and on what grounds have these lessons been formed? Finally, there is the question of proliferation. Why do nations begin, halt or see through to completion their weapons development programmes? Under which conditions might those who have weapons use them? On proliferation, unlike some of the other questions, there has already been some impressive research (Solingen 2007; Hymans 2006).

References

Achen, C.H. and Snidal, D. (1989) 'Rational deterrence theory and comparative case studies', *World Politics* 41, 2: 143–69.

Arms Control Association (2008) 'The U.S.–North Korean agreed framework at a glance', Washington, DC: Arms Control Association. Available online at: www.armscontrol.org/factsheets/agreedframework.asp (accessed 10 February 2009).

Brodie, B. (1947) 'The absolute weapon: Atomic power and world order', *Bulletin of the Atomic Scientists* 46, 3: 150–55.

——(1959) 'The anatomy of deterrence', *World Politics* 11, 2: 173–92.

Brown, A. (1996) *The Gorbachev Factor*, Oxford: Oxford University Press.

Chang, G.H. (1990) *Friends and Enemies: The United States, China, and the Soviet Union, 1948–1972*, Stanford: Stanford University Press.

von Clausewitz, C. (1976) *On War*, trans Howard, M. and Paret P., Princeton: Princeton University Press.

Davis, J.W. and Wohlforth, W.C. (2004) 'German unification', in Herrmann, R.K. and Lebow, R.N. (eds) *Ending the Cold War*, New York: Palgrave-Macmillan, pp. 131–57.

English, R.D. (2000) *Russia and the Idea of the West: Gorbachev, Intellectuals and the End of the Cold War*, New York: Columbia University Press.

Freedman, L. (2004) *Deterrence*, Cambridge, MA: Polity Press.

Garthoff, R. (1989) *Reflections on the Cuban Missile Crisis*, revised edn, Washington, DC: Brookings Institution.

George, A.L. and Smoke, R. (1974) *Deterrence in American Foreign Policy: Theory and Practice*, New York: Columbia University Press.

——(1989) 'Deterrence and foreign policy', *World Politics* 41, 2: 170–82.

Harrison, S. (2002) *Korean Endgame: A Strategy for Unification and U.S. Disengagement*, Princeton: Princeton University Press.

Herrmann, R.K. (2004) 'Learning from the end of the Cold War', in Herrmann, R.K. and Lebow, R. N. (eds) *Ending the Cold War*, New York: Palgrave-Macmillan, pp. 219–38.

Hopf, T. (1994) *Peripheral Visions: Deterrence Theory and American Foreign Policy in the Third World, 1965–1999*, Ann Arbor: University of Michigan Press.

Huth, P and Russett, B. (1984) 'What makes deterrence work? Cases from 1900 to 1980', *World Politics* 36, 4: 496–526.

——(1988) 'Deterrence failure and crisis escalation', *International Studies Quarterly* 32, 1: 29–46.

Hymans, J.E. (2006) *The Psychology of Nuclear Proliferation: Identity, Emotions, and Foreign Policy*, Cambridge: Cambridge University Press.

Ihlwan, M. (2008) 'U.S.–North Korea nuclear deal: Who wins?' *Business Week*, 30 June. Available online at: www.businessweek.com/globalbiz/content/jun2008/gb20080630_879728.htm?chan=top+news_top+news+index_global+business (accessed 10 February 2009).

Jervis, R. (1979) 'Deterrence theory revisited', *World Politics* 31, 2: 289–324.

——(1989) 'Rational deterrence theory: Theory and evidence', *World Politics* 41, 2: 183–207.

Jervis, R., Lebow, R.N. and Stein, J.G. (1984) *Psychology and Deterrence*, Baltimore: Johns Hopkins University Press.

Kaufmann, W.W. (1954) *The Requirements of Deterrence*, Princeton: Princeton Center of International Studies.

Kimball, J. (1998) *Nixon's Vietnam War*, Kansas: University Press of Kansas.

Kissinger, H. (1957) *Nuclear Weapons and Foreign Policy*, New York: Harper Bros.

Lebow, R.N. (1981) *Between Peace and War: The Nature of International Crisis*, Baltimore: Johns Hopkins University Press.

Lebow, R.N. and Stein, J.G. (1987) 'Beyond deterrence', *Journal of Social Issues* 43, 4: 5–71.

——(1989) 'Rational deterrence theory: I think, therefore I deter', *World Politics* 41, 2: 208–24.

——(1990) 'Deterrence: The elusive dependent variable', *World Politics* 42, 3: 336–69.

——(1994) *We All Lost the Cold War*, Princeton: Princeton University Press.

Levesque, J. (1997) *The Enigma of 1989: The USSR and the Liberation of Eastern Europe*, Berkeley: University of California Press.

McNamara, R.S., Blight, J.G. and Brigham, R.K. (1999) *Argument Without End: In Search of Answers to the Vietnam Tragedy*, New York: Public Affairs.

Matlock, J. (1995) *Autopsy on an Empire: The American Ambassador's Account of the Collapse of the Soviet Union*, New York: Random House.

Milburn, T.W. (1959) 'What constitutes effective deterrence?', *Journal of Conflict Resolution* 3, 2: 138–45.

Morgan, P.M. (1983) *Deterrence: A Conceptual Analysis*, revised edn, Beverly Hills: Sage Library of Social Science.

Schelling, T. (1960) *The Strategy of Conflict*, Cambridge, MA: Harvard University Press.

——(1966) *Arms and Influence*, New Haven: Yale University Press.

Shaw, A. (2008) 'Nuclear Weapons', *Global Issues website*. Available online at: www.globalissues.org/issue/67/nuclear-weapons (accessed 10 February 2009).

Solingen, E. (2007) *Nuclear Logics: Contrasting Paths in East Asia and the Middle East*, Cambridge: Cambridge University Press.

Zhang, S. H. (1992) *Deterrence and Strategic Culture: Chinese-American Confrontations, 1949–1958*, Ithaca, NY: Cornell University Press.

37

Coercive diplomacy

Scope and limits, theory and policy

Bruce W. Jentleson[1]

The relationship between force and diplomacy is among the most difficult questions in international security, both as a field of study and in policy. Are they distinct choices – pursue diplomacy or use force? Or, at least in some instances, is it a matter of striking a balance between them? Coercive diplomacy, as reflected in the very terminology, manifests the latter approach. Scholars who study it as well as policymakers who practise it seek to determine how best to strike the balance between coercion, including the threat or use of limited military force, and diplomacy. The objective is to understand the scope and the limits of its utility at both the theoretical and the policy level.

This chapter starts with a core definition of coercive diplomacy, drawing especially on the work of Alexander George as well as others. Distinctions between coercive diplomacy and other force–diplomacy concepts and strategies are then drawn; major theories are reviewed that explain its success and failure, including pertinent case data and other empirical information; and the implications for policy and further research are considered.

Defining coercive diplomacy

In his classical definition, Alexander George (1971) defines coercive diplomacy as a strategy geared towards pressuring an opponent to change policy that emphasizes diplomacy, but also entails the threat and/or limited use of military force or other forms of coercion (e.g. economic sanctions). The three key elements in the core definition of coercive diplomacy are: limited objectives, coercive but limited means and the possible use of carrots along with sticks. These elements are derived from the coercive diplomacy literature, which – while being marked by some conceptual and methodological disputes and permutations – has been developed to an unusual degree in the spirit of refinement and cumulation, rather than refutation and nullification.

Limited objectives

Coercive diplomacy is a strategy for policy change, not conquest. George originally set the parameters at defensive rather than offensive objectives, or preventing gains by the target as distinct from making gains of one's own. This included a 'Type A' coercive diplomacy, to force an opponent 'to stop short of the goal'; and 'Type B', to get an opponent 'to undo the action' (George 1971; George and Simons 1994: 7–11; Art and Cronin 2003: 389f., 394f.). This was expanded in the second edition of *Limits of Coercive Diplomacy* to include a 'Type C' of 'cessation of the opponent's hostile behaviour through a demand for change in the composition of the adversary's government or in the nature of the regime' (George and Simons 1994).[2] While Type C coercive diplomacy still involves pressure rather than direct intervention for regime change, George acknowledged that this type of objective 'stretches coercive diplomacy to its outer limits' in terms of being a defensive objective (George and Simons 1994: 8f.). Art and Cronin push further, arguing that even in some type A and B cases, what is defensive

> is in the eyes of the beholder. The coercer views its attempt to change the target's behavior as defensive because it wants to stop the target's objectionable behavior. The target, however, does not view its behavior as objectionable because it is trying to alter a situation that it considers unjust or unacceptable; consequently, from its standpoint the actions it is taking are also defensive.
>
> (Art and Cronin 2003: 19)

Art and Cronin thus drop this internal differentiation, but keep the parameter that the objectives must still be limited in scope. Other authors argue similarly.

Coercive but limited means

Again going back to George, coercive diplomacy is 'forceful persuasion'. It is coercive, not just the diplomacy of demarches, but as part of a strategy that 'seeks to *persuade* an opponent … rather than bludgeon him into stopping' (George and Simons 1994: 10). It seeks to influence, but not deny choice to the target. The main original distinction was from 'compellence' as developed by Thomas Schelling (1960), based on a view of the latter as exclusive or heavy reliance on coercive threats to influence an adversary (George 1991: 5).[3] The importance of this distinction arose in part from the Cold War context, where escalation of lower-level conflicts to the nuclear level was an overarching concern. On the one hand, with the transition to the post-Cold War era, there is less concern about escalation. On the other hand, it remains important to distinguish the limited nature of coercive diplomacy from 'full-scale compellence … the use of whatever amount of force it takes to get the adversary to change its behavior' (Art and Cronin 2003: 9).

Sticks and carrots

The constant across all major coercive diplomacy studies is that albeit within this limited force parameter, cases must include the threat or use of force as a defining element. This criterion has two variations. One is the degree of emphasis on other coercive measures such as economic sanctions. Many coercive diplomacy cases, though, involve both types of coercive instruments. However, if a case involves sanctions, but not the threat or use of military force, it does not qualify as a case of coercive diplomacy. The other variation is in the use of positive inducements, or 'carrots'. Positive inducements are not required in the definition. For example, positive inducements were used in only four of the 16 cases analysed in the study by Art and Cronin. Moreover, as Jakobsen states, 'a strategy does not qualify as coercive diplomacy if the carrot employed is greater than the stick' (Jakobsen 1998: 79). Still, as discussed further below, positive inducements do appear to be a key causal factor in successful coercive diplomacy.

Coercive diplomacy's distinctiveness along the force–diplomacy continuum

Positing the overall force–diplomacy relationship as a continuum, coercive diplomacy falls in the middle. On the one end is *diplomacy* in the classical sense, as defined by Nicolson, as 'the management of international relations by negotiation' (Nicolson 1980/1939: 4).[4] William Zartman and Jeffrey Rubin develop this further, defining international negotiations as 'joint decision making under conditions of conflict and uncertainty, in which divergent positions are combined into a single outcome' and '[e]ach of two or more sides attempts to obtain what it wants through the exchange of information, typically in the form of offers and counteroffers' (Zartman and Rubin 2000: 12). This is a rich and varied literature that encompasses work on mediation, conflict resolution and conflict prevention, as well as a range of other strategies, and which discusses both bilateral and multilateral formats (e.g. Druckman 1997; Zartman 1978). While force is always there as a backdrop, the emphasis is largely on dialogue and other peaceful means.

At the other end is *war*. While acknowledging the Clausewitzian definition of war as 'politics by other means', those other means are principally military and are not just confined to limited uses of military force (von Clausewitz 2007). War is, as Schelling puts it, the use of 'brute force' to 'take what you want' (Schelling 1966: 2); to 'bludgeon' rather than persuade an opponent, as George puts it (George 1991: 5); or 'the deadliest instrument of conflict resolution', as defined in a leading International Relations text (Kegley and Wittkopf 1997: 347). Negotiations are not necessarily inconsistent with brute force, but to the extent that they are present, they are a result of, rather than an alternative to or accompaniment of, the use of military force. As Art and Cronin point out, the important point is that '[w]herever one draws the line between limited and full-scale use, if the coercer has to cross that line to achieve its objectives, then, by definition, coercive diplomacy has failed. In this case, war, not coercive diplomacy, produced the change' (Art and Cronin 2003: 10).

Lawrence Freedman poses his approach as 'strategic coercion', a concept that he acknowledges 'is very close' to coercive diplomacy but which he prefers for stressing the coercive component more and the diplomatic one less (Freedman 1998: 17). But while he is right in identifying some of the conceptual uncertainties that coercive diplomacy has, his effort to keep to the distinction does not hold up in the cases studies, two of which carry 'coercive diplomacy' in their titles and others of which are shown in the index to use the concept extensively (Jakobsen 1998; Holoboff 1998). Daniel Byman and Matthew Waxman's *Dynamics of Coercion* goes further in de-emphasizing the diplomatic dimension yet still staying short of war, i.e. 'getting the adversary to act in a certain way via anything short of brute force' (Byman and Waxman 2002: 3). But while this principal focus on force has its value, its single-dimensionality in dealing with multidimensional dynamics seems to be one of the reasons why they have to use cases illustratively and sporadically rather than as intensive, cohesive case studies.

A further distinction is that between coercive diplomacy and deterrence. George's original conceptualization of coercive diplomacy was based heavily on differences in the nature of the objectives, with deterrence being geared 'to dissuade an adversary from undertaking a damaging action not yet initiated' and coercive diplomacy being 'a response to an action already taken' and an effort to get the adversary either 'to stop short of the goal' or 'undo the action' (George and Simons 1994: 7ff.). This distinction works best with regard to standing deterrence, i.e. the development of military capabilities and the projection of political will as part of a largely explicit strategy to convey on an ongoing basis a credible retaliatory threat that is sufficient to deter attack or other acts of aggression or expansion (Morgan 1977; George and Smoke 1974; Schelling 1966). The differentiation becomes more blurred with regard to immediate deterrence, meaning not just the standing posture, but a more active invocation of threats prompted by a crisis or other particular issue. Either way, the strategy of deterrence aims more at intimidation than at persuasion – and if it fails, it risks escalating beyond coercive diplomacy and other more limited uses of force and ending up as war (see also Chapter 36 on deterrence in this volume).

Explaining success and failure

Two largely consensual analytic points characterize the literature on coercive diplomacy. One is the difficulty of successful coercive diplomacy. George's books are about the *limits* of coercive diplomacy; Art and Cronin calculate only a 32 per cent success rate; Freedman states up front that his variant of strategic coercion 'is not an easy option' (Art and Cronin 2003: 405; Freedman 1998: 17). Among the policy change successes cited in these studies are the 1961–62 Laotian ceasefire and neutrality; the 1962 Cuban missile crisis; the 1995 ending of the Bosnian war; some crises involving Iraq during the 1990s, in between the 1991 and 2003 wars; and Libya's agreement to end support for terrorism and its WMD programme, negotiated in the years 1998–2003 (Jentleson and Whytock 2005/06).

The other generally agreed analytic point is the difficulty of theorizing and strategizing in anything more than conditional and probabilistic terms. George and Simons have five contextual variables, nine conditions and four variants (George and Simons 1994: 270–74, 279–91). Art and Cronin build on the framework developed by George and Simons, agreeing with some of their variables and disagreeing with others, adding three factors of their own and providing additional reasons why coercive diplomacy is inherently difficult (Art and Cronin 2003: 361–74, 383–402). The value of such approaches is in bringing out the 'context-dependence' of coercive diplomacy. Too often models, equations and theories are developed to a degree of abstraction where they gain parsimony, but at the heavy price of empirical accuracy, analytic reliability and policy relevance. Still some sorting out among these many explanatory factors and/or identification of other more powerful ones would be helpful for at least a relatively more parsimonious causal chain as well as for relevance to policy.

In my own work, drawing on the literature as well as challenging it, I posit two sets of variables, one focusing on the strategy of the coercer state and the other on the target state's domestic political economy, as key (Jentleson and Whytock 2005/06).

Coercer state strategy

Strategy, as Freedman so aptly defines it, 'constitutes the creative element in any exercise of power. It involves the search for the optimum relationship between political ends and the means available for achieving them' (Freedman 1998: 15). As Richard Betts points out, 'strategies are chains of relationships among means and ends that span several levels of analysis ... strategy is a distinct plan between policy and operations' (Betts 2000: 6f.). For coercive diplomacy, the crucial condition for success is a relationship between ends and means that leads the target state to assess the costs of non-compliance or the benefits of compliance as outweighing the benefits of non-compliance or the costs of compliance. Whether or not a particular coercive diplomacy strategy strikes this balance depends on its meeting three key criteria: proportionality, reciprocity and coercive credibility.

Proportionality refers to the relationship within the coercer's strategy between the scope and nature of the objectives being pursued and the instruments used in their pursuit. The main source of imbalance arises when the objectives go beyond policy change to emphasize regime change. It is hard enough to seek to compel changes in the target's policy as described above, either as Type A (stopping short of a goal) or as Type B (undoing an action). It is even harder with Type C objectives of regime change as distinct from policy change.[5] This objective in particular manifests 'asymmetry of motivation', which is one of the main variables stressed by George and Simons, and how 'the strength of the opponent's motivation not to comply is highly dependent on what is demanded of him' (George and Simons 1994: 281f.). While it is not strictly the case that the more limited the objectives the more likely they are to succeed, the policy change/regime change differentiation demarcates a crucial proportionality threshold.

Reciprocity involves an explicit or at least mutually tacit understanding of the link between the coercer's incentives and the target's concessions. Given that coercive diplomacy is a strategy for influencing, but not denying the target's choices, there have to be terms of exchange based on a shared belief that if you do x, I will do y. Art and Cronin give particular emphasis to the utility of positive inducements (Art and Cronin 2003: 388f.; Baldwin 1971). This link may be explicitly designed as a gradual process, as in George's conception of conditional reciprocity and Robert Axelrod's tit-for-tat (George 1993; Axelrod 1984). It does not have to be, though, so long as it is sufficiently definite and robust that the target does not think it can get the benefits without having to reciprocate. Conversely, if the target is too unsure that reciprocal measures will follow, it may question whether the concessions being demanded are worth the return. The balance lies in neither offering too little too late or for too much in return, nor too much too soon or for too little in return.

Coercive credibility means that in addition to these calculations about the costs and benefits of cooperation, the target knows that non-cooperation has consequences. Threats and uses of force and other coercive instruments (e.g. economic sanctions) must be sufficiently credible to raise the target's perceived costs of non-compliance and defiance. This adds an element of intimidation to the reassurance cultivated through reciprocity, a complementarity that can establish a force–diplomacy balance that is lacking in either alone. It is not enough, though, just to have superior military force or economic position. The US is the coercer state in all the cases cited by Art and Cronin and by George and Simons (in some cases unilaterally, in others as a coalition leader, but always in a principal role), all against targets less militarily powerful, but with the varying degrees of success noted earlier (Art and Cronin 2003: 402; Holoboff 1998: 179–211; O'Sullivan 2003; Hufbauer et al. 1990; Pape 1997; Jentleson 1999). Art and Cronin stress the inherent difficulty of credibly conveying denial capacity with limited military force; and George has great concerns about the risks in using ultimata.

All three elements of a balanced coercive diplomacy strategy are more likely to be achieved if other major international actors are supportive and if opposition within the coercing state's domestic politics is limited. Thus, not only substantive strategy, but also the domestic and international contexts are important. In the case of Libya, for example (Jentleson and Whytock 2005/06), the key international actors were Western Europe, due to both its diplomatic weight and its economic capacity as a potential alternative trade partner for Libya; the United Nations; and regional actors such as Saudi Arabia and South Africa. On the domestic side, a new type of actor – terrorism victims' families, in this case families of the Pan Am 103 Lockerbie bombing victims – were the major domestic constraint on US policy. Victims' families, be they the Lockerbie families or the families of victims of the terrorist attacks of 11 September 2001, do not fall neatly into the usual typology of economic, ethnic and ideological pressure groups. Yet, given the post-September 11 threats to personal and national security, their influence is likely to continue as part of the US foreign policy debate.

The domestic political economy of the target state

The second main set of variables involves the target state and its domestic political economy. Relational factors such as asymmetry of motivation give us some sense of the target as not just an object to be acted upon, and indicate that the success or failure of coercive diplomacy is not just a function of the relative distribution of power. But they still leave questions about how and when the target state does or does not secure a favourable motivational asymmetry and compensate for unfavourable power balances. This requires more systematic and direct analytic emphasis on the target state's domestic political economy.

The starting point for such analysis is Johan Galtung's classic formulation in the economic sanctions literature assailing 'naïve theories of economic warfare' that 'do not take into account the possibility that value deprivation may initially lead to *political* integration and only later – perhaps much later, or even never – to political disintegration' (Galtung 1967: 407). The same could be said for coercive diplomacy theories that too readily equate the capacity of the coercer state to impose costs with the likelihood of target compliance without 'equal emphasis on [the] adversary's countermoves' (Byman and Waxman 2002: 42). The same point is made by Robert Keohane and Joseph Nye in their distinction between the sensitivity and vulnerability dimensions of interdependence, with the former being a measure of susceptibility to disruption by external forces but the latter taking into account a state's capacity to counter such disruptions and blunt their effects, whether economically or through mustering the political will to resist (Keohane and Nye 2001).

While regime type affects the capacity and strategies for self-defence, it is not determinative. The George–Simons and Art–Cronin case studies almost all involve non-democratic target states, yet show successes as well as failures, including success in one instance and failure in another against the same non-democratic regime. Conversely, the case on which Galtung based his theory, the multilateral sanctions imposed by the United

Nations in the mid-1960s against Rhodesia, involved a target that, at least for its white minority, was democratic yet showed plenty of will to resist.

Regime-type distinctions based on 'rogue state' status have had some, but limited analytic utility. Such regimes share common characteristics, such as highly repressive rule and resort to direct and indirect aggression in their international behaviour. But the differences have been sufficient to engender definitional, predictive and prescriptive problems. First, the definitional parameters are extremely imprecise. How much and how many types of behaviour that are considered 'beyond the pale' must a state display in order to be included, and what is the definition of 'beyond the pale'? Second, to the extent that there are agreed-upon definitions, they define the nature of the state in terms of its actions and policies, and are thus tautological. Regime type and state behaviour are conflated, making it problematic to use the former as the predictor of the latter. Third, the very terminology is highly charged politically. It is used very little outside American political discourse, and is seen in Europe, the Arab and Muslim world, and elsewhere to manifest both American moralism and domestic political pressures (Litwak 2000: 47–56, 242ff.; Nincic 2005). Fourth, the empirical record is weak. Distinctions based on the 'rogue' nature of the regime have not been a consistent predictor of behaviour for a particular state over time or for the category as a whole. So while there can be some generality of approach, policy must be 'differentiated' to fit the particulars of the state and circumstances in question (Litwak 2000: 224ff., 252–55).

We thus need to look beyond regime type at two key factors that affect the target state's susceptibility to coercive diplomacy. One is the regime leadership's calculus of whether its own self-perpetuation in power is better served by resistance or by compliance. Among other things, this may depend on the ability of the regime to use resistance to outside coercion as a way of rallying national support in the integrative manner stressed by Galtung or, alternatively, the potential to reap domestic political gains by improving relations with the coercer. That assessment may also depend on the resources available to the regime to absorb the costs of resistance, resources that may be limited depending on whether it faces domestic political threats or economic challenges. The other and inter-related factor is the role of elites and other domestic political and societal actors and the question of whether their interests lead them to be 'short-circuiters' of coercive diplomacy efforts, pressuring the regime to resist the external pressures, or 'transmission belts' that see their interests as being better served by the policy concessions demanded, and thus transmit the pressure.[6] For both the regime leadership and these other political and societal actors this is in part an economic calculation of the costs that military force, sanctions and other coercive diplomacy 'sticks' can impose and the benefits that trade and other economic 'carrots' may carry.[7]

In sum, the analytic focus is on assessing the substantive soundness of the coercer's strategy and the political and economic factors that determine the susceptibility of the target state to it. This brings both more of the elements of diplomacy and more of the domestic political economy of the target into the analysis. The interactive–relational nature is maintained, but with greater emphasis on establishing the general parameters for a balanced coercive diplomacy strategy and then tailoring that strategy to the target's domestic political economy in a manner likely to activate elite 'transmission belts' and otherwise affect the regime leadership's cost-benefit calculations. Our Libya case study both elaborates and bears out this framework involving the coercer state's strategy and the domestic political economy of the target state (Jentleson and Whytock 2005/06).

410

Implications for policy and further research

Six main policy implications follow, as developed more extensively elsewhere (Jentleson and Whytock 2005/06; Jentleson 2006) and summarized here:

1 *Balancing coercion and diplomacy.* There is greater potential complementarity between coercion, including threats or limited uses of force, and diplomacy than the more singular advocates of one or the other strategy tend to convey.

2 *Deft diplomacy.* Skilled statecraft matters. That may sound like a truism, but it is too often taken for granted. Major coercive diplomacy successes such as the 1962 Cuban missile crisis and the 1998–2003 Libya case could well have gone the other way had it not been for the deftness of the diplomacy.

3 *Policy change, not regime change.* That policy change is possible without regime change is a crucial point. But another point is even more important: pursuing regime change can be counterproductive to achieving policy change. In the case of Libya, for example, taking regime change off the table early in the negotiations was crucial to building the trust needed to achieve the quite substantial policy changes of ending WMD programmes and support for political violence movements.

4 *Sanctions re-revisionism.* Economic sanctions can be an effective part of coercive diplomacy strategy when imposed multilaterally and sustained over time. The undifferentiated debate over whether sanctions do or do not work needs to be focused more on establishing the conditions under which they are most likely to be effective.

5 *Multilateral support crucial.* Multilateral support not only gives coercive diplomacy greater coercive capacity (whether through sanctions or other coercive measures), it also confers a degree of legitimacy that no nation can claim while acting on its own. At the tactical level, the target state needs to see that it cannot split the international coalition.

6 *Know the target.* Conditional generalizations about applicable lessons that are transferable from one case to another are important as long as unique aspects of each case are also taken into account, particularly the dynamics of 'circuit breakers' and 'transmission belts'.

The agenda for further research follows similar lines. Theories and analytic frameworks identifying key variables need to be both refined and deepened. How well does the framework offered herein of coercive state strategy and its three key elements (proportionality, reciprocity and coercive credibility) hold up to further testing, analysis and elaboration? Work along these lines not only addresses coercive diplomacy per se, but it also, even more fundamentally, draws on and contributes to an understanding of the nature of power and influence in international affairs.

Additional case studies can add to the empirical bases. Cases like Iranian and North Korean proliferation, while having other dimensions, do fit the coercive diplomacy parameters. They have begun to be studied and need to be further addressed as they develop further. Other examples include Russia and Georgia.

In these and other ways, coercive diplomacy studies can be a major part of efforts to think more strategically about diplomacy. For on the one hand, while the need for military force has not gone away, many factors in twenty-first century international affairs inherently limit its utility. On the other hand, along with successes achieved

411

through diplomacy, the failings also have to be acknowledged. To the extent that scholars help develop the greater understanding and strategies for effective diplomacy, coercive as well as other forms, we will be making an important contribution to a safer and more secure world.

Notes

1 I wish to acknowledge Professor Christopher A. Whytock, who while a Duke graduate student was my research assistant and co-author, and on whose work this article also draws.

2 Type C was added in the second edition largely based on my case study of the Reagan strategy against the Nicaraguan Sandinistas (Jentleson 1994: 175–200). While the Reagan policy does get some credit for the fall of the Sandinistas, it 'came at a very high immediate and long-term cost. Especially when one considers that other policy options were possible, the U.S. involvement in Nicaragua can hardly be held up as a model of success' (p. 188). George also concludes from this case that while absolute statements are not warranted, 'type C coercive diplomacy in particular carries little prospect for success' (George and Simons 1994: 269).

3 Gary Schaub, in a chapter in the Freedman volume, argues for 'resuscitating' compellence and criticizes coercive diplomacy for inconsistency and lack of clarity (Schaub 1998); Peter Jakobsen, also in the Freedman volume, makes the case for the validity of the distinction and the preferability of coercive diplomacy (Jakobsen 1998).

4 Nicolson later refers to this as 'the British type of diplomacy' distinguished from the 'warrior' conception of 'Machtpolitik or Power Policy' as developed in the late nineteenth century by Prussia-Germany with its 'belief that force, or the threat of force, are the main instruments of negotiation' (Nicolson 1980/1939: 78f.).

5 Art and Cronin (2003) question whether regime change is that much more difficult an objective, but they do so largely based on an analysis of the 1991–94 Haiti case study (ending the military coup and restoring to power the democratically elected President Jean-Bertrand Aristide), which mistakenly attributes the success to coercive diplomacy, when in fact it required not just a limited use of force, but a fully fledged US military intervention force; and not just the threat of intervention, but the actual launching of an airborne and naval invasion force on its way to Haiti. However blurry the line between coercive diplomacy, limited use of force and the more extensive uses of coercion and warfare may be, it was crossed in this case.

6 The image of 'transmission belts' is from Jentleson (2000):

> The key element is not just the formal domestic political structure but ... the permeability of the regime as indicated by the degree of independent activity of domestic actors that can act as "transmission belts," carrying the economic impact of the sanctions into the target's core political structures.
>
> (Jentleson 2000: 135f.)

Jonathan Kirshner offers a similar formulation, stressing the importance of identifying not only central government actors, but also

> the core groups whose political support allows the regime to remain in power ... Pressure on core support groups creates indirect incentives by motivating those groups to pressure the government to change course, and by raising fears that dissatisfaction among such groups will cause them to conclude that their interests can be better served under new leadership. ... One way that coercive instruments work is by motivat[ing] the most influential groups, who act relatively promptly, pressuring (or jettisoning) the government in order to protect their own interests.
>
> (Kirshner 1997: 42, 45)

7 For related arguments on WMD, see Etel Solingen's conceptions of 'liberalizing' and 'nationalist-confessional' coalitions (Solingen 1994: 127f.); Levite (2002–03: 75) on the importance to a government of having a domestic consensus in favour of a nuclear reversal decision, 'whether cultivated

entirely indigenously or, as is commonly the case, with some external support and (at times) prod-ding, [which] typically requires the sophisticated use of offsets and incentives'; and the case studies in Campbell, Einhorn and Reiss (2004). Paul acknowledges that domestic factors may be relevant, but argues that security considerations are more powerful determinants (Paul 2000: 26).

References

Art, R. and Cronin, P. (eds) (2003) *The United States and Coercive Diplomacy*, Washington, DC: United States Institute of Peace Press.

Axelrod, R. (1984) *The Evolution of Cooperation*, New York: Basic Books.

Baldwin, D. (1971) 'The power of positive sanctions', *World Politics* 24, 1: 19–39.

Betts, R.K. (2000) 'Is strategy an illusion?', *International Security* 25, 2: 5–50.

Byman, D. and Waxman, M. (2002) *The Dynamics of Coercion*, Cambridge: Cambridge University Press.

Campbell, K., Einhorn, R. and Reiss, M. (2004) *The Nuclear Tipping Point*, Washington, DC: Brookings Institution Press.

von Clausewitz, C. (2007) *On War*, trans. Howard, M. and Paret, P., New York: Oxford University Press.

Druckman, D. (1997) 'Negotiating in the international context', in Zartman, W. and Rasmussen, J.L. (eds) *Peacemaking in International Conflict: Methods and Techniques*, Washington, DC: United States Institute of Peace Press, pp. 111–62.

Freedman, L. (ed.) (1998) *Strategic Coercion*, Oxford: Oxford University Press.

Galtung, J. (1967) 'On the effects of international economic sanctions', *World Politics* 19, 3: 378–416.

George, A.L. (1971) 'Coercive diplomacy: Definitions and characteristics', in George, A.L. and Simons, W.E. (eds) *The Limits of Coercive Diplomacy*, Boulder: Westview Press, pp. 7–11.

——(1991) *Forceful Persuasion: Coercive Diplomacy as an Alternative to War*, Washington, DC: United States Institute of Peace Press.

——(1993) *Bridging the Gap: Theory and Practice in Foreign Policy*, Washington, DC: United States Institute of Peace Press.

George, A.L. and Simons, W.E. (eds) (1994) *The Limits of Coercive Diplomacy*, 2nd edn, Boulder: Westview Press.

Holoboff, E.M. (1998) 'Bad boy or good business? Russia's use of oil as a mechanism of coercive diplomacy', in Freedman, L. (ed.) *Strategic Coercion*, Oxford: Oxford University Press, pp. 179–211.

Hufbauer, G.C., Schott, J.J. and Elliott, K.A. (1990) *Economic Sanctions Reconsidered*, Washington, DC: Institute for International Economics.

Jakobsen, P.V. (1998) 'The strategy of coercive diplomacy: Refining existing theory to post-Cold War realities', in Freedman, L. (ed.) *Strategic Coercion*, Oxford: Oxford University Press, pp. 61–85.

Jentleson, B.W. (1994) 'The Reagan Administration versus Nicaragua: The limits of "Type C" coercive diplomacy', in George, A.L. and Simons, W.E. (eds) *The Limits of Coercive Diplomacy*, 2nd edn, Boulder: Westview Press, pp. 175–200.

——(1999) *Economic Sanctions and Post-Cold War Conflict*, Study commissioned by the National Academy of Sciences, National Research Council, Commission on Behavioral and Social Sciences.

——(2000) 'Economic sanctions and post-Cold War conflicts: Challenges for theory and policy' in Stern, P.C. and Druckman, D. (eds) *International Conflict Resolution After the Cold War*, Washington, DC: National Academies Press, pp. 123–77.

——(2006). *Coercive Diplomacy; Scope and Limits in the Contemporary World*, Stanley Foundation Policy Brief. Available online at: www.stanleyfoundation.org/policyanalysis.cfm?id=57 (accessed 10 February 2009).

Jentleson, B.W. and Whytock, C.A. (2005/06) 'Who "won" Libya? The force–diplomacy debate and its implications for theory and policy', *International Security* 30, 3: 47–86.

Kegley, C. and Wittkopf, E.R. (1997) *World Politics: Trend and Transformation*, 6th edn, New York: St. Martin's Press.

Keohane, R.O. and Nye, J.S. (2001) *Power and Interdependence*, 3rd edn, New York: Longman.

Kirshner, J. (1997) 'Microfoundations of economic sanctions', *Security Studies* 6, 3: 32–64.

Levite, A.E. (2002/03) 'Never say never again: Nuclear reversal revisited', *International Security* 27, 3: 59–88.

Litwak, R. (2000) *Rogue States and U.S. Foreign Policy*, Baltimore: Johns Hopkins University Press.

Morgan, P. (1977) *Deterrence: A Conceptual Analysis*, Beverly Hills, CA: Sage Library of Social Science.

——(1997) 'Deterrence', in Jentleson, B.W. and Paterson, T.G. (eds) *Encyclopedia of U.S. Foreign Relations*, Volume II, New York: Oxford University Press, pp. 11–18.

Nicolson, Sir H. (1980/1939) *Diplomacy*, New York: Oxford University Press.

Nincic, M. (2005) *Renegade Regimes*, New York: Columbia University Press.

O'Sullivan, M. (2003) *Shrewd Sanctions: Statecraft and State Sponsors of Terrorism*, Washington, DC: Brookings Institution.

Pape, R. (1997) 'Why economic sanctions do not work', *International Security* Vol 22 (Fall 1997): 90–136.

Paul, T.V. (2000) *Power versus Prudence: Why States Forgo Nuclear Weapons*, McGill: Queen's University Press.

Schaub, G. (1998) 'Compellence: Resuscitating the concept', in Freedman, L. (ed.) *Strategic Coercion*, Oxford: Oxford University Press, pp. 37–60.

Schelling, T. (1960) *The Strategy of Conflict*, Cambridge, MA: Harvard University Press.

——(1966) *Arms and Influence*, New Haven: Yale University Press.

Solingen, E. (1994) 'Political economy of nuclear restraint', *International Security* 19, 2: 126–69.

Zartman, I.W. (1978) *The Negotiation Process*, Newbury Park, CA: Sage.

Zartman, I.W. and Rubin, J. (2000) *Power and Negotiation*, Ann Arbor: University of Michigan Press.

38

Peace operations

Oliver Ramsbotham and Tom Woodhouse

In UN Secretary-General Boutros Boutros-Ghali's *Agenda for Peace* (1992), the term 'peace operations' was seen to cover traditional peacekeeping, peace enforcement and post-conflict peacebuilding. Preventive diplomacy was a further category. All of these were interpreted as fulfilment of UN Charter provisions in the aftermath of near-universal international support for enforcement action to reverse Iraq's occupation of Kuwait in 1991, and the sudden flurry of non-forcible UN peace operations between 1989 and 1992 to manage transitions from war to peace in a number of long-standing conflicts on almost every continent. It seemed that a new era for UN-sanctioned – and, in the latter case, UN-managed – forcible and non-forcible peace operations had dawned. However, these distinctions have not corresponded to consistent or generally accepted conceptual categories in the evolution of international practice since then.

Originally associated mainly with UN deployments, peace operations (or what purport to be peace operations) today are now also conducted by or under the aegis of regional organizations (EU, AU, OSCE and OAS), sub-regional groupings (ECOWAS), politico-military alliances (NATO) and a variety of ad hoc coalitions led by militarily powerful states (Russia, the US, Britain, France, Nigeria and Australia). This has even at times encompassed a role for private military companies. In the literature, peace operations featured prominently in chapters on conflict prevention, peacekeeping, peacebuilding, peace enforcement and humanitarian intervention. As with Wittgenstein's rope, which is a continuous whole although no single strand goes through the entire cord, no one definitional element runs consistently through the whole length.

This chapter describes the nature of peace operations (history, functions, authorization, spectrum of force and definition); peace operations and post-war peacebuilding; the measurement of success in peace operations; and possible future directions for peace operations.

What counts as a peace operation?

The UN Department of Peacekeeping Operations (UNDPKO) listed 20 'UN Peacekeeping Deployments by Mission' in October 2008 with 75,512 troops, 12,125 police officers and 2,606 military observers (United Nations Department of Public Information 2009). When the Center on International Cooperation (CIC) produced its first *Annual Review of Global Peace Operations 2006*, its 'data sections concentrated heavily on the United Nations'. In 2007, however, after criticism, the data set was expanded to include figures on EU, AU, NATO and 'other operations'. This resulted in a further 30 'non-UN missions', to give 'a richer picture of the evolving international architecture for peace operations, within and beyond the UN' (Center on International Cooperation 2007: ix; see also Center on International Cooperation 2008: vii; 137–94). It is this shift to include increasing numbers of non-UN missions in the definition of peace operations that causes most of the current difficulties.

For example, the CIC list, and other peace operations lists such as those updated every three months by the ZIF Center for International Peace Operations (Center for International Peace Operations 2008), include the 150,000-strong US-led Multinational Force in Iraq (MNF-I) and Russian-led forces in the 'near-abroad' on the one hand, and almost entirely civilian OSCE missions and small UN Peacebuilding and UN Special Representative missions on the other. Unlike the situation in the early 1990s, where a single mission like the UN Transitional Authority in Cambodia (UNTAC) could be seen as constituting a comprehensive peace operation in itself, in the more complicated and varied contemporary combinations several of the missions listed separately (together with others not listed) combine – often indeterminately – in a single undertaking, as in Iraq, where there is a noticeable imbalance between the contributions of MNF-I, NATO's 162-strong Training Mission in Iraq (NTM-I), the UN's 229-strong Assistance Mission in Iraq (UNAMI) and the EU's small Rule of Law Mission in Iraq (EUJUST LEX).

A brief history of peace operations

These complications are the result of the rapid and unpredictable evolution of peace operations over the past 20 years. A glance at mission inception dates shows how, despite abrupt discontinuities, current peace operations reflect their historical origins. Once again, there are variations as to how specialists categorize different 'phases' or 'generations' of peace operations (Durch 2006 borrows the term 'surges'). It seems simplest to distinguish three phases:

- UN peacekeeping up to the end of the Cold War (Phase 1)
- The period of expanded UN missions between the initiation of UNTAG (UN Transition Assistance Group for Namibia) in 1989 and the withdrawal of UNOSOM II (UN Operation in Somalia) in 1995 (Phase 2)
- The more diverse and complex changes that have attended the emergence of 'third-generation peace operations' since then (Phase 3).

This evolution has been precipitated by three main convulsions. First, the end of the Cold War opened up the whole possibility of large-scale international interventions of this kind. Second, some key UN peace operations towards the mid-1990s were overwhelmed by crises that temporarily seemed to call the whole undertaking into question. The third break was the result of the US response to the 11 September 2001 attacks and the 'war on terror' that threatened to sideline or co-opt the enterprise into what could no longer be called peace operations.

Phase 1

During the Cold War, despite exceptions such as the United Nations Operation in the Congo (1960–64), the 13 UN peacekeeping missions were largely restricted to inter-position activities. Their main function was to monitor borders and establish buffer zones after the agreement of ceasefires. The missions were typically composed of lightly armed national troop contingents from small and neutral UN member states. UN peacekeeping came to be defined in terms of a few basic principles famously, if unofficially, formulated by UN Secretary-General Dag Hammarskjöld and UN General Assembly President Lester Pearson to guide the work of the United Nations Emergency Force (UNEF I), created in response to the Suez Crisis in the Middle East in 1956. The UNEF I principles served to define the essence of UN peacekeeping at least until the mid-1990s and were based on:

- the consent of the conflict parties
- the non-use of force except in self-defence
- political neutrality (not taking sides)
- impartiality (commitment to the mandate)
- legitimacy (sanctioned and accountable to the Security Council advised by the Secretary-General).

One of the key questions is how many, if any, of these principles survive in definitions of current peace operations, and whether this matters.

Phase 2

Phase 2 was ushered in by two linked developments. The first was the unexpected transformation of decolonization arrangements for Namibia in 1989 into a template for an unprecedented burst of multidimensional UN-led peace operations. Since most of these were in support of agreed ceasefires or peace accords (for example in Nicaragua, Angola, El Salvador, Cambodia and Mozambique), it was at first supposed that the Hammarskjöld/Pearson principles still applied. UN peacekeeping expanded and merged into UN post-settlement peacebuilding without fundamentally changing its character.

Second, and at this point clearly conceptually distinct, was the collective security operation to reverse Iraq's occupation of Kuwait in 1991 – only the second large-scale UN-authorized 'coalition war', as Michael Pugh calls it (2007: 372). Since the first was the Korean war, which only received UN endorsement as a result of the Soviet Union's ill-judged absence from the Security Council in 1950, the 1991 Iraq war seemed to be the first genuinely international 'peace enforcement operation' by the international community, and appeared to herald a new era – a 'new world order', as US President George H. W. Bush somewhat reluctantly described it – in which the UN might be able at last to make real some of the ideals of its founders. In the absence of what had originally been intended as a UN peace enforcement capacity (UN Charter article 47), however, as Operation Desert Storm demonstrated, the UN through the Security Council could authorize enforcement operations, but plainly could not conduct them.

It is this discrepancy that has generated much of the continuing controversy about peace operations, as what was originally a relatively clear distinction between UN-authorized and UN-managed non-forcible peacekeeping/peacebuilding operations on the one hand and UN-authorized but non-UN-managed peace enforcement operations on the other has subsequently collapsed.

Phase 3

The collapse ushered in a deeply ambivalent 'third generation' of peace operations. This was precipitated by a loss of confidence in the UN's ability to manage major conflict-related peace and security challenges in the wake of failure in Bosnia (1992–95), Somalia (1992–95) and by reflex Rwanda (1994), and the converse attempt by major military powers and alliances to use the UN Security Council to authorize forcible intervention and its aftermath as in Kosovo (1999), Afghanistan (2001) and, most notoriously, Iraq (2003) – if necessary *retrospectively* (as pioneered earlier in the 1990s by Nigerian-led interventions in Liberia and Sierra Leone). This blurred the middle ground as UN peacekeeping missions were now usually conducted under a Chapter Seven enforcement mandate (which often necessitated cooperation with non-UN forces), while the most powerful military states and alliances were – or claimed to be – working with UN acquiescence or tacit cooperation, if not explicit authorization.

The evolving functions and mandates of peace operations

In addition to changes over time, it is also worth noting differences in the initial conditions and functions of peace operations, particularly as articulated in mission mandates, because the context is often highly influential in setting the parameters for expected results, or should be. Initial declared functions often overlap, are the result of political compromise and may subsequently change as the operation proceeds. Nevertheless, they play a more significant role in determining the scope and outcome of peace operations than is often acknowledged.

Six different initial contextual functions for peace operations can usefully be distinguished (Ramsbotham 2006).

- *Interposition and monitoring operations* are traditional 'phase one' functions, some of which, such as UNDOF (Israel–Syria), are holdovers from the Cold War period. A more recent example is UNMEE (2000–2007), which was tasked with monitoring the cessation of hostilities in the Ethiopia–Eritrea conflict. UNIFIL (Lebanon) changed its character after the 2006 Israel–Hezbollah war and is now seen by some as a prototype for possible future interposition and monitoring missions in the region.
- *Decolonization operations* are mounted to assist the transition to self-rule after wars of national liberation (Namibia, East Timor). In these cases, the fact that the respective 'colonial' powers (South Africa, Indonesia) have already agreed to withdraw evidently makes the task of the interveners easier.
- *Democracy restoration operations* are tasked with defending an already existing democracy or restoring an ousted democratically elected leader (Haiti, Sierra Leone). Although resistance from the usurper is likely to be strong, the existence of an already elected alternative improves prospects, so long as this changeover of power is generally seen to have been legitimate ('free and fair elections').
- *Peace support operations* are interventions to help manage the transition from war to peace after a ceasefire or some form of already agreed peace arrangement (Cambodia,

El Salvador, Mozambique, Burundi). This is the *locus classicus* for peace operations – indeed, peace support operations are sometimes conflated with peace operations in general. A prior peace agreement greatly increases the chances of success, but since making peace between undefeated conflict parties in civil wars does not end the conflict, but merely transmutes it into intense political rivalry, the post-agreement period is often the most dangerous. The collapse of agreements in Angola and Rwanda in the 1990s subsequently engulfed the peace operations intended to support them (UNAVEM II, UNAMIR). This is where the advocates of post-war international intervention have had to – and to some extent, did – learn some important lessons.

- *Humanitarian intervention operations*, unlike during the Cold War period, are now usually interventions in ongoing internal conflicts or civil wars, initially mainly driven by concern for the welfare of civilian populations (Bosnia 1992–95, Somalia 1992–95, Kosovo 1999, Darfur 2007; there are also humanitarian interventions that are not peace operations, such as *Operation Provide Comfort* in support of the Kurdish population in northern Iraq after 1991). This contextual function should be clearly distinguished from peace support operations (see above). Failure to make this distinction led to the 'wrong lessons' being learned from debacles in Bosnia (the massacre in Srebrenica) and Somalia (the deaths of 25 US soldiers). UN peace support operations in general were wrongly implicated in the failure of what were not peace support operations. Conversely, when as a result no action was subsequently taken by the most powerful members of the Security Council in the first weeks of the Rwanda genocide (1994), it was again UN peace operations in general that were mistakenly discredited.

- *Regime change operations* are an explicit attempt to topple an existing government seen to threaten international peace and security, and in particular the national interests of the most powerful interveners (Afghanistan 2001, Iraq 2003). Another major shift in contextual functions occurred as international peace operations were co-opted into what the administration of US president George W. Bush called the 'war on terror'. Weak or failed states were seen as actual or potential havens for terrorism (US *National Security Strategy* 2002), and US defence and foreign policy requirements expanded to encompass forcible democratization and 'nation-building' as a national security priority. 'Stability, security, transition and reconstruction (SSTR) operations' became a 'core US military mission' (US Department of Defense 2005).

There is no suggestion that these are watertight distinctions (if a forcible operation were to be mounted to remove a corrupt dictatorship in a country with severe economic problems, for example, it would probably straddle the 'restoration of democracy' and 'humanitarian intervention' functions). But it is helpful to bear them in mind when it comes to assessing the success and effectiveness of peace operations, as indicated below.

The authorization, coordination and implementation of peace operations

What are 'officially endorsed and accepted' peace operations? Clearly, a UN Security Council resolution is a sufficient mandate (although the UNSC is a political body reflecting the national interests of the most powerful states). But, as already suggested, this is now not generally regarded as a necessary condition – for example, in circumstances where the UNSC cannot agree.

Linked to this is the highly challenging issue of coordination. No matter what their origins, major peace operations usually end up as post-conflict peacebuilding or reconstruction operations. This has required intervening nations to sustain 'nation-building' and 'transitional administration' capacities of exactly the kind that had, somewhat ironically, just been relinquished by the UN with the winding down of the Trusteeship Council and by erstwhile imperial powers through the merging of former colonial offices into foreign ministries. The result was a 'post-war planning gap' filled by a number of ad hoc arrangements. The penalty of failure was graphically illustrated in Iraq in 2003 with the almost instantaneous collapse of the original post-intervention administration planned from the US Department of Defense. The consequences were dire in the extreme. The UN voted in December 2005 to set up a UN Peacebuilding Commission (PBC) in an attempt to help remedy this at international level.

The spectrum of force in peace operations

Robust third-generation peace operation missions, therefore, have usually been mounted, not under UN command, but by a small number of regional security organizations and coalitions of the willing and capable such as NATO forces in Bosnia and Kosovo (IFOR, SFOR and KFOR); Nigerian peacekeeping forces (ECOMOG) in West Africa; a British-led IMAT (International Military Advisory Team) in Sierra Leone working alongside, but independently of the UNAMSIL force; and the Australian military providing the leadership of the force in East Timor (INTERFET/UNTAET).

According to the UK *Military Contribution to Peace Support Operations* doctrine (UK Ministry of Defence 2004), UK peace operation planning no longer separates combat operations from 'operations other than war' (OOTW), but envisages the use of military capabilities across the full 'spectrum of tension' from traditional peacekeeping duties through to combat against spoilers and enemies of the peace. At the tactical level 'where action actually takes place' and where formation and unit commanders 'engage directly with adversaries, armed factions and the civil population', there is a similar – and very demanding – requirement to combine combat skills with those of negotiation, mediation and the generation of consent. In addition, there is continuing controversy about whether it is possible to 'gear up' from traditional peacekeeping to combat level, as well as to 'gear down' in the other direction.

Conclusion: peacekeeping, peace operations, and war

Given its great complexity and variability, and the magnitude of the different interlocking tasks currently undertaken by such a diverse range of actors, it is simplest to contrast peace operations with traditional peacekeeping on the one hand and traditional war fighting on the other (cf. Table 38.1).

The five criteria that define traditional peacekeeping are the five Hammarskjöld/Pearson principles. As shown above, only one of these still applies unchanged (in theory) to peace operations – the criterion of impartiality, although even this can be watered down in cases where the 'international mandate' is seen to be compromised or even non-existent. Nevertheless, the contrast with traditional war fighting remains reasonably clear – again in theory. If there is no clear dividing line between peace operations and traditional war fighting, then most would conclude that the whole idea of international peace operations has lost its purchase.

Table 38.1 Contrast between peace operations, traditional peacekeeping and traditional war fighting

Traditional peacekeeping	Peace operations	Traditional War
Universal consent	General consent of target populations, not of spoilers	No consent
Political neutrality between main conflict parties	No neutrality if a conflict party opposes the mandate	No neutrality
Impartiality in fulfilling mandate	Impartiality in fulfilling mandate	No impartiality
Non-use of force except in self-defence	Full spectrum of force needed to fulfil mandate	Full spectrum of force
International mandate	Normally uphold UN Charter purposes and principles, if possible with international mandate (perhaps retrospective)	National interest

Source: Ramsbotham, Woodhouse and Miall (2005): 143.

Peace operations and post-war peacebuilding

Irrespective of the different initial functional contexts for major peace operations – decolonization, democracy restoration, post-agreement support, humanitarian intervention and regime change – or even of who the lead actor(s) may be, given the prevalence of internal conflict and breakdown in the target states, the core challenge in major peace operations is to create the sustainable conditions needed to underpin the desired outcome and enable the interveners to withdraw (Ramsbotham et al. 2005: 185–214). Evidently, the details of how this aim can be achieved vary from case to case, but a recognizable pattern of requirements can be discerned with a surprising degree of consistency. From the sectoral tasks identified in the 1992 UN *Agenda for Peace* and its successors ('actions to identify and support structures which will tend to strengthen and solidify peace in order to avoid a relapse into conflict' (Boutros-Ghali 1992: 11)) to the various 'pillars' identified in the 2004 US template for successful post-conflict reconstruction *Winning the Peace* (Orr 2004).

A summative sector/phase framework can be constructed from an extensive literature to illustrate the main points (cf. Table 38.2).

Much of this is controversial, for example, the nature and merits of democracy as a requirement, or what the role of the World Bank should be in 'conflict-sensitive economic adjustment policies', or how to manage human rights issues. Some, like Elizabeth Cousens, advocate a minimalist approach that does not raise excessive expectations through over-ambition and concentrates on encouraging 'authoritative and, eventually, legitimate mechanisms to resolve internal conflict without violence' (Cousens and Kumar 2001: 4). But it is hard to see how even this can be achieved without the interlocking elements that help to secure the phase 2 requirements:

- national armed forces under home government control stronger than challengers
- sufficient indigenous capacity to maintain basic order impartially under the law
- adequate democratic credentials of elected government with system seen to remain open to those dissatisfied with the initial result
- a reasonably stable relationship between centre and regions

421

- a formal economy yielding sufficient revenue for government to provide essential services (with continuing international assistance), economic capacity to absorb many former combatants and progress in encouraging general belief in better future employment prospects
- adequate success in managing conflicting priorities of peace and justice, protecting minority rights, and fostering a reasonably independent, yet responsible media.

Table 38.2 An indicative sector/phase matrix for post-intervention transformation and withdrawal in peace operations

Sector A	Security
Phase 1	International forces needed to control armed factions; supervise DDR; help reconstitute national army; begin demining.
Phase 2	National armed forces under home government control stronger than challengers.
Phase 3	Demilitarized politics; societal security; transformed cultures of violence.

Sector B	Law and Order
Phase 1	International control of courts etc; break grip of organised crime on government; train civilian police; promote human rights/punish abuse.
Phase 2	Indigenous capacity to maintain basic order impartially under the law.
Phase 3	Non-politicised judiciary and police; respect for individual and minority rights; reduction in organized crime.

Sector C	Government
Phase 1	International supervision of new constitution, elections etc; prevent intimidation; limit corruption.
Phase 2	Reasonably representative government; move from winner-takes-all to power-sharing system; stable relationship between centre and regions.
Phase 3	Manage peaceful transfer of power via democratic elections; development of civil society within genuine political community; integrate local into national politics.

Sector D	Economy
Phase 1	International provision of humanitarian relief; restore essential services; limit exploitation of movable resources by spoilers.
Phase 2	Formal economy yields sufficient revenue for government to provide essential services; capacity to reemploy many former combatants; perceived prospects for future improvement (esp. employment).
Phase 3	Development in long-term interest of citizens from all backgrounds.

Sector E	Society
Phase 1	Overcome initial distrust/monitor media; international protection of vulnerable populations; return of refugees underway.
Phase 2	Manage conflicting priorities of peace and justice; responsible media.
Phase 3	Depoliticize social divisions; heal psychological wounds; progress towards gender equality; education towards long-term reconciliation.

International Intervention Transitions	
Phase 1	Direct, culturally sensitive support for the peace process.
Phase 2	Phased transference to local/civilian control avoiding undue interference/neglect.
Phase 3	Integration into cooperative and equitable regional/global structures.

Source: Ramsbotham, Woodhouse and Miall (2005): 199.

Unless something like this is envisaged, it is difficult to imagine that the outcome will be sustainable and allow intervening forces to be withdrawn securely.

When it is remembered that the transformation needed to deliver phase 2 conditions must be achieved at the same time as the immediate fulfilment of phase 1 requirements (the phases are 'nested'); undefeated parties to the conflict have not given up their political ambitions; the material and institutional infrastructure is usually greatly debilitated; there are 'spoilers' intent on undoing the process; transitions to democracy, market economy, and the rule of law increase instability *en route*, an idea may be gained of the daunting dimensions of the peacebuilding or reconstruction undertaking that large-scale peace operations imply.

How can success in peace operations be measured?

In view of the challenge posed by the scale of the crises that international peace operations attempt to address, it is not surprising that the overall record for the last 20 years has been mixed. Certainly, excessive expectations have not been helpful, and it is wise from the outset to be realistic about chances of success. But in evaluating peace operations (including peace and conflict impact assessments, lessons learned and best practices identified), the problem goes deeper. What criteria should be used, and how can they be measured? Failure to agree over this issue can explain discrepant conclusions – for example, why the peace operation in Cambodia 1992–93 is classed as a 'success' by Doyle and Sambanis (2000), a 'partial success' by Hampson (1996) and a 'failure' by Durch et al. (2003).

The two most common criteria used are subsequent levels of violence, because these can be measured, and whether post-intervention 'free and fair' elections have been held and a legitimate government is in place, which is also easily verified (Downs and Stedman 2002). But as Michael Lund notes, while there are many studies 'that take an interest in the restoration of minimum physical security, it is much harder to find rigorous, data-based analyses of the other desired outcomes of macro-level peacebuilding, especially using comparative data across several countries' (Lund 2003: 31).

This does not apply to meticulous analysts like Doyle and Sambanis (2006), who use a data set of 145 civil wars between 1945 and 1999 to determine criteria for determining success in post-war peace processes. Here, there is clear statistical evidence that in difficult cases, a peace treaty combined with a 'transformative' UN intervention 'are crucial in maintaining the probability of success', and that without them the likelihood is 'very low' (see also the similar conclusion in Fortna 2008). There have also been attempts to compare the relative success of different types of peace operations – for example, the RAND Corporation's comparison between UN-led and US-led 'nation-building' efforts (Dobbins et al. 2004; although see criticism of this by Durch 2006: 26f.).

Controversies: on the very idea of peace operations

Peace operations are a litmus test for the evolution of the international collectivity. Does an 'international community' really exist? In that case, do peace operations represent emerging norms that serve the interests of peoples rather than states, and do they, however unevenly, progressively leaven the behaviour of states accordingly? Or is there still only an international system of states? In the latter case, are peace operations merely an expression of the interests and values of the most powerful among them, and a mechanism by which the capitalist centre continues to police and control the periphery?

Controversy about peace operations is best seen as articulated along a spectrum defined by answers given to these questions. The spectrum includes views about what the prevailing nature of the international collectivity *is at the moment*, and about what it *should be in future*. These usually go together (cf. Table 38.3).

At one end of the spectrum is a neorealist position that is dismissive of the UN, shows scant interest in international law and refuses to use 'peace' language at all. The US version, exemplified in Bobbitt (2002), looks instead to coalitions of the willing led by the US in defeating international terrorism. What is needed from this perspective is not peace operations, but 'stability, security, transition, and reconstruction' operations. There are Russian equivalents. The future position of China will be increasingly significant here. Furthermore, if China's mounting economic challenge to the US should change into global political–military rivalry, the entire post-Cold War impetus behind the expansion of international peace operations may be abruptly put into reverse.

Others, like David Chandler (2004), follow Robert Jackson (2000) in interpreting contemporary world politics as being no more than a limited society of states with a common interest in preserving collective order, but not enough to underpin universal interventionary principles. Sovereignty preserves plural values and is best left to do just that. Intervention always serves the interests of the powerful. Traditional UN peacekeeping principles are still the most appropriate.

Others adopt a more extended view of international society along Grotian lines, such as Nicholas Wheeler in the humanitarian intervention debate (2000). They interpret the society of states in a more expansive manner to include universal humanitarian values that trump state sovereignty when civil government is contested to the point of breakdown, or proves incapable of fulfilling its prime task of protecting citizens' basic rights. Wider international society is then seen to have a legitimate interest in intervening, so long as this is ultimately interpreted as 'human security' and can be seen to be internationally sanctioned (United Nations 2000; International Commission on Intervention and State Sovereignty 2001: 15). It is probably true to say that most current specialists writing on peace operations are located somewhere within this broad category.

There are others again who see the logic behind peace operations only as being properly met when a further stage is reached – as it were, a 'fourth generation' – in which the universal principles underlying genuine peace operations are reflected in global politics (cosmopolitan democracy, global civil society, equitable economic arrangements and universal values that are recognized cross-culturally) as well as operational capability and practice. The conceptual underpinning is provided by theorists like Richard Falk (1995), David Held (1995) and Mary Kaldor (2003), who advocate a decisive evolution of global order towards cosmopolitan governance. At the operational level, this implies a move in

Table 38.3 Peace operation theory and practice: a spectrum

	1	2	3	4	5
Theory	realist	pluralist	solidarist	cosmopolitan	critical
Practice	stabilization forces	traditional peacekeeping	current peace operations	'fourth generation' peace operations	not defined

the direction of 'cosmopolitan peace operations' (Woodhouse and Ramsbotham 2005). Among the most innovative ideas here are the quite detailed proposals now on the table for the development of a military intervention capability specifically owned by the UN, according to which designated forces will train and serve entirely as UN forces, not national troops. Plans for a United Nations Emergency Peace Service (UNEPS) were presented to the UN in 2006 (Johansen 2006), and Michael Codner has elaborated requirements for a United Nations Intervention Force (UNIF) of some 10,000 troops in the first instance (Codner 2008).

The fifth, and final, category in this schema is loosely headed 'critical theory', but also encompasses post-structural Foucauldian (Duffield 2001) and radical feminist (Fetherston 1995) viewpoints (see Bellamy and Williams 2004). This school of thought refers to various possibilities of purely civilian, non-violent, or gendered peace operations, but no operational implications are seriously discussed. The implication is that if critical criteria are properly met, then peace operations themselves are no longer needed (Pugh 2004: 54).

In conclusion, the complexity and variability of the evolution of peace operations over the past 20 years has not been accidental. It has been a function of the fact that the 'international community' is moving into uncharted waters in the post-Cold War world. It is hardly an exaggeration to say that in the continual reinterpretation of peace operations as a key element of what is meant by 'restoring and maintaining international peace and security', the international community has been redefining itself. The relation between the UN (chief legitimizer of peace operations) and the US (chief enforcer) is still being worked out, with the UN currently navigating its way between the twin dangers of marginalization and cooptation. Clear principles to supplement traditional 'just war' criteria are needed, such as principles of impartiality, universality, consistency, and the key requirement that peace operations must serve the interests of those in whose name the intervention is carried out, not the interests of interveners (Ramsbotham and Woodhouse 1996; Ramsbotham 2006). Interventions that do not meet these requirements should not be called 'peace operations'.

References

Bellamy, A.J. and Williams, P. (eds) (2004) *Peace Operations and Global Order: International Peacekeeping*, Cambridge: Polity Press.

Bellamy, A.J., Williams, P. and Griffin, S. (2004) *Understanding Peacekeeping*, Cambridge: Polity Press.

Bobbitt, P. (2002) *The Shield of Achilles: War, Peace and the Course of History*, London: Allen Lane.

Boutros-Ghali, B. (1992) *An Agenda for Peace*, New York: United Nations.

Center for International Peace Operations (2008) *International and German Personnel in EU, UN, OSCE, NATO and Other Field Missions as of August 2008*. Available online at: www.humansecuritygateway. info/documents/CIPO_ZIF_intlgermanpersonnel_Aug2008.pdf (accessed 20 February 2009).

Center on International Cooperation (2007) *Annual Review of Global Peace Operations 200*, Boulder, CO: Lynne Rienner.

——(2008) *Annual Review of Global Peace Operations 2008*, Boulder, CO: Lynne Rienner.

Chandler, D. (2004) 'The responsibility to protect? Imposing the liberal peace', in Bellamy, A.J. and Williams, P. (eds) (2004) *Peace Operations and Global Order, International Peacekeeping*, Cambridge: Polity Press, pp. 59–81.

Codner, M. (2008) 'Permanent United Nations military intervention capability: Some practical considerations', *Royal United Services Institute Journal* 153, 3: 58–67.

Cousens, E. and Kumar, C. (eds) (2001) *Peacebuilding as Politics: Cultivating Peace in Fragile Societies*, Boulder, CO: Lynne Rienner.

Dobbins, J., McGinn, J.G., Crane, K., Jones, S.G., Lal, R., Rathmell, A., Swanger, R.M. and Timilsina, A.R. (2004) *The US Role in Nation-Building: From Germany to Iraq*, Santa Monica, CA: RAND.

Downs, G. and Stedman, S.J. (2002) 'Evaluation issues in peace implementation', in Stedman, S.J., Roth-child, D. and Cousens, E.M. (eds) *Ending Civil Wars: The Implementation of Peace Agreements*, Boulder, CO: Lynne Rienner, pp. 43–69.

Doyle, M.W. and Sambanis, N. (2000) 'International peacebuilding: A theoretical and quantitative analysis', *American Political Science Review* 94, 4: 779–801.

——(2006) *Making War and Building Peace: United Nations Peace Operations*, Princeton, NJ: Princeton University Press.

——(2007) 'Peacekeeping operations', in Weiss, T. and Daws, S. (eds) *The Oxford Handbook on the United Nations*, Oxford: Oxford University Press, pp. 323–48.

Duffield, M. (2001) *Global Governance and the New Wars: The Merging of Development and Security*, London: Zed Books.

Durch, W.J. (ed.) (2006) *Twenty-First Century Peace Operations*, Washington, DC: United States Institute of Peace.

Durch, W.J., Holt, V.K., Earle, C.R. and Shanahan, M.K. (2003) *The Brahimi Report and the Future of UN Peace Operations*, Washington, DC: Stimson Center.

Falk, R. (1995) *On Humane Governance: Toward a New Global Politics*, Cambridge: Polity Press.

Fetherston, B. (1995) 'UN peacekeepers and cultures of violence', *Cultural Survival Quarterly* 19, 1: 19–23.

Fortna, V.P. (2008) *Does Peacekeeping Work? Shaping Belligerents' Choices After Civil War*, Princeton: Princeton University Press.

Hampson, F. (1996) *Nurturing Peace: Why Peace Movements Succeed or Fail*, Washington, DC: USIP Press.

Held, D. (1995) *Democracy and the Global Order: From the Modern State to Cosmopolitan Governance*, Cambridge: Polity Press.

International Commission on Intervention and State Sovereignty (2001) *The Responsibility to Protect*, Ottawa: International Development Research Centre.

Jackson, R. (2000) *The Global Covenant: Human Conduct in a World of States*, Oxford: Oxford University Press.

Johansen, R.C. (ed.) (2006) *A United Nations Emergency Peace Service to Prevent Genocide and Crimes Against Humanity*, New York: World Federalist Movement.

Kaldor, M. (2003) *Global Civil Society*, Cambridge: Polity Press.

Lund, M. (2003) *What Kind of Peace is Being Built? Taking Stock of Post-Conflict Peacebuilding*, Ottawa: International Development Research Agency.

Orr, R.C. (ed.) (2004) *Winning the Peace: An American Strategy for Post-Conflict Reconstruction*, Washington, DC: CSIS Press.

Paris, R. (2004) *At War's End: Building Peace After Civil Conflict*, Cambridge: Cambridge University Press.

——(2007) 'Post-conflict peacebuilding', in Weiss, T. and Daws, S. (eds) *The Oxford Handbook on the United Nations*, Oxford: Oxford University Press, pp. 404–26.

Pugh, M. (2004) 'Peacekeeping and critical theory', *International Peacekeeping* 11, 1: 56–82.

——(2007) 'Peace enforcement', in Weiss, T. and Daws, S. (eds) *The Oxford Handbook on the United Nations*, Oxford: Oxford University Press, pp. 370–86.

Ramsbotham, O. (2006) 'Cicero's challenge: From just war to just intervention', unpublished paper presented at Iserlohn Conference, Germany, October.

Ramsbotham, O. and Woodhouse, T. (1996) *Humanitarian Intervention in Contemporary Conflict*, Cambridge: Polity Press.

——(1999) *International Peacekeeping Operations*, Santa Barbara, California: ABC-CLIO.

Ramsbotham, O., Woodhouse, T. and Miall, H. (2005) *Contemporary Conflict Resolution*, 2nd edn, Cambridge: Polity Press.

Stedman, S.J., Rothchild, D. and Cousens, E.M. (eds) (2002) *Ending Civil Wars: The Implementation of Peace Agreements*, Boulder, CO: Lynne Rienner.

426

UK Ministry of Defence (2004) *The Military Contribution to Peace Support Operations* (JWP 3.50), 2nd edn., Shrivenham: Joint Doctrine and Concepts Centre.

United Nations (2000) *We the Peoples: The Role of the United Nations in the Twenty First Century* [The Millennial Report of the Secretary General], New York: United Nations Department of Public Information,.

United Nations Department of Public Information (2009) *Monthly Summary of Troop Contributors [January]*, New York: United Nations Department of Peacekeeping Operations.

United Nations General Assembly (2004) *A More Secure World: Our Shared Responsibility – Report of the Secretary-General's High Level Panel on Threats, Challenges and Change*, New York: United Nations.

United Nations General Assembly and Security Council (2001) *Report of the Panel on United Nations Peace Operations* (Brahimi Report), A/55/305-S/2000/809, August 21, 2000.

United States (2002) *The National Security Strategy of the United States of America*, Washington, DC: Office of the President of the United States.

United States Department of Defense (2005) 'Military support for stability, security, transition and reconstruction operations', Directive No. 3000.05, Washington, DC, November 28.

Weiss, T. and Daws, S. (eds) (2007) *The Oxford Handbook on the United Nations*, Oxford: Oxford University Press.

Wheeler, N. (2000) *Saving Strangers: Humanitarian Intervention in International Society*, Oxford: Oxford University Press.

Woodhouse, T. and Ramsbotham, O. (2005) 'Cosmopolitan peacekeeping and the globalisation of security', *International Peacekeeping* 12, 2: 139–56.

39

Humanitarian intervention

Alex J. Bellamy

In the 1990s, genocide in Rwanda (1994) killed at least 800,000 people, and war in the former Yugoslavia (1992–95) left at least 250,000 dead and forced thousands more to flee. Protracted conflicts in Sierra Leone, Sudan, Haiti, Somalia, Liberia, East Timor, the Democratic Republic of Congo (DRC) and elsewhere killed millions more. As of 2008, conflict in the Darfur region of Sudan has cost the lives of around 250,000 people and has forced more than three million people from their homes (Coebergh 2005). Significantly, approximately 90 per cent of the victims in these conflicts were civilians. In what Mary Kaldor famously described as 'new wars' (1999), civilian deaths are a direct war aim, not an unfortunate by-product. Although most of these slaughters involved non-state militia groups, typically, the worst perpetrators of crimes against civilians are states. Although the precise figures are contested, according to R. J. Rummel, in the twentieth century, around 40 million people were killed in wars between states, whilst 170 million were killed by their own governments (Rummel 1994: 21). Historically, genocides have ended in one of two ways: either the *genocidaires* succeed in destroying their target group, or they are defeated in battle. This cold fact is borne out by recent cases. The Rwandan genocide ended with the defeat of the Rwandan government and *interahamwe* militia at the hands of the Rwandan Patriotic Front (RPF); the carnage in Bosnia came to an end when the military balance turned in favour of a Croat–Muslim coalition backed by NATO airpower; and the bloodshed in Darfur has declined primarily because the *Janjaweed* militia and their government backers have succeeded in forcing their civilian victims into exile.

Facts like these pose a major challenge to world politics. Contemporary international order is based on a society of states that enjoy exclusive jurisdiction over a particular piece of territory and have rights to non-interference and non-intervention that are enshrined in the Charter of the United Nations. This system is in turn prefaced on the assumption – drawn from the famous Hobbesian 'state of nature' analogy – that states exist primarily to protect the security of their citizens. In other words, the security of the state is considered important, and worth protecting, because states provide security to individuals. It should be clear from the proceeding paragraph that this assumption is wrong. In the past century, threats to individual security have tended to come more from one's own state than from other states. This raises the question of whether there are circumstances in which the security of individuals should be privileged over the security of states? Should a state's right to be secure and free from armed attack be dependent on its fulfilment of certain responsibilities to its citizens, not least a responsibility to protect them from mass killing? Or, should the imperative of maintaining an international order with a basic degree of harmony between states override concerns about human security? It is these questions that animate the contemporary debate about humanitarian intervention.

This chapter provides an overview of the evolution of the debate between those who believe that the protection of civilians from genocide and mass atrocities ought to trump the principle of non-intervention in certain circumstances and those who oppose this proposition. I argue that since the end of the Cold War, a broad international consensus has emerged around a principle called 'responsibility to protect' (R2P), first developed by the International Commission on Intervention and State Sovereignty in 2001 (ICISS 2001). R2P holds that states have a responsibility to protect their citizens from genocide and mass atrocities and, when they fail to do so, that responsibility transfers to the international community, primarily as represented by the Security Council. This leaves unresolved the thorny question of what should happen when the Security Council chooses not to intervene in cases of genocide and mass atrocities – a theme discussed in detail by the ICISS in 2001, but omitted entirely from the international commitment to R2P in 2005 (United Nations General Assembly 2005). It is one thing to recognize the Security Council's responsibility and right to act in such cases, it is quite another thing to persuade it to do so. This chapter begins by evaluating the arguments put forward by both sides of the debate before focusing on the debate about the NATO intervention in Kosovo, which acted as a catalyst for the development of R2P. The chapter ends by examining the extent to which R2P has succeeded in finding a middle road between these different positions.

The case for intervention

The case for intervention is typically premised on the idea that external actors have a *duty* as well as a *right* to intervene to halt genocide and mass atrocities (e.g. Rawls 1999: 119). For advocates of this position, sovereignty should be understood as an instrumental value because it derives from a state's responsibility to protect the welfare of its citizens. As such, when states fail in their duty, they lose their sovereign right to non-interference and non-intervention (Tesón 2003: 93, 1998; Caney 1997: 32). There are various ways of arriving at this conclusion. Some liberal cosmopolitanists draw on Kant to insist that all individuals have certain pre-political rights that deserve protection (Caney 1997: 34). Many advocates of the Just War tradition writers arrive at a broadly similar position, but ground their arguments on theology. Paul Ramsey (2002: 20), for instance, used Augustine's insistence that force be used to defend or uphold justice to argue that intervention to end injustice was 'among the rights and duties of states until and unless supplanted by superior government'.

Political leaders who adopt this position tend to maintain that today's globalized world is so integrated that massive human rights violations in one part of the world have an effect on every other part, and that social interconnectedness itself creates moral obligations. The leading proponent of this view was former British Prime Minister Tony Blair. Shortly after NATO began its 1999 intervention in Kosovo, Blair gave a landmark speech setting out his 'doctrine of the international community' and endorsing the concept of sovereignty as responsibility (Blair 1999). Blair maintained that sovereignty should be reconceptualized because globalization was changing the world in ways that rendered traditional views of sovereignty anachronistic. He argued that global interconnectedness created two sets of responsibilities. First, paraphrasing John F. Kennedy, Blair argued that enlightened self-interest created international responsibilities for dealing with egregious human suffering, because in an interdependent world 'freedom is indivisible, and when one man is enslaved, who is free'. Second, sovereigns had responsibilities towards the society of states, because problems caused by massive human rights abuse in one place tended to spread across borders.

A further line of argument is to point to the fact that states have already agreed to certain minimum standards of behaviour and that humanitarian intervention is not about imposing the will of a few upon the many, but about protecting and enforcing the collective will of international society. Advocates of this position argue that there is a customary right (but not duty) of intervention in supreme humanitarian emergencies (Wheeler 2000: 14). They argue that there is agreement in international society that cases of genocide, mass killing and ethnic cleansing constitute grave humanitarian crises warranting intervention (see Arend and Beck 1993; Tesón 1997; Donnelly 1998). They point to state practice since the nineteenth century to suggest that there is a customary right of humanitarian intervention (Lepard 2002; Finnemore 2003). In particular, they point to the justifications offered to defend the US- and British-led intervention in Northern Iraq in 1991 to support their case. In that case, the British argued that they were upholding customary international law, France invoked a 'right' of intervention and the US noted a 're-balancing of the claims of sovereignty and those of extreme humanitarian need' (see Roberts 1993: 436–37).

This movement towards acceptance of a customary right of humanitarian intervention was reinforced by state practice after Northern Iraq. Throughout the Security Council's deliberations about how to respond to the Rwandan genocide in 1994, no state argued that either the ban on force (Article 2(4)) or the non-intervention rule (Article 2(7)) prohibited armed action to halt the bloodshed (see Barnett 2002), suggesting tacit recognition that armed intervention would have been legitimate in that case. Throughout the 1990s, the Security Council expanded its interpretation of 'international peace and security' and authorized interventions to protect civilians in safe areas (Bosnia); maintain law and order and protect aid supplies (Somalia); and restore an elected government toppled by a coup (Haiti) (see Roberts 1993; Findlay 2002; Morris 1995). These instances prompted Richard Falk (2003) to describe the 1990s as 'undoubtedly the golden age of humanitarian diplomacy', whilst Thomas Weiss (2004) argued that 'the notion that human beings matter more than sovereignty radiated brightly, albeit briefly, across the international political horizon of the 1990s'. Progress did not stop, however, at the turn of the century. Since 2000, the Security Council has on several occasions mandated peacekeepers to protect civilians under threat in the Democratic Republic of Congo, Burundi, Cote d'Ivoire, Liberia and Darfur (see Holt and Berkman 2006). What is more, since 2002, the UN's standard rules of engagement have permitted peacekeepers to use force for this purpose.

Although appealing, several aspects of this defence of humanitarian intervention are problematic. First, it is not self-evident that individuals *do* have pre-political rights. Parekh (1997: 54f.), for example, argues that liberal rights cannot provide the basis for a theory of humanitarian intervention because liberalism itself is rejected in many parts of the world. Second, critics argue that any norm endorsing the use of force to protect individual rights would be abused by powerful states, making armed conflict more frequent by relaxing the rules prohibiting it, but without making humanitarian intervention any more likely (Chesterman 2001; Thakur 2004).

Above all, however, is the charge that advocates of humanitarian intervention exaggerate the extent of consensus about the use of force to protect human rights. There is a gap between what advocates would like to be the norm and what the norm actually is. We should remember that the putative 'golden era' of humanitarianism included the world's failure to halt the Rwandan genocide; the UN's failure to protect civilians sheltering in its 'safe areas' in Bosnia; and the failure to prevent the widely predicted mass murder that followed East Timor's referendum on independence in 1999. The world stood aside as Congo destroyed itself, taking four million lives and – more recently – failed to halt the mass killing in Darfur. Moreover, closer inspection of the relevant cases from the 1990s suggests that the advances were more hesitant than implied by advocates of intervention. Most notably, the Security Council has still yet to authorize intervention against the wishes of a fully functioning sovereign state. The only instance of humanitarian action in such a case was NATO's intervention in Kosovo, and this was conducted without the consent of the Security Council. Finally, with the partial exceptions of Douglas Hurd's claim that the British were upholding customary international law in Northern Iraq, and Belgium's International Court of Justice defence of NATO's intervention in Kosovo, humanitarian interveners themselves have typically chosen not to justify their actions by reference to a new norm of humanitarian intervention, lest they encourage others to do likewise (see Wheeler 2000).

The case against intervention

Nowadays, only a handful of marginal states (Cuba, Iran, Venezuela and Zimbabwe) are prepared to argue that humanitarian intervention is *never* warranted. Even China (2005), the state most closely associated with the principle of non-interference, publicly acknowledges that massive humanitarian crises are a 'legitimate concern' for international society and that the Security Council is entitled to take action in such cases. Largely, therefore, contemporary opposition to humanitarian intervention focuses not on this, but on the questions of who can *legitimately authorize* intervention and *in what circumstances*.

Whilst advocates of intervention are prepared to acknowledge its legitimacy in certain cases even when it is not authorized by the Security Council, opponents maintain that international order requires something approximating an absolute ban on the use of force outside the two parameters set out by the UN Charter – Security Council authorization (Chapter VII) and self-defence (Article 51). The starting point for this position is the assumption that international society comprises a plurality of diverse communities, each of which has different ideas about the best way to live. According to this view, international society is based on rules – the UN Charter's rules on the use of force first among them – that permit coexistence (see Jackson 2002). In a world characterized by radical disagreements about how societies should govern themselves, proponents of this view hold that unfettered humanitarian intervention would create disorder as states waged wars to protect and violently export their own cultural preferences.

What is more, a right of unauthorized humanitarian intervention would open the door to potential abuse. Historically, states have shown a distinct predilection towards 'abusing' humanitarian justifications to legitimize wars that were anything but humanitarian. Most notoriously, Hitler insisted that the 1939 invasion of Czechoslovakia was inspired by a desire to protect ethnic German citizens of Czechoslovakia whose 'life and liberty' were threatened by their own government (in Brownlie 1974: 217–21). More recently, some commentators have argued that the US and UK abused humanitarian justifications in an ill-fated attempt to legitimize the 2003 invasion of Iraq, emphasizing the humanitarian case for war as it became clear that the other reasons given (the existence of Iraqi weapons of mass destruction or WMD) were fictitious and insufficient (cf. Morris and Wheeler 2006). It was precisely because of the fear that states would exploit any loophole in the ban on the use of force that the delegates who wrote the UN Charter issued a comprehensive ban with only two limited exceptions – force used in self-defence and under the authority of the Security Council. According to Chesterman, without this general ban, there would be *more war* in international society, but not necessarily more genuine humanitarian interventions. Chesterman argues that states do not refrain from intervening in humanitarian emergencies because they are constrained by law, but 'because states do not want them to take place' (Chesterman 2001: 231). Creating a humanitarian exception to the ban on force would not enable more humanitarian interventions, but it would make it easier for states to justify self-interested invasions through spurious humanitarian arguments. 'On balance', Franck and Rodley concluded in 1973, 'very little good has been wrought' in the name of humanitarian intervention (Franck and Rodley 1973: 278).

Finally, it is important to note that a majority of states continue to oppose humanitarian intervention – seeing it as a dangerous affront to another core principle, self-determination, which underpinned post-war decolonization. The General Assembly's 1970 Declaration on Principles of International Law Concerning Friendly Relations stated categorically that:

> No state or group of states has the right to intervene, directly or indirectly, for any reason whatever, in the internal or external affairs of any other state. Consequently, armed intervention and all other forms of interference or attempted threats against the personality of the state or against its political, economic and cultural elements, are in violation of international law.

This position was clearly in the ascendancy during the Cold War. In 1977, when Vietnam invaded Cambodia and ousted the murderous Pol Pot regime, which was responsible for the death of some two million Cambodians, it was condemned for violating Cambodian sovereignty. China's representative at the UN described Vietnam's act as a 'great mockery of and insult to the United Nations and its member states' and sponsored a resolution condemning Vietnam's 'aggression'. The US agreed. Its ambassador argued that the world could not allow Vietnam's violation of Cambodian sovereignty to 'pass in silence', as this 'will only encourage Governments in other parts of the world to conclude that there are no norms, no standards, no restraints' (Wheeler 2000: 90f.). France argued that 'the notion that because a regime is detestable, foreign intervention is justified and forcible overthrow is legitimate is extremely dangerous. That could ultimately jeopardize the very maintenance of law and order'. Norway, among others, agreed, admitting that it had 'strong objections to the serious violation of human rights committed by the Pol Pot government. However the domestic policies of that government cannot – we repeat cannot – justify the action of Viet Nam' (Chesterman 2001: 80).

And these sentiments persist today. More than 30 years after the Vietnamese experience, the Non-Aligned Movement (NAM) reaffirmed its commitment to the 1970 Declaration on Friendly Relations. In the Outcome Document of the movement's 2006 conference, the NAM's heads of state pledged to conduct their external relations in accordance with the principles set out by the 1970 Declaration (Non-Aligned Movement 2006: §§16.2 and 22.2).

Unsurprisingly, there are also a number of problems with these positions and alternative perspectives. First, its overriding assumption that states protect their citizens and cultural difference does not hold in every case, as the examples offered at the beginning of this chapter attest. Second, critics argue that this perspective overlooks the wealth of customary practice suggesting that sovereignty carries responsibilities as well as rights (see Tesón 1997). Third, although there are a number of notorious historical cases, the fear of abuse is exaggerated (Weiss 2004: 135). It is fanciful to argue that denying a state recourse to humanitarian justifications for war would make them less war prone – it is unlikely that either Hitler in 1939 or Bush and Blair in 2003 would have been deterred from waging war by the absence of a plausible humanitarian justification. In the case of Iraq, for instance, the coalition's legal defence rested on Iraq's non-compliance with past UN Security Council resolutions (see Bellamy 2003). Humanitarian justifications only came to the fore once this legal argument had been proven fallacious by the absence of Iraqi WMD. Fourth, this position overlooks the wide body of international law relating to basic human rights and the consensus on grave crimes such as genocide (see Scheffer 1992; Mertus 2000).

Almost all governments recognize that crimes such as genocide and mass killing are a legitimate concern for international society. Some governments, international officials, activists and analysts argue that sovereigns have a responsibility to protect their citizens from mass killing and other abuses, and when they fail to do so, others acquire a right to intervene. A majority of the world's governments, however, argue that this responsibility does not translate into a right of humanitarian intervention without the authority of the UN Security Council because that would contradict other cherished principles of international order, including the rule of non-aggression and the right to self-determination. Since the end of the Cold War, the UN Security Council has authorized collective intervention to protect populations from mass killing. In this sense, there is a norm of UN-sanctioned humanitarian intervention (Wheeler 2000), but it is heavily circumscribed in practice to cases where the host state has collapsed or where the recognized government is not the target of intervention and lends its support. This presents a dilemma about what to do in cases where some governments believe that intervention is warranted to save people from genocide and mass atrocities, but where there is no consensus in the Security Council. This dilemma was exposed by NATO's decision to intervene in Kosovo in 1999. The debate sparked by this constellation provided a catalyst for a fundamental reconsideration of the way that international society conceptualizes the problem of sovereignty and the protection of citizens.

Towards responsibility to protect

On 24 March 1999, NATO launched *Operation Allied Force* to prevent a humanitarian catastrophe in Kosovo caused by Serbian oppression. The intervention was not authorized by the Security Council, and NATO chose not to present a draft resolution because

433

Russia threatened to veto any resolution authorizing the use of force. NATO's intervention in Kosovo was therefore a significant test of the legitimacy of humanitarian intervention because it involved a group of states stepping outside the UN framework and using force to end a humanitarian emergency. A commission of experts found the intervention to be 'illegal but legitimate' (Independent International Commission on Kosovo 2000: 4), meaning that whilst it was not strictly legal, it was 'sanctioned by its compelling moral purpose' (Clark 2005: 212). Most NATO members chose not to defend the intervention on legal grounds, arguing instead that the ethnic cleansing of Kosovar Albanians by Serbian forces created a moral imperative to intervene.

The critical test came at the beginning of the intervention, when Russia introduced a draft Security Council resolution condemning the intervention. Surprisingly, given the widespread hostility to intervention detailed in the previous section, the draft resolution was emphatically rejected by 12 votes to three (Russia, China and Namibia). Although five of the 12 states that rejected the draft were NATO members, seven were not. What is remarkable is that those seven, which included states such as Malaysia that were traditionally sceptical about humanitarian intervention, chose to actively side with NATO rather than abstain (S/PV.3989, 26 March 1999). Although the failure of the Russian draft did not constitute retrospective authorization (see Wheeler 2001: 156), it did add credence to the claim that there is an emerging moral consensus about the right of intervention in extreme situations.

Significantly, support for NATO's action came from a variety of different states. The Organization of the Islamic Conference – normally a staunch defender of state sovereignty and the principle of non-interference – communicated its support for the intervention in a letter to the Security Council stating that: 'a decisive international action was necessary to prevent humanitarian catastrophe and further violations of human rights' in Kosovo (S/1999/363, annex, 31 March 1999). It should not be overlooked, however, that many, if not most, of the world's states rejected this view. In addition to the well-recorded hostility of Russia, China and India, the Non-Aligned Movement responded to Kosovo by declaring its rejection of 'the so-called right of humanitarian intervention, which has no legal basis' in its 2000 Cartagena Declaration.

The intervention sparked fierce debate at every level of the UN. Even the UN Secretariat was deeply divided. Some, such as UN Secretary-General Kofi Annan's special advisor John Ruggie, speechwriter Edward Mortimer and deputy Iqbal Rizza supported NATO. They argued that the Serbs and their supporters were using sovereignty as a veil to protect their gross human rights abuses. Others, such as Kieran Prendergast – the head of the Department of Political Affairs – and Sashi Tharoor – a future candidate for Secretary-General – criticized NATO's violation of Article 2(4) of the UN Charter banning the use of force (Traub 2006: 97). After the crisis had passed, Annan tackled the issue in his opening address to the 1999 General Assembly. Annan used the address to set out the problem and challenge world leaders to find a solution. It is worth citing the speech at length:

> To those for whom the greatest threat to the future of international order is the use of force in the absence of a Security Council mandate, one might ask … in the context of Rwanda: If, in those dark days and hours leading up to the genocide, a coalition of States had been prepared to act in defence of the Tutsi population but did not receive prompt Council authorization, should such a coalition have stood aside and allowed the horror to unfold?

To those for whom the Kosovo action heralded a new era when States and groups of States can take military action outside the established mechanisms for enforcing international law, one might ask: Is there not a danger of such interventions undermining the imperfect, yet resilient, security system created after the Second World War, and of setting dangerous precedents for future interventions without a clear criterion to decide who might invoke these precedents, and in what circumstances?'

(Annan 1999)

The Secretary-General argued that the state was the servant of the people and that the 'sovereignty of the individual' was enhanced by growing respect for human rights. State sovereignty therefore implied a responsibility to protect individuals. The role of the UN was to assist states in the fulfilment of their responsibilities and the achievement of their sovereignty. This much was clearly set out in the UN Charter, Annan reiterated. The question, however, was one of how to determine the 'common interest' in particular cases? In a case such as Kosovo, did sovereignty as a responsibility require intervention and, if so, who was entitled to decide? Answering his own questions, Annan developed three benchmarks. First, a principle of intervention should be 'fairly and consistently applied'. Second, it should embrace a 'more broadly defined, more widely conceived definition of national interest'. Third, the proper authority was the Security Council, but the Council should accept its responsibilities and make a commitment to respond to humanitarian emergencies. Repeating his warning to those who would stand in the way of genuine collective humanitarian action, Annan told the Assembly that 'if the collective conscience of humanity ... cannot find in the United Nations its greatest tribune, there is a grave danger it will look elsewhere for peace and for justice'.

Answering Annan's challenge, the baton was picked up by the Canadian government, which in 2000 announced the creation of the International Commission for Intervention and State Sovereignty (ICISS) charged with the task of finding a global consensus on humanitarian intervention. In 2001, the Commission – chaired by Gareth Evans and Mohamed Sahnoun – delivered a landmark report, called *The Responsibility to Protect*. The Commission argued that states have the primary responsibility to protect (hereafter R2P) their citizens. When they are unable or unwilling to do so, or when they deliberately terrorize their citizens, the 'the principle of non-intervention yields to the international responsibility to protect' (ICISS 2001: xi). R2P was intended as a way of escaping the irresolvable logic of 'sovereignty versus human rights' by focusing not on what interveners are entitled to do ('a right of intervention') but on what is necessary to protect people in dire need and the responsibilities of various actors to afford such protection. The ICISS argued that R2P was about much more than just intervention. In addition to a 'responsibility to react' (intervene) to massive human suffering, international society also had responsibilities to use a wide range of non-violent tools to prevent such suffering and rebuild polities and societies afterwards. The Commission also set out criteria for evaluating when intervention was warranted and a process for resolving the thorny question of authority in cases where the Security Council is blocked by a veto. It argued that Council members should refrain from vetoing humanitarian operations except when their vital national interests are involved and identified other potentially legitimate sources of authority (General Assembly, regional organizations) that could be turned to in cases where the Council was deadlocked.

After four years of intense lobbying and careful diplomacy, at the 2005 World Summit, the UN General Assembly unanimously committed itself to the principle of R2P (see

Bellamy 2006). Every government admitted that they had a responsibility to protect their citizens from genocide, war crimes, crimes against humanity and ethic cleansing, and that this responsibility transfers to the society of states as a whole in cases where the host government is unwilling or unable to discharge its duty. At their core, the World Summit's paragraphs on the Responsibility to Protect amounted to four commitments:

1 All states accept that they have a responsibility to protect their own citizens from genocide, ethnic cleansing, war crimes and crimes against humanity.
2 The international community [however defined] will encourage and assist states in the fulfilment of their responsibility, including by helping states to build the necessary capacity and assisting states under stress.
3 The international community has a responsibility to use diplomatic, humanitarian and other peaceful means to protect people from genocide, ethnic cleansing, mass atrocities and war crimes, through either the UN or regional arrangements.
4 The UN Security Council stands ready to use the full range of its Chapter VII powers, with the cooperation of regional organizations where appropriate, in cases where peaceful solutions are inadequate and national authorities manifestly fail to protect their citizens from genocide, war crimes, ethnic cleansing and crimes against humanity.

A year later, R2P was unanimously reaffirmed by the Security Council in Resolution 1674, which stated the Council's determination to protect civilians. Missing from the paragraphs of both texts, however, were the ICISS recommendations about criteria to guide decision-making on intervention and any acknowledgement of the possibility that unauthorized intervention might sometimes be legitimate. These are likely to remain controversial questions that can only be resolved on a case-by-case basis into the future (see Bellamy 2009). What the principle of R2P does, however, is to recalibrate the whole discussion about the best way of responding to genocide and mass atrocities away from the rights and wrongs of intervention towards questions about which measures are most likely to have the best protective effects in different circumstances.

The future challenge

The challenge now, as the current UN Secretary-General Ban Ki-moon has argued, is to translate R2P from words into deeds and to change the practice of how the world responds to genocide and mass atrocities. If the principle continues to develop and gain momentum, chapters about humanitarian intervention might become obsolete as global institutions, regional organizations and individual states develop the capacities to better prevent and respond to such crimes. It is not yet clear, however, whether changing the terms of debate has altered its fundamental logic. The test will come partly in how the world responds to new and emerging crises – and the slow, inadequate and half-hearted response to Darfur does not bode well in this regard – and partly in how successful UN reform is in building the necessary capacities and decision-making capabilities.

In relation to this latter issue, R2P has helped to move the agenda forward in at least three ways. First, by replacing old debates about 'humanitarian intervention' with a broad continuum of measures aimed first and foremost at preventing genocide and mass atrocities and, if that fails, protecting vulnerable populations, R2P can contribute to reducing 'moral hazards' associated with intervention (Kuperman 2008). When it is fully operational, R2P will enable international society to respond to crises before they descended into violence, thereby reducing the likelihood of international efforts inadvertently encouraging violent rebellion. Second, by incorporating political and diplomatic strategies alongside legal, economic and military options, R2P points towards holistic strategies of engagement that can overcome the temptation to conceive complex problems in exclusively military terms. In relation to Darfur and elsewhere, the almost exclusive focus on military solutions has inhibited efforts to build peace through political processes grounded in practical solution to local disputes (de Waal 2007). Third, by turning attention to the protection of civilians from genocide and mass atrocities, R2P provides a stimulus for new thinking about the practicalities of protection in the form of military doctrine and guidance for humanitarian agencies (e.g. Holt and Berkman 2006). If translated 'from words into deeds', these three contributions could deliver better protection to vulnerable populations and significantly advance the practice and politics of humanitarian intervention.

References

Annan, K. (1999) 'Annual Report of the Secretary-General to the General Assembly', 20 September.

Arend, A.C. and Beck, R.J. (1993) *International Law and the Use of Force: Beyond the UN Charter Paradigm*, London: Routledge.

Barnett, M. (2002) *Eyewitness to a Genocide: The United Nations and Rwanda*, Ithaca, NY: Cornell University Press.

Bellamy, A.J. (2003) 'International law and the war in Iraq', *Melbourne Journal of International Law* 4, 2: 497–520.

——(2005) 'Is the war on terror just?' *International Relations* 19, 3: 275–96.

——(2006) 'Whither the responsibility to protect? Humanitarian intervention and the 2005 World Summit', *Ethics and International Affairs* 20, 2: 143–69.

——(2009) *Responsibility to Protect: The Global Effort to End Mass Atrocities*, Cambridge: Polity Press.

Blair, T. (1999) 'Doctrine of the international community', speech to the Economic Club of Chicago, Hilton Hotel, Chicago, 22 April.

Brownlie, I. (1974) 'Humanitarian Intervention', in Moore, J.N. (ed.), *Law and Civil War in the Modern World*, Baltimore: Johns Hopkins University Press, pp. 217–21.

Caney, S. (1997) 'Human rights and the rights of states: Terry Nardin on non-intervention', *International Political Science Review* 18, 1: 12–37.

Chesterman, S. (2001) *Just War or Just Peace? Humanitarian Intervention and International Law*, Oxford: Oxford University Press.

China, Government of (2005) 'Position paper of the People's Republic of China on the United Nations reforms', 8 June.

Clark, I. (2005) *Legitimacy in International Society*, Oxford: Oxford University Press.

Coebergh, J. (2005) 'Sudan: The genocide has killed more than the tsunami', *Parliamentary Brief* 7, 9, London, February.

de Waal, A. (2007) 'Darfur and the failure of the responsibility to protect', *International Affairs* 83, 6: 1039–54.

Donnelly, J. (1998), *International Human Rights*, 2nd edn, Boulder: Westview.

Falk, R. (2003) 'Humanitarian intervention: A forum', *Nation*, 14 July.

Findlay, T. (2002) *The Use of Force in UN Peace Operations*, Oxford: Oxford University Press for the Stockholm International Peace Research Institute (SIPRI).

Finnemore, M. (2003) *The Purpose of Intervention: Changing Beliefs About the Use of Force*, Ithaca, NY: Cornell University Press.

Franck, T.M. and Rodley, N.S. (1973) 'After Bangladesh: The law of humanitarian intervention by military force', *American Journal of International Law* 67, 2: 275–305.

Holt, V.K. and Berkman, T.C. (2006) *The Impossible Mandate? Military* Preparedness, *The Responsibility to Protect and Modern Peace Operations*, Washington, DC: The Henry L. Stimson Centre.

Independent International Commission on Kosovo (IICK) (2000) *Kosovo Report: International Response, Lessons Learned*, Oxford: Oxford University Press.

International Commission on Intervention and State Sovereignty (ICISS) (2001) *The Responsibility to Protect*, Ottawa: International Development Research Center.

Jackson, R.H. (2002) *The Global Covenant: Human Conduct in a World of States*, Oxford: Oxford University Press.

Kaldor, M. (1999) *New and Old Wars: Organized Violence in a Global Era*, Cambridge: Polity Press.

Kuperman, A.J. (2008) 'The moral hazard of humanitarian intervention: Lessons from Bosnia', *International Studies Quarterly* 52, 1: 49–80.

Lepard, B. (2002) *Rethinking Humanitarian Intervention: A Fresh Legal Approach Based on Fundamental Ethical Principles in International Law and World Religions*, University Park: Pennsylvania State University Press.

Mertus, J. (2000) 'The legality of humanitarian intervention: Lessons from Kosovo', *William and Mary Law Review* 41, 4: 1743–87.

Morris, J. (1995) 'Force and democracy: The US/UN intervention in Haiti', *International Peacekeeping* 2, 3: 391–412.

Morris, J. and Wheeler, N.J. (2006) 'Justifying Iraq as a humanitarian intervention: The cure is worse than the disease' in Sidhu, W.P.S. and Thakur, R. (eds) *The Iraq Crisis and World Order: Structural and Normative Challenges*, Tokyo: United Nations University Press, pp. 163–75.

Non-Aligned Movement (2006) *Final Document of the 14th Summit Conference of Heads of State or Government of the Non-Aligned Movement*, Havana, Cuba, 11–16 September.

Parekh, B. (1997) 'Rethinking humanitarian intervention', *International Political Science Review* 18, 1: 49–69.

Ramsey, P. (2002) *The Just War: Force and Political Responsibility*, Lanham: Rowman and Littlefield.

Rawls, J. (1999) *The Law of Peoples*, Cambridge, MA: Harvard University Press.

Roberts, A. (1993) 'Humanitarian war: Military intervention and human rights', *International Affairs* 69, 3: 429–49.

Rummel, R.J. (1994) *Death by Government*, London: Transaction Press.

Scheffer, D.J. (1992) 'Towards a modern doctrine of humanitarian intervention', *University of Toledo Law Review* 23, 2: 253–93.

Tesón, F.R. (1997), *Humanitarian Intervention: An Inquiry into Law and Morality*, 2nd edn, New York: Transnational Publishers.

——(1998) *A Philosophy of International Law*, Boulder: Westview Press.

——(2003) 'The liberal case for humanitarian intervention' in Holzgrefe, J.L. and Keohane, R.O. (eds) *Humanitarian Intervention: Ethical, Legal and Political Dilemmas*, Cambridge: Cambridge University Press, pp. 93–129.

Thakur, R. (2004) 'Iraq and the responsibility to protect', *Behind the Headlines* 62, 1: 1–16.

Traub, J. (2006) *The Best of Intentions: Kofi Annan and the UN in an Era of American World Power*, London: Bloomsbury.

United Nations General Assembly (2005) *2005 Summit Outcome* A/60/L.1, 20 September.

Weiss, T.G. (2004) 'The sunset of humanitarian intervention? The responsibility to protect in a unipolar era', *Security Dialogue* 35, 2: 135–53.

Wheeler, N.J. (2000) *Saving Strangers: Humanitarian Intervention in International Society*, Oxford: Oxford University Press.

——(2001) 'The legality of NATO's intervention in Kosovo', in Booth, K. (ed.) *The Kosovo Tragedy: The Human Rights Dimensions*, London: Frank Cass.

40

Global governance

Thomas J. Biersteker[1]

Global governance is a permissive concept. Like globalization, with which it is often associated, the frequency with which global governance is invoked in the scholarly literature and in policy practice far exceeds the number of times it is precisely or carefully defined. As a result, the term 'global governance' is applied to a wide variety of different practices of order, regulation, systems of rule and patterned regularity in the international arena. It is permissive in the sense that it gives one license to speak or write about many different things, from any pattern of order or deviation from anarchy (which also has multiple meanings) to normative preferences about how the world should be organized.

This chapter begins, therefore, with an attempt to provide a general definition of the concept of global governance, with particular reference to the governance of security affairs. It then considers Inis Claude's classic three-fold typology for addressing the subject of power and international relations (Claude 1962), in which he distinguished analytically between balance-of-power systems, collective security arrangements and world government. It illustrates the application (and complex integration) of these general analytical frameworks, with specific reference to different historical periods of order and global governance over the course of the past two centuries. Next, it discusses how global governance is managed, from the international society of states (Bull 1977), to arguments about the importance of hegemony for order and governance (Gilpin 1975, 1981), international regimes (Keohane and Nye 1977), institutions (Keohane and Martin 1995; Martin 1992), international law (Abbott and Snidal 2000), global norms (Katzenstein 1996; Keck and Sikkink 1998; Finnemore and Sikkink 1998), or private authority (Cutler et al. 1999a; Hall and Biersteker 2002). The chapter concludes with a consideration of the increased salience of different institutional actors, particularly non-state actors, involved in contemporary global governance, and a comparison of different bases of governance.

Defining global governance

Global governance is often defined in terms of what it is not – neither a world government nor the disorderly chaos and anarchy associated with a Hobbesian 'state of war of all against all'. In one of the pioneering studies of global governance published in 1992, James Rosenau defined global governance in general terms as 'an order that lacks a centralized authority with the capacity to enforce decisions on a global scale' (Rosenau 1992: 7). His conception of global governance was that of a purposive order that exists for the management of interdependence in the absence of a global state. His definition is very broad and has relatively little to say about who or what makes decisions, or precisely how enforcement takes place.

Governance is derived from the Latin word *gubernator*, which is described both as a person who steers, and as a 'self-acting contrivance for regulating' to ensure an even and regular motion (Oxford English Dictionary 1971: 1182). This is an important distinction, and we will return to these two different aspects of how governance is accomplished in the discussion below. The Oxford English Dictionary (OED) defines governance as:

1   the idea of controlling, directing or regulating influence, as well as being subject to the control of another (a relational aspect);
2   the office, function, or power of governing;
3   the manner in which something is governed or regulated; and
4   the general conduct of life or business, demeanour, and 'discrete or virtuous behaviour', which adds a normative component to governance (Oxford English Dictionary 1971: 1181f.).

Drawing on the origin of the concept and the different aspects of governance identified above, it is possible to define global governance in general terms. Global governance requires first, some form of *patterned regularity* or order at the global level. Patterned regularity is a necessary, but not a sufficient, condition for global governance.

Second, following Rosenau, and with acknowledgement of Hedley Bull's important contribution (Bull 1977), global governance must be *purposive* and/or oriented toward the achievement of some goal or goals. In this sense, and integrating it with the first element, global governance is order, plus intentionality, at the global level.

Third, governance connotes a *system of rule*, or rules. Either these rules can be formal and embodied within formal institutions, or they can be informal and reside inter-subjectively among a population or a set of key institutional actors. Global governance entails decisions that shape and define expectations ('controlling, directing, or regulating influence') at the global level. There can be different degrees of institutionalization associated with different forms of governance, and there is much debate about whether formal or informal institutions are necessary for governance.

Fourth, the system of rule implied by global governance is *authoritative*, in the sense that there is a social relationship between the governed and some governing authority. Governance requires acceptance by a significant portion of some relevant population and therefore is 'as dependent on inter-subjective meanings as on formally sanctioned constitutions and charters' (Rosenau 1992: 4). Governments can persist without widespread popular support, but governance requires the performance of functions necessary for systemic persistence. Governance should not be equated with government, but with the functions of government.

Fifth and finally, as indicated above, given that the word governance is derived from the Latin word *gubernare* (both 'to steer' and 'to regulate'), it connotes some agent who *steers* the process and it also allows for *self-regulation*. In this sense, a market or set of market mechanisms can be said to govern.

Thus, global governance is an inter-subjectively recognized, purposive order at the global level, which defines, constrains and shapes actor expectations in an issue domain. It is a system of authoritative rule or rules (with varying degrees of institutionalization) that functions and operates at the global level. For a system of authoritative rules to operate at a global level, they do not need to be universally practised or universally recognized as legitimate. It merely requires that they be widely shared and practised on a global scale (on multiple continents) by relevant and important actors (Alker et al. forthcoming).

Types of global governance arrangements in security affairs

In *Power and International Relations*, Inis Claude differentiated between three heuristic ways to manage power in international relations – balance of power systems, collective security arrangements and world government (Claude 1962). He placed the three alternatives on a continuum, ranging from the least formally institutionalized arrangement (balance of power) on one end of the spectrum, to the most formally institutionalized (world government) on the other. Collective security arrangements were placed in the middle of the continuum. Each of the ideal types he sketched provides a basis for global governance of security affairs. They each entail an inter-subjectively recognized, purposive order at the global level, which shapes and defines actor expectations. Each is a system of authoritative rule or rules that functions and operates at the global level. They differ primarily according to their degrees of formal institutionalization.

In his analysis of the evolution of international society, Adam Watson developed a similar continuum to describe the spectrum of international systems, from the absolute independence of individual states at one end of the spectrum to absolute empire at the other (Watson 1992: 13). Following in the tradition of Hedley Bull, Watson argued that order promotes peace, but it does so at the price of independence and constraints on freedom of action of states (due to its association with greater degrees of institutionalization). Independence, however, also has its price, in terms of economic and military insecurity and as a result, states must form and rely upon alliances to provide for their security. Hegemony – where some power (or small group of powers) is able to 'lay down' the law – and suzerainty – where members of international society accept that hegemony as legitimate – are intermediate forms of global governance. Dominion and empire exist at the other end of Watson's continuum.

The principal basis for differentiation in both of these conceptions is the degree of institutionalization entailed in the governance arrangement. They are also differentiated by the principal mechanism of governance. Thus, both balance-of-power systems and state independence as arrangements for global security governance at one end of the continuum have relatively low levels of formal and informal institutionalization and are essentially regulated by a form of market mechanism. They are governed or regulated principally through the separate actions of individual state actors pursuing their own security interests. Kenneth Waltz, in *Theory of International Politics*, draws an explicit analogy to the market mechanism when he describes states interacting in the international system as analogous to firms in a market (Waltz 1979: 90f.). Like firms, states are in constant competition with one another, and pursue individual survival in a system without hierarchy, which he defines as anarchy.

At the other end of the continuum – whether it is in the form of dominion, empire or a world government – the systems of governance are essentially hierarchical, top-down

441

and highly institutionalized. They entail governance principally by governments (a single state in cases of dominion or empire, or a unitary government in the case of the world state). In dominion, imperial authority determines the internal government of other communities, but they maintain their identity. Empire exists when the direct administration of others is carried out from a unitary imperial centre. Both require high levels of institutionalized authority. The same would obviously be true of world government.

In between these two extremes of complete state independence and world government are a large variety of informal institutions, complex combinations of formal and informal institutional arrangements, and a wide range of different social networks. Rather than being regulated principally by market mechanisms or hierarchical institutions, these systems of governance are regulated by networks composed of key institutional actors, who share a common concern with a particular issue domain, but not necessarily a common approach or method for addressing it. Their authority is sometimes contested and different governance arrangements can often contradict one another. Networks are ideally 'forms of organization characterized by voluntary, reciprocal, and horizontal patterns of communication and exchange' (Keck and Sikkink 1998: 8), but there are also aspects of hierarchy in many networks. The recent popularity of the idea of public/private partnerships in global governance constitutes one contemporary form of network governance.

The period of US hegemony immediately following the Second World War was an example of a form of global governance situated in the space between state independence and formal hierarchy. In this case, a single power was able to shape and mould the primary institutions of global governance for most of the world, many of which persist, in revised form, to this day. Hegemony can be provided by a single state or by a relatively small group of states, such as the P-5, G-7, G-8 or G-20, which have adapted and extended the system originally developed under US hegemony over the course of the past 60 years. As will be discussed in more detail below, hegemony is only one basis for this intermediate form of global governance between independent states and a world state.

Hierarchical governance is probably the most efficient, but it is actually relatively rare in the international system. Market governance is more widespread, but less guided, steered or reliable. Network governance is the most common form of contemporary global governance, but its effectiveness and reliability are also highly variable and uncertain. Table 40.1 summarizes this analytical framework for characterizing different global governance arrangements.

Different periods in time may be associated with the general predominance of one or another of these forms of global governance. At a very general level, balance of power systems (in at least two different forms) are often associated with the nineteenth century (Schroeder 1989), while collective security arrangements are associated with the twentieth century, from their initial articulation and introduction immediately following the First World War in the League of Nations to their broadened institutionalization after the Second World War in the form of the collective security mechanisms of the UN Security Council. This characterization is highly over-simplified and can be somewhat misleading, however. In any given period, there is a complex blend of overlapping forms of global security governance, with different systems and elements of different systems co-existing in complex, and sometimes contradictory, ways.

Thus, the balance-of-power systems of the nineteenth century should be differentiated by their degree of informal institutionalization. The Concert system of the first half of

Table 40.1 Analytical Framework for Characterizing Types of Global Governance Arrangements

Inis Claude	Balance of Power Systems	Collective Security Arrangements	World Government
Adam Watson	Independent States	Hegemony Suzerainty	Dominion Empire
Degree of Formal and Informal Institutionalization	Low	Medium	High
Principal Mechanism of Governance	Market	Network	Hierarchy

that century with its periodic meetings and assemblies of representatives of the Great Powers was far more institutionalized than the competitive balance-of-power system that emerged at the end of the century (Schroeder 1989). The post-First World War period cannot be equated with the idea of collective security, since several major powers used the League of Nations for maintaining the post-war distribution of power and never fully accepted its mechanisms for collective security (Wolfers 1966). Similarly, the post-Second World War period is best characterized as a fusion of elements of institutionalized collective security (the UN Security Council and its mandate to maintain international peace and security) with balance-of-power considerations that acknowledged power differentials at the time of its creation (the designation of Permanent Members of the UN Security Council and the veto power granted to them). Because of its institutionalization of balance-of-power considerations, the UN did not operate as it was originally intended to function in the security domain – as an effective institution of collective security imposing sanctions and authorizing peacekeeping operations – until after the end of the Cold War, when the bipolar confrontation between the US and Russia came to an end.

Different bases of global governance

Global governance in the security domain exists largely within the broad area between market-regulated systems of balance of power (with sharply articulated state independence) and formal hierarchical systems associated with empire or world government. Much of the theoretical and policy debate about forms of global governance revolves around the different (and often interconnected) bases of governance: the society of states, hegemony, international regimes, institutions, international law, global norms or private authority. Indeed, much of the scholarly literature in International Relations is devoted to debates about the bases of global governance. Below, the broad outlines of each are briefly sketched.

The international society of states

For Hedley Bull, the principal basis of global governance is to be found in the evolving institution of the *society of states*. He terms this 'the anarchical society', because its core units are independent states coexisting in a situation of anarchy (defined as the absence of a central authority). He draws on the work of Hugo Grotius to argue that 'that states and the rulers of states in their dealings with one another were bound by rules and together formed a society' (Bull 1977: 72). The definition of global governance presented above is built on the foundation provided by Bull. He defined order in terms of a relationship, pattern and regularity, and stressed its purposive nature (that is, the way it promotes certain primary goals and/or values).

Global governance for Bull refers principally to the system of informal diplomatic rules and practices that regulates interstate interaction. The existence of interstate communication and diplomatic envoys does not constitute international society. International society requires reciprocal recognition of rules and of like rights and duties, such as diplomatic recognition, diplomatic immunity and the exchange of ambassadors. The society of states is differentiated from the system of states in that it involves more than states in regular contact with each other. Rather, it entails states in regular contact, but also conscious of, and bound by, common interests, values and/or rules in their relationships (Bull 1977: 16).

Christian Reus-Smit develops Bull's concept of the international society of states (Reus-Smit 1997), arguing that contractual international law and multilateralism constitute deep structural elements underlying contemporary international society. Constitutional structures at the international level originate within the domestic cultures of dominant states (like the US after the Second World War), but once embedded in the practices of other states, the values inherent within those constitutional structures condition the behaviour of all states and provide a basis for global governance. For Reus-Smit, 'constitutional structures' (1997: 556) are coherent ensembles of inter-subjective beliefs, principles and norms that define both what constitutes a legitimate actor and the basic parameters of rightful state action. They incorporate three inter-subjective normative elements: (1) beliefs about the moral purpose of the state, (2) an organizing principle of differentiation (sovereignty) and (3) a norm of pure procedural justice (Reus-Smit 1997: 566ff.).

The principal goals of the society of states are to preserve the society of states; maintain the survival, independence and sovereignty of the individual states that constitute the society; limit state violence; and provide for global public goods, such as the protection of property rights. The form of global governance provided by the society of states does not require formal, international institutions, but international law plays a central role as an institution of international society. The international society of states is historically grounded in Western Europe, and one of its principal contemporary challenges is the expansion of international society to the rest of the world (Bull and Watson 1984).

Hegemony

State *hegemony* provides the basis for another form of global governance. Both the hegemony of England in the nineteenth century and the hegemony of the US in the twentieth century provided global leadership and underwrote the provision of collective goods, backed by their considerable political, economic and military resources. State hegemony is a relatively hierarchical basis for global governance that is maintained by structural power (Strange 1986), indicated by leadership and, occasionally, operated with ideological hegemony, where direct coercion is rare and the leadership of the hegemon is widely accepted by other states (Cox 1987). Thus, hegemony has three facets of meaning: capabilities, leadership and ideological dominance.

For Charles Kindleberger, writing about the governance of the global economy (Kindleberger 1973), and for Robert Gilpin, who extended Kindleberger's conception to the governance in the global security domain (Gilpin 1981), the essence of hegemony is political leadership of the hegemonic state and is indicated by its willingness to underwrite the costs of maintaining the governance of the economic, political and/or military order. Among the different things a hegemon can do in the security domain is to use coercion (based on a predominance of power), employ persuasion (with credibility), provide leadership in the form of public goods and subsidize transaction costs. In the economic sphere, the hegemon is expected to prevent others from constructing trade and investment barriers, manage the world economy and perform as an engine of growth for the rest of the global economy.

Hegemonic stability theory developed in the context of a widely shared consensus in the 1970s that the US was in relative decline from its position of global hegemony established in the immediate aftermath of the Second World War. There was a broad concern among hegemonic stability theorists that as a hegemon declines, the order and global governance it provided would naturally begin to break down (Kindleberger 1973; Gilpin 1975, 1981).

Because of its central focus on power and power relations, looking to hegemony as the basis for global governance has special appeal for analysts in the tradition of political realism. As Gilpin and others associated with hegemonic stability theory clearly realized, however, relative power distribution is constantly undergoing change (both in perception and in reality). The difficulty of accurately gauging the significance of US decline in the 1970s was emphasized by critics in the 1980s (Strange 1986; Nau 1990), and the idea of US hegemonic decline seemed almost anachronistic following the end of the Cold War in the 1990s. In addition, as liberal institutionalists argued, international regimes could provide an alternative basis for global governance, even after hegemony.

International regimes

The concept of international regimes cannot be fully understood outside the context of the debate about hegemonic decline and hegemonic stability. While Robert Gilpin worried about the consequences of US decline and/or the potential temptation for the US to become a rogue hegemon, liberal institutionalists like Robert Keohane argued that international regimes could persist even without a hegemon (Keohane 1984). Processes of path dependence ensured that once the institutions of global governance had been created under hegemonic authority, it would take a great deal to dismantle them. As long as the demand for regimes was sustained, they would continue. It is easier to maintain existing international regimes than to create new ones, but it was possible to imagine that new regimes could also be created to govern different issue domains, even after hegemony.

Regimes are defined as 'sets of implicit or explicit principles, norms, rules, and decision-making procedures around which actors' expectations converge in a given area of International Relations' (Krasner 1983b: 2). Principles are beliefs of fact, causation and rectitude. Norms are standards of behaviour defined in terms of rights and obligations. Violation of norms is frowned upon, even though they are occasionally broken. They are not inviolable, but there is a general sense that they ought to be followed. Rules are specific prescriptions or proscriptions for action, and decision-making procedures are prevailing practices for making and implementing collective choices. International regimes tend to be far broader in scope than individual international organizations because they entail norms, legal conventions, general beliefs, a variety of different practices and the presence of other institutional actors.

International regimes are widely associated with the governance of the global economy, but the concept has been extended into the security domain, with consideration of the non-proliferation, arms control, peacebuilding and counterterrorism regimes. International organizations, such as the International Atomic Energy Agency (IAEA), may institutionally embody many of the central concepts, norms and practices associated with the non-proliferation regime, but they cannot be equated with it.

There has been a great deal of debate about the direct and indirect influence of international regimes, measured principally in terms of their effects on individual states (Haggard and Simmons 1987). They are said to function by lowering the costs of cooperation, providing a forum for bargaining, increasing information, providing links that enable trade-offs (for example, trade access for alliance participation) and affecting the reputation of states. Regimes constrain states by increasing the costs of defection from agreements enforced by regimes, and they therefore provide an institutionalized basis for global governance.

Institutions

Institutions are closely related to the operation of international regimes, and when defined broadly (Keohane 1988; Young 1992), they are nearly identical to them. Robert Keohane defines institutions as 'related complexes of rules and norms, identifiable in space and time' (1988: 383). Institutions provide a system of authoritative rules at the global level and can provide a basis for governance by defining, constraining and shaping actor expectations in different domains.

Individuals associated with the tradition of political realism contend that institutions have no direct effect on state behaviour and operate largely at the margins of International Relations (Mearsheimer 1994: 7). Institutions are viewed as the product of the most powerful states, and they tend to reflect the prevailing distribution of power in the world. States choose to obey them, if they wish.

Institutionalists argue that institutions provide an important basis for global governance. Institutions such as multilateralism can provide solutions to a variety of different dilemmas of strategic interaction (Martin 1992: 766). States demand institutions because they solve collective action problems. One of the best indicators that institutions matter to states is that governments continue to invest in them (Keohane and Martin 1995: 40f.). Institutionalists do not restrict their claims to the international political economy and argue that the division between security and economics is largely specious (Keohane and Martin 1995: 43f.). Institutions play a critical role in providing information in both domains. The salience of relative gains is contextual – it depends on the number of major actors in the system and on the question of whether military advantage favours offence or defence. Institutions reduce incentives for states to cheat, lower transaction costs, link issues and provide focal points for cooperation.

International law

Although they are widely viewed as principal components of international regimes, both international law (which represents a formalization of rules) and global norms (which approximate informal rules) can serve as bases for global governance.

International law represents a codification of rules governing the behaviour of major institutional actors, particularly that of independent states. In their work on law in international governance, Kenneth Abbott and Duncan Snidal distinguish between what they term 'hard' and 'soft' law (Abbott and Snidal 2000). Hard law refers to legally binding obligations that are precise and restrict behaviour and sovereignty. EU human rights law, which is backed by the European Court of Justice, is an example of hard law. Soft law refers to a weakening of hard law along one (or more) of three dimensions: obligation, precision or delegation (Abbott and Snidal 2000: 422). If obligation, precision and/or delegation are absent, as they often are in practice, there is still a form of legalization present. Abbott and Snidal make this distinction not only to illustrate the variety in degrees of legalization, but also to illustrate how widespread legalization has become globally. The UN Charter's injunction against state aggression, the international Convention on the Prevention and Punishment of the Crime of Genocide, the Non-Proliferation Treaty and the activities of the International Criminal Court are all examples of soft international law that govern the security domain.

Legalization is a distinctive form of institutionalization. It is also one of the principal methods by which states increase the credibility of their commitments to each other. Powerful states can resist international law, but they often have a significant stake in (and benefit from) hard legalization. They can also benefit from soft legalization because contracting costs can be lowered; sovereignty costs can be limited; uncertainty can be reduced; bargaining problems can be eased; compromises can be achieved over time; and compromises can be facilitated between strong and weak states.

Global norms

Global norms are another central component of international regimes. They constitute the ideational or normative underpinnings for governance. Adherence to norms is one of the best empirical indicators of the presence of global governance. Norms are standards of appropriate behaviour for actors with a given identity (Finnemore and Sikkink 1998: 891). Finnemore and Sikkink distinguish between different categories of norms: regulative, constitutive and prescriptive. Regulative norms both order and constrain behaviour and are most closely associated with conceptions of global governance. Constitutive norms create new actors, interests, identities or categories of actors. Prescriptive norms establish what 'ought' to be done. Neta Crawford makes a distinction between norms as common practice and normative beliefs based on ethical prescriptions, but she also notes that 'international relations theorists frequently use "norms" to denote both senses' (Crawford 2002: 40).

Norms can provide a basis for global governance, because they define, constrain and shape actor expectations in an issue domain. If norms are internalized within major players, they become an authoritative base for a system of rules that operate at the global level. Finnemore and Sikkink argue that norms emerge at the global level through a multi-stage process: from the phase of norm emergence, where norm entrepreneurs frame issues and use organizational platforms to articulate norms, to the phase of norm cascade, where imitation, threshold points, contagion, peer pressure, conformity and self-esteem all play a role in norm dissemination. Once norms develop to a stage where they are taken for granted, where they become naturalized or unquestioned, where institutions embody them in their rules and structures, and where they take on the force of law, they can be said to be internalized (Finnemore and Sikkink 1998: 895).

International norms are widespread and increasingly visible in the governance of the security domain – from justifications for the use of force and proportionality in war (derived from just war theory and practices) to proscriptions against the use of torture, norms against the first use of nuclear weapons, and in support of the idea of sovereign responsibility to protect. These norms are often contested and reside at different places in Finnemore and Sikkink's three-stage process described above. Even before they are internalized, however, they provide a basis for global governance (considered as an inter-subjectively recognized, purposive order at the global level).

Private authority

Most of the forms of global security governance considered up to this point (with the possible exception of global norms), are based on relations between states or evaluated exclusively in terms of their influence on state behaviour. Private sector actors also provide forms of governance, typically in association with states, but occasionally on their own. Private authority in the global political economy has received the most attention, from self-binding codes of conduct and standards setting schemes to coordinated lobbying efforts, independent rating and assessment agencies, and private regimes (Cutler et al. 1999a). These are all instances where private-sector actors take the lead in establishing norms, rules and institutions that guide (or steer) behaviour (Cutler et al. 1999b: 4).

The idea of private authority in global governance has also been extended into the global security realm (Hall and Biersteker 2002; Avant 2005). A great variety of non-state actors are engaged in multilateral global governance, from advocacy networks like the International Campaign to Ban Landmines to public policy think tanks, private military companies, militia groups and warlords, transnational movements engaged in the commitment of acts of terrorism and, in some instances, even mafias and vigilante groups. They can be said to be authoritative because they establish standards, provide social welfare, enforce contracts, maintain security for certain populations and offer an alternative basis for global governance. Authority requires both the consent of, and recognition by, a part of the population governed by that authority. It entails a social relationship.

Advocacy networks and think tanks establish their authority through the operation of transnational advocacy networks (Keck and Sikkink 1998) and through the authority of their expertise (Hall and Biersteker 2002: 14). Transnational movements committing acts of terrorism on a global scale also legitimate themselves on the basis of their claims of 'expertise' in interpreting different religious texts. Private military companies typically have authority delegated to them by states (Avant 2005: 87), though there can be instances when they operate without it. Militias and warlords function at times like quasi-states or emergent states, taxing local populations and providing public goods such as security. Vigilante groups and criminal organizations operate in the shadowy world between coercion and legitimate authority. It is often difficult to draw the line between them, but the extent to which vigilantes and criminal organizations provide public security, reinforce contracts and create employment opportunity provides a base from which they can establish public recognition and consent.

Private authority in the security domain emerges when states delegate it, enable it or passively allow it to develop. It can also develop in spaces where the state has abdicated from its responsibilities, and in some instances, it can be seized from the state. Although private actors are increasingly playing authoritative roles in the security domain, their role in global governance is most apparent in transnational advocacy networks and the articulation of an alternative basis for global governance.

Conclusion

Although the realm of global governance has traditionally been occupied predominantly by states and inter-governmental organizations, a variety of different institutional actors, particularly non-state actors, are increasingly playing a salient role in contemporary global governance. They articulate alternative forms of governance, play active roles in formulating the agenda and create spaces where a purposive order of authoritative sets of rules can be articulated and established. They are altogether absent in the form of governance provided by the international society of states and largely invisible in the governance provided by state hegemony, but they are principal players in the production of international norms and obviously in the realm of private authority. Other bases of governance – regimes, institutions and international law – tend to be composed of a mixture of the two, with states predominating in most.

With regard to the mechanisms of governance, there is again a range – from hierarchy in hegemonic systems to networks in governance by global norms and international society. Private authority, international law, regimes and institutions as bases of governance tend to be governed by a combination of both hierarchy and network.

With regard to the degree of formal institutionalization, there is again wide variation, both between different bases of governance and within them. International society and private authority operate with relatively low levels of formal institutionalization at the global level, while most forms of hegemony are associated with high degrees of formal institutionalization. Regimes, institutions, law and norms tend to operate at an intermediate level of formal institutionalization, with a mix of formal and informal institutional arrangements. Table 40.2 compares and contrasts different bases of global governance.

The variety of different bases for identifying and comprehending forms of contemporary global security governance – the society of states, hegemony, regimes, institutions, law, norms and private authority – illustrate well the complexity of the subject, as well as the range of institutional players involved. Global governance in most issue domains is provided by a complex combination of these different bases, rather than by any single one of them. In spite of all of the disorder and complexity associated with global security issues, however, there is a great deal of purposive and authoritatively rule-governed order present in the contemporary international system. It is not always a very a just or efficient system of governance, but it is governance nevertheless, and is central to any understanding of attempts to address contemporary security challenges.

Table 40.2 Comparing different Bases of Global Governance

What Governs?	International Society	Hegemony	Regimes & Institutions	Law & Norms	Private Authority
Who Governs?	States (exclusively)	State(s)	States (primarily)	States & NGOs	Firms, NGOs, Non-State Armed Groups
Principal Governance Mechanism	Network	Hierarchy	Hierarchy & Market	Hierarchy & Networks	Networks & Hierarchy
Degree of Formal Institutionalization	Low	High	Medium	Medium	Low

Note

1 I would like to thank Myriam Dunn Cavelty, Victor Mauer and Georg von Kalckreuth for their comments on an earlier draft of this essay. I would also like to acknowledge and thank the students of Multilateral Governance and International Organizations at the Graduate Institute, Geneva in 2007 and 2008 for posing challenging questions that shaped some of the ideas contained in this essay.

References

Abbott, K. and Snidal, D. (2000) 'Hard and soft law in international governance', *International Organization* 54, 3: 421–56.

Alker, H., Amin, T., Biersteker, T. and Inoguchi, T. (forthcoming) *The Dialectics of World Orders*.

Avant, D. (2005) *The Market for Force: The Consequences of Privatizing Security*, Cambridge: Cambridge University Press.

Bull, H. (1977) *The Anarchical Society: A Study of Order in World Politics*, New York: Columbia University Press.

Bull, H. and Watson, A. (eds) (1984) *The Expansion of International Society*, Oxford: Clarendon Press.

Claude, I. (1962) *Power and International Relations*, New York: Random House.

Cox, R. (1987) *Production, Power, and World Order: Social Forces in the Making of History*, New York: Columbia University Press.

Crawford, N. (2002) *Argument and Change in World Politics: Ethics, Decolonization, and Humanitarian Intervention*, Cambridge: Cambridge University Press.

Cutler, C., Haufler, V. and Porter, T. (eds) (1999a) *Private Authority and International Affairs*, Albany, NY: State University of New York Press.

——(1999b) 'Private authority and international affairs', in Cutler, C., Haufler, V. and Porter, T. (eds) *Private Authority and International Affairs*, Albany, NY: State University of New York Press, pp. 3–28.

Finnemore, M. and Sikkink, K. (1998) 'International norm dynamics and political change', *International Organization* 52, 4: 887–917.

Gilpin, R. (1975) *US Power and the Multinational Corporation: The Political Economy of Foreign Direct Investment*, New York: Basic Books.

——(1981) *War and Change in World Politics*, Cambridge and New York: Cambridge University Press.

Haggard, S. and Simmons, B. (1987) 'Theories of international regimes', *International Organization* 41, 3: 491–517.

Hall, R. and Biersteker, T. (eds) (2002) *The Emergence of Private Authority in Global Governance*, Cambridge and New York: Cambridge University Press.

Katzenstein, P. (ed.) (1996) *The Culture of National Security: Norms and Identity in World Politics*, New York: Columbia University Press.

Keck, M.E. and Sikkink, K. (1998) *Activists Beyond Borders: Advocacy Networks in International Politics*, Ithaca, NY: Cornell University Press.

Keohane, R. (1984) *After Hegemony: Cooperation and Discord in the World Political Economy*, Princeton: Princeton University Press.

——(1988) 'International institutions: Two approaches', *International Studies Quarterly* 32, 4: 379–96.

Keohane, R. and Martin, L. (1995) 'The promise of institutionalist theory', *International Security* 20, 1: 39–51.

Keohane, R. and Nye, J. (1977) *Power and Interdependence: World Politics in Transition*, Boston: Little, Brown and Co.

Kindleberger, C. (1973) *The World in Depression, 1929–1939*, Berkeley: University of California Press.

Krasner, S. (ed.) (1983a) *International Regime*, Ithaca, NY: Cornell University Press.

——(1983b), 'Structural causes and regime consequences: Regimes as intervening variables', in Krasner, S. (ed.) *International Regimes*, Ithaca, NY: Cornell University Press, pp. 1–22.

Martin, L. (1992) 'Interests, power and multilateralism', *International Organization* 46, 4: 765–92.

Mearsheimer, J. (1994) 'The false promise of international institutions', *International Security* 13, 3: 5–26.

Nau, H. (1990) *The Myth of America's Decline: Leading the World Economy into the 1990s*, Oxford: Oxford University Press.

Oxford English Dictionary (1971) *Complete Text, Volume I (A-O)*, Oxford: Oxford University Press.

Reus-Smit, C. (1997) 'The constitutional structure of international society and the nature of fundamental institutions', *International Organization* 51, 4: 555–89.

Rosenau, J. and Czempiel, E.-O. (eds) (1992) *Governance without Government: Order and Change in World Politics*, Cambridge: Cambridge University Press.

Rosenau, J. (1992) 'Governance, order and change in world politics', in Rosenau, J. and Czempiel, E.-O. (eds) *Governance without Government: Order and Change in World Politics*, Cambridge: Cambridge University Press, pp. 1–29.

Schroeder, P. (1989) 'The nineteenth century system: Balance of power or political equilibrium?' *Review of International Studies* 15, 2: 135–54.

Strange, S. (1988) *States and Markets*, London: Pinter.

Waltz, K. (1979) *Theory of International Politics*, Reading: Addison-Wesley.

Watson, A. (1992) *The Evolution of International Society: A Comparative Historical Analysis*, London and New York: Routledge.

Wolfers, A. (1966) *Britain and France Between Two Wars: Conflicting Strategies of Peace from Versailles to World War II*, New York: W.W. Norton.

Young, O. (1992) 'The effectiveness of international institutions: Hard cases and critical variables', in Rosenau, J. and Czempiel, E.-O. (eds) *Governance without Government: Order and Change in World Politics*, Cambridge: Cambridge University Press, pp. 160–94.

41

The study of crisis management

Arjen Boin, Magnus Ekengren and Mark Rhinard

It has become a staple of conventional wisdom to note that long-standing security paradigms are no longer adequate for explaining our rapidly changing world. As traditional military threats take a backseat to 'new' threats ranging from suicidal terrorism to climate change, conventional conceptions of security are rethought and refashioned. This new thinking is prompting national and international security organizations to reform, retool and recast.

This chapter summarizes key findings of crisis management research and explores the relevance of these findings for the security community. Scholars in this community have traditionally focused on existential threats to the nation-state. With its strong foundation in International Relations theory, the discipline of Security Studies has investigated how stability and peace depends on the levels of mutual confidence among nations. Since the early 1990s, they have begun to study other threat agents and other referent objects of security. The interdisciplinary field of crisis management research concentrates on a society's efforts to prepare for, and deal with, urgent threats to its core values and life-sustaining systems. It comprises theoretical and empirical findings that help us understand how societies can protect themselves against a wide variety of hazards, be they man-made or natural in origin.

The overview of this research area follows three steps: Section 1 briefly reflects on the concept of 'crisis' and presents an overview of the various schools of thought on crisis development and crisis management. Section 2 discusses the various *causes* of crisis. Section 3 offers a framework for understanding the *response* to emerging threats. This chapter concludes by considering the complementary nature of crisis management research and Security Studies.

Studying crisis: schools of thought

There are many definitions of crisis, but most contain three elements: threat, urgency and uncertainty. Using these elements, we define a crisis as 'a serious threat to the basic structures or the fundamental values and norms [of a society], which under time pressure and highly uncertain circumstances necessitates making vital decisions' (Rosenthal et al. 1989: 10).

This definition of crisis covers a wide variety of adversity: natural disasters and environmental threats; financial meltdowns and surprise attacks; terrorist attacks and hostage-takings; epidemics and exploding factories; infrastructural dramas and organizational decline. What these events have in common is that they create impossible conditions for those who seek to manage the response operation and to make urgent decisions – all while essential information about causes and consequences remains unavailable.

In the field of crises and crisis management studies, a variety of perspectives or 'schools' can be discerned. We will briefly mention the schools that appear relevant for the security field.

Crisis has been a key concept in sociology since Durkheim founded the discipline. In sociological terms, crisis marks the phase during which order-inducing institutions stop functioning – the threat of anomie lurks in the background. The empirical and theoretical findings of disaster research are particularly relevant. The thorough understanding of collective behaviour, disaster myths and the pathologies of top-down coordination in times of adversity has proved particularly fruitful to understanding crisis dynamics (Rodriguez et al. 2006).

Another subfield of sociology – organization theory – has produced one of the most powerful theories informing crisis studies. In *Normal Accidents*, Charles Perrow (1999) applied two wholesale sociological concepts (complexity and coupling) to explain organizational breakdown. This and other similar work in organization theory helped raise a fundamental debate about the feasibility and desirability of entrusting dangerous technology to large-scale bureaucracies (Sagan 1993; *Journal of Contingencies and Crisis Management* 1994; Chiles 2001).

Scholars working within the field of International Relations (IR) have studied crises and crisis management from two different angles. The first angle uses a decision perspective to study international crises. This body of richly documented studies has taught us much about leadership behaviour in times of crisis (Hermann 1972; Craig and George 1983; Janis et al. 1987) as well as dynamic interaction between parties (Brecher 1993). In explaining the escalation and outcomes of international conflicts, IR scholars study how pervasive perceptions, bureau-politics and small-group dynamics affect the critical decisions made during a crisis (Allison 1971; Jervis 1976; Lebow 1981; George 1991).

A second group of IR scholars has conceived of crises as part of a growing number of problems that threaten national security. Even before the end of the Cold War, scholars within the field of Security Studies began to criticize the exclusive focus on military issues (Buzan 1983; Ullman 1983). They argued that attitudes on the nature of security differed dramatically across peoples and countries; in many areas, contingencies like severe weather or energy shortages created as much insecurity and posed as great a threat to the viability of societies as foreign armies.

When the prospect of a global nuclear conflagration faded after the Cold War, a litany of pre-existing problems stood out in sharper relief. Scholars turned their attention to what might be loosely called 'new security' challenges, ranging from civil or ethnic conflict, resource scarcity, environmental degradation and uncontrolled migration to organized crime, international terrorism and drug trafficking (Walt 1991; Baldwin 1995). Scholars in this field studied how security policy elites struggle to design an effective policy response to such threats (Stares 1998; Bigo 2000), why such threats become subjectively 'securitized' (Buzan et al. 1998; Huysmans 1998) and how governments prepare for the prospect of crises and 'failed security' (Relyea 2003). This development provides a clear parallel with the field of crisis research, where the crisis concept encompasses a wide variety of threats.

Another group of scholars from the discipline of social psychology study how crisis managers make critical decisions under stress (Janis and Mann 1977; Holsti 1979). Their work shows that group decisions do not necessarily compensate for the shortcomings in the decision-making process of the stressed individual (Janis 1982; 't Hart 1994; 't Hart et al. 1997). In addition, psychologists have done important work that helps us understand the relation between human error, technology, organizational culture and the development of crises (Reason 1990). The natural decision-making perspective shows that well-trained operators make crisis decisions in a very particular way (Flin 1996; Klein 2001): they compare their situational assessment with mental images of similar situations (they select the decision that comes with the slide that matches their assessment). This tells us that crisis decision-making differs quite dramatically from the incremental, semi-rationalistic way in which routine decisions tend to be made.

In the field of communications studies, interesting work is being done on the relation between crisis actors, political stakeholders, the media and civilians (Fearn-Banks 1996; Seeger et al. 2003). This body of research helps us understand why sound decisions may or may not help to manage a crisis, depending on the way they are communicated. It helps us understand how media 'frames' shape crisis reports, which, in turn, affect general perceptions of the crisis and the authorities managing it.

Our *tour d'horizon* would not be complete without mentioning the field of risk studies, itself an interdisciplinary social-scientific endeavour (Pidgeon et al. 2003). It studies why and how people act on negligible risks (avoiding flying) while they ignore others (smoking, driving without seatbelts). The cutting-edge researchers in this field try to calculate risks in order to help policymakers make decisions on baffling issues such as genetically modified food, environmental pollution or space travel. The risk field is thus complementary to crisis research: risk researchers map potential threats, whereas crisis researchers are more concerned with how society can prepare for, and cope with, risks that actually materialize.

These various schools have built an impressive body of theoretical and empirical research findings. In the following sections, we will explore how these findings enhance our understanding of the *causes and patterns* of crises. In addition, we will use these findings to construct a framework that helps us analyse governmental *responses* to all kinds of crises.

Causes of crisis

Crises are the result of three types of causes. First, there are threat agents. It suffices to note here that these agents may take all kinds of forms (ranging from earthquakes to human errors). The second cause lies in the characteristics of complex and tightly coupled systems, which allows traditional threat agents to escalate in unforeseen and often incomprehensible ways. The third cause of the crisis lies in the inability of a social unit (an organization, town or country) to recognize the emerging threat and nip it in the bud.

Threat agents typically remain unnoticed, or key policymakers fail to attend to them (Turner 1978). In the process leading up to a crisis, these seemingly innocent factors combine and transform into an undeniable threat to the system. These factors are referred to as pathogens, as they are present long before the crisis becomes manifest (Reason 1990).

As socio-technical systems become more complex and increasingly connected (tightly coupled) to other (sub-)systems, their vulnerability to disturbances increases (Turner 1978; Perrow 1999). The more complex a system becomes, the harder it is for anyone to understand it in its entirety. Tight coupling between a system's component parts with those of other systems allows for the rapid proliferation of interactions (and errors) throughout the system.

Complexity and lengthy chains of accident causation do not remain confined to the world of high-risk technology. Consider the financial crises that have rattled the global markets in recent years (Eichengreen 2002). Globalization and ICT have tightly connected most world markets and financial systems. As a result, a minor problem in a seemingly isolated market can trigger a financial meltdown in markets on the other side of the globe. Structural vulnerabilities in relatively weak economies such as Russia, Argentina or Turkey may suddenly 'explode' on Wall Street and cause worldwide economic decline.

All this makes a crisis hard to detect. As complex systems cannot be easily understood, growing vulnerabilities go unrecognized. Ineffective attempts to deal with seemingly minor disturbances 'fuel' the lurking crisis. Only a minor 'trigger' is needed to initiate a destructive cycle of escalation, which may then rapidly spread throughout the system. Crises may have their roots far away (in a geographical sense) but they can rapidly snowball through global networks, jumping from one system to another and gathering destructive potential along the way.

One might argue that modern society is better equipped than ever to deal with routine failures: sophisticated hospitals, computers and telephones, fire trucks and universities, regulation and funds – these factors have helped to minimize the scope and number of crises that were once routine events (Wildavsky 1988). Others argue that the resilience of modern society – its capacity to bounce back and return to normalcy – has deteriorated: when a threat (e.g. an electrical power outage) does materialize, the most modern systems suffer most. Citizens and organizations in modern Western cities are not used to coping with a sudden absence of amenities. It remains unclear what can be done to enhance a society's capacity to be resilient in the face of disaster. This is a matter of concern: modern society continues to build houses, factories and supporting infrastructures in places that are proven from historical experience to be fraught with risk, while scenarios of future crises promise more mayhem (Quarantelli et al. 2006).

A different but equally important cause of a crisis lies in the inability to recognize emerging threats in time. There are at least three reasons why many potential crises fail to be recognized.

First, threats to shared values or life-sustaining functions cannot always be recognized before their disastrous consequences materialize. In many cases, as the crisis process begins to unfold, policymakers fail to notice anything out of the ordinary. Everything still seems to be in order, even though hidden interactions eat away at the underlying pillars that uphold a system. It is only when the crisis is in full swing and becomes manifest that policymakers can recognize it for what it is.

The second reason is found in the contested nature of crisis. A crisis rarely, if ever, 'speaks for itself'. The definition of a situation is, as social scientists say, the outcome of a subjective process. More often than not, people will differ in their perception and appreciation of a threat. In fact, we might say that crisis definitions are continuously

455

subjected to the forces of politicization (Edelman 1977). Crises can have a discrediting effect on policies and institutions, as the perceived underperformance of government agencies undermines their legitimacy. This creates opportunities for opponents of the status quo to propose reforms that in normal times would be politically unfeasible (Boin et al. 2008).

Even if there were a consensus that a serious threat is emerging, the status of this new problem is far from assured. Governments deal with urgent problems every day; as such, attention devoted to one problem detracts attention from another one (Jones and Baumgartner 2005). For a threat to be recognized as a crisis and placed on the urgent policy agenda, it must clear many cognitive, political and institutional hurdles (Bovens and 't Hart 1996; Birkland 1997).

All this has clear implications for a society's ambitions and efforts to prevent crises. While societies can and should try to prevent crises that are to be expected (building levees to prevent flooding, for instance), it would be an illusion to think that a society can be made 'crisis free'. New threat agents will develop in unforeseen ways and will not be recognized until their consequences are felt. Therefore, societies have to invest in crisis management capacities. We turn to this topic in the next section.

Crisis management: crucial challenges for leadership

The challenges of crisis management appear to be increasing. This is not necessarily because the mechanisms of crisis have changed. Crisis management has become more challenging because the democratic context has changed over the past decades. Analysts agree, for instance, that citizens and politicians alike have become at once more fearful and less tolerant of major hazards to public health, safety and prosperity. At the same time, citizens and politicians routinely and collectively ignore seemingly 'objective' threats such as global climate change, nuclear proliferation, energy shortages and political violence.

In contemporary Western society, crisis management should not be viewed just in terms of the coping capacity of governmental institutions and public policies; it should be considered a deeply controversial and intensely political activity (Habermas 1975; Edelman 1977; 't Hart 1993). This section presents a framework for understanding and analysing what are considered the five critical challenges for crisis management: sense making, decision-making, meaning making, terminating and learning (Boin et al. 2005).

Sense making

In the previous section, it was noted that policymakers often find it hard to recognize (from vague, ambivalent and contradictory signals) that something out of the ordinary is developing. Crisis scholars have identified a variety of reasons that explain why these officials fail to 'make sense' of information that in hindsight appears painfully obvious.

The bewildering pace, ambiguity and complexity of a crisis tends to overwhelm normal modes of situation assessment. Stress may further impair sense-making abilities. The organizations in which crisis managers typically function tend to produce additional barriers to crisis recognition. In fact, research shows that organizations are unable to detect even the simplest incubation processes, i.e. those processes in which a threat emerges based on just a few causal factors, along a predictable pattern and given a long lead-time (Wilensky 1967; Turner 1978; Kam 1988).[1]

Some researchers also point to organizations that have developed a proactive culture of 'looking for problems' in their environment. These so-called high reliability organizations have somehow developed a capacity for thorough yet fast-paced information processing under stressful conditions. The unresolved question is whether organizations can design these features into existing organizational cultures (Weick and Sutcliffe 2002).

Critical decisions and coordination

Crisis decisions involve tough value tradeoffs and major political risks (Janis 1989; Brecher 1993). Interestingly, many pivotal crisis decisions are *not* taken by individual leaders or by small informal groups of senior policymakers. They emerge from various alternative loci of decision-making and coordination ('t Hart et al. 1993). In fact, the crisis response in modern society is best characterized in terms of a network comprising a wide variety of response organizations that rarely work with each other.

An effective response therefore requires interagency and intergovernmental coordination: only when response organizations work together is there a chance that critical decisions will be implemented effectively. Getting public bureaucracies to adapt to crisis circumstances is a daunting – some say impossible – task. Most public organizations were originally designed to conduct routine business in accordance with such values as efficiency, fairness and lawfulness. The management of crisis, however, requires flexibility, improvisation, redundancy and the breaking of rules. These are skills that may be acquired through training and simulations (Boin et al. 2004).

Coordination is not a self-evident feature of crisis management operations. The question of who is in charge typically arouses great passions. In disaster studies, the 'battle of the Samaritans' is a well-documented phenomenon: agencies mobilizing different resources for coping with a crisis find it difficult to align their actions. Sensitivities and conflicts that governed the daily relations between authorities and others before the crisis do not simply disappear (Rosenthal et al. 1989).

A truly effective crisis response is to a large extent the result of a naturally evolving process.[2] It cannot be managed in a linear, step-by-step and comprehensive fashion from a single crisis centre, however well endowed it may be with top-level decision-makers and state-of-the-art information technology. There are simply too many hurdles that separate a leadership decision from its timely execution in the field ('t Hart et al. 1993).

Meaning making

Once a crisis has materialized, leaders are expected to reduce uncertainty and provide an authoritative account of what is going on, why it is happening and what needs to be done. Once they have arrived at a situational appraisal and made strategic policy choices, leaders must get others to accept their definition of the situation. They must impute 'meaning' to the unfolding crisis in such a way that their efforts to manage it are enhanced. If they do not, or if they do not succeed at doing so, their decisions will not be understood or respected. If other actors in the crisis succeed in dominating the meaning-making process, the ability of incumbent leaders to decide and manoeuvre is severely constrained.

Two problems often recur. First, public leaders are not the only ones trying to frame the crisis. Their messages coincide and compete with those of other parties, who are likely to espouse various alternative definitions of the situation and advocate different

457

courses of action. Censoring them is hardly a viable option in a democracy. Second, authorities cannot always provide accurate information right away. They struggle with mountains of raw data (reports, rumours, pictures) that are quickly amassed during a crisis. Turning data into a coherent picture of the situation is a major challenge in its own right. Communicating such a picture to the public in the form of accurate, clear and actionable information requires a major public relations effort. This effort is often hindered by the aroused state of the audience: people whose lives are deeply affected tend to be anxious if not stressed. Moreover, they do not necessarily see the government as their ally. Pre-existing feelings of distrust towards a government do not evaporate in times of crisis (Rosenthal et al. 1989).

Terminating a crisis

Governments – at least democratic ones – cannot afford to stay in crisis mode forever. A sense of normalcy will have to return sooner or later. It is a critical leadership challenge to make this happen in a timely and expedient fashion. Crisis termination must be managed on two levels. It is done by shifting back from emergency to routine mode. This requires some form of downsizing of crisis operations. At the strategic level, it is about rendering an account of what has happened and gaining acceptance for that account.

The burden of proof in accountability discussions lies with leaders: they must establish beyond doubt that they cannot be held responsible for the occurrence or escalation of a crisis. These accountability debates can easily degenerate into 'blame games' with a focus on identifying and punishing 'culprits' rather than discursive reflection about the full range of causes and consequences.

Crisis leaders can be competent and conscientious, but that alone says little about how their performance will be evaluated when the crisis is over. Crises have winners and losers, and it is all too easy to fall on the losing side. Policymakers and agencies that have failed to perform their duties prior to or during critical moments need not despair, however: if they 'manage' the political game of the crisis aftermath well, they may prevent losses to their reputation, autonomy and resources. The political (and legal) dynamics of the accountability process determines which crisis actors end up where (Brändström and Kuipers 2003; Boin et al. 2008).

Learning

The final challenge consists of drawing political and organizational lessons. A crisis offers a reservoir of potential lessons for contingency planning and training for future crises. One would expect those involved in crises to study these lessons and feed them back into organizational practices, policies and laws.

Lesson drawing is one of the most underdeveloped aspects of crisis management (Lagadec 1997; Stern 1997). In addition to cognitive and institutional barriers to learning, lesson drawing is constrained by the fact that the question of *which* lessons are drawn influences how the crisis affects a society. Crises become part of collective memory, a source of historical analogies for future leaders (Khong 1992; Sturken 1997). The political depiction of crisis as a product of prevention and foresight failures would force people to rethink the assumptions on which pre-existing policies and rule systems rest. Other stakeholders in the game of crisis-induced lesson drawing might seize upon the lessons to advocate measures and policy reforms that incumbent leaders reject. Leaders thus have a big stake in steering the lesson-drawing process in strategic directions. The crucial challenge is to ensure that feedback streams generated by a crisis are channelled to support pre-existing policy networks and public organizations.

The documentation of these constraints has done nothing to dispel the near-utopian belief in crisis *opportunities*, an assumption found not only in academic literature but also in popular wisdom (Boin and 't Hart 2003). A crisis is seen as a good time to clean up and start anew. Crises represent discontinuities that must be seized upon – a true test of leadership, the experts claim. US President George W. Bush is a good example: in the wake of the 2001 attacks, the president introduced several reforms (the Uniting and Strengthening America by Providing Appropriate Tools Required to Intercept and Obstruct Terrorism (USA PATRIOT) Act of 2001, the new Department of Homeland Security) that would prove revolutionary and redefine the US's approach to security threats. Crisis research suggests, however, that crises generate just as many constraints as opportunities in their aftermath.

Conclusion: the crisis approach reconsidered

The crisis approach outlined in this chapter provides a framework for understanding the dynamic evolution of crises and the challenges of public crisis management. The past years (notably since 11 September 2001) have brought a wider understanding by policymakers of the intersecting challenges of public crisis management and security policy, prompting scholars to follow suit. Several conceptual overlaps and opportunities for dialogue across scholarly disciplines are worth summarizing here.

First, crisis scholars remind us that even the wealthiest and most competent government imaginable can never guarantee that major disruptions will not occur. Policymakers cannot rely on crisis prevention alone. Crisis prevention is a necessary and indeed vitally important strategy, but it pertains only to known emergencies – those that have already occurred. Complex, unknown crises require a strategy of resilience and preparation (Wildavsky 1988). This type of thinking is fairly new in the Security Studies community, and could usefully inform analyses of how governments address complex security threats (and how governments might avoid the 'failures of imagination' that can afflict their approaches to security policymaking). At a more practical level, crisis management scholars help to complement security policy scholars by identifying with greater precision the mix of policies, organizations and tools (both military and civilian) needed to manage today's complex threats.

Second, crisis scholars, not unlike some security policy scholars, propose that the concept of 'crisis' is a label, or a semantic construction used to characterize situations or epochs that are somehow regarded as extraordinary, volatile and potentially far-reaching in their negative implications. The intensity or scope of a crisis is thus not solely determined by the nature of the threat, the level of uncertainty or the time available to decision-makers. A crisis is to a considerable extent what people make of it. Policymakers cannot focus solely on 'objective' threats. They will have to take into account the perceptions of citizens, which may not correlate with threats as suggested by 'experts'. Security studies scholars working in a constructivist vein will see affinities between this approach and their own. The crowded security agenda following the end of the Cold War, and its increased complexity after 11 September 2001, means that public crisis management scholars and traditional security policy scholars interested in threat perceptions are studying the same empirical 'threat space'.

Third, crisis management research has remained fairly agnostic about power relationships in the making and implementation of policies designed to protect people (some of the classic IR studies of crisis decision-making during the Cold War have much to say about this topic). Although a number of studies have examined the political dynamics that unfold during a crisis, less attention has been paid to the more fundamental social interests that 'win' or 'lose' as part of a governments' approach to modern crisis management. As a consequence, public crisis management analysis sometimes smacks of a technocratic approach. Moreover, proposed solutions may appear 'technically' sound, but may be difficult to apply in practice and divorced from questions of the distribution of authority and power in a society. Security researchers, with their traditional focus on power and trust in the highly unpredictable international arena, can provide valuable insights to the field of crisis management research.

Scholars on both sides should be encouraged to borrow tools and concepts from one another to enrich their analysis. The erosion of the traditional distinction between domestic and international politics, between internal and external security, and between threats 'at home' versus those 'abroad' are likely to facilitate closer interaction between the two disciplines. This will not come a minute too soon, as security policy and crisis management are becoming increasingly alike in a world of globalized threats and challenges.

Notes

1 Some categories of people are known for their ability to keep their cool and to stay clear-headed under pressure. They have developed a mode of information processing that enables competent performance under crisis conditions (Flin 1996; Klein 2001). This quality is often seen in veteran military officers, journalists, and fire and police commanders.
2 See, for instance, the improvised response in New York City to the attacks on the World Trade Center on 11 September 2001 (Kendra and Wachtendorf 2003).

References

Allison, G.T. (1971) *Essence of Decision: Explaining the Cuban Missile Crisis*, Boston: Little Brown.
Baldwin, D.A. (1995) 'Security studies and the end of the Cold War', *World Politics* 48, 1: 117–41.
Beck, U. (1992) *Risk Society: Towards a New Modernity*, London: Sage Publications.
Bigo, D. (2000) 'When two become one: Internal and external securitizations in Europe', in Kelstrup, M. and Williams, M. (eds) *International Relations Theory and the Politics of European Integration*, London: Routledge, pp. 171–204.
Birkland, T. (1997) *After Disaster: Agenda-Setting, Public Policy, and Focusing Events*. Washington: Georgetown University Press.
Boin, R.A. and 't Hart, P. (2003) 'Public leadership in times of crisis: Mission impossible?', *Public Administration Review* 63, 6: 544–53.
Boin, R.A., Kofman-Bos, C. and Overdijk, W.I.E. (2004) 'Crisis simulations: Exploring tomorrow's vulnerabilities and threats', *Simulation and Gaming: An International Journal of Theory, Practice and Research* 35, 3: 378–93.
Boin, R.A., McConnell, A. and 't Hart, P. (eds) (2008) *Governing after Crisis: The Politics of Investigation, Accountability and Learning*, Cambridge: Cambridge University Press.
Boin, R.A., 't Hart, P., Stern, E. and Sundelius, B. (2005) *The Politics of Crisis Management: Public Leadership under Pressure*, Cambridge: Cambridge University Press.

Bovens, M. and 't Hart, P. (1996) *Understanding Policy Fiascoes*, New Brunswick: Transaction Publishers.

Brändström, A. and Kuipers, S.L. (2003) 'From "normal incidents" to political crises: Understanding the selective politicization of policy failures', *Government and Opposition* 38, 3: 279–305.

Brecher, M. (1993) *Crises in World Politics: Theory and Reality*, Oxford: Pergamon Press.

Buchanan, M. (2000) *Ubiquity: Why Catastrophes Happen*, New York: Three Rivers Press.

Buzan, B. (1983) *People, States and Fear: The National Security Problem in International Relations*, Brighton: Wheatsheaf.

Buzan, B., Waever, O. and de Wilde, J. (1998) *Security: A New Framework for Analysis*, Boulder: Lynne Rienner.

Columbia Accident Investigation Board (CAIB) (2003) *Columbia Accident Investigation Report 1*, Burlington: Apogee Books.

Chiles, J.R. (2001) *Inviting Disaster: Lessons from the Edge of Technology*, New York: Harper Business.

Craig, G.A. and George, A.L. (1983) *Force and Statecraft: Diplomatic Problems of Our Time*, Oxford: Oxford University Press.

Edelman, M.J. (1977) *Political Language: Words that Succeed and Policies that Fail*, New York: Academic Press.

Eichengreen, B. (2002) *Financial Crises: And what to do about them*, New York: Oxford University Press.

Fearn-Banks, K. (1996) *Crisis Communications: A Casebook Approach*, Mahwah: Lawrence Erlbaum Associates.

Flin, R. (1996) *Sitting in the Hot Seat: Leaders and Teams for Critical Incidents*, Chichester: Wiley.

George, A.L. (ed.) (1991) *Avoiding War: Problems of Crisis Management*. Boulder: Westview Press.

Habermas, J. (1975) *Legitimation Crisis*, Boston: Beacon Press.

't Hart, P. (1993) 'Symbols, rituals and power: The lost dimension in crisis', *Journal of Contingencies and Crisis Management* 1, 1: 36–50.

——(1994) *Groupthink in Government: A Study of Small Groups and Policy Failure*, Boston: Johns Hopkins University Press.

't Hart, P., Rosenthal, U. and Kouzmin, A. (1993) 'Crisis decision making: The centralization thesis revisited', *Administration and Society* 25, 1: 12–45.

't Hart, P., Stern, E.K. and Sundelius, B. (eds) (1997) *Beyond Groupthink: Political Group Dynamics and Foreign Policymaking*, Ann Arbor: University of Michigan Press.

Hermann, C.F. (ed.) (1972) *International Crises: Insights from Behavioral Research*, New York: The Free Press.

Holsti, O.R. (1979) 'Theories of crisis decisionmaking', in Lauren, P.G. (ed.) *Diplomacy: New Approaches in History, Theory, and Policy*, New York: The Free Press, pp. 99–136.

Hughes, E.C. (1946) 'Institutions in process', in McClung Lee, A. (ed.) *New outline of the Principles of Sociology*, New York: Barnes & Noble, Inc., pp. 236–47.

Huysmans, J. (1998) 'Security! What do you mean? From concept to thick signifier', *European Journal of International Relations* 4, 2: 226–55.

Janis, I.L. (1982) *Groupthink*. Boston: Houghton Mifflin.

——(1989) *Crucial Decisions: Leadership in Policymaking and Crisis Management*, New York: The Free Press.

Janis, I.L. and Mann, L. (1977) *Decision-Making: A Psychological Analysis of Conflict, Choice and Commitment*. New York: The Free Press.

Janis, I.L., Herek, G.M. and Huth, P. (1987) 'Decisionmaking during international crises: Is quality of process related to outcome?', *Journal of Conflict Resolution* 31, 2: 203–26.

Jervis, R. (1976) *Perception and Misperception in International Politics*, Princeton: Princeton University Press.

Jones, B. and Baumgartner, F. (2005) *The Politics of Attention: How Government Prioritizes Problems*, Chicago, IL: University of Chicago Press.

Journal of Contingencies and Crisis Management (1994) 'Systems, organizations and the limits of safety: Symposium', 2, 4: 205–40.

Kam, E. (1988) *Surprise Attack*, Cambridge: Harvard University Press.

Khong, Y.F. (1992) *Analogies at War: Korea, Munich, Dien Bien Phu, and the Vietnam Decisions of 1965*, Princeton: Princeton University Press.

461

Kendra, J.M. and Wachtendorf, T. (2003) 'Elements of resilience after the World Trade Center disaster: Reconstituting New York City's emergency operations center', *Disasters* 27, 1: 37–53.

Klein, G. (2001) *Sources of Power: How People make Decisions*, 7th edn, London: MIT Press.

Lagadec, P. (1997) 'Learning processes for crisis management in complex organizations', *Journal of Contingencies and Crisis Management* 5, 1: 24–31.

Lebow, R.N. (1981) *Between Peace and War: The Nature of International Crisis*, Baltimore: Johns Hopkins University Press.

Perrow, C. (1999) *Normal Accidents: Living with High-Risk Technologies*, 2nd edn, Princeton: Princeton University Press.

Pidgeon, N., Kasperson, R.E. and Slovic, P. (eds) (2003) *The Social Amplification of Risk*, Cambridge: Cambridge University Press.

Reason, J. (1990) *Human Error*, New York: Cambridge University Press.

Relyea, H.C. (2003) 'Organizing for homeland security', *Presidential Studies Quarterly* 33, 3: 602–24.

Rodriguez, H., Quarantelli, E.L. and Dynes, R.R. (eds) (2006) *Handbook of Disaster Research*, New York: Springer.

Rosenthal, U., Boin, R.A. and Comfort, L.K. (eds) (2001) *Managing Crises: Threats, Dilemmas, Opportunities*, Springfield: Charles C. Thomas.

Rosenthal, U., Charles, M.T. and 't Hart, P. (eds) (1989) *Coping with Crisis: The Management of Disasters, Riots and Terrorism*, Springfield: Charles C. Thomas.

Sagan, S.D. (1993) *The Limits of Safety: Organizations, Accidents and Nuclear Weapons*, Princeton: Princeton University Press.

Schwartz, R. and Sulitzneanu-Kenan, R. (2004) 'Managerial values and accountability pressures: Challenges of crisis and disaster', *Journal of Public Administration Research and Theory* 14, 1: 79–102.

Seeger, M.W., Sellnow, T.L. and Ulmer, R.R. (2003) *Communication and Organizational Crisis*, Westport: Praeger.

Stares, P.B. (1998) *The New Security Agenda: A Global Survey*, New York: Japan Center for International Exchange.

Stern, E.K. (1997) 'Crisis and learning: A balance sheet', *Journal of Contingencies and Crisis Management* 5, 2: 69–86.

Sturken, M. (1997) *Tangled Memories: The Vietnam War, the AIDS Epidemic, and the Politics of Remembering*, Berkeley: University of California Press.

Turner, B.A. (1978) *Man-Made Disasters*, London: Wykeham.

Ullman, R. (1983) 'Redefining security', *International Security* 8, 1: 129–53.

Walt, S. (1991) 'The renaissance of security studies', *International Studies Quarterly* 35, 2: 211–39.

Weick, K.E. and Sutcliffe, K.M. (2002) *Managing the Unexpected: Assuring High Performance in an Age of Complexity*, San Francisco: Jossey-Bass.

Wildavsky, A.B. (1988) *Searching for Safety*, Berkeley: University of California Press.

Wilensky, H. (1967) *Organizational Intelligence: Knowledge and Policy in Government and Industry*, New York: Basic Books.

Bibliography: selected readings

Part I: Theoretical approaches to security and different 'securities'

Adler, E. (1997) 'Seizing the middle ground: Constructivism in world politics', *European Journal of International Relations* 3, 3: 319–63.

Adler, E. and Barnett, M. (eds) (1998) *Security Communities*, Cambridge: Cambridge University Press.

Aradau, C. and van Munster, R. (2007) 'Governing terrorism through risk: Taking precautions, (un) knowing the future', *European Journal of International Relations* 13, 1: 89–115.

Ayoob, M. (1995) *The Third World Security Predicament: State Making, Regional Conflict, and the International System*, Boulder, CO: Lynne Rienner.

Baldwin, D.A. (1995) 'Security studies and the end of the Cold War', *World Politics* 48, 1: 117–41.

——(1995) *Neorealism and Neoliberalism: The Contemporary Debate*, New York: Columbia University Press.

——(1997) 'The concept of security', *Review of International Studies* 23, 1: 5–26.

Bellamy, A.J. (ed.) (2005) *International Society and its Critics*, Oxford: Oxford University Press.

Bigo, D. (2008) 'International political sociology', in Williams, P. (ed.) *Security Studies: An Introduction*, London: Routledge, pp. 116–30.

Booth, K. (1991) 'Security and emancipation', *Review of International Studies* 17, 4: 313–26.

——(ed.) (2005) *Critical Security Studies and World Politics*, Boulder, CO: Lynne Rienner.

——(2007) *Theory of World Security*, Cambridge: Cambridge University Press.

Brooks, S.G. and Wohlforth, W.C. (2005) 'Hard times for soft balancing', *International Security* 30, 1: 72–108.

——(2009) *World Out of Balance: International Relations Theory and the Challenge of American Primacy*, Princeton, NJ: Princeton University Press.

Bull, H. (1977) *The Anarchical Society: A Study of Order in World Politics*, London: Macmillan.

Buzan, B. (1991) *People, States and Fear: An Agenda for International Security Studies in the Post-Cold War Era*, Hemel Hempstead: Harvester-Wheatsheaf.

——(2004) *From International to World Society? English School Theory and the Social Structure of Globalisation*, Cambridge: Cambridge University Press.

Buzan, B., Wæver, O. and de Wilde, J. (1998) *Security: A New Framework for Analysis*, Boulder, CO: Lynne Rienner.

Campbell, D. (1992) *Writing Security: United States Foreign Policy and the Politics of Identity*, Minneapolis, MN: University of Minnesota Press.

C.A.S.E. Collective (2006) 'Critical approaches to security in Europe: A networked manifesto', *Security Dialogue* 37, 4: 443–87.

Clark, I. (2005) *Legitimacy in International Society*, Oxford: Oxford University Press.

——(2007) *International Legitimacy and World Society*, Oxford: Oxford University Press.

Der Derian, J. (1995) 'The value of security: Hobbes, Marx, Nietzsche, and Baudrillard', in Lipschutz, R.D. (ed.) *On Security*, New York: Columbia University, pp. 24–45.

Der Derian, J. and Shapiro, M.J. (eds) (1989) *International/Intertextual Relations: Postmodern Readings of World Politics*, Lexington: Lexington Books.

Dillon, M. (1996) *The Politics of Security: Towards a Political Philosophy of Continental Thought*, London: Routledge.

Doyle, M.J. and Ikenberry, G.J. (1997) *New Thinking in International Relations Theory*, Boulder, CO: Westview Press.

Doyle, M.W. (1997) *Ways of War and Peace: Realism, Liberalism and Socialism*, New York: W.W. Norton.

Dunne, T. (1998) *Inventing International Society: A History of the English School* London: Macmillan, St Antony's Series.

Dunne, T., Kurki, M. and Smith, S. (eds) (2007) *International Relations Theories: Discipline and Diversity*, Oxford: Oxford University Press.

Elshtain, J.B. (1987) *Women and War*, New York: Basic Books.

Enloe, C. (1990) *Bananas, Beaches and Bases: Making Feminist Sense of International Politics*, Berkeley, CA: University of California.

Galtung, J. (1984) *There are Alternatives: Four Roads to Peace and Security*, Nottingham: Spokesman.

Gilpin, R.G. (1982) *War and Change in World Politics*, Cambridge: Cambridge University Press.

Hansen, L. (2006) *Security as Practice: Discourse Analysis and the Bosnian War*, London: Routledge.

Hoffmann, S. (1987) *Janus and Minerva: Essays in the Theory and Practice of International Politics*, Boulder, CO: Westview Press

Huysmans, J. (1998) 'Security: What do you mean? From concept to thick signifier', *European Journal of International Relations* 4, 2: 226–55.

Jervis, R. (1976) *Perception and Misperception in International Politics*, Princeton, NJ: Princeton University Press.

——(1986) 'Cooperation under the security dilemma.' *World Politics* 30, 4: 167–214.

Katzenstein, P.J. (ed.) (1996) *The Culture of National Security: Norms and Identity in World Politics*, New York: Columbia University Press.

Kaufman, S.J., Little, R. and Wohlforth, W.C. (eds) (2007) *The Balance of Power in World History*, Basingstoke: Palgrave Macmillan.

Keohane, R.O. (1984) *After Hegemony: Cooperation and Discord in the World Political Economy*, Princeton, NJ: Princeton University Press.

——(ed.) (1986) *Neorealism and its Critics*, New York: Columbia University Press.

Keohane, R.O. and Nye, J.S. (1977) *Power and Interdependence: World Politics in Transition*, Boston, MA: Little Brown.

Krause, K. and Williams, M.C. (eds) (1997) *Critical Security Studies: Concepts and Cases*, London: UCL Press.

Legro, J.W. and Moravscik, A. (1999) 'Is anybody still a realist?' *International Security* 21, 2: 5–55.

Mearsheimer, J.J. (2001) *The Tragedy of Great Power Politics*, New York: W.W. Norton.

Onuf, N. (1989) *World of Our Making: Rules and Rule in Social Theory and International Relations*, Columbia: University of South Carolina Press.

Organski, A.F.K. (1968) *World Politics*, New York: Alfred A. Knopf.

Rousseau, D. (2005) *Democracy and War: Institutions, Norms, and the Evolution of International Conflict*, Stanford, CA: Stanford University Press.

Schweller, R.L. (1996) 'Neorealism's status-quo bias: What security dilemma?' *Security Studies* 5, 3: 90–121.

Smith, M.J. (1986) *Realist Thought from Weber to Kissinger*, Baton Rouge: Louisiana State University Press.

Thomas, C. (2000) *Global Governance, Development and Human Security: The Challenge of Poverty and Inequality*, London: Pluto Press.

Tickner, J.A. (1992) *Gender in International Relations: Feminist Perspectives on Achieving Global Security*, New York: Columbia University Press.

United Nations Development Programme (1994) *Human Development Report 1994*, New York: United Nations.

Wæver, O. (1993) '"Societal security": the concept', in Wæver, O., Buzan, B., Kelstrup, M. and Lemaitre, P. (eds) *Identity, Migration and the New Security Agendas in Europe*, London: Pinter, pp. 17–40.

——(1995) 'Securitization and desecuritization', in Ronnie, D.L. (ed) *On Security*, New York: Columbia University Press, pp. 46–86.

Walker, R.J.B. (1993) *Inside/Outside: International Relations as Political Theory*, Cambridge: Cambridge University Press.

Walt, S. (1991) 'The renaissance of security studies', *International Studies Quarterly* 35, 2: 211–39.

Waltz, K.N. (1979) *Theory of International Politics*, New York: Random House.

Weldes, J. (1999) *Constructing National Interests: The United States and the Cuban Missile Crisis*, Minneapolis, MN: University of Minnesota Press.

Wendt, A. (1992) 'Anarchy is what states make of it: The social construction of power politics', *International Organization* 46, 2: 391–425.

——(1999) *Social Theory of International Politics*, Cambridge: Cambridge University Press.

Williams, M.C. (2007) *Culture and Security: Symbolic Power and the Politics of International Security*, London: Routledge.

Wolfers, A. (1952) 'National security as an ambiguous symbol', *Political Science Quarterly* 67, 4: 481–502.

Wyn Jones, R. (1999) *Security, Strategy, and Critical Theory*, Boulder, CO: Lynne Rienner.

Zehfuss, M. (2002) *Constructivism in International Relations: The Politics of Reality*, Cambridge: Cambridge University Press.

Part II: Contemporary security challenges

Abrahamsen, R. and Williams, M.C. (2006) *The Globalization of Private Security: Country Report Nigeria*, Aberystwyth: University of Wales.

Alibek, K. (2009) *Biohazard*, New York: Delta.

Allison, G., de Carmoy, H., Delpech, T. and Lee, C. (2006) *Nuclear Proliferation: Risk and Responsibility*, Washington, DC: Brookings Institution Press.

Anand, S., Peter, F. and Sen, A. (2006) *Public Health, Ethics, and Equity*, Oxford: Oxford University Press.

Andreas, P. and Nadelmann, E. (2006) *Policing the Globe: Criminalization and Crime Control in International Relations*, Oxford: Oxford University Press.

Andreas, P. and Price, R. (2001) 'From war fighting to crime fighting: Transforming the American national security state', *International Studies Review* 3, 3: 31–52.

Aradau, C. (2008) *Rethinking Trafficking in Women: Politics out of Security*, Hampshire: Palgrave.

Arquilla, J. and Ronfeldt, D.F. (eds) (1997) *In Athena's Camp: Preparing for Conflict in the Information Age*, Santa Monica: RAND.

Bächler, G. (1999) *Violence through Environmental Discrimination*, Dordrecht: Kluwer Academic.

Barlow, E. (2008) *Executive Outcomes: Against All Odds*, Alberton, South Africa: Galago Publishing.

Barnett, J. and Adger, N. (2007) 'Climate change, human security and violent conflict', *Political Geography* 26, 6: 639–55.

Berdal, M. and Serrano, M. (eds) (2002) *Transnational Organized Crime and International Security: Business as Usual?* Boulder, CO: Lynne Rienner.

Bertram, E., Blachman, M., Sharpe, K. and Andreas, P. (1996) *Drug War Politics: The Price of Denial*, Berkeley, CA: University of California Press.

Braun, C. and Chyba, C.F. (2004) 'Proliferation rings: New challenges to the nuclear nonproliferation regime', *International Security* 29, 2: 5–49.

Buhaug, H., Gleditsch, N.P. and Theisen, O.M. (2008) *Implications of Climate Change for Armed Conflict*, Washington, DC: World Bank Group.

Cameron, S. and Newman, E. (eds) (2007) *Trafficking in Humans: Social, Cultural, and Political Dimensions*, Tokyo: United Nations University Press.

Campbell, K.M., Einhorn, R.J. and Reiss, M.B. (2004) *The Nuclear Tipping Point: Why States Reconsider their Nuclear Choices*, Washington, DC: Brookings Institution Press.

465

Castles, S. and Davidson, A. (2000) *Citizenship and Migration: Globalization and the Politics of Belonging*, New York: Routledge.

Chesterman, S. and Lehnardt, C. (eds) (2007) *From Mercenaries to Markets: The Rise and Regulation of Private Military Companies*, Oxford: Oxford University Press.

Cincotta, R.P., Engelmann, R. and Anastasion, D. (2003) *The Security Demographic: Population and Civil Conflict after the Cold War*, Washington, DC: Population Action International.

Collier, P. (2007) *The Bottom Billion: Why the Poorest Countries are Failing and What can be done About it*, Oxford: Oxford University Press.

Collier, P. and Hoeffler, A. (1998) 'On the economic causes of civil war', *Oxford Economic Papers* 50, 4: 563–73.

Crenshaw M. (ed.) (1983) *Terrorism, Legitimacy and Power*, Middleton, CT: Wesleyan University Press.

——(1995) (ed.) *Terrorism in Context*, University Park: Pennsylvania University Press.

Der Derian, J. (2001) *Virtuous War: Mapping the Military-Industrial-Media-Entertainment Network*, Boulder, CO: Westview Press.

Duffield, M. (2005) 'Getting savages to fight barbarians: Development, security and the colonial present', *Conflict, Security and Development* 5, 2: 141–59.

Dunn Cavelty, M. (2008) *Cyber-Security and Threat Politics: US Efforts to Secure the Information Age*, London: Routledge.

Dunn Cavelty, M. and Kristensen, K.S. (eds) (2008) *The Politics of Securing the Homeland: Critical Infrastructure, Risk and Securitisation*, London: Routledge.

Elbe, S. (2006) 'Should HIV/AIDS be securitized? The ethical dilemmas of linking HIV/AIDS and security', *International Studies Quarterly* 50, 1: 119–44.

Eriksson, J. and Giacomello, G. (eds) (2007) *International Relations and Security in the Digital Age*, London: Routledge.

Euben, R. (1999) *Enemy in the Mirror: Islamic Fundamentalism and the Limits of Modern Rationalism – A Work of Comparative Political Theory*, Princeton, NJ: Princeton University Press.

Friesendorf, C. (2007) *US Foreign Policy and the War on Drugs: Displacing the Cocaine and Heroin Industry*, London: Routledge.

Guild, E. and van Selm, J. (eds) (2005) *International Migration and Security: Opportunities and Challenges*, London: Routledge.

Guillemin, J. (2005) *Biological Weapons: From the Invention of State Sponsored Programs to Contemporary Bioterrorism*, New York: Columbia University Press.

Hamilton, A. (2003) 'Resource wars and the politics of scarcity and abundance', *Dialogue* 1, 3: 27–38.

Hoffman, Bruce (2006) *Inside Terrorism*, New York: Columbia University Press.

Homer-Dixon, T. (1999) *Environment, Scarcity, and Conflict*, Princeton, NJ: Princeton University Press.

Huysmans, J. (2000) 'The European Union and the securitization of migration', *Journal of Common Market Studies* 38, 5: 751–77.

——(2006) *The Politics of Insecurity: Fear, Migration and Asylum in the EU*, London: Routledge.

Ingram, A. (ed) (2004) *Health, Foreign Policy and Security: Towards a Conceptual Framework for Research and Policy*, Nuffield Trust/Nuffield Health and Social Services Fund.

Kaldor, M. (1999) *New and Old Wars: Organized Violence in a Global Era*, Cambridge: Polity Press.

Kalicki, J.H. and Goldwyn, D.L. (2005) *Energy and Security: Toward a New Foreign Policy Strategy*, Washington, DC: Woodrow Wilson Center Press.

Klare, M.T. (2001) *Resource Wars: The New Landscape of Global Conflict*. New York: Metropolitan.

——(2008) *Rising Powers, Shrinking Planet: The New Geopolitics of Energy*, New York: Metropolitan Books.

Koblentz, G. (2003/04) 'Pathogens as weapons: The international security implications of biological warfare', *International Security* 28, 3: 84–122.

Laqueur, W. (1976) 'Post-modern terrorism', *Foreign Affairs* 75, 5: 24–36.

——(2003) *No End to War: Terrorism in the Twenty-First Century*, New York: Continuum.

Lavoy, P.R. (2006) 'Nuclear proliferation over the next decade: Causes, warning signs, and policy responses', *The Nonproliferation Review* 13, 3: 433–54.

Lomborg, B. (2001) *The Skeptical Environmentalist. Measuring the Real State of the World*, Cambridge: Cambridge University Press.

McInnes, C. (2005) *Health, Security and the Risk Society*, London: Nuffield Trust.

Migdal, J.S. (1988) *Strong Societies and Weak States: State–Society Relations and State Capabilities in the Third World*, Princeton, NJ: Princeton University Press.

Milliken, J. and Krause, K. (2002) 'State failure, state collapse, and state reconstruction: Concepts, lessons and strategies', *Development and Change* 33, 5: 753–74.

Münkler, H. (2005) *The New Wars*, Cambridge: Polity Press.

van Munster, R. (2009) *Immigration, Security and the Politics of Risk in the EU*, Basingstoke: Palgrave.

Newman, E. (2007) 'Weak states, state failure and terrorism', *Terrorism and Political Violence* 19, 4: 463–88.

Newman, E. and van Selm, J. (eds) (2003) *Refugees and Forced Displacement. International Security, Human Vulnerability, and the State*, Paris: United Nations University Press.

O'Hanlon, M. (2000) *Technological Change and the Future of Warfare*, Washington, DC: Brookings Institution Press.

Pape, R. (2003) 'The strategic logic of suicide terrorism', *American Political Science Review* 97, 3: 343–61.

Percy, S. (2007) *Mercenaries: The History of a Norm in International Relations*, Oxford: Oxford University Press.

Perovic, J., Orttung, R.W. and Wenger, A. (2009) *Russian Energy Power and Foreign Relations: Implications for Conflict and Cooperation*, London: Routledge.

Richardson, L. (2006) *What Terrorists Want: Understanding the Enemy, Containing the Threat*, London: Random House.

Sagan, S.D. (1996) 'Why do states build nuclear weapons? Three models in search of a bomb', *International Security* 21, 3: 54–86.

Sagan, S.D. and Waltz, K.N. (2003) *The Spread of Nuclear Weapons: A Debate*, New York and London: W.W. Norton.

Sageman, M. (2004) *Understanding Terror Networks*, Philadelphia: University of Pennsylvania Press.

Salama, S. and Hansell, L. (2005) 'Does intent equal capability? Al-Qaeda and weapons of mass destruction', *Nonproliferation Review* 12, 3: 615–53.

Schneider, G., Barbieri, K. and Gleditsch, N.P. (eds) (2003) *Globalization and Armed Conflict*, Lanham, MD: Rowman & Littlefield.

Simons, A. and Tucker, D. (2007) 'The misleading problem of failed states: A "socio-geography" of terrorism in the post-9/11 era', *Third World Quarterly* 28, 2: 387–401.

Singer, P.W. (2003) *Corporate Warriors: The Rise of the Privatized Military Industry*, Ithaca, NY and London: Cornell University Press.

Sterling, C. (1994) *Thieves' World: The Threat of the New Global Network of Organized Crime*, New York: Simon and Schuster.

Stern, J. (2003) *Terror in the Name of God: Why Religious Militants Kill*, New York: HarperCollins.

Tilly, C. (1985) 'War-making and state-making as organized crime', in Evans, P.B., Rueschmeyer, D. and Skocpol, T. (eds) *Bringing the State Back in*, Cambridge: Cambridge University Press, pp. 169–91.

Walker, W. (2004) *Weapons of Mass Destruction and International Order*, Adelphi Paper No.370, New York: Oxford University Press.

Wenger, A. and Wollenmann, R. (eds) (2007) *Bioterrorism: Confronting a Complex Threat*, Boulder, CO and London: Lynne Rienner.

Yergin, D. (2006) 'Ensuring energy security', *Foreign Affairs* 85, 2: 69–82.

Zimmermann, D. and Wenger, A. (eds) (2006) *How States Fight Terrorism: Policy Dynamics in the West*, Boulder, CO: Lynne Rienner.

Zureik, E. and Salter, M.B. (eds) (2005) *Global Surveillance and Policing: Borders, Security, Identity*, Devon: Willan Publishing.

Part III: Regional security challenges

Abrahamian, E. (2008) *A History of Modern Iran*, Cambridge: Cambridge University Press.

Anastasakis, O. and Koppa, M. (2009) *Democratisation in the Postcommunist Balkans*, Basingstoke: Palgrave Macmillan.

Anderson, L. and Stansfield, G. (2009) *Crisis in Kirkuk: The Ethnopolitics of Conflict and Compromise*, Philadelphia, PA: University of Pennsylvania Press.

Ansari, A. (2006) *Confronting Iran: The Failure of American Foreign Policy and the Next Great Crisis in the Middle East*, New York: Basic Books.

Baev, P.K. (2008) *Russian Energy Policy and Military Power: Putin's Quest for Greatness*, London: Routledge.

Barrios, H., Beck, M., Boeckh, A. and Segbers, K. (eds) (2003) *Resistance to Globalization: Political Struggle and Cultural Resilience in the Middle East, Russia, and Latin America*, New Brunswick, NJ: Transaction Publishers.

Basrur, R. (2006) *Minimum Deterrence and India's Nuclear Security*, Stanford: Stanford University Press.

Beeman, W.O. (2008) *The Great Satan vs. the Mad Mullahs: How the United States and Iran Demonize Each Other*, Chicago, IL: University of Chicago Press.

Ben-Ami, S. (2006) *Scars of War, Wounds of Peace: The Israeli–Arab Tragedy*, Oxford: Oxford University Press.

Bleiker, R. (2005) *Divided Korea: Toward a Culture of Reconciliation*, Minneapolis, MN: University of Minnesota Press.

Caplan, R. (2005) *Europe and the Recognition of New States in Yugoslavia*, Cambridge: Cambridge University Press.

——(2005) *International Governance of War-Torn Territories: Rule and Reconstruction*, Oxford: Oxford University Press.

Cha, V.D. and Kang, D.C. (eds) (2003) *Nuclear North Korea: A Debate on Engagement Strategies*, New York: Columbia University Press.

Chadha, V. (2005) *Low Intensity Conflicts in India: An Analysis*, New Delhi: Sage.

Chan, S. (2008) *China, the U.S., and the Power-Transition Theory: A Critique*, London: Routledge.

Chinoy, M. (2008) *Meltdown: The Inside Story of the North Korean Nuclear Crisis*, New York: St. Martin's Press.

Chubin, S. (2006) *Iran's Nuclear Ambitions*, Washington, DC: Carnegie Endowment for International Peace.

Cordesman, A. and Kleiber, M. (2007) *Iran's Military Forces and Warfighting Capabilities: The Threat in the Northern Gulf*, Westport, CT: Praeger.

Crampton, R.J. (2002) *The Balkans since the Second World War*, New York: Longman.

Diamond, L., Plattner, M.F. and Brumberg, D. (eds) (2003) *Islam and Democracy in the Middle East*, Baltimore, MD: John Hopkins University Press.

Dodge, T. (2003) *Inventing Iraq: The Failure of Nation-Building and a History Denied*, London: Hurst & Co.

Funabashi, Y. (2007) *The Peninsula Question: A Chronicle of the Second North Korean Nuclear Crisis*, Washington, DC: Brookings Institution Press.

Ganguly, S. and Hagerty, D.T. (2006) *Fearful Symmetry: India Pakistan Crises in the Shadow of Nuclear Weapons*, Seattle: University of Washington Press.

Gill, B. (2007) *Rising Star: China's New Security Diplomacy*, Washington, DC: Brookings Institution Press.

Gilley, B. (2004) *China's Democratic Future: How it will Happen and Where it will Lead*, New York: Columbia University Press.

Goldman, M.I. (2008) *Petrostate: Putin, Power, and the New Russia*, Oxford: Oxford University Press.

Goldstein, A. (2005) *Rising to the Challenge: China's Grand Strategy and International Security*, Stanford, CA: Stanford University Press.

Herring, E. and Rangwala, G. (2006) *Iraq in Fragments: The Occupation and its Legacy*, London: Hurst & Co.

Hussain, R. (2005) *Pakistan and the Emergence of the Islamic Militancy in Afghanistan*, London: Ashgate.

Indyk, M. (2009) *Innocent Abroad: An Intimate Account of American Peace Diplomacy in the Middle East*, New York: Simon & Schuster.

Kang, D.C. (2007) *China Rising: Peace, Power, and Order in East Asia*, New York: Columbia University Press.

Katouzian, H. and Shahidi, H. (eds) (2008) *Iran in the 21st Century: Politics, Economics and Conflict*, London: Routledge.

Keddie, N.R. and Richard, Y. (2006) *Modern Iran: Roots and Results of Revolution*, revised and updated edition, New Haven, CT: Yale University Press.

Kennedy, P. (1987) *The Rise and Fall of Great Powers: Economic Change and Military Conflict From 1500 to 2000*, New York: Random House.

Kurtzer, D.C. and Lasensky, S.B. (2008) *Negotiating Arab–Israeli Peace: American Leadership in the Middle East*, Washington, DC: United States Institute of Peace.

Little, D. (2008) *American Orientalism: The United States and the Middle East since 1945*, 3rd edition, Chapel Hill, NC: University of North Carolina Press.

Malik, V.P. (2006) *Kargil: From Surprise to Victory*, New Delhi: HarperColllins.

Mankoff, J.A. (2009) *Russian Foreign Policy: The Return of Great Power Politics*, Lanham, MD: Rowman & Littlefield.

Miller, A.D. (2008) *The Much Too Promised Land: America's Elusive Search for Arab–Israeli Peace*, New York: Bantam Dell.

Nasr, V. (2006) *The Shi'a Revival: How Conflicts Within Islam will Shape the Future*, New York: W.W. Norton.

Nawaz, S. (2008) *Crossed Swords: Pakistan, its Army, and the Wars Within*, Karachi: Oxford University Press.

Orttung, R. and Latta, A. (eds) (2008) *Russia's Battle with Crime, Corruption, and Terrorism*, London: Routledge.

Panagariya, A. (2008) *India: Emerging Giant*, New York: Oxford University Press.

Pollack, K.M. (2004) *The Persian Puzzle: The Conflict Between Iran and America*, New York: Random House.

Pond, E. (2006) *Endgame in the Balkans: Regime Change, European Style*, Washington, DC: Brookings Institution Press.

Quandt, W.B. (2005) *Peace Process: American Diplomacy and the Arab–Israeli Conflict Since 1967*, 3rd edn, Berkeley, CA: University of California Press.

Rashid, A. (2008) *Descent into Chaos: The United States and the Failure of Nation Building in Pakistan, Afghanistan, and Central Asia*, New York: Viking.

Ross, R.S. and Feng, Z. (eds) (2008) *China's Ascent: Power, Security, and the Future of International Politics*, Ithaca, NY: Cornell University Press.

Saikal, A. (2006) *Modern Afghanistan: A History of Struggle and Survival*, London: I.B. Tauris.

Shambaugh, D. (ed.) (2005) *Power Shift: China and Asia's New Dynamics*, Berkeley, CA: University of California Press.

Shambaugh, D. and Yahuda, M. (eds) (2008) *International Relations of Asia*, Lanham, MD: Rowman & Littlefield.

Shirk, S.L. (2007) *China: Fragile Superpower: How China's Internal Politics Could Derail Its Peaceful Rise*, Oxford: Oxford University Press.

Shlaim, A. (1995) *War and Peace in the Middle East: A Concise History*, London: Penguin.

——(2000) *The Iron Wall: Israel and the Arab World*, New York: W.W. Norton.

Stansfield, G. (2007) *Iraq: People, History, Politics*, Cambridge: Polity Press.

Takeyh, R. (2006) *Hidden Iran: Paradox and Power in the Islamic Republic*, New York: Times Books/ Henry Holt.

Trenin, D.V. (2007) *Getting Russia Right*, Washington, DC: Carnegie Endowment for International Peace.

Part IV: Confronting security challenges

Art, R. and Cronin, P. (eds) (2003) *United States and Coercive Diplomacy*, Washington, DC: United States Institute of Peace.

Avant, D. (2005) *The Market for Force: The Consequences of Privatizing Security*, Cambridge: Cambridge University Press.

Axelrod, R. (1984) *The Evolution of Cooperation*, New York: Basic Books.

Bellamy, A.J. (2009) *Responsibility to Protect: The Global Effort to End Mass Atrocities*, Cambridge: Polity Press.

Boin, R.A., 't Hart, P., Stern, E., and Sundelius, B. (2005) *The Politics of Crisis Management: Public Leadership under Pressure*. Cambridge: Cambridge University Press.

469

Boin, R.A., McConnell, A. and 't Hart, P. (eds) (2008) *Governing after Crisis: The Politics of Investigation, Accountability and Learning*, Cambridge: Cambridge University Press.

Brecher, M. (1993) *Crises in World Politics: Theory and Reality*, Oxford: Pergamon Press.

Bretherton, C. and Vogler, J. (2006) *The European Union as a Global Actor*, 2nd edn, London: Routledge.

Chesterman, S. (2001) *Just War or Just Peace? Humanitarian Intervention and International Law*, Oxford: Oxford University Press.

Crawford, N. (2002) *Argument and Change in World Politics: Ethics, Decolonization, and Humanitarian Intervention*, Cambridge: Cambridge University Press.

Cutler, C., Haufler, V. and Porter, T. (eds) (1999) *Private Authority and International Affairs*, Albany: State University of New York Press.

Finnemore, M. (2003) *The Purpose of Intervention: Changing Beliefs About the Use of Force*, Ithaca, NY: Cornell University Press.

Freedman, L. (2004) *Deterrence*, Cambridge: Polity Press.

——(ed.) (1998) *Strategic Coercion*, Oxford: Oxford University Press.

Fukuyama, F (2004) *State-Building: Governance and World Order in the 21st Century*, Ithaca, NY: Cornell University Press.

George, A.L. and Smoke, R. (1974) *Deterrence in American Foreign Policy: Theory and Practice*, New York: Columbia University Press.

George, A.L. and Simons, W.E. (eds) (1994) *The Limits of Coercive Diplomacy*, Boulder: Westview Press

Haftendorn, H., Keohane, R.O. and Wallander, C.A. (eds) (1999) *Imperfect Unions: Security Institutions over Time and Space*, Oxford: Oxford University Press.

Hall, R. and Biersteker, T. (eds) (2002) *The Emergence of Private Authority in Global Governance*, Cambridge and New York: Cambridge University Press.

Hill, C. and Smith, M. (eds) (2005) *International Relations and the European Union*, Oxford: Oxford University Press.

Holzgrefe, J.F. and Keohane, R.O. (eds) (2002) *Humanitarian Intervention: Ethical, Legal and Political Dilemmas*, Cambridge: Cambridge University Press.

Hopf, T. (1994) *Peripheral Visions: Deterrence Theory and American Foreign Policy in the Third World, 1965–1999*, Ann Arbor, MI: University of Michigan Press.

Lebow, R.N. (2005) 'Deterrence: Then and now', *Journal of Strategic Studies* 28, 5: 765–73.

Mérand, F. (2008) *European Defence Policy: Beyond the Nation State*, Oxford: Oxford University Press.

Moravcsik, A. (1998) *The Choice for Europe: Social Purpose and State Power from Messina to Maastricht*, Ithaca, NY: Cornell University Press.

Neumann, I.B. and Sending, O.J. (2009) *Governing the Global Polity: Governmentality in World Politics*, Ann Arbor, MI: The University of Michigan Press.

Rosenau, J. and Czempiel, E.-O. (eds) (1992) *Governance without Government: Order and Change in World Politics*, Cambridge: Cambridge University Press.

Smith, M.E. (2004) *Europe's Foreign and Security Policy. The Institutionalization of Cooperation*, Cambridge: Cambridge University Press.

Snyder, G.H. (1997) *Alliance Politics*, Ithaca, NY: Cornell University Press.

Solingen, E. (2007) *Nuclear Logics: Contrasting Paths in East Asia and the Middle East*, Cambridge: Cambridge University Press.

Wallace, H., Wallace, W. and Pollack, M.A. (eds) (2005) *Policy-Making in the European Union*, 5th edn, Oxford: Oxford University Press.

Walt, S. (1987) *The Origins of Alliances*, Ithaca, NY: Cornell University Press.

——(2009) 'Alliances in a unipolar world', *World Politics* 61, 1: 86–120.

Webber, M., Croft, S., Howorth, J., Terriff, T. and Krahmann, E. (2004) 'The governance of European security', *Review of International Studies* 30, 1: 3–26.

Weiss, T.G. (2007) *Humanitarian Intervention: Ideas in Action*, Cambridge: Polity Press.

Welsh, J. (ed.) (2000) *Humanitarian Intervention and International Relations*, Oxford: Oxford University Press.

Wheeler, N.J. (2000) *Saving Strangers: Humanitarian Intervention in International Society*, Oxford: Oxford University Press.

470

Index